The
Frozen
Echo

THE
FROZEN
ECHO

Greenland and the Exploration of
North America, ca. A.D. 1000-1500

KIRSTEN A. SEAVER

Stanford University Press
Stanford, California

Stanford University Press
Stanford, California
© 1996 by the Board of Trustees of the
Leland Stanford Junior University

Printed in the United States of America

CIP data are at the end of the book

This book is dedicated to the memory of my parents, Signy Monrad Andresen and Olaf Emil Andresen

Acknowledgments

It is a truth universally acknowledged that anyone writing a book must be in need of a supportive spouse. I am unusually lucky, for my historian husband, Paul S. Seaver, provided me with encouragement and expert help and forsook his Elizabethans long enough to travel with me in Iceland, Greenland, Norway, and all around the British Isles. Above all, he patiently suffered the epiphanies I experienced—and endlessly communicated— while writing this book.

Our daughter Hannah has my lasting gratitude for her good advice and for working hard since the age of two to improve my English. Son David entered into this project with enthusiasm and contributed his skills as a graphic artist, providing several maps and the drawing of a medieval Norse turf-and-stone house in Fig. 11.

I have also benefited from the advice of friends at Stanford University and elsewhere. My longtime friend Barton J. Bernstein read part of my early draft and made valuable suggestions about how to focus my presentation. Kari Ellen Gade at Indiana University taught me Old Norse and helped me over countless linguistic and literary hurdles. I owe more than I can express to her lively interest in my topic and to her uncompromising eye for detail. Various notes bear testimony to the help I got from many others unfortunate enough to find themselves in my path, including the historian David Harris Sacks, known in both Britain and the United States for his ability to deliver capsule explanations of difficult problems when buttonholed between sessions at a conference, and the astronomer Kevin D. Pang, who provided valuable information about his research on the 1453 eruption of the Kuwae Caldera.

While doing research in England, I received the encouragement and support of two valued friends. I could not have had a better pilot in tricky waters, nor a better example of erudition and scholarly energy, than Helen Wallis, the former Keeper of Maps at the British Library. Despite her busy schedule of writing and lecturing she found time to answer my questions, settle me in at the British Map Library, and give me down-to-earth advice. I mourn her death on February 7, 1995. Our mutual friend Sarah Tyacke, Director of Special Collections at the British Library before she went on to head the Public Records Office and also an expert on early maps and related subjects, is much concerned with the problem of transporting scholarly knowledge from lesser-known languages into English. Her optimism and drive, and her interest in my project, cheered me on through difficult periods.

Other scholars' horror stories of uncooperative librarians, archivists, and museum curators only increase my gratitude for the fine treatment I have received everywhere. When I asked Irmelin Martens at The University Collections of Ancient Artifacts in Oslo about Norwegian medieval iron production, her reply came within a week, with up-to-date scholarly details not easily available elsewhere. I got equally prompt help from the Scottish Public Record Office when I requested information about the Campbell clan, and from the Canadian Museum of Civilization concerning the use of the illustration in Fig. 8. In addition, I am grateful to all the staff members in the British Library who helped me find elusive items, always with the greatest courtesy and good humor. My special thanks go to super-sleuth Karen Cook in the British Map Library. I also owe great thanks to William Mills and Shelley Sawtelly at the Scott Polar Institute Research Library, Cambridge University, who enabled me to make maximum use of their fine collections on my visit. Closer to home, the Stanford University Library has been an invaluable resource, and I am particularly grateful to the staff in Interlibrary Loans and in the Earth Sciences Library for making my life easier.

I owe many Danish and Greenlandic scholars and institutions warm thanks. Jette Arneborg, Jørgen Meldgaard, and Christen Leif Vebæk have been especially liberal with their time and expertise, and the majority of the illustrations in this book bear witness to their personal generosity as well as to the cooperation of their departments at the Danish National Museum. I also thank Hans Christian Gulløv at the Danish National Museum's Ethnographic Section for his help and for permission to use his exquisite drawings of Norse and Inuit carvings, and Bent Fredskild at the Greenland Botanical Survey, University of Copenhagen, for timely advice as well as for permission to reproduce his paleobotanical diagrams.

The Danish Polar Center responded generously in allowing the reproduction of several illustrations from old volumes of their journal *Meddelelser om Grønland*, and during an interview in Copenhagen, Hans Kapel at the Greenland Secretariat provided valuable information about current Greenland Inuit research. He took the beautiful photograph of Herjolfsnes, reproduced here as Fig. 3 with his permission. Jens Fabricius, Head of the Greenland Ice Patrol, gave permission to use the satellite photo in Fig. 7. Søren Thirslund at the Maritime Museum in Elsinore, an expert on the ancient sun compass, gave me the picture shown in Fig. 4. I also owe great thanks to Joel Berglund personally, as well as to the Qaqortoq Museum and the National Museum and Archives in Nuuk, Greenland, for their generosity in making the illustrations in Fig. 15a and Fig. 21 available.

By sending me reprints and bibliographical information, Arneborg and Vebæk in particular have enabled me to keep up with developments in Norse Greenland research. Nobody could ask for better teachers, for between them they have participated in Greenland excavations from before the Second World War to the present. Vebæk's death in January of 1994 was a great loss to his many friends and to the scholarly community, and I feel it acutely. Both Vebæk and Arneborg have read and commented on my manuscript, correcting mistakes and asking trenchant questions without disputing my freedom to suggest new interpretations. I would have found it difficult indeed to write this book without these two friends. My conclusions and any lingering mistakes about the archaeological material are entirely my responsibility.

Some practical considerations in producing this book need mention here. In keeping with the current trend of limiting the use of accents and other diacritical marks, I have left out such marks in personal names and place names in the main text whenever they would confuse, rather than enlighten, an English-speaking reader unfamiliar with the Scandinavian languages. An exception is made for the 'á' in Icelandic and Old Norse, which corresponds to the modern Danish, Swedish, and Norwegian 'å' (pronounced 'aw'). In the Notes and Works Cited, diacritical marks have been preserved.

A related problem concerns the continually changing spelling of Inuit place-names in Greenland. I have used the latest style (e.g., replacing the diacritical mark ^ with double vowels) as much as possible, with much help from Arneborg, but these later versions are not so fundamentally different from various earlier spellings as to make them unrecognizable when consulting older maps. Naturally, new maps of Norse and Inuit archaeological sites in Greenland show the latest spelling of place-names. They also have a new numbering system for ruin sites that is not yet available to the general public, so I am using the old one; the sites are easy to locate on both older and newer maps. Each new map edition can also be expected to show a greater number of ruin sites than its predecessor, for fresh discoveries are made all the time.

The master files of up-to-date archaeological map transparencies at the Greenland Secretariat have not been printed since the publication of Knud Krogh's *Erik den Rødes Grønland* in 1982, which therefore remains the best currently available source of detailed maps for both the Eastern and Western Norse Settlements in Greenland. The maps in Figs. 1 and 2 show only the chief locations mentioned in this book.

Growing up in Norway shaped my view of the world and of terms such as "Nordic" and "Scandinavian." In modern usage, the "Nordic" countries are Denmark (including Greenland and the Faroes), Finland, Iceland, Norway, and Sweden, but historically the term is not clear-cut either geographically or politically. For example, Finland does not figure in the present book at all. Although people in the five Nordic countries now often use the term "Scandinavian" when referring to themselves, the word has been imposed from the outside and is loosely based on the Scandinavian Peninsula, a definable geographical (but not political) feature. Those of us who grew up in those five northern countries do not think of ourselves as "Scandinavians"—we are Norwegians, Danes, and so on, and we tend to say "the Far North" or "the Nordic countries" when referring to the general region.

The credit for making me aware of these and other cultural quirks goes to my Stanford University Press editor, Peter J. Kahn. Any work that wants to marry two widely different historical traditions while adopting offspring from several related fields gives an editor two options: correcting for style and language while leaving everything else alone, or correcting for style and language while asking the author to clarify concepts and agruments. Peter took the latter approach with such patience, sensitivity, and skill that a potentially painful process became a real pleasure.

I dedicate this book to the memory of my parents, who were not particularly patient, and who were as disparate as two people could be. But together they created a summer paradise on an island in the Oslofjord during the blackest years in Norway's recent history, and there the seeds of *The Frozen Echo* were planted. We had no electricity at the summer house, and all radios had been confiscated both in town and in the country. The timeless quality of our simple, solitary life on the island made Norway's isolation from the rest of the world during the German occupation (1940–45) seem less sinister and more bearable, at least to us children. The local farmers and fishermen led the same harsh lives they had always endured, and from Midsummer Eve until the end of August of every year, we, too, were ruled more by the sun and the weather than by the Wehrmacht.

I picked wild berries at four in the morning, with the sun already high in the sky and the terns screaming as if they wanted to crack the mirror of the fjord. After a heavy sou'wester I watched heaving masses of water thunder against the pink granite shore and pull away again, sucking and gurgling and wringing the seaweed, while I licked the salt off my lips and marveled that the sea pinks still clung to their cracks. I read endlessly when the evenings were long and light, and I accepted the inexorableness of seasons when August gave us back the night and the stars, and the aurora borealis flickered in the northern sky. The ground smelled of mushrooms, and the air gave warning of winter's chilly grip. It was a comforting, familiar cycle that seemed to say: "Things will not get much better, but not much worse, either." They could not possibly end.

Some years after the war, a Greenlander visited there and said: "This reminds me of home." And my curiosity was born.

K. A. S.
Palo Alto, California

Contents

Illustrations   xv

Introduction   1

One   Greenland and Vínland: North Atlantic
Exploration Five Hundred Years Before
the Cabot Voyages   14

Two   Social and Economic Conditions in Norse
Greenland Before 1350   44

Three   Church and Trade in Norse Greenland
Before 1350   61

Four   Ivar Bárdarson's Greenland   91

Five   The Western Settlement Comes to
an End   113

Six   Rumors of Trouble in the Eastern
Settlement   139

Seven   England and the Norwegian Colonies,
1400–1450   159

Eight   Sailing out of the Middle Ages,
1450–1500   192

Nine   Greenland, 1450–1500   225

Ten   The Age of Discovery   254

              Appendix A   315
              Appendix B   323
              Appendix C   329

         Notes   331
         Works Cited   377
         Index   393

Illustrations

Fig. 1 Map of the Eastern Settlement in Norse Greenland 3

Fig. 2 Map of the Western Settlement in Norse Greenland 4

Fig. 3 Photo of Herjolfsnes (Ikigaat) 10

Fig. 4 Reconstruction of the tenth century bearing dial found by
C. L. Vebæk 17

Fig. 5 Photo of Brattahlid 20

Fig. 6 The site of the Norse farm Sandnes in the Western
Settlement 22

Fig. 7 Satellite photo showing Greenland south of 72°N 30

Fig. 8 A. A. Bjørnbo's depiction of the medieval Norse world
circle 35

Fig. 9 Photo and drawing of carving found by Debora Sabo on
Baffin Island 40

Fig. 10 Carvings of Norsemen found by T. Mathiassen on Inussuk
Island 41

Fig. 11 A medieval turf-and-stone Norse house. Illustration by
David O. Seaver 49

Fig. 12 Floor plan of a modest house block for man and beast
(Roussell) 52

Fig. 13 Floor plan of a medieval Thule winter house cluster 106

Fig. 14 "The farm beneath the sand," Western Settlement 116

Fig. 15 Early representations of Campbell clan shield 121

Fig. 16 Portraits by medieval Greenland artists 125

Fig. 17 Crucifixes from about A.D. 1300, Western Settlement 129

Fig. 18 Hvalsey (Ø83) farm and church in the Eastern Settlement   154

Fig. 19 A. A. Bjørnbo's map based on the works of Claudius
Clavus   166

Fig. 20 Remains of a fifteenth century dress found in a grave at
Herjolfsnes   171

Fig. 21 A pewter cross to be worn around the neck, found at Ø83
(Hvalsey)   173

Fig. 22 Late fifteenth century European table knives   174

Fig. 23 Detail from a Catalan chart in the Biblioteca Ambrosiana,
ca. 1480   212

Fig. 24 Map of the North Atlantic. By David O. Seaver   215

Fig. 25 The northwestern Atlantic region from Ruysch's 1507–8
mappamundi   216

Fig. 26 Eskimo carvings of Europeans, 15th or 16th centuries   227

Fig. 27 Large fragment of cast metal cooking pot, circa
17 cm. high   228

Fig. 28 Medieval headgear found in Herjolfsnes graves   230

Fig. 29 A fifteenth century man's high-necked overgown found at
Herjolfsnes   231

Fig. 30 Unworked iron found by C.L. Vebæk during excavations in
Vatnahverfi   233

Fig. 31 Palæobotanical diagrams from Brattahlid (Fredskild)   244

Fig. 32 Section of the map commissioned in Lisbon by Alberto Cantino
in 1502   278

Fig. 33 Detail from the King-Hamy world map, ca. 1502   286

Fig. 34 Section of the map by Robert Thorne the Younger   289

**The
Frozen
Echo**

"Earth is but the echo of the silent voice of God."
Samuel Miller Hageman, "Silence"

Introduction

It is now generally accepted that Eirik the Red's son Leif (as well as one or two of his brothers) sailed from Greenland across the Davis Strait and made landfalls on the North American continent almost a thousand years ago. Those familiar with the so-called Vínland sagas also know that a small but intrepid group, led by the Icelander Thorfinn Thordsson, set out from Greenland and made an abortive attempt to settle new land in the west. They gave up because they were outnumbered by hostile natives. From then on, native North Americans supposedly enjoyed another five hundred years of peace and quiet until John Cabot found them in 1497.

There is some evidence, however, that the Norse Greenlanders continued to cross the Davis Strait occasionally for lumber and—most likely—fur. This should come as no surprise, for since the eighth century at least, the Norse had sailed long distances in clinker-built, open ships with square sails; they had colonized Iceland in the ninth century, Greenland at the very end of the tenth, and attempted North America early in the eleventh; and they continued for a long time to sail across vast stretches in the North Atlantic to maintain sporadic contact between Greenland and both Iceland and Norway.

Historians of the North Atlantic rim countries nevertheless disagree on the extent to which the Greenlanders explored and exploited North America after Eirik the Red's son Leif had headed the first organized expedition to explore the new lands that Bjarni Herjolfsson sighted when he drifted off course on his voyage to join his father in Greenland.[1] I shall address that problem and introduce another, namely whether there is a connection between the Norse Greenlanders' disappearance and the voyages of exploration that took place in the North Atlantic around A.D. 1500, marking the start of modern European exploitation of the Norsemen's Vínland and Markland.

Documentary and archaeological evidence suggests that such a connection exists, and that it is the logical result of a complex web of contacts and travels covering the North Atlantic throughout the entire Middle Ages. Despite the dearth of written records in the mariners' world of tall tales and practical knowledge, of hearsay and personal experience, it is possible to trace the routes by which information must have traveled and been preserved. Sketching those routes is another purpose of this book.

Appendixes A and B show the tight connections among the handful of North Iceland families who provide the link between the last recorded sailings from Greenland and the already swelling influx of English fishermen and merchants in Iceland. These last known travelers to Norse Greenland, and their descendants, governed Iceland from the end of the fourteenth century right through the fifteenth and formed the bridge between the "known" and the "unknown" Greenland—a bridge wide and strong enough to ensure that knowledge of Greenland and the route there never could be entirely lost. It was built of kinships and marriages, of old traditions and new developments, and of the relentless quest for profit that drove English and Norse alike into the farther reaches of the North Atlantic.

Central to the question of how much John Cabot and others knew about lands in the west in the 1490s is the riddle of the Norse Greenlanders' fate. After five centuries of scratching a living as farmers, hunters, and fishermen at the edge of the habitable world, all the colonists were gone by about 1500, even from their southernmost and longest-lasting toehold, called the Eastern Settlement despite its west coast location (see Fig. 1). About a century and a half earlier the Norse Greenlanders had abandoned their northernmost colony, the so-called Western Settlement (see Fig. 2) in the present-day Nuuk region.[2] The Greenlanders' disappearance remains a puzzle to historians, and providing at least a partial answer to that puzzle will be one more goal of the present work.

Combining Norse Greenland research with scholarship focused on North Atlantic explorations in the late fifteenth and early sixteenth centuries is not a new idea. The British historian James A. Williamson, who spent fifty years expanding our knowledge of John and Sebastian Cabot's voyages, concluded in 1962 that the fate of the Greenland colony is more important in the story of Atlantic discovery than used to be supposed.[3] The last recorded sailing from Norse Greenland took place in 1410, but Poul Nørlund's 1921 excavations of the churchyard at the Norse settlement of Herjolfsnes (now Ikigaat) in southwest Greenland showed that even in the late fifteenth century, the colonists in the Eastern Settlement still had visi-

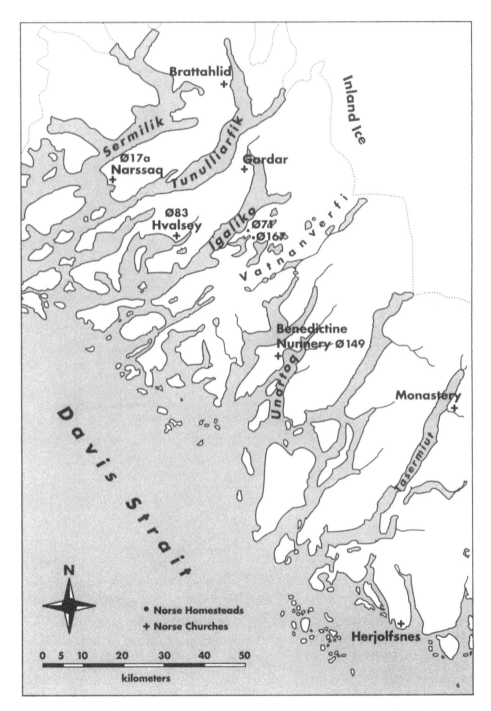

FIG. 1. Map of the Eastern Settlement in Norse Greenland, showing the major sites discussed in this book. Source: David O. Seaver.

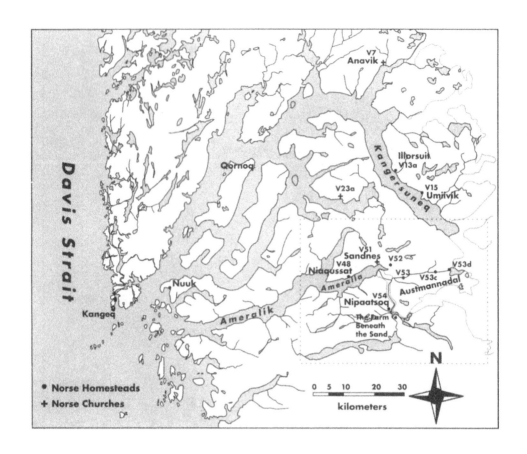

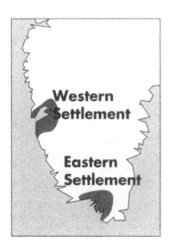

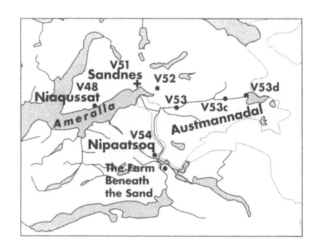

tors from abroad who enabled them to keep up with clothing fashions in Europe.[4] Williamson based his assessment on a good overview of what was then known in the field of Norse Greenland studies, as well as on his own knowledge of early voyages in the North Atlantic. Later work in both fields supports his view, but as yet there has been no attempt to follow up his suggestion that research on early English and Portuguese discoveries in the North Atlantic include a stronger focus on Norse Greenland.

In order to evaluate the situation in Norse Greenland at the end of the fifteenth century, when documented Portuguese and English voyages of northern exploration began, it is necessary to follow the colony's development from its inception and look at a number of commonly held views that so far have gone unchallenged.

Many of my conclusions are based on detailed reevaluations of well-known sources, such as the sagas, Ivar Bárdarson's "Description of Greenland," reports of ships "drifting off" to Greenland, documents about a wedding at Hvalsey (Greenland) in 1408, and papal letters from 1448 and 1492. But I have also based my interpretations on less frequently studied documents in *Diplomatarium Islandicum* and *Diplomatarium Norvegicum*. The latter collection in particular is often passed over in favor of the more convenient *Regesta Norvegica*. While extremely useful, the résumés in the *Regesta* necessarily represent the more commonly accepted views of what is significant about any given document and sometimes stand in the way of new interpretations.

New interpretations require that we question old and often unchallenged assumptions, such as that the Greenland colony was doomed to failure because of the unique hardships associated with life in that faraway land. Comparisons of Norse Greenland with Iceland or Norway during the same five hundred years repeatedly demonstrate the need for caution in assuming that life was always harder in Greenland.

Throughout the Middle Ages, many Norwegians battled starvation every day of their lives. For example, in a late-twelfth-century letter from Pope Alexander III to the Norwegian archbishop, the pope says he knows that many people in the archbishop's country are so poor that they ought to be allowed to fish herring even on Sundays and most other holidays if the fish run near land. Also, those who have no bread may sustain themselves on fast days by eating legumes, fish, or whatever else is at hand.[5] The Norwegians endured, however, and so did the Icelanders, despite the fact that both of their countries were buffeted by disasters and offered general

---

FIG. 2 (*opposite*). Top: Map of the Western Settlement in Norse Greenland. Below left: Greenland, showing the locations of the two Norse settlements. Below right: Inset showing the dotted area on the main map in greater detail. Source: David O. Seaver.

living conditions that only the fittest could survive. Were the Norwegians and the Icelanders made of sterner stuff than their Greenland cousins, or did something occur to make it impossible for the descendants of Eirik the Red and his followers to sustain life in the end?

We cannot hope to understand the end of the Greenlanders' tale without knowing the beginning, so I shall start with the voyages of Eirik the Red and his sons. Subsequent chapters will sketch the economic growth of the Norse colony to the point where it could support a regular episcopal establishment, and will examine the role played by the church in the religious, economic, and administrative life of medieval Greenland, as well as in the colony's demise.

It is commonly thought that the Greenlanders were abandoned by internally disorganized Norwegian lay and ecclesiastical authorities (upon whom they supposedly had come to depend) because Greenland suffered from a rapidly deteriorating economy in the mid-fourteenth century and thus was not worth troubling over. In fact, however, the evidence challenges this view. The Greenlanders themselves, acting from a position of strength rather than weakness, appear to have been instrumental in severing some of their ties with the Norwegian church and crown *before* economic and political problems in Norway and practical consequences of the Great Schism in the Catholic Church completed the rupture. There is also reason to think that Greenland remained an attractive destination for some Icelanders well into the fifteenth century, long after the country had ceased to be an active concern of Norwegian officials.

There are nevertheless indications of serious problems in Greenland during the colony's last period. We shall examine various potential causes of trouble besides those generated by relations with church and crown: climatic and ecological changes, the extent and effects of isolation, Norse-Eskimo relations, the possibility of epidemics or foreign marauders, failure of trade due to the deteriorating situation in Norway, and deep-seated sociological shortcomings so severe that they prevented the Norse settlers from adapting to the challenges posed by their harsh environment and their isolation at the edge of the known world. Considering how long the Greenland colony lasted, this final theory is a curious one, but with permutations it has been espoused by scholars such as Christian Keller, Kirsten Hastrup, and Thomas McGovern, and it influences current thinking in the field.

Samuel Eliot Morison in 1971 weighed in with his own explanation for the Greenlanders' demise:[6]

The question of what became of the Norse Greenlanders is argued in all the general works, in varying degrees of acrimony; I have discussed it pleasantly and profitably with Dr. Helge Larsen of the National Museum, Copenhagen. . . . Whilst not denying that the Eskimo may have moved in on Brattahlid when its survivors were too weak to resist, Dr. Larsen and I regard any such attack as a mere coup de grâce to a dying community, dying from isolation, and undernourishment.

This kind of a priori reasoning has a long tradition in Greenland studies. The Norwegian explorer, scientist, and humanitarian Fridtjof Nansen thought the Norse Greenlanders had sickened and died because they no longer received grain shipments from Norway. In his judgment, grain-based nutrition was essential to people of European extraction, and a lack of it would result in reduced fertility and poor health.[7] His opinions about the Greenlanders influenced people's thinking for a long time and contributed to such grotesqueries as F. C. C. Hansen's analysis of the skeletal remains from Nørlund's excavations of the Herjolfsnes churchyard.[8] Dr. Hansen had already made up his mind that the last of the Greenlanders must have been in a sad state, so he found deformities and signs of malnutrition at every turn. Decades after Dr. Hansen's verdict we learned that a new examination of the same material, as well as analyses of bones from other Norse graveyards in Greenland, showed no such degeneration.[9]

Both North Atlantic exploration and major theories about Norse Greenland's demise will be discussed in the light of current research both in English and in the Scandinavian languages. My aim has been to create a bridge not only between the two language groups, but between the rather different scholarly traditions and methods governing Greenland research in particular and that of North Atlantic exploration and colonization in general. I want not to create further controversy in an already difficult field, but to encourage a broader approach to solving several vexing problems.

Historians of early North Atlantic exploration have a number of English and Continental texts and documents to guide them, as well as a wealth of early maps. I have used the same pool of material. Those who write about Norse Greenland must rely to a large extent on archaeological reports and minute philological analyses of the very few documents and Old Norse manuscripts that specifically concern Greenland. Danish and Norwegian scholars, to whom we are indebted for much of our present knowledge about medieval Greenland, have usually focused on that huge island as a unique problem—related to what went on elsewhere in the north at the same time, to be sure, but somewhat detached from English and American research on North Atlantic exploration.[10] Conversely, since many of the reports and analyses used in this study are in Danish, Norwegian, or Icelandic and not always accessible to English-speaking historians of late-fifteenth-century Atlantic exploration and colonization, some of the latter scholars have drawn conclusions based on insufficient knowledge of what their Scandinavian colleagues have uncovered.[11]

This is an appropriate time to ask new questions about several old problems, because we are at a crossroads of scholarly information and interpretation. Cartographical research has made great strides generally, and the
controversy over Yale University Library's so-called "Vinland Map" has focused attention on the area with which the present book is concerned.[12] Ice
core research, oceanographic research, botanical investigations, and other
studies have improved our understanding of the interplay between climatic
changes and the food resources in Greenland and its surrounding waters.
We also know much more than we did twenty years ago about the Black
Death and its consequences, and those same twenty years have seen the
publication of valuable source material as well as of important historical
analyses, of which I shall mention just a few.

The Discovery of the Sea by J. H. Parry, with its clear explanations of a
number of technical problems related to navigation, is one such valuable
tool, and in the difficult field of cartography no scholar should have to make
do without *Cartographical Innovations,* compiled by Helen Wallis and Arthur H. Robinson. Ólafur Halldórsson's *Grænland í Miðaldaritum* provides a useful collection and lucid analysis of medieval source material
about Greenland and deserves the frequent mention Gwyn Jones gives it in
his own new and expanded edition of *The Norse Atlantic Saga,* which despite some weaknesses is another good compendium for those interested
in early Atlantic exploration.

I have also made much use of the work of the British historian David
B. Quinn, whose careful research and scholarly courage have greatly advanced our understanding of North Atlantic exploration in the fifteenth
and sixteenth centuries. Samuel Eliot Morison, who in 1971 completely
rejected the idea of pre-Columbian European discovery of America in the
fifteenth century, earned a gentle rebuke from Quinn:[13]

This rejection of any pre-Columbian movement across the Atlantic apart from the
Norse voyages leaves the ocean peculiarly empty for many centuries, but it is a justi-
fiable reaction in an outstanding historian whose great merit is that he sees sharply
in black-and-white terms and is therefore uniquely qualified to expound what is
already known. He is perhaps too impatient to study the nuances of pre-
Columbian enterprise.

One of Quinn's recent gifts to those who want to study the nuances of
both pre- and post-Columbian Atlantic enterprise is a five-volume collection of documents pertaining to the discovery and early colonization of
North America.[14]

Documents are still turning up that shed light on English and Portuguese explorations in the North Atlantic in the decades just before and after
1500. Quinn noted in 1976 that much remains to be done in connection
with the early Newfoundland cod fishery; that French notarial records have

just been scratched in a few locations; and that "[t]he great treasurehouse in northern Spain is only now being investigated on behalf of the Canadian Archives department, and the first reports are promising. . . . Nothing has been done, to my knowledge, to locate and search similar records in Portugal."[15]

Valuable work on early Basque whaling in Newfoundland is being done by Selma H. Barkham and by Canadian archaeologists working both above and under water.[16] Archaeologists and anthropologists tracing indigenous populations in North America and Greenland have also dispelled many of the uncertainties with which scholars had to contend a generation ago, and Norwegian archaeologists have recently made discoveries about their own country's medieval culture and economy that also illuminate the Norse Greenlanders' situation.

Thirty years ago, after reasoning that bold and able sailors with sturdy ships and in perennial search of new land were bound to cross the Davis Strait once they had gained a foothold in Greenland, the Norwegian explorer Helge Ingstad succeeded in locating a Viking site at L'Anse aux Meadows in northern Newfoundland. Excavations at the site have settled a long-simmering controversy by proving conclusively that the Norse did pass that way around A.D. 1000.[17]

Fresh interest in Greenland Norse archaeological remains was kindled in 1990 when a mudslide revealed a deep-frozen and seemingly well preserved Norse farm in the southernmost reaches of the Western Settlement, the northernmost Greenland Norse colony.[18] In addition, the number of listed Eskimo and Norse archaeological sites in Greenland has increased greatly in recent years, in part because burgeoning sheep populations have grazed away the scrub obscuring many ruins.

It is a long step from knowing about these ruins to excavating them, however. Summers in Greenland are short, and permafrost often lurks right below the surface. A microwave scanner invented by Jeppe Møhl, capable of thawing the ground without damaging archaeological artifacts, is therefore an exciting technical development.[19] In some places, the land has subsided as much as five or six meters since the Norse settlement period, leaving large areas underwater, and the transportation of people, equipment, and artifacts in that huge island is dauntingly cumbersome.[20] In short, research in Greenland is extremely expensive, and Denmark is a small country. Our knowledge of the island's history may seem woefully inadequate, but it has been achieved through heroic efforts by modern investigators.

Poul Nørlund's 1924 account of his Herjolfsnes (Ikigaat) excavations should be required reading for anyone studying Norse Greenland. The report shows how Nørlund's quick thinking and the inventiveness of support staff back in Copenhagen salvaged an amazing collection of medieval gar-

FIG. 3. Herjolfsnes (Ikigaat), the Norsemen's first port-of-call in southwest Greenland. Source: Photograph by Hans Kapel, 1993, reproduced by permission.

ments, and it is so scrupulously detailed, right down to footnotes with polite disagreements with "authorities," that it is as useful today as when it was written. It also gives chilling examples of amateur archaeology. The problems caused by unskilled early investigators haunt modern Greenland archaeologists to this day.

At Herjolfsnes (Fig. 3), these problems began in the 1830s, when it became increasingly obvious that the site contained an ancient Norse graveyard. In 1839, a commercial assistant named Ove Kielsen excavated for two and a half days and found several coffins, a skull with blond hair still attached, a couple of wooden crosses, and some other articles, including a "sailor's jacket" which turned out to be part of a medieval man's gown. Kielsen was then given a stipend of £4, which enabled him to hire 24 men to dig for five more days and turn up a large part of the churchyard to a depth of two or three feet. Neither he nor the experts back in Copenhagen found the salvaged bits of garments, crosses, soapstone, and tombstones particularly interesting. Nørlund's 1921 expedition provided the first professional archaeological excavation of the site.[21] It is a wonder he found anything left to explore.

Until 1968, all archaeological investigations in Greenland were under Danish leadership. Since 1968, research decisions have been made jointly by the National Museum in Nuuk and the appropriate authorities in Copenhagen. Since 1969, there has been great emphasis on illuminating the cultural contacts between Eskimos and Europeans after Dano-Norwegian recolonization began in 1721 with the arrival of the Norwegian missionary Hans Egede, but during 1976–77 an Inuit-Norse Project carried out a study of selected medieval and (it was thought at the time) contemporaneous Norse and Eskimo sites in the the Nuuk region.[22] Jørgen Meldgaard, head of the Inuit Section at the Danish National Museum, led the project and considered it an opportunity to encourage cooperation between Norse and Inuit archaeologists as well as between scientists in such related fields as anthropology, zoology, and paleobotany. As it turned out, none of the Eskimo sites investigated could be ascribed to the Norse period or to the period immediately afterward, but much valuable information came from the excavations nevertheless, after both middens and structures had been analyzed according to the most modern scientific methods.[23]

It is expected that future excavations in both the Eastern and the Western Settlements will also benefit from close attention to stratigraphic research and comparisons with material from other sites, and that they will incorporate a wider variety of Norse sites than has generally been the case up to now. Archaeologists have in the past tended to concentrate on the churches and the largest, best-preserved farms. An investigation of the many smaller structures that have come to light in recent years will quite likely change some of our notions about the Norse Greenland economy.[24]

Refinements in radioactive carbon dating have also contributed significant information about Greenland's Norse and Inuit past.[25] Some earlier excavations have already been reevaluated and, for example, conclusions that the Danish archaeologist Therkel Mathiassen drew from his many investigations of old Eskimo sites have had to be revised. Evidently, he consistently assigned too early a date to his Thule ("Inussuk") finds.[26]

The Danish archaeologist and historian Jette Arneborg is currently heading a project to catalog the hundreds of radiocarbon datings that have been done on Greenland samples since about 1955. There is an urgent need for consistency in these datings, so in addition to describing the material itself, the database will include the find context, the datings, and the ratio of stable isotopes.[27]

Typological analyses have also led to a readjustment of dates. For instance, both Therkel Mathiassen and Morten Porsild thought that Thule antler arrowheads with screw tang belonged to the end of the sixteenth and early seventeenth centuries, but they are now thought to belong to the latter half of the seventeenth century and the first half of the eighteenth.[28]

About twenty years ago, Henrik M. Jansen complained in the Danish journal *Meddelelser om Grønland* that none of the Greenland excavations since 1945 had been published as a scholarly paper, and that it was impossible to write a history of medieval Norse Greenland based on currently available information.[29] The bad news is that articles on Greenland research appearing both before and after Jansen's plea have not always been as exhaustive or as profusely illustrated as in earlier days, and they have been published in such a wide variety of journals in Denmark, Norway, England, Canada, and the United States that they are not always easily accessible. The good news is that analyses of data acquired decades ago are now joining new technology and new research to provide additional knowledge.

In the spring of 1991, the Danish archaeologist C. L. Vebæk published "The Church Topography of the Eastern Settlement and the Excavation of the Benedictine Convent at Narsarsuaq in the Uunartoq Fjord," a detailed account of his excavations in 1945–46 and 1948, which he had no time to write up in full while he was a Keeper of Department I of the Danish National Museum from 1946 until 1983. Among the artifacts Vebæk recovered from the convent at Narsarsuaq was half a wooden disk that turned out to be a sun compass (pelorus or bearing dial) from the tenth century.[30] It took him about forty years to gain scholarly acceptance for his interpretation of this find, which changes our view of Viking navigation.[31]

Despite his illness, Vebæk managed to finish a report on his excavations in Vatnahverfi and a book about his research on Norse site Ø17a in the Eastern Settlement, the oldest dated farm found in Greenland, where he excavated in 1954, 1958, and 1962. He was also able to report on his work in the northernmost section of the Eastern Settlement, often referred to as the Middle Settlement.[32]

Jørgen Meldgaard of the National Museum is reviewing the many ancient artifacts collected in Greenland by the Danish scientist Morten Porsild some seventy to eighty years ago. In addition, we can look forward to the results of a reanalysis of all Norse skeletal remains found in Greenland and transported back to Copenhagen, and Hans Kapel at the Greenland Secretariat hopes that there will eventually be sufficient funding to undertake a thorough typological study of beads found in Greenland excavations.[33]

The fresh approaches made possible by modern science and technology form only a part of the observable changes in studies of Norse and Inuit settlers in medieval Greenland. Just as important is a gradual shift in our attitudes toward other societies and cultures. Perhaps the realization that our own technology and industrialization have at times placed us dangerously at odds with our natural environment enables us to acknowledge that non-industrial societies may be advanced in ways that serve their unique needs. The Norse, for instance, thoroughly understood the intricacies of rigging a ship; they developed a complex legal system; and they finely honed the portable art of poetry. And the Inuit evolved tools, weapons, clothing, and traditions that enabled them to survive in a very harsh environment.

Two traditional attitudes nevertheless dominate Norse Greenland research to this day and warrant a critical look. One, already mentioned, is the foregone conclusion that something happened to make the colony no longer viable. It is hard to find a serious analysis that does not assume a disaster of some kind. The other assumption, related to the first, is that the Greenlanders were unable to control their own destiny to any reasonable degree.

In my view, the archaeological and documentary evidence suggests that the Norse Greenlanders functioned well enough individually and communally to be able to make decisions as momentous as those their ancestors had made when settling Greenland.

The last chapters of this book will be devoted to considering late-phase evidence and to exploring the chief current theories about the Greenlanders' ultimate fate: a slow petering out in total isolation, slow or rapid emigration, or a final violent attack by outsiders. Early English and Portuguese voyages in those waters will likewise be discussed in detail, to see if it was more than a coincidence that the Norse Greenland colony came to an end just when North Atlantic exploration touched it closely. This material is so suggestive that it has led me to formulate a new hypothesis for the demise of Norse Greenland.

European maps and documents from the late fifteenth and early sixteenth centuries make it clear that Greenland became more isolated in the first few decades *after* 1500 than before. Those intent on exploiting the Newfoundland fisheries and other aspects of the New World soon learned the quickest and most reliable route, completely avoiding Greenland just when Denmark and Norway were in such economic and political turmoil that officialdom had only sporadic thoughts for an old colony far west in the ocean.

Archaeological and literary evidence suggests that a few Norse Greenland stragglers may have lasted well into the sixteenth century. It is easy to imagine the growing despair of those remaining few when—after a sudden but short-lived increase in navigation right past their front door—no more ships came.

Greenland and Vínland: North Atlantic Exploration Five Hundred Years Before the Cabot Voyages

The Norse colonies in Greenland were evidently successful from the start, and the settlers soon exploited areas far to the north and, probably, to the west of their farming settlements, on at least a seasonal or "commuting" basis. They may conceivably also have had one or more encampments in North America, however small. On this last subject the scant literary sources at our disposal are not very useful, though they do provide us with tantalizing information in other respects.

The medieval Icelandic work "Landnámabók" (The Book of the Settlements) principally addresses the early history of Iceland, but it also contains information about Greenland and the even newer lands to the west. Its genesis is not known. Among the five extant redactions are two complete, but rather different, versions—one in Sturla Thordarson's *Sturlubók* (approximate date 1260–80), and the other in *Hauksbók* (1306–8).[1] Other old Icelandic manuscript material still extant contains additional accounts of the colonization of Greenland, namely Chapter 6 of "Íslendingabók" (The Book of the Icelanders), which also mentions Vínland; "Grænlendinga saga" (The Saga of the Greenlanders); and "Eiriks saga rauða" (The Saga of Eirik the Red).[2]

The two latter sagas are often referred to jointly as the Vínland sagas, because they are our principal sources of information about the first Norse voyages to North America. These two sagas and "Íslendingabók" are not contemporaneous with the events they describe, so their historical accuracy is the subject of continuing debate.

The earliest of the three works, "Íslendingabók," was written by the historian Ári Thorgilsson the Learned (1068–1148) sometime before 1133 and most probably between 1122 and 1125, as a revision of a somewhat earlier work by him. Gwyn Jones finds "Íslendingabók" "critical, accurate, based on reliable sources of information, and much concerned with chronology" and gives equally high marks for accuracy to the two extant seventeenth-century transcripts from which we know it. Jakob Benediktsson also stresses the lengths to which Ári went in order to secure trustworthy information, but Olafur Halldorsson argues that "Íslendingabók" is not reliable about dates, and that Greenland was probably settled somewhat later than the commonly accepted date of 985 or 986.[3]

The antecedents of "Grænlendinga saga" and "Eiriks saga rauða" are difficult to establish. Among the contents of the late-fourteenth-century codex called *Flateyjarbók* is an expanded version of the saga of King Olaf Tryggvason (king of Norway 995–1000), in which there are three interpolations adding up to what we now call "Grænlendinga saga." We know nothing about the provenance or original date of the information in these three interpolations. Jon Johannesson reasons that the original saga was written down no later than about 1200, while Halldorsson is convinced that both "Grænlendinga saga" and "Eiriks saga rauða" were first written down at the beginning of the thirteenth century, although independently of each other. In 1986, Gwyn Jones agreed with Halldorsson's arguments. He had previously argued that "Eiriks saga rauða" was probably composed sometime after 1263 (a couple of generations after "Grænlendinga saga" was first committed to vellum), but that quite possibly there had also been an earlier version of "Eiriks saga rauða."[4]

"Eiriks saga rauða" emphasizes the part played by the Icelander Thorfinn Thordsson *karlsefni* ("The-Stuff-a-Man-Is-Made-of") in the exploration of North America, rather than the prowess of Leif Eiriksson and his brothers, and it is therefore sometimes called "þorfinns saga karlsefnis." Five seventeenth-century versions of this saga derive from two extant vellum codexes, *Hauksbók* and *Skálholtsbók*. The former collection was written for, and partly by, Hauk Erlendsson (d. 1334), who was a ninth-generation descendant of Karlsefni's and therefore tempted to polish the tale somewhat. The *Skálholtsbók* codex, while considerably more recent than *Hauksbók*, is thought to be the more reliable of the two. Halldorsson thinks that *Skálholtsbók* was quite possibly written by Olaf Loptsson around 1420.[5] This is an argument with potentially wide implications that will be discussed in Chapter Seven.

If we accept Halldorsson's judgment that both sagas were first written down in some form at the beginning of the thirteenth century, we are left with a gap of two centuries between the time of the Vínland voyages and the time the sagas were composed on the basis of oral tales still in circulation. The question then becomes, How reliable is oral history?

There are almost as many answers to this question as there are people asking it. It is a commonplace, however, that for as long as oral history is the main form in which a society passes on vital information, people's ability to remember may develop to a remarkable degree. That this was taken for granted among the medieval Norse is demonstrated by a runic "graffito" in the megalithic tomb at Maeshowe in the Orkneys. Inscribed with a bold and steady hand, and as clear when I saw them a few years ago as if they had been carved the previous year, the runes boast: "*þessar rúnar reist sá maðr er rynstr er fyrir vestan haf með þeirri öxi er átti Gaukr Trandilssonr fyrir sunnan land*" (These runes were carved by the best rune-master in the western ocean, with the axe that belonged to Gauk Trandilsson in the southern part of the country [Iceland]).[6]

It took the combined efforts of Hermann Pálsson and Aslak Liestøl to interpret the runes and to unravel the identity of the proud fellow who had seen no need to identify himself, so sure was he that those who could read the inscription would understand the reference. The runes had been carved during the winter of 1153–54 by Thorhall Ásgrimsson, the great-great-great-grandson of Ásgrim Ellida-Grimsson who killed Gauk Trandilsson, as told in Chapter 26 of "Njál's Saga." Liestøl notes: "In other words, Gaukr's axe had stayed in his slayer's family for six generations—about 200 years. This is a wonderful illustration of strong family tradition, and it is also a reminder to archaeologists of just *how* burials can be precisely dated by objects found in the tombs."[7]

Besides demonstrating the durability of oral tradition, this story shows the interdisciplinary nature of research on the medieval Norse. Archaeology and linguistic analysis combined can also tell us about the navigational and time-keeping devices that such Norsemen as Eirik the Red and his sons were likely to have possessed at the end of the tenth century, including the so-called sunstone or *sólarsteinn*. Knowing what skills and information we may assume on these long-distance travelers' part is essential to interpreting their exploits.

The Norse were experts at latitude sailing, guided by the sun and the North Star and aided by a wealth of knowledge about such natural phenomena as currents or bird and fish migrations, as well as by familiarity with the coastlines they sailed to and from. Gwyn Jones wrote in 1984 that it would be reasonable to assume that Norse mariners also used a simple but effective kind of bearing dial, "though the only indication of this is the half of a round disc of wood . . . discovered by C. L. Vebæk in 1948. . . . Had it been whole the notches would number thirty-two, offering a sophisticated division of the horizon reminiscent of the late Middle Ages rather

FIG. 4. Carl V. Sølver's reconstruction of the tenth-century bearing dial found by C. L. Vebæk at the Norse nunnery in Greenland. Drawing upon his knowledge of the sun's positions, a skipper could steer by the thin, radial shadow cast on the disk held level in his hand. For a detailed description, see Vebæk and Thirslund, *Viking Compass*. Source: Photograph by Søren Thirslund, reproduced by permission.

than Viking times, when an eight-point dial conforming to the eight named points of the Old Norse horizon would appear more natural."[8]

Jones is needlessly cautious here. The wooden sun compass (made of spruce or larch) that the Danish archaeologist C. L. Vebæk discovered at the Benedictine convent in Narsarsuaq has proved datable to the turn of the millennium, so it is fair to conjecture that Eirik the Red and his contemporaries had a similar compass at their disposal.[9] A bearing dial would not only have helped them set their course to a known destination, but more importantly would have been an aid in finding their way home from previously unknown places, as well as in giving others information about their discovery. For example, the cool demeanor ascribed to Bjarni Herjolfsson in Chapter 2 of "Grænlendinga saga" suggests that Bjarni knew approximately where to find Greenland—although neither he nor his crew had ever sailed that way before—and that he had no great problem returning to the proper latitude after having drifted off southwest to North America.

As Fig. 4 shows, the bearing dial was notched to correspond to east, north, south, and west, with several stages in between. It had a hole in the middle to accommodate a wooden stick, with a thinner twig pushed through it to cast a radial shadow on the disk, as on a sundial adjusted for telling time. Various other marks (gnomon curves) on this ancient sun compass show that its owner allowed for seasonal and other variations. Drawing upon his knowledge of the sun's positions, a skipper could stand aft with the disk held level in his hand and make the shadow cast by the twig point to the appropriate notch in the dial. The helmsman would then use this thin shadow to hold his course.[10] Kari Ellen Gade at Indiana University has suggested the need to take a fresh look at the current interpretations of the Old Norse word *sólarsteinn* or "sunstone" in the light of what we now know about this wooden bearing dial.[11]

In a summary of the controversy among Norse scholars over this word, Peter Foote presented an interesting theory that the *sólarsteinn* was a crystalline rock capable of polarizing the sun's rays so a mariner could take a solar observation even in cloudy weather. Though this is a seductive theory, and some other scholars have endorsed it, ultimately it fails to convince because it relies on material having little or nothing to do with the culture in question.[12] Foote's notion is not supported by Søren Thirslund at the Danish Maritime Museum at Elsinore, and Gwyn Jones is also among those who express doubts about it, although he offers no countersuggestion. As Jones sees it, the question is chiefly how early the Norse may be supposed to have known about such a stone's optical properties.[13]

Since an object may be made from more than one kind of substance—a beaker is a beaker whether it is made of wood, glass, pottery, pewter, or the ubiquitous Norse material soapstone—the Greenland bearing dial may have been a wooden version of an object more frequently made of soapstone. The latter material is cheap, easily carved, and will not burn if dropped into a fire, but it is also easily broken and sinks if it falls overboard.[14] A bearing dial incised on a carefully shaped crystal or other very hard rock, and incorporating the owner's or artist's accumulated knowledge of solar navigation, would be a treasure of the sort indicated by Foote, and it would certainly be round and smooth.

The King's Mirror, which was written around 1260, well before the advent of the mechanical clock, suggests a close association in the medieval northern mind between the time of day and the points of the compass:[15]

As to how long an hour should be I can give you definite information, for there should be twenty-four hours in . . . a night and a day, while the sun courses through the eight chief points of the sky: and according to right reckoning the sun will pass through each division in three hours of the day.

Conceivably, the word *sólarsteinn* fell into disuse when the mechanical clock and the magnetic compass came into fairly general use later in the fifteenth century, and people no longer relied on the sun's radial shadow on a disk. Had this word been used to describe a burning-crystal or a magnifier of some kind, as Foote suggests, the linguistically conservative Icelanders would probably have retained the word *sólarsteinn* along with the perennially useful object itself. A dual interpretation of *sólarsteinn* does not contradict the information in the *þáttr* quoted by Foote, according to which Saint Olaf was able to get a *geisli* (beam, ray, or radial) from his *sólarsteinn* even in overcast weather.[16] In a saga so intent on glorifying King Olaf Haraldsson, we should not wonder at such an example of his prowess; we are probably supposed to marvel at the king's ability to defy the weather rather than at the usefulness of his *sólarsteinn*.

In a dial used on land to tell time by an extension of the same knowledge employed in the solar compass, stone would be far preferable to wood. Significantly, Icelandic church inventories list *sólarsteinn* several times, the earliest in 1318 and the latest in a 1408 inventory from Reynistead nunnery.[17] The reason a *sólarsteinn* appears among cups, bed linen, vestments, and other useful and valuable articles is probably that it is any kind of sundial—either a bearing dial or a device for telling time—usually made of stone, but occasionally of wood. In religious establishments, with their need to keep track of the time for prayers, a good sundial would have been both valuable and useful; we see the close connection between time-keeping and church rituals in the more modern Icelandic word *klukka*, which means both "bell" and "clock."

The ability both to take a bearing from the sun's position and to tell time by the sun was quite likely a part of the knowledge Eirik the Red and his followers carried with them to Greenland; it may have been common even as early as when (according to both "Grænlendinga saga" and "Eiriks saga rauða") Eirik the Red and his father Thorvald Ásvaldsson left their home in southwestern Norway sometime in the second half of the tenth century "because of some killings" and went to Iceland.[18]

By that time, Iceland had been settled by the Norse for the better part of a century. Eirik and his father supposedly had to make do with hardscrabble land, so that when Eirik married the well-connected Thjodhild Jörundsdaughter after his father's death, he went to live with her in the more fertile Haukadale. After a couple more killings (his temper appears to have matched his hair color) he was forced out of Haukadale and eventually settled on one of the many windblown islands in nearby Breidafjord.[19]

In a neighborly gesture, he lent his ornamented high seat posts to a man named Thorgest, who refused to return them when Eirik wanted them back. The ensuing deadly quarrel caused Eirik to be made an outlaw for three years. Determined to put his period of banishment to good use, he readied his ship and crew and sailed west to explore the land and islands Gunnbjörn Ulfsson had sighted when his ship drifted off course sometime in the first half of the tenth century.[20] Gunnbjörn's family also lived in northwestern Iceland, and he and Eirik the Red were both descendants in the fifth generation of the Norwegian chieftain Öxna-Thorir, brother of the Viking Nadd-Odd who reportedly had been blown off course to Iceland in the days before its colonization.[21]

The islands Gunnbjörn had sighted were named Gunnbjarnarskerries after him. We do not know exactly which islands they were, except that they lay off the east coast of Greenland, probably in the Ammassalik area. This impression is strengthened by the story about the Icelander Snæbjörn Galti, who reportedly went west to "Gunnbjarnarskerries" around 978 and was killed there by a shipmate under conditions that smack strongly of the inhospitable climate on the east coast.[22] This Snæbjörn Galti and Eirik the Red's wife, Thjodhild, were both great-grandchildren of another renowned traveler, Eyvind the Easterner. Furthermore, Snæbjörn, Thjodhild, and Eirik had all been living in the same part of Iceland at about the same time. Given Gunnbjörn's and Snæbjörn's kinship with Eirik the Red and his wife, we should probably assume that when Eirik in his turn set out for "Gunn-bjarnarskerries," he carried much family sailing lore in his head and was fairly confident of where he was heading.

According to both "Grænlendinga saga" and "Eiriks saga rauða," Eirik chose the alluring name "Greenland" for the country he found beyond "Gunnbjarnarskerries" because it would make people want to go there. If the story is true, the stratagem must have worked, for the summer after Eirik returned to Iceland, he led a colonizing expedition said to have numbered 25 ships, fourteen of which made it to their destination.[23]

Eirik the Red built his chieftain's seat Brattahlid ("Steep Slope") in prime pastureland on the western shore of the inner Eiriksfjord, or Tunulli-arfik as it is now called. The site (Fig. 5), which eventually developed into a large complex of at least three farms, has been the subject of several excavations, each one demonstrating that Brattahlid was important in the Eastern Settlement from the very beginning until the colony ceased to function.[24]

The other survivors also made their homes at the heads of sheltered

F I G. 5. Eirik the Red's property at Brattahlid in the Eastern Settlement. Source: Photograph by Jette Arneborg, 1980, reproduced by permission.

fjords in southwestern Greenland. Located between latitudes 60°N and approximately 61°30′N, the Eastern Settlement region lies far enough south of Iceland to provide additional hours of winter daylight while still giving the settlers the "white" summer nights they were used to. The settlers found that Eirik had not lied—green pastures did await their seasick, hungry livestock. Thick willow scrub provided both fodder and fuel; in many places there were sizable groves of birch and rowan trees; and bluebells, buttercups, and fireweed brightened the summer landscape just as they do now. In the rivers swam fat char; in the sea were fish and seal for the taking along with the occasional whale; and birds of sea and land provided eggs, meat, and feathers. Large herds of reindeer were a bonanza to people who came from Iceland, where there are no large land animals. Soon the colonizers found their way to seasonal hunting grounds where walrus, narwhal, and polar bears provided them with valuable commodities for trade. In short, the newcomers must have felt well rewarded for their dangerous voyage, especially since they probably had not turned their backs on the best farmland in Iceland.

The rather continental climate at the heads of the Greenland fjords alternates brief and reasonably warm summers with long and icebound winters, but the Norse were no strangers to harsh seasons. Furthermore, the colonizers arrived at what we now know was a climatically optimal time in Greenland, and they appear to have had the country to themselves when they came. The first colonizers in Iceland had been equally fortunate, having apparently been preceded by only a few Irish monks.[25] The Norse settlers' lack of competition for homesteads in both cases is worth noting, for it contrasts sharply with what they experienced when they reached North America a few years after they had arrived in Greenland.

Ári Thorgilsson's "Íslendingabók" says that Eirik and his people found only ruins and remnants of stone tools and boats from the *Skrælings*—a contemptuous term, loosely translatable as "scruffy wimps," which the Norse used to describe the natives of Greenland and North America. These mementos were presumably left behind by the Dorset Eskimos, who deserted South Greenland around A.D. 900 and were eventually replaced by the Thule Eskimos from whom the modern Greenlanders are descended. But long before the Thule culture reached the Norse settlements in the south, the Norsemen had encountered them, and probably some remaining Dorset people, when they went far north to hunt.[26] This topic will be discussed in more detail later in this chapter, in conjunction with the settlers' push far to the north of their second colony, the so-called Western Settlement.

The small, but initially thriving Western Settlement must have come into existence at about the same time as the Eastern Settlement. Radiocar-

FIG. 6. The site of the Norse farm Sandnes (V51) in the Western Settlement. Source: Photograph by Jette Arneborg, 1984, reproduced by permission.

bon (C-14) datings from the Norse farms at Niaquusat and Nipaatsoq in the Nuuk district show that those farms had already been built by about A.D. 1000, and the midden at Niaquusat in particular proved very deep.[27]

Right from the start, the principal farm in the Western Settlement appears to have been Sandnes (Kilaarsarfik) at the sheltered head of Ameralik fjord. Like Eirik the Red's farm Brattahlid in the Eastern Settlement, Sandnes has been excavated several times in this century, and a later chapter will recount some of the results in greater detail.[28] Here we need note only that the region around Sandnes farm was both fertile and lovely (Fig. 6), and that the Norse colonists, with their eye for usable land, would surely have wasted no time in spotting it.

It may seem odd that with such favorable conditions from the start— plenty of pasturage in both settlements, a comparatively benign climate, and no competing Inuit in the neighborhood—the push westward across the Davis Strait continued almost immediately. Most likely, Leif Eiriksson and his brothers were propelled by the lure of forests as well as by the momentum of success and curiosity. Helge Ingstad, who has explored both sides of the Davis Strait in a small craft, writes:[29]

Near Holsteinborg [Holsteinsborg] the Davis Strait is at its narrowest, no more than 200 sea-miles across, and a crew would not need to sail far out to sea before sighting the lofty mountains of Baffin Land. . . . From the higher mountains near Holsteinborg one may also glimpse the loom of the Cumberland Peninsula. In short, it is more than probable that at quite an early period the Norsemen had knowledge of the coasts of Baffin Land, and these pointed the way to other parts of North America.

"Grænlendinga saga" tells us that Leif Eiriksson successfully retraced an involuntary voyage made by Bjarni Herjolfsson several years earlier.[30] In other words, the Norse appear to have first spotted North America through a combination of accident and inevitability. Vikings venturing farther and farther into the Atlantic, in fair weather and foul, had also sighted Iceland and Greenland by chance before those countries were methodically explored and settled. The history of fifteenth- and early-sixteenth-century Atlantic exploration is likewise dotted with tales of vaguely known lands and islands that became the objects of systematic exploration. There is nothing surprising in this. It would be far stranger if at any point in history a party of explorers had set out to investigate something they could not reasonably have expected to find.

Another similarity between the explorations of Iceland and Greenland and the first Norse investigations of the New World is that all were spearheaded by people with close local and familial ties to one another, who were able to keep potentially lucrative information about new lands within the confines of a small group at first. Again, this pattern is equally evident among the late-fifteenth- and early-sixteenth-century explorers of the North Atlantic who will be discussed in later chapters.

The first expanse of coastline Leif and his crew saw on the other side was an unprepossessing display of rocks and glaciers, now assumed to have been Baffin Island. They named it Helluland or "Slab-Land."[31] Rocks and ice were in good supply back home in Greenland, so the party kept heading south. The next stretch of land was a more welcome sight, with vast forests inland from sandy beaches. This the Norse named Markland, or "Forest Land"—presumably Labrador south of Hamilton Inlet.[32] The present limit for all forests on the northeastern coast of America is at 58°N, Napartok Bay, and is practically identical with the +10°C July isotherm.[33]

According to "Grænlendinga saga," Leif said about the second land he found: *"Af kostum skal þessu landi nafn gefa ok kalla Markland* (I'll name this country for its advantages and call it Forest-Land)." Concerning the third land, the saga notes: *"Ok gaf Leifr nafn landinu eptir landkostum ok kallaði Vínland* (And Leif named the country for its quality [produce] and called it Wineland)."[34] Put differently, Markland and Vínland were named for the *best* those two areas had to offer, not for their *only* qualities.

There is no agreement concerning either the location of Vínland or

Leif's ostensible reason for giving that name to the third country he sighted. The Vínland sagas were written over two hundred years after the events they tell about, and the accounts of these early voyages show the writers grappling with descriptions of places they had never seen and for which they had no maps. The old Norse language did not even have a word for maps.[35]

The notion that the first syllable was *vin* with a short vowel (meaning "green meadow") has been so thoroughly discarded that we are left with the incontrovertible, long-vowelled *vín* or "wine."[36] Archaeological investigations begun by Helge and Anne Stine Ingstad proved beyond any doubt that the site they found at L'Anse aux Meadows on northern Newfoundland Island was Norse and C-14 datable to around A.D. 1000, and that it therefore may well have comprised the wintering houses built by Leif and used by his immediate successors in those waters.[37] The site's location is strategically perfect, but not by any stretch of the imagination is it in a lush, grape-growing region, even allowing for the warmer climate a thousand years ago. As late as in the 1530s, the explorer Jacques Cartier claimed to have found grapes on both sides of the St. Lawrence; today it is considered necessary to look south of the 45th parallel to find wild grapes.[38] As for the "self-sown wheat" that Leif Eiriksson found in Vínland according to "Eiriks saga" (and to which Adam of Bremen alluded in his description of the "island" Vínland), some scholars think the grain was lyme grass seeds, while others refer to the wild "corn" or rice (*Zizania aquatica*) that Cartier found on various islands in the Gulf of St. Lawrence, and that grows as far north as Newfoundland.[39]

Discoveries recently made by Canadian archaeologists should soon settle the question of what region Leif had in mind when he so boldly named it Vínland. Continued excavations at the L'Anse aux Meadows site have revealed large amounts of storage space and specialized work areas of the kind normally associated with transshipping stations. This arrangement suggests that during the Norsemen's brief stay here, they brought in valuable goods from elsewhere and stored them until they could be shipped back to Greenland. We now know that "elsewhere" was at least as far down the American coast as the south shore of the St. Lawrence, for in the Norse artifacts concentration layer were three butternuts (*Juglans cinerea*, also known as "white walnut"), as well as a burl of butternut wood worked with metal tools. The butternut tree has never grown north of the St. Lawrence Valley and northeastern New Brunswick, and its northern limit in fact corresponds quite well with that of North American wild grapes.[40]

It is well to remember that Leif's father was said to have named *his* country "Greenland" on what many consider flimsy grounds. Yet that huge island is green in places if one keeps looking. The sagas make it clear that the Norse also kept looking when they found themselves in North America. Most likely, they explored for quite a distance down the mainland coast and some way up the St. Lawrence, just as Eirik the Red had explored considerable stretches of Greenland before deciding to settle there.[41]

The presence of wild grain and of grapes were not the only attractions in Leif's Vínland. "Grænlendinga saga" notes that the days there were satisfyingly long even at midwinter: "*Sól hafði þar eyktar stað ok dagmála stað um skammdegi*."[42] Magnusson and Pálsson translate this as: "On the shortest day of the year, the sun was already up by 9 A.M. and did not set until after 3 P.M." They note that this would locate Vínland between 40°N and 50°N, or anywhere between New Jersey and the Gulf of St. Lawrence. Gwyn Jones cautiously translates the passage as: "On the shortest day of winter the sun was visible in the middle of the afternoon as well as at breakfast time." In a footnote he gives the literal translation: "The sun had there *eyktarstað* and *dagmálastað* on the shortest day (or days)."[43]

The word *stað* ("place" or "location") is worth noting in this passage from "Grænlendinga saga" from which so many scholars have tried to wrest information about the latitude of Vínland. Jones says: "The Norsemen had no clock time in the early eleventh century, but the period indicated was more or less that extending three hours each side of noon."[44] But if the Norse of a thousand years ago could both tell approximate time and take their bearings by means of sundials, *stað* could just as easily mean "location on the dial" as "location on the horizon."

Leif's account of what he had found led his brother Thorvald to organize a new expedition.[45] He and his men made it safely across the Davis Strait and had sufficiently detailed sailing directions to find Leif's houses, where they wintered. Two summers were spent in exploring, and all was well until they ran into Skrælings. The Native Americans in that general region a thousand years ago were the ancestors of the Micmacs of New Brunswick, the Beothuk of Newfoundland, and the Montaignais of southern Labrador. There may also have been some Dorset Eskimos in the more northerly parts, especially during summer hunting. Helge Ingstad believes that Dorset Eskimos coexisted with the Beothuk in Newfoundland at the time of the first Vínland voyages, but veteran Canadian archaeologist Robert McGhee notes: "It seems certain that the Dorset people had abandoned Newfoundland and southern Labrador by the time of the Norse explorations." Two things appear clear, however: there were no Native Americans actually living at the L'Anse aux Meadows site while the Norsemen used it, and the Skrælings referred to in the Vínland sagas were not Inuit.[46]

The Norsemen conscientiously dispatched eight of the first nine Skrælings they saw, but the ninth got away, and the friends to whom he presumably told his tale turned out to be more numerous and adept at fighting than the Greenlanders had counted on. Both "Grænlendinga saga" and "Eiriks saga rauða" agree that Thorvald Eiriksson was killed and buried in the New World. The latter saga, however, reports in the fine tradition of medieval travelers' tales that the malefactor was a Uniped, not a Skræling.[47]

The voyage of the third Eiriksson, Thorstein, evidently was abortive. The accounts in "Grænlendinga saga" and "Eiriks saga rauða" differ, but in both we are told that Thorstein drifted about in fog all summer and barely made it ashore back in the Western Settlement. And there he died, leaving a young widow named Gudrid Thorbjarnardaughter.[48]

Through Gudrid, Sandnes farm in the Western Settlement joins Brattahlid as a key location in the saga of North American exploration, for Thorstein Eiriksson apparently owned a half share of Sandnes, which Gudrid would have inherited.[49] When Nørlund and Roussell excavated at Sandnes in the 1930s, they found near the churchyard an arrowhead so far unknown in Greenland Eskimo finds, but shaped rather like those used by Indians in Labrador and a little farther south. It is unlikely that there was a church at Sandnes when the earliest Vínland explorers passed through the farm, but McGhee thinks that because the style is "consistent with that of points used by the Indians of southern Labrador and Newfoundland in the period between A.D. 1000 and 1500," this arrowhead may well be evidence of later Norse contact with the New World. Its ethnic origin is nevertheless uncertain, and the chert from which it is made could also be Greenlandic, according to Jette Arneborg.[50]

Gudrid returned south to her in-laws at Brattahlid, where she met the wealthy Icelandic merchant Thorfinn Thordsson Karlsefni. Karlsefni arrived with grain, malt, and other luxuries with which to tempt the Greenlanders, as well as with a reputation for doughtiness and excellent family connections, and he married the still young and attractive Gudrid. Together, they headed another Vínland expedition setting out from Brattahlid, this time with colonizers on board. Gudrid is said to have been one of only five women on that expedition.[51] They may well have broken their voyage at her Sandnes farm to take on fresh provisions and livestock before heading north toward Disko Island and then west, following the ocean current as it veers away from the Greenland coast and eventually heads south along the North American coast.

There is little point here in speculating on exactly where Karlsefni, Gudrid, and the others went during the couple of years they spent in the New World. As with the voyages of Leif and Thorvald, it is more useful to focus on the evident variety of locations and situations experienced by Karlsefni and his colonizing party. They clearly spared no effort in scouting for attractive havens for themselves and the animals they had brought.

The colonists appear to have managed fairly well until repeated Skræling attacks made them decide to pack up and sail home. This decision surely was the better part of wisdom for so few people far away from help of any kind. And it was early days yet in the Greenland colonies; there cannot have been a need for more land at any cost. In addition, Gudrid had given birth to a son in the New World, and Karlsefni's family farm in the fertile Skagafjord region of northern Iceland must have seemed a more promising patrimony for his little Snorri than the doubtful possibilities of Vínland.

It would be a mistake to regard this colonizing venture as a total failure, for the settlers stayed long enough and traveled around enough to collect priceless information about Greenland's nearest neighbor to the west—information that there is every reason to believe was cherished and used, rather than promptly forgotten.

After wintering in Greenland on their return, Karlsefni, Gudrid, and their small son went to Norway for a year and then settled for good in northern Iceland.[52] What they did with Sandnes farm is not known, but the most likely arrangement would have been for Leif Eiriksson to buy it. Leif would have known the value of the farm itself, and he was better able than anyone to appreciate its strategic position, both for northern hunting and for the further voyages we know took place across the Davis Strait to Markland and possibly farther south.

Karlsefni's descendants kept his fame alive, but we do not know that they ever again sailed for the sake of gain from Iceland to the coasts *beyond* Greenland. It was easier for the Icelanders to go to Norway for lumber as well as for commodities the New World could not provide at all. Also, for reasons that will be discussed in later chapters, wealthy and ambitious Icelanders became increasingly drawn into the orbit of Norwegian power politics and in the end appear to have lost all interest in their Greenland cousins.

While detailed sailing directions to North America may have faded among most Icelanders, the lore of so many different and wonderful lands in the far western ocean survived and gave rise to tales of such fabled countries as Hvítramannaland ("White Men's Country"), supposedly near "Vínland the Good" and said to have been involuntarily visited around the year 983 by Ári Marsson, another kinsman of Eirik the Red's wife Thjodhild.[53] For as long as Iceland kept in touch with Greenland, and the Greenlanders continued to cross the Davis Strait, the Icelanders would have heard from their Greenland friends about such actual rather than fanciful places as Markland.

The latest documentary evidence we have for a voyage to Markland is in the *Icelandic Annals*, a series of annals begun at the end of the thirteenth century, using Bede's chronological system and a number of foreign sources as well as native Icelandic ones.[54] The "Skálholt Annals" (echoed here by "Gottskálk's Annals" and "Flatey Annals") note that in 1347, a storm-battered small ship from Greenland fetched up at Straumey in Iceland with a crew of seventeen or eighteen. The ship had lost its anchor and been driven off course on its way back from Markland. No further explanation for its recent destination was given in the annals, quite likely because none was needed. Jette Arneborg suggests that this 1347 voyage may have been a sign that the Greenland Norse had resumed Markland voyages because they now were desperate for lumber.[55]

Some results from analyses of wood types in archaeological material from Norse Greenland excavations were published in 1993. They suggest that the Greenlanders had *never stopped* crossing the Davis Strait for lumber. Of ten specimens of ship's parts found in the Western and Eastern settlements, six were found to have been made of larch (*Larix*), two of spruce (*Picea*), and two of either spruce or larch. While plentiful elsewhere in the northern hemisphere, neither species grew in Greenland, and the larch is not indigenous to Norway. The authors of the 1993 article conclude "that the ship's parts of larch and spruce were probably made out of Siberian driftwood, while it is less likely that the wood employed was felled in Markland (Labrador) or in Vinland (Newfoundland)."[56]

The trouble with logs long soaked in salt water, however, is that they lose their resilience and become hard to work with.[57] They would therefore have been less desirable for shipbuilding than seasoned lumber that could be made to take a proper curve. The Greenlanders had every reason to retrace their route at least as far as to Markland to cut their own gratis lumber, especially for shipbuilding, but also for other uses. They did not skimp on wood when it was available; for example, the newly discovered site in the Western Settlement now being excavated shows lavish use of both shaped wood and logs.[58] Barring a costly shipload all the way from Norway, the only decent-sized logs at the Greenlanders' disposal were those washed up by the sea—or those known to be available across the Davis Strait.

There are other compelling reasons for believing that the Greenland Norse continued their voyages across the Davis Strait for several centuries once they were familiar both with the route and with the rewards waiting on the other side. The voyage itself was also apt to be lucrative, for it would have taken the Greenland Norse through the summer hunting and fishing grounds which they called Norðrseta. This name is generally seen as referring to the area from the present-day Holsteinsborg District north to the Nussuaq Peninsula, whose rich wildlife was as vital to the Eskimos as to

the Norse hunters from both settlements.[59] This seems too limited an interpretation. Our chief sources of information about Norðrseta—Björn Jonsson from Skardsá (*Annálar,* ca. 1643) and the anonymously compiled
Grænlandsannáll (ca. 1623)—supply two names in the northernmost
reaches of Norðrseta: "*Greipar*" (a "grip" or a span connecting two points,
as between forefinger and thumb) and "*Króksfjarðarheiði*" (the "hooked-
fjord-plains" or "hooked-fjord-wilderness"), and we are told about this region that "*Grænlands var þar bygðar sporðr*" ("this was Greenland's end
[tail]").[60] Vaigat, which stretches in a splendid curve right above Disko Island, has long been considered the Norse hunters' "*Króksfjarðarheiði.*" But
"*Greipar*"—which connotes a curved stretch bridging two points and capable of exerting pressure—may well refer to the ice closing off the upper
Davis Strait (see Fig. 7). It would force a sailing ship to head west along
its U-shaped curve to Baffin Island, instead of continuing north along the
Greenland coast with the risk of being caught in the chilly, crushing grip
of that vast plain of ice connecting Greenland with North America. Quite
possibly the Norse extended their walrus hunts clear across the Davis Strait,
which they had to cross anyway in order to obtain wood for shipbuilding
and—very likely—for charcoal with which to smelt bog iron into crude
"blooms" subsequently brought back to Greenland.

A 1993 report on the Meta Incognita Project's investigations of the Baffin Island sites associated with Martin Frobisher's three voyages (1576–78)
noted two archaeological riddles of special interest to Norse scholars. One
problem was posed by several crude iron blooms of the type obtained from
medieval hearth furnaces. Now scientifically studied for the first time since
Charles Francis Hall found the initial specimens in 1860–61, these blooms
have been carbon-dated to a period coinciding with Norse habitation in
Greenland. Since the publication of the 1993 study, additional examination of one bloom showed that Frobisher's men had attempted to resmelt
it with coal, succeeding only in giving a high sulfur content to the bloom
and making it more brittle. This also interfered with the carbon-dating of
the bloom's outer layers. The Smithsonian team now advises using the
bloom's core readings, which date the bloom to the first half of the fifteenth century.[61]

In the absence of convincing archaeological and literary evidence to the
contrary, I find it unlikely that the technologically advanced Frobisher party
took up precious cargo space with crude iron lumps from England, which
they then subjected to a treatment that rendered the iron brittle and useless.
The express purpose of Frobisher's last two voyages was to find ore containing precious metals, so it is more probable that Frobisher's men found
these strange, heavy rocks already on the site and—out of curiosity—shat-
tered one and tried to smelt others. This explanation still does not tell us

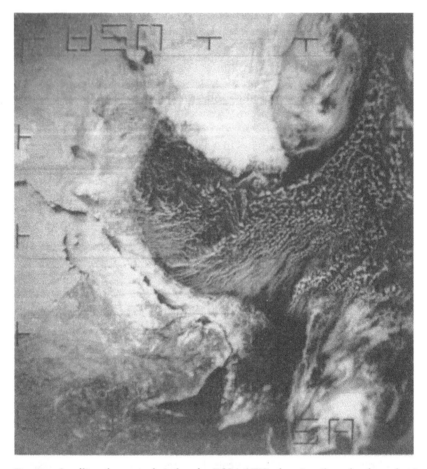

FIG. 7. Satellite photograph (taken by ESSA-VIII) showing Greenland south of 72°N, with the waters between Iceland and Greenland as well as the Davis Strait and the coast of Labrador south to the Gulf of St. Lawrence. Source: Greenland Ice Patrol, reproduced with permission.

who had left the blooms behind, however, and the thin soil cover on the sites used by Frobisher's three expeditions has not yielded up any traditional Norse objects that might clear up the problem. Instead, American and Canadian archaeologists found another puzzle.

Near the ruin of an ancient Dorset Eskimo winter house on Willows Island, a string of 25 walrus mandibles protruded from the soil near an alignment of whale vertebrae. All the teeth had been extracted from the mandibles before they were nestled tightly together, tooth side up, in an east-west alignment five meters long. At a site dubbed "Anvil Cove" archaeologists discovered another partially buried alignment of walrus mandibles, again with all the teeth extracted. This neatly arranged series of 95 walrus jaws stretched over about 25 meters. Hall had also found such a deliberate arrangement of walrus mandibles in 1861 and had asked his Inuit companions what they knew about this feature, but they had no idea. The Smithsonian expedition was made none the wiser in 1991—Fitzhugh observes that "[t]hese unusual bone deposits appear to represent a previously undescribed form of Thule or Dorset hunting ritual."[62]

The archaeological literature on Greenland has interesting parallels to both the iron blooms and the walrus jaws encountered in Baffin Island and provides reason to suppose that the answer to the riddles arising from these discoveries may lie in the Norse Greenlanders' continued voyages across the Davis Strait in search of the things their economy cried out for: iron, wood, furs, and walrus products. When Poul Nørlund and his team excavated the Norse Greenland bishop's former site at Gardar (Eastern Settlement), they found a number of walrus skulls in and around the church. Buried directly outside the east end of the chancel, in fill which the Norse had deliberately brought in to create good burial soil, were twenty or more walrus skulls with their teeth extracted. According to Nørlund, they "lay so closely together and at such a uniform depth that they would seem to have been buried with a purpose. . . . It is perhaps not impossible that religious or demoniacal ideas have been attached to these strange animals . . . hunted so far away from the settlement and . . . of such great value to the population."[63] These carefully arranged walrus jaws had so obviously been buried by the Norse and not by Eskimos that the existence of ritualistically buried walrus jaws on the American side may conceivably also be ascribed to Norse Greenland hunters.

During those Gardar excavations, a smithy and many pieces of slag were also uncovered. Although similar finds have been made at innumerable Greenland Norse sites both before and after 1926, the archaeologists have yet to discover a hearth pit for the actual smelting of iron from bog ore according to well-known medieval practice in both Norway and Iceland. After examining the slag pieces from Gardar and a couple of nearby sites and finding them commensurate with slag resulting from the further refinement of crude iron blooms, the Danish scientist Niels Nielsen concluded that the Norse Greenlanders must have smelted their own bog ore in hearth pits, because it would have made absolutely no sense to import unworked blooms from Norway or Iceland to a country as short of fuel as Greenland appeared to him to have been. We now know that there are no iron bogs in Greenland, so the Norse Greenlanders would have had to import the blooms they reforged in Greenland. North America's resources were a great deal closer than those of Norway.[64]

Since Nielsen's time, a Norse hearth pit furnace has been uncovered on the American side of the Davis Strait, at the Viking site Helge and Anne Stine Ingstad discovered at L'Anse aux Meadows in Newfoundland.[65] In this case, the Norse had houses to shelter them through the winter season and would have had ample time to refine the crude blooms on the spot, but this would not have been true of seasonal voyagers between Greenland and America. By the time they had burned the charcoal and produced one or more crude blooms from bog iron, it would be time to head back home during the brief season when the Davis Strait was reasonably navigable. Safely back in Greenland, a crew could then smash the brittle iron bloom and share out or trade the pieces for further refinement and use in home forges. The Baffin Island blooms may bear witness to at least one Norse ship that did not return safely to Greenland.

It would have been natural for the Greenlanders to increase their profit on voyages for lumber, iron, and walrus by hunting North American land animals such as marten, lynx, black bear, and wolverine. Ingstad and others have therefore reasoned that the list of desirable Greenland produce which the Norwegian Archbishop Erik Valkendorf drew up around 1516, in anticipation of a Greenland voyage that came to nothing, was based on real knowledge of products the Greenlanders had brought to Bergen in their trading heyday. We should be careful about reading too much into Valkendorf's list, however. Lars Hamre is probably closer to the mark when he notes that Valkendorf simply imagined Greenland as a very rich country from which one might reasonably expect not only cod, salmon, walrus ivory, and seal blubber, but also the various kinds of valuable furs obtained from Russia and northernmost Norway, both of which countries were still seen by Valkendorf and his contemporaries as part of a continuous landmass that included Greenland.[66] Silver and gold were also on the archbishop's list—quite in keeping with the high hopes of sixteenth-century explorers, but not with the reality known to the Greenlanders at any point.

Almost as good as gold and silver, however, were the precious furs, walrus ivory, and other commodities for which the Greenlanders quickly became known. As noted above, Sandnes farm in the Western Settlement was strategically located for activities both in the Norðrseta region (the region from the present-day Holsteinsborg district north to the Nussuaq Peninsula) and in North America. It is therefore not hard to believe the mid-fourteenth-century Norwegian priest Ivar Bárdarson, who said about Sandnes church ("Stensnes kircke") that for a while it had been a cathedral and a bishop's seat. This statement gave rise to the speculation, still unproved, that the Icelander Eirik Gnupsson *upsi*, who left Iceland to serve as Greenland's first bishop in 1112, had his seat at Sandnes church—a speculation the Danish archaeologist Aage Roussell fueled by tentatively connecting Bishop Eirik with an exceptionally ornate chair arm he found in one of the very early layers at Sandnes.[67] "Gottskálk's Annals" say that "*Eirik Grænlendinga byskup leitade Vínlands* (Bishop Eirik went in search of Vínland)" in 1121. No news of Bishop Eirik was recorded after that, but the same annals note that three years later, in 1124, Arnald was consecrated Bishop of Greenland.[68] We are left with the impression that Eirik Gnupsson had not resumed his episcopal duties in Greenland.

The mystery surrounding Bishop Eirik and Vínland has set imaginations roaming as freely as the Norsemen's ships. First of all, there is the verb *leitade* to contend with. *At leita* means "to go in search of" or "to go and find" and is just as ambiguous in Old Norse as it is in modern English. We are faced with a similar riddle in "Laurentius's Saga": "*Á öðru ári prestdóms sira Lafranz gjörðist þat til tíðinda, at Eirekr konúngr sendi Hrólf til Íslands, at leita Nyjalands* (It happened in the second year *sira* Laurentius was bishop, that King Eirik sent Hrolf to Iceland to go and find New-Country)."[69] Hrolf died in 1295, evidently without having carried out his errand, and leaving geographers with yet another vague story of islands or lands west in the ocean.

Did Bishop Eirik sail off searching for a Shangri-la he had only heard mentioned, or did he know where he was going? Given the likelihood that sailings from Greenland to North America had continued after Karlsefni abandoned his attempt to colonize Vínland, it is reasonable to suppose that the bishop had a more concrete destination than poor Hrolf, and that he cannot have had unrealistic expectations from such a voyage if he lived among people who on occasion crossed the Davis Strait themselves.

The next question must therefore be, Why would Bishop Eirik want to go to Vínland? He may have wanted to increase his income by means of lumber and fine American furs, for whether he lived in the Western or Eastern Settlement, the local farmers probably did not pamper him, if the experience of early Icelandic bishops is anything to go by. But how could he turn his back on spiritual sheep who must have been so badly in need of a shepherd's care?

There have been suggestions that Bishop Eirik's flock included some strays in the New World, and that these were the reason for his voyage.[70] Such ideas are easily hatched and just as easily smothered, particularly in a prevailing climate of doubt about further Norse attempts to settle in the New World. Before dismissing the possibility altogether, let us look at some arguments advanced by the Norwegian medievalist Eirik Vandvik in connection with a letter Pope Alexander III (r. 1159–81) wrote to the Norwegian archbishop in Trondheim. The archbishop had evidently asked how to apply the church's restrictions on consanguinity in marriage to a small population living in extreme isolation. The pope's letter began:

Through the diligent report of your messengers We have learned that there is supposed to be an island lying at a distance from Norway of twelve days journeying or
more, and said to belong under your authority as Archbishop. The parishioners on
that island are said to be so closely related to one another that they are hardly able
to enter into a legal marriage in accordance with canonical rules.

The pope also said he was not sure he had the authority to issue a general
dispensation from church rules in this matter, but he was willing to let the
Norwegian archbishop grant dispensation for marriage in cases of fifth,
sixth, or seventh degree consanguinity, though certainly not in the fourth
degree. And such dispensation would be justified only "if, as We are told,
the above-mentioned island lies twelve days' journeying away from other
countries, and you are certain that the people are in such great difficulty on
this account. . . ."[71]

Vandvik argues that the island in question (*insula quedam*) cannot have
been Iceland or Greenland. When the Nidaros (Trondheim) archbishopric
was founded in 1154, just a few years before Alexander III was elected
pope, the bishoprics of Iceland and Greenland were listed under specific
Latin names, as was the practice of the Papal Curia. The Curia would not
employ a term as vague as "said to belong under your authority as Archbishop" except to distinguish between what was definite and what was *said*
to be the case. Had the *insula quedam* been Iceland or Greenland, the Pope
would have known for certain that it was under the Nidaros archbishop's
authority and would have said so.

A second argument by Vandvik, that twelfth-century Norwegian clerical messengers would probably not have regarded Greenland as an island,
also deserves consideration. Although Adam of Bremen (about 1075)
thought of both Greenland and Vínland as islands, to him and his contemporaries the term "island" implied barbarity and remoteness, not necessarily a smallish piece of land surrounded by water on all sides. A century after
Adam, the *Historia Norvegiæ* (written around 1170 by a Norwegian cleric)
saw Greenland as part of a large northern landmass, and *The King's Mirror*
(about 1250) likewise assumed that Greenland was part of that mainland.[72]
A geographical survey in an Icelandic manuscript, *Veidarvísir ok borgaskipan* (composed about 1300 and partly based on a guidebook written in
Iceland before 1150), tries to locate Helluland, Markland, and Vínland in
the ocean south of Greenland and hypothesizes that while Vínland may be
an African peninsula, the other two names refer to islands.[73] On the basis
of these and other literary sources, A. A. Bjørnbo drew a map of how the
medieval Norse saw their geographical world.[74] This map (Fig. 8) shows
Greenland as part of a vast, solid, eastward-connected northern landmass.
Both Helluland and Markland are islands, while Vínland merges with the

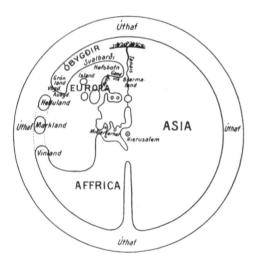

FIG. 8. A. A. Bjørnbo's depiction of how the medieval Norse imagined the world circle. Source: "Cartographia Groenlandica," p. 82; reproduced by permission of Dansk Polarcenter, Copenhagen, publisher of *Meddelelser om Grønland*.

African continent. The stretch of northwestern Norway still known as Hålogaland was also at the time widely thought to be an island.

Later sources and common sense lend some support to Vandvik's argument. Greenland is huge and extends so far into the polar regions that circumnavigation was impossible until the twentieth century. As late as 1741, the Norwegian Greenland missionary Hans Egede wrote:[75]

The western side [of Greenland] is known to a latitude of seventy-some degrees. Whether Greenland is a big island, or borders in the north on other countries, nobody has yet been able to ascertain; but we may safely conclude that it must border on America on the northwestern side, for between America and Greenland stretches the . . . bay which the sea charts call Strat-David after an Englishman, who Anno 1585 is supposed to have been the first who found [it], and which is still visited annually by them and other nations for the sake of the whale-fishing.

On the generally recognized periphery of the medieval Norwegian archbishopric, no territory *known* to be an island was as distant as a twelve days' journey from Norway. Nor could Greenland be said to be a twelve days' journey both from Norway and from all other countries (*ab aliis terris*)—Iceland was much closer to Greenland than Norway was. But the voyage of some 1,900 nautical miles from the Norse site at L'Anse aux Meadows (on Newfoundland Island) to the Eastern Settlement, hugging the coast via Cape Porcupine, Cape Chidley, and Cape Dyer before crossing the Davis Strait, would have taken the Greenland Norse about twelve days and nights if they covered a reasonable 150 nautical miles in 24 hours, according to calculations made by Helge Ingstad in a different context from Vandvik's.[76]

Unless Pope Alexander III's letter was perfunctory, it is therefore conceivable that, as Vandvik argues, the *insula quedam* was a Norse outpost in North America some twelve days' voyage from Greenland, where Bishop Eirik Gnupsson may have been headed in 1121, and where the population would undoubtedly have been both isolated and small enough to make the Norwegian archbishop worry about consanguinity.

A presumption of continued sailings from Greenland to North America for the sake of logging and hunting forces the question of whether the Greenlanders made further attempts to settle in Labrador, Newfoundland, or points even farther south. The few and vague surviving hints of isolated Norsemen staying in Markland or Vínland in the twelfth century must be treated cautiously. Unfortunately, accounts of blond, blue-eyed Indians, wonderfully informative runic inscriptions, or remains of Norse buildings on the North American continent find adherents among a few enthusiasts like Hjalmar R. Holand while exasperating other scholars in the field to such a degree that common sense evaporates at the other end of the spectrum as well.[77]

We must leave the door open for future knowledge and continue to ask not only *did* some Norse Greenlanders put down roots in North America but also *could* they have? The answer to the latter must be yes—the voyage itself was clearly not an insurmountable problem. But they would have needed good reasons to take such a step. What might have compelled them? And even if small Norse encampments can be proved to have existed in America in the twelfth century, did they survive into the next couple of centuries? How much information about such experiences was relayed back to Greenland? Last but not least, Did they find an area where they could get along with the local Skrælings?

The so-called Maine Penny provides tantalizing evidence of contact between American natives and Norsemen in the *second* half of the eleventh century, decades after the events in the Vinland Sagas. The small Norwegian coin, minted during the reign of Olaf Kyrre (1065–80), was found during excavations of a twelfth-century Indian site on the Maine coast, along with objects indicating trade with the Dorset Eskimos of northern Labrador. McGhee surmises that the coin had been brought south after first being obtained by Dorset Eskimos, whose ancient sites have yielded other evidence of Norse contact during that period. In his judgment, Norse traders—necessarily few in number—would have felt fairly safe exchanging goods with the Dorset people in the kind of open, northern coastal country with which they were familiar, while their initial experiences with hostile Indians in the densely forested areas to the south would have discouraged them from going farther down the American coast than necessary to find lumber. Besides, the furs and the tusks from narwhal and walrus that they could obtain from the Eskimos were of far greater value than anything the Indians to the south had to offer.[78]

McGhee's analysis of the probable relationships between North American natives and the medieval Norse makes good sense. In Greenland, where there were neither deep forests nor Indians to contend with, it is reasonable to suppose that the Norse managed to get along with the Eskimos to some degree, just as on the other side of the Davis Strait. But it is far from clear whether their first Greenland contacts were with lingering Dorset or early Thule Eskimos. Encounters with indigenous peoples would at any rate have taken place eventually, as a result of the Norse Greenlanders' summer hunting in the Greenland part of Norðrseta.

We have tangible and touching proof of at least one such Norðrseta voyage. Sometime in the mid-thirteenth century, three Norsemen found themselves on the island of Kingittorsuaq (latitude 72°57' N) so early in the spring that they had possibly spent the winter there. They left a message— a silent testimony to calloused hands going about their work skillfully and meticulously despite bitter cold. Neat runes on a small, beautifully shaped and smooth stone announce that "*ellikr. sikvaths:son:r. ok.baanne: tortarson: ok: enrithi: osson: laukardak.in: fyrir.gakndag vardate. ok rydu: xxxxxx* (Erling Sighvatsson and Bjarni Thordarson and Eindridi Oddsson on the Saturday before the minor Rogation Day [April 25] piled these cairns and . . .)."[79]

There are indications of Norse forays beyond this region as well, but it is impossible to know just how far north the hunters pursued their game in any given period. Jette Arneborg's forthcoming book on Inuit-Norse interaction, which provides a systematic coverage of key Norse and Inuit archaeological sites, makes it clear why archaeologists are cautious about dating Norse (or presumed Norse) objects relative to the age of Eskimo ruins in which they have been found.[80] Radioactive carbon dating, designed to reveal the approximate date when an organic substance stopped growing, is especially tricky in situations involving marine creatures, driftwood, or wool.[81] In addition, distinctions must be made not only between Dorset and Thule houses and artifacts, but among three definable Thule periods. Both scholarly opinions and the results of carbon datings vary for each site.

According to the Canadian archaeologist Peter Schledermann, C-14 tests indicate that the Thule people arrived in the Eastern High Arctic sometime after A.D. 900 and in due course colonized the northern part of West Greenland, after about 1000. He notes that in this estimate he differs from Danish archaeologists, who favor a pre-Norse arrival date of the Thule culture in Greenland.[82] Thule habitations on Ruin Island (Inglefield Land) have been dated anywhere from the tenth to the early thirteenth century, while an Eskimo site at Nuulliit in the more southerly Thule district has been dated to sometime in the eleventh century.[83] Associated radiocarbon dates show that bits of chain mail and other pieces of iron, found by Peter Schledermann in the eastern Ellesmere Island region in 1977–79, stem from "somewhere in the 13th to 15th centuries A.D., well within the period of Norse activities on the west coast of Greenland." It is worth noting, too, that in Schledermann's judgment the two cairns discovered on a small, steep island right off the east coast of Ellesmere Island (about 79°33′N) by the British explorer Captain G. S. Nares in 1875 could only have been raised by the Norse, whereas McGhee thinks that these and some other large cairns in the area were more likely built by Dorset Eskimos.[84]

Pieces of a wooden barrel made in the European manner turned up among the earliest Thule remains at the Quajaa site in Jakobshavn Icefjord, where the latest C-14 dating is A.D. 1255.[85] There is no way of knowing where these or other typically Norse mementos such as bits of metal pots, combs, iron rivets, gaming pieces, and pieces of chain mail and woven cloth originated, and how they were obtained. Although some Norse articles found in far outposts may just have been pilfered from abandoned Norse sites and traded among the Eskimos themselves, McGhee observes that "the number and distribution of such finds suggests that [Norse-Eskimo] contacts must have occurred more frequently than recorded in the Norse historical accounts."[86]

The lack of unanimity about Dorset and Thule Eskimo migrations joins a general disagreement on the timetable for the Norse exploration northward along the west coast of Greenland. Gwyn Jones accepts that the Norse Greenlanders continued to exploit North America at least on a commuting basis and also acknowledges the evidence for their forays into Arctic Greenland, but with this qualification: "That the Greenlanders moved up their own coast as far as Disco and Upernavik, and once to Melville Bay, we know—but the full process took time."[87]

It makes no sense that they should have been slow to explore their own coast northward, given both the swiftness with which the first generation of settlers crossed the Davis Strait and the recent archaeological evidence confirming that the Western Settlement was founded at about the same time as the Eastern one. The distance between the Western Settlement and the Disko Bay region is not appreciably greater than the distance between the two settlements, and there were plenty of good reasons to continue north. Not only is the Holsteinsborg coastal region the most extensive ice-free continuous land area in western Greenland and a reindeer hunter's mecca, but marine game abounds there as well.[88] The availability of export goods such as walrus hide for strong ropes, walrus tusks for ivory, narwhal horns for magic and medicine, and polar bear hides (or even live polar bears) must have drawn the settlers from the start and surely was the cause, rather than the consequence, of their trade with Norway.

Trade with the Eskimos is implied by the piece of a bronze scale found by Pat Sutherland on a Thule tenting site on the west coast of Ellesmere Island.[89] It is suggested, too, by the wide variety of Norse articles found in old Eskimo sites, as well as the occasional Eskimo artifact located in Norse archaeological sites. A number of small carvings representing Norsemen—and possibly other Europeans—also show that the Eskimos had many opportunities to observe these strange visitors at close quarters.

Among the more interesting and hotly disputed carvings is the small wooden figure in Fig. 9, found by Debora Sabo in 1972 at a thirteenth-century Thule site on the south side of Baffin Island, at approximately 61°N. A mere 5.5 centimeters tall, the carving shows a man wearing a one-piece, long tunic with a border following the lower edge into a split in front, and with a pectoral cross. Hans Christian Gulløv says we should not assign too much significance to the cross, but taken together with the rest of the unusual costume, it has led to speculation about whether other Europeans besides the Norse used those far northern waters in the Middle Ages. Schledermann says the carving was probably made by an Inuk, "undoubtedly" represents a Norseman, and "strongly suggests Inuit/Norse contact on the Baffin Island coast." Gulløv thinks it is "most likely" Norse and from the thirteenth or fourteenth century.[90] Gwyn Jones is less specific, saying it "appears to represent a man dressed in European clothes." McGhee agrees that it apparently represents "a person in European clothing" and believes that it was almost certainly carved on Baffin Island, because it is very different from the conventional style in which Greenland Eskimos depicted Norsemen. Guy Mary-Rousselière notes that this kind of long, hooded robe was common enough in the thirteenth and fourteenth centuries, also in Greenland, but that the horizontal line drawn just below the shoulders suggests chain mail. As for the cross, he says that Scandinavian Christians sometimes wore one on their chests in the period A.D. 1000–1300, while medieval religious or ecclesiastical costumes in Western Europe rarely included a cross, except for the religious and military orders such as the Templars.[91]

On the so-called Skræling Island off Ellesmere Island, Peter Schledermann's team in 1979 found a crudely carved wooden head, said to be datable to about A.D. 1100. Schledermann thinks it is either a Dorset or a Thule representation of a Norseman, but Gulløv judges it to be a Norse self-portrait. A copper blade was found in the same house. Pieces of wool

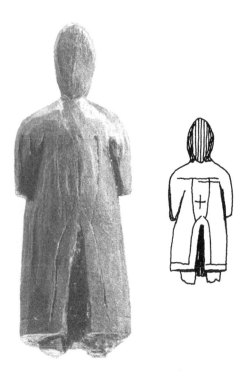

FIG. 9. Photograph of an ivory carving 5.5 centimeters tall (left) found by Debora Sabo in 1972 at a Thule site on the south side of Baffin Island. The carving shows a man wearing a one-piece, long tunic with a border following the lower edge into a split in front, and with a pectoral cross. These details show up clearly in the drawing (right) by Hans Christian Gulløv. Sources: carving photograph reproduced by permission of the Canadian Museum of Civilization (negative no. 91–72); drawing from Gulløv, "Eskimoens syn," fig. 17, reproduced with the author's permission.

cloth (one of them radiocarbon dated to 1190), chain mail, an iron boat rivet, and a number of other Norse items were also found in or around the four Thule ruins excavated on Skræling Island.[92]

When the Danish archaeologist Therkel Mathiassen excavated on Inussuk Island, at latitude 72°55′N, in 1929, he found two small wooden dolls carved by Thule Eskimos (Fig. 10), the carving of a face with obviously European features and a "leaf" ornamentation on the flip side, a piece of bell metal, some coarsely woven cloth, and a spinning top of bone. Rather deep in the Thule midden of nearby Sermermiut he also located a number of Norse objects, including half of a pair of iron shears, the handle of a bronze spoon, and several oblong sharpening stones. The bottom layer of the Sermermiut midden has since been C-14 dated to about 1100–1200.[93] A Thule grave at Nuugaq (in the northern Disko Bay region) contained a small piece of Norse cloth along with Thule (or "Inussuk") artifacts, which could mean that the cloth had been considered either expendable enough for use as a ground covering or precious enough to rate as grave goods. At Illorssuit, in a Thule house ruin, Mathiassen found a rusty iron knife blade as well as half of a bronze cooking pot of a type well known from Scandinavia in the later Middle Ages.[94]

The problem is that we do not know whether these Norse objects changed owners close to the place in which they were found, or whether they were brought to these outlying spots by itinerant Inuit who had also traded the objects among themselves. Nor is there any way to determine which of these articles the Norse had given away of their own free will.

We know the Eskimos appreciated iron, but it is difficult to guess what relative values they assigned to Norse articles made of cloth or soapstone. Knives and cooking pots were obviously useful objects in themselves and therefore subject to trade, as were the numerous Norse spoons and whetstones that have also been found quite far north. Some articles, such as

FIG. 10. Photographs of carvings found by Therkel Mathiassen on old Thule sites, Inussuk Island, West Greenland, in 1929, with drawings by Hans Christian Gulløv. Both carvings are Eskimo representations of thirteenth- or fourteenth-century Norsemen. (A non-Thule carving of a European from about the same period is shown in Fig. 16c.) Sources: carving photographs reproduced from Mathiassen, "Inugsuk," plate 22: 3 and 4, with permission of the National Museum, Copenhagen; drawing from Gulløv, "Eskimoens syn," figs. 3 and 4, reproduced with the author's permission.

chess pieces, iron ship rivets, woven cloth, and bits of chain mail, dating from about A.D. 1270 and found on both the Canadian and Greenlandic side of Smith Sound, may well have reached the Eskimos by other means. McGhee's reflections on this subject suggest that barter was a part of Norse-Eskimo relations in this region, while another recent expert opinion holds that most of the non-Eskimo articles found were unlikely objects for trade, and that the Norse probably did not part with them willingly.[95]

Any of the objects mentioned above, which are only a small sampling of modern archaeological discoveries, may have come from pilfering in ships, shipwrecks, or settlements. The frequency with which barrel staves or even whole coopered vessels have turned up in medieval Eskimo sites all along the northern perimeter of Smith Sound and the west coast of Greenland emphasizes the possibility of shipwrecks as a source, for ships customarily carried barrels for everything from fresh water to fish and butter. Because examples of the Norse coopers' art at Eskimo sites grow more frequent with greater proximity to the Norse farms, some seasoned archaeologists, such as Therkel Mathiassen and Erik Holtved, have been convinced that the Eskimos must have learned coopering from the Norse. Hans Kapel at the Greenland Secretariat in Copenhagen assured me, however, that the Eskimos had their own distinct brand of coopering, in which the wood was carefully shaped and fitted together to form small vessels.[96]

One voyage to the far north in about 1266 did definitely not end in a shipwreck. It is recounted in the "Greenland Annals" by Björn Jonsson of Skardsá, which Gwyn Jones calls "a collection of great though irregular value of 1623." A Greenland priest named Halldor reported in a letter to a colleague that some people returning from Norðrseta had been farther north than any before them and had seen signs of Skrælings, but not the Skrælings themselves. Greenland churchmen had then sent another expedition even farther north (possibly into Melville Bay), where they had a good look around without going ashore, before returning to Gardar all the way down in the Eastern Settlement.[97]

We should keep this daring voyage in mind when evaluating both the tiny carving in Fig. 9 and the pieces of chain mail that have been found scattered over such a wide northern area. Chain mail is usually worn for military purposes, not by hunters, fishermen, and farmers intent on their daily pursuits. It may have been worn by Norse Greenlanders fearing attacks by Eskimos or others, on either side of the Davis Strait and Smith Sound. It may also have been worn by other medieval Europeans exploring in those waters, however, for the northern sea lanes appear to have been busier throughout the Middle Ages than is generally supposed. The problems attached to finds of chain mail in Greenland, and the possibility that others besides the Norse explored in Greenland waters well before the end of the fifteenth century, will be discussed later.

With or without chain mail, the Greenlanders no doubt did their share of fighting, but their primary concern was with their farms. Their voyages of exploration, their far-flung hunting trips on land and sea, and their incessant quest for land were necessary to farming as they knew it: animal husbandry supplemented by fish, game, and trade in surplus products. The skills they brought to their new country had been finely honed in Iceland and Norway and served them well. In the colony's prime, some 4,000–5,000 Norse people in the Eastern Settlement and 1,000–1,500 in the Western one called Greenland home.[98]

CHAPTER TWO

Social and Economic Conditions in Norse Greenland Before 1350

The establishment of the church as an institution in Norse Greenland required a proper financial basis as well as sufficient social organization. Forming an idea of these elements is necessary but also difficult given the fragmentary nature of the literary and documentary evidence.

Many sources about medieval Greenland are irretrievably lost. Finn Magnusen, the nineteenth-century compiler of *Grønlands Historiske Mindesmerker*, noted that a number of manuscripts disappeared in the seventeenth century, not only in Iceland, where a fire at Skálholt Cathedral in 1630 destroyed a large part of the church archives, but also in Norway and Denmark. We are left with such teasers as this one by Peder Clausen Undal in 1632: "The following was found in the old Icelandic book . . . Anno 1344: Thord Eigilsson sailed to Greenland and the same year returned to Norway with a richly laden ship and much goods. . . . And much of this book had been torn away, otherwise there would no doubt have been more noted down about Greenland." We shall probably never know how this item relates to a 1346 entry in the *Icelandic Annals*.[1]

Documents actually written in Greenland are not known to exist in any archive, and among all the Eddic poems preserved in the *Codex Regius*, only the *Atlakviða* ("Lay of Atli") mirrors Greenlandic topography and social conditions. Archaeological investigations in Greenland have not turned up a single vellum manuscript, nor any useful runic inscriptions along the lines of "I, Halldor, the last of my people, take up my chisel to tell of the Greenlanders' fate. . . ."

We may hope for future discoveries; the Vatican Library, for example, is not yet picked clean. Presumably some letters were written by officials of church and crown in Greenland, but the degree of non-runic literacy among lay Greenlanders, or their need for written communications and documentary evidence of property transactions and other legal concerns, can only be conjectured.[2] While *Jónsbók* (1281) is the first Icelandic law code referring to the use of letters as proof of contracts, we know for certain that in Iceland, letters were being issued by about 1185, if not earlier, although the oldest dated Icelandic letter that still exists in the original is dated June 23, 1311.[3]

The earliest known document referring to Greenland by name is Pope Leo IX's bull of January 6, 1053, in which he makes Adalbert, the archbishop of Hamburg-Bremen (and his successors) *"episcopus in omnibus gentibus Suenonum seu Danorum, Noruuechorum, Islant, Scrideuinnum, Gronlant et uniuersarum septentrionalium. . . ."*[4] How firm a foothold Christianity had in Greenland by 1053 has been the subject of much debate, but Greenland itself had evidently been implanted on the continental consciousness in some fashion, despite Pope Leo's vague reference to *"uniuersarum septentrionalium."* The latter phrase was repeated in a similar bull issued two years later, but was absent in the 1133 confirmation of the Hamburg archbishop's authority by Innocent II—an authority that now included not only Greenland but the Faroes.[5]

Twenty years after the first papal bull concerning Rome's northernmost province, Adam of Bremen, a canon of Bremen Cathedral since 1066 or 1067, wrote his four-volume *Gesta Hammaburgensis ecclesiæ pontificum*, in which he referred to both Greenland and Vínland as islands and made a number of observations about the Scandinavian countries. In these accounts, Adam demonstrated a conviction that when gathering, processing, and retailing information about unfamiliar places, one must pay proper attention to monsters and marvels.[6] What better homes for such exotica than countries at the edge of the known and habitable world? Most scholars have assumed that Adam's chief informant about the far north was King Sveinn Estridsson of Denmark, but Henrik M. Jansen is more inclined to credit Isleif Gizurarson, who became the first native bishop of Iceland in 1056 under the Hamburg-Bremen archbishopric, and who had been educated in Westphalia. Whoever Adam's informant was, he does not appear to have had firsthand knowledge about Greenland, for Adam wrote that this country got its name because the inhabitants turned green from all the salt water to which they were continually exposed. He added: "They live like the Icelanders, except they are more savage and threaten seafarers with piracy. It is said that Christianity recently winged its way to them as well."[7]

Another surviving medieval source of information about Norse Greenland is the fifteenth-century manuscript of *Historia Norvegiae* discovered in Edinburgh in 1849 by the Norwegian historian P. A. Munch.[8] Originally composed at the end of the twelfth century, *Historia Norvegiae* has its share of fanciful tales about giants and about maidens who become pregnant from drinking water, but the author clearly has also had access to more sober travelers' tales:[9]

Beyond the Greenlanders to the north, hunters have found small people whom they call *Skrælings*. They are thus made that when they receive a wound that is not life-threatening, their wounds turn white without bleeding; but when they are mortally wounded, their bleeding scarcely stops. They completely lack iron; they use walrus tusks for throwing-weapons and sharp stones as knives.

This is a good description of how the Norse must have perceived the Eskimos.

Like the *Historia Norvegiae*, the work known as *The King's Mirror* (*Konungsskuggsjá* or *Speculum regale*), written around 1260 in the form of a sage father's advice to his son, assumes that Greenland is connected in the north to a great Eurasian landmass.[10] *The King's Mirror* is a more practical compendium for medieval Greenland-farers than the *Historia Norvegiae*, however. Some of its advice addresses the threat posed to navigation by the various forms of ice along the Greenland coasts. When Eirik the Red sailed to Greenland, and for quite some time thereafter, it was customary to sail from northwestern Iceland until sighting the first glittering Greenland snowcaps in the Ammassalik region, and then to follow the East Greenland coast around Cape Farewell and up the southwest coast until Herjolfsnes (Ikigaat) appeared as the first outpost of the Eastern Settlement. The advice in *The King's Mirror* suggests that the climate may have become colder by the middle of the thirteenth century:[11]

There is more ice to the northeast and north of the land than to the south, southwest, and west; consequently, whoever wishes to make the land should sail around it to the southwest and west, till he has come past all those places where ice may be looked for, and approach the land on that side.

Papers presented at a University of East Anglia conference in 1979, as well as more recent work by Knud Frydendahl, suggest that indeed there was a cooling trend in the northwestern Atlantic as early as the beginning of the thirteenth century. Sailing directions given a century later by the Norwegian priest Ivar Bárdarson also stress that Greenland must now be reached by a different route from the one used in earlier days.[12] Fig. 7 (in Chapter 1) shows that modern mariners are equally well advised to worry about ice in Greenland waters, and it illustrates why early sailors and mapmakers assumed that the Davis Strait was closed off to the north.

How much the climate may have changed in the period A.D. 1000–1500 will be discussed in various contexts later, but it is important to note here that even the Western Settlement survived for more than a century after these new and troublesome ice conditions had become part of the Greenland sailing lore in the thirteenth century. The Eastern Settlement held on for another two hundred and fifty years or so and was visited by at least occasional ships throughout that period.

A modern traveler, looking from an airplane down on the chilly vastness of the North Atlantic, will understand why people sailing in open ships did not crowd the farther reaches of those sea lanes just for the pleasure of an outing. Daredevils and pirates some of those medieval sailors may have been, but mostly they balanced the daunting risks of the voyage all the way to Greenland from Norway against the promise of profit from trade. *The King's Mirror* noted that men went to Greenland for three reasons: to win fame, to satisfy their curiosity, and to gain wealth. Those who braved the dangers of the voyage could look forward to profitable trade, "for this land lies so distant from other countries that men seldom visit it."[13]

Grain and iron, for which there was a perennial market in Greenland, could be turned to good advantage by an enterprising trader. Malt, honey, pitch, and other luxuries no doubt also found buyers among the more well-to-do Greenlanders. We do not know the extent to which the Greenlanders (especially the early generations, who were still unburdened by tithes and foreign taxes, and some of whom probably also had loot left from their own or their ancestors' Viking raids) were able to indulge the well-known Norse love of ostentation. Although the brownish, homespun wool cloth so often found by Greenland archaeologists conjures up an image of drably dressed people going glumly about their business, reality may have been somewhat different.

Recent laboratory tests performed on similar cloth found during the excavations of Viking sites in York show that the wool had originally been brightly colored with natural dyes, many of which were also available to the Greenlanders.[14] Experts at the National Museum in Copenhagen have reached similar conclusions about some Greenland finds from both settlements. During the 1984 excavations at Sandnes farm, a piece of homespun cloth was found that had been dyed indigo blue with either woad or indigo, and from Herjolfsnes there is even an example of polar bear fur having been dyed red.[15]

People who took the trouble to dye their clothing, and who were known to value ostentatious display at feasts, were likely to covet both silk and linen if available, but these materials do not survive well in the ground, especially in Greenland with its cycles of freezing and thawing and its gravelly soil, so proof is hard to come by. In Viking York, however, archaeologists have found remains of silk, most likely from Byzantium. Recent excavations at farm V48 (Niaquusat) turned up flax pollen from the bottom layers right up to the recent ones, and another research team found flax pollen and seeds at Sandnes. Flax, which needs a growing season of only four to five months, was thus cultivated even at this northernmost settlement throughout the period of Norse occupation.[16]

The Greenlanders' daily lives were no doubt every bit as hard, frugal, and monotonous as those of their Icelandic and Norwegian contemporaries, but it would be a mistake to assume that at the height of their prosperity and independence, Greenland chieftains and their families trudged off to feasts and midsummer assemblies dressed in thick, brown, woolen garments and smelly furs, with not a shred of imported cloth to call their own—particularly when we know that excavations in both settlements have revealed such imported luxuries as Rhenish stoneware.[17] Many Greenland products were coveted abroad, so the inhabitants had the means with which to pay.

As *The King's Mirror* noted, a man could become wealthy from the Greenland trade. For the European luxury market, the Greenlanders for several centuries provided white falcons, walrus ivory, narwhal horns, and the furs of polar bears, white and blue polar foxes, weasels, and perhaps various North American mammals. Caribou skins were less luxurious but widely used, as were strips of tough walrus hide for heavy-duty anchor and mooring ropes. Eiderdown, sealskins, and blubber were appreciated by the Greenlanders themselves and also in demand abroad. All three products made excellent staples for trade, as did oil from the livers of cod and Greenland shark. Blubber and oil provided light and heat even in households that did not rely on them as a food supplement.

To any northerner who could afford it, butter, rather than blubber, was the fat of choice, whether it was spread on bread or on dried fish. Properly aged butter was more desirable still, and along with cheese it was a valued form of payment all over medieval Scandinavia. Other products from domestic animals, such as hides from horses, cattle, and sheep, were in constant demand all over Europe and would have been among the articles a thrifty, stock-raising Greenlander put by for trade if he could possibly spare them.[18]

Last, but not least, the coarse, warm wool spun and woven by the women in Norse Greenland was well received abroad. The Greenland sheep, *Ovis aries*, had coarse outer hairs and soft under hairs, and the climate encouraged thick fur.[19] A flock of sturdy sheep and goats was probably a medieval Greenland farmer's most useful asset as far as his and his family's needs were concerned. In this he did not differ from his Icelandic cous-

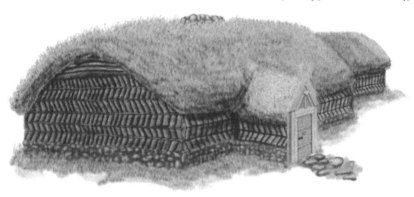

FIG. 11. Artist's rendering of a medieval turf-and-stone Norse house. Note how the turf strips are made to form a chevron pattern. Source: David O. Seaver.

ins and most of his Norwegian ones. Adam of Bremen (who also recognized the cultural affinity between Iceland and Greenland) relayed this information about the eleventh-century Icelanders:[20]

> They live only on what their cattle produce and dress in their skins; no grain grows there, and there is very little wood. Therefore they live in underground burrows, and enjoy the same roof, food, and bedding as their cattle. Therefore they also live in holy innocence, since they do not covet more than nature gives them, and gladly may they say with the Apostle: "When we have food and clothing, we are content." They have mountains for castles and springs for slaking their thirst. Blessed are these people, I say, who in their poverty have not a covetous man among them, and most blessed in that they now have all converted to Christianity.

Whether it was Bishop Isleif or someone else who had painted this rosy picture of the Icelanders' blessed state of bucolic simplicity, Adam's informant had clearly tried to describe Icelandic farms and farming to him. The thoroughly urban canon must have struggled to picture what life must be like in a turf-and-stone house with a low and sloping turf roof. Although the turf strips could be made to form a handsome pattern such as shown in Fig. 11, and although a well-to-do farmer might have a stone-set façade to his dwelling, such a house probably sounded to Adam like an animal's burrow; and like animals the Icelanders must therefore live, lacking as they did both grain and fuel, and reportedly eating both moss and seaweed.

Icelandic architecture in particular reflected that country's lack of timber. Although the Norse Greenlanders would have had to cross the Davis Strait for a steady supply of good-sized logs, it is not at all certain that they ever were as desperately short of wood for both building and fuel as the

Icelanders became. Quite large birch trunks surviving from the Norse period have been found in some of the Eastern Settlement fjords, and archaeologists have been struck by the fact that the Greenlanders seem to have
wasted the woodchips produced by shipbuilding, house construction, and
the fashioning of household objects.[21]

The Greenlandic building style was nevertheless rather similar to the
Icelandic one. Thick walls of turf and stone, resting on a sill of large stones,
were capped by a sloping turf roof on a foundation of beams and branches.
A series of upright poles inside helped shore up the roof. There was no chim-
ney, only a smoke-hole in the roof with an adjustable stone cover allowing
some protection against rain and snow. On festive occasions, those who
could afford it covered the inside turf walls of the communal room with
woven and embroidered hangings. To the extent that wood was available,
it was also used in wall panels, doors, loom frames, bed frames, and high
seat posts; in covering the banked-up soil for the pallets and benches on
which people slept and sat at their work or meals; and in a number of other
useful or ornamental capacities. There is even occasional evidence of
wooden floors, but generally the floor would consist of packed-down soil
and gravel, on which there might be a cover of twigs and heather for
warmth during the winter. Occasionally floors might be paved with flat
stone slabs. Although the Norse had their fireplaces in shallow pits in the
floor and had to be circumspect about their floor covering, flagstones appear to have been more common in barns than in rooms for people, as is
apparent in Fig. 12, Roussell's drawing of a modest house block at Brattahlid.

The Greenland settlers wisely brought with them their Norse culinary
traditions as well as their architecture. Iceland moss has both nutritional
and medicinal value and is not unpalatable. The reddish seaweed dulse—
which in its preferred dried form smells like the inside of an old fish barrel—
was considered a taste treat, as was the big, umbelliform plant angelica (to
this day Icelandic children may be seen chewing on angelica stems). An especially tasty variety, alpine angelica, already grew in southern Greenland
when the settlers arrived, and since Norse farm sites often are recognizable
by a concentration of angelica plants, we must suppose that the colonizers
also cultivated it. They appear to have encouraged the existing stands of
lyme grass (*Elymus mollis*) as well. A modern visitor to the ancient episcopal farm at Gardar (Igaliko) is usually struck by the rich growth of this
plant, which provided some edible grain in a country where even barley
would not ripen. Flax seeds, as well as the seeds of knotgrass (*Polygonum
aviculare*), chickweed (*Stellaria media*), and other common weeds, have
turned up in Norse Greenlandic samples containing human feces, so it is
clear that such seeds were used as a food supplement.[22]

It is safe to assume that the Norse knew and used every edible plant on sea and land in their northern environment. We know that they seasoned their food with juniper berries and wild herbs, and that they knew that scurvy-wort was good for them.[23] They must also have been delighted with the mountain cranberries, bilberries, blueberries, cloudberries, and crowberries available in Greenland. Many of the berries growing in far northern latitudes keep exceptionally well (crowberries will keep under a layer of snow and be the sweeter for it), and they often have a high vitamin C content. These food supplements must have helped the Norse Greenlanders stay healthy to the very end of their settlement.

Dwarf willow, birch, and the occasional rowan tree grew as dense scrub when the first settlers arrived, as it still does in places today. It would have had many uses to the Greenlanders as fuel and suitable material for roof supports and other building needs. While the colonists were still few in number, they appear to have treated it somewhat cavalierly, at times burning it off to clear land for their farm buildings and pastures. Anyone faulting them for this should spend a day trying to walk through this Greenland scrub, which often reaches to the height of a man and is almost impenetrable, as many an archaeologist can testify.

It is uncertain how soon the Greenlanders began to adapt their building style and farms to suit their climate and manner of living. Until recently, scholars have usually deferred in this matter to the study published in 1941 by the Danish architect-turned-archaeologist Aage Roussell, who noted three distinctive building styles: (1) the *longhouse*, incorporating one or more rooms in a row; (2) the *passage house*, consisting of several rooms lying in rows behind each other and connected by one or more passages; and (3) the *centralized farm*, a large house block incorporating both the human dwelling and the various barns for the animals.[24]

In the past decade, Claus Andreasen has redefined this typology.[25] He defines the *longhouse* as a structure that may have one or two rooms added to the back of a whole row of rooms. The *passage house* has rooms both in an extended line and in rows behind each other, the rooms connected to each other by one or more passages. The conglomerate of rooms making up Roussell's *centralized farm* varies from the other two categories only in that it performs an additional function by housing animals as well as people, not in any real difference of construction.

Therefore, Andreasen argues, there are only *two* architectural categories in Norse Greenland. If the criterion is function, the difference is whether the dwelling and barns are separate or joined under one roof. If the criterion is style, the choice is merely between a longhouse and a passage house. He stresses that these divisions preclude any attempt to date the styles relative to each other. Roussell, on the other hand, thought the cen-

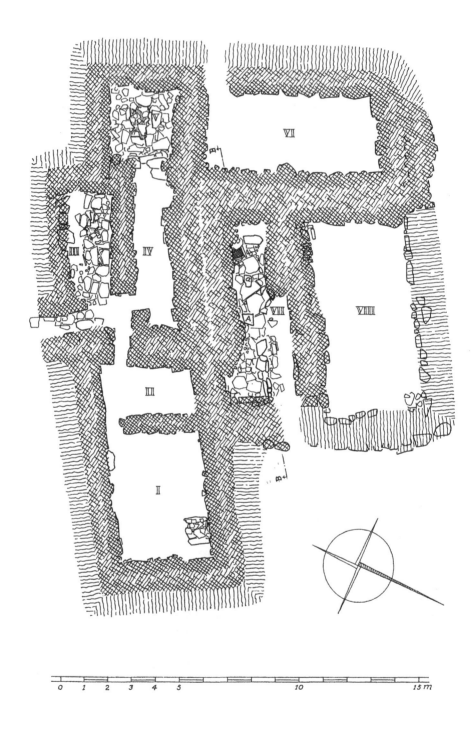

0   1   2   3   4   5   10   15 m

tralized farm may have been a relatively late response to a worsening climate, because in his experience this architecture was peculiar to inland farms, which he reasoned must have been brought into use later than the more desirable sites right on the coast. He also thought this type of construction was natural for medium-sized and small farms, rather than for larger ones.

Andreasen says that no such chronology of architectural change has been demonstrated on any farm excavated in the Western Settlement, where all coastal *and* inland sites appear to have been exploited within the first century or so. The picture we have is far from complete, because the sites excavated in both the Eastern and Western Settlements have generally been the largest and most obviously important ones, but there are clear indications among these larger farms that even some rather recent ones had a longhouse dwelling—and that these farms were connected to churches. In other words, a longhouse with its often impressive, stone-set façade and fastidious distance from stables and barns became a mark of status. In both settlements, the church farms commanded large, relatively level sites on the coast, with ample room to spread the buildings. Other farmers, with precarious toeholds along the coast or in the valleys, had to be much more thrifty with their potential grassland and therefore concentrated their buildings in combined quarters for man and beast.

Given what we now know about the architecture of large, coastal church farms, smaller coastal farms, and inland farms, as well as about the kinds of bones their middens contain, Andreasen theorizes that an interdependent, hierarchical economic system involving all three types of farms evolved early in the colonization period. First, there was the wealthy farm with a church, a large dwelling, and many stables and barns, whose owner exchanged services and cattle products in return for caribou from the inland farmers and seals from the smaller coastal farmers. Second, there was the inland farm with just enough grazing for some sheep and goats and maybe a cow or two. The farmer stabled them in a small barn that formed part of his passage house block and obtained seals either directly from the coast or via the owner of the local church farm. Midden analyses have

FIG. 12 (*opposite*). Floor plan of a modest house block for people and livestock, from ruin 47 at site Ø29, Brattahlid. Source: Reproduced from Roussell's original drawing ("Farms and Churches," p. 160) with permission of the National Museum, Copenhagen. To an untrained eye, the ruins of both Figs. 12 and 13 would appear in the landscape as an irregular pattern of stones and raised turf, so we should not be surprised that early investigators in modern Greenland sometimes confused Norse and Eskimo sites.

shown that even on these inland farms, about one-third of the bone material came from seals. The next biggest category of bones was from caribou, while domestic animals were the smallest source of bones. Third, there was the kind of coastal farm whose owner is still called a *kystbonde* in Danish and Norwegian, with all that word implies of dependence on hunting and fishing. He and his household subsisted mostly on fish and seal meat, supplemented by some meat from caribou, sheep, or goats, and very little meat or produce from cattle.[26]

Stratigraphic studies, which would enable us to compare the domestic economy of the first Norse settlers in Greenland with that of their descendants some centuries later, have been in short supply so far. Archaeologists have been bedeviled not only by the dislocations in the ground from countless seasons of freezing and thawing, but also by the disturbances resulting from Eskimos looking for iron, the efforts of early amateur archaeologists, and the activities of the Norse settlers themselves. The Greenlanders periodically swept the twig floor covering of their living rooms (with whatever lost objects it contained) out on the midden, and they often would level a midden or a house in order to build a new structure there.

More recently, however, some stratigraphic studies have been possible, in part due to the excavations of the Eastern Settlement site Ø17a at Narsaq, led by the Danish archaeologist C. L. Vebæk in 1954, 1958, and 1962. In 1976–77, Thomas McGovern and G. F. Bigelow analyzed animal bones from Ø17a, from "well-defined strata within and immediately around the main structure . . . [which] show both continuity and some important changes in subsistence patterns between occupational strata."[27] The farm features at least ten ruins, of which one is a longhouse, and was occupied continuously from the start of the settlement period until late in the history of the colony. We may be certain that it was settled at the time of Eirik the Red, for on the site was found a rune stick carved in a style the Danish runologist E. Moltke has dated to the period 985–1025.[28] Vebæk also found Viking-period arrowheads, as well as a half-moon-shaped piece of soapstone with a central hole and various incisions, which may or may not have been a bearing dial. The markings resemble compass divisions, but Vebæk is cautious about ascribing navigational use to this stone.[29]

McGovern and Bigelow's analysis of Ø17a gives evidence of a varied, protein-rich diet—a picture McGovern corroborates in a later and very useful article placing observations about Ø17a in the wider context of material obtained from many other Norse Greenland sites. Cattle, sheep, and goats dominate the bones from domestic animals at Ø17a, and in both older and newer layers the ratio of sheep and goat bones to cattle bones is the rather typical one for Norse Greenland of 1.5:1 to 2:1. The cattle at Ø17a were of the small medieval type, while the goats and "goat-horned" sheep were more like the modern Icelandic breeds. Interestingly, there were lots of bones of very young animals; there is no way of knowing whether they had perished by themselves or been slaughtered. In his most recent study, McGovern concludes that all the evidence available so far suggests that cattle were kept for their milk, rather than for their meat, in both settlements.[30]

Bones of both very young and adult pigs were found at Ø17a, suggesting that Norse Greenlanders raised their own pigs. It would actually be quite surprising if they had not done so, for pigs are hardy, omnivorous, intelligent creatures, and pork was and is considered a delicacy all over Scandinavia. The Norse also ate horses, and at Narsaq horse bones were found in the midden, as were dog bones. It is not clear whether the dogs had been eaten by people, or had just been tossed on the midden when they died, to serve as fodder for pigs and other scavengers.

Wild creatures of land and sea were well represented at Ø17a, especially caribou and various species of seals. McGovern and Bigelow nevertheless noted that studies of five Eastern Settlement farms have shown caribou bones making up only about 3.5 percent of the wild species bones, while the average on eight Western Settlement farms was over 23 percent. There seems to be evidence of declining caribou hunting in the later phase at Ø17a, while a small Western Settlement farm (V48) studied during the Norse-Inuit Project showed no particular drop in caribou hunting between the bottom layer (C-14 dated to about A.D. 1000) and the uppermost layer (A.D. 1350–80). Nonetheless, the Danish archaeologist and historian Jette Arneborg recently cautioned against making too much of the data from the latter study, since the stratigraphy at this site is not as regular and decided as was thought at first.[31] We know only what we knew before: the Norse ate caribou.

As already noted, various kinds of seal formed an important part of the Norse Greenlanders' diet, even on the most inland farms. However, bones of ringed seal, which the Eskimos hunted so efficiently in the open sea and through breathing holes in the ice, are apparently rare or absent in the Norse middens.[32] McGovern and Bigelow, who believe that the Norse Greenlanders lacked harpoons, surmise that they had communal hunts of seals (and small whales) similar to modern Faroese pilot whale drives, in which the animals are forced into shallow water where they can be butchered, rather than speared in the open sea. Vebæk agrees with McGovern and Bigelow that the medieval Greenlanders appear to have lacked harpoons throughout the duration of the colony, despite being able to watch the Inuit technique for hunting both whales and ringed seals, but he warns against drawing rash conclusions based on the mere absence of evidence for harpoons. For example, although we know that the polar bear was highly valued by the Norse, and that they hunted it successfully (probably in groups), only a single heavy spearpoint suitable for bear-hunting has so far been found by Norse Greenland archaeologists.[33]

Vebæk's is surely the voice of common sense here. We know that the Greenland Norse had big spears; that they understood the principle of barbs; and that they hunted and killed bears, seals, whales, and walrus. In the Thule Eskimo culture, no significant difference has been found between equipment used to hunt whales and that used to hunt seals and walrus, although these people have hunted whales in the open sea for many centuries. The anthropologist Allen P. McCartney says: "Whaling procurement in all Eskimo societies seemingly stressed skill and technique, not technology *per se*; this skill applied also to elaborate ceremonial preparations and management of supernatural powers."[34] It is quite possible that the Norse, too, "stressed skill and technique, not technology *per se*."

Fresh mussels were widely enjoyed by the Greenlanders, judging from generous shell collections in their middens. Bird bones, mostly from seabirds, made up only a small part of the collections at Ø17a, however. As in other Norse sites, there were also very few fish bones here. Cod-sized cranial and vertebrae bones would have been recognized if present, according to McGovern and Bigelow, who observe that the rather small number of Norse fish hooks and line sinkers found in Greenland also indicates that fish played a smaller part in the Norse Greenlanders' diet than in that of their contemporaries elsewhere in the North Atlantic. McGovern made a similar observation in his recent detailed analysis of Greenland midden material.[35]

This position is open to question on several grounds, especially given the quantities and variety of fish available. Vebæk says firmly, with regard to Ø149 (the convent at Narsarsuaq), where McGovern found a similar lack of fish bones, that "it is quite unbelievable that the Norsemen of this locality would not have fished."[36] Moreover, the large number of net sinkers found suggests that the Greenlanders often used *nets* to catch fish. Before the fish were hung up to dry down by the shore or taken fresh up to the houses, they would have been decapitated and cleaned; often, the backbone would have been removed as well. The guts would either have been thrown in the sea to crabs and other scavengers or used as homefield fertilizer. Hungry ravens would have competed with cats, dogs, and pigs for any remaining scraps on the farm middens.[37] Thus the paucity of fish remains does not of itself prove that the Norse Greenlanders were dilatory fishermen.

Recent studies by modern Norwegian archaeologists in their own country suggest that the likely reason for the lack of backbones and crania from large fish in medieval Greenland's Norse middens is that those scraps were too valuable to throw out. They were dried, crushed, and used as food for cattle, horses, and maybe people. This is what medieval farmers did on coastal farms in northwestern Norway, which are now being excavated, and which show surprisingly few fish remains considering the residents' known reliance on fishing.[38] The shared culture of these medieval Norwegian coast-dwellers and their Norse Greenland contemporaries included how to use the similar resources available to both countries. Remembering how useful fish meal was to man and beast alike in Norway during my wartime childhood, I suspect that the surprisingly large number of small millstones found in Norse Greenland sites were used more for grinding dried fish scraps and moss, to be made into porridge or soup for human consumption, than for the rare batch of imported grain.[39] This would not have been the last resort of desperately hungry people, but a sensible use of available foodstuffs in a diet that already was rather fish-flavored.

McGovern and Bigelow are surely right in assuming that walrus, polar bear, and arctic fox contributed to the Greenlanders' "cash economy" rather than to their normal diet. The walrus at Ø17a (and elsewhere in Norse Greenland) were represented by jawbone chips and penis bones—the latter apparently considered trophies. Although the walrus had probably been killed in the Holsteinsborg–Disko Bay region, the valuable tusks were evidently not extracted until the hunters returned home with the heads. Interestingly, the upper levels of Ø17a show a decline in walrus bones, which in turn may reflect declining access to the northern hunting grounds following the end of the Western Settlement.[40]

Even close to home, hunting and fishing would have been seriously curtailed in the cold season, when the Greenlanders must have drawn on stored dairy products and dried or smoked fish and meat until the harp seals arrived in May or June. Among the best preserved ruins in both settlements are large, well-built storehouses of stone that bear clear witness to the need for hoarding. Gathering hay and other fodder to see the domestic animals through the long winter also added to the hectic pace of securing food and trading supplies during the summer months.

When shorter days and increasing cold forced people indoors, there was plenty to do besides looking after the animals. The women still had their children, cooking and some dairying, spinning, weaving, sewing, and mending, while the men had to see to their boats, add to their fishing and hunting equipment, and fashion tools and household objects from bone, soapstone, wood, and sometimes iron. Their tools varied as much as their raw materials. A good, sharp knife was probably a Greenlander's best companion, but wooden bowls have been found that show lathe marks, and at the settlement-period site of Ø17a there are antler chips showing signs of sawing as well as of cutting.[41] Scholars still argue about whether or not the Greenlanders extracted bog iron themselves, or whether they were entirely dependent on imports.[42] They certainly were skilled smiths.

Given the number of hours required just to supply everyday needs, it is a wonder the Greenlanders had time for leisurely pursuits, but chessmen and other gaming pieces found in ruin sites from every period testify to the popularity of board games. The farms also frequently had a bath house, where people could relax while sweating themselves clean and trading tales and gossip. In such leisure hours, the people no doubt passed on to their descendants stories of how Greenland was settled, how Eirik the Red's sons found a good route to the lands in the west, and how people lived in other countries.

We have no way of knowing if the Greenlanders had exaggerated notions about blessings to be found abroad. One blessing they were more likely to possess than their contemporaries elsewhere was relatively good health in themselves and their animals, thanks to a secluded and originally uncontaminated environment. Studies of a group of feral sheep (from modern herds of the Icelandic-Faroese breed) in the inner part of Nuuk, where some of the most prosperous farms in the old Western Settlement lay, show that these sheep's only parasites were very small numbers of the intestinal worm *Nematodirus spathiger*, capable of surviving cold winters and short summers. No lice or other ecto-parasites were found in their wool. On the old Norse farms, however, the sheep louse and sheep ked have been found, along with evidence of human fleas and lice.[43]

Although the Norse usually cooked their meat, hungry hunters in remote regions may conceivably have fallen victim to trichinosis. Widespread in both the Arctic and temperate zones, and able to survive in dead or rotting meat for a long time, trichinae form part of an ancient ecological complex found in polar bears, walrus, seals, dogs, and pigs. Excepting the pork, Eskimos have also depended on these food sources since time immemorial, and it is interesting to note that the East Greenland Eskimos have long had something they call "walrus sickness," with a variety of clinical symptoms reminiscent of typhoid or meat poisoning.[44]

The Norse Greenlanders' diet was on the whole a healthy one, except in famine years, and they lived on separate farms, each of which had a supply of fresh water, so most forms of contagion would have spread more slowly than in villages or towns. By contrast, the entire Viking population of urban York appears to have suffered from intestinal parasites assured of a continuing life cycle by the proximity of cesspits and garbage pits to the community wells.[45] Judging from the joyful stanzas spoken by the future Earl Rognvald Kali of Orkney (d. 1158) after he had spent five weeks in the English town of Grimsby, the Norse themselves were well aware of the drawbacks to town living:[46]

Five weeks we waded
through wetness and filth,
mud wasn't missing
in the middle of Grimsby:
. . . .

Despite the Greenlanders' environmental advantages, Gwyn Jones questions their ability to withstand epidemic disease and other disasters. In his view, their existence was so marginal in every way that the slightest change might tilt them toward disaster, and he estimates that "their numbers were dangerously small, probably never more than four thousand souls." Such a small population, he reasons, had no recovery margin in the face of a depopulation similar to the one experienced by the Icelanders, who numbered around 80,000 in the year 1100, but only about 47,000 in 1800, thanks to "Fire, ice, pestilence, and neglect."[47]

It is inadvisable to explain conditions in Greenland by extrapolating from the situation in Iceland. Not only was Iceland much closer to other European countries than Greenland was, and hence more vulnerable both to contagion and to the exploitation by outsiders that fill the pages of Icelandic history, but Iceland's extraordinary geological conditions heaped natural disasters on the population, as Jones himself describes so eloquently elsewhere.[48] While the *Icelandic Annals* repeatedly noted volcanic eruptions, earthquakes, and mudslides, or skies so darkened by ash that the sun was powerless even during the summer, causing birds and beasts to die and preventing grass from growing, the Greenlanders lived considerably more safely among their stable granite mountains.

The Norse colonists probably were not proof against leprosy, however, which was endemic in the far north from the eleventh century until the modern period.[49] We must also assume that visitors from time to time brought contagious diseases to Greenland. Medieval sagas and annals alike often refer to epidemics in both Iceland and Greenland—both of the Vínland sagas contain such references for the earliest period of the Greenland settlement. Typhus, transmitted by body lice and apt to occur when another disaster like famine was already present, is equally ancient in that part of the world, and influenza and dysentery would also have been on the list of nasty surprises a visiting ship might bring the Greenlanders.[50]

Norse Greenland gravefinds of parents and children buried together, in both the Eastern and Western Settlements, also suggest invasions of virulent disease. What the archaeologists have *not* found is evidence that a devastating epidemic put an end to either colony. C. L. Vebæk has cautiously suggested that some of the skeletons he found placed very close together in Gravefield I at the Narsarsuaq convent may constitute a mass grave after an epidemic of some kind, but he also notes that so far, neither anthropological analyses nor C-14 datings have proved or disproved this theory, which involves a graveyard he estimates was in use for several centuries.[51]

Other graveyards have also been examined, but none of the material has been fully analyzed, including the earliest Norse Greenland skeletal material available for study, which comes from the graveyard surrounding the first small church at Eirik the Red's homestead Brattahlid. Now called "Thjodhild's church," it is thought to date from about the year 1000 and to have been in use for just a short time, until a new church was built nearby. The remains of 144 people were found, 15 small children among them. Preliminary investigations found grooves in the bones showing that both the men and the women had been very muscular. Many of the elderly people showed signs of arthritis, a common disease all over Scandinavia at the time. Ten of the women and 23 of the men had been between 30 and 50 years old when they died; two women were older than 50. Two women and one man were between eighteen and 22 years old when they died; fifteen women and fourteen men had died between twenty and 30 years of age; and another fifteen men had died some time after their twentieth year. The average height of the women was 5′1½″, while the average height of the males was 5′7½″ (although several men had been taller than 6′1″).[52]

These statistics are not startling in any way, but they provide a baseline against which we may compare, for example, the teeth and height of later generations of colonists to find an answer to the much-asked question: Was malnutrition an endemic and increasing problem in Norse Greenland? Even here, there are no simple answers. Recent dental studies of Greenland Norse skulls suggest there was a slight decrease in the size and development of teeth over time, and there are also indications of shorter stature, but these changes are not necessarily signs of degeneration, according to the Danish physician and anthropologist N. Lynnerup. Instead, they may be proof of the Norse settlers' efficient adaptation to their Greenland environment. Dr. Lynnerup is only surprised that—according to Thomas McGovern—there was no parallel *cultural* adaptation.[53] Other scholars have also noted the discrepancy between McGovern's adaptation theories and the fact "that those aspects of the teeth used to indicate stress fail to show any significant differences between early and late period samples."[54]

So far, the skeletal remains of some 350 Norse Greenlanders have been made available for study, and all known data about them are now being entered into a computer. These remains are not necessarily a representative selection either geographically or chronologically, however, and they constitute a very small percentage of the approximately 70,000 Norse estimated to have lived in Greenland over a span of 500 years.[55] However much those ancient graveyards may eventually contribute to our knowledge of how average Norse Greenlanders lived and died, and of how they adapted culturally, the real bones of contention lie elsewhere.

CHAPTER THREE

Church and Trade in Norse Greenland Before 1350

The story of the growth of the church in Greenland, from a hazy beginning with the first generation of settlers at Brattahlid to seeming robustness at Gardar see in the thirteenth and early fourteenth centuries, is also the story of the Greenlanders' trade and contact with Norway during the same period. There are three major reasons for this: first, the archbishop and bishops back in Norway were actively engaged in trade, since their tithes and other income were paid in naturalia; second, ships went to Greenland rather infrequently even at the best of times, so church business and private enterprise were usually shipmates; and third, the church kept better records than anybody else. It is well to keep in mind, however, that while the later absence of records about Greenland indicates church indifference, it does not mean the sudden end of private trade or of contact with the rest of the world.

Historia Norvegiae credits the Icelanders with having brought Christianity to Greenland, while "Eiriks saga rauða" and "Kristni saga" claim that Leif Eiriksson went to Norway and was charged by King Olaf Tryggvason (d. 1000) with bringing the Christian faith to Greenland. Eirik the Red was supposedly reluctant to convert to Christianity, but his wife embraced the new faith, "and she had a church built not too close to the farmstead. This building was called Thjodhild's Church, and there she and many others who had accepted Christianity would offer up their prayers."[1]

Because the story of Leif's visit to King Olaf was manufactured much later by the Icelandic monk Gunnlaug, who wrote a flattering biography of Olaf Tryggvason, there has been a tendency also to discount both the possibility that Leif sailed to Norway and that his mother Thjodhild built a church at Brattahlid.[2] Common sense nevertheless suggests that Leif must have sailed to both Norway and Iceland, perhaps several times, to be as skilled a navigator and organizer as his voyage to Vínland shows he must have been. It is likely, too, that he wanted to take his place alongside Icelandic chieftains' sons paying court to the Norwegian rulers. As for Thjodhild and her church: in 1961 a small church consisting of a wooden shell protected by thick turf walls, and surrounded by a circular churchyard, was found on a knoll just south of Eirik's old farm houses.[3] A modern visitor will find only the horseshoe-shaped outline of the three turf walls; the west wall with the entrance had been entirely of wood. But the view east across the iceberg-dotted fjord can scarcely have changed in the almost thousand years since the first tiny Greenland congregation enjoyed it before and after prayers.

It is fitting that the first church in Greenland was built on the colony's principal farm. In the early settlement period, nobody ranked above Eirik the Red. Scholars usually assume that he was also the lawspeaker of the colony, and that he and his settlers perpetuated the Icelandic system of an *Alþing* (general assembly) with both legislative and judicial powers. Eirik's chieftaincy passed to his son Leif and then to Leif's son Thorkell, according to "Fóstbræðra saga" ("The Fosterbrothers' Saga").[4] We cannot trace Eirik's direct heirs further, and we do not know if or when the position of lawspeaker became separated from the chieftaincy of Brattahlid. In Greenland, just as in Iceland, the office of lawspeaker was probably elective and not hereditary, except in the sense that high office had a tendency to be passed around in a very narrow circle.

"Fóstbræðra saga," whose action takes place in the early eleventh century, says that the *Alþing* or annual assembly was held at Gardar in Einarsfjord, not at Brattahlid.[5] The Icelandic sagawriter may of course have superimposed what he knew about Greenlandic practice during his own time, but the large farm at Gardar was so conveniently located in the most densely populated part of the Eastern Settlement that it would have been sensible to hold the assembly there from early on.[6] Einarsfjord lies immediately southeast of Eiriksfjord, and by Greenland standards it is but a short sail from Brattahlid to an isthmus across which a short and pleasant walk leads to the sheltered Gardar plain in the inner Einarsfjord. Gardar would have been equally accessible to the many people living in the lake-strewn inland district known at the time as Vatnahverfi.

The Icelandic skald Helgi Thordsson, whose ship drifted off to Greenland sometime in the first half of the eleventh century, and who wed the suspiciously oft-married widow of Skeggi at Herjolfsnes, eventually became the lawspeaker. Sometime after his marriage he moved to Brattahlid, with no explanation given for the move. A mid-fourteenth century account by the Norwegian priest Ivar Bárdarson says that the "lawman" always lived at Brattahlid.[7] By Ivar's time, the old office of lawspeaker had given way, both in Iceland and in Norway, to a system allowing the Norwegian king more power and the *Alþing* and chieftains less, by replacing the lawspeaker with first one and then two royally appointed lawmen. These lawmen in turn had the power to appoint judges to sit in the *lögretta* that replaced the old lawcourts.[8] We have no way of knowing if these or other administrative changes affecting post-republican Iceland were brought to bear in Greenland, however. Modern excavations have demonstrated that Eirik's old farm eventually developed into three separate complexes, and one of these may have accompanied the newer office of lawman, but we cannot be sure.[9]

When the powerful farmer Sokki Thorisson was the chieftain of Brattahlid around 1123, he must also have been the lawspeaker, for he summoned and presided over a general assembly to discuss what he considered an urgent need to have a proper episcopal diocese in Greenland. If we may believe the story told in "Grænlendinga þáttr" (preserved in the late-fourteenth-century compendium *Flateyjarbók*), Sokki got the other farmers to agree that his son Einar should go to Norway and petition King Sigurd "Jerusalem-Farer." They were evidently also willing to help share the cost of supporting a bishop. To aid his negotiations with the Norwegians by demonstrating the Greenlanders' ability to pay, Einar took with him plenty of walrus tusks and hides.[10]

As mentioned in a previous chapter, the Greenlanders appear to have had one bishop already, the Icelander Eirik Gnupsson *upsi*, who had gone to find Vínland in 1121. This was just a couple of years before Sokki Thorisson at Brattahlid sent Einar off on his mission to Norway. Sokki either may have wanted Greenland to have the status of a regular episcopal establishment, as the Icelanders had after the establishment of the Skálholt and Holar bishoprics, or he simply may have wished to make certain the Greenlanders had a hand in the next appointment. He would surely have been aware of Bishop Eirik's disappearance, whether Eirik had set out from the Eastern Settlement, from Sandnes in the Western Settlement, or even from Iceland as Jette Arneborg has suggested, for the account in "Grænlendinga þáttr" indicates comparatively frequent communication both between the Eastern and Western Settlements and between Greenland and Iceland at the time.[11]

The Bishop of Skálholt at the time Sokki summoned his assembly was Thorlak Runolfsson, whose mother was the granddaughter of Karlsefni of Vínland fame. Continued contact between Karlsefni's kin and the people at Brattahlid may have contributed to Sokki's ambition. It is also likely that Sokki and some of the other chieftains expected financial advantage, as well as prestige, from having a bishop and regular clergy in their country. By this time, tithing had been mandatory in Iceland for about twenty years (Iceland was the first of the Scandinavian countries to pass such laws), and Sokki may have figured that as the chieftain of Brattahlid and the owner of a church, he might be entitled to a full half of the tithe—the fourth that was meant for the upkeep of the church building (*kirkjutíund*) and the fourth that paid for the priest's services (*preststíund*)—if he emulated some of his Icelandic peers and had himself or a member of his household ordained. The bishop and the poor could then share the remaining half.[12]

A live polar bear that Einar had also brought with him from Greenland helped smooth his relations with King Sigurd, and the rest of Einar's valuable cargo must have convinced the king and others that the Greenlanders were prosperous enough to support a bishop. A Norwegian clerk named Arnald was appointed bishop to the Greenlanders in 1124 and was consecrated in Lund that same year.[13] Arnald may have been a braver and more adventurous man than many of his clerical colleagues, but it is worth noting that for him, at least, being the bishop of Gardar did not mean professional death at the back-of-beyond. In 1152 he was made Bishop of Hamar back home in Norway, having been succeeded in Greenland by Bishop Jon *knútr* ("knuckle" or "knot").[14]

After his consecration to the Gardar see, Bishop Arnald sailed to Iceland with Einar. Here they spent the winter of 1125–26, allowing the new bishop to become acquainted with his two Icelandic colleagues, Thorlak of Skálholt and Ketil of Holar. The *Icelandic Annals* proudly noted that in 1126, three bishops were present at the *Alþing* at the same time.[15] Presumably, as the son of the chieftain at Brattahlid and the protector of the Greenland bishop, Einar Sokkason also consorted with the chief men of Iceland, exchanging news and renewing old connections.

According to "Grænlendinga þáttr," Bishop Arnald maintained good relations with Einar Sokkason and his father at Brattahlid when safely arrived in Greenland, although he decided to establish his episcopal residence at Gardar in Einarsfjord. Jette Arneborg has argued convincingly against the generally held notion that the large farm at Gardar, one of the best farms in the settlement, at any time was simply handed over to the church. This makes particular sense when we consider that Bishop Arnald was a foreigner.[16] Developments that will be discussed later suggest that Arneborg's analysis is correct, as is her supposition that continued secular control helps explain the reluctance to stay in Greenland that many later bishops displayed.

During Arnald's long tenure at Gardar, he taught the Greenlanders to reckon with his office. He had a keen appreciation of money and played a major part in the central controversy reported in "Grænlendinga þáttr," which resulted from a treasure found in a deserted place near a ship (and its dead Norwegian owners) by some Greenland hunters. Bishop Arnald encouraged the hunters to turn over much of this treasure to the church at Gardar, so that masses could be said for the dead men's souls. The rest of the loot was distributed among the finders, as was customary. Enraged Norwegian heirs sailed to Greenland to demand their money, but the bishop stood firm and as usual counted on Einar Sokkason and his father to support him. Einar and several others lost their lives in the protracted quarrel, but Bishop Arnald weathered the crisis so well that it did not even prevent his later advancement in Norway, where the tale had been told by the foiled heirs and their men.

Arnald's successor, Bishop Jon *knútr*, was followed by Jon *smyrill* ("sparrow-hawk") Sverrifostri, who was consecrated in 1188 and arrived in Greenland the following year, after a stopover in Iceland to meet Bishop Brand of Holar and the aging Bishop Thorlak of Skálholt—and perhaps to see how they implemented church directives among the Icelanders.[17] Thorlak had already become known for his statutes aimed at improving the morals of both churchmen and laymen in his country, apparently a daunting task. He was also the first Icelandic bishop to demand that both the churches and their income should belong to the church, rather than to the chieftains—an issue that remained unsettled in Iceland for at least another 120 years, and one that there is little reason to suppose was ever settled in Greenland.[18]

Whatever Jon *smyrill* may have learned from his Icelandic colleagues, he no doubt also had his own ideas about what was due to his office and to himself. When he arrived at his see, a large episcopal farm and a cathedral of sorts already awaited him, but a new, cruciform cathedral (Gardar II) dedicated to St. Nicholas was built around A.D. 1200. Both Poul Nørlund and later scholars therefore think that it was raised at Jon's initiative, and that the remains of a strongly built man found in 1926 under the floor of the north chapel were his. A bishop's gold ring and a fine crozier made of ashwood and carved walrus ivory were found buried with him.[19]

Though no match for the ambitious ecclesiastical edifices going up elsewhere in Europe at that time, Gardar cathedral distinguished itself by size and shape from the surrounding stone-and-turf houses. It was built of blocks of the local red sandstone, which had a handsome pattern of white dots and circles, and it had molded soapstone trim. Huge sandstone slabs paved the way from the sacristy to the main door of the episcopal dwelling. We also know that the cathedral had a separate bell tower and windows of opaque, greenish glass. Such windows would have been compatible with the period of Jon *smyrill*'s tenure, for in 1195 Bishop Thorlak's successor at Skálholt, Bishop Páll, brought two glass windows back to his cathedral in Iceland when he returned from being consecrated abroad.[20]

Bishop Páll of Skálholt and Bishop Jon *smyrill* of Gardar were good friends, so Jon spent the year 1203 in Iceland visiting Páll before going on to Norway and Rome. After a few more years back in Greenland, he died there in 1209. Such a catalog of one man's travels makes voyages in those waters seem easy and commonplace, but they were demonstrably dangerous and, as mentioned earlier, neither particularly frequent nor regular even between Iceland and Norway. The *Icelandic Annals* note, for instance, that in 1187 no ship arrived in Iceland from Norway, and again in 1219: "*Kom ecki skip til Islands.*"[21]

Throughout the entire life of the Norse Greenland colony, the dangers of the route and the infrequency of sailings were important obstacles to maintaining tight administrative ties between that colony and the Norwegian ecclesiastical and secular authorities. Especially when early missionary zeal waned, priests and bishops had to balance the dangers of the voyage against whatever advantages awaited them in remote Greenland, just as did the merchants described in *The King's Mirror*. It added to the danger that not every ship in those waters was a sturdy, Norwegian-built *knarr*, for the Greenlanders were building their own ships from at least the 1180s and sailing them boldly wherever they needed to go.[22] In 1189, a man named Ásmund *kastanrassi* ("Wriggle-Ass") sailed from Greenland via the uninhabited east coast and fetched up in Iceland with his small, Greenland-made ship held together with wooden pegs and baleen or sinew lashings. It was clearly a sight to behold, since the Icelanders took special notice of it. Aage Roussell found evidence of exactly this type of shipbuilding during his 1934 excavations at Umiviarssuk, not far from Sandnes farm in the Western Settlement. Unfortunately, Ásmund went down with his ship the following year on the next leg of his voyage to Norway.[23]

Of course, even well-built Norwegian ships were also lost in the treacherous North Atlantic. A ship named *Stangarfóli*, which had set sail from Bergen in Norway on a course for Iceland at about the time Ásmund was heading east, also disappeared. In the year 1200, hunters found its wreck on the inhospitable east coast of Greenland, along with the skeletons of six men and the undecomposed body of a seventh, the Icelandic priest Ingimund Thorgeirsson. Next to Ingimund lay several wax tablets on which he had carved runes to tell about his death from starvation. It is not in itself odd that he chose to write his story in runes, since runes were used concurrently with the Roman alphabet for a long time in both Iceland and Greenland, and even in Norway. But Ingimund was not only a priest; he had been the Norwegian archbishop's first choice as bishop of Gardar when Bishop Jon *knútr* died. Ingimund had declined the honor, and Jon *smyrill* had been appointed in his stead.[24] Ingimund ended in Greenland whether he liked it or not, and the service over his remains may well have been performed by Jon himself.

By this time there were several other churches in the two settlements, but we have no way of knowing how many priests there were. Old documents suggest that priests were spread thinly in several parts of the Norwegian archdiocese. In 1206, for instance, the pope wrote sternly to Archbishop Thorir that it did not constitute a proper baptism if, for lack of both priest and water, a dying infant was anointed with spit on the forehead and chest and between the shoulders.[25] Under circumstances that problematic, a priest might have charge of several churches, especially if they were "half-churches" or chapels.

A map in C. L. Vebæk's recent account of the known churches in the two Greenland settlements shows the thirteen Eastern Settlement church sites that archaeologists had located by 1989, including several small churches from the early period, with round or oval churchyards. Vebæk notes that these "undoubtedly belonged to the very farms near which they were situated." They are not likely to have been parish churches, for they are not named in Ivar Bárdarson's list of Greenland churches, nor in the other lists provided by the late-fourteenth-century *Flateyjarbók* and in the seventeenth-century writings of Björn Jonsson of Skardsá and Arngrimur Jonsson. Most likely, they were chapels without a regular priest attached.[26] Excavations of some of the bigger churches indicate that several of them were built in the late twelfth or early thirteenth centuries, and that none appears to have been built later than about A.D. 1300, when the famous Hvalsey church was erected.

No church has so far been located in the so-called Middle Settlement (now considered the northernmost part of the Eastern Settlement). That there must have been at least one church in that area, however, is suggested by a tombstone with a runic inscription that had been used as building material in an Eskimo house on Napassut Island, south of Ivittut. In the Western Settlement as well, the youngest of the three churches found (V7 at Ujarassuit) also dates from about 1300, although Roussell notes that the church at Sandnes, the principal farm in the Western Settlement, had a Gothic chancel with a nave added later.[27]

During this expansion of the Roman Church in Greenland, to which Jon *smyrill* must have contributed until he died in 1209, an Augustinian monastery was founded in Tasermiut fjord (Norse: Ketilsfjord) and a Benedictine convent in Uunartoq fjord (Norse: Siglufjord, or in Ivar Bárdarson's account, Ramsnesfjord). A church was attached to each religious establishment. In 1926, when Poul Nørlund and Aage Roussell examined the church believed to be associated with the monastery (Ø105), they ventured an early date of about 1200 for that building.[28]

The nunnery at Narsarsuaq (Ø149) with its church and large farm, which Nørlund discovered in 1932, was excavated by Vebæk during the summers of 1945, 1946, and 1948. He estimates the church to have been among the most recent ones, built around 1300, but he found signs of at least one earlier church on the site. This is not surprising, since the Benedictine nunneries in Iceland and Norway were founded in the twelfth century, and there is no reason to suppose that Greenland was very different in this respect.[29]

The many surviving homilies from twelfth-century Iceland show that the Icelandic clergy, at least, kept in touch with mainstream European Catholicism. Sermons in the vernacular were not unknown, but the Mass and other services were conducted in Latin. Jon *smyrill*'s friend Bishop Páll of Skálholt had gone to school in England, and Páll's predecessor, Bishop Thorlak, had studied in Paris and at Lincoln for six years.[30] Even so, we must ponder against the backdrop of later events how much book learning was shipped all the way to Greenland, and to what degree the congregations in either Iceland and Greenland were influenced by gentle scholarship and Christian instruction.

Letters from Pope Innocent III during the opening years of the thirteenth century certainly suggest that Norse bishops in those days faced a certain amount of physical risk. For example, in 1202 Bishop Bjarni of Orkney's tongue was cut out on orders from Earl Harald of Orkney, and in 1206 the pope wrote to the Norwegian archbishop, Thorir, about complaints that priests in Thorir's diocese had engaged in lay business, gone to war, spilled blood, and taken off their priestly habit, to name a few irregularities.[31] It would be surprising if the clergy in Greenland during that period could not give as good as they got, or if the laity there constituted a model of sober respect for God's work. They certainly did not do so in Iceland, where the first quarter of the thirteenth century witnessed bloody controversies between powerful northern farmers and Gudmund Árason, the bishop of Holar from 1203 until 1237. After Gudmund had been forced to take refuge with the famous saga-writer Snorri Sturluson at Reykholt, Gudmund's enemies killed his supporters, and fully armed they entered Holar Cathedral, drove people out into the churchyard, and killed them. Two chieftains took over the bishop's farm, fields, and tithes and forced the remaining priests to conduct services.[32]

Despite irregular shipping connections, news of the struggles and changes in both Norway and Iceland must eventually have reached the ears of Bishop Jon *smyrill*'s successor, Bishop Helgi of Gardar.[33] Bishop Helgi had come to Greenland around 1212, after his ordination and the customary stopover in Iceland on the outbound voyage. We know nothing about his tenure in Greenland. Three years had passed between Jon *smyrill*'s death and Bishop Helgi's arrival, and after Helgi's death in 1230 there was an interval of ten years before the next bishop came to Gardar.[34] During such interims, the church probably was in at least as vulnerable a position vis-à-vis powerful and unruly laymen in Greenland as in Iceland.

A man named Nicholas was consecrated in 1234 as Helgi's successor but did not finally arrive at his see until six years later, and died only two years after that, in 1242.[35] We know too little to say whether the delay in filling the post had been due to difficulty in finding someone willing to go to Greenland, to power struggles in Norway, or to a slowness in communications that not only delayed the bishop-elect's voyage to Greenland but may even have kept the archbishop ignorant of Helgi's death for a year or two. Communications were certainly slow, especially since distant Rome had to be informed of vacancies and proposed appointments, but we must look elsewhere for an explanation of the increasingly long intervals between Greenland appointments.[36]

We can probably rule out the threat of piracy, for it was not yet a serious problem north of the Faroes—although some people may have imagined that it was. For example, Pope Innocent IV decided in 1244 that the archbishop of York should henceforth consecrate future bishops of Man, to save the bishops-elect from having to cross the dangerous ocean in order to be consecrated by the Norwegian archbishop in Nidaros (later Trondheim).[37] This danger—if real and not a convenient political ruse—probably reflected reluctance to go through the notoriously pirate-infested inside passage west of Scotland, not new or unusual perils in the North Sea or the Atlantic.

A shortage of qualified people is one possible reason for a lack of Gardar aspirants. An indication of the deficit in ecclesiastical manpower in Norway can be seen in the fact that Pope Innocent IV in 1253 gave Archbishop Sörle dispensation for 100 ecclesiastics in the Nidaros archdiocese, making it possible for them to be promoted to all degrees within the church despite having been born out of wedlock.[38]

More important, probably, was the growing Norwegian indifference to the needs of the Atlantic colonies, which must have affected episcopal appointments in Greenland at least as severely as in Iceland. Because medieval Icelandic sources are far more plentiful than those we have for Greenland, it is instructive to look at how developments in Norway influenced church appointments at this time in Iceland.

When the two Icelandic bishops Gudmund of Holar and Magnus of Skálholt both died in 1237, their vacant seats were filled the very next year. This speed was in part owing to the fact that the Norwegian archbishop's hand was forced because Icelandic candidates had been put forward even before the two bishops' deaths. Old Bishop Magnus picked Magnus Gudmundsson to succeed himself, while people in the north of Iceland chose Björn Hjaltason as Gudmund's successor at Holar. When the two *electi* went to Norway in 1236 to be consecrated by Archbishop Sigurd, however, the latter refused, insisting that since the Lateran Council of 1215, episcopal appointments were to be made by the Chapter in Norway. The Icelanders had no say in the matter. Both of the replacement bishops, Sigvard of Skálholt and Botolf of Holar, were Norwegian and Archbishop Sigurd's personal choice.[39]

But once those two substitutes had been ordained and packed off to Iceland, the archbishop evidently considered them off his hands, for when Bishop Botolf wrote and complained that people up north in Iceland showed him disrespect and said nobody could tell from his hands and head that he was a bishop, Sigurd curtly replied that he was obligated only to consecrate the bishops in his province, not to equip them with ring and mitre.[40] If Sigurd cared so little about the figure his bishops cut in Iceland, Greenland was probably lower still in his priorities.

The Greenlanders' greater distance from Norway meant that it was even harder for them than for the Icelanders to influence the center of power. By the same token, however, Greenlandic chieftains and bishops were probably less apt than their Icelandic colleagues to keep an eye on Norway during their domestic struggles for dominance.

Sigvard and Botolf arrived in Iceland to take up their episcopal duties in a country torn by local power struggles and quarrels between Icelandic farmers and Norwegian traders, and by the feud between King Hákon Hákonsson and Skuli Bárdarson for supremacy in Norway. The two bishops supported King Hákon's liege man in Iceland, Gizur Thorvaldsson, who in 1241 killed his former father-in-law Snorri Sturluson, the famous Icelandic chieftain and saga-writer.[41]

Snorri's nephew Sturla Thordarson (1214–84), who followed in his uncle's footsteps as a historian, politician, and skald, provided much of our present information about those turbulent days. It is unfortunate that he gave us only glimpses of developments in Greenland during his lifetime, for his social position, his regard for accurate information, and his personal knowledge of many of the chief characters make his long "Hákonar saga Hákonarsonar" a good source of information about events in Norway and Iceland. The saga was written during 1264–65, or just a couple of years after the Icelanders had yielded to Hákon's relentless efforts to end Iceland's republican independence and make it a tribute country of Norway.[42]

One of Sturla's rare references to Greenland touches on the still unanswered question of whether King Hákon succeeded in making the Greenlanders submit to him. Sturla notes that in the summer of 1247, a new Gardar bishop named Olaf went to Greenland with instructions to persuade the Greenlanders to submit to kingly rule "as was done in all other countries." Another nephew of Snorri Sturluson's, Thord *kakali* ("buffoon"), and Bishop Heinrek, Botolf's replacement at Holar, carried a similar brief with them to Iceland that summer. King Hákon distrusted Thord *kakali* and ordered him back to Norway for good in 1250, but Bishop

Heinrek stayed, and with the help of many Icelanders he eventually succeeded in paving the way for the country's submission to King Hákon.[43]

In the *quid pro quo* of the 1263 covenant of union (*Gamli sáttmáli*) between the Icelanders and the Norwegian king, the Icelanders were promised peace and non-interference in domestic legislation in return for paying taxes and swearing allegiance to the crown, and six supply-ships were to come from Norway every year unless circumstances prevented their sailing.[44] It has been widely assumed that the Greenlanders got a similar arrangement when they seemingly agreed in 1261 (see below) to the principle of paying royal compensation, but the Danish historian Finn Gad demonstrates that this assumption has a flimsy base. It is founded on extrapolation from the Icelandic agreement and on a ludicrous letter from 1568, in which King Fredrik II of Denmark and Norway addressed the royal subjects he imagined were still living in Greenland and said he regretted the discontinuation of an "old agreement" that two ships with supplies were to leave Norway for Greenland each year.[45]

Jette Arneborg finds good reasons for supposing that the Greenlanders did not bow graciously to the demands by the Norwegian king, especially since they demonstrably had the ships and skills necessary to sail to Iceland or Norway and to procure their own goods without waiting for the royal ships, but she also has a weighty argument for the Greenlanders' eventual compliance: without a formal agreement, they might perhaps risk having their ships impounded by royal ombudsmen in Iceland or Norway.[46]

For kingly rule in Greenland to be effective, however, it would also have required a resident royal ombudsman there. The only two surviving sources that mention a separate royal ombudsman for Greenland date from the last quarter of the fourteenth century, and neither tells us anything useful about the royal ombudsman's place in Greenlandic society. According to the first document, dated July 20, 1374, King Hákon VI ordered the confiscation of some property in Bergen which his ombudsman in Greenland, Sigurd Kolbeinsson, had bought in defiance of the king's right to first option. Within two weeks of receiving his summons, Sigurd was to present himself to the lawman in Bergen—a circumstance that shows Sigurd was in Bergen already. Presumably he had also been there when he bought the disputed property, so it is fair to wonder how much time he had actually spent in Greenland.[47] In the second document, dated May 20, 1389, the Greenland ombudsman's name is not even mentioned. In the course of a trial in Bergen, he is said to have acted in accordance with his duties when a party of Icelanders had drifted off to Greenland in the early 1380s and been forced to trade there. We have no other proof of that ombudsman's existence than the sailors' say-so.[48]

These are important documents for other reasons and will be discussed again in Chapters Four and Six, but neither they nor other sources provide any evidence at all that a covenant similar to the Norwegian-Icelandic one was made with Greenland. It is doubtful that it was even *possible* for the Norwegian authorities to exercise meaningful control over Greenland either before or after the 1260s, given bishops who absented themselves from their see for years at a time and communications so attenuated that an exchange of messages could take four years. Furthermore, royal power had already peaked in Norway when Hákon died in 1263. His heir, Magnus Hákonsson "Law Mender" (d. 1280), had been in power for only three years when he ceded the Western Isles and the Isle of Man to Scotland.[49] The power of the crown steadily diminished in Norway until the middle of the fifteenth century and was certainly not going to increase in faraway Greenland.

We must be equally skeptical about the success of ecclesiastical oversight in Greenland, especially by the Norwegian archbishop. To outward appearances, the church remained vigorous in Greenland well into the fourteenth century, with the construction of new churches peaking around the year 1300, but organizational cracks were showing in both Norway and Greenland even before the end of Bishop Olaf's long tenure at Gardar.

We have little information about Olaf and do not know if his appointment was as blatantly political as Bishop Heinrek's in Iceland, or if he had been chosen for other reasons and had merely been ordered to take King Hákon's demand for subjection to Greenland. "Gottskálk's Annals" tell us that Olaf was consecrated in 1246, went to Greenland in 1247, was shipwrecked in Iceland in 1262, and died in 1280. By the time he left Iceland after a stay of two years, the republic was no more, and King Hákon—who had engineered its demise—was dead.[50] It is not clear whether Olaf went straight from Iceland to Norway in 1264, or whether he briefly returned to his see before going abroad again. In any event, the *Icelandic Annals* report that he was shipwrecked again at Hitarnes in Iceland in 1266, in a ship coming from Greenland.[51]

This was the ship carrying the Greenlandic priest Halldor mentioned in Chapter One. Halldor described an expedition that had recently returned to Gardar, having been sent by "the priests" (which presumably included Bishop Olaf) to explore the far north of Greenland.[52] The date of that northern expedition is as unclear as its purpose. It may, for example, have been undertaken to see if the Eskimos could be taxed like the people in the extreme north of Norway. The recipient of Halldor's letter, a Greenland priest named Arnold, had just become chaplain to King Magnus Hákonsson, so the expedition may have been instigated by the crown, with Halldor duly filing a report. In that case, the venture could have involved the same three Norwegians who (according to "Hákonar saga Hákonarsonar") in the fall of 1261 returned home from Greenland after an absence of four years and reported that the Greenlanders had agreed to pay compensation for murder (*þegngildi*) to the Norwegian king, whether the victim was a Norwegian or a Greenlander, and even if the killing had taken place as far north as Norðrsetr or beyond.[53]

This concession has been interpreted as evidence that the Greenlanders submitted completely to King Hákon. If that is true, it is conceivable that when Bishop Olaf left Greenland in 1262 and went to Norway a couple of years later, he sought praise for having helped bend the Greenlanders to the crown's will. It is not a likely scenario, however, because if he anticipated approval on that score, he would have been more likely to accompany the three Norwegians who returned to Norway in 1261 with their good news for the king. Before we assume that the Greenlanders, too, had been worn down by external threats, internal intrigue, and their bishop's injunctions to become the Norwegian king's obedient and taxpaying servants, we should ask if the three returning Norwegians had been sent to Greenland because Bishop Olaf had proved *ineffective* as a royal emissary. In other words, the concession they reported may have been the most the Greenlanders would agree to, rather than an indication of complete subjection to King Hákon.

Both the northern voyage described by Halldor the priest and the return of the three Norwegians to King Hákon fell squarely within Bishop Olaf's tenure at Gardar, and he surely knew at least as much as later chroniclers about everything that might influence his career. The length of his stay in Norway suggests that the real purpose of his trip was to put himself forward for a bishopric at home. Therefore, if he had reason to think King Hákon dissatisfied with him, he was well advised to wait for the king's death before returning to Norway, for Hákon espoused the principle of royal consent in appointing bishops and archbishops.[54]

On his arrival in Norway, Olaf found not only a new king, but a new archbishop, whose consecration in Nidaros he attended in the spring of 1267.[55] However amicable his relations may have been with King Magnus, Archbishop Hákon, and Hákon's almost immediate successor Jon *rauð* ("the Red"), and whatever his hopes for promotion may have been, back to Greenland Olaf went in 1271, to people who had managed without him for nine years, and who probably were no better disposed than the Norwegians toward the relentlessly increasing taxes and tithes of every kind.[56]

Bishop Olaf had not been back at Gardar for very long when the 1274 Church Council of Lyon decreed that all Christians must pay Six-Year Crusading Tithes in addition to their other tithes.[57] Letters passing between Rome and Nidaros make it clear that this would be no easy task for the Norwegian archbishop and his bishops, even supposing that both the clergy and the hard-pressed laity were eager to comply. The troubling state of the Norwegian coinage, which the archbishop claimed was not worth much abroad, made matters worse. Silver coins were increasingly debased with copper, and even at the best of times they had never been used in those remote parts of the Norwegian archbishopric where people had no grain, but lived on fish and milk. On December 4, 1276, Pope John XXI breezily assured Archbishop Jon *rauð* that such people could pay their tithes in naturalia, which then must be converted into gold or silver for easy shipment to Rome. He also excused Jon from visiting his more distant sees in connection with these new Crusading Tithes and allowed him to have them collected from Gardar by "reliable men."[58]

Despite these concessions, the Norwegian archbishop felt obliged to address Rome on the subject two years later. The Six-Year Crusading Tithes had been collected without problems the first year, Jon wrote, but the second year had been one of bad harvests in Norway, so the Norwegian clergy could not pay. He therefore hoped the pope would waive their tithes for that year. Although there were great difficulties involved in reaching Gardar, he continued, two "reliable men" had just been sent off with a ship that was going out there anyway, and they had been given the power both to collect the tithes and to grant absolution to those who had not paid earlier. He hoped the pope would then permit the tithes to be converted to goods that could be traded for silver abroad. In a measured reply of January 31, 1279, the pope (now Nicholas III) approved of this arrangement and said the archbishop's representatives to the Gardar see were allowed to grant absolution there. But there could be no question of waiving any of the tithes due. Jon would, however, have eight years instead of six to collect the money.[59]

The Norwegian archbishop was hardly the pathetically poor and put-upon creature Jon projected in his letters to Rome, for in the second half of the thirteenth century he was by virtue of his office the biggest businessman in Norway, with huge investments in shipping and commerce, especially the codfish trade.[60] Furthermore, at the time of Archbishop Jon's second exchange with the pope, King Magnus was still alive and had just made major changes and concessions (with potential implications also for the Greenlanders) in the crown's relationship with the Norwegian church.

The so-called *Sættargjerð* of 1277, which superseded and redefined all old agreements between the lay and ecclesiastical authorities in Norway, recognized the part that shipping and trade played in church finances. It stipulated that any trade restrictions would exclude bishops, minor clergy, or the laymen in their service, unless the archbishop and his bishops had consented to the restrictions. Equally significant was the incorporation of expanded church taxation, which now was to include every conceivable source of income.[61] Predictably, this action hardened the resistance of those called upon to pay.

Before the extended grace period for the Six-Year Crusading Tithes was up, Bishop Olaf of Gardar died, in 1280 or 1281. It is anyone's guess how he had reacted to Archbishop Jon's two "reliable men" and their errand. It is equally a matter of conjecture whether the Greenlanders were stimulated into paying by strong-arm tactics or by relief at having been granted absolution for past nonpayment, but they must have paid up in some fashion, for Jon soon saw fit to complain about the resale value of their wares. Having so successfully painted a bleak picture for two popes already, the archbishop saw no reason to change his tune, especially since he was finding himself at loggerheads with young King Eirik Magnusson and his Council of Regency and was still smarting from having lost, in 1281, the right to coin money—a right Norwegian archbishops had enjoyed since about 1222.[62] Early in 1282, therefore, Jon *rauð* complained to Pope Martin IV that the tithes from Greenland—oxhides, sealskins, and walrus products— were difficult to sell for a "suitable" price.[63]

Martin IV replied firmly in March of the same year that Jon should sell the regular tithes for gold or silver and send the money to Rome together with the Six-Year Tithes. The pope took the additional precaution of writing to King Eirik Magnusson by the same post, urging him not to interfere with the export of the Six-Year Tithes, and canceling earlier restrictions against the sale of silver to the clergy by laymen, so that tithes paid in naturalia could be converted as easily as possible. Not leaving anything to chance, the pope then wrote to Jon again on May 15, telling him to send the Crusading Tithes for Iceland, the Faroes, Greenland, and Norway through eight named merchants in Lucca, and admonishing him to give written notice of the amount sent.[64]

Little did Martin IV know that the previous spring, while pleading both inferior tithe goods and lack of silver, the Norwegian archbishop had sent off 31 silver bars (equal to 25.5 pounds sterling) to be deposited in the Cistercian monastery Ter Doest in the bishopric of Tournai in what is today Belgium. The abbot's receipt is dated May 20, 1281. Jon *rauð* had probably intended the silver as a pension fund for himself as soon as it had become clear to him that Norway was not big enough to hold him, his young king, and the Council of Regency. Jon went into exile in Sweden in 1282 and died there soon afterwards. The money was finally paid out in the spring of 1284 to Canon Eindridi of Nidaros, who had accompanied the money to Ter Doest in the first place. He had some trouble getting the money released, however, until his patron King Eirik wrote a blunt letter explaining that Jon was dead, and that the money belonged to the Nidaros Chapter.[65]

This tale provides a framework for examining the commonly held view that Greenland's economic position had taken a decided turn for the worse by the end of the thirteenth century—a discussion we shall return to later. It also illustrates a turning point in relations between church and crown in Norway, between Norway and Rome, and between Norway and its colonies. At the fulcrum of this turning point were tithes and taxes.

We have just seen that neither the king nor the archbishops in Norway at that time had scruples about withholding funds from Rome if they thought they could get away with it. Other Norwegians were so reluctant to pay the pope that when Honorius IV in 1285 appointed his chaplain Uguccio as his tithe collector for Norway, he noted sternly that collection in that country had fallen in arrears since the death of Archbishop Jon, and that all clergy must do their part.[66] "Doing their part" chiefly meant excommunicating those who did not pay their tithes. Innumerable injunctions not to waver in this duty were sent out to Norwegian parish priests during the next few decades, which suggests that the threat of excommunication was not always sufficient to make people pay up.

If this was the case in Norway, where episcopal oversight was real and continuous, there is good reason to question Greenland's tithing compliance in the years following Bishop Olaf's death in 1280 or 1281. The Greenlanders had no bishop until Bishop Thord arrived at Gardar some eight or nine years later, in 1289.[67] Church discipline in general and the collection of tithes in particular must have suffered meanwhile, for the Greenlanders could not have predicted if or when a replacement bishop would come. We can see in retrospect that the delay was in great part caused by the confusion after the death of King Magnus "Law-Mender" in 1280, and by the even greater confusion in the Nidaros archbishopric in the time between Jon *rauð*'s flight to Sweden in 1282 and Archbishop Jörund's receiving the pallium in 1288.[68] But the Greenlanders did not know this, and if they had been aware of the confusion, it would scarcely have encouraged them to think that things were well in hand back in Norway.

The late-thirteenth-century story in "Laurentius's Saga" that tells how "King Eirik sent Hrolf to Iceland to go and find New-Country" illustrates both the confusion in Norway and the complexity of the crown's relations with its Atlantic colonies at this time.[69] King Eirik "Priest-Hater" of Denmark and Norway apparently sent Hrolf off on his fruitless search for "New-Country" because in 1285, two priests named Adalbrand and Thorvald Helgasonar had drifted off course and reported spotting an unknown coast far to the west of Iceland. In an amusing analysis of this story, Hermann Pálsson reasons that this "unknown" coast was merely the east coast of Greenland, with which the Icelanders were familiar, and that they had fed the unpopular, ever-greedy King Eirik a tall story to set him off on a wild-goose chase for fresh dominions.[70] It is certainly hard to believe that nobody in all of Iceland knew what lay to the west of their country. They were aware that the Greenlanders were still sailing to Markland, and both Norway and Iceland had sailors able to deliver a bishop to the Greenlanders, as they did again in 1289.

Once arrived in Greenland, Bishop Thord stayed for a remarkable twenty years, which helps to explain the church building boom that lasted into the beginning of the fourteenth century. Norway under Eirik "Priest-Hater" may have been uncongenial enough to make Thord grateful for his post in faraway Greenland, but his devotion to duty more likely resulted from a lack of both travel opportunity and official communications, thanks to the fresh confusion that resulted from changes occurring in Norway when Eirik died in 1299 and his brother, Hákon V Magnusson, succeeded to the throne.

Hákon's *Rettarbót* of 1302 prohibited foreigners from trading north of Bergen, to Iceland, or to any of his other tribute-paying countries.[71] This was bad news for Norway's Atlantic colonies and came on top of the stringent laws passed in the days of Hákon's father, King Magnus. The Icelanders were so troubled by Hákon V's version of the old covenant between Iceland and Norway that the chieftains wrote a letter to the king during the 1302 *Alþing*. While acknowledging Hákon's goodwill and his right to rule over them, they complained that too much wealth was now being taken out of their country and too few goods received in return. Furthermore, the old agreement, which promised six trading ships with imported goods annually, was not being faithfully observed.[72]

Whether or not the Greenlanders had ever had a formal shipping agreement with the crown, Norway's communications with Greenland were even poorer than with Iceland. This is quite evident from a letter that Bishop Arni of Bergen (in office since late 1305) wrote to Thord of Gardar on June 22, 1308. Bishop Arni surmised that Thord did not yet know that King Eirik "Priest-Hater" had been dead since 1299, and he passed on the additional news that five Norwegian bishops had died during the past few years, including the bishop of the Faroes, who had passed away in Bergen shortly before Arni wrote. Arni's studiously bland letter asked Thord to pray for the dead bishops' souls.[73] By the same post, the Bergen bishop wrote to the bishop of Skálholt to tell him that Bishop Erlend of the Faroes was dead, and to warn his Icelandic colleague to expect unrest in Norway.[74] Gifts accompanied both letters, the most interesting one being a generous personal gift to Bishop Thord of a pale blue chaperon lined with black fur, and a matching gown.[75] Either the wealthy Bishop Arni assumed that these were the sort of clothes his Greenland colleague needed at Gardar, or his gift as well as his letter constituted a veiled invitation to an old friend to come home and apply for one of the vacant bishoprics, dressed as befitted a man in his position.[76] The latter explanation seems the more likely one, for when the Bergen ship returned to Norway the following year, the Gardar bishop was on board, presumably with his fine new clothes. He stayed in Norway until both he and Bishop Arni died in 1314.[77]

Prior to Thord's arrival, his Bergen colleague had engaged in a protracted correspondence with the aging Archbishop Jörund, who had sent notice that he wished to convene a meeting of the Provincial Council in Nidaros in March of 1309 that Arni clearly had no intention of attending and to which he did not go. The correspondence between the two men grew heated after Jörund wrote (February 6, 1309) that he intended to consecrate the Norwegian priest Lodin as the new bishop of the Faroes at this meeting. In his efforts to prevent this appointment, Arni even wrote directly to Rome. Old Jörund's death in April of 1309 did not put an end to the dispute. When Thord arrived from Greenland that summer, his friend was still pursuing his delaying tactics, arguing as before that it was customary for the bishop of the Faroes to be chosen from a pool of approved Bergen candidates. Bishop Thord of Gardar would no doubt have been eligible by this standard, for he is referred to as a canon of Bergen in several documents from 1310 and 1311, most of them involving him directly in Arni's fierce fight to prevent Lodin's consecration, which continued under Jörund's successor, Archbishop Eiliv. Indeed, Arni so resented Eiliv's support of Lodin that he refused to collect money in his bishopric for Eiliv's pallium. Lodin eventually drowned in 1316 without having been consecrated, but he had been in control of the Faroese episcopal income since 1311.[78]

Such power struggles between the archbishop and the Bergen bishop were bound to echo in the Atlantic colonies. To a much greater degree than the archbishop, the Bergen bishop was directly involved in colonial affairs, because colonial trade and the collection of tithes and taxes in large measure passed through his hands. Bishop Thord of Gardar's firsthand information about Greenland must therefore have been very useful to his enterprising friend Arni, and while the latter did not succeed in making Thord bishop of the Faroes, he let Thord watch his battle skills at close quarters. Arni fought not only against the archbishop, but against lax monks, priests, and laity in his diocese; against resident German merchants who refused to pay their tithes; and even against the crown itself, by trying to diminish the authority of *Magister capellarum* Finn Halldorsson, Dean of the Royal Chapel in Bergen.

In an effort to reduce episcopal power in Norway, King Hákon V had just received the pope's permission to make the clergy in his fourteen Royal Chapels accountable only to a *Magister capellarum*, to the pope, and to himself.[79] Heading these Royal Chapels was the Church of the Twelve

Apostles in Bergen, where Finn Halldorsson was now the *Magister capel-larum*. And because all bishops were *ex officio* members of the Norwegian Council, Hákon V wasted no time in ensuring that candidates for vacant bishoprics were recruited from either his Royal Chapel in Bergen or from the second most important one, the Church of St. Mary in Oslo. This arrangement, so central to his intention of governing through patronage, had important consequences for Norway and its colonies, both during his lifetime and later, and it was a situation that ambitious clergymen could not afford to ignore.[80]

In his efforts both to protect his see's traditional perquisites and to maneuver Thord into a bishopric closer to home, Bishop Arni was thus playing a dangerous game. He lost some of his battles, but he must still have been at the height of his power when he died in 1314, for he was immediately succeeded by his brother, Bishop Audfinn of Stavanger, who continued Arni's defiant style.[81]

Thord of Gardar's death must have been anticipated, for his successor, also named Arni, was consecrated shortly before Thord died in 1314.[82] We do not know if this Bishop Arni was connected with any of the Royal Chapels, nor do we know if he stopped in Iceland on his way to Greenland in 1315. If he did, he was fortunate enough to do so during a lull in the various epidemics that had struck Iceland in 1306, 1309, and 1310, often together with exceptionally bad weather.[83]

When Arni arrived at Gardar see, it had been left to a steward for six years, but the Greenlanders evidently were none the worse for wear. If they had caught the smallpox, mumps, or other infections being passed around in Scandinavia at that time, illness failed to clip their wings, judging from two incidents that took place during the period of Arni's tenure. Both concern the value of cargoes shipped from Greenland to Norway, a subject that will shortly take us back to Archbishop Jon *rauð*'s lachrymose correspondence with the popes.

The first item is a grievance that seems to have involved several private merchant ships, not just a single official one. On July 24, 1325, Bishop Audfinn of Bergen complained in a letter to the archbishop of Nidaros about the tithes due on wares "from those Trondheim merchants who are now arriving on the Greenland *knarrs*." Archbishop Eiliv replied the very next month that according to the law, Greenland merchants need not pay tithes until they had decided where to spend the winter, so if these travelers were not going to spend the winter in Bergen, they should probably pay their taxes back home in Nidaros.[84]

The second item provides a partial answer to the question of whether Greenland by this time was capable of contributing significantly to the economy of the church. In 1327, just two years after Bishop Audfinn's complaint about the Trondheim merchants who had arrived with private trading goods from Greenland, there arrived in Bergen "127 *lisponsos ad pondus Norwege*" of walrus ivory from Greenland. This shipment, equal to some 800–1100 kilos (depending on one's reference source), constituted Peter's Pence and Crusading Tithes. A merchant from Flanders bought the cargo for "*12 libris & 14. sol. turon argenti,*" said to equal about 28 lbs. of pure silver.[85] Scarcely three years earlier, Archbishop Eiliv had advised the Papal treasury at Avignon of the payment of Peter's Pence from his entire archdiocese: 55 pounds sterling and five solidos, or the equivalent of 331 and a half gold guilders.[86] Although the Greenland ivory covered both Peter's Pence and Crusading Tithes, the money contributed was not inconsiderable when compared with this second sum. It is even more significant in the present context that in a two-year period, the Greenlanders could pay church dues *and* make the long voyage worthwhile for private merchants.

Finn Gad assumes that the crown had little profit from its distant tribute country by this time, because a royal document of August 16, 1328, seems to indicate that the year before, Gardar see had contributed only a sixteenth of the total Crusading Tithes collected by the Norwegian archbishop, or a tenth of the sum contributed by Bergen.[87] Such figures may be proof of the Greenlanders' reluctance to pay, or they may merely demonstrate the great wealth and relatively large population of Bergen and its surrounding area. It is difficult to know the exact amounts paid in Peter's Pence or other levies by *any* medieval Norwegian bishopric, particularly during periods of rapid inflation in Europe. There are many gaps in the extant documents; the sums are given in such a variety of coinage and weights that we cannot be sure we are dealing with the same payment in different sources; and even when the sums are quoted in Norwegian marks, we do not always know if we are dealing with counted or weighed silver.[88] We also lack reliable population figures for the various dioceses and cannot estimate the taxes and tithes supposedly due from each.

It is more useful to our Greenland study to focus on some verifiable aspects of the complex economic picture in Norway in the first half of the fourteenth century. First, Bergen was so busy, rich, and important that a document from 1316 refers to not just one but two *féhirðir* (royal ombudsmen) in Bergen, responsible for calling in taxes and keeping accounts.[89] The king's men did not readily submit to the authority and taxing power of the church. At the beginning of 1328, for example, Bishop Audfinn of Bergen complained to his archbishop that when he tried to collect tithes for some Bergen property, he was threatened by no fewer than three royal officials: the lawman as well as the sub-ombudsman and the seneschal.[90] Second, while Pope John XXII (r. 1316–34) enjoined the archbishops of both Nidaros and Lund to collect Peter's Pence vigorously, and to present proper accounts rather than allow business practice to slide as in the past, the records show that in Sweden the collectors ran into considerable resistance in the 1320s, and the situation in Norway was clearly no better either then or in the next decade. For example, in 1335, King Magnus ordered all who owed old or new debts and fees to the Bergen Cathedral and to the bishop to pay those debts within a month.[91] Third, at the end of 1328, Archbishop Eiliv of Nidaros prohibited the collectors of papal tithes from collecting more than half of those tithes, for Pope John XXII had given the other half to the Norwegian king for fighting the heathen Russians, and those funds were to be supervised by the archbishop.[92] Fourth, as noted earlier, ships were still arriving from Greenland in 1325 with cargoes valuable enough to invite additional squabbles over tithes and taxes. This last circumstance is generally overlooked in the prevailing dark view of the Greenlanders' situation. This view is succinctly expressed by Gwyn Jones:

At the end of the [thirteenth] century the Crown made the Greenland trade the monopoly of the Norwegian merchants of Bergen. We can trace the consequences for Iceland with fair exactitude: in the years 1326, 1350, 1355, 1374, and 1390 no ship reached Iceland from Norway; and in 1324, 1333, 1357, 1362, 1367, and 1392 one ship only. The consequences for Greenland would be even more severe, as trading developments in Norway erased so remote, perilous, and unprofitable a route from the merchant's portolan. Bergen had become glutted with cheaper furs and hides and walrus tusks raked from nearer hunting grounds; Martin IV in Rome and the Archbishop of Nidaros wag sad heads at each other over the resultant devaluation of the Greenland tithe, payable in such commodities. . . . And this as early as 1282, before the bottom fell out of the market. (p.102)

Jones neglects to cite his sources for the 1282 reference, although it clearly points to the correspondence growing out of Archbishop Jon *rauð*'s reluctance to part with money for the pope's coffers. Similarly, no evidence is cited for his information on shipping, but it has to come from the *Icelandic Annals*. Nor does he allow for the feast-or-famine aspect of shipping in periods notable for extreme weather variations—if the *Icelandic Annals* are any guide.

Jones treats the entire fourteenth century as a continuation of the late thirteenth. The failure of his analysis to differentiate between the periods before and after the Black Death struck Norway in 1349 is troubling in such a blanket statement about pivotal events. It is even more disturbing that it is impossible to trace any solid information underlying his general statement about the devaluation of Greenland staples. These staples included a great variety of products, ranging from walrus ivory, eiderdown, and precious furs to hides and homespun.

In other words, Jones's view that the Greenland economy was already showing signs of decline by the end of the thirteenth century has a shaky foundation. If we want to understand what happened to the Greenlanders around the year 1500, we must first be clear about their position a couple of centuries earlier. This includes returning to Archbishop Jon's complaints to see if the economic situation in Greenland immediately before 1300 warrants such a bleak conclusion. In fact, I believe it does not. The archbishop's correspondence can be understood not as proof of a precarious Greenland economy but as crafty maneuvering on the part of a greedy cleric confronted with popes as rapacious as himself, against a background of growing tensions among various branches of authority in Norway. The devaluation of the Norwegian coinage (noted by the archbishop) accelerated in the 1340s and caused severe problems in Norway, but it would not have affected the Greenlanders adversely, since they never used coin, but paid for everything—including their tithes—in naturalia. The Norwegian medievalist Grethe Authén Blom points out that since silver for coins was not mined in Norway during the Middle Ages, the king's income was also almost entirely paid in kind. She notes that "apart from cattle hides, stockfish and butter, the products of medieval Norway were of inferior quality and little was suitable for sale. It was essential that the king obtain other articles that could be easily changed into money, or goods that were not available in his own country."[93]

Several Greenland products filled that bill. For as long they had buyers, they would fetch the going market price elsewhere, and—since devaluation and inflation go together—they would be more valuable in stockpiles than any coin of the realm. Medieval Norwegian kings and archbishops knew that perfectly well and relied on it in their relentless quest for money. Our next question must therefore be whether there still were buyers for Greenland produce after the end of the thirteenth century.

In Chapter One we noted that as late as 1516, Archbishop Valkendorf was making plans to sponsor a trading voyage to Greenland. It would be hard to explain the archbishop's eagerness to cash in on Greenland wares if the bottom had dropped out of the market for most of what Greenland had to offer as early as the beginning of the fourteenth century.[94] It would be equally hard to explain why Hákon V Magnusson made a five-year trade treaty with Flanders in 1308 if Norway no longer needed to market luxury goods.[95] What were the most important luxury goods that came from Greenland? Walrus ivory was one, and we have already seen that it was a Flanders merchant who bought the walrus ivory that came in from Greenland in 1327. The other was the white gyrfalcons called Greenland falcons because they were almost never found elsewhere. It is probably safe to assume that neither ivory nor gyrfalcons were *ever* traded cheek-by-jowl with codfish and sheepskins in the Bergen market.

Difficult to catch even in Greenland, gyrfalcons were worth a fortune by the time they reached Europe; the duke of Burgundy is said to have ransomed his son from the Saracens as late as in 1396 for twelve Greenland falcons.[96] In 1276, just when Archbishop Jon was fine-tuning his laments, the Norwegian king sent the English king a princely gift of three white and eight grey gyrfalcons, a large number of ermine pelts, and a complete whale's head with all the baleen still attached. In the spring of 1315, Edward II of England sent a man to Norway to buy falcons and hawks— hardly a sign that these birds were now a glut on the international market.[97]

On the contrary, by 1337 gyrfalcons had grown in such short supply that Bishop Hákon of Bergen was obliged to write to King Magnus that he had not been able to obtain for him either white or grey falcons from an unnamed "Scottish page," and the situation was no better three years later. When the Bergen bishop wrote in November of 1340 to report to King Magnus about tax collections, he noted that Raimundo de Lamena, who was supposed to receive falcons in payment for apothecary goods, had not been able to get more than two or three birds from the royal palace in Bergen.[98] These incidents strongly suggest that both white and grey gyrfalcons, which had been a prized Greenland export since the beginning of the settlement, were as valuable as ever in the second quarter of the fourteenth century. If anything, there was a shortage of supply.

There is good reason to suppose that other Greenland exports also retained their value. Plain homespun wool cloth (*vaðmál*) was so central to the medieval Scandinavian economy that after the union with Norway in 1263, the Icelanders' tax to the Norwegian king was assessed in that commodity.[99] Greenland wool was prized for its high quality. Walrus hide continued to be unmatched for strength, and walrus ivory was still widely used for liturgical and other purposes throughout the fourteenth century. Narwhal tusks, although brittle and therefore not as suitable for carving as walrus ivory, were peddled as unicorn horns and kept their European reputation for medicinal and magical properties well into the sixteenth century and even later, and they were very expensive.[100]

High-quality furs were so important to the Norwegian economy that from early on traders had exploited such resources high above the arctic circle. The most famous of these was Ohthere (Ottar), a chieftain from Hålogaland who visited the celebrated Anglo-Saxon King Alfred toward the end of the ninth century, and who boasted of exploiting the Finnmark-Kola region. In the fourteenth century Norwegian kings still paid their debts in furs from the far north.[101] Helge Ingstad comments—unfortunately without citing his evidence—on the changes in the Bergen pelt and fur market in the mid-fourteenth century, when the well-entrenched Hanse became the middlemen for the Novgorod fur trade "to the detriment of exports from Greenland and Norway."[102] As in the case of other Greenland commodities, however, the adverse economic consequences here would have affected Norway, especially Bergen, rather than Greenland.

The Hanse no doubt made life difficult for the Norwegian merchants in Bergen, especially after the Germans formally established an office there in 1343 following several decades of increasingly liberal concessions from the crown.[103] But Greenland merchants may well have avoided the situation in Bergen by taking their wares elsewhere, or by trading with English, Scottish, or other non-Scandinavian merchants—a subject that will be discussed later in a different context. There may also have been changes in first ports-of-call resulting from adjustments in North Atlantic sailing routes due to the widening belt of sea ice brought by a cooling climate. Ivar Bárdarson's "Description of Greenland," which included directions for the best sailing routes to Greenland from both Iceland and Norway in the mid-fourteenth century, noted that it had become too dangerous to use the earlier direct route between Snæfellsness in Iceland and the islands off the east coast of Greenland. He recommended instead a more southerly route around present-day Cape Farewell before aiming for Herjolfsnes in the Eastern Settlement.[104]

It is important to stress here that while later navigators also described the ice belt as both daunting and variable, ice cannot be blamed for mid-fourteenth-century problems with Greenland trade. Ivar was describing a *workable* route. Furthermore, in 1344, three years after Ivar had left Norway, Thord Eigilsson "sailed to Greenland and the same year returned to Norway with a richly laden ship and much goods."[105] Normally, a ship would make the outward voyage one year and sail home the following summer after wintering in Greenland or Iceland, so if Thord accomplished the round-trip voyage in one season, he cannot have encountered too much trouble that year. The *Icelandic Annals* noted for 1346, right after observing that Thord Eigilsson ceased to be lawman for South Iceland that year, that the Greenland *knarr* arrived safely (presumably in Iceland) with much goods.[106] This information may belong with the 1344 voyage; the point is that there were countless voyages about which we know nothing at all, especially direct voyages between Norway and Greenland that were of little interest to the Icelandic annalists or to the church.[107]

No less important were the Norwegian monarchs' reiterations of their trade monopolies with the Atlantic colonies throughout the fourteenth century, along with their increasing wish to turn a profit and to exercise control through the sale of licenses.[108] Both of these developments encouraged evasiveness and secrecy and put a premium on illicit Greenland trade, with results that will be discussed more fully in Chapters Five and Six.

Ecclesiastical and secular authorities in Bergen supposedly monitored colonial tax collection and trade, but they did not necessarily have shared goals or loyalties.[109] The picture of Greenland trade in Bergen in the mid-fourteenth century is further clouded by a change in that city's accounting practices. When Bishop Hákon of Bergen wrote to Magnus in the summer of 1340 asking the king to approve the decisions he, the archbishop, and others had made concerning the value and minting of new money, he also requested that the Bergen bishop no longer be responsible for accounting for the king's tax receipts. The money he—Bishop Hákon—earned from this privilege did not compensate him for the trouble caused by the present unfavorable and confused state of the tax-collecting system.[110]

Additional correspondence between the bishop and the king during the 1340s makes it clear that the ombudsman's office in Bergen was in a state of disarray during this period. Some of the responsibility for collecting and accounting for secular taxes devolved on the ombudsmen, some on the bishop, and some was left to others to deal with.[111] It would therefore not be surprising if accounts of import taxes and tithes on Greenland goods went missing. There are strong indications, however, that it was the goods themselves that went missing—at least those intended for church and crown.

The Norwegian king's lack of white and grey falcons by 1337 is just one indication of this development. Greenland imports intended for the payment of tithes and taxes became conspicuously absent in accounts for the second quarter of the fourteenth century, while Bishop Arni was still at Gardar. In the Norwegian tithe collections of 1333, Gardar is not mentioned at all, and in 1340, the Bergen bishop complained to Magnus *smeyk* that people "coming from the West" would not pay their taxes to the king's fiscal representative (*féhirðir*) there, but only to the king himself.[112] Jette Arneborg thinks it quite likely that the Greenlanders were among these recalcitrant people, and that this was the reason the Bergen bishop, who must still have profited from administering the king's income, decided the following year to send the clergyman Ivar Bárdarson as *officialis*, or episcopal ombudsman, at Gardar see in Greenland.[113]

Such an office had been known in Norway since 1290, and Archbishop Eiliv had decreed in 1327 that every bishop should have an *officialis* to look after the finances of his bishopric, but there had clearly been no hurry to provide one for the Gardar bishop until now, when the archbishop of Nidaros was Páll Bárdarson, former Royal Chancellor and Dean of the Royal Chapel in Oslo, and the Bergen bishop was Hákon Erlingsson, an equally sturdy broom in royal service.[114] The wish to establish firmer control over Gardar was the natural consequence of clear indications that the Greenlanders were now balking at paying tithes and taxes, as well as of the blurred line between royal and ecclesiastical finances, particularly in the Bergen diocese.

Bishop Hákon was a busy man. He reported directly to King Magnus in Sweden on the state of the royal coffers, and he wrote stern admonitions to priests in his diocese who did not show sufficient talent for collecting money. For example, the year before he issued Ivar Bárdarson's "passport" for Greenland, he warned a priest in Bøfjord to assert his fiscal rights even if his parishioners continued to object.[115] When the tough-minded bishop sent Ivar to Greenland in 1341, he equipped him with a letter in Latin asking everybody to assist this priest from the Bergen diocese, whose errand in Greenland was on behalf of both Bishop Hákon himself as well as the church generally.[116] This implied duality of Ivar's mission is worth noting, for his long stay in Greenland was so important that it will be discussed at length in the next two chapters.

Bishop Arni, who had soldiered on at Gardar meanwhile, was confronted first with the 1341 arrival of the Bergen bishop's emissary and then with the news that, in 1343, Jon Eiriksson *skalli* ("the bald") had been consecrated bishop of Gardar.[117] Although Arni did not breathe his last until 1348, Archbishop Páll of Nidaros claimed he simply had no idea that old Arni was still alive out there in Greenland.[118] Given the number of ships that continued to arrive with goods and news from Greenland and Iceland, the archbishop's obliviousness seems odd, and it is downright suspicious when seen in conjunction with the drying-up of Greenland tithes. The ship that had brought Ivar out to Greenland would have had time to report back on Bishop Arni's failure to fleece his flock and send the wool back to Norway.

The "Skálholt Annals" note both Jon *skalli*'s consecration as bishop of Gardar in 1343 and his failure to go out to his diocese, and it is from the Skálholt archives that Bishop Gisli Oddsson (1593–1638) supposedly got the information that in the year prior to Jon's consecration the Greenlanders had joined with "the folk of America" after having willingly abandoned Christian faith and virtues.[119] Gisli wrote:

The inhabitants of Greenland of their own free will abandoned the true faith and the Christian religion, having already forsaken all good ways and true virtues, and joined themselves with the folk of America. Some consider too that Greenland lies closely adjacent to the western regions of the world. From this it came about that the Christians gave up their voyaging to Greenland. (p. 2)

At the time of Gisli's writing, the European colonization of America was well under way, and the demise of the old Norse colonies in Greenland had been known for some time. Gisli may have attempted—as others after him have done—to explain the disappearance of the Norse Greenlanders in terms of their proximity to America, basing his theory on the Greenlandic "un-Christian" and hostile attitudes to authority that had been noted in mid-fourteenth century Skálholt archives. His statement is neither proof of the Greenlanders' wholesale exodus to the New World in the mid-fourteenth century, nor a lamp by which we may study the fate of Christianity in Greenland. Later developments show that the Greenlanders had incorporated the church into their social fabric and had no particular reason suddenly to reject its teachings and rituals, provided they could control how the church affected their lives and their economy.

Withholding tithes in order to limit expenses connected with the church would have been relatively easy for people so far removed from the centers of authority. That may be one reason why the Provincial Council in Bergen decided in 1345 both to ask for reduced Crusading Tithes and to request complete exemption for the Faroes and Greenland, only a year after Thord Eigilsson supposedly arrived from Greenland with a large and valuable cargo that seems not to have been destined for the church.[120]

The immediate reason for this 1345 petition was Pope Clement VI's demand for a Three-Year Tithe from all ecclesiastical offices in Norway. That same summer, Canon Botolf of Bergen had brought 700 gold guilders in Norwegian Peter's Pence to Avignon, and the pope's new request appears to have strained the Norwegian archbishop's patience. He met with his bishops to determine what each diocese could reasonably offer to contribute, such as six *libras* from Oslo and Nidaros, three from Hamar, and from Gardar and the Faroes *"pro quolibet quatuor libras."*[121] Given the bias of the Norwegian archbishop and his bishops at that time, the petition may be more an indication that the clergy wanted to salvage what they could for themselves than a sign that they had already given up on those colonies, only four years after sending Ivar off on his errand. The pope might find it comparatively easy to credit the Faroes and Greenland, so distant and so poorly known to the Curia, with inability to pay.

Whatever the reason why tithes and taxes failed to arrive in Norway from Greenland, this failure was not the result of extreme poverty among the colonists or of a crippling lack of shipping opportunities, any more than it was due to rejection of the Christian faith. Poul Nørlund has noted that the many fourteenth-century garments he found in the graves at Herjolfsnes were the height of fashion, with elaborate gores and pockets, and so demanding of both cloth and labor that they were hardly a sign of poverty. Bits of Rhenish stoneware found at various Norse Greenland sites are of a type that was popular in Denmark from the middle of the fourteenth century, the very period in question here; even more recent is the fifteenth-century piece that Nørlund found in the depths of the foundation of the great hall at Herjolfsnes.[122] If traders brought such items to Greenland, they must have known they would receive enough payment to make the voyage worth their while.

Jette Arneborg also argues that the halt in the Greenlanders' payment of various tithes cannot have been due to lack of ships, for in 1346, just one year after the Provincial Council in Bergen asked that Greenland and the

Faroes be exempted from paying Crusading Tithes and two years after Thord Eigilsson's reported voyage, the *Icelandic Annals* say that the Greenland *knarr* arrived safely and with a great deal of goods.[123]

The year 1347 was an especially busy one in Icelandic harbors. Thirteen oceangoing ships arrived that year, joining six that were already there, so that when the small, anchorless Markland-ship with seventeen Greenlanders on board also bobbed in, there were twenty foreign ships in all wintering in Iceland.

With so many visitors, it is no coincidence that epidemics of various kinds raged all around Iceland that year and the next, starting in the south.[124] We have no way of knowing if the contagion spread to Greenland, but it is certain that Ivar Bárdarson did not succumb to either illness or accident during his twenty years in Greenland, for he returned safely to Norway with a strange tale to tell. As for the slighted Bishop Arni of Gardar, there is some evidence that he may have been bishop of the Faroes for a brief period in 1348, the same year he died.[125] With Arni gone, Ivar was in sole charge of the bishopric as the Gardar *officialis*, while Arni's supposed replacement, Jon *skalli*, remained in Norway until he was made bishop of Holar many years later, in 1357.[126]

Bishop Jon *skalli* "of Gardar" and Orm of Holar (who was also in Norway at the time) were the only bishops left alive in all of Norway after the Black Death struck that country in 1349 with results every bit as dreadful as those in England, Denmark, and elsewhere in Europe the year before.[127] Cattle and fields were left untended, with terrible economic consequences, at least in the short term. During the peak of this crisis, which also involved Shetland, the Orkneys, the Hebrides, and the Faroes, shipping in the North Atlantic seems to have come to a virtual standstill. The Skálholt bishop's ship *Thorlakssuden* had arrived in Norway in 1347 on what was supposed to be its annual trading voyage, but it was not able to sail home again until 1351. For lack of altar wine, mass was canceled in all church annexes throughout Iceland in 1350.[128]

For the Icelanders and Greenlanders, this lack of communication was nevertheless a blessing in disguise. Another half century passed before the Black Death ravaged Iceland, in 1402–4, and it is unlikely that it ever reached Greenland.[129] For the bubonic, rather than the pneumonic, form of the Plague to take hold in Greenland, a ship would have had to bring both infective rats and sailors still well enough to manage the ship, and the rats would have needed a favorable climate for the survival and reproduction of the flea vectors, which require heat and humidity to breed and flourish. The rat species in question at that time would have been the black rat (*Rattus rattus*), also known as the ship rat, for the brown rat (*Rattus norvegicus*) did not invade Europe from Asia until some three centuries later. The brown rat is adept at exploiting natural habitats away from human dwellings, but the black (or ship) rat is not.[130] The cold and rather arid Greenland climate did not encourage cozy flea-and-rat colonies outside, and no rat bones have been found inside the Norse houses there so far (only the bones of house mice).

When we read the blunt description of the Plague in the "Lögmannsannáll," it seems especially unlikely that the Black Death reached Greenland via voyages that at best took a couple of weeks, and usually much longer: "It was the nature of the pestilence that men lived no more than a day or two, with sharp, stabbing pains in the chest, after which they hemorrhaged and expired."[131] We now know that this is an accurate description of the Plague in its pneumonic and most virulent form, which is transmitted through direct contact rather than through rodents' fleas, and which therefore spreads particularly fast. Pneumonic plague, which is 95–100 percent fatal, was the most common form in northern cold and damp climates.[132] Under such circumstances, it is doubtful that a ship's crew could have lasted long enough to reach Greenland alive.

Some scholars have thought that perhaps the Plague helped finish off the Western Settlement, but archaeologists have found no signs there of large-scale pestilence.[133] In addition, later investigations have shown that although at least parts of the Western Settlement were viable for some decades beyond the first outbreak of the Plague in Norway, this northernmost colony apparently did not last long enough to have been affected by the Icelandic outbreak.[134] The Plague finally reached Iceland in 1402, possibly brought by sailors who had developed full or partial immunity to the disease in one or another form. If it then spread to the Eastern Settlement in Greenland, several prominent Icelanders who spent the years 1406–10 in Greenland (Chapter Six) would not have brought back the rosy report they did about conditions in the Eastern Settlement.[135]

It is easy to assume that the lasting reduction in the number of ships going out to Iceland and Greenland was due to the blow that the Black Death gave the Norwegian economy, but as subsequent events show, this is at best a partial explanation. Private and official shipping enterprises were equally hard hit, and yet it is obvious to any reader of the *Icelandic Annals* and the *Diplomatarium Islandicum* that after the initial shock of the Plague, ships continued to plow the northern seas on both public and private business in the second half of the fourteenth century. For people with money and power, it was a question of priorities and of where their interests lay, not of whether they would be able to travel at all.

But the havoc wreaked by the 1349 arrival of the Black Death in Norway, and the subsequent lull in long-distance sailing, must have had a profound impact on the life of at least one man in Greenland—the priest Ivar

Bárdarson. Having gone there in 1341 to remind the Greenlanders of their responsibilities to church and crown, he might reasonably have expected to go home after a tour of duty of eight to ten years, but instead he stayed for almost twenty years and left a remarkable legacy that ever since has shaped people's ideas about Norse Greenland.

CHAPTER FOUR

Ivar Bárdarson's Greenland

When Ivar Bárdarson arrived at Gardar, old Bishop Arni was alive and presumably still looking after the spiritual needs of his flock. Had Bishop Hákon of Bergen been worried on that score in 1341, he would surely have arranged to find the Greenlanders a better episcopal substitute than a man of business like Ivar. The latter's long stay as the Gardar bishop's *officialis* was evidently dictated not by anyone's tender concern for the Greenlanders' Christian instruction, but by a wish to determine parish boundaries and tithing districts and to restart the flow of goods back to Bergen.[1]

Modern scholars such as Jette Arneborg and Christian Keller also surmise that Ivar's job in Greenland was in part to provide new registrations of the churches and their property, and to claim the king's rights.[2] Both their interpretation and my own arguments below are supported, first, by Ivar's "Description of Greenland"; second, by what we know about the duties of an episcopal *officialis* in general and the blending of royal and ecclesiastical finances in the Bergen diocese in particular; and third, by the fact that Ivar returned to Norway to become a canon at the Royal Chapel in Bergen (the Church of the Twelve Apostles)—an appointment that shows his close connection with the crown as well as with the church.[3]

We do not have Ivar's original report. Finnur Jonsson based his 1930 edition of Ivar's "Description of Greenland" mainly on a seventeenth-century copy of a manuscript he judged to have been written in the early sixteenth century and to have formed part of the collection of documents and information about Greenland gathered by Archbishop Erik Valkendorf prior to 1516. Ivar's description was written down by another party to whom he had told his tale, and it appears to have suffered later interpolations, but Jonsson nevertheless was convinced that most of the information handed down to us came directly from Ivar himself.[4] Despite the shortcomings of its provenance, the account is still considered so reliable in locating and identifying church and farm sites that Ivar's statements about land and tithes "belonging" to Gardar see and to various churches in the Eastern Settlement have not been as seriously queried as they should have been.

Interpreting Ivar's account literally, some scholars have estimated that the church owned about two-thirds of the best pastureland in Greenland by the mid-fourteenth century. The great number of cattle and large pastures belonging to the big farms with churches suggested to Thomas McGovern, for instance, that people on the smallholdings eventually were reduced to "alms status" from the church in bad times.[5] Such claims must be carefully weighed not only against what Ivar seems actually to have said, but against strong indications that land remained under predominantly lay control in Norse Greenland, and against the inescapable fact that Ivar came to Greenland just when the parish system was being put into effect in both Norway and Iceland. In Iceland especially, this was such uphill work that it warrants a close look, for the situation there may tell us something about conditions in Greenland.

It had been decided in 1297 that the dean and Chapter of Nidaros in Norway would have a say in selecting the bishops for the Faroes, Greenland, Iceland, and the Hebrides.[6] This law was intended to prevent the chieftains in those colonies from pushing their own preferences, but it was not particularly effective. In a painstaking analysis of lay versus ecclesiastical privilege in the medieval Icelandic church, the Danish scholar Inge Skovgaard-Petersen argued that while the new Christian law code accepted by Skálholt see in 1278 had been an attempt to adjust Icelandic conditions and the country's approximately 220 churches to fit the canonical framework—in great part by converting to the system of ecclesiastical patronage common elsewhere in Europe—this change did not succeed in Iceland, because it ran counter to the whole system of private church ownership that had distinguished both Iceland and Greenland since the introduction of Christianity in those countries.[7]

In Germanic law, Skovgaard-Petersen notes, only persons, not institutions, could own property and enjoy the privileges and the right of advocacy before the courts that went with ownership. By the same token, the responsibility for construction and maintenance also devolved on the legal owner of a property. All these aspects of ownership came into play when wealthy farmers erected churches on their own land and had either themselves or someone of their choice ordained as priests. When tithing became law, these church farmers (who had physical wardship over the church) became responsible for collecting and distributing the tithes, so the tithes were effectively divided into three parts rather than four: one part for the poor, one for the bishop, and the third and biggest one for the church farmer as compensation for collecting the tithes, keeping up the church, and paying the priest (often himself)—with the additional sweetener of not having to pay tithes on any of his land said to belong to the church.

Until the introduction of Norwegian-inspired new laws in 1278, the Icelanders had not been allowed to give landed property to the church without the consent of their heirs, and there were also strict limits to other kinds of donations. Even after 1278, when the consent of heirs was no longer required for a bequest, most transfers of real property to the church were in name only, and wardship over a given church was often inherited, so the position of the big farmer with a church on his family land scarcely changed. Although the new laws stipulated that the bishops should have sole power over the churches and their property—including the appointment of priests, the tithes, and all other gifts to the church—laymen could continue to administer church property. Therefore, the only advantage the church farmer lost, sometime toward the end of the Middle Ages, was the right to choose the priest.

According to Skovgaard-Petersen, the power of the individual church-farmer-cum-chieftain in Iceland began to yield to the unified church only when the parish system became effective in the course of the fourteenth century, and people were obliged to have all church services performed by the church to which they owed tithes.[8] It is certainly clear from the copious rules laid down by Bishop Jon of Skálholt in 1345 that the parish system was not functioning well in Iceland at the time the Bergen bishop sent Ivar Bárdarson to Greenland. And if Icelandic church farmers were so reluctant to give up their ancient chieftain privileges, despite persistent pressure from Norway, it is unreasonable to suppose that their Greenland peers had meekly turned over their farms and fortunes to a handful of priests and sporadic bishops.

Jette Arneborg has presented strong arguments for why the secular owner of Gardar farm retained control over the farm and its income even after it had become the episcopal seat.[10] If we broaden her conclusion and suppose that also the parish churches (all of which were connected with large farms) remained under mainly secular control just as in Iceland, Ivar's detailed description of land and tithes associated with each church, including the Gardar cathedral, would remain accurate, but actual land *ownership* in Greenland would be very different from that envisioned by McGovern. Both the control of tithing income and the legal authority over church property would have been in the hands of secular church owners, not relinquished to the clergy, and those church farmers would have dealt with smaller farmers according to traditional secular rules and would also have been in a position of considerable power vis-à-vis the church.

One passage from Ivar's "Description" suggests precisely such a connection between secular ownership of a church farm and the advowson of its church.[11] The "splendid church dedicated to St. Nicholas" is the new cathedral church (Gardar II) dating from about 1200: "between it [Einarsfjord] and the aforementioned Rampnes Fjord lies a large royal farm, which belongs to the King, and that farm is called Foss [Waterfall], and there stands also a splendid church dedicated to St. Nicholas, of which the King has the endowment. . . ." Other passages in the "Description" deal with land that belongs to (*hører till*) a certain church, or with a certain church that owns (*eger* or *æger*) a specified stretch of land. The phrase "belongs to" (and its Danish and Norwegian counterparts) signals a need to look closely at the word "owns," for both expressions may refer to the *population* of a specified area—that is, to the congregation belonging to a given parish—rather than to the land owned by a particular church. The people of a parish may certainly be said to "belong to" the church that has the cure of their souls. The following passage illustrates the need for circumspection:[12]

Item next comes Eiriksfjord, and outermost in the fjord lies an island called Henø [Renø? = "Reindeer Island"], of which half belongs to [*hører till*] the Cathedral and the other half to Dyrnes Church. Dyrnes Church is the biggest parish in Greenland, and said church lies to the left as one sails into Eiriksfjord. Dyrnes Church owns [*æger*] everything all the way as far as Midfjord, Midfjord branches out straight northwest from Eiriksfjord, and farther into Eiriksfjord lies Sun Mountain Church. She owns [*æger*] all of Midfjord.

If this actually described church-owned real estate, the Greenlanders had indeed been reduced to the virtual serfdom imagined by McGovern. But for this to come to pass, landowners would have had to turn over their land in neat parcels surrounding each church, rather than in the ancient, haphazard pattern of land ownership—someone's dowry here and another's inheritance there. The tidy demarcations repeatedly described by Ivar show that he saw it as his job to establish *parish boundaries* for tithing purposes. Furthermore, he reports: "Dyrnes Church is the biggest parish in Greenland." Why introduce this information here unless his concern had been with parishes all along?

It is likely that Ivar had to make his peace with chieftain-owners of large church farms who did not willingly submit to control by either kings or bishops, or their representatives. It is equally likely that independent farmers spanning the economic spectrum were the dominant class to the end. This interpretation does not question Ivar's truthfulness, but it runs counter to the theory of a hierarchical, ecclesiastically controlled society that McGovern and others think evolved from the early system of privately owned churches and independent farmers.[13] A social system based on secular control would, by contrast, fit well with Claus Andreasen's analysis of the economic interplay among three types of farms (discussed above in Chapter Two). Intractable lay control was probably also a major reason why Gardar bishops were increasingly reluctant to live in Greenland.[14]

The archaeological record, too, testifies to the survival of secular power in Greenland for many decades after Ivar's time. It shows that not only big churches but also large festal halls were attached to the four most important farms in the Eastern Settlement: Brattahlid, Gardar, Hvalsey, and Herjolfsnes. Indeed, Nørlund has concluded that the large, well-constructed festal hall at Herjolfsnes was built so late that the piece of early-fifteenth-century Rhenish stoneware found in the depth of the foundation "lay at such a considerable depth compared with the building that it cannot date from the last Norse period at Herjolfsnes. . . ."[15] The festal hall at Hvalsey is equally a late addition, and so is the biggest of the four halls, at Gardar, which architecturally resembles the ones at Hvalsey and Herjolfsnes.[16]

By the early fifteenth century, Greenland had been without a resident bishop for some decades, so this late evidence both of trade and of expensive and essentially secular structures again conflicts with McGovern's vision of a fatal ecclesiastical chokehold on the Greenlanders: "Baldly put, a society whose administrators (as well as its peasants) believe that lighting more candles to St. Nicholas will have as much (or more) impact on the spring seal hunt as more or better boats is a society in serious trouble."[17] No Greenland midden has yet revealed such abject belief in the efficacy of candles, nor evidence of a society so cowed by the church that it failed to function properly to the very end.

While separation from the Norwegian mother church—and hence from Rome—in the late fourteenth century may be said to have spelled "moribund isolation" for the Greenland church, Nørlund's excavations at Herjolfsnes showed that secular trade was maintained with Europe right up until about 1500, so it is clear that indifference by the church hierarchy did not spell doom for the Greenlanders as a people, any more than earlier efforts to dominate them (through Ivar, for instance) had done.[18] Since the inception of established Christianity in Greenland, the colonists had managed their affairs *despite* church interference in their economic, social, and political life, not *because* of it.

The Greenlanders nevertheless seem to have adapted to ritual Christianity without too much struggle, so that long after the last episcopally ordained priest had died, many Christian rituals endured in Greenland because they had become such a part of the social fabric. We cannot blame revulsion against Christian practices for the Greenlanders' penchant for lay ownership, nor for their growing opposition to tithing in the mid-fourteenth century. There is thus no reason to take literally Gisli Oddsson's claim (noted in Chapter Three) that the Greenlanders had made heathens of themselves and gone to America by 1342, Ivar Bárdarson's first year in Greenland.

Unfortunately, Gisli's statement has such curiosity value that it continues to muddy discussions of religious attitudes in Greenland during the colony's last century and a half, as do two frequently quoted fifteenth-century papal letters of appointment for ostensible Gardar bishops. The first, written by Pope Nicholas V in 1448, refers to "the fervent piety of the peoples of this island," and the second, from Pope Alexander VI in 1492, paints a sad picture of a people abandoned by the church for so long that they have reverted to heathen practices.[19] Both letters were written when the Greenland church had already been abandoned by the church hierarchy for several generations, and they will be discussed in later chapters in the context of other problems. I refer to them here only to make the point that even in the late Middle Ages, the popes' knowledge of Greenland was as flimsy as Gisli's, and that the papal letters and Gisli's statement are equally useless as indicators of either religious or material conditions in Greenland at any time.

The spiritual life of the Greenlanders whom Ivar was supposed to attach more firmly to the Norwegian church hierarchy seems to have lain somewhere between "fervent piety" and "heathen practices." It is impossible to determine the fulcrum of a lever so long and badly broken, but this should not deter us from accepting the evidence that a lever did exist—the Greenlanders had accepted the Christian religion along with much or most of everyday church practice.

The common pairing of the words "faith" and "practice" shows that we find it useful to anchor the ephemeral and personal "faith" in the more tangible and universal "practice" when we speak of religion. Unfortunately, we cannot measure anyone's religious faith, divorced from symbols and rituals, unless we have access to private thoughts expressed in visual art, in speech, or in writing. The medieval Greenlanders did not leave us any such testimonies, except for occasional formulaic tombstone inscriptions such as "God rest his soul," which may express either simple and unquestioning faith or mere obedience to form.

Church buildings and funeral customs do tell us something about religious faith and practice in medieval Greenland, but most of our information comes from the various pagan and Christian symbols recovered by archaeologists. The Christian symbols range from simple crosses or runic inscriptions carved on loom weights, spoons, and other everyday objects, to tombstones and the numerous crosses and crucifixes found in Norse Christian graves in both the Eastern and Western Settlements. The latter finds will be discussed in conjunction with the demise of the Western Settlement; what they reveal is in this respect no different from the discernible story in the Eastern Settlement.

Two religious houses were still in existence when Ivar described Greenland for the Norwegians. Unfortunately, we have no archaeological reports at all about the supposed Augustinian monastery in Tasermiut fjord, which housed "*canonicus regulares*" and was dedicated to the saints Olaf and Augustine.[20] Vebæk's patient efforts at the Benedictine nunnery at Narsarsuaq in the Uunartoq fjord yielded much interesting information, especially about the settlement-period farm that preceded the religious house, but he found few guides to determining when the last Norse lived there, and whether the site had been a convent to the last or had reverted to being a regular lay farm. All the buildings were dauntingly collapsed, including the most recent church (from around A.D. 1300), but Vebæk concluded that this virtual obliteration was most likely due to the incessant foehn winds sweeping across the plain. Surprisingly, none of the numerous fragmented artifacts found at the site denotes religious use, and grave crosses are conspicuously absent from the many graves excavated in the church and churchyard. One fragment of a bronze church bell was found in the churchyard, in addition to what was probably a piece of a church bell clapper.[21]

We have no way of knowing when or how the bell was broken, nor whether someone had felt free to tinker with an object that had once been hallowed by a priest. Fragments of medieval church bells have turned up in innumerable Greenland archaeological sites, both Norse and Eskimo. Nørlund reports, for instance, that while he and Roussell were excavating the churchyard and church at Gardar in 1926, "hardly a day passed when we did not find one or more pieces of bell-metal, and the Greenlanders [modern Greenland Inuit] often find fragments here and there in the fields when digging or removing stones." Almost a hundred years ago, Daniel Bruun brought back to Copenhagen a bell cannon that had also been found at Gardar, by the gate in the fence enclosing the north side of the homefield rather than near the church or the bell-towers.[22]

We cannot assume that church bell fragments became available to the Eskimos only after the Norse were gone. Metal scraps could have been used for trade with the Eskimos in return for narwhal horns, walrus tusks, food, or other commodities.[23] The bells, which had to be imported, may have broken by accident at any time, and the Norse would not have been able to recast them as bells. To the Eskimos, metal casting was an unknown process altogether, so Nørlund stresses that the many half-smelted bell fragments found at Gardar must represent Norse attempts to reuse the metal. The sites he excavated gave him the overall impression that, besides making the best of accidental breakage, "in their last days the Norsemen, for want of other metal for weapons or other necessities, have themselves broken their bells into pieces. They were at any rate better able to do it than the Eskimos."[24]

Thousands of archaeological finds show that the Greenlanders were not desperate for metal, for right from the beginning of their settlement they substituted soapstone, antlers, baleen, and bone for iron or bronze in weapons as well as in ornaments and household objects. Claus Andreasen and Jette Arneborg recently noted that iron occurs surprisingly often in Norse Greenland finds, and that the worn-down blades on most of the knives are actually no different from those found on contemporaneous knives elsewhere in Scandinavia.[25] It does not seem likely that the last generation or two of Norse Greenlanders deliberately smashed their own church bells —and at Gardar, of all places. If they did, we must ask not only what prompted them to do it in the absence of dire necessity, but how they *dared* do it. Did they eventually lose the last vestige of awe for the power which the church demonstrated in its sacraments as well as through exorcism, excommunication, holy water, and the blessing of everything from churches and bells to fields and people?

The writer Frank Delaney, recalling his childhood and youth in a largely agricultural Irish community, describes the interaction between priest and parishioners, as well as between paganism and the Catholic faith and its rituals, in an isolated Atlantic peasant community. He reminds us that "[i]n a rural society, the man who interpreted the elements, who had access to the gods, held power."[26] The fear and awe surrounding Delaney's parish priest stemmed, we are told, both from the priest's commanding physical presence and from his sense of his own power. This sense was nourished by the terrifyingly intimate knowledge he had of his parishioners' lives and thoughts through the confessional, and by his and his flock's faith in his sacred office and its rites.

In Greenland, the chain of sacred ritual power reaching directly from God to the pope and thence to the archbishops and bishops, and which a bishop continued when ordaining a priest, was frequently stretched, and it finally broke within fifteen years of Ivar's departure from Greenland. When the last ordained priest had died and his teachings were a dim memory among the settlement elders, the Greenlanders may have found that they need neither fear retribution for smashing already damaged church bells, nor otherwise reckon with the mystic power of the church. That is not the same as saying they lost all capacity for religious belief.

A certain detachment may well have prevailed even at the peak of church authority, for had the church's power over the supernatural been at the very core of the Greenlanders' existence, their communities would have suffered cycles of devastating spiritual deprivation or fear during the increasingly long periods when there were no bishops maintaining the links to Nidaros and Rome. Faith in the Trinity or in redemption through Christ does not vanish the minute the Eucharist is unavailable, but a person who fully believes that only through priestly ministrations can he or she be assured of salvation is in a quandary when the priest goes missing or his link with the Divine is demonstrably tenuous.

Greenland grave finds suggest that the pragmatic colonists did not readily abandon old heathen safeguards, and that even the symbolic use of the cross did not invariably denote piety and a strong belief in Christian redemption. A blizzard of crosses does not proclaim a dyed-in-the-wool Christian population any more than peace symbols sprayed on every wall testify to pacifism in an entire people, or the hoisting of a flag guarantees unquestioning loyalty to a government. But the extensive Greenlandic use of the cross does prove beyond a doubt that the church had successfully supplanted most heathen symbols with Christian ones. This was important in a society so accustomed to believing in the power of symbols and charms.

It is unlikely that the church met with insurmountable cultural resistance when it asked people to believe in the power of the words spoken over the sacraments, or of the symbols accompanying the words, for the Norse had long believed that spells could be worked through the power of the spoken word or of carved runes.

The medieval church encouraged belief in church magic in popular devotion and often made the line between magic and religion difficult to draw.[27] The sagas repeatedly make it clear that the Norse believed in sorcery both before and after the introduction of Christianity; and as late as 1407, say the *Icelandic Annals*, an unfortunate fellow named Kollgrim was burned at the stake in the Eastern Settlement after having been found guilty of seducing another man's wife through black arts.[28] The blurring of the line between religion and magic in Norse culture, as well as between Christianity and heathendom, is obvious when, for instance, a Thor's hammer and a cross were made simultaneously to be used as amulets.[29]

Poul Nørlund found that many people in the Herjolfsnes churchyard, including a number of children, had been buried with crosses differing widely in artistic quality and style. Marie Stoklund has noted that all but three of the 58 crosses found there terminated in a point at the lower end, as if they had been made to be set in a turf wall, for example, when not being carried about. Comparing them with finds from medieval Bergen, she found the crosses from both places so similar that she thinks they must have been similarly used as devotional crucifixes (*andaktskors*)—personal tokens of piety—during prayer and eventually buried with the owner.

Stoklund also points out that the Herjolfsnes crosses are not like medieval English or French funeral crosses, nor are they like the medieval lead crosses found elsewhere in Scandinavia, which had a magic purpose.[30]

The most finely executed, interesting, and best preserved Herjolfsnes cross is no. 150, whose transverse limbs are inscribed with runes of two different types, showing that they did not originally belong together. The vertical limb is conventional enough: "*Maria: mikai amik Brigit* ("Maria: Mikae(l) owns me Brigit"). The transverse limb says, chiefly in Latin in the form of a magic formula: "*ma(ria) au(e) agla tetragramma Iesus so(ter) a-(don)ai on lo de(us) pater k(ristu)s r(ex) adoni(ia) filii iat.*" Finnur Jonsson told Nørlund that it must have been written by a priest with a good knowledge of both Latin and the mystic formulae. This inscription with its blend of religion and magic cannot be from earlier than around A.D. 1300, and probably is somewhat later, in Nørlund's judgment.[31]

Throughout the entire period represented in Nørlund's Herjolfsnes excavations—late twelfth century to about 1500, but mostly fourteenth century and later—even the infants had been buried as carefully and in as Christian a manner as in Europe, in shrouds or in the occasional coffin, and with their heads facing west. The wood used for coffins was both driftwood and imported timber, including larch that may have stemmed from the American continent. Nørlund said unequivocally about his finds overall: "On the whole neither dresses nor other objects bear the stamp of a culture that is degenerating into barbarism." He was equally convinced that the dresses found there generally reflected a higher social level than the ordinary dresses of the common people known from European representations.[32]

These indications of continuing community responsibility and adherence to ritual, coupled with evidence of prosperity and late-fifteenth-century contact with Europe, show that while the church had left a lasting mark on Greenlandic life, the Greenlanders remained in control of their lives despite permanently severed contacts with Nidaros and Rome. Nørlund's conviction that he had seen no evidence of descent into barbarism or deprivation lends special significance to another of his observations: although a very simple cross was found in a Herjolfsnes grave dating from no earlier than the beginning of the fifteenth century, grave crosses were not much used after about 1400, and as they grew rarer, they were more carelessly made.[33] In other words, what we consider Christian burial customs lasted until the end of the colony, but reliance on the Christian symbol, the cross, seems to have faded along with the supply of priests. Had it been part of a veneer only?

The retention of lay control over church property suggests that the Greenlanders had been slow to toss out old customs. A couple of examples from Nørlund's work confirm this. Inside the Herjolfsnes church (approximate date 1200), Nørlund was surprised to find only two graves in the nave and none at all in the chancel. More odd still—since burials inside the church were theoretically reserved for clergy—one of those graves contained a bear's tooth amulet and the other the remains of a dagger, as well as of the kind of oval box with baleen sides and wooden bottom so frequently found at Thule Eskimo sites. The box had been placed under the dead person's head and contained some sort of animal substance, perhaps food for the journey beyond in the heathen manner.[34] Nobody has yet been able to explain these finds in the context of Christian piety in Greenland.

Nørlund encountered much less favorable conditions for preservation when he excavated the Gardar churchyard, but it was clear that the burial customs here had corresponded to those at Herjolfsnes. As discussed in Chapter One, twenty or thirty walrus skulls with broken-out teeth were found carefully buried either inside or around the Gardar church in such a manner that Nørlund thought they might have been connected with some kind of religious ritual involving these animals that were so valuable to the Norse Greenlanders.[35] This discovery throws a unique light on religious practice in medieval Greenland, for whether the Gardar priests and bishops allowed the Norse to combine ancient luck-in-hunting rituals or walrus worship with church ritual, or the Greenlanders decided they did not need permission, the walrus skulls in sacred soil suggest that the Greenlanders did things their own way.

The ancient, heathen ways had a better chance of surviving if Greenlandic chieftain church owners doubled as priests, the way their peers did in Iceland, especially during the establishment phase of the Greenland church. Temporal and spiritual power had long been combined in the ancient Norse office of the chieftain-priest, the *goði*. Under the new Christian order, too, Norse chieftains for a long time considered it natural (and profitable) to continue presiding over religious observances in churches on their own farms. We have seen that large church farms were a feature of the Greenlandic system as well as of the Icelandic one, and that they probably remained under lay ownership and control. Under such circumstances, especially given Greenland's great distance from Norway, the church farmer—ordained or not—would have retained considerable influence. Even when going along with the approved new religion and its immense power, he would have been conscious of his own power base among the farmers—a group accustomed to passing on accumulated skills, customs, and lore, and usually slow to give them up for new ones.

In a traditional peasant-based society of the kind that evidently prevailed in Greenland long after the church had imposed its own mores in Norway and Iceland, people expected observable value in return for gifts and loyalty to a chieftain.[36] If they failed to obtain this value, they would find a different leader. This ancient and deep-seated cultural reservation may be a major reason why the Greenlanders stopped paying tithes and taxes to a church and crown that provided precious little in return. Conflicts between Greenland chieftains and representatives of the church would have mounted whenever the ecclesiastical and royal authorities in Norway demanded increased tithes and taxes.

Ivar came to Gardar as the ombudsman of the Bergen bishop, with a share in the latter's office as royal tax collector. In Norway, the office of royal ombudsman or tax collector, called either *syslumaðr* or *féhirðir* ("guardian of goods"), had evolved from the privileges and responsibilities belonging to the offices of *ármaðr* and *lénsmaðr*. By about 1300, the royal ombudsman had a designated seat and was a powerful presence in his district, and in 1308 Hákon V Magnusson decreed that if an ombudsman discharged his office well, his son could inherit the office if he was not disqualified for other reasons. By the time Ivar left Bergen for Greenland in 1341, however, the ombudsman system was already beginning to lose its clear definition in Norway, and we do not know if any of this system had ever applied to Greenland.[37]

Ivar noted in his "Description" that there were two royal farms in the Eastern Settlement: "Foss" (Waterfall) and "Thiødhijllestad" (Thjodhild's Place), but he mentioned no relationship between these two farms and a royal ombudsman in Greenland.[38] As noted in the previous chapter, only two late-fourteenth-century documents mention a royal ombudsman for Greenland. Since both sources date from several years *after* Ivar's return to Norway, it is conceivable that he had instituted the office there as part of an effort to tighten up tax collection and to implement Bishop Hákon's wish to separate royal tax collection from the duties of the Bergen bishop. But whether the royal ombudsman's office was already well established in the Eastern Settlement or new with Ivar's arrival, in a crisis the incumbent would have found it safer to side with local chieftains than to rely on support, advancement, and privileges from a distant and increasingly impotent monarch.

Ivar's "Description" said that the Greenlanders had a lawman who lived at Brattahlid (not at one of the designated royal farms) and implied that this lawman had been the instigator of an expedition to the Western Settlement led by Ivar himself. These statements raise questions about the lawman's authority in Greenland relative to a royal ombudsman's or to Ivar's own.

Post-republican Iceland had followed the changes that took place in Norway in the first half of the fourteenth century, where the functions of the king's ombudsmen or *féhirðir* had encroached on the old office of the lawman and now included calling together the assembly and the courts, nominating the lawmen, filing suits, supervising the courts, and carrying out sentences ranging from fines to capital punishment. Besides being the king's chief tax collectors, the royal ombudsmen in Norway were also responsible for military preparedness in their districts.[39]

If the office of the Greenland ombudsman in Ivar's time combined that much judicial, fiscal, military, and general police authority, the lawman at Brattahlid would have been serving at the pleasure of the ombudsman and would probably not have taken the initiative in calling out an expeditionary force against Skrælings or anybody else. It is likely, however, that the royal ombudsman's office in Greenland in the mid-fourteenth century did not carry nearly the power enjoyed by royal ombudsmen in Norway or Iceland, regardless of whether Ivar or someone else had charge of it. In fact, it may have been common knowledge in Norway that the Greenland lawman had kept much of the lawspeaker's old power and standing as the elected leader of a society of independent farmers, for we should note that Ivar (or the person writing down and relaying his information) evidently thought people would find it plausible that the Greenland lawman had the authority to organize an expedition to defend the Western Settlement against Skrælings.

Given these doubts about the official chain of authority in mid-fourteenth-century Greenland, it is hard to know how much to believe of either Ivar's reasons for the expedition to the Western Settlement or his report of finding that northernmost colony deserted. If the lawman, untrammeled by any royal ombudsman's authority, had actually learned of trouble between Eskimo and Norse hunters in the Western Settlement area and wanted to send assistance north, Ivar may, for purposes of his own, have seized an opportunity to have both ships and armed men placed at his disposal. He was a priest and the Gardar bishop's *officialis*, and it was only against heathens and infidels that a clergyman was allowed to carry arms.[40]

It is more likely, however, that Ivar himself took the initiative in the expedition and later chose to hide behind the local authorities and the excuse that the expedition was intended for fighting the heathen Skrælings, for such pious locutions were in the spirit of the times. Ivar's voyage to the Western Settlement was practically contemporaneous with a letter King Magnus wrote in 1354, giving Powell Knutsson, the lawman of *Gulaþing* (the assembly and court that included the city of Bergen) permission to outfit a ship and sail to Greenland in order to "protect" the Christians there.[41]

Arneborg notes that if Ivar's "Description" contains interpolations from the fifteenth or sixteenth centuries, they may have been occasioned by then-current descriptions of Skrælings as very dangerous people. If the interpolations were added somewhat later, they may have been inspired by a wish similar to Gisli Oddsson's of finding an explanation for the Norse Greenlanders' disappearance.[42] Assuming that Finnur Jonsson was right about the provenance of the manuscript he used, *any* interpolations would have been from the fifteenth or early sixteenth century at the latest, since Archbishop Valkendorf had collected his documents on Greenland in anticipation of a 1516 voyage that came to nothing.

In the last part of his "Description" Ivar recounts what he found when he and a number of others sailed up to the Western Settlement. The brief account is given *twice*, with very slight variations, as if to drive home the eeriness of the scene the party encountered:[43]

In the Western Settlement stands a large church, named Stensnes Church. That church was for a time the cathedral and bishop's seat. Now the Skrælings have destroyed all of the Western Settlement; there are left some horses, goats, cattle, and sheep, all feral, and no people either Christian or heathen.

All the foregoing was told us by Ivar Bárdarson Greenlander, who was the superintendent of the Bishop's establishment at Gardar in Greenland for many years, that he had seen all this, and he was one of those who had been appointed by the lawman to go to the Western Settlement against the Skrælings, in order to drive the Skrælings out of the Western Settlement, and when they arrived there, they found nobody, either Christians or heathens, only some wild cattle and sheep, and they slaughtered the wild cattle and sheep for food, as much as the ships would carry, and then sailed home therewith themselves, and the aforementioned Ivar was along.

We do not know exactly when Ivar made this voyage up north. It could have been anytime during his more than twenty years in Greenland, but most likely took place before 1349, just before Ivar could reasonably have expected to return to Norway had the Black Death not interfered. His report of finding a deserted colony is made no less interesting by mounting evidence that the Western Settlement effectively ended sometime between 1360 and 1400, from what various archaeological reports from the area tell us.[44]

Excavations at the late-abandoned Western Settlement site at V54 (which will be discussed in some detail later) show that the people there were not suffering from an inadequate diet, nor were they isolated from their Western Settlement neighbors or from the Eastern Settlement. An unused sharpening stone of Igaliko (Gardar) sandstone found in the uppermost layer of room VIII indicates communication with the Eastern Settlement right up until the final phase.[45] Furthermore, there were no signs here of a pestilential or violent end; it seems highly unlikely that the last people died unburied; they did not leave too hurriedly to take personal objects with them; and they probably had the means to leave when the fancy took them, since the owners were not poor people by local standards.

The big questions that the reports on V54 fail to answer are: when and

why did the people leave, and where did they go? And did Ivar tell a sani-
tized version of his expedition to the Western Settlement, or does the form
in which his report survived suffer from too many later "explanations"?
Ivar's ostensible reason for going up to the Western Settlement was to drive
out the Skrælings said to be threatening the community. Had deadly
friction developed after at least a couple of generations of peaceful coexis-
tence since the Eskimos began migrating south along the west coast of
Greenland?

Chapter One relates that the Norse from both settlements had made
early contact with the Eskimos in the northern hunting regions. For instance, the Inuit site at Sermermiut in the middle of the Norðrseta produced
a C-14 dating of roughly A.D. 1240 for the Thule layer in which several
Norse objects were found.[46] There must have been skirmishes between the
two peoples, especially if they found themselves competing for fish and
game, but even after the Eskimos established permanent settlements near
the Norse colonies, the possibilities of friction were probably lessened because the Eskimos tended to occupy the outer coasts. Gulløv, who has studied the evidence carefully, has concluded that relations overall appear to
have been amicable or at least neutral.[47] Eskimo lore written down by Europeans tells of both fights and friendships between the Eskimos and the
Norse, but it is not a very reliable historical source, especially since the Eskimos telling the tales may wittingly or unwittingly have adjusted their stories
to the stranger's ear. More will be said about Norse-Eskimo relations later,
but Jette Arneborg has made it clear that modern scholars in this field do
not believe the Eskimos caused the demise of the Norse in either settlement.[48]

What are we to make of Ivar's claim that he saw *no people at all*, "either
Christians or heathens," in the Western Settlement? We do not know exactly when the Thule Eskimos started building winter settlements in the
Nuuk district, as opposed to just visiting the region for summer fishing and
hunting. None of the Eskimo sites investigated near the Norse sites in the
Western Settlement region during the Inuit-Norse project of 1976–77
could be ascribed to the Norse period or to the period immediately afterward.[49] But C-14 datings made in 1982 from Thule winter houses (of the
type shown in Fig. 13) on Kangeq Island in the *outer* part of Nuuk district
suggest Eskimo presence there in the first half of the fourteenth century—
in other words, by the time Ivar sailed in those waters. Norse artifacts, including two honing stones of red sandstone all the way from Igaliko
(Gardar), were found deep in the Eskimo midden at Kangeq, and the earliest evidence of Thule culture demonstrated in C-14 dating of bones at Aasivissuit is ascribed to around 1280.[50] As far south as Nuuk, the number of
Thule people probably was not very large in the mid-fourteenth century,

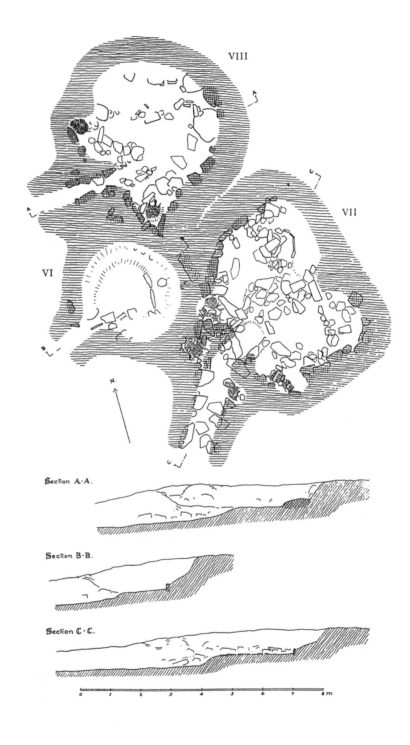

VIII

VII

VI

N.

Section A·A.

Section B·B.

Section C·C.

0   1   2   3   4   5   6   7   8 m

however, and whether they were away hunting farther north or chose to stay out of sight when Ivar and his men sailed past, they may very well have been missed.

The Norwegian explorer Fridtjof Nansen was the first to note that had the Eskimos killed the settlers, they would promptly have dispatched the livestock for food, the way Ivar and his companions did. Helge Ingstad agrees with Nansen in this, but differs in his explanation for what did happen to the Western Settlement Norse. Nansen thought they were away hunting, but did not say why that would also have involved women, children, and old people. Helge Ingstad is of the opinion that they had decided to opt for a better life in North America; that they did not have space for all their animals on their ships; and that the Markland ship drifting off to Iceland in 1347 may actually have been an emigrant ship.[51]

Given the constant Norse preoccupation with food supplies, any Western Settlement people who set out across the Davis Strait for good could have been expected to slaughter for provisions those animals they could not take with them live or sell to neighbors, but we should note that abandonment of livestock was not unheard-of in medieval Norse culture. "Landnámabók" tells of the Icelandic settler Helgi *magri*, who put a boar and a sow ashore at Galtarhamar in Eyjafjord and sailed off. That story has a happy ending—three years later, 70 pigs were found in a nearby valley. Another story, less happy and more closely related to our discussion here, surfaced during the 1993 excavations of the "farm beneath the sand" in Greenland's old Western Settlement. It became clear that the last inhabitants of the farm (whose date of abandonment is not yet settled) had left some animals behind to shift for themselves and seek shelter in the empty house. But there is one very important difference between the situation here (and at Galtarhamar) and the scene described by Ivar: neither cows nor horses were among the abandoned animals.[52] Cows and horses were both more valuable and more vulnerable than pigs, goats, or sheep.

Gisli Oddsson's statement that the Greenlanders had forsaken the Christian faith and joined the people of America in 1342 is no more proof of emigration than it is of apostasy. It is unlikely that Ivar could have assembled his expedition so soon after arriving in Greenland, and we now know that 1342 is too early a date for the complete end of the Western Settlement.

FIG. 13 (*opposite*). Floor plan of clustered late-medieval Thule winter houses at Illorssuit in Disko Bay. Source: Reproduced from an original drawing in Mathiassen and Holtved ("Contributions," Fig. 56) with permission of the National Museum, Copenhagen. Hans Christian Gulløv at the Museum's Ethnographic Section points out that the three-legged metal pot shown in Fig. 27 was found in the north fireplace of House VIII, at top.

Nor need we pay much attention to Jon Duason's theory (espoused by his Canadian intellectual heir Tryggvi Oleson and by nobody else) that the Norse, far from feeling menaced by the natives, eventually intermarried with the Thule Eskimos on both sides of the Davis Strait and produced the "inland people" (or Tunit) of Inuit lore. There is no evidence that such an intermixture took place on either side of the Davis Strait, while there is much to suggest that the Tunit were Dorset Eskimos.[53]

Had the Norse in the Western Settlement felt so mortally threatened by the Eskimos that they had evacuated the settlement by the time Ivar got there, they surely would not first have sent a delegation to the Eastern Settlement and then sat back waiting for help to arrive. Ivar's claim that news had reached Gardar about such threats is in itself enough to argue against the supposed helplessness of the people in the Western Settlement, for if there were ships to carry such news, there were ships to carry people to safety without waiting for help. Ingstad's emigration theory at least has the merit of being feasible, for the arrival of the Markland ship in Iceland in 1347—six years after Ivar had come to Greenland—shows that the Greenlanders still had ships capable of sailing considerable distances. In addition, the Western Settlement Norse were in an even better position than their cousins farther south to fetch Markland lumber for more ships.

Ivar's report also reveals that ships were still available in Greenland, for at least two ships were involved in his expedition. He must have anticipated trouble with *somebody* when he went to the Western Settlement with such a sizable force, but chances are slim that he came north to deal with hostile Skrælings. It would better explain both his expedition and the absence of local Norse if Ivar represented a menace that the people of the Western Settlement had anticipated.

The deserted scene obviously took Ivar by surprise. If the residents had abandoned practically all their farms before his expedition set out from home, word would have reached the Eastern Settlement somehow, and Ivar would not have been surprised to find the colony depopulated. Indeed, there would not even have been any reason to send an expedition. Furthermore, the archaeological evidence suggests that the settlement was viable for some time after Ivar's visit, and that a few farmers must have stayed on even if the majority of the inhabitants had left, so somebody would surely have come forward and told the men from Gardar what had happened—*if those men had looked friendly.* But the armed Gardar men must have looked menacing both aboard their approaching ships and while slaughtering the animals they found, so the locals would have been wise to stay out of sight until the visitors were gone. The horses, goats, sheep, and cattle that Ivar found grazing were not likely to have been untended for long, for one winter out in the open would have killed the cows even if the sheep had been able to survive.

Most likely, people in the Western Settlement had a good idea of why Ivar and his company were honoring them with a visit. Since Ivar's errand in Greenland evidently was to assess and collect tithes and taxes for crown and church, he would expect money from both settlements and would want an explanation if none came. If the people in the Western Settlement had stopped sending their share of hides and tusks, butter and eiderdown to Gardar, they would soon have deduced that the tax collector or related trouble was coming their way when they spotted Ivar's ships.

Ivar probably sailed up the Ameralik fjord with course for Sandnes (which his "Description" called "Stensnes"), the center of both ecclesiastical and secular power in the Western Settlement, and the ships would have been visible from land long before they scraped against the shore. The residents would have had plenty of time to gather their valuables, and perhaps some animals, and head for secluded inland valleys, leaving the rest of the animals to fend for themselves meanwhile.

While Ivar's professed reason for going to the Western Settlement is suspect, his description of what he saw seems truthful in at least one respect. He and his men landed in a deserted place. But nowhere in Ivar's account is there any hint that he had found farmsteads in ruins; that he had found or looked for dead bodies from an attack or other disaster; or that he and his companions had searched for clues all the way up and down the settlement. All but one of the known farms in the Western Settlement lay deep inside the two large fjords Nuup Kangerdlua (Godthåbsfjord) and Ameralik with its extension Ameralla; many of the homesteads were hidden from view or else far inland; and most of them lay some five to ten kilometers from their nearest neighbors.[54]

If Ivar and his men had spent all the time and energy necessary to make sure they did not overlook a hapless, Skræling-menaced farmer or two, his report would most likely have claimed credit for it. But this was no mission of mercy. Achaeologists have had little help from Ivar's "Description" in locating more than 80 Western Settlement farm sites, three of them with churches.[55] His account of the Western Settlement's topography is so perfunctory, especially compared with his detailed description of the Eastern Settlement, that one strongly suspects he and his men contented themselves with observing the area immediately surrounding "Stensnes" (Sandnes) before sailing home with their fresh meat. But why such lack of curiosity when the expedition had taken the trouble to sail up from the Eastern Settlement?

The facts that Ivar was chosen for the Greenland assignment in the first place, that he survived there for a long time, and that he went on to a sinecure in Norway afterward suggest that he was an astute and practical fellow who knew his limits. Certainly he would have been well advised not to overdo the pursuit of his object if most of his companions were hired hands from the Eastern Settlement, who were willing to help with tax collection, and who might tolerate cattle-rustling, but who would draw the line at terrorizing fellow Greenlanders at a Norwegian's command. But Ivar would have been especially wise not to press his men to investigate further if, as seems likely, both he and they were terrified by the deserted scene confronting them.

We are told twice in the "Description" that the members of the expedition saw neither Christians nor heathens, as if Ivar's lasting shock and bewilderment had been impressed upon his listener and scribe in Norway. The mention of "heathens" may account for a later interpolation about Skrælings, but the wording could also be a guide to Ivar's own thinking. In the minds of Ivar and his people, heathens and black magic would have been closely connected. The sight of eerily deserted homesteads where they had expected barnyard bustle, barking dogs, and children playing may well have been so frightening that they left as fast as they could. No business of Ivar's in the Western Settlement could be important enough to warrant the risk of falling victim to evil, supernatural powers. Nor would he have been eager to return to the scene later. Safely back in Norway, he would have had to tell his story in a way that justified his failure to collect taxes and tithes from the people in the Western Settlement.

Arneborg has pointed out a possible connection between the Greenlanders' continuing recalcitrance about paying taxes and the fact that in 1354–55, King Magnus Eiriksson *smeyk*, still fancying himself king of Norway as well as of Sweden, resumed the machinations he had begun in 1348 when he had been preparing for another Christian confrontation with the heathen Russians.[56] King Magnus had asked the pope to help him finance his pre-Plague expedition by taxing the clergy and promising the king half of the income for fighting the heathen—and the other half as a papal "loan." The pope obliged him in 1351 and ordered the Swedish and Norwegian clergy to pay a four-year tax on all income, and the impoverished Magnus pounced on his right to this money, despite reaching a peace treaty of sorts with the Russians that same year.[57]

In this 1351 tax, Arneborg sees an explanation for the letter King Magnus wrote ordering Powell Knutsson to outfit a ship and sail to Greenland in order to protect the Christians there. Arneborg reasons that despite Ivar Bárdarson's presence, the Greenlanders had also refused to pay the four-year special tax that expired in 1355, and that Powell Knutsson's errand was to collect the tax.[58] Ruthless money extraction would certainly have been in line with King Magnus's decision the previous year to place Iceland under a royal governor who, in return for a lump sum paid to the king, was given the right to collect all the taxes from Iceland into his own pocket for three years.[59] And Arneborg is on firm ground in assuming that Magnus (whose career as king of Norway took an abrupt downward turn in 1355 when his son Hákon came of age) was in a bind over the pope's loan, for in 1358 he was excommunicated for failure to pay it back, and two years later he was obliged to pawn large areas of southwestern Sweden to cover his war losses.[60]

But there is no further record of Knutsson's voyage. It is doubtful that it ever took place and even more doubtful that Magnus had ever intended for it to take place. Most likely, he was merely putting on a pious perfor-mance as a serious Defender of the Faith who deserved whatever money he could lay his hands on. Magnus was not new to laying holy paper trails, for in 1347 he and Queen Bianca had made out their "will" so they could show good intentions toward innumerable Norwegian hospitals and churches, including Gardar Cathedral in Greenland. At that time, Christianity was presumably in the best of health out there, and to be rewarded: "*Item eccle-sie cathedrali jn Grænelande centum marchas denariorum, jn vestibus pro ornatu ecclesie preciosis.*"[61]

Arneborg is probably on safe ground in assuming that Greenlanders and their handful of ecclesiastics (still untouched by the Black Death) had no intention of honoring the pope's 1351 demand for special taxes. Bishop Arni of Gardar had the best excuse possible: he was dead. We do not know for certain whether he died in Greenland or returned to Norway some time after Jon *skalli*'s consecration as bishop of Gardar in 1343, but there is some reason to believe that he had returned to Norway and been appointed bishop of the Faroes just before he died in 1348.[62] The Greenlanders greeted their first resident bishop in nineteen years in 1368. Bishop Alf, who had been consecrated in 1365, very soon after Ivar's return to Norway, came from the Munkeliv monastery in Bergen and must therefore have been well aware of both Ivar Bárdarson's return to that city and the 1364 appoint-ment of Ivar Vigfusson *holm* as the pope's new subcollector in the islands belonging to Norway. This famous Icelandic chieftain's authority thus of-ficially encompassed Greenland, although he was primarily supposed to collect tithes and taxes from Skálholt and Holar bishoprics.[63]

It is hard to believe that Ivar *holm* was not equally aware that a new Gardar bishop was being sent out, or that he did not make at least some effort to collect, from next door, wealth that would so directly benefit him-self. Despite believing that the Western Settlement was no more, Ivar Bár-darson must have held out hope of gain from the Eastern Settlement, since Bishop Alf had been appointed.

Although the Church hierarchy in Norway had long reflected the growing confusion and contention surrounding the papacy, neither this situation nor the Great Schism beginning in 1378 are entirely to blame for the fact that no more bishops came out to Greenland after Alf of Gardar died, some time during 1376–78. Corruption and favoritism dictated episcopal appointments, but that would not have prevented later Gardar bishops from going out to Greenland if they thought the voyage would bring them greater wealth or social status than they could command by staying put in Norway or Denmark. They must have known that they would be able to function in Greenland only on the inhabitants' own terms—and that those were no longer acceptable.

We have seen that the Greenlanders apparently stopped sending tithes and taxes to Norway after the first quarter of the fourteenth century, and there is no reason to suppose that they paid up more readily when the power of both church and crown in Norway had become significantly weakened. But their increasing reluctance to pay appears to have had its roots in alienation from a distant and demanding authority rather than in a suffering domestic economy; there are no grounds for thinking that the Greenlanders were barely scraping by around 1400. It is very unlikely that they simply decided to cut all connection with the church, however, for they still thought of themselves as Christians.

They could not foresee that their refusal to pay ever-larger sums to church and/or crown would eventually contribute to the Norwegian authorities' loss of interest in Greenland, or that this situation would be exacerbated by other circumstances completely beyond the Greenlanders' control, such as pestilence and other disasters in Norway. They could not know, for instance, that by 1371, things would be so bad in Norway that Archbishop Thrond of Nidaros would receive papal dispensation to ordain and promote twenty men born out of wedlock, and ten sons of priests, because a fresh outbreak of the Black Death had reduced the former 300 or so ecclesiastics in his see to about forty old and decrepit priests.[64]

The Greenlanders were used to waiting many years for their bishops and could not have known that Alf would be the last one to come their way. By the time they woke up to this possibility, the 1,000–1,500 souls who had inhabited the Western Settlement at its peak were gone.

CHAPTER FIVE

The Western Settlement
Comes to an End

If Ivar Bárdarson's motive for going to the Western Settlement was to collect taxes and tithes, and the central and most vulnerable part of the population took cover on his arrival, this still does not explain why the whole settlement was deserted within a few decades, nor does it tell us what became of the people. Poul Egede, son of the eighteenth-century Norwegian pioneering missionary in Greenland, thought that only some great disaster could have made the Norse leave such lovely country.[1] He and his family had endured several years of extreme hardship in the Nuuk region, ranging from starvation and cold to isolation and unpredictable relations with the Eskimos, but clearly he did not think any one of those conditions sufficient reason for leaving the place.

Either a great disaster or several smaller ones could have brought about the end of that self-sufficient medieval community, comprising perhaps 90 families at its peak. The population may already have shrunk by the time of Ivar's visit around 1350, but in the sheltered, fertile inland valley Fridtjof Nansen dubbed Austmannadal (Valley of the Norwegians; now Kuussuaq), several farms have been found that show signs of having been successfully occupied until late in the fourteenth century, perhaps, as Berglund has put it, by "a remnant population which gradually died out as a community of old people." Berglund notes that parallels of such community dynamics are known to have occurred in Western Scandinavia.[2]

North America was a feasible destination, at least, for Western Settlement people anxious to leave. They would have known at least as much as their eleventh-century ancestors about havens in the hunting and logging regions to the west. At Sculpin Island (north coast of Labrador, 56°48′N,

61°16′W), for example, where icebergs may be stranded offshore even in August, Barry Matthews has noted that in "sheltered canyons away from the influence of the cold Labrador current, there is one of the tallest and most luxurious forests in the whole of the Labrador-Ungava Peninsula, with spruce trees up to 22 metres, and paper birch . . . up to 12 metres tall, and fruits such as raspberry, . . . squashberry . . . and skunkcurrant. . . ."[3] And farther south, the country was suitable for cattle farming in precisely those spots first favored by later European colonists, where any traces of sporadic Norse habitation would have been wiped out almost at once. Helge Ingstad reasons that the Viking site at L'Anse aux Meadows was left undisturbed only because the water there was too shallow for later whale boats.[4]

For those Western Settlement inhabitants who wanted to remain cattle farmers in a settled Norse community, the Eastern Settlement would have been a more logical alternative once Ivar had returned to Norway. Some adventurous souls probably had a chance to leave the country on non-Greenlandic ships, but the Greenlanders must have been aware that deteriorating conditions in both Iceland and Norway spoiled those countries as havens for people wanting to improve their lives. In addition, after almost four centuries, neither country could have been regarded by the Greenlanders as "home" any more than England is considered "home" by present-day New Englanders.

Regardless of where they went, the Western Settlement Norse would have needed a strong inducement to abandon their farms. In a recent article, Claus Andreasen and Jette Arneborg noted that several big Western Settlement farms at Kilaarsarfik (Sandnes) and Nipaatsoq and in Austmannadal, which have been extensively investigated by archaeologists and found to have been built more or less contemporaneously, also show evidence of having been abandoned at about the same time. This would indicate that the depopulation of the Western Settlement resulted from adverse conditions affecting everyone.[5] We might add to this interpretation a related possibility, namely that the people collectively had an opportunity to go elsewhere which they could not refuse.

It would have been a serious blow to both the economy and the spirits of the local population to return home from hiding and find a large number of their livestock slaughtered by Ivar's men, and some may have decided to emigrate at that point rather than wait for more visits of a similar nature. But Ivar's visit may have been only one in a series of adverse events. For instance, archaeologists have found evidence of attacks by the caterpillar *Agrotis oculta* in various Western Settlement sites from the fourteenth century, which would have done damage to some pastures, but not on a scale to ruin the settlement as a whole.[6] The infestation may just have added to economic problems already severe enough to help explain why taxes and tithes were not forthcoming, and to make leaving a reasonable option, especially for people who lived on very marginal land.

A deteriorating climate may have hastened the erosion caused by Norse farming practices, in which case a growing number of farms would fall into the "marginal" category. Much more research is needed, however, before we can say with any certainty what the weather conditions were in various parts of Greenland at any given time in the past. It does seem that there was a North Atlantic cooling trend both around 1250 and then again around 1350, and that about A.D. 1400 there was a pronounced deviation from overall mean values in Greenland coinciding with a period of destructive weather patterns both in Iceland and in the rest of Scandinavia.[7] According to the Danish meteorologist Knud Frydendahl, such cooling trends tend to start up around Franz Josef's Land and spread westward, reaching the east coast of Greenland and producing vast quantities of the sea ice that menaces navigators between Iceland and Greenland. This pattern occurs long before these conditions cause problems in the Davis Strait. He also notes that the Ellesmere Island ice shelf appears to have started growing at a relatively recent date. Studies of icebergs calving off its glacier suggest that it was around 1370 that summer melt-off no longer kept up with cold-season accumulations.[8] The deepening chill may have threatened the grass crop and the settlers' comfort ashore and caused problems for both sea hunting, fishing, and navigation—a situation that could certainly have speeded the departure of the Western Settlement colonists.

Unfortunately, we are still a long way from understanding either the climate fluctuations themselves or their ecological and demographic impact. For example, even during an overall cooling trend there may be milder spells, or vice versa. And from recent archaeological work on marginal or abandoned medieval farms along Norway's rocky, weatherbeaten North Atlantic seaboard, we have learned that "marginal farms" were not always abandoned because they became uninhabitable, but very often because they were less desirable to begin with, so they were the last to be settled and the first to be left during population expansions and contractions.[9] Even so, we cannot preclude the possibility that people in the Western Settlement suffered from ecological disasters caused by climate changes or by man himself, but it is hard to track environmental problems in an already marginal area across a span of six or seven hundred years.

The Norse farm recently found buried near the large plain east of Nipaatsoq (site V54, illustrated in Fig. 14) was dubbed "the farm beneath the sand" when preliminary investigations showed that it had been partly buried in drifting sand deposited by the wind. Initially, it was impossible to tell whether the farm had been abandoned *because* of the flying sand, or

FIG. 14. "The farm beneath the sand" in Norse Greenland's Western Settlement. Recently discovered by chance, it is being excavated in a race with time. Source: Photographs by Jette Arneborg, 1994, reproduced by permission.

whether erosion originally caused by grazing Norse sheep had precipitated the sand problem later. Because the site was underwater when it was first discovered, an alternative hypothesis was that a catastrophic flood had caused the people to leave. Test excavations in the summer of 1991 showed that the farm site (occupied from around A.D. 1000 until late in the settlement period, when a fire possibly caused the people to flee) had been abandoned before flying sand covered the turf directly above the large house ruin sometime in the mid-fifteenth century. It was not until several centuries later that the site was flooded and left under mud and gravel deposits.[10] The progression of these estimates by experienced archaeologists vividly illustrates the difficulties imposed by the Greenland landscape.

When Roussell excavated a big church farm at V7, he noted that part of the homefield had been eroded down to the gravel by foehn winds, and that a row of flagstones had been laid down between the house and the church in an area too dry to require stepping-stones now. Similarly, at V15 (Umiivik) in Kangersuneq fjord, the upland is poor today, but the farm was large and had housing for about fifteen cows, so the vegetation must have been better in the Middle Ages. Farm V13a (Illorssuit) farther up the Kangersuneq is another of several sites here that are now as barren and desolate as V15, but that once sustained a good number of cattle and sheep through the summer grazing and produced enough fodder for the long winters.[11] In none of these places is it possible to tell which came first—erosion resulting in poor grasscover, or the abandonment of the farms.

Recent studies of soil erosion in the Eastern Settlement show that despite the so-called "Little Ice Age" that began around A.D. 1600, the area eventually recovered from the extensive damage suffered during the Norse period. Recolonization and large-scale sheep farming in the modern period have led to new and severe erosion. The scientist Bjarne Holm Jakobsen notes that environmental destruction is almost unavoidable in low-arctic landscapes and will accelerate, and that dramatic short-term climate oscillations in our own time have triggered crucial degradation processes.[12]

Iceland has always had the same problem: tourists are frequently reminded that it may take fifty years for some plants to reestablish themselves in fragile areas. Iceland never had an interim recovery period, yet a large number of Icelandic farmers and their livestock managed to survive in their unpredictable, low-arctic climate. So did the struggling coastal farmers above the Arctic Circle in Norway, who to this day pasture their animals on narrow, grassy shores that were stripped of their trees so many thousands of years ago that they are—wrongly—perceived to be in their "natural" state.[13]

Even if cooler temperatures did not substantially prevent regrowth of pastures, other effects from deteriorating weather may have created insurmountable problems for the Western Settlement residents. For example, Kangersuneq fjord in our own time is filled with calving glacier ice most of the summer, making access difficult, and the heads of both Ameralik and Ujarassuit fjords are made shallow and inaccessible by river silt. We do not know when these problems started, nor how they would have affected people if they were occurring in the fourteenth century, but if ice in the fjords and permafrost ashore *had* become a problem by then, some people may certainly have been induced to leave. At several Western Settlement archaeological sites, Aage Roussell's progress was hampered by frozen soil right below the surface even in summer; but again there is no telling which came first, the frozen ground or the depopulation of the community.

The history of human occupation of the high arctic fits with the theory that summer sea ice was relatively less extensive during the whole period from about A.D. 1000 to 1600, when the whale-hunting Thule culture spread southward. But the climate in the high arctic is not necessarily synchronous with conditions farther south in Greenland, and local weather patterns do not always follow the broader patterns.[14] For instance, around 1920, temperature anomalies in the Nuuk (Western Settlement) region ran counter to the general warming trend that began then in the northern hemisphere. And when the ice off West Greenland was so extensive during the winters of 1982–84 that they were named the worst ice winters of the century, this was again a local phenomenon unknown elsewhere in the northern hemisphere. Ecological variations observed during 1982–84 in the present-day Nuuk region may provide a guide to troubles the medieval Norse may have experienced during a similar bout of cold weather. Fishing, except for icefishing, became impossible for many months during each of those years. Very cold winters will cause both fish and shrimp to die in shallower waters, while the effects on salmon and cod populations are less immediate. Especially critical to cod are spring and early summer temperatures, when the eggs hatch and the larvae begin to drift with the current, which at that point apparently must be above a critical point of 1.8°C. As for adult cod, their kidneys fail at 2°C.[15] The feeding and breeding patterns of sea mammals would be affected by unfavorable temperature changes, and so would the grazing available to both caribou and domestic animals. M. C. Parry has noted that in areas of marginal farming under a maritime regime, a long-term climatic fluctuation of 1°C "would have a pronounced effect on the length of the growing season."[16]

"Marginal farming under a maritime regime" describes the Western Settlement well. Located 400 kilometers north of the Eastern Settlement, where the average temperature of 1°C is reached a month earlier in the spring and lasts a month longer in the fall, the Western Settlement had a considerably shorter growing season for grass. Other factors also influence pasturage, however, and it complicates the picture further that even inclement weather may have some benefits. Damper and cooler weather with lots of rain at the right time may well yield better vegetation than dry, warm summers and may benefit domestic animals as well as caribou.

It probably is not useful to focus on long-term warming or cooling trends when the aim is to discover why an entire community closed down over a relatively short period. Joel Berglund speculates that both the Eastern and Western Settlements may have experienced really destructive deviations in the weather for several years in a row, resulting in emigration from fringe areas and in loss of livestock in central areas. Modern climatologists agree with Berglund that two or three consecutive seasons of inclement weather would cause greater dislocation than a gradual cooling or warming trend.[17]

The Greenland Norse experienced both short-term and long-term climatic fluctuations many times during their tenure, and they adjusted to them well enough to last for half a millennium. The inhabitants of the Western Settlement may nevertheless have faced a breaking point some time in the second half of the fourteenth century. Because they depended on a certain number of able-bodied men for communal hunts on land and sea, their small communities would suffer if too many people moved away in response to a shrinking subsistence margin or other problems. Seals were the mainstay of the economy and were hunted communally, as were caribou. Therefore, we should expect that seal and caribou remains would diminish over time and then fall off sharply in the middens if a gradual decline in the availability of able-bodied hunters brought the Settlement to an end. In fact, however, analyses of the bone material from the small Western Settlement farm at Niaquusat (V48), excavated during the Norse-Inuit Project of 1976–77, show an *increase* in seal bones relative to those of sheep, goats, cattle, and caribou, in analytic unit AU 3 (C-14 dated to A.D. 1250–1350) compared with analytic unit A 1 (C-14 dated to A.D. 1000–1100). Caribou bones show no great drop relative to those of domestic animals.[18] If these analyses are reliable, they suggest increased dependence on seal in the final phase, and an end to the farm when communal hunting ended, which agrees well with Andreasen and Arneborg's observation that the last farmers in the community appear to have left more or less simultaneously.

The Niaquusat farm, located just a few kilometers from Kilaarsarfik (Sandnes) on the north coast of Ameralla, has long interested archaeologists, both because of its deep midden and because some Eskimos told Daniel Bruun in 1903 that Norse skulls with Eskimo arrows still stuck in them had been found there.[19] The midden excavations of 1976–77 produced no evidence of a Norse-Eskimo fight, nor any explanation for the farm's abandonment at an obviously late date. One human bone was found in the uppermost midden layer, and two badly preserved skeletons turned up in the slope near the coast. These bones have recently been identified as Eskimo. Across the fjord from V48 lies Eqaluit Bay, where archaeologists have found Norse farm V59, as well as a number of Eskimo winter houses which Jørgen Meldgaard judges to be from the period immediately after the Norse left the area.[20]

V54 at Nipaatsoq, also studied during the Norse-Inuit Project of 1976–77, lies to the southeast of V48 on the other side of Ameralla, about eight kilometers from the inland ice cap and close enough to Sandnes that the latter can be clearly seen from a hill behind the farm. Contrary to V48, where the focus was on the midden, at Nipaatsoq almost the entire complex of interconnected rooms for people and animals (including a room in the middle of the house that contained large quantities of sheep manure) was excavated. This farm had also been in use from the very beginning of the eleventh century until the end of the settlement; it had been rebuilt at least once, after a fire around A.D. 1225, and in its last phase it had featured a handsome stone façade.[21]

The archaeologist in charge of the 1976–77 excavations here, Claus Andreasen, had the overall impression that the farm had been left after a somewhat sloppy tidying-up, in which useful personal articles were taken along, while heavier articles of soapstone and whalebone were left behind. In the pantry (room IV) were found the remains of a number of whole mussels, four beheaded ptarmigans, three capelins and one big codfish, seal flippers, a hare, the hind piece of a reindeer, parts of ox, sheep, and goat, and some clotted milk in a barrel. In a corner by a fireplace were the toe joints of four cow's legs.[22] Clearly, ample food supplies from both wild and domestic animals, including seal and fish, were available at this inland farm at some point, but the date of this larder relative to the abandonment of the farm is not clear, preventing conclusions about the farm's final phase. The stratigraphic problems chiefly arise from the Norse practice of cutting turf from a building site over which they may have spread the levelled remains of an older house.[23]

Other mysteries surround the people on this medium-sized, inland farm in its last phase besides the dating of the well-stocked larder. In the midden, of which only the most recent layer remained, were rivets, iron nails, some rings that may have come from a coat of mail, and a goat's knuckle with an engraved pattern that was found repeated both on a couple of soapstone shards and on a small silver shield found in the uppermost layer of room VI. Andreasen reasons that the silver shield was actually made on the farm, especially since Meldgaard and his team had found a small lump of silver during trial excavations there in 1952. The shape of the shield (shown in Fig. 15a) is generally associated with the first half of the fourteenth century,

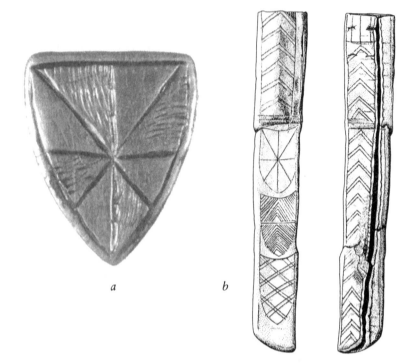

a   *b*

FIG. 15. Probable early examples of the Campbell family's coat of arms. *a*: Small silver coat of arms, 1.4 × 1.8 cm., found at Nipaatsoq in the Western Settlement. Source: The original is in the collection of the Greenland National Museum and Archives in Nuuk; this photograph, taken by Erik Holm, is reproduced here with their kind permission. *b*: Knife scabbard with coat of arms, early to mid-fourteenth century, found in London. Source: Drawing by Nick Griffiths (in Cowgill, De Neergaard, and Griffiths, *Knives and Scabbards*, p. 139, item 429), reproduced by kind permission of the Museum of London.

but the engraved pattern with eight wings (in heraldic terms a "gyronny of eight") has a counterpart only in the coat of arms of the Scottish Campbell clan around A.D. 1330, according to a London authority consulted by the National Museum in Copenhagen.[24] Such a date agrees well with an early- to mid-fourteenth-century leather scabbard found during excavations in London (Fig. 15b), displaying the same coat of arms.[25]

The Scottish Record Office said in response to my own inquiry that the presence in Greenland of this small silver coat of arms is as big a mystery to them as to everybody else. Although the gyronny of eight is particularly associated with the Campbells, and the Record Office is not aware of any other family using this device—at least in the United Kingdom—recent research indicates that the Campbells were Strathclyde Britons and not Gaels as assumed earlier, and that there is thus little reason to suppose that as a family they were notable seafarers.[26] Yet some of the early Campbells had so many legitimate and illegitimate sons that it would have been strange if some of them did not seize any adventure that offered and left to make their way in the world.[27] A member of the Campbell clan (which by this time had several branches, all of whose coats of arms used the gyronny of eight in some fashion) may well have stayed at V54 long enough to carve the symbol of his heritage on several different objects—unless a Norseman on the Nipaatsoq farm had taken a fancy to the shield pattern after seeing it abroad or in a visitor's possession.

David B. Quinn, unaware both of the silver coat of arms and of some other objects that will be discussed in later chapters of this book, and far from convinced that even the Eastern Settlement was "viable in the middle and late fifteenth century," writes judiciously:[28]

Without explicit evidence of a single English artifact from either the Eastern or the Western Settlement, it is hard to believe that we can meaningfully discuss English voyages to Greenland—which, however, might have taken place, more plausibly perhaps than direct transatlantic passages at a relatively early date, but on which we are so far totally uninformed.

The archaeological evidence shows that somebody living at V54 during its final phase was a long-distance traveler, or knew someone who was. Already noted are the ship rivets (which may of course also have come from flotsam) and the possible pieces of chain mail found in the midden. Other likely late-phase finds on the farm include an arrowhead made from meteoric iron that stems from Savissivik (south of Thule, but far north of the Western Settlement), as well as an unused sharpening stone of Igaliko sandstone found in the uppermost layer of room VIII, indicating communication with the Eastern Settlement right up to the final phase. By the door of room VI lay many pieces of coniferous wood, which may have been either driftwood or Markland wood.[29]

The Campbell coat of arms is one more piece of evidence that the Western Settlement had contact with distant places in the mid-fourteenth century. It also points specifically toward Scotland during the period 1337–40 discussed in Chapter Three, when the Greenlanders had stopped paying tithes and Bishop Hákon of Bergen was so hard put to procure white and gray gyrfalcons for King Magnus that he had turned, though in vain, to "the Scottish page." Scotland evidently was a reasonable place to inquire about such commodities at the time—King David II of Scotland is said to have sent a single peregrine falcon to Edward III of England in 1335.[30]

The Scots had ships and hardy sailors accustomed to the northern seas, and they must have been as aware as everyone else that Greenland had long been the source of white gyrfalcons fit for kings. Moreover, they would have been well-informed about developments in Norway, for the connection between Norway and Scotland was ancient and still important to both sides. The Shetlands and Orkneys belonged to Norway until 1468, when Christian I of Denmark and Norway pawned both groups of islands to the Scottish king.

It is unlikely that mid-fourteenth-century Scottish authorities monitored all ships coming and going in their adjoining groups of islands, or that they would have been concerned enough to put obstacles in the way of a ship going to or returning from Greenland on a route that was hardly a secret among sailors. The only secret involved in a private enterprise to fetch falcons and other goods from Greenland would have been the one made necessary by the Norwegian royal monopoly on trade with the colonies. By the second quarter of the fourteenth century, however, the supervision of colonial trade was breaking down in Norway, and in Scotland such central authority as there had been was suffering from dynastic disorder and English aggression.[31]

The slowly accumulating physical evidence that there must have been voyages from Britain and the Western Isles to Greenland during the Middle Ages is supported by common sense. *For people capable of sailing from the British Isles to Iceland and northern Norway, there was no invisible barrier in the North Atlantic preventing them from reaching Greenland as well.* Moreover, the Icelandic laws in *Grágás* contain detailed provisions (which may date from as early as 1170) governing inheritance in case an Icelander died while in Norway, Sweden, Denmark, England, Dublin, Greenland, Shetland, or the Western Isles, or if a man from any of these countries died while in Iceland.[32] Together with physical evidence and common sense, these laws are proof that from early on the North Atlantic was crisscrossed by men of various countries in their open ships. There is no reason to suppose that northern sailors became more squeamish or less able to navigate as marine technology progressed.

Throughout the Middle Ages, involuntary voyages between the British Isles and Greenland were not only possible but probable, given the unpredictable sailing conditions and the contact between England and Iceland that is known to have existed well before the first recorded English sailings there in 1412.[33] But there are also indications of deliberate sailings, such as a voyage to Greenland in 1360 by an English Minorite friar said to have written *Inventio fortunatae* to record his experiences. The Minorite's contemporary who retold the story at no point expressed surprise that the voyage from England to Greenland had taken place; the centerpiece of the account (which will be discussed at the end of this chapter) was the friar's explorations farther north once he had reached Greenland. This implies that going there from England was not in itself a novelty. What made the Minorite's voyage stand out in posterity is that it involved a scientist and scholar, rather than a rough-and-ready trader or fisherman whose entire life was spent plying those northern seas. The friar had the ear of the English king and court, as well as the ability to write down his story. It is worth remembering the story of Ohthere at King Alfred's court several centuries before: Ohthere may have been unusually enterprising and lucky, just like the Minorite explorer, but the real reason we know about him and his north Norway exploits is that he happened to capture Alfred's interest. Ohthere had many colleagues in Norway who were never written up in history.

The possibility that well-equipped foreigners may have sailed far up the Davis Strait in the high Middle Ages is signaled by the pieces of chain mail found at medieval Eskimo sites, although they are usually seen as evidence of Norse-Eskimo contact. The traces of chain mail found in the midden at V54 may also point to foreign visitors. Chain mail, whether the long mail shirt or the separate, tight-fitting mail hood with a shoulder piece that came into use around A.D. 1300 (see Fig. 9), was cumbersome to wear and of little use to people who fished and hunted, and who usually were dressed as in Fig. 10b. Armor of any kind was for warriors, and only for those warriors who could afford it. It was expensive, and it rarely turns up in archaeological excavations even in the other Scandinavian countries.[34] If the various Greenland and Baffin Land finds of chain mail are indeed Norse and not from other Europeans, we must at least ask what kind of business made the Norse need such equipment in those waters.

The problem of distinguishing between Norse and other European archaeological traces confronts us again at V51 (Sandnes or Kilaarsarfik), the large Western Settlement farm known to have been in existence since the Vínland voyages. When Daniel Bruun made the first systematic investigations here in 1903, he found a piece of walrus tusk carved to represent a man's head (see Fig. 16a) down by the shore. He assumed it represented a Norseman. Aage Roussell, who excavated at Sandnes in 1930–32, thought that neither this carving nor the one of wood (Fig. 16b) which he himself found on Norse farm V52a, Umiiviarssuk, could have been made "for any serious purpose." Hans Christian Gulløv in 1982 called both carvings Norse self-portraits, not Eskimo work.[35]

During my visit to the Danish National Museum in 1991, Jørgen Meldgaard assured me that the Sandnes carving in Fig. 16a is most certainly not Eskimo work. On the rare occasions that Thule carvings included facial features, they were indicated by simple, *incised* lines for nose and eyes. To illustrate his point, Meldgaard brought out an Eskimo wood carving of unknown provenance from Morten Porsild's Disko Bay collections. In startling and exquisite detail, the tiny bust depicts a mid-fourteenth-century European dandy, wearing a tight-fitting cap with rolled brim on carefully curled, earlobe-length hair, and with incised lines indicating facial features. According to Meldgaard, the lack of proof that other Europeans sailed in those waters at such an early date is all that prevents both the carving of the dandy and the one shown in Fig. 16a from being said to represent a non-Norse European.[36]

Both 16a and 16b are quite different from each other as well as from 16c, which Therkel Mathiassen found in the Inussuk midden farther north. Gulløv ascribes 16c to the thirteenth or fourteenth century, with the lifelike facial features indicating either Norse or Dorset Eskimo work.[37] No clear inferences can be drawn from these three portraits, but it is interesting that Roussell thought carving 16a "makes no attractive impression." He continued:[38]

The large, drowsy eyes, lacking in completed details, the short nose and the long upper lip over the large, wide mouth, together with the coarse chin all make a picture which, for the Norsemen's own sakes, we hope is a caricature. Above the brow the roughly worked ivory continues . . . almost in the form of a flat-crowned cap, though it is hardly that, partly because the unfinished carving contrasts strongly

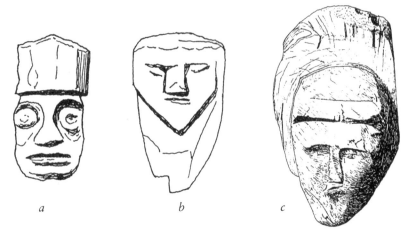

a   *b*   *c*

FIG. 16. Portraits by medieval Norse Greenland artists. *a*: Walrus tusk carving found by the Sandnes shore and generally supposed to represent a Norseman. *b*: Wood carving, also of a Norseman, found at Umiiviarssuk. *c*: Wood carving found in the Inussuk midden. Source: Drawings by Hans Christian Gulløv, reproduced with his permission. Gulløv, in "Eskimoens syn," ascribes the carving shown here as *c* to the thirteenth or fourteenh century; it represents a Norseman or other European from approximately the same period as the carving shown in Fig. 9.

with the face itself, and partly because these caps did not come into use in Europe before the close of the 14th century, which means after the West Settlement is supposed to have been destroyed.

Roussell's reasoning here is dictated in large part by lack of knowledge at the time he was working that the settlement had lasted beyond Ivar Bárdarson's visit, and also by an instinctive unease bordering on aversion. I have a similar reaction. Face 16a is no coarser than the carelessly carved, bearded face 16b, but while both 16b and 16c look comfortably familiar to a Scandinavian, the face in 16a looks alien and faintly menacing even on well-groomed display at the National Museum in Copenhagen. It is as if the artist wanted to record a feeling of unease after an encounter with a stranger. It is hard to believe that someone able to carve these features would get the proportions of the cap to the face so wrong that the hat could not be shown properly. The general indication is of a close-fitting crown with a wide, turned-up brim in a style so practical that it was widely used in both the fourteenth and fifteenth centuries. It is also striking that the man's face appears clean-shaven, while the Norse until about A.D. 1400 favored beards and mustaches, as in face 16b (face 16c may be the portrait of a man too young to have a beard).[39]

Portrait 16b appears to have been carved in an idle moment at V52a, Umiiviarssuk, where Roussell and his team also unearthed four small stoneware shards, judged to be from at least two dark red Rhenish stoneware jugs of the fourteenth century.[40]

As noted in Chapter Three, such imports would most likely date from the *mid*-fourteenth century or later; therefore, these stoneware pieces point to trade and contact with other countries right up to the last phase of the Western Settlement. The jugs may have reached the Western Settlement on a Norwegian or other European ship, or they may have been brought home by a venturesome Norse Greenlander, but they certainly were not left behind by the receding tide for the people at V52a to find.

This farm, which Roussell says that "we cannot consider . . . in its last phase as being earlier than the middle of the fourteenth century," lies rather high up in an inland valley, about two kilometers from the fjord, with a splendid view over the Ameralla and Ameralik fjords out toward the Davis Strait.[41] A striking feature of V52a, apart from the quantity of wood used in the houses and furnishings, was a well-preserved bathhouse with a platform made of old ship's planks and barrel tops. Roussell remarks: "It is clear from the different profiling of the eight planks that it was not merely one ship that was broken up here at the head of Lysufjord [the Ameralik-Ameralla fjords], a circumstance that opens up rich possibilities for conjecture. . . ." A handsome toy boat, found under the platform, suggests easy familiarity with the sea among the people on the farm. The little ship was marked to indicate three or four strakes and could represent anything from a small coastal vessel to a large cargo ship. It was among the artifacts recently studied by Danish wood specialists, but they were unable to indicate the provenance of the wood. There is no wood-diagnosis.[42]

The building complex at V51, Sandnes, had a handsome stone façade and an enclosure with room for six to eight cows. In several other rooms there were quantities of sheep dung and tethering pegs for small animals, but even in room XIV, where firmly trampled sheep dung was mixed with tufts of animal hairs, there were no bones indicating that the animals had died inside from lack of care.[43] Nor have we any indications of what may have caused the last owners to leave; there were no bones or artifacts suggesting that they had died in situ.

No human bones, but an unusually large number of artifacts, were found on some of the late-phase farms in Austmannadal that Roussell excavated in 1937. At site V53, which appears to have partly fallen into the river from its steep bank, a well-preserved pair of smith's tongs—not something a Norse Greenlander would leave behind under most circumstances—was found in one of the remaining rooms. Almost directly east of V53, surrounded by lush, green slopes, lies the large farm V53c, which it was possible to excavate in its entirety. A soapstone bowl with an intricately carved handle was found here, along with the usual plethora of soapstone shards. Closely grouped by a wall lay 63 loom weights, presumably from an upright loom that had been left to slow disintegration. Bits of cloth, a belt buckle and a couple of buttons of bone, carved chessmen, and a gaming die of walrus tusk provide glimpses of daily life on the farm, but nowhere is there any sign that people and animals were actually left to die here.[44]

The most interesting results in this region came from excavations of the large farm at V53d, which is the innermost ruin in Austmannadal and so hidden that one is almost on top of the site before spotting it. A desire for concealment from late-phase outside threats cannot have been the reason for locating all the way in here, however, for the farm clearly evolved over a very long period, and the farmhouse, a block of 22 rooms, sat conspicuously on top of a hill. Furthermore, seal and whale evidently were on the menu to the last, which required extended and presumably communal hunting trips away from home, in full view of whoever else frequented those waters.[45]

Just as was the case at V52a, plenty of wood had been available for construction and furnishings; and here too, as at V53c, at least one large loom had been left to disintegrate. In room XXI were 98 loom weights and a heald-stave from a loom at least 160 centimeters long. Three loom stays were found in room XIX as well, along with more loom weights and a great number of artifacts (including a rune stave) mixed into the thick carpet of twigs on the floor. Other finds in this room included a large iron hunting spear with a long screw tang, as well as a sickle and a leaf knife of iron. Both here and elsewhere were innumerable whale bone spades and shovels, obviously not used much in room XVII, where the archaeologists encountered the powerful odor of freshly thawed sheep droppings from a layer almost three feet deep over the original flagstoned floor. Undaunted, Roussell and his team located several artifacts in this dung, including an ornamented and well-preserved horn spoon.[46]

At V53d, among the remains of the crossbench in room XXI lay a crucifix carved in relief, dated by Roussell to around A.D. 1300 and shown in Fig. 17a. It was made of driftwood, probably locally, and terminated in a point like so many of the Herjolfsnes crosses.[47] We cannot guess to which parish the owners of the lovingly carved crucifix belonged; none of the three churches found in the Western Settlement lies particularly close to V53d either by land or by sea.

One of these churches is at Pisissarfik fjord, just above the ruins of farm V23a at Quasinguaq. Sample excavations of the churchyard here revealed up to five strata of interments, with the skeletons very decomposed. The farm site proper, described by Daniel Bruun as "rather large and overgrown," shows signs of Eskimo habitation both on top of and next to the Norse ruins.[48]

The cemetery at the church called Anavik at V7 (Ujarassuit) also had many interments in its gravelly soil, and a sample excavation outside the southeast corner of the church showed that in the deep, very wet, and frozen sand beds there one may yet find well-preserved bodies and even burial clothes. Roussell estimated the church to have been built around A.D. 1300, as late as the most recent churches down in the Eastern Settlement. The large farm itself was too collapsed for anyone to ascertain its general floor plan, but a corner fireplace belonging to the mid-fourteenth century was found here, again suggesting that people were prospering until the last, thanks in part to the farm's favorable location in excellent caribou-hunting country. The impression of prosperity is strengthened by the size of the farm's storehouse, a dry-stone structure that is still prominent in the landscape, and that may have had two full stories and a loft separated by wooden floors.[49] It was probably also intended for the storage of tithes.

At neither of these two church farm sites are there any significant artifacts or other clues to how, when, or why the people disappeared. K. Fischer-Møller analyzed the bones brought back from the V7 churchyard (including a male skull with reddish blond, wavy hair still attached),

a

FIG. 17. Two crucifixes from about
A.D. 1300, found in the Western Settlement by Aage Roussell. *a*: Found in
Room XXI at V53d, Austmannadal.
b: Found at V51, Sandnes. Source:
both photographs from the National
Museum, Copenhagen, and reproduced with their permission.

b

from 1300 or later in Roussell's estimate. There was evidence of arthritis, but otherwise there were no signs of disease, dental caries, or malnutrition in any age group. The same general good health was evident in the skeletal material brought back from the third and oldest church known in the Western Settlement, V51, Sandnes (Kilaarsarfik), although graves I-III there contained the remains of a couple and their two children who may have been victims of an epidemic.[50]

Here at the head of the Ameralik fjord, archaeologists must contend with both a 5–6 m. rise in the water level since the Middle Ages, and with an inner fjord so shallow from silt deposits that large sections now lie dry at low tide. The former problem means that the sea has taken most of Sandnes church and large parts of the churchyard, while the latter phenomenon prevents even umiaks from landing at V51 or neighboring coastal sites at low tide.[51] In addition, a haphazard pattern of freezing and thawing and a continuously moving midden make dating at Sandnes especially difficult. Roussell nevertheless reasoned that the interments he examined at this site dated from around 1300, because a crucifix (Fig. 17b) found in the most crowded part of the churchyard was very similar to the one found at V53d in Austmannadal (Fig. 17a).

The Sandnes crucifix appears to have been imported rather than made locally, as does a handsome wooden pax found buried close by. It begs the question of why, and with whom, these elaborate pieces were buried; they may well have been the personal property of a priest. They contrast starkly with the small and crudely made wooden cross placed next to the family buried in graves I-III, in the manner of the Herjolfsnes graves. Pieces of several other crosses of varying quality were also found at Sandnes. Aside from crosses carved on various household utensils, there were no other religiously oriented finds at V51, unless we include a rune stick found in the living room of the dwelling. One side said: "*emanuel sabaoth atho/nai usion agios othan/nathos ælæison/alfa th o.*" On the other side was carved: "*filæhs artifæhs/deus iesus saluat/or agios othonna/thos ælæison ææl/ kaagelai agela.*" And on the edge for good measure: "*Mæssias sother.*" The runologist Erik Moltke calls this "a typical holy quack inscription" by someone with just a smattering of Greek, Latin, and Hebrew, and with a facility for magic formulae.[52]

Conditions for preservation were so poor at Sandnes that Roussell found no garments in the churchyard or elsewhere on the farm, but excavations in 1984, mostly between the dwelling and the beach, turned up several pieces of homespun cloth, including one piece dyed bright blue. Evidence of linen cultivation was found in the midden. This recent excavation also revealed many more bones and tooth fragments from walrus than are com-

monly found on the Norse farms, which testifies to the central importance
of Sandnes church farm both in the community and with regard to the
Norðrseta hunts. Arneborg noted recently that the distribution pattern of
walrus products in the Western Settlement points to their having ended up
on the three church farms, probably as tithes.[53]

Many farm implements and weapons made of whalebone were found
in the 1930s by Roussell and his team, as well as leaf knives and other knives
made of iron, and innumerable objects made of soapstone or wood. Notable among the latter were shoe lasts in several sizes, so carefully made that
they distinguished between the right and the left foot. Together with meticulously carved shank buttons and other ornamental objects of bone and
ivory found both at Sandnes and elsewheré, these shoe lasts bear witness
to a way of life that was far removed from brute subsistence.[54]

A businesslike whalebone axe found at Sandnes is a sobering reminder
of grimmer aspects to pastoral life in medieval Greenland. Properly helved,
Roussell notes that it would have been "capable of making an impression
upon the thickest of skulls." Here as elsewhere, axes, bows, arrows, and
spears were used for hunting and—if necessary—for fighting. No remains
of a crossbow have been found in the Western Settlement, but the skull of
a young reindeer found in the midden at Sandnes, and two human skulls
(presumably of Christians) from the Sandnes churchyard, all had holes that
looked as if they had been caused by a crossbow bolt.[55]

We cannot conclude on the basis of such finds that the demise of the
settlement was due to hostile visitors, for various sagas make it clear that
the Norse were perfectly capable of fighting each other. Although the possible traces of chain mail in the V54 midden and the somewhat menacing
carved face (Fig. 16a) found at Sandnes suggest that not everybody who
sailed in these waters came to trade, hunt, or fish peacefully, it would have
required a determined army to inflict more than limited damage on a community of such scattered and secluded farms.

Not one of the discoveries so far made in the Western Settlement permits
conclusions about any single threat sufficient to kill the settlers or put them
to flight. Rather, one is left with the impression that enough problems developed to make people increasingly ready to consider relocating, given an
opportunity and a final shove. The shove could have been anything from
a couple of years of disastrous weather to hostile visitors, including Ivar
Bárdarson and his men. The only practical requirements for emigration
would have been a feasible destination and space on board a ship (their
own or someone else's), and we know that both were available to the inhabitants of the Western Settlement. The shards of Rhenish stoneware at V52a,
Umiiviarssuk, and the Campbell coat of arms at V54, Nipaatsoq, show that

around the time of Ivar Bárdarson's expedition, the Western Settlement's contacts extended beyond Greenland.

In the account of Ivar Bárdarson's journey to the Western Settlement in Chapter Three, we noted that the cooler weather of the time evidently brought so much drift ice to southern Greenland that changes in the sea routes to the Eastern Settlement had become necessary. This may have meant that those voyaging to the Eastern Settlement—both Norse and other explorers and adventurers—would have found ice blocking the entrances there until late summer. Rather than attempting to break through, they may have continued to explore further, eventually reaching the Western Settlement, which though farther north had different currents and local climate conditions.

While there are great annual variations in the two currents moving Polar Ice from the east coast of Greenland around Cape Farewell to the southwest coast, as well as in the amount of so-called West Ice drifting southward in Baffin Bay and the Davis Strait in the summer, the former *generally* veers away from the west coast around Arsuk (just north of the Eastern Settlement), while the south-moving West Ice is carried out into the Davis Strait around Kangaamiut in the Sukkertoppen district north of the Western Settlement.[56] Under those conditions, the Eastern Settlement region is harder to reach than the Western one, except for a short period in late summer. What T. V. Garde noted a century ago is revealing: sailing ship skippers who had made a successful run into Julianehaab (the heart of the old Eastern Settlement) were paid a bonus on their return to Copenhagen because they had been forced to go north to Arsuk before sailing south again in the narrow, dangerous passage between the ice belt and the land.[57]

Ice conditions fluctuate widely from year to year, however. They may not have been that bad in 1360, for example, when the mysterious Minorite friar and explorer came to the Eastern Settlement before proceeding northward in the Davis Strait. Or perhaps his crew members were familiar with the south Greenland waters—we simply do not know. Like most other material about medieval Greenland, the story of this expedition and the evidence for it are sketchy and bewildering and reach us in a roundabout way, but that should not discourage us from trying to extract what information we can from them. Here we draw on the work done on this topic by the English scholar E. G. R. Taylor.[58] In Taylor's account, a medieval world traveler from the Low Countries reported that in 1364, eight people who had come from Greenland were visiting the Norwegian king and his court in Bergen. Among those eight were two priests, one of whom (said to be a fifth-generation descendant of a "Bruxellensis") was carrying an astrolabe, which an English Minorite had given him in Greenland in exchange for a Testament. The priest with the astrolabe told the king that this English Minorite, an accomplished astronomer and mathematician from Oxford, had come to Greenland in 1360, and that

leaving the rest of the party who had come to the Island, he journeyed further through the whole of the North . . . and put into writing all the wonders of the is- lands, and gave the King of England [Edward III] the book, which he called in Latin *Inventio fortunatae*, which book began at the last climate, that is to say latitude 54° continuing to the Pole.

According to the Belgian, the priest from Greenland let his king (who would have been Hákon VI Magnusson) know that in *Inventio fortunatae*, the Minorite wrote of such wonders as a circle of mountains to the north where no people lived, except "on the last side where in that narrow land [isthmus] there were 23 people not above 4 feet tall . . . whereof 16 were women." Where these "pygmies" lived, there was an "Indrawing Sea" of five channels. In two places farther inland, the English explorer had found "a great piece of ship's planking and other balks which had been used in big ships, besides many trunks of trees which at some earlier date had been hewn down." From this he inferred "with certainty" that people had lived there formerly, but were now gone. And "right under the Pole there lies a bare rock in the midst of the Sea . . . all of magnetic stone. . . . And the Mi- norite himself had heard that one can see all around it from the Sea: and it is black and glistening. . . ."

Perhaps thinking that some firsthand information was called for as well, the priest told the king that where he himself had been living, it rained scarcely six times a year, and then only for six or seven hours. It never blew hard enough "to drive a corn mill," and the air was always cool. The priest's seven companions are reported to have said that "they had also heard such things said by their elders, but had never seen them."[59] If this last statement refers to "corn mills," these native Greenlanders could truthfully say they had neither seen nor needed one.

Several elements of this tale have a familiar ring. The world map that Geraldus Mercator (a native of Flanders) published in 1569 had an insert showing just such a polar region with its terrifying "Indrawing Seas."[60] Mercator said his source for this and the story outlined above was the writ- ten account in the "Belgic language" by one Jacobus Cnoyen of Herzogen- busch. Cnoyen himself may have got the story about the eight Greenlanders while on a 1364 business trip to Bergen, a Staple of the Hanseatic League. Mercator gave an account of it all in a letter to the English mathematician and occultist John Dee, who presumably was not himself able to read Cnoyen's "Belgic language"; Dee then wrote his own version of the story as told in Mercator's letter. Dee's manuscript (later damaged by fire) incorporating the Cnoyen-Mercator information was dated June 8, 1577. Just three years later, as Taylor reconstructs the sequence of connections in her article "A Letter Dated 1577 from Mercator to John Dee," Richard Hakluyt also referred to Cnoyen's story.[61]

Hakluyt accepted Dee's conclusion that the English Minorite and author of *Inventio fortunatae* must have been Nicholas of Lynn, a famous Oxford mathematician and explorer who was the undisputed author of a *Kalendarium* begun in 1386. The assumption that Nicholas of Lynn also wrote *Inventio fortunatae* has been slow to die, although the friar described in Cnoyen's account was a Franciscan, while Nicholas of Lynn was a Carmelite, and although there is nothing to connect Nicholas of Lynn with voyages in the far north. When doubts about the Nicholas connection eventually arose, so did doubts about the existence of *Inventio fortunatae*, aided by misgivings due to obscure or fantastic passages in the Dee-Mercator-Cnoyen account. The consequence was a tendency to throw out the baby with the bathwater. Striking a compromise, a recent editor of Nicholas of Lynn's *Kalendarium*, Sigmund Eisner, writes that "even if the *Inventio fortunatae* should prove to be genuine, no proof has risen so far to identify its author with Nicholas of Lynn."[62]

Approaching the problem from a different angle, E. G. R. Taylor, Alwyn Ruddock, and David Quinn believe that *Inventio fortunatae* was as real as Nicholas himself, but that the book and Nicholas had no connection with each other. According to Taylor, "we cannot doubt that the travelling monk existed or that he wrote *Inventio fortunatae*." Ruddock assumes that the work existed in manuscript form only and notes that the *Travels of Marco Polo* had not been printed in England even as late as the end of the fifteenth century and was almost unknown there before the sixteenth century. Quinn agrees, arguing that most early maps also remained in manuscript form and therefore were virtually unknown, and he takes it for granted that only a few manuscript copies of *Inventio fortunatae* circulated among people interested in geography and exploration.[63]

Evidence for the existence of at least one work by that name is found in several references besides the Dee-Mercator-Cnoyen one. Three are associated with Christopher Columbus. Las Casas mentions *Inventio fortunatae* in his *Historia de las Indias*, and so does Ferdinand Columbus in his biography of his father. In a letter (to be discussed later) written during the winter of 1497–98 to Christopher Columbus, the English merchant John Day regretted that he had been unable to find the book "Ynvincio fortunati." Quinn reasons that the copy which Day mislaid in 1497 may well have been the only surviving copy in England, and he also notes that Day's letter is the earliest English reference to the work. It was already known to

Martin Behaim of Nüremberg, however, when he wrote near the North Pole on his globe of 1491–92: "In the book *De inventione fortunata* it may be read that there is a high mountain of magnetic stone . . . surrounded by the flowing 'mare sugenum' which pours out water like a vessel through an opening below. Around it are four islands, of which two are inhabited. . . ." The well-traveled German Johann Ruysch, whose world map was published in the Rome edition of Ptolemy's *Geographia* in 1508, also quoted from *Inventio fortunatae*.[64]

Both *Inventio fortunatae* and its unknown Minorite author thus seem to have been genuine enough. Nor is there any reason to distrust the existence of a late-fourteenth-century report penned by an educated, observant, well-traveled Belgian and read by Mercator, who then gave the information to John Dee. What is unclear from Dee's manuscript, our only available version of Cnoyen's account, is whether it contains interpolations by Mercator or Dee (such as a garbled reference at the beginning to the army which conquered the "Northern Islands" for King Arthur, and to nearly 4,000 people who "entered the indrawing seas [beyond Greenland] who never returned"), and whether Cnoyen blended the Greenland priest's report (which he had heard) with extracts from *Inventio fortunatae* (which he had read), knowing that the two were related.

The latter explanation is the more likely one, for otherwise there is no accounting for these words following the description of the magnetic rock: "This was the writing and words of the Minorite, who has since journeyed to and fro five times [where?] for the King of England on business. . . . They came to be found in a book called *Inventio fortunae* [*sic*—Dee's amendment], of which the Minorite himself was author."[65] Furthermore, it is not likely that the priest, who had known the friar in Greenland in 1360 (the year of the latter's explorations), would have reported in Norway just four years later both what the friar had seen and that he had written a book about it, which he had given to the king of England. Such a timetable would be a tall order for any explorer-author, and it would also imply that the priest and the friar had met again *after* the king of England had received *Inventio fortunatae*.

We may never learn the name of the Minorite explorer and writer, but we can make a good guess at the identity of the astrolabe-toting priest from Greenland. He and his companions are said to have reported to king and court in Norway in 1364, the same year we know that Ivar Bárdarson was back in Bergen, stepping into a sinecure at the Royal Chapel after his long service as the Gardar bishop's *officialis*. The number of priests in Greenland was never very great; Finnur Jonsson estimates that there were twelve parish churches and two monastic churches in all of the Eastern Settlement during its peak.[66] If two priests had recently arrived in Norway from Green-land in 1364, the probability is high that one of them was Ivar Bárdarson returning home.

Further evidence lies in the similarity between Cnoyen's report that the two priests had come to Norway accompanied by six lay Greenlanders, and the beginning of Ivar's "Description of Greenland," which says that "wise men who have grown up in Greenland and *who have recently come from Greenland*" contributed to the detailed sailing directions provided in the account.[67]

Some of the specific information that the priest is reported to have given the king of Norway also suggests that the priest was none other than Ivar. Who but a native Bergen-man would comment on the lack of rain in Green-land? Compared with the rainy city of Bergen, Greenland is indeed dry. And who had greater need than Ivar to pass on the Minorite explorer's tale about deserted human habitations far north in Greenland? It corroborated his own story of the depopulated Western Settlement he had found on his supposed errand of mercy.

But the Minorite was not describing the farming areas of the Western Settlement, where we know that some people were still living at the time. Even if they had temporarily taken to the hills again at the sight of another large ship, their farms would have been there for the Minorite to see. He cannot have sailed alone, so those who went north with him must have been Norse Greenlanders, familiar with the location of the Western Settlement. If the ship called in there and found everybody going about their business as usual, our explorer would not have found anything odd enough to com-ment on at all.

What the friar noted was "a great piece of ship's planking and other balks which had been used in big ships, besides many trunks of trees which at some earlier date had been hewn down," from which he deduced "with certainty" that people had lived there formerly, but were now gone. He made this discovery farther inland from a place where he had encountered Eskimos; his description of male and female "pygmies" is clearly based on personal experience. There is no telling where the friar encountered either these Eskimos or the evidence of ship-building, however. It may have been either in Greenland or on the American side of Davis Strait, in the Markland region, but most likely the latter. Any ship-building taking place on the Greenland side would have involved either drift timber or laboriously im-ported logs; only in Markland would there would have been evidence of trees "which at some earlier date had been hewn down." We may assume the Greenlanders went there from time to time to get lumber, and stumps as well as felling-marks on the logs would have told their tale. Both the well-traveled Minorite and his crew would have been able to distinguish between driftwood and trees "which at some earlier date had been hewn down."

Although the friar's route cannot be retraced from the available text, it is safe to say that since no fourteenth-century European had been to the North Pole, "the Pole" in the account by Dee-Mercator-Cnoyen must refer to impenetrable ice somewhere in the Davis Strait or maybe even Smith Sound. The magnetic rock could be a description of Disko Island—or it could be a sop to contemporary geographical lore, just like the reference to the terrible "Indrawing Seas," which resembles all early descriptions of the Far North, as Taylor points out.[68]

We do not know whether the English friar used his own ship or a Greenlandic one when "leaving the rest of the party who had come to the Island, he journeyed further through the whole of the North. . . ." It deepens the mystery that he left the rest of his party behind (presumably at the Eastern Settlement) when he continued his voyage, and that we have no idea who was in his original traveling party and why they had come to Greenland. And it is anyone's guess whether the Minorite's northern expedition afforded an opportunity for some young Western Settlement men to leave aboard his ship, or whether the Eskimo carving that Porsild found, of a mid-fourteenth-century dandy, had any connection with this party.

In sum, unknowns and uncertainties abound in three interwoven areas: in the description in *Inventio fortunatae* of deserted ship-building and logging sites in the far north; in Ivar Bárdarson's "Description of Greenland" and his account of finding neither Christians nor heathens in the Western Settlement; and in modern archaeological clues to the Western Settlement's demise. It is nevertheless possible to draw a few conclusions, which concern the Eastern Settlement as well as the Western one since they focus on the Greenlanders' contact with the rest of the world and on the choices available to them by the second half of the fourteenth century.

First, a Greenland-built ship is recorded as having been to Markland in 1347, close to the time when Ivar Bárdarson made his trip to the Western Settlement and only thirteen years before the Minorite visited Greenland. In other words, the Greenlanders at that time were just as able to build ships, and to sail them where they wanted to go, as they had been three centuries earlier. Nor was being at the mercy of the wind and the weather a peculiarity of the mid-fourteenth century.

Second, in 1360, while Ivar was still in Greenland and—as we now know—there still were people living normally in the Western Settlement, the English Minorite explorer came to Greenland and proceeded far north into the Davis Strait. This demonstrates that ships were reaching Greenland not only from Norway and Iceland, but from England as well.

Third, various objects found by archaeologists confirm such outside contacts, without revealing with whom the contacts were made or whether foreign contact may have harmed the Western Settlement.

Fourth, recent research points to temporarily cooling temperatures in the second half of the fourteenth century, but there is no evidence that people in the Western Settlement starved to death as a consequence. Nor do they seem to have died en masse from other causes, such as pestilence or Eskimo aggression.

It is conceivable that the Western Settlement Norse in particular suffered the consequences of conflicts between Dorset Eskimos and the Thule people who were taking over Baffin Island and continued to move south along both sides of the Davis Strait while cooling temperatures favored their hunting methods for large sea mammals.[69] The Norðrseta hunting region as well as the American forests and opportunities for smelting iron were more easily reached from the Western than from the Eastern Settlement, and if being a transshipment point for American products had been vital to the Western Settlement economy, it would have had dire consequences for the members of this small community if they no longer dared send ships across the Davis Strait, where a small ship's crew far from home would have been uniquely vulnerable.

The Norse could presumably continue to hunt walrus and narwhal on the Greenland side, where the Dorset Eskimos had long since disappeared, but where even relatively friendly competition with the Thule people probably would have resulted in a reduced catch. Less walrus ivory, fewer valuable pelts and furs, and no more iron blooms would have meant reduced income and curtailed trade with the Eastern Settlement, resulting in greater isolation. Even more serious in the long run would have been the effect of lost access to the lumber needed to build ships, the lifeline of any medieval Norse economy.

It seems unlikely that people who appear to have been in control of their lives to the last, and who had ships as well as occasional news from the outside, would allow themselves to perish quietly and patiently as a group. A few may have stuck it out to the last, hoping for better days or perhaps not even thinking that they needed better days. The rest must have relocated in response either to worsening conditions for cattle farming, or to competition with the Eskimos at the best hunting and fishing grounds, or to unfriendly callers, or to a wish for less isolation, or to the lure of the American coast—we cannot tell. All we know is that Ivar Bárdarson was probably somewhat premature in announcing the end of the Western Settlement, and that later historians are likely to have been precipitous in dating the beginning of the Greenlanders' isolation to the second half of the fourteenth century.

CHAPTER SIX

Rumors of Trouble in the Eastern Settlement

Ivar Bárdarson returned to Norway after more than twenty years of service to church and crown in Greenland, leaving behind an episcopal see that still had no bishop. Even on the Scandinavian peninsula itself a number of ecclesiastical benefices had been vacant for so long during the last years of King Magnus's reign that they were claimed by the Curia.[1] But while episcopal appointments in Iceland during the last half of the fourteenth century and the beginning of the fifteenth certainly reflected confusion and carelessness in high places (Skálholt, for instance, had either foreign bishops or no bishop at all from 1345 to 1413), neither church nor crown in Norway was prepared to relinquish its grip on Iceland—despite the poverty from natural disasters and other causes that characterized that country in the later Middle Ages.[2] But Greenland, which was spared similar disasters, and which in some ways offered its inhabitants a broader base for food and trade than the Icelanders had ever known, soon lost its place with Dano-Norwegian officialdom altogether.

The growing neglect of Norway's Atlantic colonies by both crown and church sometimes reflected circumstances beyond anyone's control, such as pestilence, periods of unusually bad weather, and other disasters, which together might spell major trouble on both land and sea, but which separately appear to have caused only temporary setbacks. For example, in the spring of 1393 eighteen German warships, carrying some 900 men, attacked Bergen, burned all the churches, and terrorized the population for eight days before sailing off with as much loot as they could carry on their own and stolen ships. Despite this blow struck at the heart of Norwegian shipping and trade, Bishop Vilchin of Skálholt sailed out to Iceland the very next year.[3]

Similarly, two major outbreaks of the Black Death in the fourteenth century interrupted sailings from Norway to her colonies, but those interruptions were also temporary. Nor did smallpox epidemics or the ravages of the Black Death in Iceland, which killed most of the country's priests and perhaps one-third of the population between 1402 and 1404, keep a good number of Icelandic chieftains from sailing off to Norway in 1405, as we shall see later. On the contrary, many of them were among the sizable number of people called *hinn ríki* (the rich) in fifteenth-century Iceland, after the Plague had caused many farms to fall into a few hands.[4] For survivors able to turn a grim situation to advantage, life not only went on, it went very well.

Faced with losses from pestilence, tempests, and pirates, beleaguered Norwegian officials and institutions did what they had always done when balancing investments against expected profits: they ordered their priorities.[5] Greenland, whose great distance from Norway had always made it the most difficult of the colonies to dominate, had now also become the least cost-effective and was low on the list for people whose promotion, power, and wealth had come to depend more on monarchs embroiled in European warfare and intrigue than on the Norwegian Atlantic hegemony.

It bears repeating that there is no evidence that poverty in Greenland was the reason the Norwegians at this point lost interest in their distant colony. Ivar's report on the Western Settlement probably caused it to be removed from the church and crown tax ledgers, but his account of the Eastern Settlement was studded with references to "countless" whales and reindeers, lakes and fjords full of fish, and a large forest across the fjord from Gardar Cathedral in which the episcopal cattle grazed. Ivar's "Description" altogether gives the impression that in the Eastern Settlement, the church was still well set up in an established community with a sound economic base, and his report must have been encouraging enough to warrant the appointment of another incumbent at Gardar, Bishop Alf.[6]

Bishop Alf braved the long voyage and reached Greenland in 1368, three years after his ordination and some four years after Ivar had been debriefed by king, court, and church back in Norway. The Greenlanders had by this time been without a bishop for nineteen years.[7] We have no information about Bishop Alf's years at Gardar. We know only that he died at his post in 1377 or 1378, and that no resident bishop succeeded him, although bishops nominally "of Gardar" or "of Greenland" were appointed right down to the time of the Reformation. If Alf had met with violent death at the hands of either Norse Greenlanders or Eskimos, it would surely have been mentioned in an annal, for in the same entry noting that a ship had come from Greenland to Norway in 1383 with reports of Bishop Alf's demise some six years earlier, both "Lögmanns-annáll" and

"Flatey-annáll" contain the "sorrowful news" that the bishop of Orkney had been killed.[8]

Unless the former Brother Alf of Munkeliv monastery had proved exceptionally troublesome at home in Bergen, it is hard to believe he would have been sent to Greenland if Ivar had reported, officially or unofficially, that the Eastern Settlement was in danger of insurrection, or had been threatened by Eskimos or foreign marauders, or could now scarcely sustain itself, let alone a bishop. Nor was Alf such a poor man that he would have grasped at any opportunity for improvement. For example, in 1366 (after his consecration as the Gardar bishop) he swore an affidavit that the houses he had built outside the churchyard of Nordnes church in Bergen, with his own money and with help from Munkeliv monastery, should revert to Munkeliv after his "son" (actually his sister's son) had used them for as long as he wanted.[9]

The question then becomes whether the people who finally brought back the news of Bishop Alf's death also passed around word that since Ivar's time in Greenland, life there had taken a turn for the worse, for example due to troubles with Thule Eskimos establishing year-round settlements in the Eastern Settlement region.

"Gottskálk's Annals," which lists the year of Bishop Alf's death as 1378, records that in 1379, Skrælings attacked the Greenlanders and took two boys away as slaves after killing eighteen men. Neither "Lögmanns-annáll" nor "Flatey-annáll" mentions any Skræling attack in 1379, although both note the 1383 arrival in Norway of men who had spent a couple of winters in Greenland, and who carried the news that Bishop Alf had died at Gardar six years earlier.[10] It seems odd that they would not have mentioned such a serious and recent attack on the colonists, and odder still that the peripatetic Eskimos would have bothered to capture two Norse boys, unless they intended to use them as hostages. Jette Arneborg, who believes that 1379 is too late for news of a Skræling attack to involve the Western Settlement, nevertheless thinks that the entry in "Gottskálk's Annals" must be taken seriously as an indication of trouble.[11]

That leaves two possibilities: either the Eskimos attacked the farmers in the Eastern Settlement, or there was a serious skirmish with Eskimos during a Norse hunting expedition to a distant area. The latter is more likely, considering that the settlement lasted another century or more despite the proximity of the Skrælings, and that Tissaluk in the so-called Middle Settlement is the only known instance of Eskimos having taken up residence in the deserted buildings of a Norse farmstead.[12]

Relations between the Norse and the Eskimos appear to have been friendly overall, but we still cannot rule out problems close to the Norse settlements, for the two cultures were so different that even if no quarrel arose over trading, fishing, driftage rights, and hunting, either taunts or misunderstandings may occasionally have had grave consequences between two groups so reliant on weapons.

An Eskimo tale that Henry Rink claimed was unique to West Greenland may have its roots in a real, though undatable event. Its subject is reminiscent of incidents in Norse sagas, and Robert McGhee has pointed out that indeed there is an Icelandic version of the same story, told from the Norse point of view, but containing Eskimo words. According to the Eskimo version, in the Qaqortoq (Hvalsey) fjord, in the heart of the Eastern Settlement, a Norseman was gathering shells on the shore when an Eskimo kayaker came by. The Norseman repeatedly challenged the Eskimo to try to hurt him with his lance. The Eskimo resisted at first, but at last he did as he was told, killing the Norseman. The Eskimo's chief, Ungurtoq, told him not to worry about the Norseman's death, and indeed there was no revenge for two summers. At the end of the third winter, however, the kayaker decided to kill another Norseman, and this time the Norse turned out in numbers and killed many Eskimos. The Eskimos retaliated by burning many of the Norse in their houses, and there were several more murders before tempers cooled off.[13]

The battles supposedly centered on Arpatsivik, the island which the Norse called Hvalsey, or "Whale Island," and which lent its name to the whole fjord area with its many farmsteads. Excavations at Hvalsey have not shown signs of fire, but that does not exclude a confrontation, in Joel Berglund's view. The ruins of a small Norse farm (Ø86) have been found on the island, but have not been excavated.[14] The Danish archaeologists Therkel Mathiassen and Erik Holtved found no sign of medieval Eskimo habitation in the vicinity when they examined the area in 1934, but they did not rule out the possibility that the traces had merely vanished. During their excavations that summer in the former Eastern Settlement, they found a number of other Thule Eskimo sites which Mathiassen judged to date from the mid-fourteenth to the fifteenth century. A map accompanying the report shows that these earlier sites were in the outer parts of the fjords, not at the heads where the Norse farms tended to cluster, so fights over homesteading seem unlikely.[15]

Norse artifacts, ranging from cloth and spindlewhorls to knife blades and bell metal, were found in a number of these Eskimo ruins and middens, but since the dating of the ruins themselves is very problematic, it is difficult to say which objects may have been obtained from the Norse while they were still living in the area, and which were pilfered from abandoned farms. Mathiassen noted, however, that there were Norse artifacts in even the earliest of these Eskimo houses. Those objects could have come to the Eskimos through trade, which presupposed peaceful relations.

Mathiassen evaluated his and Holtved's discoveries at a time when it was taken for granted not only that the arrival of Eskimo settlements eventually spelled the end for the Greenland Norse, but that Ivar Bárdarson's report should be interpreted literally in all respects, and that the last hundred years or more of the Norse Greenland colony had been spent in virtual isolation from the outside world. This is the background against which we must see another of Mathiassen's observations, namely that the small number of Eskimo settlements from that period makes it surprising "that so few people were able to force the Norsemen away from their 190 farms in the East Settlement."[16] Actually, 444 Norse sites had been registered in the Eastern Settlement as of 1990.[17] Whatever the ratio of Norse to Eskimos may have been at any given time, modern scholars do not believe that the Eskimos killed or forced out the Norse in the Eastern Settlement any more than in the Western one.

Nor is a "Skræling threat" either before or after 1379 a likely explanation for why Gardar bishops were increasingly slow to be appointed, reluctant to live at their see, and eventually nonresident altogether. As argued earlier, some of this development probably was the result of strong lay control of church property and growing reluctance among the Greenlanders to honor and remunerate their bishops and the church sufficiently—although they did not themselves lack for food and trade goods. Another part of the explanation lies in the international situation, for the Greenland bishopric inevitably suffered the consequences, first, of growing indifference among Norwegian secular and ecclesiastical authorities, second, of the medieval Curia's rapid growth and consequent need for money, and third, of the church's descent into the secularism and greed that caused upheavals in distant Rome and Avignon.

It shows the remarkable strength of the Roman Church that despite its growing secularization and its relentless requests for money, it had survived even to 1378 without open rebellion everywhere, including in Norway. In May of 1372, for instance, Pope Gregory XI, worried about his empty coffers, had ordered his collector for Scandinavia to call in and receive all the debts and personal property of Archbishop Olaf of Nidaros, claiming that Olaf, who had died in 1370, had agreed during his lifetime to earmark his property as payment for his debts to the pope. In July of the same year, the collector was told not only to demand tithes from all ecclesiastical benefices that had not been on the tax list up to that point, but to make the demand retroactive. No potential source of income was overlooked, so it is not surprising that there was growing resistance to paying, or that as late as 1402, Gardar diocese was still included among the Norwegian bishoprics from which Boniface IX in Rome expected papal tithes to be collected.[18]

For Norway and her colonies, the deterioration in social and economic

conditions due to the greed, indifference, and infighting among those holding secular power added to the difficulties caused by the unstable ecclesiastical situation at home and abroad. King Hákon VI Magnusson of Norway
had married Princess Margrethe of Denmark in 1363. When Hákon died
in 1380 and his young son Olaf succeeded him on the Norwegian throne,
it was the prelude to a debilitating union with Denmark, for Olaf died suddenly in 1387 and his mother, now queen of Denmark, came to rule Norway as well. The Swedes also chose her for their queen, and the 1397
Kalmar Treaty formalized the union of all three countries.

The Norwegian nobles, fearing the worst, had refused to sign the draft
of the Kalmar Treaty. Their fears were well founded, for Margrethe deliberately set about infiltrating the Norwegian nobility with foreigners; put
Danish bishops in charge of Norwegian sees; had the Norwegian tax
money sent to Denmark; and allowed the Hanseatic League to tighten its
hold on Norway (primarily through Bergen) and on Iceland.[19] Margrethe
ruled over all three countries until her death in 1412, and she ensured the
continuation of her policies through her niece's young son, Eirik of Pomerania (born 1383), who had been chosen as her successor when he was still
a child. As an adult, Eirik at every turn underscored Norway's position as
an unequal partner in the union.

When Bishop Alf died in about 1378, just as the Great Schism exploded
in Europe, the Greenlanders had no way of knowing that henceforth they
would be on their own as far as the church was concerned, and that by
1417, when the Schism ended with the election of Pope Martin V, they
would long since have lost touch with the Norwegian king and the archbishop alike.

The confusion caused by the Schism (the longest in the history of the
papacy) was great, and "all evils which had crept into ecclesiastical life
were infinitely increased." Accompanying the loss of respect for the Holy
See was the popes' greater-than-ever dependence on temporal power, "for
the Schism allowed each Prince to chose which Pope he would acknowledge."[20] Nordic royalty made full use of that choice.

King Eirik, Margrethe's successor, favored the three Pisan antipopes
Alexander V, John XXIII, and Martin V, and after the Council of Basel he
and his successor cast their lot with the Council's pope, while the English
stayed with the pope in Rome.[21] Through the appointment of English bishops in Iceland, this difference in allegiance may have contributed to the
growing English hegemony in the North Atlantic that will be discussed in
Chapter Seven.

It is doubtful whether any of these popes could count on much increase
in their temporal power from their association with King Eirik, and in matters spiritual Eirik's interest was at best spotty. The priorities of his mentor,

Queen Margrethe, shine through in a 1401 letter from Pope Boniface IX, who granted her (and any visitors she might have) the right not to fast on fast days. The pope's letter also granted her the right to have returned to her land and property that had formerly belonged to her realms, and to name candidates to ecclesiastical benefices and ranks for which the crown had had the right of patronage in the past.[22]

A Danish Bishop Henrik "of Gardar" is known to have been on hand in Oslo in 1388 for the celebration of Queen Margrethe's assumption of sole power in Norway. He had been consecrated some time before 1386, presumably soon after the Norwegian authorities had learned about Bishop Alf's death when the ship *Olafssúðinn* arrived in Norway in 1383 after spending two winters in Greenland.[23] Having been appointed at a time when the legitimacy of the Norwegian archbishop was as uncertain as the volatile Urban VI's tenure in Rome, it is doubtful that Henrik had been hand-picked to serve in Greenland. He never went there, but spent his time in Denmark and Norway until he went to Rome in 1391 to see Pope Boniface IX. By 1394, Henrik had become bishop of the Orkneys, switching sees with the incumbent Bishop Jon. Like his predecessor, Jon "of Gardar" never went to Greenland, and Henrik (who died in 1396) was hardly keen on going to the Orkneys, where Bishop William had been killed just a few years earlier.[24]

Once the Gardar appointment no longer carried an expectation that the incumbent would go to Greenland, there was no shortage of applicants. Nor was there a lack of popes willing to appoint them so long as their fees were paid. Applications for the Gardar office kept the name on the Curia's books, which probably helps to explain why Boniface IX was still expecting tithes from Gardar in 1402. He had just appointed a Minorite named Berthold as the Gardar bishop, claiming he had reserved the appointment for himself even while Bishop Alf was still alive. Soon (1402) he gave Gardar to Bishop Peter of Strengnes, but he changed his mind six months later and let the Greenland office revert to Berthold.[25]

Archbishop Askell of Nidaros, whose own tenure was also somewhat dubious, is said to have appointed a Bishop Anders to go to Greenland in 1406 "in case Henrik [dead since 1396!] was dead."[26] Askell surely was aware of Bishop Berthold's current claim on the title, for scarcely two years later, in 1408, Bishop Berthold "of Gardar" and Archbishop Askell signed a letter of indulgence together. Meanwhile, the antipope at Avignon, Clement VII (r. 1378–94) had shown his own tender concern for the Greenlanders by appointing first a Bishop Georgius of Gardar and then, in 1389, a successor named Peter Staras.[27] If either of those two bishops ever set foot on shipboard, it was not to go to Greenland.

After the 1409 Council of Pisa, the Pisan Antipope Alexander V expressed his satisfaction that Eirik of Pomerania, king of Norway, Denmark, and Sweden, had been persuaded to leave the obedience of Gregory XII of Rome.[28] When John XXIII succeeded Alexander in 1411, he lost no time in appointing the Minorite friar Johannes Petersson as bishop of Gardar, but he too changed his mind almost immediately and favored another Minorite, Jacob Treppe, with this plum. He filled other idle moments of 1411 by urging diligence in the collection of Peter's Pence in the north and by asking his Danish nuncio to preach Crusade in the three Scandinavian countries.[29]

Just as the confusion in Rome, Avignon, and Nidaros lent itself well to episcopal musical chairs, so it created ideal conditions for certain kinds of private enterprise. As soon as the lack of administrative oversight in Greenland (always chiefly provided through the church) became apparent, there was a marked increase in the number of Icelanders doing business in Greenland, despite the breach of royal prerogative that such trade entailed. Clearly, they were gambling on being able to negotiate a face-saving deal with the Norwegian authorities if their activities were discovered. Evidence will show the tacit acknowledgment among powerful people that subterfuge was not only called for, but was central to their gamble with Greenland trade.

Queen Margrethe's husband, Hákon VI Magnusson, during his reign had shown himself extremely jealous of his royal privileges, as the incident noted in an earlier chapter in which he went after the Greenland ombudsman in 1374 for having bought Bergen property in defiance of royal first option makes clear. His son Olaf (r. 1380–87) increased the taxes on ships trading with his colonies, and he also stipulated that no man should engage in trade unless he owned 15 marks in ready silver.[30] The 1397 Kalmar Union under Queen Margrethe did nothing to keep legal trade with Norway's Atlantic colonies from deteriorating further, for it, too, perpetuated the policy of royal trade monopolies that had been in effect since Viking times, and Margrethe herself brooked no interference with her privileges.[31]

As restrictions on private enterprise grew in step with the crown's determination to guard its privileges and licensing policies through increasingly harsh measures, the premium swelled on illicit trade with Greenland, the most obviously neglected colony. It cannot have taken experienced merchants long to figure out that they could make a very good profit off people who had not seen a trading vessel for several years. They had to call their trading voyages by some other name, however, and since the people to be discussed below had friends in high places, and some who were annal writers, their enterprises have ever since been known by that other name: "drifting off."

The time has come to examine the bottle so long concealed beneath this label with its implication that Greenland no longer was a place anyone would sail to voluntarily. In the process, it is also important to acknowledge that sailing in the North Atlantic was still so dangerous and unpredictable that a crew claiming to have drifted off to Greenland would have been both believable and—at times—truthful. In skilled hands, this was a very useful combination, as the last four recorded sailings to Norse Greenland show: those of the *Olafssúðinn* in 1381, of the *þorlákssúðinn* in 1382, of four ships led by Björn Einarsson in 1385, and of a group led by Thorstein Olafsson in 1406.

When the good ship *Olafssúðinn* arrived in Norway in 1383, the crew said they had been forced to spend two winters in Greenland after drifting off there while Iceland-bound. The ship brought back survivors from another Iceland-farer, Skálholt see's own vessel, the *þorlákssúðinn*. The latter had also been carried off toward Greenland and been shipwrecked there the year before (1382), the men narrowly escaping in their ship's boat. They were presumably much relieved to find the *Olafssúðinn* already waiting in Greenland.[32] The shipwreck of the *þorlákssúðinn* may have been a genuine disaster, although a churlish historian might wonder if that, too, had been invented to cover up the profitable sale of the ship itself when the death in Greenland of several crew members (reported by the annalists) enabled all the Icelanders to leave in just one ship. Whether a truthful story or merely a plausible one, it could handily serve for *both* ships when the surviving *Olafssúðinn* arrived in Norway without bothering to stop off in Iceland on the way. Luckily for the crew, the *féhirðir* (royal tax collector) in Bergen just then was Erlend Philippusson, who will also appear later as a man adept at circumventing the crown's representatives.[33]

There are several good reasons for supposing that at least the *Olafssúðinn*'s Greenland voyage was planned. First of all, it is obvious that the men were familiar with the direct route from Norway to Greenland, since they so confidently sailed straight back to Norway in 1383 without stopping in Iceland first. Second, it is equally obvious that when leaving Norway two years earlier, after a year of acquiring goods and news in and around Bergen, the *Olafssúðinn* crew must have known that the Greenlanders had not seen a Norwegian merchant ship for years—perhaps not since the Greenland royal ombudsman Sigurd Kolbeinsson had returned to Norway to purchase Bergen real estate some time before 1374, if indeed he had ever been in Greenland. If even one small ship had come from Greenland during those years, the news would have spread all over the small city of Bergen. Greenland could be expected to welcome imported goods after so many years, and a voyage to a trade-starved country, where valuable barter goods had been accumulating, would have been well worth risking. And third, the *Olafssúðinn*'s Norwegian cargo would fetch greater profits if traded for

Greenland goods and then exchanged in Norway for wares that would have high value back in Iceland when they finally got there, than if bartered in Iceland in the first place. Greenland had several luxury products not available in Iceland, and it produced all the same staples as Iceland except sulfur. We know that the men aboard the *Olafssúðinn* did in fact exchange their Norwegian goods bought in 1380–81 for Greenland products, rather than save them for belated barter back home in Iceland. Had the men been dismayed about overshooting Iceland on their outward voyage, we might expect them to have stopped in Iceland two years later to reassure worried relatives, but they failed to do so. All the evidence suggests that these men were sailors and merchants for whom profit came first.

The *Olafssúðinn* crew's pious version of their Greenland barter story appears in a document written in Bergen in May of 1389, which reports on a trial (to be discussed below) during which "two reliable men" from the *Olafssúðinn* had served as witnesses for the defense.[34] They swore on the Bible that they had been present at a Greenland *Alþing* where the residents present had agreed that no Norwegians coming to Greenland would be allowed to buy food unless they bought other Greenland wares as well. These *Olafssúðinn* crewmen also testified that the Greenland royal ombudsman had not allowed them to take crown goods away with them, because they lacked a license to do so. This last statement, which may conceivably have referred to produce from the two royal farms in Greenland, was no doubt intended to reassure the Norwegian royal authorities that the Greenlanders were following proper procedure, at the same time as it neatly explained why the *Olafssúðinn* had carried no goods belonging to the crown. The testimony said nothing about who had taken over the office of royal ombudsman in Greenland when Sigurd Kolbeinsson left, if indeed anyone had—these royal appointments required official communications of a sort evidently lacking by this time.

The Greenland *Alþing*'s vote to make expanded trade the condition of the visitors' food purchases probably was a face-saving device in which both parties colluded, and from which everybody—with the likely exception of the monarch—stood to benefit. Besides preserving friendly local relations at the time, it was an excuse that could be used by other merchants as well, and that therefore allowed the Greenlanders to hope that others would make the illegal voyage on purpose. The device certainly enabled the visitors to swear to the Norwegian authorities that they had been hostage to their situation. Having to pay the usual taxes when selling their Greenland wares in Norway would have been much more agreeable to the *Olafssúðinn* men than paying heavy fines, or having their cargo confiscated. Norwegian officials more interested in collecting money they could control than in defending the monarch's prerogatives at any cost would also have welcomed an excuse to collect duty in the regular way, and to avoid a situation that would have entailed fines or confiscation if handled by other officials. In Bergen, the issue of fiscal control had always bubbled close under the surface of any controversy involving either church or crown with the local power elite.

So much for the voyage of the *Olafssúðinn*. Let us turn now to the circumstances surrounding the 1389 trial in which the *Olafssúðinn*'s crewmen testified. As noted earlier, Erlend Philippusson was the Bergen *féhirðir* in 1383, when the *Olafssúðinn* arrived in Bergen. He held that post still in 1389, for he was by all accounts a remarkable man, trusted by successive monarchs both for his many services and for his adamant refusal to be knighted.[35] He could be expected to bring both independent opinions and common sense to court with him when he (and the judges appointed by him) sat in judgment of those with goods to dispose of and pay duty on. The suit he was asked to decide in 1389 involved two principals, the plaintiff and filer, Hákon Jonsson, and the defendant, Björn Einarsson, called "the Jerusalem-Farer" because of the wide scope of his travels.

Hákon Jonsson, shrewd and tough, with long experience as a ruthless collector of money for the crown, accused Björn and his companions of having gone to Greenland in 1385 willingly and on purpose; of having traded in Greenland without royal license; and of having bought crown goods illegally. With the help of testimony from the two *Olafssúðinn* men, the defendants refuted all the charges and convinced the 1389 court that they had drifted off to Greenland in 1385 without any intention of violating royal privilege by trading with the Greenlanders.[36] In reporting the acquittal to Queen Margrethe, Erlend Philippusson was careful to note that he had properly calculated and collected duty on goods from both Greenland and Iceland, where the 1389 defendants had stopped before coming to Norway.[37]

Though Erlend and his court may have been convinced, further examination of the details of the case suggest a different conclusion. To begin with, Björn's story would be more believable if it had not followed so soon on the heels of the *Olafssúðinn* incident. Moreover, Björn and his companions "drifted off" with a fleet of *four* ships, after having set out from Norway with holds full of desirable trade goods. They then spent *two* winters in Greenland instead of one, which suggests a planned trading visit rather than an accidental one. But the most important datum is the character of Björn the Jerusalem-Farer himself, for he was a wily and wealthy Icelandic chieftain who would just have had time to learn his predecessors' story back in Iceland before setting out for Norway in 1384.[38]

Björn Einarsson the Jerusalem-Farer is said to have written, or caused to have written, a book about his many travels, including his stay in Greenland, but nothing is known of the original. A seventeenth-century version called *Reisubók Bjarnar Jorsalafara* seems to have confused Björn and his wife Solveig with their grandson Björn Thorleifsson and his wife Olöf. It sounds convincing, however, when we are told that when Björn the Jerusalem-Farer arrived in Greenland, the bishop of Gardar had recently died, and an old priest was attending to the diocese and performing all the episcopal functions.[39] The recently dead bishop would have been Alf. As his cognomen indicates, Björn the Jerusalem-Farer's travels encompassed countries far to the south of Greenland. He had already visited Rome twice when he and his wife Solveig Thorsteinsdaughter (see Appendix A) went all the way to Jerusalem via Rome and Venice in 1406. After their return to Venice, Solveig went to Norway, but Björn went first on a pilgrimage to Compostella, where he lay ill for half a month. He then proceeded to France, Flanders, and Canterbury in England, before finally rejoining his wife in Norway.[40] His evident willingness to tell about his experiences suggests that he spread information about Greenland and Iceland to many English and Continental ears, including some that had also heard the tale of the Minorite friar and *Inventio fortunatae*.

When Björn went to Norway in 1405 on the first leg of his voyage to Jerusalem, he had just arranged for his only surviving child, a daughter named Kristin (Vatnsfjord-Kristin), to marry the young Icelandic chieftain Thorleif Arnason, who later became a prominent figure in Anglo-Icelandic politics. Kristin's first husband had just died in the Black Death, which struck Iceland for the first time in 1402–4.[41] Many lucky survivors of this great scourge besides Björn set out for Norway that summer of 1405, probably hoping to attend the wedding of Queen Margrethe's heir, young King Eirik, to Princess Philippa of England. Negotiations for the marriage had begun in 1401, and in the autumn of 1404 the groom was fully expecting to meet his bride the following spring in Bergen while conducting business in Norway on behalf of the queen. The Icelanders who set out from home in 1405 could not have known that at almost the last minute the royal wedding would be postponed until the summer of 1406.[42]

Shortly before King Eirik's departure for Norway, Queen Margrethe wrote him a long letter with detailed advice on how to receive his wife-to-be and how to deal with his Norwegian subjects. She advised him to grant requests and privileges sparingly and noted that the last time the bishop of Bergen visited her, she had ordered him to recall all licenses for sailing to Iceland. Those who wanted them (or other privileges) would have to get new ones from her or from Eirik.[43] Anyone with an interest in colonial trade, or concerned with staying in the good graces of royalty, would therefore have been well advised to be present in Bergen during King Eirik's visit in 1405.

Along with several of his friends, Thorstein Olafsson, an enterprising young Icelandic chieftain who was Björn's nephew by marriage, joined his aunt and uncle in Bergen in 1405. It would have been surprising indeed if Björn and Solveig, either in Bergen or back home in northern Iceland where they all lived, had not told Thorstein about the likely advantages of a trading voyage to Greenland, if coupled with successful pleading that the trip had been accidental and not intended as a defiance of Norwegian laws. Thorstein had everything to gain and little to lose from such an enterprise. Although he was the grandson of the lawman Thorstein Eyjolfsson, one of the most famous and powerful men in late medieval Iceland, and his own connections were with the rich and famous, he still had to make his fortune by his wits. His father had drowned when Thorstein was very young, and he appears not to have inherited much land of his own. As luck would have it, however, he married Sigrid Björnsdaughter, the daughter of one of the wealthiest men in northern Iceland, and got prime farmland with her. What is interesting from our point of view is that he married her at Hvalsey in Greenland.

For the remainder of this chapter I want to explore in considerable detail the circumstances surrounding this last recorded voyage to Greenland, paying particular attention to the implications of the kinship networks among the participants. Appendixes A and B show the tight kinship bonds between Björn the Jerusalem-Farer, his wife Solveig, and the company of Icelanders under Thorstein Olafsson's leadership who claimed to have suffered the ill fortune of being carried off to Greenland in 1406, following their visit to Norway in 1405 for the anticipated wedding of King Eirik. This last group of people known to have sailed between Norway and Greenland were members of the most powerful families in Iceland—so powerful that, as we shall see in the next chapter, they were at the center of events when the English succeeded in establishing their cod fishing and trading outposts in Iceland. Their tight kinship web also provides the key to the Greenlanders' connection with both Iceland and Norway just at the start of the fifteenth century.

In 1406, the people in the Eastern Settlement played host to Thorstein Olafsson and several of his equally well-born friends, who had spent the winter in Norway and—they claimed later—been caught in such dense fog that they drifted off course to Greenland.[44] Here they stayed for four whole years and generated enough excitement to warrant several entries in the *Icelandic Annals*, from which we catch glimpses of life in Greenland in the early fifteenth century. Even by the flexible standards of the time, their absence from home was a long one. Gudrun Styrsdaughter, wife of Thorstein's friend Snorri Torfason, acted in accordance with the careful timetables drawn up in the old laws addressing the death of travelers abroad when she considered herself a widow back home in Iceland and married a chieftain named Gisli Andresson in 1410.[45] Beyond this single incident, not one of all the surviving Icelandic documents dating from the minimum of six years that Thorstein and his friends were away from home brought up the issue of inheritance—and this among families that normally missed no opportunity to squabble over land and goods. One is left with the distinct impression that the absence of these men, the cream of northern Iceland's young manhood, was expected, and that the reason for it was known among those who needed to know.

Since these Icelanders had their own transportation and therefore could have left the first year after their arrival, their visit in Greenland must have proved both congenial and profitable. It is unthinkable that they would have left Norway without loading up on iron bars, grain, honey, and other goods coveted in both Iceland and Greenland, so they would have been able to barter with their Greenland hosts for room and board as well as for walrus tusks and other export items. A stay of four years would also have allowed them to go hunting themselves. When they finally left in 1410, they went straight to Norway rather than home to Iceland.[46] This suggests that they, too, knew the route perfectly well, and that they had on board articles that were more suitable for trade in Norway than in Iceland.

This group of prominent Icelanders had every reason to expect a good welcome in Greenland, for one of their own circle was already living there, probably at the big Hvalsey farm. The cumulative evidence for this is in the *Diplomatarium Islandicum* and involves complex family ties that have been detailed with source notations in Appendix B. These old documents show that Sigrid Björnsdaughter, the woman Thorstein Olafsson married a couple of years after arriving in Greenland, was the daughter of Björn Brynjolfsson, a rich and powerful landowner in Skagafjord in the north of Iceland, where Thorfinn Karlsefni had settled after his Greenland-to-Vínland venture in the early eleventh century. Those of Thorstein's companions whom we know by name were also from that area and familiar with each other—Brand Halldorsson, Jon Jonsson, Snorri Torfason, Sæmund Oddsson, Thord Jörundarson, Thorbjörn Bárdarson, Thorstein Helmingsson, and Thorgrim Sölvason.[47]

Every one of them enjoyed positions of wealth and power at home after their return from Greenland, Thorstein most of all, in part because of the wealth he acquired through Sigrid. It is clear that they took power for granted also while in Greenland, much in the manner of English gentry expecting to serve as local magistrates. They had learned the law from their chieftain fathers and uncles and by attending local and national assemblies and law courts since puberty.

Thorstein Olafsson was not only literate and able to write his own letters, but evidently commanded the respect of his peers. When he was appointed by Bishop Jon of Holar in 1419 to serve as the only lay judge on a panel otherwise consisting of five priests, his experience dated back at least twelve years, to a court that convened in 1407 at Hvalsey in Greenland in order to save the reputation of Thorstein's cousin Steinunn.[48]

Steinunn Hrafnsdaughter, the daughter of an Icelandic lawman, had come along on the 1406 voyage from Norway to Greenland as the wife of the well-born Icelander Thorgrim Sölvason. They must both have been quite young at the time, since Thorgrim was still flourishing in 1438.[49] Within a year of their arrival in Greenland, Steinunn had been seduced by a Greenlander named Kollgrim. The seduction was a crime, and her husband, her cousin, and their friends seem to have been invited by their Greenland peers to help deal with it in a local lay or lay-dominated court. Kollgrim was accused of having used black arts to lure her, and after the trial he was sentenced to be burned at the stake. Whether Steinunn had been in love with him, was terrified by the thought that witchcraft had touched her, or just lacked the stomach for watching a man being burned for her sake, she reportedly lost her wits and died not too long afterward.[50]

This story tells us that in 1407, black magic was acceptable to both the annal-writer and the Greenlanders as a believable explanation for seduction; at the same time, it probably was a face-saving device for a high-born Icelander whose wife had succumbed to the charms of a social inferior. Furthermore, we learn that although witchcraft presumably was an offense against the church, Kollgrim was not tried and executed at Gardar, but at Hvalsey (see Fig. 18), one of the four big Eastern Settlement church farms with a festal hall.[51]

Ever since Eirik the Red's cousin Thorkell *farserkr* ("travel-shirt") had first claimed the land around Hvalsey (Qaqortoq) fjord, farm Ø83 had been a big and prosperous establishment, with one of Norse Greenland's best harbors inside the shelter of the large island blocking the outer fjord. We know that it attracted ships and trade right up to the end of the colony, for a piece of fifteenth-century Rhenish stoneware, similar to the ones found at Herjolfsnes and at Ø167 in Vatnahverfi, has been found in front of the Hvalsey church wall.[52] It would have been a logical place for Thorstein and his friends to stay, as well as an important public venue for a trial, although for reasons other than those suggested by Joel Berglund. Berglund believes the probable reason Kollgrim was judged and executed there was that Hvalsey *church* was important in the legal system of the Greenland church because it was so wealthy—taking Ivar Bárdarson's descriptions of ecclesiastical landownership literally, he assumes that the church at Hvalsey owned all the land between the two main fjords, corresponding closely to the original land-take.[53]

As argued in Chapter Four, it is likely that Ivar's description of land as-

FIG. 18. Hvalsey (Ø83) farm and church in the Eastern Settlement. Hvalsey church, the best-preserved medieval church in Greenland, was the site of the wedding of Thorstein Olafsson and Sigrid Björnsdaughter in the fall of 1408. Source: Photograph by Jette Arneborg, 1980, reproduced by permission.

sociated with Hvalsey church referred to the *tithing* district of that church, which, like the original land-take, would have been apt to follow natural topographical boundaries. Hvalsey church, still remarkably well preserved (as Fig. 18 shows), was a fine building denoting both wealth and status. According to Roussell, the rectangular stone building was constructed in a recognizably Anglo-Norwegian style of the early 1300s and probably was one of the very last Norse churches built in Greenland. More significant in the present and future contexts, however, is the fact that Hvalsey *farm* had a festal hall. Though small (40.8 square meters), this hall was so well constructed that it remains the best-preserved medieval festal hall in all the Nordic countries. It was built up against an earlier hall, partly on the site of the demolished west wall of room IX of the dwelling. Roussell, who excavated the hall in 1935, noted that it must be regarded as a separate structure of a late—perhaps very late—date, just like the halls at Gardar and Herjolfsnes which it resembles architecturally, and which are thought to have been built in the early fifteenth century.[54]

If we may assume that Ivar Bardarson cataloged parish boundaries rather than actual church ownership of land, and that the secular chieftains had retained their authority over both the churches and the other farmers, the Hvalsey festal hall should be seen as an early-fifteenth-century secular monument to the same wealth and power that had found expression in a splendid church about a century earlier, at the peak of the church's power in Greenland. Thus the fact that Kollgrim's trial took place at Hvalsey probably reflects Hvalsey's status as a center of *secular* power in 1407, rather than the farm's prominence within an ecclesiastically dominated hierarchy. The trial's venue is also another indication that the farm served as head-quarters for the visiting Icelanders, as is the fact that Thorstein Olafsson's marriage to Sigrid Björnsdaughter took place in Hvalsey church. The central part played by Hvalsey during the four years Thorstein and his friends stayed in the Eastern Settlement suggests, furthermore, that Hvalsey was Sigrid's current home, where she welcomed her old Icelandic friends.

Several questions arise because of the close ties between Sigrid's and Thorstein's families long before the Hvalsey wedding of 1408, as well as between Björn Einarsson the Jerusalem-Farer and the families of both Sigrid and Thorstein. Just how close were these relationships at the time of Björn's Greenland soujourn in the 1380s? Had he been instrumental in arranging a match between Sigrid, the daughter of Björn Brynjolfsson "the Rich" of Great Akrar in northern Iceland, and the wealthy heir or owner at Hvalsey farm in Greenland? And had Sigrid just reached the marriage-able age of fifteen in 1392, when her father specified that she should have the farm called Thorleiksstead as her inheritance after her mother, in addition to equal shares with her siblings in the inheritance after himself?

Thorstein did not marry Sigrid until the autumn of 1408. She cannot have been aboard the ship (or ships) leaving Norway in 1406, for unless she was on a pilgrimage or on her way to be married, a well-born woman would not have been traveling such long distances on her own if single. The sources available to us would surely have mentioned it had Sigrid been married to one of the other Icelandic chieftains on the expedition and become widowed while in Greenland, for that would have raised the all-important issue of inheritance back in Iceland. The likely reason she was in Greenland when the visitors arrived was that she had been married off to a Greenlander soon after 1392. At the end of that year, Björn Brynjolfsson had formally granted his children Olaf, Sigrid, and Málfrid equal shares in their inheritance.[55] The long document drawn up at that time specified that Sigrid was also to have the sizable farm of Thorleiksstead, which had belonged to her mother. No maternal inheritance was noted for her two siblings, although there is no reason to suppose they had different mothers. Her father was not ill; he appears to have died about ten years later in the Black Death. There was no discernible reason for drawing up such a document at all unless it was done as part of Sigrid's dowry arrangements.

Having to determine a daughter's dowry before she left the country would have been a good reason for Björn Brynjolfsson to draw up his 1392 document, and Björn the Jerusalem-Farer's very recent trouble with the Norwegian authorities over the claim that he had violated royal trade pre-rogatives in Greenland would have provided Sigrid's father with an equally good reason *not* to have a written and publicly witnessed marriage contract

drawn up between him and a Greenland chieftain. Icelanders and Greenlanders were not supposed to trade directly with each other, and a marriage
contract between wealthy people was above all a carefully negotiated business deal. Nobody knew that better than Björn Brynjolfsson the Rich of
Great Akrar, who had arranged a detailed, written wedding contract when
he married off his sister Jorunn several years earlier.[56]

If a wealthy Icelandic farmer considered a Greenlander suitable for a
son-in-law, it shows that conditions in the Eastern Settlement were normal
and prosperous, and that they were *known* to be so because there was still
communication between the two countries. We have written evidence that
good conditions still prevailed in the Eastern Settlement when Sigrid married Thorstein, for in an affidavit of their wedding which Thorstein took
the precaution of obtaining before he left Greenland with his bride and
companions in 1410, the Gardar *officialis* Eindride Andreasson and *sira*
Páll Hallvardsson attested that three lawful banns had been published before Thorstein's and Sigrid's marriage in the autumn of 1408, and that
many people had been present at their wedding, which took place on an
ordinary Sunday.[57] The document reveals that social intercourse and customs were the same as under normal conditions elsewhere in the North at
that time. Had the Black Death reached Greenland from Iceland, or had
there been widespread fear of Eskimos or foreign marauders, people would
have hesitated to travel long distances to meet their friends at church, and
Thorstein and his company would not have stayed to enjoy the hospitality
of the Greenlanders for so long, even knowing how grim conditions were
back in Iceland after the recent devastations from the Plague there.

Thorstein and several members of his group had lost family members
in the Black Death, and Thorstein probably told Sigrid that her father was
one of the Plague victims. It is likely that her sister and brother had also
perished, leaving her the sole heir to Björn Brynjolfsson's multifarm estate.
This, too, Thorstein would have known before he left Iceland, and it cannot
have made the thought of marrying Sigrid any less attractive. The letter
from the Gardar *officialis*, as well as two affidavits (1414 and 1424) by
Thorstein's friends after their return to Iceland, assured their peers that the
marriage had taken place in accordance with both church procedure and
civil law, which would prevent it from being challenged. Both the 1414 and
the 1424 documents noted that the chieftain Sæmund Oddsson had not
only been present at the wedding, but had approved it as Sigrid's kinsman.[58]

It was no thanks to the official incumbents of Gardar see that the Greenland church had carried on sufficiently to give Thorstein and Sigrid a proper
wedding. Of the three or four bishops currently holding the title, Bishop
Berthold was busy in Norway, where as late as in 1426 he affixed his seal
to a transcript in Trondheim (along with those of Jon Torerson and a priest

intriguingly named *sira* Peder "Greenlander");[59] Bishop Jacob evidently preferred Denmark to either Norway or Greenland, for until his death he contented himself with issuing documents from there in the name of "Bishop Jacob of Greenland";[60] and of the mysterious Bishop Jon and the even more mysterious Bishop Anders we know nothing. We also have no way of knowing how the various Gardar claimants were perceived by people still involved in Greenlandic affairs.

Nor is there any record of the reaction in Norway when Thorstein, Sigrid, Snorri, Thorgrim, and the other Icelanders arrived there in 1410, straight from Greenland. The modern Icelandic historian Björn Thorsteinsson surmises that they went directly to the trading hub of Bergen, where they would have exchanged tales with other sailors and merchants, including the many Englishmen who came to the Bergen Staple to buy cod.[61] The Icelanders' whereabouts for the past four years would have been no secret to anybody, officialdom included.

Theirs was the very last Greenland voyage recorded in the medieval Icelandic annals. Although any notice by the annalists suggests an event of some public significance, the entry here seems to have attached only to the travelers' high rank, not to any dispute or other public concern over their voyage. The same annalist ("New Annals") had taken care to note for 1406 that the party had drifted off course on their way to Iceland and thus were not to be blamed for fetching up on forbidden shores.[62] There are no records suggesting that there was even a pro forma public inquiry, although their going directly to Norway, rather than stopping in Iceland after so many years away, suggests that they had a good Greenland cargo to trade. The reason they got off so much more easily than the preceding groups of Greenland traders may have been due in part to administrative confusion in Bergen at the end of Queen Margrethe's reign, but it is also likely that Thorstein and his companions had their way paved by his two brothers and their powerful friends.

At the 1409 *Alþing* in Iceland, the year before Thorstein and his companions left Greenland, his brother Hall Olafsson (see Appendix A) was one of the many chieftains who signed a document confirming in general terms that the Norwegian crown owned one quarter of the space aboard any ship going from Iceland to Norway, after having made its first voyage *from* Norway. More significantly, the document makes it clear that exceptions might be made if, for instance, the ship belonged to one person but had been rented to another, or *if the king or his representatives had granted an exemption.*[63] Such an exemption could easily be a hole big enough for several men to sail through.

At least one man who signed this document was in a position to grant such exemptions in Iceland, namely the *hirðstjóri* (royal administrator)

Vigfus Ivarsson, a friend of Björn the Jerusalem-Farer's and a member by birth of the powerful group of chieftains that consisted of the latest Greenland-farers' kinsmen. Others who signed this document were in positions of power in Norway: Jon Biartzson and Jon Eigilsson, who both were members of the city council in Bergen but at present in Iceland. By September 13, 1409, all three Icelandic versions of the document (July 3, 7, and 13) had been transcribed and properly witnessed back in Bergen.[64]

Communications and influence-peddling between Bergen and Iceland were clearly in good working order still. When Hall's brother Thorstein and the other Greenland-farers arrived in Bergen the following summer, in 1410, they could count on powerful family friends to help them avoid unpleasantness of the sort Björn the Jerusalem-Farer had encountered in 1389. Had they come via Iceland, the exemptions allowed for in the 1409 document could have been brought into play.

Brother Arni Olafsson, a member of these latest Greenland-farers' own circle and soon-to-be bishop of Skálholt, was also living on the west coast of Norway at the time. Though there has been no scholarly agreement on Arni Olafsson's pedigree, I present arguments in Appendix A that show why I believe he must have been Thorstein's brother. Thorstein and his friends would in any case have been able to count on help from Arni, who, it is generally agreed, was of North Iceland chieftain stock and had close connections both with the crown and with two of Norway's great families.

Queen Margrethe, as conscious of her rights as any Nordic monarch before or since, was just as active in 1410 as she had been in 1389 when Björn the Jerusalem-Farer and his partners faced Hákon Jonsson's accusations and were acquitted with the help of the independent-minded Erlend Philippusson. It was fortunate for Thorstein and his friends that when they arrived in Norway, Margrethe's trusted retainer Magnus Magnusson had just married Erlend Philippusson's daughter Sigrid, the widow of Hákon Sigurdsson at Giske whose chaplain Arni Olafsson had been. The personable young churchman was on very good terms with Sigrid and remained the chaplain at Giske under Magnus, so he was in a good position to prevent trouble for Thorstein and his friends.[65] Sigrid of Giske's ties with the crown also extended to Queen Margrethe's appointed heir, Eirik, who trusted Sigrid's brother Eindridi Erlendsson so well that he sent him with Bishop Jacob of Oslo to negotiate with King Henry V of England in the fall of 1415.[66]

Those negotiations, and the role of Thorstein Olafsson and his friends in the conflicts that were building between the English and Dano-Norwegian kings over trade and fisheries in Iceland, will form the subject of the next chapter.

England and the Norwegian Colonies, 1400-1450

The Black Death (1402–4) was a watershed in Iceland's history. As the learned North Icelander Jon Espolin reflected after closing Part One of his *Árbækur* with this event, the Plague caused a great deal of land to fall into a few hands, creating many rich people who had no incentive to gain further wealth through work, but sought promotion and power by other means. There were great feuds among the chief families, and Norwegian interests were replaced, first by English and then by German ones. Even worse from a historian's point of view: people soon forgot how things used to be; learning was neglected; and nobody bothered to write down various events as they occurred.[1]

There is more to fifteenth-century Icelandic history than Espolin's analysis allows for, but he points to important issues that also affected Greenland during this period, and his plaint suggests why Icelandic sources provide no further direct information about the country's nearest neighbor to the west. Icelandic sources of any kind are spotty for the early fifteenth century, and the last medieval annals end in 1430.

English sources connected with North Atlantic sailings in that period are mostly concerned with power politics and relations with the Dano-Norwegian crown, not with exploration or the peregrinations of lowly fishermen.[2] Research into fifteenth-century English expansion in the north-western Atlantic is further hampered by serious gaps in the records from Bristol, the English city that became most closely associated with this expansion. In the Bristol Corporation archives, no medieval port books or brokerage books are extant, and only fragments survive of the customs accounts ("Particular Accounts") for 1415–61. We must also allow for smuggling (by definition unrecorded), as well as for the fact that Bristol ships often loaded and unloaded much of their cargo elsewhere. In addition, many of the goods sold in Bristol had come in through other harbors, such as London and Southampton.[3]

There are nevertheless English records enough to show that the deteriorating political, economic, and cultural situation in Iceland was closely related to developments elsewhere. And documents in the *Diplomatarium Islandicum* and *Diplomatarium Norvegicum,* combined with archaeological reports about fifteenth-century Greenland, demonstrate that a lack of record-keeping need not signify a lack of activity or a breakdown of contemporary communication networks. This is especially true of Iceland and Greenland in the first half of the fifteenth century, the period of British ascendancy in the northwestern Atlantic. By 1415, there were innumerable contact points in Iceland between the English who came to Iceland to trade and fish, and the rich and powerful Icelanders who had firsthand knowledge of Greenland and considerable codfish interests of their own.

Those English fishermen and codfish merchants had just as good reasons to keep a low profile as did the Icelanders who had maintained contact with Greenland. David B. Quinn reminds us that fishermen at that time were often "fanatically secretive and did not easily share their discoveries of new grounds." Furthermore, in their quest for cod the English were defying the royal Norwegian trade monopoly not only in Iceland, but also in the Faroes.[4] English fishermen and merchants would not have trumpeted it about if some of them in time dealt profitably with Greenland, another potentially good source of both fresh and dried cod, as well as of traditional Greenland export goods.

Thorstein Olafsson and Sigrid Björnsdaughter had been back on their North Iceland farm for just a year when Queen Margrethe's death in 1412 marked the start of another downturn in Norway's economic situation and her relations with the Atlantic colonies. King Eirik, now 30 years old, was in sole charge of Norway, Denmark, and Sweden. Noting Eirik's energy and many personal accomplishments, Thorsteinsson sums him up as a "splendid knight" who had grand notions about himself and his Baltic empire.[5] Eirik perpetuated Queen Margrethe's trade policies for 30 more years while engaging in a succession of fruitless foreign wars, which caused an endless drain on the state coffers, plunged the king into ever more desperate efforts to raise money, and diverted his attention from the plight of his Norwegian subjects. And a portent of Eirik's attitude toward the Atlantic colonies can be found in the fact that news of his accession was not even promptly relayed: "Lögmanns-annáll" notes that no news reached Iceland from Norway in 1412.[6]

The same annal entry tells us that right after Margrethe's death, Brother Arni Olafsson and his employer, Magnus Magnusson of Giske, rode off in search of King Eirik and finally found him in Hälsingborg. King Eirik had just had his *hirðstjóri* hanged and a counterfeiter shot, but being in the royal presence paid off handsomely for Thorstein's brother. The monarch took such a liking to Arni that by the time the latter returned to his native land in June of 1415, aboard his very own ship, he was—with the approval of the Pisan Antipope John XXIII—both bishop of Skálholt and *hirðstjóri* of all Iceland, with all the incomes and privileges accompanying those offices. In addition, the Bergen merchants asked him to collect their debts in Iceland for them; the monastery at Munkeliv in Bergen wanted him to collect its tithes in the Westman Islands; and he was appointed *visitator* for all of Iceland.[7]

Bishop Arni of Skálholt was at first also the *officialis* at the vacant Holar see in North Iceland, near his brothers Thorstein and Hall and other kin. His being the brother of Thorstein and Hall Olafsson explains a number of property transactions that took place in the north of Iceland during the next few years, and since this kinship also made him the nephew of Solveig Thorsteinsdaughter and her husband Björn the Jerusalem-Farer, it explains why Arni wrote Björn asking him to be his ombudsman as *hirðstjóri* in 1414, a year before Arni could get out to Iceland himself.[8] (Björn had arrived home fit and well in 1411 after spending a winter in the Shetland Islands.[9])

Is it just coincidence that Björn, who probably told stories about both Greenland and Iceland abroad as freely as he dispensed stories of his foreign ventures at home, should have arrived home just a year before the first recorded appearance of an English fishing vessel in Iceland? We know that he was crafty as well as ambitious, but we need not suspect him of having invited the Englishmen on the ship that quietly appeared off Dyrholaey in 1412, the year Queen Margrethe died.[10] The *Annals* do not say that the Dyrholaey vessel was the *first* English ship to reach Iceland. Björn Thorsteinsson agrees with such earlier scholars as Jon Johanneson that the ham-fisted "foreign merchants" who visited the Westman Islands in 1396 or 1397 had most likely been English as well.[11] That is a safe assumption, given the centuries-old sailing traditions between Iceland and the British Isles discussed in Chapter Five and the fact that by about A.D. 1400 the English were building two- or three-masted ships with high pointed bows able to resist strong head seas, and with rigging that made it possible to stay a course within six or seven points of the wind.[12] This improved shipbuilding technique brought profound changes not only in the reach, speed, carrying capacity, and maneuverability of fishing and merchant vessels, but in the pattern of seasonal sailing that had prevailed in the North Atlantic since time immemorial. Prior to 1400, sailings from Norway to Iceland and Greenland, and between England and Iceland, had taken place almost exclusively during the summer, between the stormy seasons of late winter and autumn. The English could now sail to Iceland and home again in one extended season, beholden to no one for winter quarters, at the very time when the Icelanders' needs were mostly ignored by the Dano-Norwegian authorities and contact with Greenland was left entirely to clandestine private enterprise.[13]

Finding themselves increasingly dependent on imported fish, the English had at first sailed to the Staple in Bergen in growing numbers, but when King Eirik allowed the Hanse stranglehold on Norwegian trade to tighten in step with the crown's restrictions on trade with Norway's Atlantic colonies, the English were forced to explore other sources of cod. They soon had additional reason to go elsewhere, for in 1413, a house in Bergen belonging to Englishmen from Lynn was burned to the ground, thanks to the Hanse—and to the competition for cod.[14]

Cod was a major source of protein in all the northern countries. The codfish trade had made medieval Bergen and its bishops wealthy, and for centuries it had been a steady source of revenue for the crown as well. In the late Middle Ages the Norwegian archbishop worked to expand and secure his own central position in the stockfish (dried cod) trade, and codfish fueled the Hanse enterprises in Norway.[15] Greenland may have been too distant to benefit from the rapid expansion of the Norwegian codfish trade that began in the early fourteenth century.[16] But large English ships already in Icelandic waters could easily provide a fifteenth-century link between Greenland and the growing English market for cod, aided at first by allies among Icelandic chieftains who wanted to benefit from English needs. These chieftains were accustomed to having things their own way, and several documents suggest that during those early years they were confident that they could maneuver both the English presence and the crown's demands to their own advantage.

The Icelanders of six hundred years ago quite likely thought that the cod supply was endless and that they were perfectly capable of hauling the fish up themselves from the fragile boats at their disposal. In a good fishing year, one may even today watch the small, one-man codfishing boats arrive in Olafsvik from the open sea, with their silvery cargo piled high and already gutted with lightening speed by the same hands and eyes that set the lines, handle the boat, and monitor the sea. But the Plague of 1402–4 killed so many Icelanders that the survivors could neither supply the English with all the cod they wanted nor protect and defend their own fishing grounds when the English decided to catch much of the fish themselves. Nor were the supplies inexhaustible. Soon competition for cod among the English became so fierce that some resorted to outright violence and others looked for new fishing grounds farther and farther west. The temptation to become involved in Icelandic life and politics also arose, as we shall see.

As far as we know, English fishermen first visited the Iceland Banks in the spring of 1408 or 1409 and soon started searching for other fishing grounds farther to the east and west of Iceland, arriving in ever greater numbers.[17] There were more than 30 English fishing doggers in Iceland in 1413, just two years after the return of both Björn the Jerusalem-Farer and Thorstein Olafsson with his company of Greenland-farers. Thorstein and his magisterial kinsmen and friends must have become involved with the English starting in 1413 at the latest, for English fishermen also arrived in the north of Iceland that year and peremptorily took some cattle for which they "left behind some money."[18]

Also in 1413, an English merchant named Richard arrived in the south, bearing a letter from King Eirik of Denmark-Norway permitting him, Richard, to trade in King Eirik's realm without paying toll. Eirik also sent letters to Iceland later that summer forbidding the Icelanders to trade with foreign merchants other than those they had traded with in the past, which suggests that Richard must either have been a veteran on the circuit (perhaps even able to manage without an interpreter), or else had paid a particularly handsome fee to King Eirik for his permission.[19] While Richard rode off to Skálholt to place his letter patent before the *hirðstjóri* Vigfús Ivarsson *holm* (Bishop Arni, we recall, did not arrive until 1415, and did not name his kinsman Björn his ombudsman as *hirðstjóri* until 1414), his ship was taken along the coast to Eyjafjöllum, where the rich and powerful Gisli Andresson had his farm. Gisli had married Gudrun Styrsdaughter in 1410 when she had supposed herself the widow of Snorri Torfason, as described in Chapter Six. But in that memorable year of 1413, Snorri finally reappeared in Iceland, after four years in Greenland and three in Norway. Gudrun rode to meet him when she heard of his return, and she resumed living with him. Thorsteinsson assumes that some of the triangular reunion negotiations must have taken place under Gisli Andresson's roof while Richard the Englishman was still there after joining up with his ship, in which case Richard would have heard about Snorri's Greenland adventures firsthand.[20] Snorri was probably still in the south of Iceland in May of 1414, because had he returned to his home we would have expected to find his signature on the affidavit stating that the Hvalsey marriage between Thorstein Olafsson and Sigrid Björnsdaughter had been legally witnessed. This affidavit, signed at Great Akrar in Skagafjord, included the names of Snorri's fellow Greenland-farers Thord Jörundarson, Thorbjörn Bárdarson, Jon Jonsson, and Brand Halldorsson.[21]

The last-named of the Greenland-farers, Brand Halldorsson, was rich and wellborn, and like Thorstein Olafsson he was able to act as his own scribe.[22] We know that he had close dealings with the English from the time of their arrival, despite being loyal to King Eirik.[23] He later married the lawman Hrafn Gudmundsson's daughter Ragna and became brother-in-law to Olaf Loptsson, quite likely the man who in about 1420 summed up, through "Eiriks saga rauða" in *Skálholtsbók*, the local lore regarding the Vínland voyages that had taken place from Greenland some four centuries earlier.[24] After his voyage to North America and Norway, Thorfinn Thordsson *karlsefni* had settled in the Skagafjord region, where Olaf Loptsson, Brand Halldorsson, and Thorstein Olafsson were now living. Local stories of those events must have been as plentiful as when Karlsefni's descendant Hauk Erlendsson wrote his own version of "Eiriks saga rauða" a century earlier.

Olaf Loptsson, though not himself a Greenland-farer, had other reasons besides his kinship by marriage with Brand to be *au courant* with contemporary Greenland. Through his paternal grandmother he was a cousin of Sigrid Björnsdaughter, recently of Hvalsey. Furthermore, his uncle Jon Guttormsson had been the first husband of Björn the Jerusalem-Farer's daughter Vatnsfjord-Kristin, and Kristin's son Björn Thorleifsson (by her second husband) married Olaf Loptsson's sister Olöf.[25] A strong interest in Greenland on Olaf's part is thus easily explained, and whatever his motives may have been for writing down both the good and the bad concerning lands on the other side of the Davis Strait, it is worth noting that this information was revived just at a time when the English were pushing farther and farther west in the ocean, using Iceland as their base. Thus we can see that the English had contacts with the Greenland-farers from the beginning of the information chain linking England with Greenland via Iceland.

It is as well to stress here that no attempt at a map accompanied the *Skálholtsbók* version of "Eiriks saga rauða," just as there was none in the *Hauksbók* version written by Karlsefni's descendant a century before—or in any other surviving medieval version of either of the Vínland sagas. The medieval Norse did not use cartographical representations to convey their sailing lore. This is one of several reasons why it makes no sense to claim that the so-called "Vinland Map" at Yale had medieval Scandinavian cartographical antecedents, or that "the Norse discovery of America was represented in cartographic form and transmitted to southern Europe at least once within the first half of the fifteenth century."[26] Another reason is that throughout the fifteenth century (the Yale Map supposedly dates from circa 1440), those who claimed any knowledge at all of the farther reaches of the northwestern Atlantic were convinced that Greenland was a large peninsula connected with Europe (see Fig. 19) and reaching down from the polar wastes.[27] A third historical reason for rejecting the map's claim to authenticity is that the Icelanders who kept the stories of the first Vínland voyages alive would have known that voyages to the other side of the Davis Strait had continued in some fashion, at least intermittently, just as they knew that more people than Bjarni Herjolfsson and Leif Eiriksson had been involved even in the voyages of saga note. The dubious provenance of the "Vinland Map," its hybrid cartographical style, the composition of its ink, and its strangely uneven vellum surface are troubling, and so is the note accompanying an island west of Greenland: "Island of Vinland discovered by Bjarni and Leif in company." There is also a longer legend describing this discovery and a visit made to Vínland circa 1118 by Bishop Eirik of Greenland.[28] This last is the sort of information Europeans feasted on long after the Middle Ages—not the kind of descriptions the Icelanders would have given either to their fellow countrymen or to foreign visitors in the first half of the fifteenth century. The three late-fourteenth-century interpolations in *Flateyjarbók*'s saga of King Olaf Tryggvason, forming what we now call "Grænlendinga saga," made much of Eirik the Red and his sons, while sending Bjarni Herjolfsson down in history as an affectionate son and doughty sailor whose complete lack of curiosity about those unknown lands in the west Leif Eiriksson made up for years later—*not* in the physical or spiritual company of Bjarni. And to Olaf Loptsson and his North Iceland circle, Karlsefni the colonizer was the most notable performer in those early enterprises. I was therefore not greatly surprised when I recently found the source of the map legend to be David Crantz's *Historie von Grönland*, first published in 1765. As far as I can tell, Crantz's "information" was used by a retired German Jesuit priest playing a complicated joke aimed at the culture bearers of Hitler's Third Reich, who persecuted Jesuits while extolling their own supposed Norse antecedents.[29]

Olaf Loptsson, Brand Halldorsson, Thorstein Olafsson, and their friends were joined in 1415 by Bishop Arni Olafsson. Björn Thorsteinsson sardonically notes that the "New Annals," covering the years 1393–1430 and written by someone close to Skálholt see, are as curiously silent about the *hirðstjóri*'s concerns while Arni held this office as they are about the dealings he and his successor at Skálholt had with the English during the years leading up to 1430, when the annalist stopped writing altogether.[30]

Bishop Arni was well disposed toward the English merchants and fishermen who continued to arrive in Iceland in large numbers, although King Eirik did not share Arni's friendly attitude toward people who abused both his royal monopoly and the privileges of the Bergen Hanse. In 1415, Eirik sent his chief Bergen official Eindridi Erlendsson to England, accompanied by the bishop of Oslo and carrying a letter to Eirik's brother-in-law, King Henry V, complaining of the damage done by English fishermen in Iceland

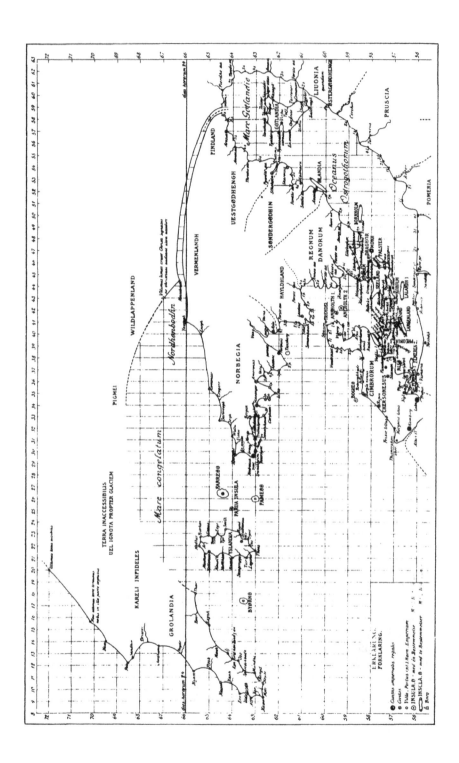

"and the adjoining islands." Henry V was busy at Agincourt, so the Duke of Bedford replied on his behalf, promising that English ships would sail to Iceland only via the Bergen Staple. Parliament supported this course.[31] Unable now to get letters patent from either King Eirik or King Henry, the English contented themselves with procuring licenses in Iceland from the *hirðstjóri* (now Bishop Arni Olafsson) and went on as before.

When Bishop Arni arrived in 1415 he replaced Vigfus Ivarsson, the *hirðstjóri* who had given Richard the Englishman his blessing to stay and trade in 1413. When Vigfus lost his office to Arni, his amicable relations with the English evidently made it natural for him to load his wife, his mother, and his many children aboard one of the six English ships lying in Hafnarfjord in 1415, and to go with them to England, bringing along much goods, including some 40 or 60 lests of cod and "much burned silver."[32] His precautions show a nice understanding of contemporary English values.

Bishop Arni Olafsson's lucrative career at home lasted just a few years. His departure was so abrupt that most scholars have assumed he fell out of favor with King Eirik over money or politics, but Thorsteinsson argues that this cannot have been the case. An acknowledgment of debt which Arni wrote on June 22, 1420, while he was at Laaland in Denmark, was signed by five of the most important people in the Dano-Norwegian realm (including King Eirik's trusted chamberlain Benedict Pogwisch), all of whom acted as guarantors. Arni had evidently brought goods earmarked for the king with him from Iceland, which he sold in Bergen because he feared they might be stolen by the pirates who frequented the waters between Denmark and Norway in increasing numbers, thanks to King Eirik's quarrels with Schleswig.[33]

Bishop Arni died abroad, probably shortly before 1425. Before he left

---

FIG. 19 (*opposite*). The Danish geographer A. A. Bjørnbo drew this map based on information from the so-called Vienna text (ca. 1430) of the works of Claudius Clavus. Source: Bjørnbo, "Cartographia Groenlandica," reproduced by permission of Dansk Polarcenter, Copenhagen, publisher of *Meddelelser om Grønland*. Ehrensvärd ("Cartographical Representations," p. 552) reports that "According to tradition . . . Erik of Pomerania, who was in Venice in 1424, charged Claudius Clavus (b. 1388) to draw a geographical map of 'Tota Dania,' that is to say, all of the Nordic countries." Bjørnbo's map incorporates several of the features in Clavus's 1427 "Nancy Map" of the north as well as some later additions in Henricus Martellus's reworking of Clavus's delineations and nomenclature, found in later editions of Ptolemy's *Geographia*. Karl Ahlenius argued (*Olaus Magnus*, pp. 30–32) that later permutations on northern names such as Vermelandi, Gentelandi, and Engromelandi had their origin in the Swedish districts of Värmland, Jämtland, and Engrommanaland (= Ångermannsland). Clavus's Icelandic and Greenlandic place-names are pure fabrications.

Iceland by way of the Westman Islands in the summer of 1419, never to return, he appears to have made his and Thorstein Olafsson's uncle Arnfinn his ombudsman as *hirðstjóri,* and he may also have agreed to act as messenger for a letter addressed to King Eirik and signed on July 1 that summer by a number of North Iceland chieftains at the *Alþing.* Both that letter and a document dated two weeks later, in which Arnfinn Thorsteinsson now refers to himself as *hirðstjóri* of all Iceland, are still in Danish archives.[34]

Although Icelandic chieftains' relations with royalty continued with the same blend of opportunism and personal loyalties that governed their dealings with each other, the summer of Bishop Arni's departure marked a turning point in the Icelanders' relations with King Eirik as well as with the English. This historians' bear-garden may, for the purposes of the present study, be profitably entered through the 1419 *Alþing* letter, both because of its contents and because of what the document suggests about Thorstein Olafsson and his circle.

We know that Thorstein was a full-fledged member of the North Iceland power elite by December of 1419, when he served as the only layman on a panel of judges appointed by the bishop of Holar. He was on the 1420 list of the most important North Iceland chieftains, and as *hirðstjóri* he supervised a property dispute between his wife's aunt by marriage and his cousin Vatnsfjord-Kristin in the spring of 1421.[35] But his name appears neither on the 1419 letter, nor on one written at the *Alþing* a year later to complain to King Eirik about the English. Both his brother Hall and his uncle Arnfinn signed the letters of 1419 and 1420. (Both his brother and his uncle had signed the 1419 letter as well, and so had his wife's kinsman Sæmund Oddsson, who had brokered his and Sigrid's 1408 Hvalsey marriage.) Thorstein's failure to sign the 1420 document may well be due to divergent opinions about the threat posed by the English, but the omission of his name from the 1419 letter is harder to explain. Although this earlier document also makes passing reference to English violence in Iceland, it mainly reflects the Icelanders' mixed feelings about their Dano-Norwegian masters as well as their English visitors. Having opened with a formal statement of allegiance to King Eirik, the chieftains who signed the document complained that while six annual trading ships had been agreed upon in the Norwegian crown's old covenant with Iceland, this agreement was now abused by the crown to such a degree that the Icelanders found themselves forced to trade with foreigners who had come peacefully on legitimate business. The chieftains duly noted that fishermen and owners of fishing doggers had robbed Icelanders ashore and caused disturbances at sea, but they were also careful to state that the miscreants had been punished by the Icelanders.

The 1419 message to the king was clear: the Icelanders wanted him to permit peaceful trade with the English, which Iceland so sorely needed due to the neglect of the Norwegian authorities. Stressing that this situation was not of the Icelanders' own making, and that they themselves had taken measures against the more violent among the English fishermen, the letter-writers showed their political acumen, for in conjunction with the deferential opening these statements made it difficult for the king to accuse them of deliberately acting against his wishes, or of being unable to maintain law and order on their own.[36]

What could possibly have been Thorstein's objection? The written sources are so silent about him between May of 1417 and the autumn of 1419 that at least one explanation offers itself: he may not have been present at the 1419 *Alþing*. He may not even have been in Iceland, but off on another quiet business trip to Greenland, safe in the knowledge that his brother Arni was the most powerful representative of both church and crown in Iceland, and that his brother Hall and his uncle Arnfinn were as usual seeing to the finer strategic points in dealing with the crown in Norway and Denmark.

It is hard to believe that Sigrid and Thorstein never gave Greenland another thought once they had sailed away. Sigrid could not have predicted the coming isolation of Greenland from Iceland and may well have retained property in the Eastern Settlement, entitling her to accumulations of stockfish and other goods. She may even have left behind a child as the heir to Hvalsey farm (she and Thorstein had only one child together) and gone back to be present when the child came of age or got married, either of which events would have involved property transactions or affirmations requiring witnesses.

We do have a hint that Sigrid may have retained property interests in Greenland. Ten years after the 1414 testimony that Thorstein's and Sigrid's Hvalsey wedding had been proper and legal, another affidavit was signed at Great Akrar. While both documents must have been concerned with property, there is one important difference: in 1424 it was *Sigrid's kinsman Sæmund* who testified that he had been present at the Hvalsey wedding, while Thorstein's friends merely witnessed Sæmund's testimony.[37] This suggests that the 1424 document was prompted by concern about property belonging to Sigrid alone, not by a transaction or dispute involving land she owned jointly with Thorstein.

Having come away from a viable community with a cargo worth taking straight to Norway in 1410, Thorstein would surely have found it profitable to return and perhaps encourage the Greenlanders to increase their production of stockfish, especially now that English merchants in Iceland were ready to act as middlemen for trade in codfish and other goods. He would certainly have known that during those years, the English merchants paid twice as much for dried cod as the Norwegians did.[38]

Thorsteinsson takes it for granted that the Norse Greenlanders at Herjolfsnes and Hvalseyfjord had some ships at their disposal and were able to trade in dried cod, and also that men from Bristol, accustomed to ranging ever farther north and west in search of fish, soon were fishing off Greenland in the late summer and probably had located the Newfoundland Banks by about 1430. He assumes that trading doggers were in the vanguard of English ships rounding Greenland's Cape Farewell, and he also argues that one reason sailings from Norway to Iceland were curtailed—and stopped altogether in the case of Greenland—was that English pirates operating in the waters around Iceland after about 1400 made the trip not worth the risk.[39]

If Thorstein went back to Greenland, his main obstacle may well have been the pervasive presence of English ships in Icelandic waters during the better part of the fifteenth century, including in the Denmark Strait between Iceland and Greenland.[40] The sparse information we have about his voyage from Greenland to Norway in 1410 gives no hint of pirates, English or otherwise, but by about 1418, Icelanders who wanted to maintain contact with Greenland would probably have been wise to arrange a deal with an English ship. It should not have been difficult to find an English merchant happy to beat the competition for fish in Iceland. After hearing the Greenland-farers' story about a country whose existence and general location had been known to northern seafarers for centuries, an English merchant may even have taken the initiative in proposing a joint venture with Thorstein and/or some of his friends. The length and risks of the additional voyage from Iceland were not negligible, however, so anyone undertaking it would be unlikely to share his information (and profit) freely with others, much less put it into the written record.

We know from Poul Nørlund's finds during his excavations at Herjolfsnes that the Greenlanders continued to have sporadic contact with foreigners until the very end of the fifteenth century, for one of his discoveries included a locally made version of a man's Burgundian-style tall cap (see Fig. 28a in Chapter 9).[41] This find is well known and is often referred to in the modern literature on medieval Greenland. One significant aspect of Nørlund's discoveries that so far has received little or no scrutiny, however, bolsters the possibility that Thorstein returned to Greenland in the company of Sigrid: the finds include examples of European clothing styles for *women*. These dresses are datable to the first half of the fifteenth century, and their prototypes would not have been worn by burly sailors. Nor would they have fit into any known inventory of English merchant ships during

FIG. 20. Drawing of the remains of an early-fifteenth-century dress found by Poul Nørlund in a grave during his 1921 excavations at Herjolfsnes. Source: Nørlund, "Buried Norsemen," reproduced by permission of Dansk Polarcenter, Copenhagen, publisher of *Meddelelser om Grønland.*

this time of English hegemony in the northwestern Atlantic. Since it is very unlikely that the English brought wives along on trading or fishing voyages that lasted for several months, aboard cramped and smelly ships, the women whose clothes inspired Greenland dressmakers in the first half of the fifteenth century were most likely Icelandic. They were certainly not Norwegian by this time.

A style-conscious Herjolfsnes woman wore to her grave an elegant dress (see Fig. 20) with stitched-down, narrow pleats shaping the bodice in front, a deep V-neck, and set-in sleeves wide at the top and tapering at the wrist. The dress was not imported, but had been made in Greenland from the local wool twill, and the style is datable to the first half of the fifteenth century.[42] Its owner had probably spent countless hours copying a dress worn by a woman arriving from abroad. The unfortunate Steinunn may have worn something like it when she arrived at Hvalsey straight from Norway in 1406. But so might Sigrid Björnsdaughter, back for a visit in Greenland and showing off the latest European fashions as became the wealthy wife of Thorstein Olafsson. The latter (and later) possibility is more likely, given the style of the dress, the circumstances of the find, and the time it would have taken for any new European court fashion to catch on elsewhere, let alone be copied in Greenland.

Nørlund, who thought the sad tales of ruptured communications with Greenland must have been greatly exaggerated, also commented that the fifteenth-century dresses he found at Herjolfsnes on the whole belong to a higher social level than the ordinary dresses of the common people we know from European representations of the period.[43] Again, this points to people like the wealthy Sigrid Björnsdaughter, and to the possibility that she and Thorstein returned to Greenland at least once.

If we aim to discover how much fifteenth-century European explorers may already have known (however vaguely) about Greenland and the lands and islands even farther west, it is essential to stress that Greenland's proven sporadic contact with non-Scandinavians throughout the entire fifteenth century has a natural flip side: *the foreigners who came there knew their way at least as far as to the west coast of Greenland, and they knew that there were Norse in southwestern Greenland with whom they could trade.*

An informant or a guide would have been useful, however—at least in the beginning. Fishermen who were merely extending their quest for cod from the waters west of Iceland to the rich banks off East Greenland may not have known that by rounding Cape Farewell and sailing deep into the fjords of southwest Greenland they would find thriving Norse homesteads, although they might eventually have found Herjolfsnes. The reason Eirik the Red had continued his own search all the way to the sheltered heads of those deep fjords was that he explored for land suited to cattle farming. And he had been able to do so without having to deal with the Eskimos. People looking to fill their ships with cod to take back to England would worry more about becoming trapped by sea ice; about being ambushed by natives of any kind (by this time the Thule people were establishing themselves on a year-round basis in the outer coastal areas); or merely about getting lost in unfamiliar areas.

A trader, on the other hand, would take further trouble if he *knew* it would put him in the way of stockfish, whose excellent keeping qualities made it such a desirable commodity that many of the English outrages in Iceland during this period were committed over stockfish.[44] English fishermen pulling up their own fish off the Iceland coast usually had to content themselves with salting their catch until they could take it home, for drying cod is a lengthy process that requires accommodations ashore. For example, at the Norwegian cod fisheries in Lofoten and farther north, fish caught in early spring could be left "round" and hung to dry after they had been decapitated and gutted, but the catch from the summer fishing had to have the backbone removed and be spread flat for quicker drying.[45] In other words, the fish would barely be dry by the end of the summer season.

Before noting two more archaeological discoveries directly related to the discussion so far, it is important to emphasize that we lack proof that Thorstein returned to Greenland, just as we lack proof of just how fifteenth-century European traders found their way to the Eastern Settlement. But there is irrefutable archaeological evidence that they *did* trade with the Greenlanders, and that European women's fashions also found their way (most likely via Iceland) in the first half of the fifteenth century. Since the English dominated the approaches to Greenland, it is reasonable to suppose that for the better part of the fifteenth century, the Greenlanders' European contact was with the cod-hungry English. It is mere conjecture, however, that Sigrid Björnsdaughter visited at Hvalsey after an absence of seven or eight years, a period just long enough for trading goods to have accumulated and warrant a voyage.

The excellent harbor belonging to Hvalsey farm obviously would have attracted even people with no connection at all to Sigrid and Thorstein, supposing they could find it. And since Hvalsey had both a sizable church and a large, late-built festal hall, the farm would have been a natural gathering point for locals and visitors alike. But Hvalsey's obvious wealth and strategic importance cannot be divorced from the farm's direct connection with Sigrid, Thorstein, and the rest of the Icelandic power elite in the first quarter of the fifteenth century. Nor should we overlook any of these factors in considering a pendant cross (see Fig. 21) found at Hvalsey. It was made of pewter of a kind that points to English origins.[46]

No firm date has been assigned either to the cross or to a distinctly European knife (see Fig. 22a) that Poul Nørlund found in a late stratum at Gardar. The knife's small size and distinctive shape, and the character of its manufacture, strongly suggested to Nørlund that it was a factory-made table knife from no earlier than the fifteenth century. This knife bears an uncanny resemblance in both size and form to a late-fourteenth-century knife (see Fig. 22b) found during excavations in London. Both knives have a whittle tang, which was the most common type in England until the early fifteenth century.[47] We must of course also bear in mind that a ship on the northern codfish route may not have carried the very latest style in cutlery.

If the central part of the Eastern Settlement had in fact made direct contact with the English by about 1418, it is tempting to assume a factual basis

FIG. 21. A pendant cross made of pewter, found at Hvalsey in the Eastern Settlement. Analysis of the metal suggests it is of English origin. Source: The original is at the Qaqortoq (Julianehåb) Museum in Greenland; this drawing by Kistat Lund is reproduced here with the Museum's kind permission.

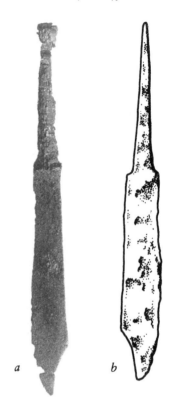

FIG. 22. *a*: European table knife found in an outdoor cooking pit at Gardar. It is single-edged and 17 cm. long, including the remnants of a wooden haft encasing a tang of the whittle type. Source: Photograph from the National Museum, Copenhagen, reproduced by permission. *b*: Late-fourteenth-century knife found during excavations in London. The combined length of the blade (ca. 12 cm.) and the whittle tang (4.7 cm.) equals that of the knife found at Gardar. Source: Drawing by Nick Griffiths (in Cowgill, de Neergaard, and Griffiths, *Knives and Scabbards*, p. 87, fig. 87), reproduced by kind permission of the Museum of London.

a   *b*

for a letter that Pope Nicholas V wrote to the bishops of Skálholt and Holar on September 20, 1448, concerning acts by "barbaric pagans" in Greenland circa 1418. Generations of historians have studied this document to see if it carries reliable evidence about the final chapter in the saga of the Norse Greenlanders.[48] It does not, and it cannot, for three main reasons.

One is that Rome's knowledge of both Greenland (to which "bishops" were still being consecrated) and Norway had eroded almost to the vanishing point by 1448. Pope Eugene in 1433 had addressed his letters of appointment for the new Gardar bishop, Bartolomeus de S. Ypolito, to "the city and diocese of Grenelandia," among others. Nicholas V's own letter of 1448 makes it equally doubtful that a delegation of Greenlanders had been on hand to enlighten the Curia about local conditions. It describes Greenland as "situated We are told at the extreme limits of the Ocean. . . ."[49]

The second reason is that the two Icelandic episcopal seats reflected the same state of abysmal confusion and corruption in 1448 that was manifest both in the other Scandinavian countries (mostly due to uncertainties about the royal succession) and elsewhere in Europe. Nicholas V himself had fled Rome because of a fresh outbreak of the Plague that summer, so "his" letter was written by a proxy who carefully avoided addressing either Icelandic bishop by name.[50] The stated reason for the letter (such a "pitiful lament" had come to the pope's ears that he wanted the two Iceland bishops to find *and* consecrate a suitable and willing bishop of Gardar) suggests blatant manipulation of the money-starved Curia by someone with scant information about Greenland, but with a will to deceive for the sake of gain. This someone was most probably the notorius Marcellus, "bishop of Skálholt," who was hustling in Rome that year, and who that same June had been given the right to collect all papal income in Scandinavia.[51] No wonder the petition failed to involve the archbishop of Nidaros in Norway, whose opinion the Iceland bishops were only advised to seek "distance permitting," and who would have been the first to focus on the doubtful nature of Marcellus's own office.

The various claims made about Greenland in the pope's letter constitute the third and chief reason for rejecting it as a source of information about that country. The Greenlanders had supposedly been Christians for nearly 600 years, and had nourished their "fervent piety" with regular divine services until "thirty years ago" (circa 1418), when[52]

barbaric pagans came by the sea from the neighbouring coasts and invaded the country, bringing low all the people established in this island with their bloody aggression, devastating their native land and its sacred edifices by fire and the sword until there was nothing left in this island (which is said to be very extensive) but nine parish churches difficult of access to the raiders because of the steepness of the mountains. The unfortunate indigenous people, men and women, particularly those who looked strong and fit enough to withstand the yoke of slavery, were deported into captivity in their own regions, as if they were under the sway of this tyrannical power.

Years later, we are told, many of the captives returned to their country and rebuilt their ruined villages. Having at long last overcome want and famine sufficiently to "supply the needs of a few priests or a bishop," they wanted to reestablish divine worship in 1448 after thirty years without the benefit of clergy, and they had sent the pope a petition asking him to "fill the spiritual void in which they find themselves." The pope's reply cautiously noted:

Touched as We are . . . by the desires expressed by the indigenous people . . . of this island of Greenland, nevertheless We do not have at Our command sufficient information about the described situation.

Some scholars think "barbaric pagans" must refer to Eskimos, the only non-Christians around at the time.[53] If literal paganism is not a requirement, and if we are persuaded that the Eskimos did not present a deadly threat to the Greenland Norse, the field is theoretically open to the English,

the Portuguese, the Basques, or the German Hanse. The Portuguese, however, were just starting their explorations and concentrated primarily on
areas to the west and southwest of the Iberian Peninsula. The Germans and
the Basques do not seem to have made their mark yet in Iceland and the
surrounding waters, so in the unlikely event that there was any truth to the
tale told in Rome in 1448 about the acts of "barbaric pagans" in Greenland
waters in about 1418, the blame would have to fall on the English.[54]

Not a single one of the letter's supposedly factual statements hold up
under scrutiny, however. Six centuries earlier (ca. A.D. 850), even the Norwegians were still firmly anchored in paganism, and the establishment of
the Greenland colony lay another century and a half in the future. Also, the
Greenlanders had been without a resident bishop since about 1378, not
1418. The nine parish churches said to have *escaped* devastation because
they were so inaccessible would have represented at least three quarters of
the total number of churches in the Eastern Settlement, most of which were
in any case conspicuously accessible. It is even more significant that archaeologists have found no sign at all of large-scale burning and destruction.
Given Greenland's topography, it would have required a sizable and determined army to inflict that much damage and to capture a large number of
people. Some of the English who reached Greenland may well have been as
violent as some were in Iceland, but there were surely many fewer foreigners
at any given time in Greenland than in Iceland, and in both places they usually had more to gain by trade and offshore fishing than by razing buildings
and abducting people.

Nonetheless, beginning in 1419 violence was a part of the English presence in Iceland, and indeed, we need look no further than to events in Iceland for the inspiration of the tale that led the Curia to express concern
about Greenland. While King Eirik's attention was focused on his quarrels
with Schleswig, large-scale English violence in Iceland erupted both on land
and at sea in 1419 and caused the chieftains to write to King Eirik from
the *Alþing*. We cannot assume that Greenland suffered a similar fate, however, for there was a very important difference between the two countries
by this time: Iceland had royal officials and sycophants whose attempts to
curb English enterprise helped spark much of the violence both in 1419
and later, but Greenland did not. And between the English and the crown's
representatives and supporters were the local power elite. These were partly
from Thorstein Olafsson's circle and partly from King Eirik's private entourage, and they did not necessarily have common goals.

As noted earlier, Thorstein's uncle, Arnfinn Thorsteinsson, had signed
the chieftains' 1419 letter to King Eirik. Less than two weeks later, now as
hirðstjóri in place of the departing Bishop Arni, he had given two English
merchants permission to trade in the Westman Islands and all over Iceland,

as well as to fish with as many men as they wished, for one year.[56] When King Eirik's nominee to replace Arnfinn as *hirðstjóri* arrived in Iceland later that same summer, this news cannot have sat well. The new *hirðstjóri* was the king's chaplain, Hannes Pálsson, and he arrived together with "many other Danes" and Bishop Jon Tofvason of Holar.[57] It is fairly clear that his brief was to keep an eye on the Icelandic chieftains as well as on the English. Thorstein Olafsson soon got to know Hannes when, as noted earlier in this chapter, Bishop Jon Tofvason asked Thorstein, Hannes, and four more clerics to review a property transaction that had taken place while Bishop Arni was the ombudsman at Holar see, and that had nothing to do with the English.[58]

The English continued to make such inroads on King Eirik's privileges in Iceland that in April of 1420, Hannes Pálsson and the royal official in the Westman Islands summoned six English merchants and their men to appear before the next *Alþing* (which they never did), on the charge that they had traded and wintered illegally, instead of leaving home between February and April and returning by September.[59] Another of King Eirik's men, a German named Stephan Schellendorp, was also in Iceland that spring of 1420. In a letter unmatched for obsequiousness, he advised the king of the bad behavior by the English merchants and fishermen in Iceland and let it be known that although both he and Hannes were working very hard, it would not hurt if more of the king's men came out to Iceland to prevent the English from taking over.[60]

These developments formed the motley backdrop for the 1420 *Alþing* and the chieftains' second letter to King Eirik, which Arnfinn, his nephew Hall, and several others of Thorstein Olafsson's kinsmen and friends also signed, though Thorstein himself did not. The chieftains' letter noted that Thorleif Arnason (Björn the Jerusalem-Farer's son-in-law) would be able to tell about the Icelanders' plight, since he and Hannes Pálsson were both setting out to see the king.[61]

Thorsteinsson finds it ironic that Thorleif was chosen to complain to King Eirik about the English, since he was one of the Icelandic chieftains who must have benefited most from the Englishmen's trade in a part of the country where he owned so much land.[62] The choice of Thorleif makes sense, however, if the chieftains thought they primarily stood to gain by trade with the English and sent Thorleif along as a counterweight to Hannes, the latter being an outsider who could not be trusted to relay the Icelanders' own concerns, and who may have bullied them into writing the letter.

Thorleif Arnason from Vatnsfjord was so wealthy that he had his own ship and traveled separately from Hannes. Near the Faroes, he was attacked by a large English vessel, in yet another demonstration on the part of the

English that they were in control of those sea lanes.[63] Having fought off the English, he went on to Norway, where people had complaints of their own about the Englishmen's illegal trade north of Hålogaland, as well as about attacks by Russians and "heathens" in the north.[64] King Eirik's secretaries must have had their hands full.

Probably because they felt threatened by the crown's countermeasures in the summer of 1420, the English in Iceland engaged in further large-scale violence. Men from Hull, including the sea captain Richard of 1413 note, killed and looted at Holar see and elsewhere in the Skagafjord region in fights described by the chronicles as "so savage" that despite having fire-arms they lost several among their own number as well.[65] During the next few years, they were said to have pillaged the countryside and burned churches, and once each year during the period 1422–24 they robbed the royal farm at Bessastaðir.[66]

Hannes Pálsson furnished a list of 37 crimes committed by the English in Iceland between 1420 and 1425, after he and another of King Eirik's men, Balthazar von Damminn, had been captured by the English in the Westman Islands—an act for which few men in Iceland were sorry, ac-cording to the *New Annals*.[67] These same annals also note that the winter of 1424 was a very bad one, and that there was little fish that year. This shortage may conceivably have fueled the fury of the Englishman John Selby, who in the summer of 1424 captured Thorstein Olafsson's wealthy associate and neighbor, Brand Halldorsson, and made him pay a ransom of four lasts of dried codfish. But it is equally possible that the rough and hot-tempered Brand either had refused to honor a business agreement with Selby or had thrown his weight around as the king's man, with conse-quences reported by the sympathetic Hannes.[68] None the worse for wear, in September of that same year Brand put his name to the 1424 affidavit stating that Thorstein's and Sigrid's Hvalsey wedding had been proper and legal.[69]

Responding to reports by Pálsson and Schellendorp, King Eirik again made it known in 1425 that all Englishmen sailing to Iceland without his permission (obviously still available for a handsome fee) were to be called to account. This decree was made public in Lynn in February of 1426, in English translation, and after Pálsson had lodged his complaint with the English Council, the Admiral (the Duke of Exeter) early in 1426 also for-bade the voyages to Iceland.[70] The Lynn merchants and fishermen therefore knew what they risked if they kept going to Iceland. Ignoring these injunc-tions, a London ship captained by John Vache put in at Lynn that same autumn after a voyage to Iceland.[71]

Hannes Pálsson's well-publicized complaints of 1425 (which Thorsteinsson judges to have been a mixture of truth and hearsay) were probably the source of the 1448 papal laments about Greenland.[72] Pálsson, too, claimed that the English had stolen many children and youths from Iceland, using force or buying them for a pittance from naïve parents. He noted that these young people had been taken to England and were living there in great misery; that the situation had become so bad that Iceland was becoming depopulated and deserted in many places; and that the English had struck similarly at other places owned by the Norwegian king, such as the Faroes.[73] Using documents from Lynn, Thorsteinsson shows that Pálsson's complaint in this case must have been at least partly based on fact. In later years, too, there were repeated claims that the Icelanders gave or sold their children to foreigners in defiance of the big landowners, who already were short of laborers.[74]

The partial solution to that problem provides another tidy parallel to the supposed events in Greenland. On August 26, 1429, just four years after Pálsson had filed his grievances against the English, it was revealed in Lynn that eleven boys and girls taken from their homes in Iceland had arrived in that city and were being offered for sale. Just at that time, Bishop Jon Gereksson of Skálholt was in Lynn; he had come to England as King Eirik's representative to negotiate with Henry VI about the continuing violations of their joint agreements to confine the English fish trade to the Bergen Staple. It is likely that it was he who extracted a promise from the Lynn merchants that the children would be sent home to Iceland the following spring.[75] In 1432, King Eirik ordered the English to free any people they had taken from the northern countries, especially from Iceland, Finnmark, and Hålogaland and "any other territory in the Norwegian realm" (*hverju öðru landi Noregs rikis*)—a capacious term that would also have included the Greenlanders in case anybody still worried about them.[76] Although many of the Icelandic children were restored to their homes, the English economic historian E. M. Carus-Wilson reasons that some must have remained, voluntarily or involuntarily, to account for the number of men and women from Iceland who crop up in the Subsidy Rolls, or those "born in Iceland" who took the oath of fealty to the English king.[77]

According to Carus-Wilson, English records show that half of Hannes Pálsson's complaints involved the same few people, many of whom proved to be mariners of Hull, which was always more of a center for piracy than cities such as Lynn and Bristol. None of the names in Pálsson's report can be traced to either Bristol or Lynn, which Carus-Wilson sees as a sign that, overall, the English "carried on a peaceful trade to the advantage of all concerned."[78]

It is right to distinguish between fishermen focused on hauling up their catch and merchants who must depend on negotiations, but "peaceful trade" was a relative term during this violent age, in which the English did not have a monopoly on looting and killing. And just how law-abiding the men of Lynn and Bristol were compared with those from Hull is also open to discussion. For example, documents for the year 1424–25 show that Bristol merchants held foreign merchants prisoners for ransom.[79] By this time, the Bristolmen had found their way to Iceland, where they soon made their presence known in earnest, particularly in Snæfellsnes ports (from which southern Greenland was a manageable next stop), and prohibitions by the Danish and English authorities were routinely violated.[80] Forty percent of the English royal licenses issued between 1439 and 1484 to trade in Iceland were to Bristol men for Bristol ships, according to Quinn, and that number represented only a fraction of those who went there without a license.[81]

Bristol was conveniently located for the route to Iceland, and the Bristolmen had no interests to maintain in Norway or the Faroes and therefore risked the least by defying King Eirik's monopoly.[82] They could hardly be expected to take a back seat to the many other English fishermen and traders who spared no effort in their pursuit of cod. In the summer of 1420, two large English merchant ships had been reported trading up north in Hålogaland in Norway, and eight years later two English ships were recorded as buying fish all the way up in Finnmark.[83] They continued to show up in these waters in the 1430s, giving rise to tales of violence and robbery, and Thorsteinsson assumes that daredevil English sailors were equally likely to set course for Greenland and North America once they were in Icelandic waters.[84]

The Bristolmen sailed by the forerunner to the modern magnetic compass known as "the needle and stone"—a needle magnetized by rubbing it with a lodestone and gingerly made to float in a dish of water.[85] Their ships were more maneuverable than those of earlier generations, but they had no better control over the weather than their predecessors in the northern seas. Soon, their ships were going to Iceland in such numbers that, by the law of averages, some of them must have drifted off to Greenland or to North America. When the English were fishing on the deep banks off western Iceland, in clear weather they would not have had to drift very far before they saw the mountains of Greenland.[86] Fishing off these Iceland banks took place in the late summer, the season with the least sea ice blocking the Greenland coasts east and west of Cape Farewell, so some fishermen may have been tempted to explore further.

Bristol ships were especially likely to head far west into the Atlantic, for to avoid Scottish pirates in the Irish Sea they were apt to sail south of Ireland and up along its west coast both going to and coming from Iceland. Quinn, who thinks that the English usually reached Iceland via the Irish Sea and western Scotland, nevertheless agrees that there is evidence of such voyages around the west of Ireland, during which vessels could more easily be swept into the ocean.[87]

A look at any modern map shows that being swept out to sea on a North Atlantic voyage between Iceland and the British Isles might as easily land a ship in Newfoundland as in Greenland. And a look at any fifteenth-century map tells us that contemporary cartography would not have helped such a mariner to locate precisely where he had been, even supposing he wanted to tell a knowledgeable audience about his experiences on his return. He might, however, add to the already existing lore about lands and islands in the Western Ocean.

If we add up (1) the indications that Englishmen with inside information traded with Norse Greenland in the first half of the fifteenth century, (2) the continuing English quest for new sources of codfish and general trading opportunities, (3) the expansion of English maritime knowledge due to both deliberate and chance ventures resulting from their involvement in Iceland, and (4) the speed with which Bristolmen came to dominate that involvement, it is hard to avoid the conclusion that at least some Bristol fishermen and merchants well before the middle of the fifteenth century had knowledge about Greenland and/or the Newfoundland Banks—knowledge they were loath to share with anyone who might interfere with their profits.

The chief lure of the Newfoundland Banks was obviously cod. The lure of the Greenland trade, at least to begin with, may have been more complex. Narwhal horns (which Europeans still thought came from unicorns) were an ancient English remedy against epidemics. For at least a century after the Black Death first struck in 1348, the population of England declined irregularly but persistently from repeated outbreaks of Plague and other epidemics, so a few narwhal horns in a merchant's cargo might enhance its value considerably.[88] Also, English sumptuary laws had, since 1337, made the wearing of furs a social privilege, which virtually guaranteed a flourishing fur trade supplying both the rich and privileged and those who merely wanted to appear rich and privileged. The thick, lustrous furs from the far north were much prized, especially various kinds of fox and ermine.[89]

Hides of various sorts, the raw material for England's second-largest urban industry in this period, would also have made a good supplementary cargo. Maryanne Kowaleski has noted that during 1435–36, Bristol's near neighbor Southampton imported as many as 1,408 large cattle hides (only 194 were exported), and that the origin of these imported hides is largely unknown. As additional evidence of the need for all kinds of raw materials, she found that during the same period in Southampton, over 38,000 skins of sheep, lamb, calf, rabbit, kid, stag, fox, and goat were imported, at least

11,000 more than were exported.[90] As for Bristol itself, we get a fair notion of its needs when we see that fish and the hides of sheep and kid were the biggest exports from Ireland to Bristol at that time. Irish furs and hawks are also said to have found a market there.[91] It is therefore doubtful that any English merchant, whether from Bristol or elsewhere, would have refused to trade for traditional Greenland goods. But we must not forget that the main reason English ships were plying the North Atlantic in such great numbers was that they wanted fish, especially cod.

However loath King Eirik was to lose control of the codfish trade, there was less and less chance that he would interfere with the Englishmen's hegemony at sea. In Denmark and on the continent, he was beset by problems resulting from his disastrous foreign policies, and the Norwegian economy was in a precipitous decline. The city of Trondheim, where the archbishop had his seat, suffered a steep drop in population throughout the entire fifteenth century, and there were scarcely any good-sized ships available. Norwegian naval power, already in a reduced state, received a heavy blow in the spring of 1428, when some 600 Hanse pirates led by Bartholomew Voet attacked the city of Bergen and the ships in its harbor. A number of Lynn merchants who habitually sailed to Bergen and were there at the time of the attack fled for their lives. Voet returned the following year with equally terrible results.[92]

For a long time afterward, the Norwegians sent out few ships, and the Bergen Staple seemed less desirable than ever to English codfish merchants. It is therefore hard to know what to make of the English government's 1429 decree on behalf of the boy-king Henry VI that in deference to King Eirik's wishes, English codfish merchants could go *only* to the Bergen Staple, where King Eirik had given the Germans and the English equal rights, and not to Finnmark or any other place in the Dano-Norwegian kingdom to which foreigners were forbidden to sail. Thorsteinsson is probably correct in thinking that the English were anxious to humor King Eirik as far as possible in this matter because they were having problems of their own with the Hanse.[93]

Recorded voyages from Iceland to Bergen ceased for a long time. A man named Ketil Snæbjörnsson and his crew, who had gone to Bergen in 1427 and who were lucky enough to survive the Hanse attack and get back to Iceland in 1428, became the last recorded Icelandic travelers sailing directly to Bergen rather than via Copenhagen in the fifteenth century.[94] Englishmen and other foreigners were appointed bishops in Iceland, with King Eirik's tacit agreement.

The first such English bishop was Jon Vilhjalmsson (John Williamsson Craxton) of Holar, who received his office from Pope Martin V in 1426, soon after the English capture of Hannes Pálsson and Balthazar von Damminn had shown who was in de facto command in Iceland.[95] We do not know who had proposed Jon Vilhjalmsson to Martin V, whose 1417 election had put an end to the Great Schism. The new Holar bishop's subsequent career is rather better known and of more interest here, especially since the Englishman's letter-book shows that during his tenure at Holar he became well acquainted with both Thorstein Olafsson and Sigrid Björnsdaughter.[96] Holar cathedral lay in the inner Skagafjord region, within easy distance of Thorstein and Sigrid at Great Akrar.

Despite the fact that Jon may have been of Norwegian stock, he seems to have made an inauspicious start as bishop. According to the "New Annals," he came out to Hafnarfjord on an English ship in 1427 and read his letter of appointment at the *Alþing*, where he was so "poorly received by the North Icelanders" that he decided to leave that same summer after consecrating four priests and a few deacons.[97] As a merchant, Jon (who evidently had no connection with Bristol) did rather better. Before going out to Iceland that summer of 1427, he had obtained a license from the English king to trade in wheat, malt, or barley in Iceland from either Lynn, Hull, or Newcastle.[98] One must suppose that when he returned home in the autumn, he had bartered his English luxuries for stockfish, and that he had collected his episcopal dues in the same commodity. In the summer of 1429 he returned to Iceland, and this time he stayed at Holar for several years.[99]

Thorstein Olafsson was then at the peak of his wealth and power, neither of which had been diminished by his daughter Kristin's marriage to another powerful and wealthy man, the lawman Helgi Gudnason, before January of 1428.[100] He was still *hirðstjóri* of northern and western Iceland when Bishop Jon of Holar arrived at his see in 1429, and he held the same office again in 1431, concurrently with being the lawman for southern and eastern Iceland.[101] It would have been impossible for the two men to avoid constant meetings over various kinds of business. Thorsteinsson takes it for granted that in the course of Bishop Jon's many dealings with Thorstein, he was entertained with stories about Greenland, and Quinn, too, assumes that the English bishops occupying both the Skálholt and Holar sees in the first half of the fifteenth century would have had an entry into chieftain households in Iceland, where they would get information about Greenland and possibly also hear the tales of the Vínland voyages of old.[102]

Having already argued that throughout the first decades of the fifteenth century, members of some of the chief families in North Iceland maintained close and deliberate connection with Greenland as well as with the leading English merchants coming to Iceland, I certainly agree that Bishop Jon Vilhjalmsson and Thorstein Olafsson probably talked about Greenland, and maybe about Vínland as well. But it is another matter how well Thorstein or his peers trusted their cod-merchant bishops during these increasingly turbulent times, and how much useful information Jon Vilhjalmsson and his colleagues received about such matters as the possibilities for trade in Greenland. Since these bishops represented outside officialdom, they were probably among the last people an Icelandic chieftain would have entrusted with information that showed him acting in violation of Dano-Norwegian trade laws.

Bishop Jon appears to have been a learned man and a good administrator, as well as a consummate politician, whom Thorsteinsson credits with helping to loosen Iceland's ties with the Norwegian archbishopric.[103] These were qualities which those North Iceland chieftains would respect, but which would also make them worry about losing control themselves, especially after 1430, when Jon Vilhjalmsson's colleague, Bishop Jon Gereksson of Skálholt, arrived in Iceland after having spent the winter in England.[104] The *New Annals*, reporting his arrival, note that he brought with him a band of roughneck foreigners as well as two priests named Matthew and Nicholas, and that Nicholas returned to England that same summer, taking much cod with him.

That year's events signaled another important shift. In a country where tithes and taxes so often were paid in stockfish, people took it for granted that their bishops and abbots would act as cod merchants, just like any other chieftains, but the blatant greed and violence exhibited—especially by Bishop Jon Gereksson, but also by his Holar colleague—were new. More troubling still, the greed and violence gave every appearance of having been sanctioned by King Eirik and the church. Thorsteinsson reasons that King Eirik probably acquiesced in ruling Iceland by way of England, given the setbacks he had suffered in his Schleswig wars and the rupture of Norwegian-Icelandic communications after the 1427–28 German attacks on Bergen.[105] Many Icelanders would have seen the increasing violence in the years after 1430 as linked not only to the growing English presence in Iceland and the shrinking supplies of stockfish, but to a foreign power play at the highest level.[106] They would have felt betrayed both by the English, whom they had befriended, and by King Eirik, to whom they had sworn fealty. This is probably the light in which we should read a resolution addressed to King Eirik and passed at the *Alþing* in 1431.[107]

The petition was signed by a broad spectrum of chieftains, officials, and lay farmers. It addressed the problem of the Englishmen and Germans who stayed the winter in Iceland, and also the troubles caused by Danish and Swedish thugs, of whom there were many in Iceland by that time, especially thanks to the new Skálholt bishop. The signatories did not think these outsiders had the right to meddle in the country's legal affairs by showing up at the *Alþing,* for example, and they stipulated that crossbows and handbows be forbidden except to check violence committed by foreigners.

Thorsteinsson is convinced that those who signed the letter (and who were almost entirely from Thorstein Olafsson's current jurisdiction) were in effect rebels against the king, and that Thorstein himself was probably the chief instigator of the petition.[108]

It would have been a logical next step for Thorstein to take this initiative in 1431 if, as previously argued, his private agenda in earlier years had been to exploit both his Greenland connections and the English presence in Iceland while building up his power base at home. By 1431, however, the Icelanders' loss of control on both land and sea would have been a powerful incentive to the chieftains to rid the country of entrenched foreigners and their weapons, as requested by the *Alþing*. Furthermore, King Eirik's power had eroded both at home and abroad because of his incessant wars and their cost. In 1431, the time was ripe for seasoned politicians like Thorstein and his allies to challenge the crown.

Thorstein's name no longer appears in the records after 1431. A smallpox epidemic ravaged Iceland in 1431–32, so it is likely that he died during that time, as did his brother Hall and many of his other kinsmen and friends.[109] In May of 1431 he had taken the precaution of getting Bishop Jon Vilhjalmsson's permission to build a chapel at Thorleiksstead, where a priest would sing mass every other Sunday.[110] Thorleiksstead is called Thorstein's own property in the bishop's letter, although it was in fact Sigrid's inheritance from her mother. Sigrid may have survived her husband and reached old age without remarrying; if she did, she clearly lived out of the public eye to such a degree that we cannot guess whether she was a partner to trade or property ventures on her own, either at home or in Greenland. Her daughter Akra-Kristin appears in the records as a tough negotiator over property rights, however.

It is uncertain whether King Eirik received the *Alþing* petition of 1431.[111] His concerns were in any event not with the Icelanders' well-being, and even less with that of the Greenlanders, despite the nomination of no fewer than *four* Bishops of Gardar in the period 1431–34, all of whom were approved by Pope Eugene IV at the beginning of a pontificate that was later ruled heretical, and that had King Eirik's allegiance.[112]

With increasingly varied success, Eirik was fighting for his political survival close to home. In August of 1432, he signed an armistice with the Hanse, and in October he began negotiations with the English king that culminated in an agreement signed on December 24, 1432. Taking advantage of the few years that the Hanse were forbidden to trade in Bergen, the English showed up there in great numbers, but the Hanse returned to Bergen in 1435, by which time King Eirik was in deep trouble with his Swedish subjects. Eirik had to leave Denmark and Sweden in 1436, after which time the Hanse became more settled than ever in Norway, while the English became further entrenched in Iceland.[113] Although the latter now had even better reasons for exploring the fisheries to the west, they had less need, if any, for Icelandic go-betweens in trade with Greenland, with which a handful of English merchants must by then have been quite familiar.

Meanwhile, the two English-backed bishops in Iceland carried on, untroubled by royal decrees. Displaying an enviable talent for business, Bishop Jon Vilhjalmsson in the fall of 1431 "helped" some hard-pressed fellow countrymen and in return received, very cheaply, half-ownership in their ocean sailer lying at anchor in Skagafjord. A couple of weeks later, when the Englishmen had to seek refuge in the Holar cathedral, the bishop again protected them and soon found himself in possession of the entire ship with crew and all the trimmings, for the price of twelve lasts of cod. Having his own ship made it easier for this servant of God and cod not only to carry on trade between Iceland and England (during 1427–40, four trading licenses were given to bishops of Holar and three to bishops of Skálholt), but to go and visit Pope Eugene IV. By January 5, 1435, Jon of Hólar was in Florence, where Eugene was living in exile as a result of his struggle with the Council of Basel. The pope, who probably had little interest in the church's most northerly outposts, had appointed a Brother Bartholomew as the latest bishop of Greenland in the autumn of 1433. When Jon of Holar reached Florence a year and half later, he appears to have had little trouble persuading Eugene to promote him to Skálholt see and let another Englishman, Jon Bloxwich, succeed him at Holar.[114]

Like Bishop Bartholomew "of Greenland," Jon Bloxwich never went out to his see. He was primed with stories about the terrors of the voyage to Iceland and was well aware that his colleague, Jon Vilhjalmsson, had found a vacancy at Skálholt see only because its most recent incumbent, Bishop Jon Gereksson, had reportedly been hauled out of his own cathedral and drowned by irate Icelanders, in 1432 or 1433.[115] Bloxwich decided on a cautious approach. He got a codfish merchant from London, Richard Weston, and a couple of other men to go to Iceland as his representatives. King Henry VI gave this sacred errand his permission, provided the captain in charge of the ship did not violate the 1429 and 1432 agreements with King Eirik concerning the Staple at Bergen. The royal patent to Bloxwich was issued on November 22, 1436, and repeated in May of 1437.[117]

Unfortunately for both Jon Bloxwich "of Holar" and his friend and colleague Jon Vilhjalmsson "of Skálholt," who also stayed in England while securing licenses to trade in both 1436 and 1438, there were too many contestants for Icelandic cod.[118] Despite at least three trading voyages made on his behalf, Bloxwich did not succeed in paying off debts he had accumulated in his quest for promotion. After Bloxwich had renounced his office, Pope Eugene IV (who in 1443 allowed him to accept an ecclesiastical benefice in the provinces of Canterbury or York) gave the Holar title to another Englishman, who never made it out to Iceland, either, and who is not even counted among the Holar bishops. Bishop Jon Vilhjalmsson fared no better in the long run. While he was in Florence petitioning the pope in 1435, the Dano-Norwegian authorities had given the Skálholt see to Gottsvin [Gozewijm] Comhaer, who had been the bishop of Bergen since 1432. Jon "of Skálholt" now sat at home in England, as desperately in debt as Bloxwich, and tried to turn Icelandic codfish into gold, but with so little success that he eventually died a pauper at St. Thomas's Hospital in Southwark.[119]

These tales of financial woe make it seem highly unlikely that either of the two bishops Jon had been in league with the Icelandic power elite, or with people who benefited from the relatively well-stocked fishing banks off Greenland or from trade with the Greenlanders. Nor is there anything in later records to suggest that the English learned anything useful about Greenland simply by providing Iceland with bishops whom they licensed for trade with England.

The shortage of fish in Iceland would nevertheless have been an additional spur for some English ships to keep pushing westward, including some of the Bristol ships descending on Iceland in ever-increasing numbers between 1437 (the year Henry VI came of age) and about 1450. The Bristolmen led the English pack in licensed trade, owing in no small part to the famous merchant William Canynges, who lent large sums of money to his king and expected favors in return.[120]

England's wars with France had depleted the state coffers, and there was increased pressure to collect taxes and customs as well as to sell licenses.[121] By 1440, when Canynges and others were making regular runs to Iceland, two English merchants acting for Bishop Gottsvin Comhaer of Skálholt had no trouble securing a license from the English king to export two shiploads of food, drink, and cloth for the bishop and his household, and to bring freight back. The bishop was said to be lacking not only bread, wine, and other necessaries, but even milk and water![122]

The irony is that the Skálholt bishop was considerably better supplied than his Bergen colleague in 1440, which illustrates both the well-oiled connection between Iceland and England and the English control of North Atlantic waters. Access to the Norwegian west coast was further limited by the political situation in Scandinavia, which was deteriorating due to the struggle for supremacy between King Eirik and Christopher of Bavaria, and which prevented any ships from reaching Bergen in the summer of 1440. The result was such a desperate shortage of grain that in September, Munkeliv monastery sent messengers overland to Hamar and Oslo bishoprics to beg for supplies.[123]

It is therefore significant that the Bergen bishop that same perilous September issued a travel pass for "his servant Jon" to go on a pilgrimage to England.[124] The pilgrim could justifiably expect to sail from Bergen on an English ship going about its regular business. The very next summer, Alderman Thomas Vanderfort of London, undaunted, sent a ship laden with trade goods to Bergen.[125] We need not view this as a philanthropic undertaking. Only half a year later, another London merchant received royal permission to export to Norway or Prussia 80 casks of old Gascony wine (". . . *versus partes Norwegie vel Prucie carcare possit et traducere*"), which had spoiled and therefore could not be sold in England.[126] Perhaps it is best not to ask what sort of wine the Skálholt bishop received in 1440, or what goods the Greenlanders were offered in trade for their own wares.

The English could continue to do as they pleased in the northwestern Atlantic while Bergen, Norway's premier seaport and supposed chief link with the Atlantic colonies, was isolated and overwhelmed, and while the two contenders for the Danish, Norwegian, and Swedish thrones thought only of their squabble with each other and of their need for revenue.

After the Norwegians had chosen Christopher as their king in 1442, he soon bethought himself of his trade privileges and the very next year announced from Copenhagen to his crown representatives in Norway, as well as to the citizens of Bergen, that he had given the citizens of Amsterdam permission to trade in Norway on condition that they pay the usual customs, but that they would not be allowed to go to Iceland or other tributary countries where foreigners were forbidden to trade.[127] We do not know if King Christopher intended to include Greenland with his "tributary countries" in 1443. But Greenland may still have been part of the general Norwegian consciousness, especially since the titular Bishop Gregorius of Gardar (circa 1440–50) seems to have been staying in various parts of Norway, including Bergen, unlike his recent predecessors.[128]

Henry VI proclaimed the following spring that his subjects were forbidden to go to Iceland, and in July of 1444 he replied to King Christopher's complaints about illegal sailings there, but the deluge of English licenses issued both before and after this announcement makes it clear that Henry's restrictions were merely intended to produce more money for his coffers.[129] Many of these licenses were so liberal that they amounted to a *carte blanche* for the owners. Even so, the latter did not always bother to secure royal permission; in 1442, for example, the Bristol merchants William Canynges and Stephen Forster sent their ship the *Katherine* to Iceland without a license. For this they were not only pardoned, but received permission to take both the *Katherine* and the *Mary Redcliff* to Iceland and Finnmark for four years—long enough to take them to Greenland and back, if they so wished. They were permitted to buy fish and "other goods" and to take their cargo to England, where they would owe the usual customs and taxes. In addition, all the merchants and sailors on board were pardoned ahead of time for any outrages they might commit while away.[130] Also in 1443, the wealthy Bristol merchant Henry May secured a license to send his ship the *Trinity* to trade in Iceland as often as he wished during the next *six* years, despite any statute to the contrary.[131]

Meanwhile, Bishop Gottsvin of Skálholt continued to enjoy his comfortable relations with the English. While he was in England late in 1445 (the same year three Englishmen were sentenced for having stolen small boys in Iceland), he and an Orkney skipper obtained royal permission to go to Iceland with servants, horses, goods, silver, and other valuable objects associated with his position; to return to England; and to make yet another voyage to Iceland.[132] Henry VI nevertheless decided in 1448 to honor the Danish king's prohibition against direct voyages to Iceland, in order to oil English negotiations with the Nordic countries after several English ships had been captured in the Sound between Denmark and Sweden.[133] Falling afoul of these new strictures, the *Christopher* of Bristol was forfeited to the crown when it returned to Bristol in the autumn of 1448 with a cargo of stockfish and saltfish, following an illegal voyage to Iceland that had been billed as a trading venture to Ireland.[134] A two-year armistice agreement between England and Denmark-Norway, specifying that English merchants would not be allowed to go to Iceland, Hålogaland, and Finnmark, was finally reached in 1449 and ratified by Henry VI in April of 1450. There was only one hitch: it was never ratified by Christian I, Christopher of Bavaria's heir to the kingdoms of Denmark and Norway.[135]

Before his death in January of 1449, Christopher had laid the foundation for the reestablisment of the crown's power in Iceland. Presiding over a larger area than any Scandinavian ruler before him, he was shrewd enough to cooperate with his nobles, at the same time as he trusted in his ability to cooperate with the Hanse, the English, and other adversaries.[136] When young King Christian I came to power, he had no compunctions about continuing Christopher's policy of increased taxation, but his statesmanship left something to be desired at first. His entourage included the infamous Marcellus de Niveriis, introduced earlier in this chapter in connection with Pope Nicholas V's letter of 1448. Because Bishop Gottsvin of Skálholt had died in Holland in 1447, Marcellus was appointed Bishop of Skálholt by Pope Nicholas the following year. The pope and his Curia may have been unaware of Marcellus's previous twenty-year career as a scoundrel and impostor of the first order.[137] That might also help explain their willingness (albeit with some misgivings) to write the 1448 letter concerning the need for a proper bishop in Greenland.

Nor does Christian I appear to have delved deeply into Marcellus's past. He loved Marcellus well, at least to begin with, and nominated him to the

Nidaros archbishopric in 1450, the year the Norwegian National Council ratified Christian's claim to the Norwegian throne.[138] Marcellus is not known to have set foot in Iceland, but he exerted considerable influence there for over a decade in ways that also involved the English, so we shall meet him again in Chapter Eight. In the interval between the death of Gottsvin and the doubtful appointment of Marcellus, the *vicarius* at Skálholt See had been Gottskálk Keneksson, the Bishop of Holar since 1442.[139] Rather than list the many confusions and disagreements within both crown and church in Norway just as the century reached its midpoint, we may use Gottskálk's experience with Christian's turbulent assumption of power as an example of how uncertain ecclesiastical office could be.

The Holar bishop and the chieftain Torfi Árason stayed with their men at the court in Copenhagen in November of 1449, but neither Gottskálk nor Torfi are reported among those who accompanied the king to Trondheim for his coronation in the summer of 1550. Instead, a Mattheus "of Holar" had a seat on the Norwegian National Council in August of 1450. On November 24, Gottskálk paid up 119 weights of silver due to the pope from Holar See, and Marcellus made him his ombudsman at Skálholt but took away the empowerments given to Gottskálk by the controversial Archbishop Aslak Bolt the previous year. Christian I then gave Gottskálk permission to sail his ship to Bergen or anywhere else in the Norwegian realm without having to pay customs. Thorsteinsson thinks Gottskálk was probably allowed to do this in order to bring the king and Marcellus their income from Iceland.[140]

Gottskálk's travel companion, Torfi Árason, had risen to prominence through power play at home and carefully cultivated relations with the Dano-Norwegian king. He was now the new husband of Thorstein Olafsson's daughter Kristin, heiress to Great Akrar and much else besides. Still in Copenhagen in November of 1450, he received a knighthood from the king and obtained the right to a coat of arms on his shield featuring a polar bear against a blue background.[141] No documents reveal Torfi's position with regard to the Dano-English treaty drawn up in the summer of 1449 (the time of his arrival in Copenhagen), nor do we know whether he looked to Greenland for any part of his income during the years he was Akra-Kristin's husband. His will, written in Bergen on August 26, 1459, ends with these words: "I wish Kristin Thorsteinsdaughter and all my friends and kin in Iceland a very good night and ask that they will pray for me."[142]

His "friends and kin in Iceland" were the great chieftains who were running things in a manner that included little time or inclination for praying. By the middle of the fifteenth century, as Thorsteinsson notes, "even bishops could not be certain of their lives."[143] The lawlessness of mid-century Iceland marked yet another turning point, not only for the English in Iceland, but also for the natives and, inevitably, for the Greenlanders. There is little reason to suppose that the descendants of those who had attended the Hvalsey wedding in 1408 had much thought to spare from their pursuit of power at home and in Copenhagen. And no ordinary Icelanders would have had the means to attempt a voyage to Greenland on their own, squeezed as they were by their chieftains' ferocious power struggles, by incessant demands for tithes and taxes, and by epidemics and natural disasters. Interception by English ships would in any case have been the likely fate of any Icelandic or Greenlandic ship capable of attempting the voyage between their two countries.

By this time, the Greenlanders had long had to make do without the Western Settlement as a convenient way-station to Markland, so they may no longer have had ships suitable for long ocean voyages. Lumber imports from Norway were also a thing of the distant past, if indeed they had ever been anything to reckon with.[144] And since those Englishmen who knew the Greenland route would no longer have needed pilots or introductions in order to trade there, the Greenlanders' direct contact with Icelandic entrepreneurs appears to have been broken, leaving them to trade solely with Englishmen or other foreigners who knew where to find them.

CHAPTER EIGHT

Sailing out of the Middle Ages, 1450-1500

In the second half of the fifteenth century, the central government in Copenhagen played an increasingly dominant and destructive part in the affairs of Norway and its colonies. The crown was narrowly focused on obtaining money for its European power politics, and in Iceland the wealthiest chieftains turned this focus to their own advantage as royal proxies who seldom were called to account for their deeds, least of all for brutality toward natives and foreigners alike.

Two aspects of the Icelandic situation are especially likely to have had a direct effect on the Greenlanders: the lack of interest in Greenland among the descendants of the powerful Icelandic families who had had a stake in their neighbor country at the beginning of the century, and the mounting pressure on the English to continue their westward search for plentiful and relatively uncomplicated sources of cod.

As before, there are no documents specifically related to English fishing and trade in Greenland, nor to pre-Cabot crossings of the Davis Strait by English or Continental Europeans, but such options must have become more attractive as the competition with other nations for Icelandic cod increased, and as the Dano-Norwegian king tried to make the most of his royal trade privileges.

A close scrutiny of these processes suggests that they led to continued interaction between the English and the Norse Greenlanders into the late fifteenth century, and that they contributed in a crucial way to the information accumulating in Bristol about the "Isle of Brazil." This information made Bristol the natural point of departure for John Cabot's expeditions, and it must also have been a major factor in the formation of the Anglo-

Azorean Syndicate whose possible part in the depopulation of Greenland will be discussed in Chapter Ten.

We have no better sources for monitoring Anglo-Icelandic trade in the second half of the fifteenth century than we have for the first half. Licenses covered only a fraction of the ships that actually sailed from England to Iceland, and a 1478 license granted to John Forster, merchant of Bristol, appears to have been the last one thought necessary for English trade to Iceland.[1] The oldest extant Bristol customs documents regarding Iceland do not begin until 1461, and only eight export shipments and fourteen import shipments are noted over the next 32 years, leaving the impression that most of the ships on that route were small fishing doggers avoiding the customs officials altogether.[2] English law exempted from subsidy (a 5 percent import duty) any fish caught in the open seas or in home waters, which resulted in spotty records of fish that had just been lightly salted before being brought home.[3] Such fish could have been caught anywhere in the North Atlantic as far as the English crown was concerned. The Icelanders took a different view, however, and so did the Danish crown.

While Torfi Árason was enjoying royal favor in Copenhagen late in 1450, King Christian I was busy amending colonial laws for his realms. On November 26, three days before he knighted Torfi and gave Bishop Gott-skálk permission to sail to Bergen and elsewhere in his Norwegian realm, he signed what became known as the *Löngurettarbót* (Long Law Code Amendment).[4] It is likely that Torfi himself brought the new laws with him when he returned to Iceland in 1451 as *hirðstjóri* of northern and western Iceland, with the additional power his knighthood gave him.[5] Greenland is not mentioned in this document, but little is beneath royal notice when it comes to Iceland. Point 14 forbids foreigners to take young or old people away from Iceland, except to go to Norway or on a pilgrimage. Nor may Icelandic parents give or sell their children to foreigners. For good measure, the king threatens all Englishmen and Irishmen who sail to Iceland with arrest and forfeiture of ships and goods.

Like their predecessors, Christian I's new laws were easily circumvented. For example, less than three weeks later in 1450, on December 16, Henry VI of England granted a license to William Canynges of Bristol to trade in Finnmark and Iceland for two years with two ships. Canynges already had a similar permit from Christian I, reportedly because people in Finnmark owed him money.[6] The English king, also in debt to Canynges, gave him another license in March of 1451, allowing him to trade to Iceland and Finnmark for five years with two ships, exporting any except Staple goods. This arrangement also had the approval of the Danish king's representative.[7]

Relations between the two monarchs were nevertheless not as smooth as this dual licensing might suggest. The two-year armistice agreement between Denmark and England was not renewed in 1551, and by 1552 Denmark had broken with England and closed the Sound. While the Hundred Years' War was winding down on the Continent, England was experiencing mounting problems at home that would lead to the Wars of the Roses, and the crown virtually abandoned any attempt to control trade with Iceland, although licenses were still being issued and bore witness to Bristol's flourishing trade with both Iceland and Finnmark. Carus-Wilson observes, however, that the number of *unlicensed* English voyages to Iceland known to have taken place around this time shows that the efficiency of the central government was at a low ebb.[8]

The Danish king, too, faced increasing turbulence in his kingdoms from the mid-1450s. He paid only intermittent attention to Norway and its colonies, as exemplified by his decision (November 29, 1454) to allow people from Holland, Zeeland, and Friesland to trade in Norway, but not in the tributary countries of "Iceland, Shetland, the Faroes, etc."[9] This "etc." included the Orkneys, which Christian I mortgaged to James III of Scotland fifteen years later as part of his daughter's dowry, and which then (along with Shetland, mortgaged soon afterwards) remained in Scottish possession.[10] For the sake of perspective, it needs stressing that while the Orkneys already in 1454 apparently had become as peripheral to the embattled and impecunious Dano-Norwegian crown as Greenland had been for decades, they obviously were very much a part of the North Atlantic landscape for other people in the region, just as Greenland still existed for those who had business there.

When the "wealthiest and wisest of the merchants of Bristol," William Canynges, had enjoyed his fifth mayoral term in 1467–68 and retired from business to join the church, his shipping empire had straddled more than two decades of mounting economic and political chaos both at home and in Iceland.[11] Except for the land-rich, powerful chieftains, the Icelanders were impoverished and decimated by epidemics, natural disasters, and relentless demands for taxes and tithes, preferably payable in stockfish. Their animal husbandry economy had slipped so badly that butter, once a common export article, was now imported on English ships.[12] Ordinary farmers, fishermen, and laborers had little or no influence on the political situation, at the fulcrum of which we find the husbands, friends, and relations of Thorstein Olafsson's and Sigrid Björnsdaughter's immediate descendants: Akra-Kristin Thorsteinsdaughter and her two daughters, Ingvild and Málfrid.

The success of Torfi Árason (Akra-Kristin's second husband) at Christian I's court has already been noted. Looming equally large in Icelandic affairs by this time was Akra-Kristin's relative Björn Thorleifsson—grandson of Björn the Jerusalem-Farer, great-grandson of Thorstein Eyjolfsson, and married to Olaf Loptsson's formidable sister Olöf. In May of 1457, Christian I extended to Björn Thorleifsson for "his faithfulness and willing service" the same honor that Torfi had received a few years earlier: a knighthood and the right to a coat of arms much like Torfi's, a white bear on a blue field.[13]

The most consistent object of Björn Thorleifsson's "faithfulness and willing service" was his own boundless ambition, and it says something about Christian I's mercurial governing style that he knighted a man whom he had recently called to account for pocketing the income of Skálholt see. Björn had ostensibly been looking after the bishopric's affairs in the continuing absence of "Bishop" Marcellus, and the sources certainly show that he plundered and debauched there. When Christian I wrote to the Icelanders in 1453 exhorting them to have no dealings with the English, who refused to pay harbor fees, he blamed this situation as well on Björn.[14]

But those two wily politicians, Christian I and Björn, clearly had more in common than otherwise, for besides obtaining a knighthood and the office of *hirðstjóri* after going to Copenhagen in late 1456 with tax moneys owed to crown and church, Björn was party to a bizarre hoax enacted by Christian I and "Bishop" Marcellus, now the royal chancellor. The Danish king complained in a letter to King Charles of France on April 10, 1457, that his Icelandic *hirðstjóri* Björn Thorleifsson, who had left home the previous winter on a royal errand, had met with bad weather, drifted to the Orkneys, and barely made it into harbor when he was set upon by Scots. Everyone aboard, including his high-born wife, and all their belongings as well as the king's, had been seized.[15] It was only 37 days after writing this letter that Christian I gave Björn his knighthood in Copenhagen, where Björn seems to have been staying for some days at his leisure. The Icelandic historian Thorsteinsson therefore reasons that either James II of Scotland had ransomed Björn from the pirates without prodding from the French king, and had given him a letter of safe-conduct to Denmark, or else the entire story (of which nothing was ever heard again) was made up to help juggle Christian's complicated relations with the Scots and the French alike. Björn had been at home still on August 7, 1456, which shows that he was late going abroad (probably in his own ship) and could count on a reasonably safe voyage as soon as autumn came and there were fewer pirates out at sea. It is also likely that he had been compelled by a special messenger named Daniel Kepken, a close associate of the king and of "Bishop Marcellus of Skálholt," to take this money to Copenhagen.[16]

Marcellus was the ideal helpmate for a monarch in need of money, because he was both completely unscrupulous and, being supposedly firmly entrenched in the church hierarchy, well positioned to funnel church money into the royal coffers. We know that Christian I was not particular about where he got his money, for in June of 1455 he had taken from the sacristy in Roskilde cathedral, for his own use, the money that had been collected for a joint Dano-Portuguese war against the Turks and for the relief of the king of Cyprus.[17] Lest his fellow monarchs think him short on valor, piety, and troubles, he wrote to King Alfonso V of Aragon and Naples in 1456, telling him of his frequent wars in Norway against Tartars, Cumanites, Lapps, and other heathens. Indeed, there was so much unrest all around that there was a danger the Norwegians might go over to the Russians. Christian then apprised Alfonso of his continuing war with the Swedish king and predicted he would also face trouble with the English king because of Iceland.[18]

In his wisdom, King Christian therefore empowered Marcellus "of Skál-holt" to license Englishmen wishing to trade in Iceland. Between the spring of 1456 and September of 1465, Marcellus issued seven such patents to men from Hull, Bristol, and London. Among those who benefited was the wealthy Bristol merchant John Shipward.[19] Shipward's licenses from various sources were both numerous and usefully vague, as were some of his accounts of where he had obtained his imported wares. On July 22, 1461, for example, he received a license from the new English king, Edward IV, to bring back to England from Iceland the *Julian* of Fowey, which he had sent from Bristol laden with merchandise on the strength of a letter-patent from the now deposed Henry VI. The *Julian* had then supposedly been re-loaded in Iceland with "other merchandise of no little value"—but when the ship actually returned to Bristol on August 25, it was entered in the Customs Accounts as having come from "Norbarn" (Bergen), along with two other ships.[20]

There would have been no reason in this period for the *Julian* to go to Norway after it had been to Iceland. Regardless of what caused these supple official records, they obviously would have allowed room for a profit-able voyage to Greenland. As before, owners of a Greenland cargo would have been foolish to publicize a trade connection known to only a few, since English import duty was due on stockfish no matter what its foreign origin, and since the Dano-Norwegian crown would have been quick to insist that any trade and fishing restrictions concerning Iceland also applied to Greenland.

For a suitable fee, both the Danish and the English crowns were willing to issue generous trading licenses, and a license as vague as the one given in 1470 to John Forster of Bristol and his partner to sail to Iceland or any other parts for fish and other goods, exporting any except Staple goods, required no subterfuge of any kind.[21] The English were also ready to sail without any licenses at all and, if necessary, to lie about the origin of their goods when they returned home. There was nothing to stop them from continuing to sail wherever they saw an opportunity to fish or trade, in the large area over which they still exercised control. This included the approaches to Greenland.

It is a fair guess that most of the English ships that went to Greenland in this period continued to fish off the east coast, rather than sail deep into the southwestern fjords where the Norse still lived. For reasons to be discussed in Chapter Nine, sailings into the Norse settlements were most likely the province of the occasional merchant ship with good connections and every intention of keeping interlopers away. Christian I certainly had no financial interest in Greenland that he was aware of, so there was no need to mention that country even *pro forma* when, for example, Anglo-Danish negotiations in 1465 produced an agreement permitting licensed English sailings to Iceland, but not to Hålogaland and Finnmark except when weather conditions interfered.[22]

It made no dent in the number of ships arriving from Bristol and elsewhere in England when Christian I on July 28, 1466, canceled *all* his Iceland sailing privileges granted to the English, because Edward IV had refused to ratify an article in the 1465 treaty concerning toll to be paid by ships passing through the Baltic Straits.[23] But the Danish king's decision brought to a head tensions that had been mounting in Iceland since he came to power and allowed his policies to be implemented in Iceland by the likes of Björn Thorleifsson, Marcellus, and Daniel Kepken.

These three men were so tightly linked in their execution of power that little can have escaped their notice. Until he died in 1465, Daniel Kepken was the king's main liaison with the Icelandic chieftains, especially with Björn. He had also been secretary and scribe to Marcellus, who continued to keep a firm hand over the Skálholt coffers and personally appointed his episcopal ombudsmen there.[24] Björn Thorleifsson had enjoyed that position in the early 1450s, as already noted.

Bishop Matthew "of Holar," whose appointment was at least as dubious as that of Marcellus, considered himself the Skálholt ombudsman in July of 1460 and threatened Bishop Andres (Anders Mus) "of Greenland" with excommunication if he performed any episcopal functions in his, Matthew's, jurisdiction without having been "cleansed" of matters raised against him before Archbishop Olaf of Nidaros.[25] But Matthew soon discovered that it took more than self-assertion to stay at the center of power—it required the right political alliances. That August, we find the aforementioned Bishop Andres "of Gardar" throwing his weight around as the Skálholt ombudsman and comfortably linking up with Björn Thorleifsson. In September of the following year, he made Björn a gift of property that had belonged to the priest Jon Jonsson, in whose ouster from office Andres had just connived. It is clear that Andres had good connections in Iceland even before he came out there, for Akra-Kristin's husband, Torfi Árason, had bethought him in his will in 1459 when both men were in Bergen.[26]

The southwest of Iceland was the closest any Gardar bishop had come to his own see since about 1378, and there is no reason to suppose that Bishop Andres ever went to Greenland either, because by 1466 he had obtained an office in Sweden. He stayed in Scandinavia until his death prompted the 1481 appointment of Bishop Jacob "of Gardar," another Dane.[27] Nor is it likely that anyone during Bishop Andres's Icelandic sojourn had boasted to his face of trading directly with his actual see, although Thorsteinsson takes it for granted that Andres had many dealings with the English merchants, since Skálholt see received a lot of its taxes in stockfish.[28]

Fees, fines, and confiscations were as much to be avoided by the English as ever, and so was Björn Thorleifsson, who had been made *hirðstjóri* of all Iceland in 1461.[29] His responsibility for maintaining the crown's trade interests included collecting customs payments from foreign merchants, and he was spurred on by the knowledge that much of the money was for his own pockets. Especially after the 1466 rift between Edward IV and Christian I, Björn's ruthless methods earned him many enemies among both the English and his fellow countrymen, but his career before that point had not won him many friends either. Eventually his luck ran out: around Michaelmas of 1467, men from Lynn killed Björn Thorleifsson at Rif in Hafnarfjord, near present-day Reykjavik. Men from Bristol were also around at the time and may have been involved as well.[30] His attackers dumped him in the sea, robbed his household of everything, captured his son Thorleif, and burned his farm. Thorleif was ransomed by his mother Olöf Loptsdaughter, and together they went to complain to Christian I in Copenhagen, after having taken furious revenge on the English.[31]

A generation or two had now passed since anyone in Iceland was likely to have had direct contact with Greenland, so strong personal ties would have shriveled along with the purely commercial ones. Given their family backgrounds and extensive contacts, however, both Björn and Olöf must nevertheless have known that the English fished off the Greenland banks. And, like their predecessors Björn the Jerusalem-Farer and Thorstein Olafsson, they must have been aware that a few Englishmen were trading with the Norse Greenlanders. It is conceivable that Björn had enraged one or two Bristol merchants by demanding a cut from their trade with Greenland, just because he felt entitled to such payments as the king's ombudsman, but nothing in the written records says so.

Until just a few years before Björn was murdered, others besides Björn and his inner circle could still obtain firsthand information about those last

Icelandic voyages to Greenland and the evident renewal of interest in Vínland, for the children of Brand Halldorsson, one of the 1408 Hvalsey wedding guests, settled their paternal inheritance as late as July of 1464.[32] Brand's sons, too, remained in the Icelandic power elite by associating themselves closely with the central government in Copenhagen and its determination to control foreign trade in Iceland. They also cemented their position at home in time-honored fashion. For example, in 1467 Hrafn Brandsson married Margret, the daughter of Thorstein Olafsson's cousin Eyjolf Arnfinnsson. That same year, the widowed Akra-Kristin Thorsteinsdaughter arranged a union between the Lawman Finnbogi Jonsson and Málfrid, her daughter by Torfi Arason, thus keeping a firm grip on power.[33]

Thorleif Björnsson (the great-grandson of Björn the Jerusalem-Farer) wasted no time in filling the power void left by his murdered father in 1467. By this time, both Daniel Kepken and Marcellus were also dead. Thorleif had served Bishop Andres "of Gardar" while the latter was Marcellus's Skálholt *officialis*, and this apprenticeship probably added to the callousness Thorleif displayed during his subsequent career as *hirðstjóri*.[34] He must have had personal charm, however, for while consanguinity long stood in the way of his legal marriage to Thorstein's and Sigrid's granddaughter Ingvild (Akra-Kristin's daughter by Helgi Gudnason), they lived together despite church disapproval and produced at least thirteen children.

Björn Thorleifsson's murder in 1467 was just one manifestation of the rift between the Danish and English kings, which resulted in a state of war between the two countries from 1468 to 1473, with renewed fighting in 1475.[35] Christian I now openly encouraged the capture of English ships at sea, starting with a 1468 seizure of four English ships in the Sound. The Englishmen involved said the capture was in revenge for the murder of Björn. Edward IV wrote to Christian I and angrily demanded his subjects' release, but in vain. Thinking that perhaps the Hanse were behind this, the English threw all the Hanseatic merchants in London in prison.[36]

English suspicions were not unfounded, for chief among the privateers employed by Christian I were Didrik Pining and Hans Pothorst, both originally from the Hanse city of Hildesheim. According to the German historian Klaus Friedland, "[t]he history of Didrik Pining's Hanseatic, Danish, and Icelandic relations appears to be significant in determining how Denmark tried to control the penetration of the North."[37] "Tried to control"— a euphemism for "failed to control"—is the key phrase when dealing with Iceland, where Anglo-Hanse relations gained a potential for disaster after Christian I gave the Hanse the right to trade there in 1468, and where Didrik Pining had close dealings with Thorleif Björnsson after 1478.[38]

Before focusing on Pining as Christian I's tool against the English in Iceland, it is necessary to clear up some common misconceptions about Pining's and Pothorst's supposed careers as North Atlantic explorers prior to 1478, and as Greenland-based pirates around 1494. While there is plenty of evidence that they were notable sea captains and privateers both before and after King Christian's death, there is nothing to show that they were engaged in a voyage of exploration at any time, nor that they conducted pirate raids from a base off the east coast of Greenland.[39] These assumptions evolved from various later sources, including Olaus Magnus's *De gentibus septentrionalis* (1555) and a letter that the Danish historian Louis Bobé found in the Danish National Archives in 1909.

The letter, written in Dutch in March of 1551 by Carsten Grypp, mayor of the old Hanse city of Kiel, was addressed to Christian III of Denmark in the obsequious tone of one flattered to serve royalty, in this case by procuring books and maps.[40] Grypp described a map of Iceland, recently published in Paris, whose legends said that Iceland was twice the size of Sicily, and that

the two sea captains Pining and Pothorst who, in the days of Your Royal Majesty's grandfather Christian I, at the request of His Royal Majesty of Portugal, etc., were sent off in some ships to seek new islands and lands in the North, have erected— on the rock Hvitserk, which lies before Greenland [*vor Gronlandth*] and directly opposite to the Snæfell Glacier in Iceland—a large structure [*eyn groidth baa*], because of the Greenland pirates who with many small ships without bottom [floorboards?—*szunder bodem*] launch surprise attacks on other ships. . . .

Extrapolating from Grypp's letter, the Danish historian Sofus Larsen in 1925 produced three interrelated theories that have enjoyed a long and vigorous life. The first is that Pining and Pothorst had been involved in a voyage of northern discovery requested by the Portuguese king, organized by the Danish king, and piloted by a Norwegian named Jon Skolp (Scolvus), said by several much later sources to have been on such a voyage in 1476. The second is that an expedition by João Vaz Corte-Real, supposedly taking place in the same period, had actually been under Pining-Pothorst-Skolp management. The third is that this joint expedition must therefore have taken place in 1473, rather than in 1476, because João Vaz Corte-Real is known to have been back home by 1476.[41]

Neither the Grypp letter, so reminiscent of medieval travelers' tales in its description of those Greenland pirates in their small boats, nor any of the other vague sources summoned to support it justify Larsen's circular reasoning. Deftly demolishing Larsen's exploration *ménage à quatre*, S. E. Morison shows that the sixteenth- and seventeenth-century sources supposedly confirming the story had merely fed off each other, sometimes in an effort to claim pre-Columbian exploration success on the part of one nation or another.[42] This last argument is one Morison often uses in various contexts, but in this case he appears to be right.

The Skolp/Scolvus story has no useful bearing on the greater picture of early North Atlantic exploration, and Grypp's letter does not mention it at all. Larsen was on flimsy ground both here and in thinking the letter constitutes evidence that Pothorst and Pining went exploring for the Danish king. Propelled by servility, and full of supposed information gained from the new map, Mayor Grypp merely gave a contemporary twist to old tales about two feisty sea rovers who were known to have served both Christian I and his successor, King Hans.

David B. Quinn, taking a moderate view, argues that we have sufficient documentary evidence of Dano-Portuguese contacts over West Africa between 1440 and 1461 to make a joint expedition around 1472 believable. He also notes that since the east coast of Greenland was exploited from Iceland both before and after 1480, Pothorst and Pining could well have made a voyage as far as to the west coast of Greenland, even if there is no evidence that he and his companions attempted to sail farther west than that.[43]

My own view is that if either Pothorst or Pining ever found themselves to the west of Iceland, it would have been in pursuit of English ships and not to explore on behalf of their king, whose focus was Baltic and Continental to such a degree that not once did he concern himself with Greenland. Not until *after* the beginning of English, Spanish, and Portuguese exploration success did a Danish monarch so much as inquire about his forgotten Norwegian colony.

Morison's spyglass has always been trained on the Iberian Peninsula rather than on the Scandinavian one, so in discarding the very notion that the Portuguese king would persuade Christian I to do his northern exploration for him and let Pining and Pothorst be in charge, he is not aware that the Scandinavian political situation also made such a voyage highly unlikely. Repeating what little mention there was in later sources about Skolp/Scolvus, Pole or Dane, Morison finds it conceivable that such a person may have rounded Cape Farewell and "looked into Davis Strait" around the year 1476 as claimed, but he makes no such allowances for the "pirate pair" Pining and Pothorst.

Neither in 1473, in 1476, nor in any other year before his death in 1481 would Christian I have had money or thought for such an exploration enterprise, whether for himself or to suit the Portuguese king—who in any case preferred to encourage voyages of exploration by his own citizens. In 1472, Christian had suffered the humiliation of seeing the bishoprics of Orkney and Shetland transferred from the archdiocese of Nidaros to that of St. Andrews.[44] It was another unwelcome distraction for Christian I that the Nordic Union was cracking, in reaction to the nationalism making itself felt all over Europe. In the fall of 1471, while Christian was already deeply embroiled in his controversy with the English, he had been wounded and had a couple of teeth knocked out during a Swedish uprising. Forced to give up his claim to Sweden, he was somewhat freer to focus on his problems with both the Hanse and the English, as well as on what he saw as the growing encroachment of papal tax collectors. A royal journey to Rome in 1474, billed as a pilgrimage, was in fact a business trip to discuss finances with the Curia, arranged by a king who saw himself as a tough international negotiator. He thought that his chance of fame and fortune lay not in the North, but in friendship with foreign princes, and it was France and not Portugal he considered his natural ally against the English, who now were showing signs of clashing head-on with the Hanse both in England and in Iceland.[45]

The Hanse did not at first appear in a hurry to establish direct trade with Iceland, although we know that men from Bremen and Braunschweig prepared to go out there in 1469. But two years later, the English in Iceland grew perturbed when two Dutch ships from Amsterdam landed in Hafnarfjord, and a German Bergen-trader also arrived.[46] The English evidently began to feel crowded, and in both 1474 and 1475 vicious fighting broke out in Hafnarfjord between the Hanse and Englishmen from Hull and Bristol. The Danish king's response was to make a royal governor (*höfuðsmaðr*) of his well-seasoned privateer Didrik Pining and send him out to Iceland in 1478.[47] Pining was the first person to hold that title; it is unclear from the sources whether he displaced or governed concurrently with Thorleif Björnsson that first year.

A peace treaty signed in Utrecht in 1473 had not solved the problems connected with English trade and fishing in Iceland, nor had Pining's piracy provided any victory or solution.[48] Specific sources about Pining's dealings with the English are few, but it is clear that he systematically forced them out of the best Icelandic harbors and precipitated a series of English raids along the coast as well as attacks against the governor's residence.[49] He may have done this with more help from people like Thorleif Björnsson than from the Hanse, but this is difficult to sort out, especially since the Hanse were divided among themselves. The Lübeck and Bergen Hanse were opposed to direct voyages between Hanse cities and Iceland, and in 1481 a letter from the Norwegian National Council to Lübeck requested that henceforth all Iceland trade should go through Bergen.[50]

The moves made by both Didrik Pining and Thorleif Björnsson in the complicated Icelandic-English-Danish-Hanse game, and supposedly directed by Christian I until his death in 1481 and afterwards by his son Hans, show neither consistency nor a master plan. King Hans is in any event said to have suffered from periodic madness.[51] Didrik Pining and Thorleif Björnsson were interested in power and wealth for themselves, in the useful guise of loyalty to the crown, but they could not control events. They wanted to keep foreign merchants trading directly with Iceland, where taxes would be payable to the local royal representatives (that is, to themselves), rather than leave that privilege to Bergen, but the foreigners had to be restrained.

Such tutorials required political manipulation and financial backing. The year Pining became royal governor (1478), he had supported Thorleif's ongoing struggle to marry his cousin Ingvild, and the following year, Thorleif gave Pining much silver and a horn made of walrus ivory to pay for a license from King Hans, the new occupant of the Danish throne, and to help ensure the legitimacy of his children with Ingvild. Thorleif and Ingvild's financial agreement, which constituted the merger of two of Iceland's greatest fortunes and political dynasties, was dated August 23, 1484. This happened only two years before Thorleif died, but while both he and Pining were still at the height of their power and influence with the Danish crown.[52]

The summer of 1484, there had been complaints that Pining and his men raped women and stole money from the farmers. The English fishermen and traders also felt threatened by recent events in and around Iceland, and Richard III must have taken their worries seriously, for that spring he told sailors and merchants from Norfolk and Suffolk that they needed a license to sail to Iceland, and that they should go in a convoy with ships from Hull. Pining had returned as *hirðstjóri* the year before, after a couple of years' absence from Iceland; he may well have spent those years privateering against the English, just as he did in 1486, when men in English port cities complained to king and Parliament that "Germans" were preventing all sailing from England to Bergen and Iceland. That year, German merchants in London wrote to their Danzig brethren that according to the English king, Pining and Pothorst were currently engaged in piracy with five ships outfitted by the Hanse. The London Hanse had been at some pains to explain that Pining was the Danish king's admiral and had nothing to do with them.[53]

It is quite clear that after 1486, Hanse trade with both Iceland and the Faroes was increasing openly, in full view of the Bergen men and the Danish king.[54] The lines are blurred, however, in the three-way struggle among the English, the Hanse, and the Danish crown, for while Pining and Pothorst were serving the Danish king, under King Hans they were going after both some of the Hanse as well as the English. But in the several battles between the English and the Germans in Iceland during the next few years—which Thorsteinsson thinks resulted from fierce competition about who would get established on shore first in the spring—the crown's representatives distinctly favored the Germans.[55]

Officially, Pining was still King Hans's chief ombudsman in Iceland, but he was absent a good deal of the time. He let the German Heinrich Mäding act in his stead, continuing his close relationship with such powerful Icelandic chieftains as Akra-Kristin's son-in-law Finnbogi Jonsson.[56] In the spring of 1490, however, Pining came out to Iceland after King Hans of Denmark-Norway and Henry VII of England had signed a new treaty about trade and fishing in Iceland. In this treaty, King Hans gave the English the right to trade and fish in Iceland as long as they obtained the necessary license every seven years, but this clause was deleted at the *Alþing* that summer, when Pining and the Icelandic chieftains confirmed the treaty and set the conditions for foreign merchants' activities in Iceland.[57]

This was the so-called *Piningsdómur* (Pining's Judgment), whose main tenets were effective for a long time, and which decreed among other things that no foreigners could spend the winter in Iceland except in an emergency, and that no Icelanders were to hire on as servants or sailors on a foreign ship. The following year saw even stricter measures against foreign fishermen, who were forbidden to operate in Icelandic waters at all unless they also engaged in trade. These restrictions of 1490 and 1491, which obviously favored the Hanse, were renewed and amplified in 1500 and 1501.[58]

Thorleif Björnsson had been dead for four years when the *Piningsdómur* was announced. Although these laws turned out to be Pining's swan song in Iceland, there was always someone ready to step into the power void. Thorleif had a brother named Einar, who in greed and ambition was a match for any man in Iceland, and who regarded himself as his brother's heir, both politically and otherwise. For example, when Thorleif's widow Ingvild inherited one-third of Akra-Kristin's property in 1490, Einar claimed he was entitled to another third.[59]

A letter written at the *Alþing* of 1491 reveals that Einar had a traditional excuse for wanting to enhance his own considerable wealth. In this letter, 25 men, led by Finnbogi Jonsson, asked King Hans to appoint Einar Björnsson *hirðstjóri* of all Iceland. Didrik Pining had reportedly died abroad, and his deputy in Iceland (a younger namesake) *had neither the money nor the property to pay fines and damages if he were to commit an injustice against another man.* In addition, the agreement with the Norwegian authorities had long been that only Icelanders (able to pay for their wrongs) should be lawmen and royal administrators in that country, unless the Icelandic farmers consented to a different arrangement. Finnbogi Jonsson, who pushed this argument with King Hans, was married to Ingvild's sister Málfrid Torfadaughter, so the remaining third of Akra-Kristin's wealth no doubt provided malpractice insurance for his own office as lawman.[60]

Despite the *Alþing*'s plea to have power returned to the natives, Hanse influence in Iceland grew along with the Englishmen's frustration. On August 6, 1489, the draft of a peace agreement was returned to the Danes by messenger from Westminster after Henry VII had made last-minute changes to it. Point four was changed to read that all English subjects should be able to sail safely to trade and fish in Iceland, against paying a stipulated annual sum to the Danish king. Henry finally signed the agreement over a year and a half later, on May 2, 1491, after further pressure from the Danish crown.[61]

Some merchants from Hull showed a copy of this peace treaty to the *hirðstjóri* Didrik Pining the Younger when they arrived in Iceland that summer, but it provided small protection against Hanse merchants also lying at anchor in Hafnarfjord. The English barely escaped with their lives and claimed to have suffered a loss amounting to £1016 sterling.[62] The attack is easier to understand if seen against events in 1486, when the *Trinity* of London had docked in Bristol after a stopover in Galway, during which they had sold a Hanse ship as well as eleven Hanse crew members seized in Hafnarfjord. At that time, Bristol already claimed to be suffering economic decline because of the deteriorating situation in Iceland, so tempers must have been running high on both sides.[63]

After three decades of instability in Iceland had made it increasingly unprofitable for the English to fish or trade there, relations between the two countries improved enough by 1500 so that English ships again flocked to the coasts of Iceland.[64] By that time, however, the English had long roamed the North Atlantic to northernmost Norway, Iceland, Greenland, and eventually beyond Greenland, and they were far less dependent on the Iceland fisheries than before. As will be discussed below, some of them must have made use of the Newfoundland and Labrador fisheries well before John Cabot came upon that region in 1497.

In consequence of their wide scope, the English had produced a class of sailors with experience of the *entire* North Atlantic, gained from sailing on many different ships and routes. This development brings an interesting light to bear on a story from *Relation du Groenlande*, the oldest known description of Greenland in a major European language. Its author, the Frenchman Isaac de la Peyrère, drew on information obtained when he was in Copenhagen around 1645. One of his sources, the Danish physician and scientist Ole Worm, told him that he had personally read an old Danish manuscript stating that in 1484, early in the reign of King Hans, some forty sailors in Bergen had claimed they made annual voyages to Greenland and brought valuable goods away with them. According to Worm's source, Hanse merchants in Bergen had been enraged at these Greenland-farers' refusal to trade with them and invited them all to a supper that ended with the hosts killing the guests. De la Peyrère took it for granted that the Greenland-farers in question were Norwegian, and since he knew that shipping between Greenland and Bergen had ceased long before 1484, he doubted the whole tale.[65] Later historians have taken their cue from him. Yet, despite the dramatic finale, the tale may nevertheless contain some truth if we allow for a different nationality among the Greenland-farers. We know that English codfish merchants continued to show up at the Bergen Staple in this period; among their crews there may well have been many who were familiar enough with the Greenland route to brag about it to the Hanse. Relations between the two rival groups were notoriously bad in Bergen at the time—in both 1475 and 1476, for example, merchants from Hull and Bristol had been accused of plundering Hanse merchants there.[66] It would not be surprising, therefore, if a record once existed of a particularly nasty brawl between some of the German merchants and English sailors with Greenland experience.

The crew on English codfishing and merchant ships did not necessarily consist only of people from the British Isles. As noted earlier, the *Lönguret-tarbót* of 1450 forbade foreign ships to carry Icelandic emigrants, and the *Piningsdómur* of 1490 stipulated that no Icelanders were to hire on as servants or sailors aboard a foreign ship. Both laws suggest that emigration and foreign employment constituted a perennial problem. This assumption is borne out by Mary E. Williams's discovery in the 1484 alien subsidy roll for Bristol that 48 or 49 Icelandic men and boys were in the service of Bristol households that year. We do not know when, how, or in what capacity they had arrived (Quinn speculates that at least some had come to learn a trade or a craft), but we do know that their masters had to pay a subsidy of two shillings per person. These householders represented a broad spectrum of people trading with France, Spain, Portugal, and Madeira, as well as with Iceland, and the list included names we shall encounter again: William Spencer, John Eliot, and Richard Ameryk.[67]

One obvious advantage to any English skipper hiring Icelandic crew members would be their knowledge of local Icelandic waters; another would be their ability to communicate with both Norwegians and Greenlanders as well as with their fellow countrymen. It is clear that at least some of the Icelanders in Bristol made themselves useful to the local merchant community, for a "William Yslond" listed as an Icelandic servant on the 1484 roll was a naturalized Englishman by 1492 and himself a Bristol merchant, trading to Lisbon with Robert Thorne, William Spencer, and John Pynke—men who, Quinn notes, "all at times come into our roster of enterprising westward-voyaging merchants."[68]

This westward enterprise was gradual but inexorable, driven by a deliberate quest for new supplies of fish that would not involve war over the cargo. The English were aided in their search by their accumulated sailing lore, by chance discoveries, and by whatever information they could pick up in various harbors. We must also take into account the likelihood that some general knowledge of earlier sailings to Greenland from the northern British and Western Isles had survived.

Quinn notes that in sailing all the way to Iceland, the Bristolmen demonstrated their ability to navigate long distances over open sea, and that they also had long experience with the far from easy voyage to Lisbon and other Iberian ports.[69] Matching their accumulated sailing experience were their contacts with foreign ports and sailors throughout the entire known Atlantic region.

Galway in western Ireland was as crucial in this information chain as Lisbon, Bristol, Bergen, or any of the Icelandic ports. As mentioned in Chapter Seven, it was reasonable for northbound Bristolmen to sail along the west coast of Ireland to avoid the pirate-infested Hebridean passage. It is clear that this was still considered a good route in 1485, when a Bristol ship wrecked on the west coast of Ireland on its return from Iceland, while in 1486 another Bristol ship sold the consignment of captive Hansemen in Galway noted above.[70] A stopover in Irish ports such as Galway could provide either additional cargo or a switch in cargo, perhaps to fool Bristol customs inspectors.[71] Extra crew might be hired for the northbound voyage—a possibility to ponder in connection with Christian I's *Löngurettarbót* of 1450, which threatened both Englishmen and Irishmen with arrest and forfeiture of ships and goods if they sailed to Iceland. Quinn surmises that Irishmen were also used as seasonal workers as soon as the Newfoundland fisheries were established in about 1502, but he cautions that we have no proof of this practice for the early period.[72]

A variety of sources, including early maps, confirm that Ireland was an integral part of the Atlantic economic network. The country's Viking heritage and its close commercial connections with Bristol virtually guaranteed not only Irish involvement in the Icelandic cod business, but the frustration of historians trying to trace the origin and destination of various types of cargo. The latter efforts are further complicated because transshipments through Irish ports were also a feature of the Bristolmen's southbound voyages, and because Galway, the center of Irish pilgrim traffic to Compostella, had constant dealings with both Spain and Portugal.[73]

Given Galway's importance as a transit point for information as well as for goods, it is of some moment that Christopher Columbus visited Galway early in his career. In a recent article, Quinn has argued that this visit probably occurred toward the end of a northern voyage that had taken Columbus as far as Iceland, and that had begun with his arrival in England aboard a Genoese trading ship, possibly in Southampton, from which he could easily have joined a Bristol ship bound for Iceland. While Quinn finds no reason to doubt Columbus's story that he went to Iceland, he nevertheless ques-

tions the explorer's statement that he had left for Iceland as early as February in 1477. Quinn claims that the fishing and trading season in Iceland
lasted at most from May to September.[74]

Actually, since time immemorial, fishermen in both Norway and Iceland had left home in February in small, open boats to begin the so-called
spring fishing season amid ice, snow, and howling gales. English fishermen
would have known when they were most likely to catch fish in Iceland and
could have left home port any time between February and May, returning
home in August and September.[75] Columbus (or his son) may have muddled
his recollections, as Quinn suggests, but the claim about the time of departure for Iceland is not suspect in and of itself.

Columbus also said that in Galway he saw a dead man and woman who
had washed ashore in their boat. Both the people and their craft were so
exotic-looking that they were immediately assumed to have come from a
country unknown to the Europeans. They may well have been Eskimos
who had drifted off course.[76] In any case, since they washed in from the
west, their arrival evidently confirmed that exotic lands and peoples existed
beyond the Ocean Sea, as already claimed by Galway sailors and foreign
visitors alike. Native pride would have kept St. Brendan's exploits fresh,
and accounts of unfamiliar land glimpsed by storm-tossed crews must have
joined both vague tales of Vínland and reports of relatively uneventful
working voyages to such well-known places as Iceland, or to fishing banks
so far away that only the best equipped and most enterprising fishermen
made use of them at this time.

The authenticity of Columbus's experiences on his Iceland voyage,
which are known to us only through the biography written by his son Ferdinand, has been the subject of much controversy. The discussion grew more
heated in 1924, when Charles de la Roncière introduced to the world the
so-called Paris Map (now in the Bibliothèque Nationale) and stoutly declared that Columbus's information about Iceland was only hearsay gar-
nered in Bristol, where Columbus had also been. De la Roncière was nevertheless certain that the map must have been made for "the Catholic Kings"
in 1491 by either Christopher Columbus or his brother Bartholomew, who
was a skilled mapmaker, and that it provided significant clues to Columbus's geographical knowledge on the eve of his first trans-Atlantic voyage.[77]

Kenneth Nebenzahl recently gave it as his opinion that the Paris Map
may just have been *commissioned* by Christopher Columbus; he finds it
too professional to be the work of either of the Columbus brothers. By contrast, the French map scholar Monique Pelletier believes that everything
about the map points to one or the other of the Columbus brothers, but she
disagrees with De la Roncière's assertion that it had been made to impress
Ferdinand and Isabella.[78] In yet another recent analysis, the English map

expert and historian Helen Wallis supports Quinn's theory that Bartholomew Columbus began the map in conjunction with his 1488–89 fund-
raising trip to England. Wallis affirms that the Ptolemy-based legends on
the Paris Map prove its close connection with Christopher Columbus, and
she believes that the map may also provide evidence that Columbus went
to Iceland. As to the map's date, she points out that since it depicts a Spanish
flag flying over Granada, it must have been completed after the expulsion
of the Moors on January 2, 1492, but before Columbus's return from his
1492 discoveries, of which nothing is shown.[79]

It is fortunate that exactly who drew the Paris Map is less important
in the present context than what the map may reveal about contemporary
knowledge of the northwestern Atlantic—knowledge considered worth
putting down on vellum. It is equally fortunate that there are useful guide-
lines for historians trying to extract information from old maps. One is to
heed R. A. Skelton, who warned against assuming that a cartographer was
cognizant of all previous work.[80] Another is to look for precedents just the
same. A third is to recognize that firsthand reports were tempered to varying degrees by cartographical theories, and that the lack of reliable surveying instruments made it difficult to assign accurate location or relative size
to an area, even when its existence was vouched for. A fourth guideline is
to estimate—if possible—how much information would have been available to an open-minded cartographer from *any* source, and to see if the
map under study corroborates evidence from other sources.

I believe the Paris Map represents knowledge that sailors and fishermen
familiar with the Bristol-Galway-Iceland route could have shared with Columbus; that there are known cartographical precedents for the map's delineations; and that those precedents are based on actual experience. I also
think Wallis is right in considering the Paris Map proof that Columbus himself was in Iceland and relayed in that map both what he saw himself and
what he heard from English crew members on the way. The kind of voyage
he described would have been a rather common one by 1477.

Exclusive of a separate *mappamundi*, the upper left quarter of the Paris
Map depicts Norway and the British Isles, with many place names shown
in Ireland. The North Atlantic is studded with smallish islands of random
shape and placement, from the Irish Sea all the way north to Iceland. The
North Atlantic *is* full of islands, as fifteenth-century mariners and cartographers would have known. West of Norway, the map shows two islands. The
nearer and smaller one, unnamed, was perhaps intended to represent Hålogaland, a well-known Norwegian destination for codfish merchants, which
even then was often thought of as an island. The next island westward is
large, deeply indented by fjords and bays, and features three big ecclesiastical buildings that probably represent Skálholt and Holar cathedrals and a

monastery. Although this island, too, is unnamed, it is clearly Iceland, which makes a fairly large island just below, "Frixlandia," baffling in its superfluousness.

De la Roncière thought Columbus had confused the location of the Faroes with that of Iceland and had compounded the confusion by believing that Ptolemy's island of "Tile" was "the one called by the moderns Frislandia." This muddle supposedly accounts for a Latin inscription near "Frixlandia."[81] The legend refers to

an island full of mountains, stone and ice, with an ever severe climate, called Iceland in the local language and Tile in Latin. There, at a great distance from the British Islands, on account of the cold, no other food is to be had than frozen fish. The islanders exchange them, in guise of money, for wheat and flour or other necessaries that the English bring them annually. It is a rugged and wild population, from what the English say, and it lives in poor subterranean abodes during the six months when the sea is frozen.

The legends on the Paris Map are taken from Pierre d'Ailly's *Imago Mundi* (Louvain, 1483), an annotated copy of which was in Columbus's library.[82] The passage just quoted, so reminiscent of Adam of Bremen's mid-eleventh-century effort to describe how the Icelanders lived, also shows an earnest attempt to relay information from an English source about this strange place.

Columbus's own notes suggest that he spent no time ashore in Iceland, for he has no information of his own about the Icelanders' "poor subterranean abodes" and diet of "frozen fish," while he juxtaposes personal experience with d'Ailly's hearsay information concerning the frozen sea:[83]

In the month of February 1477, I sailed one hundred leagues beyond the island of Tile, whose northern part is in latitude 73 degrees N. and not 65 degrees as some affirm, nor does it lie upon the meridian where Ptolemy says the West begins, but much farther west. And to this island, which is as big as England, the English come with their wares, especially from Bristol. When I was there, the sea was not frozen, but the tides were so great that in some places they rose twenty-six fathoms, and fell as much.

As already argued, February was a likely time for fishing doggers to begin leaving English ports for Iceland. Despite the flawed references to latitude and the note about the huge tides, both Columbus's account and the map legend above "Frixlandia" (obviously intended to describe the biggest island) show earnest attempts to pass on real information.[84] So does Columbus's reference to the ship's going "one hundred leagues beyond" Iceland (presumably by the captain's will and not that of Columbus), for it fits with the picture Thorsteinsson has provided of the Englishmen's relentless westward push in search of fish.

The northernmost parts of Iceland, including the large fishing banks at Bardargrunn and Deildargrunn off the West Fjords, practically touch the Arctic Circle, so Columbus could truthfully boast of having gone very far north. These banks may well have been where Columbus's skipper headed, not straight north from northern Iceland as assumed by Morison, among others.[85] Columbus claimed only to have gone *beyond* "Tile." Although "one hundred leagues" probably was a figure of speech denoting a great distance, he may conceivably have gone far enough west from the West Fjords to catch sight of the east coast of Greenland, some 287 kilometers away at the narrowest part of the strait and, in clear weather, visible from a third of the way out from Snæfellsnes.[86] Columbus's "league" represented 3.18 nautical miles of 2,000 yards.[87] If his statement is taken literally, the ship would have found itself fishing well down along the Greenland east coast, whose general aspect beyond a wide belt of sea ice would certainly have discouraged fantasies about a lush and spice-laden Asia. It is possible that Columbus got a glimpse of the islands near Ammassalik that Eirik the Red called Gunnbjarnarskerries, but not of Greenland's mainland, since those waters are often shrouded in fog. Or he may just have heard *tell* of islands to the west of Iceland.

If the Paris Map is any guide to Columbus's pre-1492 geographical knowledge of the far north, he did not associate land to the west of Iceland with a named Greenland. Way to the east, however, near "Tartary" in the thick of Asia, the map has a peninsula named "Grænlant." De la Roncière was mostly intrigued by its disassociation from Norway (with which other fifteenth-century maps connected it), and by the adjacent inscription "*Hic habitant populus monstruosus*," which he thought might imply knowledge of the supposedly defunct Greenlanders' dreadful fate.[88] To me, the most interesting aspect of this "Grænlant" is that the name is spelled more or less in the Norse vernacular, rather than in a Latinate form.

While "Frixlandia" on the Paris Map may represent a coast glimpsed by Columbus when voyaging "one hundred leagues beyond the Island of Tile," it may also just have been the cartographer's solution to a problem posed by an earlier map locating a "Fixlanda" so directly west of Ireland that it seemed an unlikely Iceland to a good navigator with personal experience of the route. At least one such map exists (Fig. 23), a portolano, or medieval navigational chart, belonging to the Biblioteca Ambrosiana in Milan. Said to be of Catalan orgin, it may date from circa 1480, about a decade before the Paris Map.[89] If the date assigned to it is correct, we must also consider the chart's relevance to the Bristol "Isle of Brazil" ventures of 1480 and 1481, which will be discussed shortly, for just like the Paris Map, the Catalan chart shows access to English information. This is hardly surprising, since the trade between Spain and England in this period was al-

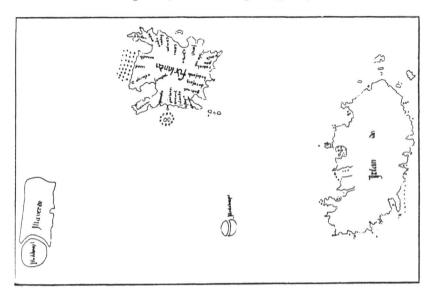

FIG. 23. Detail from a Catalan chart in the Biblioteca Ambrosiana in Milan, made ca. 1480. Greenland ("Illa verde") is correctly placed southwest of Iceland, and the location of "Fixlanda" (Iceland) relative to Ireland agrees with contemporary perceptions. Note also the double representation of "Illa de brazil." Source: Bjørnbo, "Cartographia Goenlandica," p. 125, reproduced by permission of Dansk Polarcenter, Copenhagen, publisher of *Meddelelser om Grønland*.

most entirely in the hands of Spaniards and Englishmen, who were often working together.[90]

   Thorsteinsson thinks the chart in Fig. 23 reveals firsthand knowledge of the northwestern Atlantic. The Norse Greenland colony was known among sailors to have a more southerly location than Iceland, and on this map Greenland ("Illa verde") is correctly placed southwest of Iceland, while the location of "Fixlanda" (Iceland), directly west of the northernmost part of a prominently drawn Ireland, agrees with the view King Christian I gave the cardinal of Cologne in a 1458 letter, in which he wrote that Iceland lies surrounded by ocean opposite to Great Britain. There are also signs of familiarity with Iceland itself, according to Thorsteinsson, in such placenames as "Porlana" (Portland, the Englishmen's name for Dyrholaey) and "Lavina" for the huge lavafield on the Reykjaness Peninsula.[91]

   Directly south of "Illa verde" in Fig. 23 lies a small, circular "Illa de brazil," and in mid-ocean another "Illa de brazil" is represented by facing semicircles, so stylized that they practically shout obedience to legend rather than to experience. The cartographer was obviously hedging his bets on the location of the storied "Isle of Brazil." He was also careful to delineate both "Illa verde" and its neighboring *second* "Illa de brazil" in an obviously stylized manner.

There is no single way to interpret this or any other early map, but it does seem to represent familiarity with the Iceland route as well as awareness of both an "Illa verde" (Green Island = Greenland) and another island that could be reached from Greenland, but that as yet was equally ill-defined. We do not know what maps were available to the person who drew or commissioned either this chart or the Paris Map. But we can say with fair certainty that both the Paris Map and the map in Fig. 23 grew out of the Anglo-Iberian information pool into which the Iceland trade drained during the second half of the fifteenth century, *before* John Cabot's voyages.

It is therefore worth returning to the Paris Map, which also shows an island in the extreme west of the Atlantic. No stylized pair of kidney beans this (although the map employs a similar device just east of Iceland), but a tripartite configuration, drawn with an attempt at realism and accompanied by an almost obliterated legend: "Here is the island called of the Seven Cities, a colony now peopled by Portugal; it is said from a report by Spanish ship-boys that silver is found there in the sand." De la Roncière, who deciphered the text, commented that in that same location, the Cantino Map of 1502 placed a wooded island discovered by Corte Real and named by him "Terra del Rey de Portugall." Fifty years after De la Roncière, Quinn argued that the reference may point to some kind of Portuguese discovery of land northwest of the Azores prior to 1490.[92]

We shall save a discussion of that controversy for Chapter Ten and focus for the moment on a Portuguese royal license issued in 1486, to Fernão Dulmo of Terceira and his partner Joham Affonso do Estreito of Madeira, for a voyage of discovery to "Island(s) or terra firma presumed to be the Island of Seven Cities."[93] It was an elaborately planned venture, involving two ships and expected to be of half a year's duration, for which pilots were hired and every financial and legal precaution taken. We do not know what, if anything, these men found, but it is hard to believe that such an expedition was in search of a will-o'-the-wisp, just as it seems doubtful that the islands appearing in the Ocean Sea from the first quarter of the fifteenth century onward, and variously called Antilia, the Isle of Brazil, or the Isle of Seven Cities, had no basis in maritime experience.

The Spanish and the Portuguese had gradually located and colonized archipelagoes within their reach, such as the Canaries, the Azores, the Madeira group, and the Cape Verde Islands.[94] Eventually, as the Paris Map and the portolan map in Fig. 23 demonstrate, they could also tap into the North Atlantic information network concerning islands sighted far out in the ocean. But because educated fifteenth-century Europeans thought the next continent to the west must be Asia, and because they preferred to make the unknown fit information reassuringly handed down from ancient legends, philosophers, and scientists, these sightings were judged to be of places already known through literature, whose location, subsequently forgotten, must now be ascertained again.[95]

The tripartite island of the Seven Cities in the Paris Map may represent the general Newfoundland area as perceived by Columbus from descriptions of the "Isle of Brazil" by Galway and Bristol mariners, and made to fit with lore about Antilia or the Island of the Seven Cities, where Spanish bishops supposedly settled in the eighth century after escaping from the Moors. Helen Wallis estimates the location of the map's "Seven Cities" as about 53°N.[96] This is the latitude of southern Labrador, just north of Newfoundland Island; it is also the approximate latitude of Galway. Either deliberate latitude sailing westward from Galway or a westward storm-sweep across the Atlantic could have carried a ship to Newfoundland and its rich fishing banks. But in the fifteenth century, it is more likely that the outward voyage to the Newfoundland and Labrador fishing grounds (once they had been located by English fishermen extending their activities beyond Iceland) was via Greenland, while the *return* voyage to Galway and Bristol could be undertaken on a relatively fast and easy course along latitude circa 53°N, picking up the late summer "westerlies" (Fig. 24) as well as the North Atlantic Drift, which sweeps generally eastward after the Labrador Current meets the Gulf Stream off the Newfoundland Banks.[97] Written sources suggest that this was the original procedure, and so does the Ruysch *mappamundi* published in the 1508 Rome edition of Ptolemy's *Geographia*.

There are many versions of the 1507–8 Ruysch *mappamundi*. When A. E. Nordenskiöld prepared his 1889 atlas, he used his own copy of the 1508 Rome edition to produce the facsimile of Ruysch's world map, part of which is shown in Fig. 25.[98] Nordenskiöld's Ruysch map differs from the version shown in both of the British Map Library's two copies of the 1508 Ptolemy in at least one important respect: it gives a name to the wide bay separating the large "Grvenlant" promontory from the area called "Terra Nova." The bay, which obviously represents the lower end of the Davis Strait, is named "Sinvs Grvenlantevs"—the Bay of Greenland.

Marcus Beneventanus wrote in "Orbis nova descriptio," his introduction to the section containing Ruysch's map in the 1508 Rome Ptolemy, that Ruysch reported having made a voyage to the new lands in the west, sailing on an English ship from the south of England along the 53d parallel and then "somewhat northwardly," observing many islands on the way. There is little reason to suppose that Ruysch lied about his voyage, which would have taken place around 1502–4, by which time Bristol fishermen and codfish merchants were already making regular use of the rich Newfoundland fishing banks.[99]

Ruysch's delineations of the coastlines incorporating Greenland, Labrador, and Newfoundland, and showing Iceland's relative position to Greenland, are remarkable for their attempts at realism in the midst of stylized isles and curious legends.[100] The Greenland promontory, for example, is very large; only the maps of Claudius Clavus and their progeny had so far conveyed this important and realistic feature. Claudius Clavus had no firsthand knowledge of Greenland, but he clearly had access to people who knew its approximate location relative to Norway and Iceland, and who told him that it was huge. The massive proportions of Greenland, the world's largest island, will make anyone feel dwarfed.

Where Ruysch differs radically from Clavus is in separating Greenland from the Asian-European landmass and locating it firmly to the *west* of a wide expanse of the North Atlantic. This is precisely how it would have appeared to someone approaching the region both physically and mentally from the British Isles, rather than from Norway. Ruysch, who evidently considered Greenland part of the approaches to the New World, saw the southwestern shore of the Davis Strait as a continuation of the landmass of

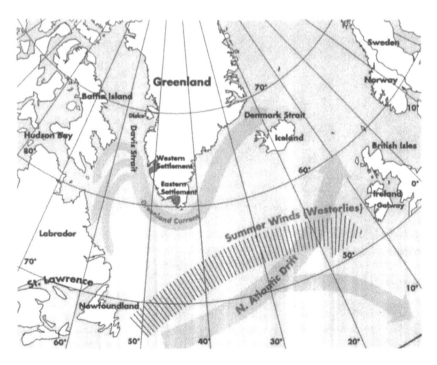

FIG. 24. Map of the North Atlantic showing prevailing currents and wind patterns. Source: David O. Seaver.

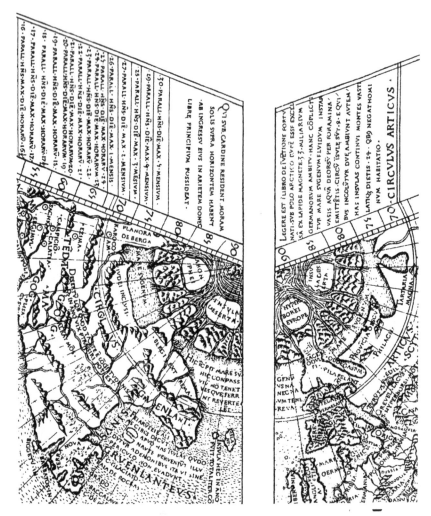

FIG. 25. The northwestern Atlantic region from Ruysch's 1507–8 *mappamundi*, showing Greenland and the Bay of Greenland. Source: Bjørnbo, "Cartographia Groenlandica," p. 187, reproduced by permission of Dansk Polarcenter, Copenhagen, publisher of *Meddelelser om Grønland*.

which the Greenland promontory was also a part. Since there is no reason to suppose that he actually went to Greenland, he must have gathered this information from the Englishmen with whom he sailed, or from people in Bristol while staying there.

Ruysch's map is evidence both of personal experience and of his having made the voyage to the New World in the company of people long acquainted with the northern codfish trade. Concerning a small island southwest of Iceland (where volcanic activity turns out to have been even more frequent than supposed), he notes that it had been "consumed by fire" in 1456.[101] And north of "Filapilant" he drew a small church named "Sancti Odulfi"—almost certainly St. Olaf's Church at Vardø, way up in Finnmark. The Norwegian archbishop had personally dedicated a church there in 1307, doubtless because that remote, codfish-rich region was as valuable to his coffers as the entire area was to the crown, both strategically and economically. Vardø and its church would have been known to English cod merchants from early on.[102]

Ruysch's English skipper probably followed a familiar route when he went from the south of England to latitude 53°N, from which he navigated "west in the direction of the east [Ruysch thought he was going toward Asia], somewhat northwardly."[103] As already noted, latitude 53°N encompasses both Galway and the southern part of Labrador; it is also the latitude Wallis assigns to the "Seven Cities" in the Paris Map. The Englishmen's name for the Isle of the Seven Cities was the Isle of Brazil—and as we shall see shortly, that was the professed destination of two Bristol expeditions that had set out in 1480 and 1481, some twenty years before Ruysch's own voyage.

Harrisse thought that Ruysch, a German, "seems never to have seen a chart made in Spain" (which would include both the Paris Map and the chart in Fig. 23), and he noted that four of Ruysch's five place-names on "Terra Nova" were new ones. Immediately southwest of the "Bay of Greenland" lies "C. Glaciato" (Icy Cape), which could represent anything from drift-ice accumulations at Cape Bauld to someplace in Labrador. "Baia de Rockas" (Rocky Bay) follows. "R. Grado," which has been tentatively translated by Harrisse as "the Large River," may indicate the St. Lawrence as described to Ruysch while he and his companions were heading north, away from Newfoundland Island.[104] The probable significance of the fourth and southernmost new name, "C. de Portogesi" (Cape of the Portuguese), will be discussed in Chapter Ten.

Ruysch's phrase "somewhat northwardly" does not tell us how far north they went. In conjunction with his map, however, the information he gave Beneventanus strongly suggests that his skipper was accustomed to fishing for cod and salmon along the Labrador coast, not just off the great banks running far into the Atlantic from the southeastern corner of New-foundland Island. Such a practice would have come naturally to Bristol fishermen familiar with a route developed as a result of a continued west-ward search for new fishing grounds, with Iceland as the original start-ing point.

The name "Bay of Greenland" for the lower Davis Strait implies that Ruysch's companions were familiar with a route that crossed this stretch of water *from* a known Greenland *to* the barely known "Terra Nova." After traversing the Denmark Strait from Iceland to Greenland's east coast, it would have been tempting for an enterprising English skipper to follow the Greenland Current (Fig. 24) down the east coast, past Cape Farewell, and up the southwest coast of Greenland, keeping clear of what remained of the sea ice in late summer. Either direct information from Norse Greenlanders or their own gradually acquired experience would eventually have caused the English to cross the Davis Strait, just as the Norse had done before them. The reward for crossing the Davis Strait would be much bigger cod—with fattier livers for coveted oil—than those to be found in the eastern At-lantic.[105]

We do not know when the first such crossing took place, but we do know that the English were no less capable, curious, or profit-oriented than their Norse predecessors in the same waters five centuries earlier. A case in point is the long and little-known voyage of the Englishman Thomas Buxer, who in 1498 sailed all the way from Iceland to San Sebastian in Spain with a cargo containing both codfish and a whale, thereby exposing himself to a Spanish fine of 150 ducats. As a sailor he was clearly a match for anyone, and yet we know about him only because his fine—still unpaid a year later—was a potential hindrance to his ambition of serving Queen Isabella, not because of his prowess at sea.[106]

After crossing the "Bay of Greenland" with a westward current, it is possible from any number of points along southwest Greenland to ride with the Labrador Current, which sweeps south at a speed of about 10 nautical miles per day and follows the *east* coast of Newfoundland Island before heading into the Atlantic, where it joins the Gulf Stream running east-northeast toward the British Isles (Fig. 24). The Norse had made good use of the same currents in the Davis Strait almost five centuries earlier. Helge Ingstad assumes that the Norse, too, would usually have avoided the Strait of Belle Isle with its fierce contrary currents and generally unpromising as-pect, just as they would have kept a wary eye out for skerries and for ice-bergs that had survived the summer melt.[107]

Long after English fishermen grew certain enough of their westward route to bypass Iceland completely, they would still have had to go far enough north to get their Greenland bearings before heading west on another reliable course, fishing down the Labrador-Newfoundland coast, and heading home along a latitude of about 53°N toward coasts so familiar that, under reasonable conditions, there was little chance of getting lost.

Northern ocean navigators still depended on knowledge of local conditions and on their ability to recognize coastlines. There were no serviceable maps comparable to the Mediterranean portolanos, and the crude navigational instruments available to fifteenth-century navigators made it difficult to measure latitude and impossible to measure longitude. Both the astrolabe and the quadrant (the latter said to have been used by the Portuguese navigator Diogo Gomes as early as 1460) depended on an artificial horizon, with which a ship's movements would interfere. Even under ideal conditions, determining latitude by observing the sun required such complex calculations that around 1485, King João II of Portugal had a commission draw up the first European manual for navigators, which included simplified tables of declination, the so-called "Rule of the Sun" and the "Rule for Raising the Pole." But in the late fifteenth century, only the ablest navigators used or understood this manual, and it was not until the sixteenth century that rough tables were introduced for calculating longitude in terms of the convergence of the meridians. Accurate timekeepers, another essential component in calculating longitude, were not available until the eighteenth century. This is J. H. Parry's assessment of the navigator's lot at the time under discussion here:[108]

By the late fifteenth century, a competent navigator could grope his way about the world with reasonable confidence. He had at his disposal a well-developed technique of dead-reckoning, and several rough but adequate methods whereby, in good weather, he could check his estimated position by observations of latitude. However long his voyage, if he escaped storms, scurvy, starvation and shoreside hostilities, he could hope to find his way home. During the voyage, he could calculate the position of his ship or of a newly discovered coast or island with some approach to accuracy. He could not, however, with anything like the same accuracy, plot these positions and the courses to them, upon a chart.

It follows from the limitations imposed on late-fifteenth-century navigators that a lengthy westward voyage (requiring reliably estimated longitudes) presented more navigational problems than a north-south one, and that an outward voyage pushing the limits of a skipper's experience was considerably more difficult than the return voyage. Also—as Quinn has observed about somewhat later westward voyages—head winds from the same "westerlies" that sped homeward-bound trips, sometimes to the point of disaster, might make an outward-bound voyage last as long as two or three months.[109] Finding new fishing grounds in the west on a triangular course via Greenland was one thing; heading straight west-northwest from Bristol via Galway into the ocean was something else entirely.

Still, by 1480 some Bristol entrepreneurs were evidently ready to try. Deteriorating opportunities in Iceland must have played a significant part in this risky venture, but it is worth noting that the merchants involved, who had a broad spectrum of trade interests, were also apt to have profited from the resurgence of Bristol's trade with France after 1475. According to Carus-Wilson, this rapidly escalating prosperity in Bristol in the last couple of decades of the fifteenth century led to striking progress in ship-building.[110]

A three-year royal license to trade, with three ships of 60 tons or less, was given on June 18, 1480, to a Bristol customs official named Thomas Croft and to three Bristol merchants: William Spencer, Robert Straunge, and William de la Fount. All three merchants were prominent in Bristol's trade with Portugal. Robert Straunge and William Spencer also had Icelandic connections; Spencer's name appears on the 1484 Bristol alien subsidy roll as the master of an Icelandic servant. Thanks to William Worcestre's *Itineraries*, we know that one of the shipowners involved was John Jay the Younger, a member of another family prominent in Iceland trade. Worcestre notes that the Englishmen's destination was the Isle of Brazil in the "western part of Ireland," and that the voyage—begun sometime after mid-July—ended with Jay's storm-tossed ship being blown back on Irish shores weeks later.[111]

Quinn interprets Croft's license as a permit to search for new fishing grounds, or for islands in the ocean where fish could be dried. Without such a permit, an official like Croft would not have been allowed to take part in commercial activity.[112] Because the ship left so late in the season, Thorsteinsson thinks her master had intended to go to Greenland for the late summer fishing, but had drifted off.[113] But fishing off Labrador and Newfoundland was also best undertaken during the later summer months; by late July or early August the problem of drift ice is usually greatly reduced, and since the codfishing season in those waters lasts from the beginning of June until well into October, there would have been plenty of time to fish for cod, salmon, and herring.[114]

The English appetite for almost any kind of fish is evident from the cargo of the *George* of Bristol, which cleared Bristol customs on September 9, 1461, and which was listed as having come from Ireland. A couple of consignments of linen, tallow, and other manufactured goods lend credence to the story, but one suspects that this had primarily been a fishing voyage to the west of Ireland, because the list of fish—herring, saltfish, hake, whiting, salmon, and pollock—is striking both in its variety and in its difference from the cargo brought in by three ships that had returned a couple of weeks earlier, on August 25. The *Christopher* and the *Marie* of Bristol, and the *Julian* of Fowey, which all claimed to have come from Bergen (as noted earlier, we know the *Julian* had not), were loaded to the gunwales with cod, and only cod: stockfish, salt fish, and the kind of small cod known as "titling"—presumably obtained entirely through trade.[115]

Underlying both Quinn's and Thorsteinsson's reasoning is the assumption that the 1480 Bristol expedition had a specific fishing target based on knowledge for which we have no written evidence. I agree and would add only that Croft and his partners probably hoped that their highly skilled captain, Lloyd, would be able to sail *to* an area he had previously sailed *from* after reaching it on a triangular course via Greenland. In a different context, Quinn has pointed out that a triangular approach was also used when sailing from either France or England to latitudes in North America between 26°N and 35°N. Until the early seventeenth century, direct sailings were rare; these destinations were usually achieved by slow coasting southward along Newfoundland, or by the even longer way via the Canaries and the Caribbean.[116] The early voyages of discovery that will be discussed in Chapter Ten also headed north for a long distance before going west.

The "Isle of Brazil" claimed as the destination of the 1480 expedition may well have been these Bristol merchants' term for a known area, while the concept of another "Isle of Brazil" retained its association with legend. We see precisely such a duality in Fig. 23, the Catalan chart. This chart, which incorporates English information from about 1480, has *two* islands called Brazil. One is in the middle of the Atlantic, and the second one lies directly south of "Illa verde"—"The Green Island."

Undaunted by their 1480 failure, Croft and his partners sent two ships off in the summer of 1481, again ostensibly "to serch and fynd a certaine Ile callid the Isle of Brasile."[117] They had the remarkable foresight to take along forty bushels of salt, belonging to Croft, who also owned an eighth share in each ship. Although any fishing or sea-trading venture was a gamble, Croft and his Bristol merchant friends are not likely to have outfitted even one expedition, much less two, just to locate a mythical island. They would have expected such a venture to serve their commercial interests, in which the codfish trade played a major part. Fish and salt went hand-in-glove, as the Hanse had discovered very early, so it is not unreasonable to suppose that Croft and his partners expected a good haul from their 1481 enterprise.

Our information about this second expedition comes mostly from the Exchequer inquiry that followed soon after the ships returned to Bristol at the end of September. The inquiry centered on whether Croft, the customs official, had acted appropriately in being a party to this expedition, so we do not learn where they went or what else was in their cargo. Quinn's research makes it abundantly clear, however, that the investigation of Croft was handled by a tight circle of his peers among wealthy Bristol merchants, who would have become privy to any knowledge obtained about the Isle of Brazil that they did not already possess. Among the jurors we find Richard Ameryk, who had an Icelandic servant in 1484, and Philip Greene, later John Cabot's landlord in Bristol.[118]

We have no reports of a Bristol expedition into the North Atlantic in 1482, but that does not mean there was none. It is quite fortuitous that we know as much as we do about the voyages of 1480 and 1481, on a license good until 1483—the year Croft became joint deputy butler for Bristol and several other ports.[119]

The hazards involved in such voyages were nevertheless so great that it would be wrong to picture a flotilla of Bristol fishing doggers heading straight for Labrador and Newfoundland every year after 1481. Knowledge obtained up to that point had been gradual, and it must have come at untold cost in ships and human lives. In addition, the seas were not so peaceful in the 1480s that the English were likely to announce it far and wide when they found substitutes for Icelandic fish.[120] It would have been impossible to keep crew members from talking, but they did not necessarily pose a security risk, for not everyone capable of baiting a hook and monitoring a sail can navigate. The tight little circle of wealthy Bristol merchants who owned the ships used for Atlantic ventures could easily require loyalty and secrecy from the *masters* they employed, however, for while experienced skippers and first-rate navigators may have been hard to find, so were lucrative berths. It is also a rare person who does not enjoy being in the confidence of the local power elite.

It was only after John Cabot's successful 1497 voyage to the "Island of the Seven Cities" that the location of the teeming Newfoundland Banks became common knowledge. Cabot's mostly English crew said there was so much fish in the new land that Iceland would no longer be needed.[121] The irony is, of course, that Cabot was on a grand quest for a short northern route to Cathay and was not at all looking for prosaic codfish. Chapter Ten will examine his voyages of exploration in the context of other high-profile ventures in those waters, but two contemporary reports on Cabot's voyages concern the issue of earlier English trans-Atlantic sailings and need mention here.

Late in 1497 or early in 1498, the English merchant John Day (also known as Hugh Say) wrote to Christopher Columbus about Cabot's discoveries. He told Columbus that the cape Cabot had found "was found and discovered in the past [*en otros tiempos*] by the men from Bristol who found 'Brasil' as your Lordship knows. It was called the Island of Brasil, and it is assumed and believed to be the mainland that the men from Bristol found."

This passage has been the subject of much debate, not just because of Day's assumption (honest or merely flattering) that Columbus already knew of earlier Bristol sailings to the "Isle of Brazil," but because *en otros tiempos* does not indicate how long ago those voyages took place.[122] Day also described Cabot's rapid homeward passage with a following wind, noting that Cabot first landed in Brittany because his crew had disconcerted him (*le ficieron desconcertar*) by claiming he was keeping too far north. If Cabot's crew, consisting mostly of Bristolmen, had the confidence to tell Cabot both then and on his abortive 1496 voyage that he was off course, they surely had previous experience with eastbound voyages from the "Isle of Brazil" fishing grounds. That would have been a good reason for Cabot to hire them.

Dom Pedro de Ayala, who in 1496 and 1497 had spent much time in Scotland as the Spanish ambassador, wrote to his monarchs on July 25, 1498: "For the last seven years the people of Bristol have equipped two, three [and] four caravels to go in search of the island of Brazil and the Seven Cities as this Genoese [Cabot] reckons."[123] While it is clear from De Ayala's letter that he had all the latest London information about Cabot's voyage, it is quite possible that it was from Scottish sources that he had learned about these other long-distance English voyages. So adept was he at gathering information during his time in Scotland that a Venetian envoy writing a major report on Britain in 1498 relied entirely on what De Ayala had told him about the northern kingdom.[124]

At the very least, De Ayala's statement in his letter to Ferdinand and Isabella suggests that, after about 1490, there were enough ships leaving Bristol for an area referred to as the Isle of Brazil and/or the Seven Cities that De Ayala was aware of them through his many connections. His letter does not preclude even earlier sailings; he may refer only to those years of which he himself has certain knowledge. If he describes a resurgence of interest in a westward quest after a brief lull, the impetus for this renewed interest may well have been the *Piningsdómur* enacted in Iceland in the summer of 1490. De Ayala shows no interest in whether Bristol shipowners would have continued to invest so much in annual westward sailings if they did not expect a tangible reward. His chief concern is that the Bristolmen had discovered land west of the demarcation line drawn up by the Treaty of Tordesillas in 1494, for that land would be Spanish territory. This territorial question is an important one that we will return to in Chapter Ten.

How far the Bristolmen had reached before Cabot's voyages or how generally known the westward route had become—indeed, how to interpret Cabot's own reports of where he had sailed—are continuing elements of uncertainty. However, they are peripheral to the problem of how Bristol voyages in the Davis Strait may have affected the Greenlanders. Here we encounter a different set of questions. Which Bristol merchants maintained trade with the Greenlanders until the end of the fifteenth century? Were they the same ones who sponsored the first English fishing ventures across the Davis Strait—and were they spurred on by information obtained from Greenlanders and/or from Thorstein Olafsson and his circle? How closely did they guard their knowledge of the Norse settlements in the inner fjords? When and why did they lose interest in these settlements? And—the biggest question of all—is there a link between the end of this trade and the end of the Norse Greenlanders? We will look at these questions in the next chapter.

CHAPTER NINE

Greenland, 1450-1500

It is certain that the Greenlanders were visited by foreign ships until sometime toward the end of the fifteenth century. We can be almost as certain that these foreigners were English, for even when they were being discouraged in Iceland by the Hanse and by the local leaders' implementation of Danish crown policies, they appear to have maintained their hegemony in the northwest Atlantic while they carried their codfish enterprises farther and farther west.

We cannot preclude German visits to the Eastern Settlement, but they seem unlikely for several reasons. When the Hanse were establishing themselves in Iceland in the last quarter of the century, they faced tough competition from the English and had their hands full without exploring westward; moreover, they did not show any interest in westward exploration later, when the English, French, Spanish, and Portuguese descended on the North American continent. The English, by contrast, contended only with the Icelanders and the crown authorities when they first gained their footing in Iceland. Equally important is the fact that they arrived just when Thorstein Olafsson and his circle possessed recent, firsthand experience with a still-prospering Greenland. We have no proof that Thorstein or his circle was directly responsible for establishing trade between the Norse Greenlanders and the English, but it is likely that this is how the connection was first made. By the 1470s, however, a similar liaison between the Hanse and the descendants of Thorstein Olafsson and his friends would have been improbable, since the Icelandic chieftains in power at that late date appear to have had no interest in Greenland. Nor is it likely that any Englishmen with information about Greenland would have passed that knowledge on to their Hanse competitors.

The Hanse were superior as cod merchants, but they did not even have sufficient naval strength to prevent English ships from reaching Iceland, and the Englishmen in their small doggers were more than a match for the Hanse when it came to fishing rather than trading. Fishermen would also have been in the vanguard of those who ventured westward on their own in search of new fishing banks, but the vessels that sometimes made their way into the heads of the Norsemen's Greenland fjords would most likely have been merchant ships, carrying pilots familiar with local waters and bringing merchandise similar to that appearing in cargo lists for Iceland-bound merchantmen. This cargo could be traded for stockfish and other commodities intended for profitable resale.

Even when merchant ships topped off their homebound cargo by catching and salting down fish themselves, they belonged to an entirely different category from the countless little fishing doggers leaving England each spring. And neither merchants nor fishermen should be confused with professional pirates—English, Hanse, or others.

There were two kinds of pirates in the North Atlantic toward the end of the Middle Ages: private entrepreneurs waiting to fall upon any hapless ship in order to make a profit of sorts, and those who were motivated by politics or by a desire for revenge. The latter would have included the Germans who attacked Bergen; Pining and Pothorst who were employed by the Danish king; and the English who retaliated both on land and at sea when they met with resistance to their activities in Iceland. Neither sort of pirate would have had much reason to go to Greenland or to bob around for weeks in the dangerous, ice-studded waters surrounding it. Especially for the Hanse, whose fulcrum lay in the Baltic, it would have made little sense to sail off toward a barely populated country on the far northwestern reaches of the Atlantic, just for the chance of some recreational killing and pillaging.

Pope Nicholas V's 1448 letter, discussed in Chapter Seven, is in large part responsible for later theories about "foreign pirates" in Greenland. These theories name the Hanse as possible suspects right along with the English. Both groups certainly produced violent and rapacious people, capable of venting their tempers on shipboard as well as on land, but to assume that any of them would go all the way to Greenland on a speculative pirate venture is to forget that they, too, had to balance probable profit against known exertion.

The merchants who knew the way to the Norse-populated areas at the heads of a few big Greenland fjords, and who most likely were English, clearly cultivated trade and did not just steal what they wanted on a hit-and-run basis. The likely reasons for this approach will be discussed later, and so will the proofs they left behind of their visits, but first let us see if

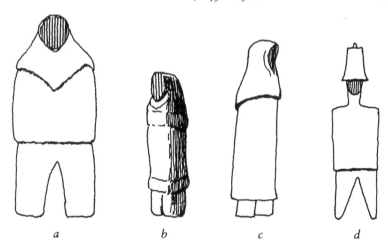

a   *b*   *c*   *d*

FIG. 26. Eskimo carvings representing Europeans of the fifteenth or sixteenth centuries, according to Hans Christian Gulløv. Source: Gulløv, "Eskimoens syn," figs. 2, 7, 11, and 15; the drawings are by Gulløv and are reproduced here with his permission.

we can find out more about the visitors themselves by looking at images left behind of them in the archaeological record.

From images the Eskimos made of the strangers they saw, we know that they observed their visitors carefully. Some of the tiny, carved figures found in Norse and Inuit archaeological sites have been discussed in earlier chapters; here we shall focus on those the Danish scholar Hans Christian Gulløv has tentatively assigned to the fifteenth or sixteenth centuries.[1] Of the four shown in Fig. 26, three (a, b, and c) were found from the southern Disko Bay region northward to Upernavik, roughly in the rich hunting area the Norse called Norðrseta, while of the fourth (d) we know only that it was found "somewhere" on the west coast of Greenland. The site where a doll was discovered is in any case not necessarily the site where it was made. The carving might have accompanied its owner on long travels to seasonal hunting grounds, or it could have been traded.

Fig. 26a was found by Therkel Mathiassen when he examined a badly collapsed Inuit site at Kissorsaq in the Upernavik district. The serviceable sailor's gear—two-piece clothing with a large, separate hood—could have been worn by a Norseman, an Englishman, or any other European, but not by an Eskimo. The same kind of clothing is evident on 26b, which was also found by Mathiassen, under the floor stones of a partly collapsed Thule (Inussuk, in Mathiassen's terminology) house ruin at Illutalik in Disko Bay.[2]

The dating of such Eskimo carvings is very difficult and often depends on the presence of datable non-Eskimo objects at the archaeological site in question. On the basis of further research by several other scholars, Jette Arneborg argues convincingly that the bottom midden layers at Thule Eskimo sites at both Illutalik and Illorssuit, in which several non-Eskimo articles were found, should probably be ascribed to the fifteenth century. She notes that cast metal pots of the type represented by a large fragment from Illorssuit (Fig. 27), which appear to have been in wide use in northern Europe toward the end of the Middle Ages, were manufactured in northern Germany in the fourteenth and fifteenth centuries. A wooden knife handle from Illutalik was from a so-called kidney dagger, known from all over central, western, and northern Europe in the Middle Ages, but particularly widespread in Scandinavia during the fourteenth and fifteenth centuries.[3] In the present context, the possibility of British provenance for both the pot and the dagger must also be considered. We know that Iceland-bound merchant ships from Bristol carried a variety of cauldrons, kettles, and cooking pots, and that cauldrons like the one known from Illorssuit and

FIG. 27. Large fragment of a three-legged cast metal cooking pot, about 17 cm high, found in a fourteenth- or fifteenth-century Thule Eskimo site at Illorssuit (see Fig. 13). Source: Mathiassen and Holtved, "Contributions," p. 157; the photograph and permission to reproduce it are courtesy of the National Museum, Copenhagen. Similar pots are known from all over northern Europe and the British Isles.

other Greenland sites were made in various parts of the British Isles in the later Middle Ages. Finds have been particularly plentiful in Ireland, where Bristol ships frequently dropped anchor.[4] Kidney daggers were also common in England over a long period; among the articles retrieved from the *Mary Rose*, which capsized in 1545, was a kidney dagger datable to the fifteenth century. At Illutalik, Mathiassen found the dagger handle, with rivet holes for the blade, near the bottom of the midden right next to a piece of walrus ivory in the Norse style; this was also the site where he discovered the doll shown in Fig. 26b.[5]

The long garment and separate headgear on doll 26c, which was found somewhere in the Egedesminde District before 1900, fall into the same sartorial category as 26a and 26b, but the style of clothing depicted in doll 26d (for which we have no other provenance than that it was found somewhere along the west coast of Greenland) is startlingly different from that shown in the other three carvings. The greatest difference lies in the tall headgear with what Gulløv describes as a "bobble" on top. He notes that while attempts to date the piece must take into account the variety of headgear worn by later Dutch whalers in Greenland, the doll's tall hat is especially reminiscent of the easily datable Burgundian cap (without a "bobble") that Nørlund found in a Herjolfsnes grave.

More than any other single object found in the Eastern Settlement, the Burgundian cap (Fig. 28a) has enabled archaeologists to say with certainty that the Greenlanders traded with Europe until the last part of the fifteenth century. The many hoods with liripipe found at Herjolfsnes (Fig. 28b) could date from any time after the mid-fourteenth century, as indicated by their use elsewhere in Europe. Cylindrical, flat-crowned caps with straight brims such as the one in Fig. 28c were used in Europe from the close of the fourteenth century until early in the sixteenth. The one pictured here reminded Nørlund so strongly of the Sandnes carving (Fig. 16a) that he suggested the need to take a second look at Ivar Bárdarson's story of finding a deserted Western Settlement already in the mid-fourteenth century. The tall (25–30 cm) conical cap shown in Fig. 28a was made of sturdy Greenland twill, in imitation of a style fashionable on the Continent at the time of Louis XI and Charles the Bold. It appears in late-fifteenth-century portraits by Hans Memling and others; farther north it was still in use at the close of the fifteenth century.[6]

Bristol's strong and ancient trade connections with France, the Low Countries, and the Iberian Peninsula were based on easy access to both the southern Channel ports and the Bay of Biscay. The city's mariners and merchants must have reflected a variety of fashion impulses in their dress. There would most likely have been a resurgence of French influence after 1475,

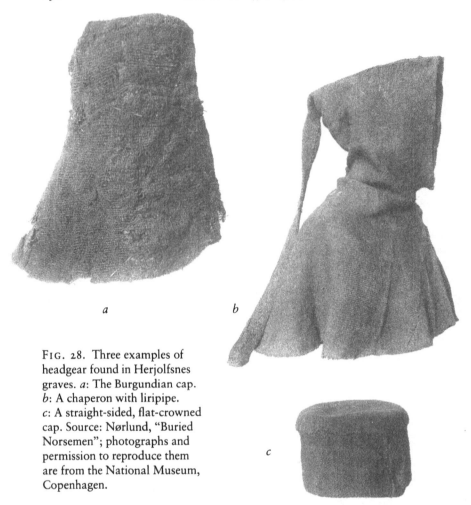

FIG. 28. Three examples of
headgear found in Herjolfsnes
graves. *a*: The Burgundian cap.
b: A chaperon with liripipe.
c: A straight-sided, flat-crowned
cap. Source: Nørlund, "Buried
Norsemen"; photographs and
permission to reproduce them
are from the National Museum,
Copenhagen.

when the Treaty of Picquigny put a formal end to Anglo-French rivalry, and
Bristol's import of wine and export of cloth quickly rose to their highest
level in many years.[7]

The Burgundian cap cannot have been practical at sea, but a merchant
stepping ashore to drive a hard bargain with the Greenlanders could do
worse than to add those impressive 18–20 inches to his height. It is also
possible that various types of headgear were brought for sale, but in that
case they have not survived in Greenland's soil, where anything above a
depth of about 55 cm in the Herjolfsnes graveyard usually was badly decomposed.[8] It is much more likely, however, that the Greenlanders pre-

ferred to trade for articles beyond their own ability to produce. All the clothes salvaged by Nørlund and his team were made from the local wool twill, often at great expense of time and effort in order to achieve a stylish effect. A case in point is the man's high-necked overgown shown in Fig. 29, with a front opening that required several dozen buttonholes. It was found in a late layer, about 45 cm below the surface, and reflects a style espoused by fashion-conscious Englishmen at the time of Henry VI (1422–61).[9] This garment made for a Greenland farmer is further evidence that Europeans visited Greenland in the middle or later part of the fifteenth century, that they came for peaceful purposes, and that their Greenland hosts did not want to appear as backwoods bumpkins.

Imported luxury goods like grain, malt, and honey would have been consumed, leaving little chance of archaeological evidence, but despite the small number of Norse sites excavated, Eskimo scavenging, the passage of

FIG. 29. A fifteenth-century man's high-necked overgown found in a relatively recent burial layer at Herjolfs-nes churchyard. This garment made for a Greenland farmer is further evidence that other Europeans visited Greenland in the middle or later part of the fifteenth century. Source: Nørlund, "Buried Norsemen," p. 124, reproduced by permission of Dansk Polarcenter, publisher of *Meddelelser om Grønland*.

five centuries, and possibly the events that will be discussed in the next chapter, there are enough traces of more durable imported objects to prove that at least some of the Greenlanders fell for the temptations the foreigners brought.

Earlier chapters have mentioned fragments of Rhenish stoneware found at Herjolfsnes and elsewhere. Vebæk's 1992 account of his earlier Vatnahverfi excavations depicts one such shard with furrow ornamentation. He found it at Ø167, a large farm snugly placed in a small, green mountain valley, which he excavated together with Jørgen Meldgaard. The shard was found in Ruin 1, which was a dwelling. In Ruin 7, a very large building complex of both dwelling rooms and barns, the excavations turned up rim pieces of three different imported bronze objects, one of them with an elegant decorative border. Human remains were found in the passage of Ruin 7, but they have since been shown to be those of a Norse male, 20–25 years old, and have been C-14 dated to no later than A.D. 1285.[10] Regardless of how those bones ended up in the passage, they cannot have belonged to the last hapless inhabitant on this large farm, which appears to have lasted well into the Eastern Settlement's late phase, judging from the imported objects found and from the buildings' generally good state of preservation. Other fascinating discoveries Vebæk made in this fertile inland area, especially at Ø71, suggest that the region as a whole prospered to the last and did not suffer too much from the erosion and sand drifts that buried some farms in the eastern part of Vatnahverfi.[11]

The dwelling (house 12) at the so-called North Farm at Ø71 was also a very large and remarkably well-preserved ruin. Advantageously located on a strip of land separating two large lakes quite far inland, in a grass-rich valley, this farm evidently produced a sufficient surplus to barter for considerable quantities of iron. A number of well-preserved knives and a nicely shaped, but damaged, axe-head were found in rooms V and VI. Particularly germane to the present discussion are the finds shown in Fig. 30: a square piece of unworked iron (room not listed) and three iron bars (room III), also semi-manufactured. With the veteran archaeologist's eye for potential significance, Vebæk grouped these pieces in his book and noted: "These bars may have been imported (perhaps from Norway), but it is not impossible that they were produced locally—that iron was produced on these farms. At least we have a small amount of slag which suggests this."[12]

Several pieces of iron slag were found in the living room (room III), where the iron bars were located, and smaller pieces of slag were found in rooms V and IX.[13] Slag is certainly evidence of iron working of some kind. The number of well-preserved knives found on this farm suggests that the last occupant may have been a smith supplying the neighborhood, but there

FIG. 30. Unworked iron found by C. L. Vebæk during excavations at Ø71 in the Eastern Settlement. The longest bar is about 12.5 cm long; all the pieces are very heavy. Source: Vebæk, "Vatnahverfi" (1992), p. 86, reproduced with permission of the author.

is no evidence of smith's tools of any kind, although the person who obtained the iron must have expected to shape it. Either his tools were eventually taken from his deserted smithy by other Norse farmers or by Eskimos, or he left the iron pieces behind when he took his tools and abandoned the farm, presumably toward the end of the Eastern Settlement's viability.

We do not yet have a termination date for this inland farm, nor for any other Eastern Settlement site. There is an almost complete lack of datings anchored in buildings and farmsteads.[14] Two things are certain, however: the owner of this semi-manufactured iron did not get around to using it all, and he had not smelted it himself, but bought it from a non-Norwegian source, which would indicate a time after the final rupture of Greenland's trade with Norway—in other words, after Thorstein Olafsson's departure from Hvalsey in 1410, and after the English had begun to trade iron and grain for Icelandic fish.

The unworked iron pieces in Fig. 30 do not look anything like the thin bars with a hole at one end and a slight, spatulate widening at the other that are normally associated with the first stage of refinement from the crude iron bloom in Norwegian bog iron production right through the fifteenth century. Irmelin Martens of the Oslo University Museum studied the picture of Vebæk's discovery and confirmed that the pieces are not of

Norwegian, Swedish, or Danish origin. Their provenance should be sought outside of Scandinavia, Martens suggests, noting also that the "wavy edge" (seen on at least two of the pieces in Fig. 30) is a distinctive feature missing in medieval Scandinavian semi-manufactured iron.[15]

The wavy edges suggest regular hammering, either to drive out slag or simply as part of the necessary process in producing shippable and salable units that a blacksmith could work with.[16] The evenness of the marks here may point to the use of a mechanical hammer, either a treadle-operated tilt hammer (known to have been in use in Britain since the mid-fourteenth century) or a water-driven hammer. Water-powered hammer-mills were already used by the textile industry when (by 1408) water was harnessed to drive bellows for English bloomeries. This improvement opened the way for blast furnaces producing larger "blooms" (chunks of molten iron), and only at that point would it have made economic sense to apply the technology of the water-driven fulling mill to power hammers that could deal with the large iron pieces.[17] Despite British production of iron for domestic use in the fourteenth and fifteenth centuries, with Forest of Dean iron from near Bristol in a leading position, good-quality iron was mainly imported from Normandy, Sweden, and especially Spain. In both the fourteenth and fifteenth centuries, Bristol was a main port for Spanish iron. Domestic production and imports of iron both increased greatly after 1450, in step with England's recovery from the Black Death.[18]

The iron depicted in Fig. 30 shows every sign of having reached Greenland from a non-Scandinavian country sometime in the fifteenth century, most likely during the second half. Whether the metal was English or Spanish (Catalan) in origin, or possibly from Burgundy or Styria, is for an expert to determine; it is in any event likely to have arrived aboard a Bristol merchantman whose cargo reflected the international nature of Bristol trade. Hanse merchants, for example, supplied the English with Baltic and Continental goods in addition to those obtained through trade with France and the Iberian Peninsula. The convergence of all these trade routes in Bristol must be kept in mind when we consider the assortment of European goods associated with late-phase Norse Greenland at Vatnahverfi, Herjolfsnes, and elsewhere.

On the large farm at the old episcopal seat of Gardar, which appears to have been viable until the end of the colony, a European table knife was discovered in a late-phase fire pit, as noted in Chapter Seven. The site is not otherwise remarkable for late-phase imported objects; the fragment of a small bronze candlestick found in room V of the bishop's residence was in the Romanesque style. Gardar is most notable for the remains of its large-scale architecture. The festal hall (room IX) of the episcopal residence, which was so wide that it may have had three aisles, had been added at a late stage, which suggests prosperity in the fifteenth century as well as during the days of contact with the church hierarchy in Nidaros and Rome. The huge capacity of the Gardar tithe barns and storehouses is also interesting, especially seen against the background of Thomas McGovern's estimates of the modest-sized livestock flocks kept by the average Norse Greenland farmer.[19] How well-filled these storage buildings were once Greenland ties with the Roman church were severed, we have no way of knowing, but they would obviously have been equally suitable for storing trade goods later on.

Eirik the Red's property at Brattahlid incorporated at least three separate farms in the fifteenth century, but the most important one must still have been that on the site of Eirik's old home, which modern archaeologists refer to as the North Farm. Both an early festal hall and a late-built church of the Hvalsey type (ca. A.D. 1300) bear witness to its wealth and importance. On the floor by the fireplace in room II of the dwelling, Poul Nørlund and Mårten Stenberger found a piece of a potbellied earthenware vessel, of pale brown clay glazed in yellow on the outside, with green patches. It is obviously of European manufacture, but Nørlund says that it "need not" be from any later than the fourteenth century.[20]

At coastal Herjolfsnes, another center of foreign trade since the start of the Norse Greenland colonies, fragments of late medieval imported artifacts have been recovered. Some Eskimos found an almost cylindrical tube of pewter, broken off at both ends and thought to be either part of a beaker or the neck of a late-medieval-style ewer, at the sea-lapped edge of the churchyard, along with three unbroken glass beads, a glass button, part of a grindstone, and a simple crucifix, all brought back to Denmark by Gustav Holm in 1880.[21] Marie Stoklund has since noted that this small crucifix was actually made of jet, a form of lignite associated with coal-rich regions such as France, Germany, and especially Yorkshire in England where the jet is of the high-grade quality needed for fine work. Many jet crucifixes and rosaries have been found during investigations of the ancient Abbey at Whitby in Yorkshire.[22]

A shard of 3 mm thin Rhenish stoneware that Nørlund found at Herjolfsnes, and that was similar to one found at Hvalsey, was of sufficiently elegant and advanced workmanship to place it firmly in the fifteenth century. As noted in an earlier chapter, this shard lay at the foundation of the well-preserved festal hall, indicating that the hall was built *after* the arrival of the stoneware.[23] This is one more proof that the Greenland community with which non-Scandinavian merchants traded was far from being on its last legs. On the contrary, Norse Greenland may at least for a time have experienced renewed vigor as a result of this change in trade—a theme to be discussed later in this chapter.

Herjolfsnes lies exposed to the open sea, so there is certainly a chance

that English fishermen might have happened on it eventually, without a pilot, but two circumstances argue strongly against European trade with
Norse Greenland having begun with a chance encounter fairly late in the
Englishmen's westward push. One is that the archaeological discoveries
discussed so far cover the better part of the fifteenth century, not just the
second half. The other is that the thick belt of summer sea ice along the
southwest coast would usually have prevented ships from coming close
enough to spot low turf-and-stone buildings in a turf-and-stone landscape,
unless they had a pilot who knew both where the farms were and how to
get inside the ice belt, or unless they arrived between late August or early
September and early April.[24]

When Nørlund and his team excavated at Herjolfsnes, a common first
port for traders during the early centuries of the colony and possibly the
final port of call in later years, it struck them as one of the most inaccessible
spots in the Eastern Settlement. The coastal ice belt excluded them from
the open sea during most of their stay. The severity of the ice problem fluc-
tuates, however, in both the long and the short term, and it clearly was not
a great obstacle in the milder climate that prevailed during the early period
of Norse colonization. As the climate grew cooler, ships arriving before the
breakup of the drift ice in late summer would very often have to sail north
to about Nunarssuit (Cape Desolation) to get *inside* the ice belt before
heading south again along the coast.[25] It is unlikely that anyone in the fifteenth century would have taken that trouble without both good reason
and a guide. Englishmen enjoying good contacts with either Icelanders or
Greenlanders in the first half of the fifteenth century probably also learned,
quite soon, that there was more land to the west of Greenland. They may
have been aware of this as early as about 1420, the time when Thorstein
Olafsson or his friends may have provided the Englishmen's first guide to
the Eastern Settlement. It is also the approximate date Olafur Halldorsson
suggests for Olaf Loptsson's version of "Eiriks saga rauða." This saga is not
confined to boasting about Karlsefni, but concentrates to an even greater
extent than the "Grænlendinga saga" on the fish, game, birds' eggs, and
other food resources to be found on the Vínland side of the Davis Strait. In
addition, the story makes it clear that the natives over there could pose a
problem, and that Karlsefni and his men had not found any grapes, the symbol of a benevolent climate. It is therefore unlikely that the English would
have had exaggerated expectations of what they might find on the other
side of the "sound," or that they would immediately have connected either
the Norsemen's stories or their own eventual experience with legendary
lands or factual reports of Asian riches.

Even the most seasoned navigators among mid- or late-fifteenth-century English fishermen and merchants would have experienced the westward voyage from Greenland as crossing a wide, northern bay with an unbroken, frozen "continent" to starboard. Furthermore, until the very end of the century, the magnetic deviation from true north would have confused even those who sailed by a compass, and the general inability to reckon longitude, coupled with the lack of calculations for the much shorter distances per degree of longitude in far northern latitudes, would have left these sailors with little communicable sense of how far north and west of Ireland they had gone in search of fish.

Before the drift ice from eastern Greenland has rounded Cape Farewell in early spring, ships already at Herjolfsnes would have been able to put to sea in fairly uncluttered waters. Theoretically, this means that an English crew could have spent the winter in Greenland and got an early start on crossing the Davis Strait, working in a good season of fishing by coasting south along Labrador before returning home on an eastward course, with salted ("wet" or "green") fish added to a cargo of Greenland stockfish obtained through trade. Over-wintering at Herjolfsnes, or elsewhere in the Eastern Settlement, would have fit comfortably within the liberal time limits of the royal licenses described in Chapters Seven and Eight, but it would also have required the cooperation of the Norse Greenlanders and enough local food resources for the extra mouths. A look at several theories and data about late-phase Norse Greenland's society and economy may tell us if either or both conditions could possibly have been met.

Scholars right up to our own time have espoused the assumption that increasing poverty, misery, isolation, and social disintegration were the Norse Greenlanders' inevitable lot once they had broken with church and crown. A review of these scholarly theories must take into account the insufficient evidence on which their claims are based, and we must be especially skeptical of the use of fifteenth-century papal letters as sources of knowledge about late-medieval Greenland. Despite the fact that the church of Rome had been the *first* medieval institution to lose complete touch with the Norse Greenlanders, Pope Nicholas V's letter about the supposedly sad conditions in mid-fifteenth-century Greenland is often paired with an equally uninformed 1492 missive from Rome, written by Pope Alexander VI (r. 1492–1503), which deserves a close look here.[26]

In the course of instructing his Chancery and Apostolic Chamber to smooth the way for a poor Benedictine named Mathias Knutsson so he could become bishop of Gardar (having been nominated for the post by Innocent VIII), Pope Alexander notes that it is believed that no ship has called in Greenland for eighty years because the sea ice permits access only in the month of August, and that it is also thought that no bishop or priest has dwelled in this country for about the last eighty years. The absence of Catholic priests has alas resulted in most of the parishioners, formerly Catholic, repudiating the baptism they had received. It is said that a communion cloth on which the last surviving priest in the country consecrated the Body of Christ, over a hundred years ago (and which is presented to the faithful once a year) is the last witness to Christian worship.

While the letter assigns only an approximate time to the disappearance of Christian instruction in Greenland, it is precise about the time the last ship is believed to have called in Greenland. Brother Mathias, who became another absentee bishop of Gardar, must have fed the Curia information easily obtainable in Bergen, where the arrival of Thorstein Olafsson and the other Greenland-farers eighty years earlier would still have been remembered. In Bergen, people would also have known that no ship had sailed from Norway to Greenland since 1410, just as they would have known that no bishop or priest had been sent there. The death of the last ordained priest could be estimated on the basis of Thorstein Olafsson's report about his Hvalsey marriage, and the problem of sea ice on the Greenland route, right down to the fact that August was a month of maximum access before autumn increased other dangers of travel, was common knowledge from a long time back.

Brother Mathias clearly did not know that other ships had visited Greenland during its supposed isolation (the pope did not worry about how the new bishop would get out to his see), nor did the monk have any other contemporary knowledge of the country beyond the fact that the Gardar office was vacant after the death of the last incumbent, Jakob Blaa. Other Vatican documents from 1492 suggest that Brother Mathias did well as a confidence-man in Rome that autumn.[27] In that capacity he would surely have known the persuasive value of such touching details as the story of the communion cloth.

The Norse Greenlanders' obviously mixed feelings about the church as an institution have been discussed in previous chapters. These earlier indications of anti-clericalism on their part make it unlikely that they despaired over their lack of ordained Catholic priests later, but we know nothing definite about their religious practices in the fifteenth century apart from what Nørlund's excavations tell us. In no way can we use as evidence the stories with which the Curia's ears were filled in 1448 and 1492.

The results of twentieth-century investigations into Norse Greenland have sometimes given rise to theories that blur the very picture they seek to clarify. A case in point is the now discarded idea (embraced by Dr. Hansen after his examination of the Herjolfsnes bones) that the last generations of Norse Greenlanders suffered from malnutrition and genetic deterioration to the point of extinction. But vestiges remain of two assumptions underlying this theory, namely that the settlers had suffered as a group because of a final, disastrous development, and that such a small, isolated community must inevitably have deteriorated genetically to the point of self-destruction.

The first assumption has yet to be proved, and the second one has recently been disproved. Studies reported at the 1993 annual meeting of the American Association for the Advancement of Science and later summarized in a *Nature Genetics* article by Alan H. Bittles and James V. Neel demonstrate that inbreeding does not greatly increase the frequency of major genetic defects in the short term, and that "insofar as consanguineous marriages expedite the elimination from the population, through homozygosity, of recessive deleterious alleles which may have minor effects in the much more common heterozygous carriers, they are from the standpoint of population genetics not undesirable."[28] In other words, a population like the Norse Greenlandic one would most likely have flushed out undesirable genetic predispositions early on.

A deteriorating climate has also been blamed for the Norsemen's ultimate failure to survive in Greenland. This approach, which entails theories about what the climate actually was like at various times, will be discussed shortly in conjunction with paleobotanical studies of the Eastern Settlement. Just as important as the climate itself would have been the Norsemen's ability to cope with any changes it produced. Despite all the evidence that the Greenlanders adjusted successfully both to their generally harsh conditions and to considerable variations in weather over half a millennium, several modern scholars have suggested that as a society the Greenlanders lost the ability to adapt to the challenges of their environment.

The American paleozoologist Thomas McGovern believes the Norse Greenland economy was "characterized by skilful co-ordination of communal labour and seasonal abundances of terrestrial and marine resources," but he also argues that it operated on too tight a margin and was so inflexibly managed that "[t]he Norse extinction . . . may be seen as a failure of human managers to select effective responses to climatic stress." He interprets the presence of cattle bones in the uppermost midden layers at the Western Settlement farm V48 as evidence of failure to adjust rather than of the possibility that there might have been no need to stop raising cattle. Considering it another defect among the Greenland Norse that they "did not produce the sort of whaling, fishing and sealing villages that characterize modern Greenland," he also faults them for not having copied Eskimo dress and hunting methods to enable them to survive.[29]

McGovern's valuable scientific work, which is mentioned several times in this book, does not provide evidence for his sociological speculations, nor do other sources. The "whaling, fishing and sealing villages that characterize modern Greenland" were encouraged by the Danes during the second colonization because such clustering of human endeavor seemed right and natural to them, but it would have been downright foolish for the Norse Greenlanders. Blessed with rich agricultural soil, the Danes have had a village system since time immemorial, unlike the Norwegians and Icelanders from whom the Greenland Norse derived their farming culture. These three more northerly countries developed a system of independent farms uniquely suited to their rocky, boggy, thin soils, where a great deal of land was needed to provide subsistence for even a medium-sized enterprise.

Kirsten Hastrup, a Danish scholar, thinks the Greenlanders were "farm-focused" and not flexible enough as a society to adapt to an environmental impoverishment she takes for granted, but whose deadly severity has never been proved. She supports her arguments by referring to Joel Berglund's 1986 essay on possible causes for the Greenlanders' decline and disappearance.[30] It is true that Berglund argues that there was a slow attrition in the population for a variety of reasons, but he offers a more optimistic view of the Norse Greenlanders' ability to adapt than Hastrup sees. He notes that they were quick to incorporate hunting and fishing with their farming, and that they were knowledgable farmers who irrigated their fields and used mountain summer farms, by which means they exploited more distant pastures while the home pastures were allowed to rest to prevent soil exhaustion. There is a note of wonder as he reflects that "some negative development must have arisen to cause the social structure to collapse." He describes his overall impression from numerous archaeological investigations into the disappearance of the Norse Greenlanders:[31]

None of the excavated ruins show signs of fleeing in panic, either from attacks or epidemics. Finally, it is also quite strange that no sacramental objects, apart from fragments of church bells, have been found in the numerous big churches in the Eastern Settlement which have been investigated. Such objects should be found in churches suddenly abandoned. Rather the evidence seems to point to a calm and orderly evacuation.

In their different ways, McGovern, Hastrup, and Berglund share an assumption that some kind of internal collapse preceded, or perhaps caused, the Norse Greenlanders' disappearance. A fourth scholar, the Norwegian Christian Keller, attributes social collapse to the effects of an isolation caused by the Greenlanders' inability to respond to changing demands in Europe. They were too distant from the burgeoning markets for cod; the value of their farm products had been declining; and the end of the Western

Settlement had quite possibly put an end to supplies of walrus tusks. Keller thinks such a course of events must have been particularly damaging to the chieftains. He reasons that the latter had probably retained their power in Greenlandic society throughout the colony's existence, and that when their position began to deteriorate, the effects were felt down through the social ranks, causing instability, violence, and an increasing failure to share and redistribute the available resources. This came on top of a supposed disaster caused by the loss of religious comfort and solace.[32]

Like Keller, Berglund assumes that the Norse Greenlanders had not adjusted their own production or economic focus to the changing situation elsewhere in Europe. He points to the survival of the Norse communities in the Faroes and Iceland (both closer to Europe than Greenland), despite their impoverishment by the end of the Middle Ages, when communications intensified because of the focus on sea fishing and trade. The population of Iceland was large enough to provide a surplus for trade, while a steadily declining population in the Eastern Settlement may at some point have fallen below the level required to produce such a surplus, and anything more than occasional ivory trading would have become impossible, Berglund reasons.[33]

In naming his own study "Vikings in the West Atlantic: A Model of Norse Greenlandic Medieval Society," Keller signals that he has no more proof for his assumptions than McGovern, Hastrup, and Berglund have for their conjectures about the social and economic collapse of Norse Greenland. The theories of all four scholars are nevertheless responses to a series of baffling physical data obtained in recent years.

Since his participation in the 1976–77 Inuit-Norse Project in the Western Settlement, McGovern has analyzed a number of bone collections from various Eastern Settlement archaeological sites. These studies, involving species classification, distribution patterns, and the proportion of wild animal bones to domestic ones in Norse middens, have yielded some results that are difficult to interpret without additional data, but also clear-cut patterns such as that even on inland farms in both Settlements, the high proportion of seal bones found shows an effective distribution system as well as a continuing ability to turn to the sea for food.

McGovern and Bigelow's investigations of the bone material collected at the Eastern Settlement farm Ø17a (discussed in Chapter Two) were especially useful because the farm was occupied for such a long time, and because the dwelling had unusually deeply stratified floor deposits.[34] The same problems that hamper other investigations of medieval Greenland nevertheless confronted the scientists at Ø17a, such as uncertainty about the midden's stratigraphy and about the climatic fluctuations, the difficulty of carbon-dating turf, and the Norse Greenlanders' penchant for splintering larger bones to get at the marrow before they let their dogs gnaw the bones.

As noted in Chapter Two, it appears that the bone ratio of domestic animals to caribou shifted from 4.43:1 in the lower Narsaq midden layers to 8.64:1 in the upper, suggesting—but not proving—that caribou hunting at Ø17a declined toward the end. And while all five seal species native to Greenland were represented at this farm, there were significant differences over time in their proportions. In the lower layer, harbor seals (common seals) dominated, followed by harp seals. In the upper layer, harbor seal bones were quite scarce; harp seals predominated along with hooded seals. Both are migratory species, either present in abundance or not at all. McGovern speculated that an increase in drift ice may have been largely responsible for a decline of harbor seals in later medieval times. Although adult harbor seals are able to tolerate ice-filled waters, modern data from the Narsaq area suggest that the pups, being less robust, have a high mortality if drift ice dominates the summer pupping grounds.[35]

Drawing upon his accumulated experience, McGovern also studied the bone collections resulting from Vebæk's several excavations in the Vatnahverfi region some forty years ago. In a recent report on these finds, he noted many similarities between these inland farms and the others he had studied previously, such as the continued reliance on various species of seal, whose bones made up about 40–50 percent of the collections, while other creatures of sea and air, as well as cattle, sheep, goats, and caribou, accounted for most of the remainder. Particularly interesting is McGovern's observation that evidence from these and other Norse Greenland farms suggests a higher-than-expected ratio of cattle to sheep and goats (around 3:1–5:1), and that average farms may have had only 10–15 head of cattle and 40–60 caprines. Multiplied by the large number of farms, however, even these relatively small flocks would have had a profound impact on the vegetation and the soil cover.[36] The question of adequate summer pasturage and winter fodder in the Norse Greenland colonies has been touched upon in earlier chapters concerning the Western Settlement. It is equally important when weighing the problems that may have beset the Eastern Settlement in its last phase.

McGovern's findings show that whatever the colonists ate at various times and locations, they had access to a great variety of food. Outright starvation of man and beast can most likely be ruled out as a factor in the Eastern Settlement's demise, but changes in climatic or other conditions may have made adjustments necessary. Much of the soil in Greenland is coarse and gravelly, with little ability to retain water. Frequent foehn winds exacerbate damage to the upper soil once the vegetation cover is broken, starting an often irreversible wind-and-water erosion. The Danish paleobotanist Bent Fredskild says flatly: "Overgrazing is, and beyond doubt was, one of the most severe threats to agriculture in Greenland." But while noting that studies of pond sediments in the Eastern Settlement show an increase of sand as soon as the Norse settlement began, and that grazing always changes the species composition in pastures, Fredskild does not think erosion from animal husbandry was solely responsible for the end of the colony. And he tersely observes that if the Norse Greenlanders had struck an ecological equilibrium in the course of rapidly exploiting all the available land, they would have been the first and only people in history to do so.[37]

The painstaking studies Fredskild made some years ago of pollen and macrofossils in various old pond sites at Brattahlid warrant a closer look, particularly because of what they suggest about the vegetation during or right after the final phase.[38] In a section cut between two small streams draining a very moist slope just above the sea cliff, the end of the zone associated with Norse habitation shows reduced human influence. Perennial weeds become more common at the expense of annuals, and the "pond" seems to have become overgrown. The changes shown in the macrofossil diagram from this site, and the differences in vegetation generally between the Norse period and the periods before and after, are very striking. The contrasts are equally great in Fredskild's diagrams from Section QD, cut from a shallow section behind one of the many raised Brattahlid beaches. Fig. 31a shows the macrofossil diagram from this site; the pollen diagram in Fig. 31b tells much the same story.

Starting from the bottom, Zone C represents the period of Norse habitation, with Layer 5 marking the beginning of the colonization, when the willow (*Salix*) and birch (*Betula*) scrub was stripped away.[39] For as long as sheep were grazing in the area, denuding bushes and other plants and cropping grass right down to the roots, this scrub would not have been able to reestablish itself. Birch in particular takes a long time to regain its ground in northern latitudes.

Especially worth noting is the obvious transition period midway through Layer 7, which marks the end of the Norse habitation. Annual weeds (III) suddenly disappear from the area, and there is also a drastic reduction in perennial weeds (IV). But before this happens, a number of moisture-loving plants have begun to predominate toward the end of Zone C, such as marsh arrowgrass (*Triglochin palustre*), common sedge (*Carex nigra*), and silverweed (*Potentilla anserina*).[40] It is uncertain to what degree these late-phase changes reflect an obviously wetter climate (also becoming evident in the soil itself) as opposed to deliberate changes in grazing and cultivation, especially since different plants regain their footing at different speeds. Many of the species Fredskild describes are familiar to me from my family's old summer home by the Oslofjord. It is now more than forty years

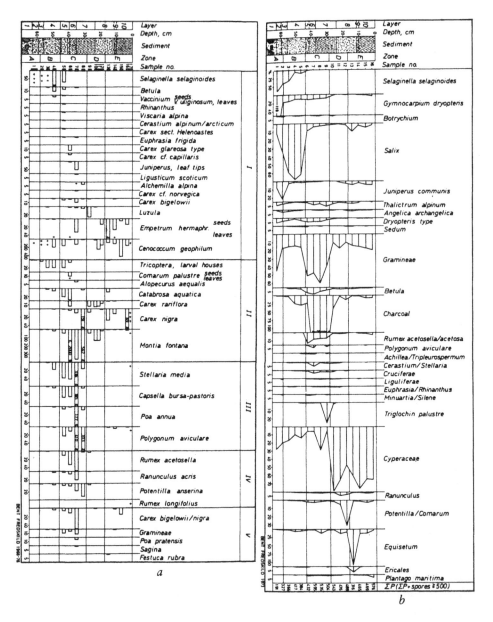

FIG. 31. *a*: Macrofossil diagram from Section QD at Brattahlid. *b*: Pollen diagram from the same site. In both diagrams Zone C, roughly layers 5 to halfway through 7, represents the period of Norse habitation. Source: Fredskild, "Palaeobotanical Investigations," pp. 28–29, reproduced with permission of Bent Fredskild.

since the last cow grazed in the sandy-soiled, marshy, and salty plain below
our house and terrorized my mother's kitchen garden, but to some degree
the area still has the look of an abandoned pasture rather than of a wild
meadow. It probably takes many seasons of snow and rain to leach out the
effects of decades or centuries of ammonia-rich animal by-products deposited on the ground. There is not much doubt, however, about what
Fredskild's diagrams show concerning the changes that the total absence
of Norse farmers and their animals brought in the Eastern Settlement
plant cover.

Climate variations were to some degree masked by the Norse farmers'
practice of irrigating their fields, but Fredskild notes that both his and earlier investigations of the Brattahlid area show that the climate was in a very
dry period when the colonization began. A later moist period was followed
by more dry weather, and then came another moist period that more or less
coincided with the disappearance of the Norse. Such a climate change could
have taken the form of more rain, or it may have been the result of lower
evaporation due to cooler temperatures, or it could indicate the formation
of a permafrost layer caused by a drop in average annual temperatures.[41]

Fredskild's data are particularly interesting in view of the American astronomer Kevin D. Pang's recent report of a cataclysmic volcanic eruption
in the South Pacific in 1453. Drawing upon the work of modern scientists
ranging from Greenland ice core experts to specialists in tree ring research,
and consulting a broad range of mid-fifteenth-century written sources from
Europe, the Middle East, and China, Pang reached the conclusion that this
volcanic explosion not only took place in the year Constantinople fell, but
that its effects were felt worldwide. For about three years, a global chill
caused widespread disaster even in normally benign climate zones. Crop
failure was common, and unusually torrential rains, strange sunsets, thick
fogs, or heavy snows earned a place in contemporary written accounts. In
both the Greenland and Antarctic ice sheets, large volcanic acid peaks have
turned up in ice core samples dated to the period 1452–60.[42]

Fredskild refers in his own report to the climatological studies made by
W. Dansgaard and others on the basis of Greenland ice core samples, which
show oscillations somewhat similar to those indicated by Fredskild's paleobotanical studies. In a 1980 study, Dansgaard and his colleagues also
showed a correlation between their Northern Hemisphere temperature index and Greenland ice sheet acidity that is strikingly in step with Pang's
1993 findings of a very cold period in the middle of the fifteenth century,
and with the changes evident from Fredskild's diagrams. Other diagrams
by Dansgaard indicate that after a chilly period in the fourteenth century
that may have coincided with the end of the Western Settlement, there was
a warming trend in the Northern Hemisphere during the first half of the

fifteenth century. By 1600, however, the "Little Ice Age" was well under way.[43]

Dansgaard and his fellow scientists nevertheless urge caution, noting that although the entire period from 1450 to 1700 is often called the Little Ice Age, this period was not especially cold either in Central Greenland or in Iceland, and that long-term climatic changes at mid-Atlantic longitudes may have been out of phase with similar changes in Europe and in North America.[44]

Scholars are still arguing over the scientific processes involved in providing a history of global climate, and research in other fields continues to turn up information that creates a need for revisions. A case in point here is the work of the Norwegian scholar Helge Salvesen and his team at Hoset, a farm located 350 meters above sea level some 40 kilometers east of Trondheim, which has long served as a marker in northern climatological research. Because the site is considered "marginal" and therefore especially vulnerable to chill and inclement weather, much like the Norse Greenland farms, climatological scholars have not questioned the long-held assumption that Hoset was deserted from about 1435 well into the sixteenth century, and that this desertion was certain proof of a long spell of worsening climate in Norway. But now a study of pollen profiles from the site reveals that the farm appears to have been occupied throughout this entire period. Salvesen reasons that Hoset farm disappeared from Archbishop Aslak Bolt's cadaster around 1435 because land had become so plentiful in the face of a shrinking population that the people at Hoset did not bother to pay rent for the land.[45] Hoset should no longer be used as evidence of an unbroken North Atlantic big chill that began well before the middle of the fifteenth century.

Quite recently, A. E. G. Ogilvie observed that in Iceland, even the early seventeenth century does not seem to have been exceptionally cold, but that there were short periods of harsh climate from the late twelfth century into the sixteenth.[46] Entries in the *Icelandic Annals* as well as other sources of information show how destructive even short periods of harsh climate could be. Modern climatologists, too, emphasize the dislocating and destructive effects of just a few bad years in succession. They also stress that a few successive years of bad weather will not necessarily change the average mean temperatures, and that the climate of *middle* latitudes may be more variable in cooler periods.[47] In the case of mid-fifteenth-century Greenland, the question is whether there was a cause-and-effect relationship between the short but deadly global chill circa 1453–56 described by Pang, and the marked paleobotanical changes Fredskild found in his samples for the end of the Eastern Settlement, along with physical proof of very damp conditions at the end of the medieval period in Greenland.

While excavating at Herjolfsnes, Poul Nørlund found support for the hypothesis that overall, the climate in southwestern Greenland did not cool significantly until *after* the Middle Ages. Although most of the really well-preserved finds in the churchyard came from layers that in 1921 were frozen all year round, masses of plant roots invading the shrouds were proof that during Norse times, the ground there must have been thawed at least in the summer.[48] The unusually wet weather for which Fredskild found evidence during the end phase of the Eastern Settlement could thus have occurred in a relatively mild period just as easily as in a cooling one, or it may have been part of a pattern alternating bad weather with good.

Even if of brief duration, a severe chill such as described by Pang may nevertheless have been enough to kill livestock and to force cutbacks in animal husbandry, and damp conditions would in themselves have exacerbated the Norsemen's perennial problem with providing enough fodder. Rain at proper intervals during the growing season is beneficial, but increased precipitation in either summer or winter in the inner fjords with their continental climate (generally on the dry side, hence the Greenland Norse irrigation systems) would have been likely to affect the Norse economy. McGovern points out that deep snow and ice crusts are very hard on the caribou as well as on domestic animals and their young. Wet weather in the haying season is equally disastrous.[49] Modern sheep farmers in Greenland know the hazards of their climate well; as noted earlier, during the winter of 1966–67, the number of sheep decreased from 47,000 to 22,000.[50] This loss of more than 50 percent was due to heavy snow, unusual cold, and a lack of winter fodder—all familiar problems to Norse Greenland farmers from the very beginning of their stay. Pastures in Greenland can be exploited for only four or five months out of the year; during the remainder of the year the animals, except perhaps the sheep, would need to be indoors subsisting on dried fodder of some kind.[51]

In the subarctic zone, where many kinds of terrestrial and marine flora and fauna exist precariously, the impact of even short-term climate variations may be severe. The scientist William G. Mattox points out that the seas off western Greenland lie in the mixing zone of arctic and temperate water masses, which means that fish populations (such as cod) existing at the northern limit of their habitat may be badly affected by even slight variations in hydrographic conditions. In modern Greenland, commercial fishing conditions off the west coast of Greenland are determined each year by changes in the relative influence of the cold East Greenland Current and the warm, salty Irminger Current as they mix in the Denmark Strait between Iceland and Greenland at about 63–64°N.[52]

Conditions must have been just as unpredictable throughout the Norse period in Greenland, not just in the fifteenth century. For instance,

Fredskild's Brattahlid study shows that the Eastern Settlement had under-
gone at least one other unusually damp period, from which the residents
recovered. We therefore cannot assume that any one period of unusually
wet weather, or a three-year chill, actually wiped out the remainder of the
Norse Greenland population in the middle of the fifteenth century. Adjustments may nevertheless have been necessary.

The Greenlanders had many resources available to them besides cattle,
sheep, and goats. If relatively mild conditions prevailed for the remainder
of the century, as Nørlund suggested, cod would usually have been plentiful
in Greenland inshore waters in the spring and summer. Colder water would
bring large numbers of capelin as well as of the huge, lethargic Greenland
shark, an arctic species with big, fatty livers used by the Norse for train oil,
just like cod livers. Train oil was a valued staple for trade as well as for home
consumption, and from the shark's flesh the Norse prepared the notorious
dish *hákarl*, with which modern Icelanders still can put tourists to flight.
The Greenland or "blue" halibut, rather higher on the taste scale, also pre-
fers cold water, and seals are more plentiful in years with greater pack ice,
providing consolation if the cod stayed away from Greenland waters in the
spawning season as a result of falling temperatures.[53]

People in the Eastern Settlement in the fifteenth century may well have
been less concerned with what kind of food was out there than with how
far out to sea they had to go to catch it. As proposed in Chapter Seven, the
end of the Western Settlement may have interfered with the Greenlanders'
ability to spend a summer season in Markland obtaining lumber of the
quality needed to build relatively large and sturdy ships, but it is impossible
to guess how soon or how strongly this change would have made itself felt.
Nor have we any idea of when—or if—the remaining Norse population
stopped going north to hunt walrus for their hides and tusks. Possibly they
found it safer to go east through Prince Christian's Sound, or they may have
stopped large-scale hunting of walrus because they no longer needed the
tusks for trade. In any event, McGovern and Bigelow thought the late levels
at Ø17a (Narsaq) showed a decline in walrus bones.[54] This may conceivably
reflect declining access to the northern hunting grounds following the end
of the Western Settlement, or it may even be a direct result of the presence
of English ships in the Davis Strait that prevented the Greenlanders from
venturing beyond their fjords to the outer coasts.

If a clear picture eventually emerges of declining walrus hunts in the last
period, we must also allow for the possibility that the Greenlanders *chose*
to spend their energy on other pursuits that had grown more profitable, for
the predominance of seal bones in all layers of inland and coastal middens
is proof that they must have had at least some kind of boats to the very end,
so they were not limited to hunting caribou or catching salmon and char

in lakes and rivers, but could fish and hunt seals for subsistence. What we do not know is whether they still turned to the sea for goods to barter.

Although seals yield fur and blubber as well as meat, all of which were wanted elsewhere in Europe, it is doubtful that fifteenth-century foreign merchants would have risked the long voyage to Greenland for seal fur and blubber, even when coupled with hides and pelts from reindeer, domestic animals, and newborn harp seals. Narwhal horns were probably welcome in Europe for the same reasons as before, but above all else, dried cod and train oil were the equivalent of money.

Fish, oils, furs, and hides could all be marketed discreetly, efficiently, and profitably through regular Bristol channels, unlike walrus ivory and "unicorn horns." From the start of the Newfoundland fisheries in the early sixteenth century, not only fish but train oil played a big part in Western European business at almost all levels (although little was written down about these lowly activities), and the cargoes of even small fishing boats were very profitable.[55]

Prior to the establishment of the Newfoundland fisheries, the English in Iceland had caught and salted fish themselves, but dried cod had to be purchased because the English lacked access to secure drying areas ashore for the considerable length of time needed to complete the stockfish process, unless the job could be contracted out to year-round residents. The cod livers may have been taken back to England for processing there, but the Icelanders would also have been able to sell their own train oil if they had a surplus. It is not unreasonable to suppose that English merchants making calls in Greenland in the fifteenth century above all wanted stockfish and train oil in return for their trade goods, and that the Norse strove to supply these goods in far greater quantities than when they had mainly fished for domestic needs and relied on very different wares, such as walrus tusks, to satisfy the Norwegian market.

If Thorstein Olafsson returned to Greenland around 1420 to collect an accumulation of Hvalsey produce belonging to his wife, he would have done so with full knowledge of the high price stockfish would fetch among English merchants, and he would have been likely to encourage the Greenlanders to step up their production of stockfish before the next merchant ship arrived. Stockfish was an eminently durable commodity, and the Greenlanders had long been accustomed to taking the long view, often storing barter goods for years between opportunities to trade. If colder currents sometimes kept the fickle cod away from their shores, there would still be enough fish, train oil, and other goods, by the time the next ship came, to exchange for luxuries such as iron bars, metal pots, and honey, and to make trade attractive enough so others would come.

Two possibilities emerge if we see the likelihood of a major switch to stockfish production in conjunction with the atypical patterns during the last phase of the Eastern Settlement that Fredskild's paleobotanical investigations and McGovern and Bigelow's paleozoological analyses suggest. Either the Norse Greenlanders voluntarily changed both their hunting patterns and the extent of their animal husbandry in order to provide more desirable goods for new market conditions, or they seized an opportunity to counter the effects of climatic conditions that were interfering with their old way of farming, but not with fishing and seal hunting. Either possibility could have brought reduced cultivation of haying fields and pastures, as well as less interest in walrus hunts.

We do not know enough about the Greenlanders' seal-hunting methods to say why they may have switched from year-round species to migratory ones that went up their fjords in huge numbers in fall and spring. If there was such a change, it may have been caused by a change in the kind of boats at their disposal as easily as by climatic changes or intimidation by English fishing doggers, but it may also have been a deliberate switch, in response to preferences for certain kinds of seal pelts in the European markets, where there was a sharp increase in the trade of furs generally during the period 1450–70.[56] It is worth noting, too, that even when the Portuguese were developing their profitable trade in exotic African commodities in the second half of the fifteenth century, the backbone of their commerce continued to be agricultural products and other traditional goods, including sealskins.[57]

A review of the available evidence thus strongly suggests that the Norse Greenlanders participated actively in the economic changes taking place all around the North Atlantic in the fifteenth century, and that outsiders considered Greenland a worthwhile place to do business with. As we have seen, written sources indicate that the last three documented voyages between Norway and Greenland almost surely were deliberate, though couched in the traditional language of "drifting off"; that Sigrid Björnsdaughter had most likely been married off by her rich father to a prospering Greenland farmer; and that Thorstein Olafsson had good reason to consider himself well married in 1408 at Hvalsey. If we add these signs that all was well in the Eastern Settlement in the early fifteenth century to the evidence that foreign merchants started arriving not so very long afterwards, and that they made at least intermittent calls until the last part of the century, it is hard to avoid the conclusion that in their modest way, the Norse Greenlanders were thriving through the better part of the fifteenth century. The late-date festal halls built at Hvalsey, Herjolfsnes, and Gardar are further indicators of continued prosperity *after* the connection with Norway and the church had been broken. One obvious explanation for this show of vigor is that the Greenlanders thought they were embarked on a promising course of trade with their new contacts.

The low profile of this barter, to which no known English or other European sources have ever alluded, is partly explained by these merchants' understandable reluctance to arouse the ire of Dano-Norwegian tax collectors and to let competitors benefit from their convenient arrangement with the Greenlanders. But the ease with which this sporadic trade could be kept quiet must have been due to the fact that the cargo brought away from Greenland was indistinguishable from that obtainable elsewhere on the Englishmen's circuit.

We need go no farther than to northern Norway for corroboration of this argument. There the population of small farming communities like the Norse Greenland ones abandoned stock raising, hunting, and other traditional forms of subsistence farming in response to the burgeoning markets for dried codfish in particular, but also for other kinds of fish. The only disagreement is over whether the change was sudden or gradual; certainly it was well established in the thirteenth century.[58]

Bergen, of course, served as the center for Norway's fish trade with England and the Continent, but the Greenlanders were too far away to benefit in a sustained way from the increased demands for cod through this Norwegian distribution system. Once the English had established themselves in Iceland, however, they could easily have become middlemen for Greenland stockfish and train oil, both of which the Norse Greenlanders were expert at producing. It would have required only knowledge of the route (which the English demonstrably gained) and a reasonably trusting arrangement with the Greenlanders to supply both commodities whenever a merchantman called. We cannot guess how long the intervals between such arrivals may have been, but they appear to have taken place throughout the better part of the century. If there is any truth behind De la Peyrère's story (noted in Chapter Eight) about the fight in Bergen between Hanse merchants and boastful English Greenland-farers around 1484, it is likely that some Englishmen were still going to Greenland at least as late as 1480.

That, in turn, suggests that the barter continued to satisfy the merchants who went there. Two major questions immediately present themselves, however. Did the trade peter out after the early 1480s, and if so, for what reasons?

Since the Dano-Norwegian crown during this period passed repeated laws to prevent able-bodied young Icelanders from leaving the country aboard foreign ships, it would be very surprising if, in succeeding generations, some adventurous and ambitious young Greenlanders had not also taken jobs aboard English ships. After all, not all Icelanders who ended up in England went there under duress, and in Greenland, where there probably never were large numbers of foreigners at any given time, the chances of abduction would surely have been slim. We need to consider a more likely problem, namely the effect even a small number of departures may have had if they involved the fittest and best hunters and fishermen from the Eastern Settlement. Some scholars, like Berglund, ascribe the Norse Greenlanders' ultimate disappearance in part to slow attrition in an already small population; the reasons given for this attrition range from murder and starvation to falling birthrates or deliberate emigration.

The inability to produce a surplus for barter would certainly have been one eventual consequence if enough able-bodied young men left the Eastern Settlement aboard foreign ships and caused a downward spiral in farming, fishing, hunting, and the making of train oil. But all the evidence suggests that there must have been able-bodied people enough in the Eastern Settlement to produce sufficient goods for intermittent trade at least up to the time, late in the fifteenth century, when a ship came on friendly business and introduced the Greenlanders to the tall Burgundy cap.

If we make the reasonable supposition that the owner of a Burgundy cap arrived sometime around 1480–90, we encounter the period when a few Bristol merchants were actively searching for a direct route to the fishing banks on the other side of the Davis Strait. These ship-owning Bristol merchants came from the same group of successful English codfish traders who had made their mark in Iceland throughout the fifteenth century, and among whose number we may reasonably expect to find some who made periodic stops in Norse Greenland. This same Bristol group also played an important part in the events that will be discussed in the next chapter.

The evidence presented in Chapter Eight suggests that the attempt to sail directly from Ireland to the Labrador-Newfoundland area, rather than going via Greenland and perhaps wintering there before crossing the Davis Strait, soon paid off for this small group of wealthy Bristol investors. If, by 1480–90, the descendants of the shipowners who led the first westward quest from Iceland had figured out how to exploit the New World fishing banks directly, without bothering with Greenland at all, people in the Eastern Settlement would have found themselves isolated, and left to eat their own stockfish stores, for the last decade or two of the fifteenth century.

The Norse Greenlanders could not have anticipated such a development. They certainly cannot be faulted for "failure to adjust" if they had done their best to take advantage of the changes brought by the fierce competition for North Atlantic fish and trade in the fifteenth century, and perhaps also to compensate for a blow to their traditional farming economy brought on by a mid-century global chill. The bitter irony is that their adjustment probably carried with it the seed of their demise. Far from being unable to adjust to economic changes elsewhere in the North Atlantic community, they may have responded too well for their own good.

The Greenlanders, who had faced so many challenges throughout their history, probably did not consider until very late, if at all, that they might be entering a terminal phase. Up to the last, they had a food distribution system that let coastal farmers eat reindeer and inland farmers rely on seal. They observed proper burial customs to the end, bought luxury goods, and copied the clothing fashions of visitors from the outside. The picture we are left with is not compatible with notions about a starving, demoralized people who were unable to adapt to their environment or to maintain reasonable relations among themselves, and who regarded themselves as cut off from the rest of the world except when someone stopped by to rob and kill.

Fredskild's botanical analyses suggest that in the Eastern Settlement's last phase, decreasing attention was paid to pastures and haying fields, presumably due to reduced stock-keeping. But as the Icelanders have repeatedly demonstrated, reductions in livestock and in the cultivation of pastures, whatever the reasons for them may be, are not in themselves irreversible processes. Both the Greenlanders and the Icelanders had recovered from adverse weather cycles in the past, and the number of people and animals had steadily increased after each colony's first fragile beginning. The flocks of animals would slowly have grown again even after a major loss, and meanwhile their pastures might have benefited from decreased use.

A Norse Greenland community that was still sufficiently viable to attract foreign traders until at least 1480 or 1490, and that left behind the orderly scene described by Berglund, is not likely to have been suddenly or violently destroyed at the turn of the century. But of the Norse Greenlanders' disappearance there can be no doubt, and it is time to explore new avenues of thought about it.

By the end of the fifteenth century, after ten or twenty years with no English ships calling, and with direct contact with Iceland an even more distant memory, many of the colonists may have felt deprived and isolated enough to welcome the chance of another change, brought by post-Columbian explorers and adventurers. Drawn by reports of new lands and opportunities far west in the ocean, these new travelers had much in common with Eirik the Red and his little band of colonists. It is perfectly possible that even after five centuries, the Greenland Norse were as capable of adventure, and as thirsty for a fresh start, as their ancestors had been when they set sail for the great unknown.

CHAPTER TEN

The Age of Discovery

The cresting wave of European exploration slammed onto the shores of the Americas in the years just before and just after 1500, leaving some men with their lives and ships intact, while others were lost at sea or cast up on beaches for which only the natives had a name. Even if nobody as yet suspected that a vast American continent separated Europe from a huge and multifaceted Asia, by 1500 Columbus and others had revolutionized educated people's view of the world. The Atlantic and Indian oceans had proved traversable, and the potential rewards for pluck and luck were great enough for men to risk their own and other people's lives in further ventures.

When Francisco López de Gómara, the official early chronicler of the Indies, in the mid-sixteenth century summed up the speculative and risky nature of these quests, he stressed the dangers that seem to have accompanied northern exploration in particular, in ventures that left practically no records:[1]

Many undertook to continue and complete the discoveries initiated by Christopher Columbus; some at their own cost, others at the King's expence, hoping thereby to become rich and famous.... But as most of those who made discoveries were ruined thereby, there is no recollection left by any of them so far as I know, particularly those who steered northward, coasting the Bacallaos region [Newfoundland and the Grand Banks] and Labrador.

Henry Harrisse quoted this passage a century ago to complement his own observation that unlicensed adventurers had every reason to keep to themselves, to stay away from places where they were most likely to run into authorized traders and seafarers, and to keep their discoveries secret. It seemed to Harrisse that Columbus's successful 1492 voyage must have raised other adventurers' ambition to such a pitch that between 1493 and 1500, a number of ships were "unlawfully equipped in the ports of Spain, Portugal, and France, for the purpose of exploiting the New World," sailing secretly and without a license.[2]

Secrecy and the failure to obtain licenses translate into a lack of written sources for both southern and northern early ventures in the Atlantic. David B. Quinn laments: "From the point of view of the sources on which it is founded, the history of North America emerges from its dark ages some time in the second decade of the sixteenth century."[3] The secrecy aspects that Harrisse and López de Gómara note—about adventuring in general and northern voyages of discovery in particular—are in keeping with the earlier Norse and English enterprises discussed up to this point. Equally familiar is another important characteristic of late-fifteenth- and early-sixteenth-century exploration, on which Harrisse also comments—namely the part played by family connections and other forms of close association.[4] This feature, which was equally prominent in earlier centuries, reflected a desire to maximize for a chosen few the benefits of information about new areas to exploit while discouraging the spread of such information through more public channels. This monopolistic approach could also lead to rather brutal treatment of those seen as interlopers. Events in Bristol in the period 1496–1506—which will be discussed in this chapter—demonstrate the ferocity with which a small group of people would defend privilege, while Christopher Columbus's voyage in 1492 is a good example of clannish business interests intertwined with exploration, since most of the money for his expedition was provided by Genoese and other Italian merchants who had migrated westward and were now living in Seville.[5]

We have seen that the first Norse explorers who colonized Iceland and Greenland before making their way to North America belonged to a small group of enterprising people benefiting from accumulated family experience and lore. Similarly, the North Icelanders who became the link between the Greenlanders and the early English codfish entrepreneurs in Iceland were closely connected both to each other and to the Norwegian power elite, and they used all the advantages available to a successful in-group while playing their high-stakes game across familiar waters.

Such a pattern also grew apparent among the fifteenth-century Bristol shippers and merchants mentioned in Chapter Eight, and it will become quite distinct in the present chapter as we focus on the Bristol enterprises most likely to have involved the Norse Greenlanders at the start of the sixteenth century. At that time, several Bristolmen crossed paths with Azorean Portuguese explorers and entrepreneurs who also enjoyed close ties from family connections and business associations, set against a background of growing familiarity with—and daring probes into—the North Atlantic.

Before we focus on the events that appear to have culminated in the Bristol connection with Norse Greenland, we shall look at the Portuguese experience in some detail.

The North Atlantic voyages so far discussed illustrate the role of "geographic destiny"—the interplay of actual distances from one country to another, ocean currents, and prevailing winds—among both the Western Norse and the English, who saw the North Atlantic as their natural sphere of operation. The Spanish and Portuguese, too, at first found their challenges in waters closer to home. Inevitably, their northerly trading and fishing routes intersected with those of the Basques, French, Dutch, and English. Just as inevitable was the Iberians' gradual expansion to the various archipelagoes within their reach, and to Africa.

It is doubtful that the Spanish and the Portuguese paid much attention to either Denmark or Norway in the late Middle Ages, except to keep an eye on the codfish trade. Historians who believe that there was a 1474 Danish-Portuguese voyage of discovery in the far northern Atlantic, under Pothorst-Pining-Skolp management, have in part supported their position with the fact that Henry the Navigator and his brother Dom Pedro were the cousins of Philippa, the English princess who finally married the Danish King Eirik of Pomerania early in the fifteenth century, and with written evidence that two Danish courtiers served the Portuguese crown some decades later. While it is most unlikely that a 1474 Danish-Portuguese venture ever took place, the earlier connection between Denmark and Portugal was real enough, but of such slight importance to later exploration in the North Atlantic that the sooner these courtiers' tales are put in perspective, the better.

According to the fifteenth-century historian Gómez Eannes de Azurara, in 1448 a Dane named "Vallarte" (probably Vollert) showed up at Henry the Navigator's court at Sagres and was appointed the leader of a Portuguese expedition to Cape Verde. "Vallarte" had evidently come to Sagres with the blessing of King Christian I of Denmark-Norway, which the Danish historian Sofus Larsen sees as further evidence that the Portuguese and Danish kings wanted to cooperate in explorations. Judging from the end of "Vallarte' "s brief career, however, he probably was an impetuous troublemaker unlikely to be missed at home. Against the explicit wishes of his Portuguese crew, who strongly questioned the wisdom of going ashore to negotiate with Guinean chiefs, he went ashore anyway, with several of his men. The natives attacked, and only one man managed to return to the ship. Of "Vallarte" and three other men nothing more was heard; it was assumed they had been taken captive.[6]

The basis for the second tale is a letter King Alfonso V wrote to Christian I on July 11, 1460, to tell him that the Danish nobleman Laaland had distinguished himself while fighting with the Portuguese against the Moors in Alcazar. Larsen supposes that since King Christian had no ambitions in Portugal or Africa, Laaland's presence in Portugal must have been at the instigation of Alfonso's uncle, Henry the Navigator.[7] That explanation makes little sense, for the Danes would have had little useful information for Henry or anyone else at that time. They had no thought of exploring anywhere and were not even sending ships to their Norwegian colony in Greenland, as we have seen.

Like the story of "Vallarte," Laaland's tale has value chiefly because it demonstrates that connections were made across national boundaries, over great distances, and for reasons that usually had less to do with exploration for its own sake than with fishing, trade, or a wish for adventure, fame, and instant wealth. The Portuguese explorers discussed in this chapter are prime examples of such ambitions—and they managed without any help from the Danish king.

The modern historian Felipe Fernández-Armesto observes that Portuguese commerce and industry had their origin in the salting and marketing of cod, and that the Portuguese, like the Dutch, "practiced shipping and piracy in neighboring seas for a long time before taking up their imperial vocations."[8] Portuguese imperialism was well under way by 1450. At that time, they were bringing malagueta pepper from West Africa, which they soon started marketing through Flanders, and after turning their attention from the Mediterranean to the Atlantic islands, they had colonized the Canary Islands, the Madeira Archipelago, the Cape Verde Islands, and the Azores. Although Corvo and Flores, the westernmost islands of the Azores, were not discovered until 1453 on the return voyage of two Portuguese who had been searching for "Antilia" (or Island of the Seven Cities, alternatively the Isle of Brazil), firm plans for Azorean settlements had been made by 1439.[9]

The nexus of European trade shifted decisively from the Mediterranean to the Atlantic in the later fifteenth century when the business climate in the eastern Mediterranean deteriorated, partly as a result of the increasing hostility of the Ottoman Turks. Italian, Catalan, Castilian, and Basque merchants, who for centuries had been trading through the Strait of Gibraltar, now intensified their efforts in the Atlantic, and Italian communities on the Iberian Peninsula grew with the influx of new settlers. As noted, the Portuguese had already long focused their activities on the Atlantic rather than on the Mediterranean basin.[10] It is no surprise that both Portuguese maps and the voyages we shall discuss here bear witness to the country's long experience with Atlantic waters.

The conquests of the Balearic Islands, Corsica, and Sardinia had been under the aegis of the House of Barcelona. The Portuguese and Castilians who were chiefly responsible for the colonization of the Atlantic islands had little Mediterranean colonial experience. Fernández-Armesto speculates that in this unfamiliar enterprise they may have been influenced "by the strength of the 'Reconquest' tradition, which habituated them to colonial exploits and provided a conceptual framework in which African and Atlantic conquests could be justified and understood."

In some respects, the colonization of these Atlantic islands was similar to that of the New World later in the century, in that slaves eventually were brought in to make a 'plantation' economy possible, while in other ways the Iberians' experience was similar to the Norsemen's in Iceland and Greenland. Unlike the Mediterranean islands, but like Iceland and Greenland, the Atlantic archipelagoes offered no competition or threat from native populations. The first Canary islands to be colonized were seriously underpopulated; the other archipelagoes were uninhabited; and until the Cape Verde Islands were developed in the 1460s, the Atlantic colonies depended on European immigrant labor.[11] It is important to keep these elements—indigent populations, imported labor, and entrepreneurial expectations—in mind when we evaluate the Portuguese efforts to find and exploit lands and islands in the northwestern Atlantic.

The widely different locations, topographies, and climates of the newly colonized Atlantic islands led to considerable diversity in their local economies as well as in their international trade connections, which may also have influenced the patterns of further Atlantic exploration. The Madeira group, where sugar production was very successful from the start, rocketed to prosperity, and both here and in the Canaries the foreign industrial and commercial elite consisted mostly of Genoese, whose banking connections were essential to the capital-intensive sugar industry. The growth of Azorean prosperity, on the other hand, was slower and due primarily to increasing Portuguese exploitation of mainland Africa, for the prevailing winds ensured that the Azores became staging posts for that trade. Wheat was the main crop in the Azores, and the foreign industrial and commercial elite was Flemish, because merchants from the rich and populous southern Netherlands were sure of a market for Azorean wheat.[12] Accustomed to a cooler climate than that of the other Portuguese islands, the Azoreans we shall meet later may have been especially apt to find promise in the chilly and austere North American east coast, even if its products were not as dazzling as sugar, African slaves and gold, or the spices of the Orient.

The Canaries were in Castilian hands by the time Christopher Columbus set out from there to find the western sea route to India. They were an ideal starting point for him, as it turned out, for attempts to reach land by sailing straight west from the Azores were at most times of year doomed to failure by the prevailing westerlies. Well into the seventeenth century, French and English ships are known to have reached southeastern North

America by deliberately going south to the Canaries so they could follow the Spanish route, first westward and then northward.[13]

These wind patterns were part of the "geographic destiny" of the people who chose to make their homes in the Azores, and who remained under Portuguese hegemony. But some thought this destiny existed only to be challenged—people already engaged in seafaring and trade, and particularly those hoping to find new regions for exploitation. The form that exploitation might take could range from the sorts of fishing voyages we have already discussed, for which licenses may or may not have been issued and become a part of the written record, to such political maneuvering as pursuit of a lucrative colonial governorship, for which extensive documentation exists. In the following, we shall focus primarily on the English and Portuguese voyages of North Atlantic discovery for which there *were* licenses and other written sources, and which were reflected in maps as well as prompted by them. These voyages, and the people who headed them, created a westward momentum that we shall see probably swept the Norse Greenlanders with it.

The Portuguese were encouraged in their search for "Antilia" by the work of the Florentine cosmographer and physician Paolo Toscanelli, who in the early 1470s became convinced that the Ocean Sea between Europe and "Asia" was not as wide as previously thought. He drew a map to show how easily "Antilia," for example, could be reached. The same miscalculation of the earth's circumference was present in the work of Ptolemy [Claudius Ptolemæus], whose second-century geographical theories were improved upon and presented to a receptive world in 1474 by Donnus Nicolaus Germanus.[14] The influence of these sanguine maps on Columbus's later plans is well known and needs no elaboration here.

In January of 1474, Fernão Telles received a charter to go from the Azores in search of new islands anywhere except in the Guinea region. A supplementary grant made in November of 1475 gave him the right to the "Island of the Seven Cities"—all he had to do was find it.[15] Telles does not appear to have been successful as an explorer, perhaps because of the problems connected with sailing west, against the prevailing wind, from the Azores. That did not discourage others from trying, however.

A sixteenth-century source, apparently eager to establish Portuguese precedence over the English in the discovery of North America, relates that the wealthy Azorean João Vaz Corte Real had made an undated voyage under the orders of Alfonso V and discovered Newfoundland, for which he was rewarded with the captaincy of Angra in Terceira in 1474. This is the Corte Real voyage Sofus Larsen linked with the fictitious Pothorst-Pining-Skolp enterprise, and whose source has proved so unreliable in other respects that Quinn observes: "If João Vaz Corte Real sighted America before Columbus, as is not impossible, it was almost certainly not in 1472 or thereabouts but much later. . . ." Quinn allows for a possible pre-Columbian voyage by Corte Real *père* because the license which Gaspar Corte Real obtained in 1500 mentions that he had already made voyages, and these voyages (accompanying his father) might go back into the 1480s. We can only be certain that Gaspar could not have gone on an unrecorded voyage in 1488, a year his father is known to have been away from home, for Gaspar was Acting Governor in his absence. In addition, there is no clear evidence of Portuguese expeditions in the decade between 1476 and 1486.[16] My own view is that Gaspar probably engaged in an independent venture after he came into his patrimony upon João Vaz's death in 1496.

The Corte Real ventures will be discussed in some detail later in this chapter, because they illustrate the extensive nature of Atlantic exploration at the turn of the century as well as the Azorean involvement in northern quests, and they act as foils to Bristol-based voyages of exploration in the same period. They are also of special interest to us because they involved a region that may have loomed large in the Norse Greenlanders' fate.

Although there is no conclusive evidence that the Portuguese made an American landfall either before the English or before Columbus, Quinn thinks the indications that Portugal made a discovery on the American mainland before 1492 "are not negligible." The maps we think the English knew were mainly the work of Italian cartographers, but the latter's information about the Atlantic came mostly from Portuguese sources, in large part as a result of Portugal's search for islands west in the ocean. This quest included Diogo de Tieve's chance discovery of the last two Azorean islands in 1453, which extended the Portuguese empire a good third of the way across the Atlantic and gave the Azoreans an edge in further Portuguese exploration efforts, however mixed the results may have been.[17]

Samuel Eliot Morison believes in an uncluttered ocean prior to 1492 and sees two main reasons why the known Portuguese attempts to locate new or mythical Atlantic islands, in the time between João Vogado's voyage of 1462 and Columbus's first voyage, were doomed to failure. In the first place, the explorers went looking for islands in a part of the ocean that contains no islands. In the second place, the prevailing westerlies during the season when those attempts were made discouraged captains and crews alike, until after Christopher Columbus had proved that such long voyages could be made successfully from the *Canaries*, "with the northeast trades on his stern."[18]

Morison's views allow no room for pre-Columbian northern probes, despite mounting evidence that at least by the early 1480s, Azoreans and other Portuguese navigators with contacts among British sailors and codfish merchants would have had access to information about the Atlantic far to the north and west of the British Isles. Columbus's own voyage to Iceland and Galway in 1477 demonstrated this Portuguese connection with England, Ireland, and Iceland.

There is a firm association of the legendary "Antilia"—which first appeared directly opposite Portugal on the Pizzi Nautical Chart of 1424—with the Portuguese concept of the "Island of the Seven Cities"; a connection that cannot be traced farther back than to Tieve's 1452–53 expedition resulting in the discovery of the two westernmost Azorean islands. The two place-names became linked with Portugal in general and with Azorean lore in particular. It is reasonable to assume, as Morison does, that Martin Behaim told the story of Antilia–Seven Cities on his 1492 Nuremberg globe because he had learned the tale in either mainland Portugal or the Azores.[19]

Martin Behaim's name is in turn connected with several Azorean persons and locations etched in the annals of early North American exploration, so he deserves some attention here. The son of a prosperous Nuremberg merchant, he is also a prime example of how difficult it is to assign nationalities to the people involved in these ventures. Opportunists would go where opportunity offered, whether they called themselves merchants, cartographers, or explorers. Seville, Lisbon, Genoa, London, Bristol—what mattered most was finding good trade connections or a king who would issue a protective charter and perhaps provide financial backing for a venture.

From at least 1486 until 1490, and again from 1494 to his death, Martin Behaim lived at Fayal in the Azores. During part of the interim period he stayed in his native city of Nuremberg, where he made his 1492 globe reflecting the same worldview, and the same underestimated circumference of the earth, that his contemporaries Toscanelli, Martellus, and Columbus espoused. Behaim, who spent most of his life as a merchant and commercial agent, is not reliably known to have had a leading role in any voyage of exploration, despite his own claims, but he traveled extensively in the course of business. His entry into the world of discovery was probably through his wife, whom he married in 1486. She was the sister of João Vaz Corte Real's son-in-law, Jobst de Hürter; their father was the Flemish governor of the Azorean islands of Fayal and Pico. João Vaz (whose younger daughter Izabel eventually married Jobst de Hürter II) appears to have acquired a reputation as an explorer by that time, and his sons, most notably Gaspar and Miguel, soon made their lasting mark in history through voyages of discovery that will be discussed shortly.[20]

There were other similarities between João Vaz Corte Real and his contemporary Icelandic chieftain peers than the belief that in matrimonial matters, the devil you know is preferable to the one you don't. He raised his sons to follow in his footsteps as a mariner; he was a ruthless businessman and administrator; and he knew the value of royal patronage. This is Morison's description of the man:[21]

João Vaz Corte Real, chamberlain to the Infante D. Fernando, showed such energy in obtaining colonists for Terceira that the king made him captain of that island in 1474, and within ten years added the island of São Jorge to his domain. He married a Spanish lady from Galicia after forcibly abducting her, and as a ruler in the Azores he had the reputation of being greedy, cruel, and unjust. Dying in 1496, not greatly regretted, he left a family of three sons: Vasco Annes, Miguel, and Gaspar.

It is probable that João Vaz, like the Norsemen and the Bristol English, played with his cards close to his chest, preferring to let his sons benefit from what he had learned from his voyages, rather than spill all he knew to Behaim, his relative-by-marriage.

The polar regions appear on Behaim's globe as a group of islands divided by channels draining into a polar ocean, in accordance with the theories of the fourteenth-century work *Inventio Fortunatae* (to which Behaim referred) and with Mercator's mid-sixteenth-century ideas.[22] Although this globe conformed very closely to the 1484 and 1486 Ulm editions of Ptolemy's *Geographia*, the Danish geographer A. A. Bjørnbo thought Behaim may have had special knowledge about the real Greenland and its actual location, because he showed a certain amount of independence in the jumble of place-names surrounding northern Norway, and because the information he provided about Iceland was "mainly correct" and in part new to cartography.[23]

If we compare Behaim's efforts in 1492 with the "Paris Map" and with the maps in Figs. 23 and 25, it is hard to credit him with any special insights that had not long been available to many Englishmen and Portuguese in the codfish business. Iceland may have been only slightly more real to Behaim than the "Antilia" he also put on the globe he made after spending several years in the Azorean island of Terceira, a hub of commerce and exploration.

Late in the summer of the year Behaim made his globe in Nuremberg, the Genoese navigator Christopher Columbus set off on his first great voyage to the "Indies" on behalf of Spain, but with navigational ideas that had been formed in the Portuguese environment of 1476–85. He sailed on Spain's behalf because he had failed to interest either the English or the Portuguese monarchs in his grand scheme.[24] Henry VII had other pressing concerns, and the Portuguese were already managing very well in the field of exploration. Four years before Columbus and his crew reached the Caribbean, Bartolomeo Dias had culminated the Portuguese probe down the west coast of Africa by rounding the Cape of Good Hope, at the same time as Pedro de Covilhã had sailed south along the east coast of Africa and sent a message that the sea route to India was feasible.[25] When word spread in Europe that Columbus's voyage had also been successful, it represented a welcome triumph for the Spanish monarchs whose charter Columbus carried.

Although reports of Spanish and Portuguese exploration success in more southerly waters often overshadowed North Atlantic quests during the last decade of the fifteenth century, these southern voyages directly affected both northern enterprise itself and the cartographical and political interpretations of what northern voyages of exploration accomplished.

Bitter rivalry developed between Portugal and Spain over the question of ownership in the newly discovered regions. Mediation by the pope resulted in the Treaty of Tordesillas in 1494, which decreed that a meridian be drawn in the Atlantic some 960 nautical miles west of the Portuguese Cape Verde Islands, corresponding in modern terms to 50° west of Greenwich. It divided the whole known world in two, giving Portugal what lay to the east of the line and Spain everything to the west of it. The line crossed the South American mainland at the mouth of the Amazon, which meant that Portugal soon gained control of both the East Indies and Brazil, although Spain otherwise obtained large parts of the Americas. The earliest extant map showing the Tordesillas demarcation is the so-called Cantino map of 1502, which celebrates the discoveries made by Pedro Alvares Cabral and the Corte Real brothers, among others, in the name of the Portuguese king.[26]

From 1494 on, the most pressing official question asked about trans-Atlantic discoveries was whether the Tordesillas line of demarcation had been violated, even though "[i]t was . . . believed for a long time, since longitude determination at sea remained wildly inaccurate, that the islands and mainland discovered within the next decade lying in the latitudes between roughly 45°N to 55°N were inside the Portuguese sphere as laid down in 1494."[27]

A cartographer's national allegiance became an issue, and simmering controversy undoubtedly contributed to the atmosphere of circumspection and concealment in which so many expeditions were planned, executed, and reported. In the past half century, historians have disagreed strongly about both the policy and the implementation of national secrecy during the Age of Discovery. These questions, and the debate about the degree to which the coastlines shown were "proof" of colonial claims rather than the result of faulty surveying, are somewhat peripheral issues here, but they cannot be ignored. Royal charters were notably and suspiciously vague about destinations, even when they were so detailed in other ways that one expects to find a feeding schedule for the ship's cat.

The Portuguese historian Jaime Cortesão, who took both Norse and pre-Columbian Portuguese discoveries in North America for granted, claimed that national economic considerations encouraged secrecy about Portuguese discoveries. He argued that in the fifteenth and sixteenth centuries, Portugal was a small and relatively defenseless country whose merchant kings pursued their economic objectives through navigation, so it was necessary to have a national policy focused on secrecy and monopoly, as exemplified by the Portuguese king's order in 1480 that the crews of foreign ships found in the Portuguese zone of navigation should be thrown into the sea. The English scholar G. R. Crone immediately refuted Cortesão's position, noting that foreign interlopers were tolerated everywhere during these years, and that the Portuguese policy of secrecy was not successful even with respect to maps. He used as an example Martellus's explicit map of Bartholomeo Dias's 1488 discoveries.[28]

One problem with this last argument is that Henricus Martellus Germanus made his map around 1489, well before the Treaty of Tordesillas.[29] It will become evident later in this chapter that maps of newly discovered land sometimes constituted very privileged information in the late fifteenth and early sixteenth centuries, and that both Spain and Portugal guarded their colonial enterprises as zealously as Bristol merchants nourished their own monopolies.

Although the Portuguese continued to oppose English trade in West Africa even after the close contact between England and Portugal had been emphasized during the Anglo-Spanish treaty negotiations in 1488, such issues do not seem to have affected trade between the British Isles and the two Iberian countries.[30] This trade continued as before, with codfish as one of the unifying agents and Bristol as a major English port. For better or for worse, those engaged in Atlantic fishing and trade constituted a supranational community paying little attention to politics and diplomatic posturing. Evidence is overwhelming that in the last two decades of the fifteenth century, the Atlantic sea lanes were long in many directions and rapidly growing longer, and that they were international to a degree we must acknowledge in order to have a proper perspective on the daring and high-profile voyages of discovery that followed, and on the new maps trailing in their wake.

Bristolmen in search of new markets, especially for their wool cloth, had started going to Madeira and other Portuguese Atlantic islands by 1480.[31] This was also the time they began experimenting with direct voyages to the fishing banks near the "Isle of Brazil." By the 1490s, Spain was granting land to Englishmen in the Canaries, which they had taken over from the Portuguese; both Lisbon and Seville had English merchant colonies; and in October of 1492, while Columbus was crossing the Ocean Sea, the naturalized Icelander William Yslond was shipping cloth from Bristol to Lisbon together with Robert Thorne, William Spencer, and other local luminaries.[32]

Columbus was following a trend when he took himself and his Genoese background to Portugal, England, Ireland, Iceland, and finally to Spain, on a quest that germinated in trade, branched into navigation and cartography, and flowered as independent exploration. His fellow Italian John Cabot, whose name became as firmly linked with the Newfoundland–Nova Scotia region as Columbus's with the Caribbean, had an equally itinerant career before he became convinced that he had the key to reaching "Cathay" (China) by sailing west. One big difference between the two men was that Cabot's career path was the reverse of the one followed by Columbus, who appears to have found his 1477 lesson about northern waters unconducive to exploring the northwestern Atlantic and eventually chose a southern route. Cabot tried to make his fortune in southern Europe before deciding to make his great westward push in the north, using Bristol as his starting point.

John Cabot was a merchant's son, again like Columbus, and may also have been born in Genoa, but by 1484 he was married to a Venetian woman, had a couple of sons, and was living in Venice where he had obtained citizenship. Here he worked as a merchant and a merchant's factor and once traveled as far as Mecca. This experience of Oriental riches, coupled with reading Marco Polo's account of his travels, had a lasting effect on Cabot's ambitions. It is probable, but not provable, that "our" John Cabot was the Venetian named Johan Caboto Montecalunya who lived in the Spanish seaport of Valencia in 1490–93, where he managed to interest King Ferdinand in some harbor improvements he thought he was qualified to take charge of, especially since he was a skilled mapmaker who could draw up proper plans. By 1493, the harbor project appeared moribund, perhaps for lack of funds. Both Williamson and Morison think it likely that just when his harbor scheme had fizzled, Cabot learned of Columbus's success in sailing westward to "India" when the latter returned to Barcelona in April of 1493 and received a tumultuous welcome.[33]

At that point, Cabot apparently reached two conclusions: he would try to go Columbus one better, and to do so he would have to interest somebody other than Ferdinand and Isabella, who were so delighted with Columbus's de facto accomplishment that they had little reason to support someone else in an untried venture. Spanish royal interest in Cabot-the-explorer appears to have been kindled only by reports from Rodrigo Gonzales de Puebla, the Spanish ambassador in London, that "one like Columbus" had arrived in England and was making plans to explore on behalf of the English king. On March 28, 1496, Ferdinand and Isabella responded that "it is . . . clear that no arrangement can be concluded in this matter in that country [England] without harm to us or to the King of Portugal."³⁴

Cabot's scheme for outshining Columbus consisted in finding a westward route to Cathay that took advantage of the known convergence of the meridians (in other words, foreshortened distances) in far northern latitudes.³⁵ Henry VII of England was therefore at least as logical a potential patron as João II of Portugal. Cabot must also have had other practical reasons for using England as his starting point. During his period as a Spanish-based merchant and cartographer, he may well have become aware, like John Day and De la Puebla's Spanish colleague Dom Pedro de Ayala, that Bristol merchants had been sending ships far into the North Atlantic for several years prior to 1497.³⁶

No Atlantic maps existed by which a mariner could plot a course to unfamiliar regions even when their general location was indicated. Not until the 1530s did Pedro Nunes lay the foundation for modern charts, "oriented by geographical north with indications of magnetic variations" and using "a rectilinear projection with mathematically consistent distortion."³⁷ In 1496, skilled pilots were still a navigator's best hope when personal experience did not suffice, and Bristol was Cabot's best chance of obtaining pilots and further information, as well as an ideal place to hire experienced crew. He would have had to provide something in return, however, such as a superior knowledge of navigational theory. This would have counted rather heavily, for the inability to establish reasonably exact longitude was a major obstacle in getting crews to accept oceanic sailing in the fifteenth century. Cabot actually suffered from the same shortcoming, but he was at least knowledgeable enough to note and record compass variations off Newfoundland in 1497, even if neither he nor his contemporaries knew exactly what to make of them.³⁸

Cabot packed up his wife, his sons, and his navigator's and mapmaker's tools and set sail for Bristol in either 1494 or 1495, where he soon made useful contacts. He eventually rented a house from Philip Greene, who had been one of the jurors from Bristol's "inner circle" when Thomas Croft had to account for his part in the 1481 expedition to the "Isle of Brazil."³⁹ Appendix C provides an overview of this group of merchants in the period 1480–1510, and of its close association with Atlantic enterprise of every kind. We see that in 1498, the year for which we have proof that John Cabot paid Greene rent for lodgings in Nicholas Street, Greene was also the landlord of John Jay (Bailiff of Bristol, 1498–99) and of the merchant John Thomas.⁴⁰

This was probably John Jay "the younger," who had been Greene's co-juror in 1481 as well as co-owner of the ships involved in the 1480 expedition into the North Atlantic, and who is thought to have been associated with Cabot's voyages in both 1497 and 1498. He and his close relatives were at the center of Bristol trade not only in the North Atlantic, including Norway, but to Iberia and Africa, and he became involved with Bristol enterprises in North America in 1501–5. John Thomas will also appear later in this chapter as a key member of the original Anglo-Azorean Syndicate in Bristol; he later had a long and profitable career as a Bristol merchant with ventures in both the New World and the Iberian Peninsula.[41] A third tenant of Greene's, William Clerk, likewise became active in Bristol enterprise in Newfoundland after 1502.

There are two main reasons why these powerful Bristol shipowners and merchants, themselves at the core of far-flung, underreported ventures into the North Atlantic, would have allowed Cabot into their circle and sufficiently into their confidence to help him assemble a crew. In the first place, Cabot was not a competitor in the fish trade, for he expressed no interest in cod. He was after the spices of Cathay. In the second place, these Bristolmen probably hoped that Cabot would acquire much useful information and succeed both in transferring the lucrative spice trade to their city and in finding urgently needed new markets for Bristol cloth.[42] They must have thought it prudent both to assist him and to keep an eye on him in an attempt to limit general access to further information about a region with which they already must have had some familiarity, judging from the English-inspired section of the Ruysch map discussed in Chapter Eight.

The men who fished near the "Isle of Brazil" in the last decades of the fifteenth century considered that area part of a continuous Greenlandic-Canadian coast, curving around the "Bay of Greenland." Those rocky, fog-shrouded coasts could hardly have fit anyone's notion of Cathay, although they still thought of this landmass as the east coast of Asia. But it is likely that Bristol navigators familiar with northwestern waters would, when approached by Cabot, allow that among all those bays and inlets there might well be a passage through which a ship might eventually reach Cathay. To find such a passage, however, someone had to invest in a venture focused on exploration rather than on fishing.

Quinn suggests that Cabot may have attempted a preliminary voyage of discovery as early as 1495 in the hope of establishing firm grounds for negotiating with Henry VII.[43] It would have been a reasonable thing to do, but we have no proof that it happened. Nor do we know what arguments Cabot used in March of 1496, when he succeeded in obtaining letters patent for himself and his three sons "Ludovicus, Sebastianus and Sanctus." Ever reluctant to part with funds, Henry VII granted Cabot and his sons the right to use five ships at their own expense "to sayle to all partes, countreys, and seas, of the East, of the West, and of the North" to find, and subsequently to govern, any countries, regions or provinces "in what part of the world soever they be, whiche before this time have beene unknowen to all Christians"—surely a convenient formula for avoiding conflict with Spain, Portugal, and Denmark. The Cabots would also have the monopoly of trade in these newfound areas. In return for all this generosity, the king would receive one-fifth of any profits, in addition to the substantial fees already paid for the license itself.[44]

Williamson is probably correct in surmising that Cabot, who had first-hand knowledge of the spice trade and secondhand knowledge from Marco Polo about the glories of Cathay, had long since deduced that Columbus had come nowhere near China. He must have managed to convince Henry VII both of this and of the merit in his own scheme for reaching Cathay via a comparatively short northwestern voyage from England.[45] Since it seems clear that he had enough reliable reports of land in the northwest to consider his goal attainable, he must have been persuasive on this point as well when he stood before the king. Neither Henry VII nor Cabot could have thought, any more than did Columbus, that the next landmass to the west was anything but the Asian continent, for the notion of an intervening American continent had not yet been born.

From John Day's letter to Columbus we know that Cabot's 1496 expedition (which consisted of only one ship) was unsuccessful. His crew confused him with their sailing directions, and bad weather, coupled with a shortage of food, forced him to turn back.[46] Undaunted, and perhaps thinking that even a negative lesson had value, he set off again the following year in the *Matthew* of Bristol, accompanied by his son Sebastian and, as before, with a mostly Bristol crew. Several scholars have speculated that the two noted Bristol merchants Hugh Elyot and Robert Thorne the Elder may also have been aboard the *Matthew*, because both men were active in the subsequent exploitation of North America, and because Thorne's son, Robert Thorne the Younger, claimed in 1527 that his father and Hugh Elyot "were the discoverers of the Newe found landes. . . ." The learned John Dee, for reasons best known to himself, assigned a date of 1494 to this event.[47]

A second look is warranted before we assume that Dee's date should have been "1497" and thus safely linked with John Cabot's first successful voyage. First of all, Thorne and Elyot enjoyed high visibility among the Bristol merchants and shipowners actively expanding their Atlantic sphere, so it is unlikely that they would have been shy about coming forward to claim a share in the glory when Cabot was feted upon his return in 1497. Secondly, we must allow for a likely connection between those two prominent Bristolians and earlier North Atlantic enterprises, including ones that periodically involved sending ships to Greenland.

The archaeological evidence discussed in Chapters Seven and Nine points to contact between Greenland and England (most likely Bristol) until at least the 1480s, possibly the 1490s. We have also seen that in 1480 and 1481, precisely the period in which Thorne and Elyot were rising professionally, ships were sent out from Bristol by members of Thorne and Elyot's circle to find a direct route to the "Isle of Brazil"—or the "Island of the Seven Cities" as John Day chose to call it in his letter reporting on Cabot's success. It is by a sheer fluke that we know about even these undertakings, for as Quinn notes, "after 1481 darkness falls over Bristol activities in the western ocean, lasting for the rest of the decade." It is possible that the discovery was made in 1494 and was not made public for several years while it was exploited in secrecy, as Quinn suggests.[48]

Both Elyot and Thorne were wealthy merchants with considerable interests in the codfish trade, and when the *Piningsdómur* of 1490 made conditions for the English in Iceland very tough, Elyot and Thorne may well have gone on one or more expeditions to the west—to what would be named the Newfoundland-Labrador region—hoping to expand the fisheries there, quite possibly in 1494, as Dee claimed. It is unlikely that they would have broadcast their knowledge of these fishing grounds, or that they would consider an area from which Ireland could be reached in two weeks as constituting a part of Asia. Only when the delineations of those new coasts became better known would it have been possible to claim, as the younger Thorne did in 1527, that the Bristolmen's distant fishing grounds and the "Newe found landes" were in the very same region, and that Elyot and Thorne had reached them before Cabot did. For reasons noted in Chapter Eight, as well as for reasons that will be discussed later in this chapter, it is likely that the two men considered their claim to include some part of Labrador (which they saw as part of a continent terminating in a Greenland promontory), rather than Newfoundland Island.

However quiet Elyot may have been about his earlier ventures, he was a litigious man whose lawsuits generated documents. Later in this chapter, his quarrels with members of the 1501 Anglo-Azorean syndicate will serve as a candle in the murk surrounding the disappearance of the Norse Greenlanders. The only way John Cabot himself contributed to that illumination was through his association with the men who must have known the Greenland route as well as the way to the "Isle of Brazil," and who continued to expand their knowledge of those unfamiliar shores in the west.

Discussions about John Cabot's own route in both 1497 and 1498 have kept scholars occupied for generations.[49] It nevertheless seems clear that Cabot bypassed Greenland, which is an indication of how well his Bristol pilots knew the more direct route to the Labrador-Newfoundland region, and which contrasts sharply with the route used by Corte Real just three years later—as we shall soon see. Cabot's expedition left Bristol on about

May 20, 1497, and headed "north and then west" from Dursey Head in Ireland, at 51°33′N.[50] We now know that the eastbound Labrador current was running against them at about one mile an hour, slowing them down, but they had smooth seas and good winds from the east-northeast most of the way, according to John Day's account of the story that Cabot himself told upon his return to Bristol.[51] The only bad weather they encountered, two or three days before sighting land, lasted for a day only. They arrived on St. John the Baptist's Day, June 24, at an unspecified North American location (which John Cabot's son Sebastian later called Prima Terra Vista, on his 1544 map). Nearby lay the big island which John Cabot named St. John, on whose modern identity scholars cannot agree either.[52]

Morison is sure "St. John" was Belle Isle, at the northern end of the strait separating Newfoundland from Labrador, and that Cabot's landfall was at Cape Dégrat, at 51°37′. In Harrisse's opinion, Sebastian Cabot in his 1544 map deliberately falsified, by some ten degrees, the latitude assigned to his father's first landfall, which corresponded to Cape Percé on Cape Breton Island. In Harrisse's own estimate, early-sixteenth-century maps placed the English discoveries between 56°N and 60°N. Arguing that Harrisse should not be trusted here because of his "personal animosity" for Sebastian, the modern Cabot expert James A. Williamson thinks Cabot's landfall was in Maine. Morison professes great wonder at this judgment, but any interested scholar is well advised to read Williamson's evaluation of the points that must be considered.[53]

The two maps that might have been able to settle this controversy—one which John Day hurriedly drew for Columbus and enclosed with his letter, and one which Cabot himself made—are lost. Questions might remain even if these maps turned up, however. Cabot went ashore only once in this new land, to erect a cross and to plant the banners of Henry VII, the pope, and St. Mark of Venice, and on that one occasion he and his small crew of eighteen or twenty men never went more than a stone's throw from their ship. This understandable precaution made it virtually impossible for John Cabot to record even the latitudes of the land he explored, for with the exception of that one landing, his measurements were roughly made from shipboard by means of quadrant and astrolabe.[54]

Quinn and others (although not Morison) assume that Juan de la Cosa, one of Columbus's pilots, had access to John Cabot's or John Day's maps when drawing his world map in 1500, but Williamson, noting that Spanish mapmakers were about fifty years behind the Portuguese in skill, warns against reading too much specific information into the La Cosa map, which he calls "primitive."[55] In general, more recent cartographical scholarship finds that although the extant version of this map is a copy made sometime between 1501 and 1510, it is true to the original, whose record of Columbus's discoveries was based on first-hand knowledge.[56]

One of the La Cosa map's many notable features is a large depiction of St. Christopher that conveniently eliminated the issue of whether the Central American isthmus might contain a passage through to Asia. Nor does the map suggest a break in the northern landmass. We have no way of knowing how much information La Cosa possessed about contemporary attempts to find a passage to Cathay in what soon (1507) became known as the North American continent, but Kenneth Nebenzahl, for example, supports Quinn in considering the La Cosa map our earliest surviving record of both John Cabot's and Columbus's voyages.[57]

In its surviving form, La Cosa's map has an odd appearance, with mismatched eastern and western halves, and it has no indications of scale or of latitudes and longitudes. On its featureless North American coast, the "English Cape" (*Cauo de ynglaterra*) lies due west of Dursey head, as Day had also noted in his letter. Quinn suggests that La Cosa's "Sea discovered by the English" (*mar descubierto por inglese*), shown just south of the coastline marked with English flags, may represent the waters between Cape Breton and southern Newfoundland, and he takes it for granted that the reference here is to Cabot's voyages.[58]

These questions are still wide open. At that early date, and especially on a Spanish map, place-names assigned to English discovery must be considered in conjunction with both Day's and De Ayala's stated belief that the English had sent ships into the distant northwestern Atlantic at least from the early 1490s. We do not know what part of eastern North America John Cabot surveyed, only that it probably lay somewhere between southern Labrador and Nova Scotia, possibly even as far south as Maine. Day noted in his letter that he was convinced that the "point of land" *first* discovered by Cabot was the Isle of Brazil and thus old hat to the Bristolmen, a statement which suggests either Newfoundland island or the Labrador-Newfoundland mainland.

One of Day's most notable observations is that *most of the new land was discovered when Cabot was coasting south*. In other words, the real significance of Cabot's 1497 voyage appears to be that he went farther south than the Bristol fishermen had ever gone, and that he surveyed a region which in balmy summer weather seemed to hold every promise of a lusher, richer "Cathay" farther on. It will shortly become evident that he managed to convince Henry VII of this as well.

Day reports that while sailing south along this new coast in midsummer heat, Cabot and his party had found a silent world of tall mast trees "and other trees underneath them," a description indicating a mixture of coniferous and deciduous trees incompatible with a very northerly site, but certainly familiar to anyone who has sailed along that coast as far south as Maine. Cabot and his party saw several signs of human habitation and observed two creatures running, but could not tell if they were men or beasts. Morison considers Cabot's failure to spot any Indians a sure indication that he was observing Newfoundland rather than Nova Scotia, for "[t]he Beothuk tribe which inhabited the big island were hunters and salmon fishermen, not particularly interested in the coast, but the Micmac of Nova Scotia . . . flocked to the shore in summer to fish and dig clams."[59]

The crew's discovery of great quantities of cod and other fish is usually interpreted as firm evidence that Cabot had located the Grand Banks off the southeastern coast of Newfoundland, and that these were a great and welcome surprise to everyone in Bristol. These assumptions do not hold up under scrutiny. Not only was there excellent fishing in the coastal waters running northward, but huge fishing banks also surround Nova Scotia and Sable Island, forming an almost continuous belt with the Grand Banks except for the deeper water in Cabot Strait leading into the Gulf of St. Lawrence. While it is true that several foreign diplomats as well as John Day and John Cabot's son Sebastian described the plethora of fish (Sebastian's 1544 map notes "sturgeons, salmon and baccalaos [codfish]"), we need to look at other elements in the most exuberant and most frequently quoted fishing forecast of them all: the long report Raimondo de Soncino sent from his listening post in England to the duke of Milan on December 18, 1497. De Soncino wrote:[60]

. . . The said Master John, as being foreign-born and poor, would not be believed, if his comrades, who are almost all Englishmen and from Bristol, did not testify that what he says is true. . . . And they say that it is a very good and temperate country, and they think that Brasil wood and silk grow there, and they affirm that the sea is covered with fishes which are caught not only with the net, but with baskets, a stone being tied in them in order that the baskets may sink in the water.

And this I heard the said Master John relate, and the aforesaid Englishmen his comrades say they will bring so many fishes that the kingdom will no longer have need of Iceland, from which country there comes a great store of fish called stockfish.

De Soncino had been present when John Cabot and his supporting cast of Bristolmen reported to Henry VII in London. Judging from de Soncino's letter, the crew verified *all* of Cabot's buoyant expectations and observations, not only the news about codfish. It obviously was a timely occasion for assuring the English monarch that England need no longer depend on Icelandic fish and the whims of the Danish king, but this passage in de Soncino's letter is in no way evidence that people in Bristol were overjoyed chiefly because Cabot had found them an overseas source of codfish. That was surely news only to people outside of Bristol, including the English king and those in his orbit.

Cabot himself did not think the road to glory was paved with codfish, although he was pleased for the moment. He had made a triumphal return to Bristol around August 6, after a fifteen-day voyage aided by favorable winds and currents, but slightly delayed by a landfall on the coast of Brittany which John Day ascribed to "confusion" brought on by Cabot's Bristol crew, who again claimed he was keeping too far north. His reception both in Bristol and in London was so gratifying that de Soncino assured the duke of Milan:[61]

... Master John has set his mind on something greater; for he expects to go further on towards the East [Levant] from that place already occupied, constantly hugging the shore until he shall be over against an island called by him Cipango, situated in the equinoctal region, where he thinks all the spices of the world, and also the precious stones originate. . . .

... I too believe in it, and what is more, the King here, who is wise and not lavish, likewise puts some faith in him; for since his return he has made good provisions for him, as the same Master John tells me. And it is said that in the spring, his Majesty . . . will fit out some ships and will besides give him all the convicts . . . that they will go to that country to make a colony. . . .

The Venetian envoy to England, Lorenzo Pasqualigo, who proudly considered John Cabot a fellow citizen, echoed these rumors in letters to his brothers, claiming that next spring the English king would let Cabot "have ten ships armed to his order, and on his request has conceded him all the prisoners except such as are confined for high treason, to man his fleet."[62]

The warrant issued on February 22, 1498, for two pension payments to John Cabot of £10 from Bristol customs revenues, was signed by Richard Ameryk (see Appendix C) and Arthur Kemys, "late custumers" of Bristol.[63] Cabot had good reason to be pleased with the king's favor and pension arrangements, as well as with his own visibility in the Bristol inner circle. Cabot received a second charter from Henry VII on February 3, 1498, to go "to the lande and isles of late founde by the said John" with up to six ships. When the expedition left Bristol in May, it consisted of four small Bristol and London ships and one larger one outfitted at the king's expense, although royal financial support seems to have been somewhat grudgingly given. We know from the letter penned by Ferdinand and Isabella's faithful Dom Pedro de Ayala on July 25, 1498, that one of Cabot's ships was driven ashore in Ireland after a storm, with at least one Italian cleric on board, to whom De Ayala referred as "another Friar Buil." In the report Raimondo de Soncino had sent to the duke of Milan on December 18, 1497, he remarked spitefully that "some poor Italian friars will go on this voyage, who have the promise of bishoprics." Despite the sneering tone of these remarks, the one clergyman we know for certain was on this voyage was a man of no little importance. He was Brother Giovanni Antonio de Carbonariis, for whom the duke of Milan's London correspondent was holding a letter in June of 1498 while de Carbonariis was away on Cabot's voyage.[64]

The presence of clergy suggests that John Cabot may have intended to establish a colony or "factory" of some kind, but we know nothing more about this 1498 venture than that Cabot intended to sail west and south in hopes of penetrating to Cathay, and that it ended in his death sometime after he had headed west from Ireland. De Carbonariis ceased to appear in documents, and John Cabot was never seen again, according to *Anglia Historia*, written circa 1512–13 by the Italian priest Polydore Virgil, who had been in England since 1502.[65] A pension was still being paid out to Cabot's family at Michaelmas of 1499, which indicates that there had been no reliable report of his death by that time.

There is some reason to suppose that other participants in the expedition had returned safely on a different ship or ships. One of them, Lancelot Thirkill, who had evidently gone on the 1498 voyage to the "new Ilande" with Thomas Bradley, was very much alive in Bristol in 1501; we just have no way of knowing if he had been on a ship marooned in Ireland early in the summer of 1498. Williamson finds it unlikely that not one ship out of a fleet of five would have survived, and he is among those who think it possible that John Cabot's own ship reached North America on that last voyage, because when the soon-to-be-discussed Corte Real expedition visited Labrador, Newfoundland, and maybe part of Nova Scotia in 1501, the crew obtained from the Indians a piece of a gilt sword that seemed to have been made in Italy, as well as a pair of silver earrings that might have originated in Venice.[66] Lest these items be seen as evidence of foul play by the Indians, it should be noted that they may simply have been left behind by a forgetful party—Cabot's or someone else's.[67]

The account of these interesting objects came from Pietro Pasqualigo, Venetian ambassador to Portugal and brother of Lorenzo Pasqualigo, the Venetian ambassador to London. Between them, these two brothers must have known most of the news and gossip circulating in European power centers at the time. Like Lorenzo, Pietro could assume that his correspondents in Venice would value the local twist to his story involving their fellow citizen Cabot, and he was obviously in a good position to report on the subsequent Corte Real ventures, all of which were chartered by the Portuguese king.

The modern historian L.-A. Vigneras assumes that Cabot's successful expedition of 1497 may have been a general reason for King Manoel's obvious interest in western as well as eastern exploration the following year.[68] The short westward passage Cabot had envisioned, from the supposed east coast of the Asian [American] continent to the known, lucrative, spice-trading centers, is not likely to have lost its allure yet for the Portuguese, for soon after Vasco da Gama had returned from Calicut to Portugal in 1498 with his heavily laden ships, it became apparent that the round trip from Lisbon around the Horn to Goa on the west coast of India could take as long as a year and a half, and at best six months, depending on the wind and the currents.[69]

Although the subsequent Corte Real voyages of discovery were confined to the North Atlantic, they were of great concern to other European maritime powers, particularly to Spain, because any new discoveries might infringe upon Spanish rights granted by the 1494 Treaty of Tordesillas. What Gaspar Corte Real originally went in search of, or what he told the Portuguese king he wanted to look for, cannot be deduced from any document. But rich, well-born, well-connected Azorean administrators like João Vaz Corte Real and his three sons were clearly welcome at court, for royal interest and protection ensured a succession of generous patents for exploration and colonization in ventures which the Corte Reals' wealth allowed them to undertake at private expense.[70]

Gaspar was 45–50 years old when King Manoel's patent of May 12, 1500, gave him and his heirs the right to own, govern, and monopolize the trade of any lands he might find on a voyage of discovery at his own cost. The charter's preamble noted that Gaspar had already been on at least one voyage of exploration in search of lands and islands.[71] Even if a previous voyage had taken place after João Vaz's death in 1496, Gaspar may also have gone exploring with his father while the latter was alive. Both in Gaspar's case and in a number of other instances, it strains credulity to argue that there cannot have been an earlier voyage if there is "no evidence" for it—in other words, if no previous charter is known. Charters were mostly needed to protect land claims and trade, not to probe unfamiliar sea routes.

Gaspar's plan in 1500 quite likely was dictated by his own experience together with information passed on by his father, as well as by other Azorean long-distance sailors. It is possible that Gaspar's aristocratic background had prevented him from access to (or faith in) people familiar with the Bristol fishing route westward, for his own account and the Cantino map in Fig. 32 both show that he must have set a course very similar to that which English (and eventually Iberian) fishermen had long been using to reach the banks off western Iceland and southeastern Greenland. From the Denmark Strait, the Corte Real expedition's two ships followed the current south along Greenland's east coast (Fig. 24), down around Cape Farewell, and up along the southwest coast until the current and the obstacle of ice directed them westward across the Davis Strait.

Gaspar evidently sighted the mountains of southern Greenland before he rounded Cape Farewell, but he made no effort to land on either coast. If it is true that Gaspar had left Lisbon at the beginning of September (which was a good time to sail in the Davis Strait, but which did not allow much time before the start of autumn storms in the Atlantic), he had no time to waste on breaking through the ice belt in order to attempt a risky landing on barren-looking, cold, and mountainous Greenland before heading west across the Davis Strait. There, Gaspar discovered a land to the north "that because it was very cool and green and with many trees, as are all the lands in that area, he called it Greenland."[72]

Corte Real's "Greenland" (*Terre Verde*) is generally thought to have been in the greater Newfoundland region.[73] The name may merely have been an inspiration akin to Eirik the Red's five centuries earlier, but it may also have resulted from the Iberian cartographical tradition that had caused the Catalan chart of ca. 1480 (Fig. 23) to show a conceptual "Illa verde" immediately north of an equally stylized "Illa de brazil." Much clearer are the indications that the extensive knowledge of the North Atlantic which the Portuguese had by 1500, and to which Gaspar and his father had probably contributed, did not include familiarity with Norse Greenland. Gaspar named his subsequent western discovery "Greenland" in apparent ignorance of the name's current employment elsewhere.

Ever since the Dane Claudius Clavus first drew Greenland on a map in 1427 and depicted it as a huge promontory reaching westward from the northern Eurasian landmass, European cartographers had been prepared to accept that a western extension of Asia might be identical with Greenland. The map (Fig. 25) which Ruysch made after his voyage with Bristol fishermen to the New World around 1502–4 shows clearly that while he also was unaware that there was an entire American continent to contend with, and imagined Greenland to be an Asian promontory, he saw it as an extreme *eastward* extension of that continent.

Gaspar Corte Real, who evidently did not associate Cape Farewell with any kind of known Greenland, liked what he saw of his own *Terre Verde* and set out from Lisbon again the following year. With a fresh patent from King Manoel, he and his brother Miguel left with three ships on May 15, 1501, allowing plenty of time for exploration. Again, the expedition followed the route via Greenland's southern cape, where they encountered so much ice that they headed straight west across the lower Davis Strait. All three ships then seem to have coasted south along Labrador before going down the outer coast of Newfoundland Island and, possibly, exploring parts of Nova Scotia. Along the way they picked up the sword and earrings thought to have been left by a member of Cabot's 1498 expedition, and which stirred the imagination of the Venetian Pietro Pasqualigo.[74]

Pasqualigo was not the only Lisbon-based diplomat to report on the Corte Real voyages. An Italian named Alberto Cantino often dispatched information from there to Ercole d'Este, duke of Ferrara, in whose service he appears to have been.[75] One of several surviving letters from Cantino, dated October 17, 1501, reports that two ships from Gaspar's expedition had returned to Lisbon between October 9 and 11 with much news, but without further sight of Gaspar after he had taken his ship on an extended probe southward along the new coast. Both Cantino and Pasqualigo reported that many natives had been brought back on the two other ships, and they provided enough details about these captives' appearance and way of life for us to be certain that they were North American Indians and not Eskimos, though we cannot be sure just where their home had been.[76]

By mid-winter there was still no news of Gaspar. On January 15, 1502, his brother Miguel obtained a charter of his own, in which the king extended the privileges he had given Gaspar (and which Miguel had inherited) to include any lands Miguel might discover for himself. Miguel had little joy of these privileges, however, for he never returned. His expedition appears to have gone straight to the Newfoundland region without a long leg via East Greenland first. All three ships reached their western destination safely and then split up to search for Gaspar. The other two ships eventually returned to Lisbon with the report that Miguel had failed to show up for their Newfoundland rendezvous on August 20. Only one Corte Real brother, Vasco Annes, now remained in Portugal. Since he was the eldest and fast approaching sixty, he may not have been in any condition to brave the North Atlantic in search of Gaspar and Miguel—or he may just have been too important a person at home. At any rate, when the king sent out an armed search expedition in 1503, Vasco Annes was not on it, and Damião de Góis in 1566 judged that "this affair was brought to an end because it was not desirable to incur any further expense in it."[77]

Taking full advantage of his Lisbon listening post, Alberto Cantino commissioned a world map (Fig. 32) for his duke. It was a state-of-the-art depiction of some Spanish but mostly Portuguese discoveries that included the voyages of Cabral and Vasco da Gama as well as the Corte Real explorations of 1500 and 1501.[78] The cartographer obviously did not know or care about the Norse Greenland colony belonging to Denmark-Norway, which is not surprising. Just a few people who quietly profited from intermittent trade there knew about the "real" Greenland's tiny European population, and those merchants were most likely from Bristol, as we have seen. Wil-

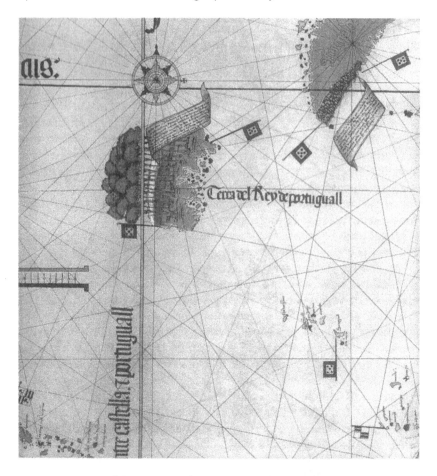

FIG. 32. Section of the map secretly commissioned in Lisbon by Alberto Cantino in 1502. The map, the earliest surviving Portuguese depiction of that country's recent probes to the east and west, is still in the Biblioteca Estensa in Modena, Italy. Source: Photograph reproduced by permission of the British Library.

liamson tartly observes that "[t]he cartographer . . . ignored Cabot and the English as if they had never been."[79]

The map is always associated with Cantino's name, while the cartographer's identity (probably an Italian working in Portugal) has remained a secret for reasons summarized by Kenneth Nebenzahl:[80]

In the political atmosphere of this period, the need for anonymity was imperative. Success in the bitter rivalry between Spain and Portugal required that the new geographical data generated by discoveries in the East and West Indies be kept secret. Information from returning mariners was assembled by cartographers to form official charts for kings and their advisors. To copy or divulge the contents of these royal maps was a capital crime.

The Cantino planisphere, drawn at such risk to the cartographer and sent off in the greatest secrecy, was received by Ercole d'Este in November of 1502 and is still preserved in the Estense Library at Modena. Its sketchy American coastline records only the areas explored through 1501, in brilliant colors that include bright orange parrots in the Brazil region. An equally prominent feature is the sturdy line that divides Spanish and Portuguese territories in accordance with the Treaty of Tordesillas, and which is clearly visible in Fig. 32. The line slices through a large chunk in the Newfoundland region that represents either an island or part of an otherwise unexplored mainland, and our attention is drawn to the larger, eastern half, which has Portuguese flags, exquisitely drawn trees, and an Atlantic coast full of inviting coves.[81]

This area, which strictly speaking should have been well over on the Spanish side, is every bit as green as one would expect of a *Terre Verde*. Here it is called "Terra del Rey de portuguall" and bears a legend linking it firmly to Gaspar's 1501 voyage:[82]

This land was discovered by order of . . . the King of Portugal D. Manuel, and the man who discovered it was Gaspar de Corte Real, gentleman of the court of said ˙King; he who discovered it sent [home] a ship with . . . men and women who belonged to that land, and he [went off] with the other ship and never returned but was lost, and he [found] many mast [trees].

Northeast of the Cantino map's "Terra del Rey de portuguall" lies the real Greenland, also marked with Portuguese flags and with a nearby legend noting that it had been discovered by order of King Manoel, and that those who discovered it did not disembark, but observed jagged mountains there, "whence, according to the opinion of cosmographers it is believed to be the peninsula of Asia."[83] It is well to remind ourselves here that Cape Farewell probably was a regular course-marker for both English and Portuguese mariners well before 1500, and that cartographers acknowledged this on maps that otherwise reflected their own preoccupations.

Chapter Eight noted that De la Roncière thought "Terra del Rey de portuguall" in the Cantino map represented the same location as the Paris Map's tripartite "island called of the Seven Cities, a colony now peopled by Portugal," where Spanish ship-boys had reported finding silver in the sand. Quinn has argued that the reference on the Paris Map points to *some* kind of Portuguese discovery of land northwest of the Azores prior to 1490 and also indicates that the Portuguese had settled what they called the Island of the Seven Cities before 1493.[84] The 1507–8 Ruysch Map (Fig. 25) prudently shows both a "Cape of the Portuguese" and, well to the south of this cape, "Antilia Insula" accompanied by a legend describing the "Seven Cities."

It is probable that other Portuguese had preceded the Corte Reals in this region by a decade or more—in which case the Venetian sword and earrings that the 1501 Corte Real expedition found among the Indians could have come from a Portuguese pre-Cabotian visitor with Venetian connections. But if there had been a pre-Columbian Portuguese *settlement* in the area, of which the creator of the 1492 Paris Map had certain knowledge, the Portuguese king would surely have been aware of it, too, and would have used it as a bargaining chip when the Treaty of Tordesillas was drawn up. Most likely, there had been any number of unofficial European visitors, but no attempted settlements, when Cabot and the Corte Reals tugged the "Asian" (North American) east coast out of the mists of myth, gossip, and the most private of private enterprise.

As Ruysch's map indicates, the legend of the "Seven Cities" was slow to die even after the real islands in the Newfoundland–Nova Scotia region became known to explorers. Tales about precious metals awaiting lucky lads—Spanish or otherwise—enjoyed an even longer life. But the length of time it took for myths to die, and for cartographers to catch up with the shape of unfamiliar regions, does not alter the fact that a real change began as soon as the new coasts became officially known. Verbal accounts and cartographical representations of the latest discoveries only made possession of a piece of that slowly unfolding world even more attractive and exciting, and there was a growing demand for royal charters to sanction and protect individual discoveries.

The Corte Reals, accustomed to landed power, preserved their family rights in the New Lands after Gaspar's first official discovery of land somewhere along the Labrador coast and the Strait of Belle Isle. After the death of Gaspar and Miguel, King Manoel assigned all those rights to their eldest brother, Vasco Annes, who renewed them several times through at least 1522.[85] Surviving members of his brothers' crews would have been able to give Vasco Annes access to detailed sailing directions and must obviously have guided King Manoel's search-and-rescue expedition for Gaspar and Miguel. Morison was nevertheless certain that the Corte Reals' hereditary captaincy of the "Terra del Rey de portuguall" was titular only, and that no member of the family bothered with those lands again, but he made this assessment before L.-A. Vigneras had evaluated documents showing that the direct descendants of another Azorean landowner and late-fifteenth-century explorer, Pedro de Barcelos, also maintained his landed interests in the vicinity of Cape Breton, including Sable Island.[86]

The lack of records for the decades immediately before and after 1500 prevents continuity in our knowledge about de Barcelos's activities either at home or abroad, but what we do know warrants a closer look, both because he was a contemporary colleague of the Corte Real brothers and because of his near connection with the Azorean João Fernandes, whose title of *"llavrador"* [landowner] became the name "Labrador"—originally assigned to Greenland.

In the course of a lawsuit in 1506, Pedro de Barcelos of Angra, in the Azorean island of Terceira, mentioned lands and privileges that had been usurped while he himself was away on a three-year voyage of northern discovery at the command of the Portuguese king. His partner in this venture had been another Terceiran landowner (*llavrador*) named João Fernandes.[87] Nobody knows when this joint voyage took place or what de Barcelos and João Fernandes had found at that time. We know that the voyage must have borne fruit, however, for when Pedro de Barcelos died in 1507, his son Diogo appears not only to have inherited his father's Terceiran lands and social standing, but to have possessed information about a certain part of North America and known where to find it again.

Within a year of Pedro de Barcelos's death, the king gave his royal *escudero* Diogo additional economic privileges back home in Terceira, the stated reason for which was that Diogo's father had rendered valuable services to the crown. And when João III succeeded to the throne, he granted a charter to Diogo and his brother Alfonso to renew the search for land started by their father. Sometime between 1521 and 1531, therefore, Diogo and his son Manoel set out with one ship at their own expense and discovered *"certas ilhas e terras"* on the other side of the Atlantic.[88]

Again, we have no proof of where those "certain islands and lands" were located, or an explanation for why it had taken him so long to go there. In fact, it seems doubtful this could have been his first trip. Nor have we any way of guessing why brother Alfonso showed so little interest in the enterprise. In 1531, when Diogo declared he was off on yet another expedition and gave his brother 30 days to make up his mind to participate, Alfonso and his wife renounced all claims in both the new land and the royal grant. Diogo may simply have bought out his brother's claim. After Diogo's death, however, his son Manoel made several voyages to the new lands in the company of his first cousin Marcos de Barcelos Machado. In a place they called Isla Barcellona de Sam Bardão, these two men left cattle, sheep, goats, and pigs, which are said to have prospered in their new habitat.[89]

In a private Terceiran archive, Baptista de Lima, Director of the Archives at Angra, discovered the documents revealing this story. He then consulted sixteenth-century Portuguese maps where the name Pinheiro (the de Barcelos's real family name) occurred in the region north of the Gulf of St. Lawrence, along the coast of southern Labrador, suggesting that this was the location of the mainland first discovered by Pedro de Barcelos and reclaimed by his son Diogo. On two maps (1560–61) by Bartolomeuo Velho, de Lima also found an island or islands called "Barcellona" in a bay that appeared to be on the south shore of Cape Breton Island. The Portuguese legend next to one of the islands noted that they were called "Barcellona Islands because those who discovered them were from Barcelos."[90]

De Lima thinks that these islands are identical not only with the "Isla Barcellona de Sam Bardão" mentioned in the 1568 Terceiran documents involving the descendants of Pedro de Barcelos, but with an identifiable island that many sixteenth-century charts called "I. de Sablo," located at 44°N and 60°W, some 100 miles southeast of Nova Scotia. Here, Sir Humphrey Gilbert and his men found plenty of fresh meat in 1582, thanks to cattle and pigs that the Portuguese had brought "above 30 years hence." Vigneras agrees with de Lima that Sable Island probably formed some part of the territory discovered by Diogo and Manoel (presumably on the basis of Pedro's early voyages), and he calls attention to yet another observation by de Lima, namely that the site is in the same region (south of the Cabot Strait) where a number of sixteenth-century maps show islands called "Fagunda," "João Alvares" and "Santa Cruz"—names that are all related to the voyages of João Alvares Fagundes.[91] This, in turn, links them with de Barcelos and his voyages with João Fernandes.

In 1521, King Manoel gave Fagundes all jurisdictional and proprietary rights over a region Fagundes had discovered the previous year. He had evidently convinced the king that this was *not* territory already spoken for by the Corte Reals, which suggests that the people most directly involved in these early land grabs were well informed among themselves and took it for granted that the land would be used by those who had taken it. There are indications that Fagundes tried (and failed) to establish a year-round fishing station on his American property some time between 1521 and 1525, but scholarly consensus on just how he used his royal grant is conspicuously absent.[92]

The cattle that the Englishmen found so useful in 1582 were reddish and large like the modern Terceiran cattle. This may seem trivial until we consider the implications of de Lima's and Vigneras's research into the tight little Terceiran circle that included (at various social levels) the Corte Real and de Barcelos families, as well as the *labrador* João Fernandes and part of the Fagundes family. De Lima notes that a branch of the Fagundes clan had settled in Terceira arcound 1500, and that members of that family then intermarried with the de Barcelos family. Collaboration on ventures to the New World, resulting in neighboring land claims, was therefore very likely.[93] And the introduction of livestock in the New World suggests an undertaking of some size and complexity.

All told there are many indications that discoveries and land claims were made in the region of southern Labrador, Sable Island, the Strait of Belle Isle, and Cape Breton Island just before and just after 1500 by Azoreans who came from around Angra in the island of Terceira; that these discoveries were so well known to some of the explorers' descendants that they made use of them; and that this use included bringing over livestock at an early point.[94]

From about 1502 on, the whole area drew record numbers of fishermen from Portugal and England, and not long afterward from France.[95] It is in the light of that keen competition and the obvious attraction of permanent shore stations that we must evaluate much of the information that comes next.

None of the later de Barcelos documents mentions Pedro's former partner João Fernandes, whose career appears to have followed a separate track by 1499. His is such a common name that we cannot be certain it was he who had traded in Bristol in 1486, when the customs records for that city refer to "ffernandus and gunsalus," or that he is the Portuguese merchant "Johannus Fornandus" who shipped sugar from Lisbon to Bristol on November 12, 1492, and took Bristol cloth back with him to Lisbon on January, 26, 1493.[96] But an early trading association with Bristol on the part of "ffernandus" in the company of "gunsalus" makes sense when we know that João Fernandes and his Azorean companion João Gonsalves became members of the Anglo-Azorean Syndicate in Bristol in 1501, under circumstances that will be discussed shortly.

We know for certain with whom we are dealing in 1499, when Manoel I's official in Lisbon wrote a charter on October 28 to João Fernandes (Joham Fernandez) of Terceira, who[97]

has informed us that for God's and our service, he was desirous to make an effort to seek out and discover at his own expense some islands lying in our sphere of influence, and we, in view of his praiseworthy desire and intention, not only thank him for it, but it is our pleasure and we hereby promise to grant him, as indeed we shall grant him, the governorship of any island or islands, either inhabited or uninhabited, which he may newly discover and find; and this with the same revenues, honours, profits and advantages we have granted to the governors of our islands of Madeira and the others; and for his protection and as a memorandum to ourselves we order this grant, signed and sealed by us, with our hanging seal, to be given to him. Given in our city of Lisbon on October 28. André Fernandes made this in the year of our Lord Jesus Christ, 1499.

This letter is short and to the point, without the ornate preamble about grand family connections and previous voyages that would be contained in the king's first patent to Gaspar Corte Real less than a year later.[98] The document nevertheless implies a previous voyage on João's part, for it reveals that he convinced the crown that he had in mind a region within the Portuguese sphere as defined by the Treaty of Tordesillas, which suggests he had a very good idea of where he was going. João would have been a fool indeed to pay good money for a charter and risk sailing "at his own expense" if he might end up causing an international incident and be forced to cede his hard-won property to Spain.

Most likely, João Fernandes had just completed his three years of exploration with Pedro de Barcelos, for such a lengthy voyage could not have been accomplished in the period between 1499—when João's time began to be otherwise accounted for in documents that never mention de Barcelos—and 1506—when Pedro de Barcelos was already in the midst of his Azorean lawsuit.[99]

The de Barcelos family's subsequent land claims in the southern Labrador–Sable Island region suggest that these were waters Pedro and João had explored together, to which João intended to return for a closer look, and to which he hoped to stake a separate claim after receiving his charter from the Portuguese king late in 1499. That does not mean he wanted to be cheek-by-jowl with de Barcelos; he may on the contrary have deemed it wiser to concentrate his own future interest somewhere on the perimeter of the area he had investigated with his partner. Unreliable though the early map evidence is, it favors a somewhat more northerly part of Labrador, closer to the Hamilton Inlet.

João himself undoubtedly knew where he wanted to go and how to get there, especially since the Portuguese at that time were far more advanced in navigational skills than the English were. By the end of the fifteenth century, the Portuguese had both the quadrant and the original sea astrolabe, which despite their shortcomings were well ahead of the primitive instruments still used by the English.[100] The English themselves were so aware of this difference that right to the end of the sixteenth century their explorers preferred to have a Portuguese pilot along.[101] João, whose Bristol connections may already have gone back ten years or more when he and de Barcelos went exploring, had probably also picked up some of the same useful information that led John Cabot to choose Bristol as his starting point for a short route in search of a westward penetration into northern "Asia."

When João and Pedro first set out, they may nevertheless, like Corte Real, have decided to follow the North Atlantic fishermen's traditional route toward Iceland and the Denmark Strait before rounding Cape Farewell in Greenland, crossing the Labrador Basin, and coasting south along the North American shore until they made their shorter way home, aided by eastbound winds and currents. In that case, their voyage may have contributed to the Cantino map's legend near the southern tip of Greenland, which does not refer specifically to the Corte Reals, but which says only that this land with the big mountains had been discovered by the authority of Dom Manoel of Portugal, and that those who discovered it had not disembarked. The cartographer may have preferred to credit no particular name with the area; he had in any case made his point by declaring the (Greenland) promontory to be Portuguese by right of discovery.

Very soon after 1500, João Fernandes's name nevertheless became directly associated with Greenland, but we do not know to the year when, or how, cartographers first became aware of the connection, or in exactly what it consisted. The few surviving maps from this period are as hard to date as their promontories and islands are tough to equate with modern delineations; they reflect the personal and national loyalties of their cartographers; and theory may often have overshadowed detailed knowledge of the new discoveries.

The anonymous sea chart known as the King-Hamy map (Fig. 33) is an intriguing piece in the puzzle of João Fernandes's voyages, for it is the earliest-known map with a reference to the *labrador* himself. Thirty years ago, R. A. Skelton judged the map to be post-1503 and Italian, rather than Portuguese, and while this assessment is open to debate, his discussion on early maps relating to Williamson's Cabot treatise is still a mine of useful information.[102] He noted the radical departure from the known Portuguese tradition in the King-Hamy chart's depiction of Greenland as an elongated, east-west tending island, rather than as the northernmost promontory of an Asian mainland. This island is clearly labeled "Terra Laboratoris."[103] Two other surviving maps, also anonymous, show a similar island named for the *labrador*.[104]

The provenance and date of the King-Hamy chart are unfortunately still unknown; a recent evaluation in the 1989 *Guide to Medieval and Renaissance Manuscripts* in the Huntington Library, the map's current owner, describes it as a portolan chart from about 1502, possibly made in Italy from an early Portuguese prototype.[105] If those assumptions are correct, they increase the chance that the maker of the 1502 Cantino map had information about João's early travels, as well as about the Corte Real expeditions, when he depicted the actual Greenland and its southernmost cape.

The King-Hamy chart (Fig. 33) shows Iceland ("Tile") as an island between "Terra Laboratoris" and a large Scandinavian peninsula crowned by a landmass named "Engloveland"—a permutation of the Greenland with

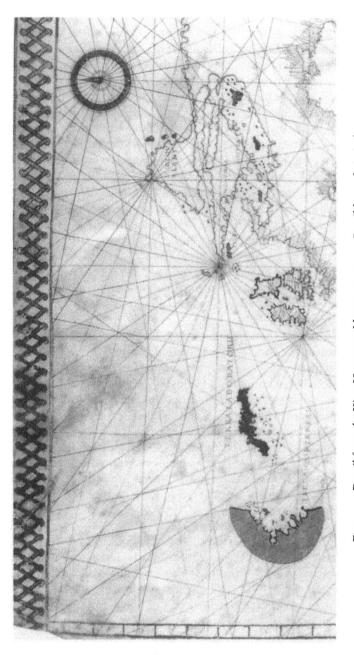

FIG. 33. Detail from the King-Hamy world map, ca. 1502. Possibly made in Italy from a Portuguese prototype, it is the earliest known map to connect João Fernandes, *labrador* from the Azores, with Greenland. Source: Photograph from, and reproduced by permission of, the Huntington Library, San Marino, California.

which Claudius Clavus had presented European cartographers about eighty years earlier. Nothing is new here. Novelty enters with the "Terra Laboratoris" island and the Newfoundland-Labrador region to the west of it, which has a number of bays and capes, including the "Capo Raso" (probably Cape Race, the southeastern termination of Newfoundland Island) at the southern tip of the area called "Terra Cortereal." In other words, the mapmaker made a firm distinction between the *labrador*'s discoveries and those made by Corte Real. This determination to distinguish João's claim from his competitor's may in part have been what made the cartographer show Greenland/"Terra Laboratoris" as an island.

The only extant non-cartographical written source linking João Fernandes with the early use of the name "Labrador" for southern Greenland must be taken with a grain of salt. Alonzo de Santa Cruz had probably seen the Spanish "Wolfenbüttel map" (ca. 1530), whose inscription near Greenland says that the Land of the Labrador was discovered by the English from Bristol, "and because he who gave the information [*el aviso*] of it was a labrador of the Azores they gave it that name."[106] De Santa Cruz clearly mixed facts with hearsay and fiction when he wrote to Charles V of Spain around 1541:[107]

This land was called labrador because a labrador [ploughman or landowner] from the Azores gave information and intelligence of it to the King of England at the time he was sent to explore it by Antonio Gaboto [*sic*, read John Cabot], the English pilot and the father of Sebastian Gaboto, your Majesty's present Pilot Major.

Had the Azorean *labrador* João Fernandes been among those who accompanied Sebastian Cabot's father to London when John Cabot reported to Henry VII on his successful 1497 voyage, we can be reasonably certain that one of the many foreign envoys present would have commented on such a separate and important discovery by a Portuguese subject. Significantly, the English-informed North Atlantic details on Ruysch's 1507–8 map (Fig. 25) do not show a "Labrador" anywhere along the curving coast of the "Bay of Greenland"; there is only a C. de Portogesi at the tip of Terra Nova, south of the islands called "Baccalauras" or Codfish Islands. The Bristolmen with whom Ruysch visited those alien shores in 1502–4 probably were not about to credit a foreigner like João Fernandes with "discovering" a Greenland whose location and existence they had taken for granted all their working lives, nor with claims to any part of the new coasts to which they assumed prior rights. Other maps discussed below also suggest rivalry between Bristolmen and the *labrador*; the likely depth of that feeling will be probed somewhat later.

At the very least, these early maps indicate that after about 1502, Portuguese and Italian cartographers credited João Fernandes with having discovered a northern territory of his own and with knowing of Greenland's existence and location. Contemporary cartography also shows that the *labrador*'s claim soon was joined by assertions that Englishmen from Bristol had known about "his" territory first. Unfortunately, it is impossible to sort out what, if any, distinction the cartographers and their informants made between Greenland and Labrador, since both were now depicted as east-tending northern promontories of a continuous continental shoreline cradling the Davis Strait.

Prior to about 1570 (when "Labrador" was moved from Greenland to its present location), inscriptions on other early maps that directly linked the *labrador*'s name with what we know as Greenland also mention men from Bristol.[108] Maggiolo's map of 1516 refers to the Greenlandic promontory's connection both with the English and with fishing: "*Terranova de pescaria inventa de laboradore de re de anglitera tera frigida*" ("New land of fishing discovered by the *labrador* for the English king, frigid country").[109] Only five years earlier, however, this Genoese cartographer had made a beautiful world map on which Greenland was labeled "land of the English"; the promontory directly to the southwest on the same continuous coastline was "the land of the Labrador and of the king of Portugal"; well to the south of this again lay the "land of fishing"; and the southernmost promontory was credited with being "the land of Corte Real and of the king of Portugal."[110]

The Italian Oliveriana map, which dates from 1508–10 or somewhat earlier, and which has both a "Cavo Laboradore" at Greenland's Cape Farewell and an island called "Insula de Labardor" to the southwest of it, is also interesting in the context of English versus Portuguese discovery.[111] Along Greenland's east coast, just below "ponta de sampaulo" (Ammassalik?), is the inscription *terra descubieri*.

Other maps of the same period give the English from Bristol at least equal billing with the *labrador* as far as Greenland's discovery is concerned, but none more interestingly than the two made by Diego Ribeiro in 1529. Both maps claim that the "Tiera del Labrador" was discovered by the English (one map adds "from Bristol"), and both state that there is "nothing of value" to be found there.[112] Was the source of this dyspeptic remark also English—or did the statement simply reflect that time's preoccupation with precious metals?[113]

The cartographer Diego Ribeiro was a native Portuguese who had succeeded Sebastian Cabot as the Spanish Pilot Major in Seville, and he penned the legends noted above just two years after Robert Thorne the Younger had sent *his* map sketch (Fig. 34) to the English ambassador in Seville and claimed that his father and Hugh Elyot had discovered the New World before Cabot. Along the coastline of "*Noua terra laboratorum dicta*" Thorne

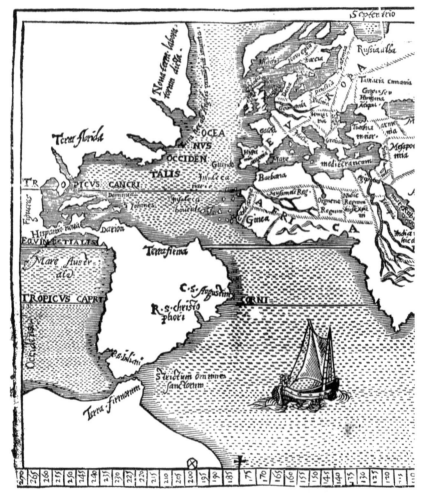

FIG. 34. Section of the world map drawn by Robert Thorne the Younger and sent to the English ambassador in Seville, 1527. From the 1903 Hakluyt Society facsimile, Maps 920 (291). Source: Photograph from, and reproduced by permission of, the British Library.

had written: "This land was first discovered by the English."[114] Because of Thorne's close link with the men directing Bristol exploration, fishing, and trade in the crucial decades before and after 1500, his map needs close scrutiny in connection with João Fernandes's experiences while he was in Bristol in 1501.

The comments Thorne made in a letter accompanying the map that he sent to the English ambassador in Seville leave no doubt that the area he claimed the English had discovered before the *labrador* was part of a mainland, "which mainland or coast goeth Northward and finisheth in the land that we found, which is called heere Terra de Labrador. So that it appeareth the said land that we found, and the Indies to be all one maine land." But we cannot overlook the possibility that the Bristol-bred Thorne included *both* Greenland and the Newfoundland region in his claims for prior English discovery, for his northwestern geography is somewhat vague, as we see from his attempt to convince the ambassador of how feasible it was to make a voyage westward through the northern polar region to the "spiceries." It is worth noting, too, that the younger Thorne's claim for English discovery began at the promontory *south* of the so-called Labrador's Land. He referred elsewhere in his letter to "the New Founde islandes that wee discovered," and he said of his father and Hugh Elyot that they were "the discoverers of the Newe found landes" that were part of a continuous coast, "as by the Carde appeareth, and is aforesaid." Moreover, he apologized for the map's being so roughly drawn, with most place-names and other details omitted for lack of space. "Many Islands are also left out, for the said lack of roome. . . ."[115]

Taken together, Thorne's letter and map make three things very clear: the large mainland territory the *labrador* was supposed to have claimed was the *northernmost* of three northern promontories along the North American east coast and could well have included southern Greenland as well as parts of modern Labrador; the thought that João Fernandes might be credited with discovering an area already known to the English was intolerable; and the English discovery of a considerable stretch of coast was due not only to John Cabot, but to Hugh Elyot and Robert Thorne the Elder—old hands at northern fisheries, trade, and exploration.

Fig. 34 shows only the western half of the younger Thorne's map, without his latitude indications that place the southernmost tip of *Noua terra* at an unlikely 60°N. It is much more significant that this point is shown to be directly west of Ireland. As suggested in Chapter Eight, at the end of the fifteenth century the "Isle of Brazil" tended to be located at about 53°N (directly west of Galway), a latitude commensurate with the northernmost tip of Newfoundland and the southern part of Labrador. Although Robert Thorne the Younger shared his contemporaries' vagueness about the polar regions, we can probably assume he was familiar with where his father and Hugh Elyot had sailed before Cabot, and with where the area lay both in relation to Ireland and to the better-known stretches of the North American east coast.

João Fernandes's own North American discoveries and the persistent linking of his name with Greenland have never been discussed in terms of the early familiarity that the English had with the Strait of Denmark, with Greenland's location, and, in due course, with the western side of the Davis Strait—the "Bay of Greenland." Nor have discussions of the *labrador* ever included the fact that some of João's fellow Terceirans retained and exploited their early discoveries in the New Lands. Evidence that a viable Norse Greenland community, however small, was known to a few outsiders has also been ignored in this context. So has the likelihood that those who traded with the Eastern Settlement in the late fifteenth century were Bristolmen from the same group that sponsored direct voyages to the "Isle of Brazil" *before* they admitted John and Sebastian Cabot, followed by João Fernandes and his companions, to their circle.

In the person of João Fernandes, who possessed considerable navigational expertise and geographical knowledge in his own right, Portuguese and English information about new discoveries and old fishing grounds must have converged. By 1499, João probably had at least as much information about eastern North America as Pedro de Barcelos, and he would certainly have been familiar with both the aims and the results of Cabot's well-publicized voyages of 1497 and 1498. Unlike Cabot, however, he seems to have had no interest in finding a westward access to exotic Asian goods; everything we know about him points to a focused interest in those new coasts just the way they were, with tall trees, green pastures, and great quantities of fish and other creatures in the sea—and to a wish to colonize a specific region. The latter required a royal charter, which João had, as well as a sufficient number of settlers and workers, which he did not have.

The charter João Fernandes obtained from the Portuguese king in 1499, which neither mentions de Barcelos nor sets any time limit, promised him as the head of his own colony the privileges and high social position he had seen others enjoy at home. It seems likely that João in the spring or summer of 1500 had returned alone to a region he had already explored on an earlier voyage with his partner—a voyage during which de Barcelos had picked out his own land claims on the strength of an earlier charter issued to him. We have no proof either of a pre-1499 de Barcelos charter or of a João Fernandes voyage in 1500, but we do know that João was in Bristol (a natural stopover after a northwestern venture) late in the autumn or early winter of that year, with two Azorean companions. By spring, they had formed a partnership with some of the Bristol merchants listed in Appendix C.

Richard Warde, John Thomas, and Thomas Asshehurst of Bristol petitioned Henry VII for a patent on March 19, 1501, together with João Fernandes, Francisco Fernandes, and João Gonsalves, "Squyers borne in the Isle of Surrys [Azores] under the obeisaunce of the kyng of Portingale." The king granted the patent to his "well-beloved subjects" from Bristol and to his "well-beloved" Azoreans that same day.[116] All six men and their heirs, attorneys, factors, or deputies were to be given complete authority, under his royal banner, to voyage to and to exploit

> any town, city, castle, island or mainland by them thus newly found, and to enter and seize these same towns, and as our vassals and governors, lieutenants and deputies to occupy, possess and subdue these, the property, title, dignity and suzerainty of the same being always reserved to us.

Their trade monopoly was granted for ten years. Tax-free import into England of one shipload of goods from the new lands for each of the first four years was to help pay for the initial investment, and shipmasters, mates, quartermasters, and common sailors were also granted incentives. Nowhere is there a specific mention of a fishery.[117]

The document is remarkable, and not only for its great length. First of all, it suggests very strongly that the group's objectives were a prospering colony and trade over which the six men would have control. Second, the charter condones the subjugation of any native population. Third, while there is a tacit assumption that such natives would not be European subjects, the charter specifies that if other Europeans tried to intrude later, they were to receive stern treatment, "even though they be subjects and vassals of some prince in league and friendship with us." A fourth undercurrent is especially worth noting: although the patent is issued to three Englishmen and three acknowledged subjects of the Portuguese king, and although it appears to grant equal rights to all six, it stresses the English king's ultimate and absolute dominion over any region they find, govern, and exploit.

Balancing Henry VII's assurance that the three Azoreans and their heirs "are for ever subjects and lieges of us and of our heirs" is the terse exception that "each of them pays to us and to our heirs so many and such customs, subsidies and other dues . . . as foreigners are held to pay and give to us." This qualifier must be seen in conjunction with a provision that appeared in the draft copy, but that was then struck through and not included in the final version inscribed on the patent roll. Williamson summarizes the clause as "to the effect that no foreigner, by virtue of any grant formerly made or in future to be made, shall expel the present grantees from their title to the new territories." [118] The clause may have been proposed by one of the three Bristolmen who knew that João Fernandes had a valid Portuguese charter; by João himself because he worried that Pedro de Barcelos and his heirs might lay claim to the same area; or by all six charter applicants in anticipation of competition from Corte Real or de Barcelos—we do not know. Nor do we know why the clause was deleted.

João Fernandes and his two Azorean companions must have understood the charter's xenophobic subtext, however. This raises the question of why, despite having their own ship and João's valid charter from the Portuguese king, they nevertheless went along with an English undertaking that might eventually discriminate against them as foreign subjects. A likely possibility is that João had proposed the joint venture to Richard Warde and the other two Englishmen, who then acted as fronts before Henry VII. Quinn has pointed out that the charter given to this Anglo-Azorean group competed with John Cabot's patents, which were still valid and might be expected to be of benefit to his heirs.[119] This gives us one more reason to suppose that the group intended to go to a different area from the one John Cabot had explored, and there are grounds for thinking that Richard Warde in particular may have wanted a chance to compete against Bristol associates now clustering around young Sebastian Cabot. Warde's name is the first one listed on the 1501 charter, and together with João Fernandes and John Thomas he was pointedly left out of a new grant in late 1502, when the Anglo-Azorean venture was derailed by the Cabot-Elyot-Thorne faction, as we will soon see.

João's own agenda gave him good reasons for seeking cooperation from his Bristol contacts. He would have had to offer solid inducements for these Bristol friends to join in a venture, however. Quinn assumes that he had made a discovery "generally to the north of the coastline explored by Cabot," and that João's information must in any event "have appeared novel and have provided alternative incentives to the hopes raised by Cabot's first voyage and so soon dashed by his failure in 1498."[120] Certainly, the greater number of people and ships available to a cooperative undertaking would have appealed to entrepreneurs of any nation in a venture of the kind described in the group's charter. In addition, the Bristolmen may well have known João to be an uncommonly expert navigator as well as the legal claimant to land already located under his Portuguese charter.

The news, received late in 1500, of Gaspar Corte Real's first successful expedition to the Newfoundland region with a charter from the Portuguese king would have been another reason for João Fernandes to seek a joint venture with his Bristol trade connections under the protection of the English king, in order to realize ambitions made quite clear in his Portuguese charter. João must have known about the Corte Real competition, whether he learned the news in Lisbon or when putting in at Bristol after a summer of western exploration. He may even have known exactly where Corte Real had been.

It is generally supposed that the entire joint Anglo-Azorean syndicate made a western voyage in 1501, soon after receiving their charter. This assumption deserves further scrutiny, for it is based solely on one short entry in the royal Household Book for January 2–7, 1502: "Item to men of Bristol that found thisle C s."[121] It seems doubtful that this entry in the Household Book had any connection with the Anglo-Azorean syndicate's activities in the summer of 1501. There is nothing here to suggest that a different part of the new coast had been explored, which is what one would have expected from a group that presumably had received its royal charter because Henry VII had been given to understand that they would *not* interfere with the area already known to and exploited by other Bristolmen.

Immediately following John Cabot's 1497 voyage, "the Isle" had become strongly associated with his trans-Atlantic discoveries. There is mounting evidence of continuing voyages based on Cabot's original charter, not on the license obtained by João and his associates. These Cabot-related voyages were all to "the new Isle," "the new Ilande," or "the new Ile" as the area is called until September of 1502, when names such as "the newe founde launde" and "the Newfound Island" join "the New Ilande" in stipulations for royal rewards.[122]

It is possible that the reward given in early 1502 "to men of bristoll that founde thisle" was intended for men from Cabot's circle who were still being remunerated for their part in the 1497–98 voyages, but it is much more likely that the recipients had returned from another Cabot-related voyage in 1501, the same summer the Anglo-Azorean group could have been expected to make use of their own charter. The Household Book entry does not name the men who shared this reward, but João Fernandes and his two Bristol friends, Richard Warde and John Thomas, were probably not among them—their names are conspicuously absent from this or any other surviving English record until another royal charter, issued December 9, 1502, specifically excluded them from western ventures that were firmly back in the hands of the men who had supported John Cabot.

Several circumstances that will be discussed suggest that the original group of six had not stayed together long enough to make even one voyage, but had fallen victim to the rivalry between the Azorean *labrador* João Fernandes and the Bristol merchant establishment, of which there is such a clear echo in Robert Thorne the Younger's letter and map of 1527 when he insisted that the "*Noua terra laboratorum dicta*" had been "first discovered by the English," more specifically by his own father and Hugh Elyot.

The three Bristolmen who had joined João and his two Azorean companions were all members of the circle that included Hugh Elyot and the Thorne family. The probable fate of one of them, Richard Warde, whose name disappeared from all known records together with that of João Fernandes, will be discussed in detail soon. There are documents showing that the second Bristol member of the Anglo-Azorean venture, John Thomas, who clearly fell afoul of the merchants' power elite for a brief period, soon was back in their good graces, for by 1504 he and Thomas Asshehurst (the third Bristol partner of the three Azoreans), together with "merchants aliens," were helping Hugh Elyot, Robert Thorne, and others to ship fish from Newfoundland.[123] This connection of Thomas Asshehurst and the "merchants aliens" (Francisco Fernandes and João Gonsalves) with the Elyot-Thorne faction's Newfoundland enterprises can be documented from at least September of 1502 until October of 1506, by which time Francisco Fernandes had also run afoul of the heavy-handed Hugh Elyot, and Elyot himself was being sued in Chancery by a longtime associate who had invested in his trans-Atlantic ventures.[124]

Given the ruthless, monopolistic business climate in Bristol in the winter of 1500–1501, it is very likely that Hugh Elyot and the equally powerful Robert Thorne the Elder had used their clout to break up the Anglo-Azorean syndicate before it could get properly started. Both men had long been linked with North Atlantic ventures in general and with the Cabot enterprises in particular. Just as important in the present context, however, is the local power their great wealth and solid connections afforded them, especially after the changes that occurred when Bristol received a new royal charter in 1499. This authorized the sitting mayor and two selected aldermen to appoint a new group of Corporation members dedicated to a properly hierarchical spirit. After these initial appointments, later members were co-opted from within the circle of power. Not wasting any time, the new Corporation members in 1500 established a fellowship of "merchant adventurers" whose members (wealthy overseas merchants) were not allowed to act as agents for nonmembers "whether stranger or citizen, either in shipping goods from Bristol or in receiving them abroad for return to Bristol."[125] The control of foreign trade was placed squarely in the fellowship's hands, for the group had the power to decide who could be a member in the first place, and those who were already members now had a big whip with which to keep fellow merchants in place.

Whatever the merchant adventurers' eventual success may have been as a group, their intention was to limit competition and to increase cohesion among themselves—a condition already much valued.[126] For example, they were expected to trade abroad together, not individually, and to share the same ships for all their overseas traffic. If disputes arose, every effort was to be made to settle them within the group rather than in the courts. Strangers and nonmembers, by contrast, were accorded a distinctly cold treatment. No records exist to tell us about the organization's eventual fate, but when João Fernandes and his two friends came to town, the membership rules were freshly hatched, including one stipulating that no Bristol merchant adventurer was allowed to join a nonmember in shipping goods to or from Bristol, or to place his own goods aboard the same vessel.[127]

It soon became evident that Hugh Elyot found internal arbitration insufficient for settling his quarrels, but that was to be expected from a man who had been involved in a Chancery action as early as 1485.[128] We need not doubt that Elyot and the elder Thorne were among the first merchant adventurers and helped draw up the rules so convenient to themselves. The same year the fellowship was formed, Hugh Elyot also became one of the two sheriffs of Bristol—a notoriously burdensome and costly office available only to the wealthiest members of the Common Council.[129] He held this office until 1501, during precisely the winter the three Azoreans spent in Bristol.[130]

The six members of the newly formed Anglo-Azorean syndicate, which was aimed solely at overseas activities, would have faced formidable opposition if Elyot, Thorne, and their circle decided that the syndicate represented just the sort of unwelcome competition they were trying to stamp out. The Azoreans were especially vulnerable as foreigners, but threats of economic reprisals and social ostracism would also have been powerful weapons against the three Bristol merchants. If Richard Warde stayed with João to the end, as it appears he did, it must have been because he had more to gain and less to lose than the others, while John Thomas may have decided to risk investing in the venture, but not to go himself. When it became clear that João's venture had ended in disaster of some kind, John Thomas was still alive and able to rejoin his former associates.

In the eyes of Henry VII, John Cabot's charter was still valid for "the Isle," so all that the six members of the Anglo-Azorean syndicate would have needed to do in 1501 was to convince him they were going somewhere else and would not be violating the rights Sebastian Cabot had inherited. But even if Henry VII did not find their venture potentially in conflict with the Cabot charter, the circle of Bristol merchants who had been involved both with John Cabot's voyages and with their own westward probes would probably have considered the Anglo-Azorean syndicate a rival undertaking and have acted accordingly.

If the younger Thorne's 1527 map approximately illustrates these Bristol merchants' perception of their rights, it would not have helped the three Azoreans any to indicate that they were heading for a section of the Labrador mainland north of Newfoundland Island. Any suggestion that the syndicate intended business with the Norse inhabitants on the eastern shore of the supposed mainland curving around the "Bay of Greenland"—that is, in southwest Greenland—would have been equally unwelcome among people who regarded this area, too, as their province.

The formation of the fellowship of merchant adventurers clearly shows that its founders did not take kindly to foreign competition of any kind, and the Anglo-Azorean syndicate would have been an obvious and vulnerable target in 1501. Some of these merchant venturers' trans-Atlantic activities in the next few years likewise demonstrate what João Fernandes and his associates were up against in Bristol; they also form a useful background against which to ponder João Fernandes's own subsequent enterprise.

Seemingly without interruption, Elyot and Thorne continued to pursue the advantages of their own early discovery, of their power and wealth, and of their continued connection with young Sebastian Cabot and his inherited charter. Bristol customs records are so spotty that we shall probably never know whether Elyot and Thorne sponsored a quiet fishing expedition to "the Isle" in 1501, but chances are good that they did, and that its success made them expand their fleet. On January 7, 1502, the king granted a ship's bounty of £20 to Robert Thorne the Elder, to his brother William Thorne, and to Hugh Elyot, for a ship bought in Dieppe and renamed the *Gabriel* when it was brought to Bristol. On May 4, Robert Thorne's nephew Thomas collected the grant, paid out of the Bristol customs receipts.[131] Thanks to A. A. Ruddock's meticulous research, we also know that the *Gabriel* was put into trans-Atlantic service that very summer and returned to Bristol in September of 1502 with a valuable cargo of salt fish belonging to Hugh Elyot, for which he evidently used the 1496 Cabot charter to avoid paying subsidy.[132] Elyot is not likely to have met with much opposition from such close associates as the Bristol collectors of customs and subsidies, Richard Ameryk and Arthur Kemys.[133]

With two or more ships set aside for "the Isle," Hugh Elyot and his partners could both fish and continue to explore further. It appears that their western venture in the summer of 1502 was successful in both respects, for in September of that year, the king rewarded two sailors who had brought back hawks and an eagle, and he paid £20 to "the merchauntes of Bristoll that have bene in the newe founde launde."[134]

Also in September of 1502, Francisco Fernandes and João Gonsalves— João Fernandes's ex-associates who were still the king's "trusty and welbeloved subgiettes"—were granted a pension of £10 each, payable from the Bristol customs income, in recognition of their service as "Capitaignes into the newe founde land."[135] With two or more ships at their disposal, their expedition had also managed to capture three natives, of whom we know only that they were originally dressed in animal skins, ate "raw flesh," and spoke an unintelligible language, and that after two years of Westminster's refining influence they were indistinguishable in looks from other Englishmen. But, adds our observer, "as to speach, I heard none of them utter one word."[136]

A new patent issued on December 9, 1502, listed Hugh Elyot first among the charter members of a group called, among other things, the Company of Adventurers into the New Found Lands.[137] The patent may have been prompted by a simple wish to protect future discovery and colo-

nization, or it may be interpreted as a safeguard against displacement by
others claiming prior discovery, such as the Corte Reals or João Fernandes.
The charter of 1502 certainly proves beyond any doubt that a deep split
had occurred within the original Anglo-Azorean syndicate of 1501, and it
clearly shows the rift-line.[138]

Elyot and the three other patentees—Thomas Asshehurst, João Gonsalves and Francisco Fernandes, all former partners of João Fernandes—
were granted wide powers over lands they might "find, recover, discover
and search out"

[p]rovided always that they in no wise occupy themselves with nor enter the lands,
countries, regions or provinces of heathens or infidels first discovered by the subjects
of our very dear brother and cousin the king of Portugal, or by the subjects of any
other princes soever, our friends and confederates and in possession of which these
same princes now find themselves.

The term of monopoly which the patentees would have against other
English subjects wishing to trade there is increased to forty years (from ten
in the 1501 charter), and there are the usual incentives, such as tax-free
freight, but the four patentees are now cautioned that they are assured of
royal protection only if the lands they find and want to exploit have not
already been claimed by "others our subjects or by any of their heirs and
assigns having authority from us in that region by other letters patent of
ours under our Great Seal. . . ." The patent specifically refers to the 1501
Anglo-Azorean charter and then goes for the jugular:

nevertheless we are unwilling that the same Richard Warde, John Thomas and John
Fernandez or any one of them, their heirs or assigns, should in any way enter or go
near any of the countries, islands, lands, places or provinces found, recovered or
discovered anew in the future under the authority and licence of any of these our
present letters, unless they shall have first obtained leave from the aforesaid Hugh,
Thomas Asshehurst, John Gonzales and Francis.
    And in case the said Richard Warde, John Thomas and John Fernandez, or any
one of them, or their heirs or assigns, may wish . . . to make their way to these islands, countries, regions and other places aforesaid with their ships and goods in
order to acquire wares in the said islands, countries and other places . . . they . . .
shall be obliged from time to time to pay, furnish and sustain all and every the costs
and charges to be arranged at each voyage with the aforesaid Hugh, Thomas Asshehurst, John Gonzales and Francis. . . .

Presumably to encourage loyalty, the charter stipulates that João Gonsalves and Francisco Fernandes henceforth are to be treated as English subjects also in the matter of customs and subsidies, provided they do not act
as cover for foreign merchants.

This last may have been aimed at their former association with João

Fernandes, whose disappearance from the scene should not be interpreted as evidence that he and Warde had already perished during a multiship Anglo-Azorean voyage in 1501 that involved all six charter members. Not only is it most doubtful that the six men had sailed out together that summer, but we must also remember that while John Thomas, too, was pushed out into the cold in December of 1502, he was soon afterward active again among his old Bristol friends and peers. In other words, the three men so pointedly excluded from the new charter of 1502 did not suffer that fate simply because they had gone missing. Instead, the lack of later news about João Fernandes and Richard Warde (except for their bad press in this 1502 charter) suggests that they had gone off on an enterprise of their own in 1501, which in some way had briefly involved John Thomas and been deeply offensive to Hugh Elyot, but which in 1502 was not known to have ended in disaster. We shall examine this enterprise as soon as we have seen the overseas consortium of Hugh Elyot and his associates to its sour finale.

Elyot's group evidently explored farther afield and may have traded with the Indians, for as soon as the Bristol ships returned from the "new found isle" in the autumn of 1503, various rewards were duly noted in public accounts: "to sir Walter Herbert's servant for bringing a brasell bowe & 2 rede arowez"; "to one that brought haukes from the Newfounded Ilande"; and to João Gonsalves and Francisco Fernandes for the continuation of their services.[139] Pension payments to the two Azoreans continued into the spring of 1504. At the same time, Hugh Elyot borrowed money from wealthy London associates and from the king to furnish his ventures, which seem to have become increasingly ambitious, for in April of 1504, the Daybook of the Treasurer of the Chamber noted a payment of 40 s. "to a preste that goith to the new Ilande."[140] We know nothing about the fate of this priest, or about his intended task—whether it was to convert Indians, scrub the souls of sailors on the voyage, or minister to an attempted settlement.

We have proof that the fishing continued to go well, with or without a permanent shore station, for late in the autumn of 1504, Bristol customs records show that the *Gabriel* and the *Jesus*, with João Fernandes's erstwhile associates John Thomas, Thomas Asshehurst, "and other merchants aliens" acting as factors, returned from Newfoundland with 20 lasts of fish and "7 tuns, 1 pipe of livers belonging to Hugh Elyott, Robert Thorne, and William Thorn, denizens, merchants." The cargo was valued at £207 10s.[141]

Other nations, such as the French, whose first datable voyage was in 1504, were already going to North America.[142] Despite this growing competition, Bristol trans-Atlantic enterprise was profitable enough that in the spring of 1505, Hugh Elyot paid back his loan to the king, and the king gave young Sebastian Cabot a pension connected with activities in "the new founde landes" (not simply in "the Isle") that probably should be interpreted as further exploration. Once again, the returning ships carried exotica as well as fish. In August of 1505, some "Portyngales [João Gonsalves and Francisco Fernandes?] brought popyngais & catts of the mountayne with other stuf to the King's grace," for which they were suitably rewarded.[143]

But something went wrong, and Elyot's syndicate fell apart. There is no known evidence that after 1505 until about 1525 (a period for which documentary material is very poor) Elyot and his associates were engaged in North American voyages, although many of them are known to have been alive and active still in Bristol in 1524.[144] There is every reason to accept Quinn's judgment that the Newfoundland fishing was maintained, and to infer from both Ruddock's and Quinn's documentary evidence that Sebastian Cabot was an active member of the syndicate of 1502-5 and had actually earned the pension granted to him on April 3, 1505, "in consideration of the diligent service and attendance . . . doon unto us in and about the fyndinge of the newe founde landes." Noting the plural "landes," Quinn hypothesizes that Sebastian had been involved in further exploration that formed the basis for later ventures on his own.[145] Waldseemüller's world map of 1507, showing the two Americas, proves that knowledgeable people were aware that the recently discovered lands were not a part of eastern Asia, and Sebastian evidently knew that, too, even if he had overly sanguine notions about what the northernmost waters were like. In 1508 he led a voyage of exploration to find a northwest passage to Asia, and he did not return to England until 1509, when he collected several accumulated installments of his pension and married a London woman.[146]

Although Sebastian's subsequent career falls outside the scope of this book, it must be noted here that he continued to have connections with the Thorne family.[147] When Robert Thorne the Younger drew his 1527 map stressing that the English had actually been the first to discover the land named after the *labrador*, he had just invested in Sebastian's expedition to the La Plata, although he failed to mention Sebastian's name when referring to this expedition in his letter to the English ambassador. Williamson interprets this as evidence that the younger Thorne shared the dislike of Sebastian that members of that expedition also expressed.[148] In that case, we might ask if this personal animosity contributed to Thorne's claim that his father and Hugh Elyot had made an independent discovery of an area north of the coast John Cabot had explored. Sebastian may already have improved his knowledge of this region while sailing in partnership with Elyot and Thorne, and that knowledge may have led him to think that a northwest passage to Asia existed. His 1508 voyage certainly increased his familiarity with the more northerly regions.

We know nothing about Sebastian Cabot's relationship with Hugh Elyot and the elder Thorne brothers, nor with João Fernandes and his associates in 1500–1501. While Sebastian may have been aware that João did not represent a direct threat to the claims he had inherited from John Cabot, it is reasonable to suppose that he wanted to make the most of his father's patent and would at least have tolerated any scheme of Elyot's that claimed to protect Sebastian's interests while the latter was still too young to manage independently. Sebastian would also have taken much of Elyot's litigiousness in his stride, for a certain amount was expected, according to David Harris Sacks, an American authority on Bristol trade in this period. Even in an enduring partnership like that of Hugh Elyot and Robert Thorne the Elder, who traded together both at home and abroad for two decades, "they reckoned their books and settled accounts after each voyage rather than maintaining their profits and losses in a joint account from year to year." A common way of settling annual accounts, says Sacks, was to file suit in Tolzey Court—it was an easy way of making one's claims public. But real disputes also arose; "long-term partnerships that lacked a strong family character seem to have been especially vulnerable to dispute and litigation when accounts could not be balanced, as happened in turn to Eliot and Thorne . . . among others."[149]

The suits in which Elyot became embroiled in 1505–6 as a consequence of his trans-Atlantic enterprise were rather nastier than seasonal rituals in Tolzey Court. His financial partner William Clerk (probably the same William Clerk who had been Philip Greene's tenant at the same time as John Cabot, and who was now living in London) filed suit in Chancery for almost £145 he had lent to Elyot to equip the ship *Michell* for a trans-Atlantic voyage. We do not know if Elyot ever paid up. Nor do we know the outcome of a feud between him and his supposed partner Francisco Fernandes. Because Hugh Elyot had sued Francisco in the Constable's Court in Bristol for £100 he said the Azorean owed him, the latter in his despair filed a countersuit in Chancery claiming that far from owing Elyot £100, Elyot owed *him* £140. Francisco asked only for a chance to present documentary evidence for the truth of his own claims, since Elyot "of his malicious mynde" had not allowed him to do this because he preferred that Francisco should remain in prison "ayenst all right and good conscience. . . ."[150]

Large enough sums are involved here to suggest that western enterprise had not proved as profitable as Elyot had hoped. The excitement certainly seems to have worn off as far as Henry VII is concerned—judging from the king's Daybook from 1506 until 1509, the year Henry died, he did not encourage trans-Atlantic voyages with a single penny during those years.[151] Other developments may also have affected Elyot and Thorne in 1505 or 1506, such as that Sebastian had come of age and wanted to be free of the

older men so he could realize his own grander ambitions, or that Elyot, the
elder Thorne, and their circle had become discouraged by the Indians' lack
of interest in wool cloth and decided they would invest in trusty codfish and
Iberian trade from now on.

More than money may have been involved if Francisco told the truth
about Elyot's brutal treatment of him, but in those circles the desire for
profit and the need to control others were never far away. If Francisco had
attempted to collect his debt from Elyot and peremptorily been thrown into
debtor's prison, it might mean both that Elyot had no more use for him and
took advantage of his vulnerability as a foreigner, and that Elyot wanted
to prevent him from becoming a competitor. Using the knowledge he had
gained from his voyages on behalf of the Bristolmen, Francisco could have
taken his money—had he got it—and entered into a partnership with a rival
fishing enterprise. Or he could have become an agent in Bristol for a Portuguese merchant, which would have been equally bad in the eyes of Elyot
and his powerful associates.

It is very likely that Francisco had ample contact with his fellow countrymen both in Bristol and in the increasingly busy Newfoundland fisheries.
So many Portuguese were now fishing off the new banks that in October of
1506 the Portuguese king began to collect a tax on Newfoundland cod.[152]
Not a scrap of news has survived of those early operations, however; one
reason for the lack of records being that "fishermen and fur traders could
leave their ports from Lisbon and Vianna north to Bristol and Galway with
little ceremony and conduct their affairs off the shores of North America
without state intervention until or unless they clashed too violently there
with men of other states."[153] We know nothing about those who succeeded
in making that fishing voyage year after year, or about those who perished.
They are as lost to history as the Norse Greenlanders, Richard Warde, and
João Fernandes, whose fates we shall now try to trace from the scattered
information available by returning to the winter of 1500–1501, when João
and his two friends from home joined forces with the three Bristolmen.

If the three Azoreans had already spent the summer of 1500 scouting
along the North American east coast, armed with João's patent from the
Portuguese king, their most important concerns besides finding a spot with
good natural resources within the Portuguese Tordesillas sphere would
have been (1) whether to choose an island or a mainland location; (2) where
to look for potential workers; and (3) whether any natives they encountered might prove too much to handle even at the point of a clumsy, but
certainly dangerous, handgun.

At the end of the fifteenth century, Newfoundland Island had a small
population of Beothuks or their immediate Algonquian ancestors, whose
number (perhaps 500) and way of life probably did not pose an inherent

threat, but who were described in sixteenth-century accounts as very hostile to Europeans. But this hostility may have been triggered by repeated offenses by the Europeans; we do not know how the Indians greeted the first English or Portuguese they encountered. On the mainland, members of a similar or related Indian culture are known to have occupied southern Labrador in the sixteenth century. Cartier's reports of his experiences in the 1530s with Indians in the region just north and south of the St. Lawrence River suggest that the Indians there were also mostly based on the mainland, but that they turned out in large numbers in their canoes to fish or to hunt seals in the more outlying areas.[154]

It therefore seems that although the Indian communities may have been fairly scattered and more apt to be on the mainland than on the islands, the natives might appear in either place in sufficient numbers that it required a fairly large expedition to control or capture them. Members of John Cabot's small 1497 expedition stayed close to their ship and did not seek out the natives even after signs of human habitation had been spotted, while ships returning from the well-equipped 1501 Corte Real venture brought back a number of captive Indians, thus helping to launch adversarial relations between natives and Europeans in North America.

Although João Fernandes and his companions would have been familiar with the methods of procuring slaves, João had grown up in the Azores, which depended on European immigrant labor until the 1460s, and he may well have rejected slave labor as unsuitable for his project and instead planned a venture calling for the skills of European fishermen, farmers, whalers, and lumberjacks. In that case, he would have been more concerned with protecting himself against the Indians than with enslaving them, and he would also have been looking elsewhere for the right kind of settlers. This was no easy task at the time.

Portuguese colonists would have been in short supply, especially for a northern enterprise. In the early sixteenth century (the first period for which there are fairly reliable figures), Portugal's population had barely risen to 1.4 million, as compared with 7 million in Spain, 14 million in France, and 4 million in the British Isles.[155] At the same time, the expanding Portuguese sea empire was siphoning off people to both Asian and African ventures.

The situation was no better in England. By 1500, England's population had barely begun its long climb out of the decline caused by repeated epidemics and famines; the crowded port cities of Bristol, Exeter, and Norwich had proved especially vulnerable to contagion introduced from London or the Continent.[156] Henry VII's offer of convicts for Cabot's ambitious 1498 expedition may in part have been prompted by his desire to rid the kingdom of criminals who had sought asylum in churches, and whose best option was to inform the magistrate that they wished to leave England, whereupon they would be stripped to the shirt and escorted down to the water's edge in hopes of finding passage on a ship.[157] But if Cabot consented to taking such rogues along, it would have been because he had no other choice. João Fernandes would not have found the situation much changed a couple of years later; England at that time had no people to spare.[158]

It is likely that before João and his two Azorean partners arrived in Bristol, they had at least decided where in North America they wanted to focus their efforts. As noted earlier, João evidently was not obsessed with the "spiceries," but instead seems to have set his sights on exploiting a stretch of southern Labrador that he had already staked out on the strength of his 1499 charter from the Portuguese king. He would have found many areas along the North American coast that were rich in products needed in Europe, and where permanent settlements of skilled workers would make exploitation easier. It was early days yet—the dismal saga of failed colonization attempts in North America had not yet begun to be written.

The huge forests in those new northern lands were a great attraction, as the Corte Real reports and the Cantino map indicate. Timber was the incentive most often mentioned in the sixteenth century, "especially among the seagoing peoples of western Europe. They were using up their best oak and other hardwoods and did not have much good coniferous timber at their disposal."[159] In addition, the hinterland supplied wild animal hides and precious furs; the surrounding seas provided fish, whales, and seals; and there were pastures that might accommodate sturdy livestock for meat, dairy products, hides, and wool.

We know that Terceiran livestock were successfully introduced to "Terra nova" early in the sixteenth century, and that when the Spaniards brought cattle, horses, and pigs to Hispaniola and Mexico, the animals thrived so that hides and tallow soon became major export articles for the trans-Atlantic trade. We also know that João's fellow Portuguese in the Atlantic islands based their economies on staple products ranging from grain, raisins, and sugar to livestock, sealskins, and wood even *after* they had become directly involved in the lucrative trade with African goods.[160] João would have seen economic opportunities wherever he explored along the North American east coast.

The three Bristolmen Richard Warde, John Thomas, and Thomas Asshehurst may originally have been attracted to João Fernandes's enterprise by the prospect of not having to find new markets for cloth, pots and pans, and other manufactured goods, concerning themselves instead with exploiting overseas primary resources and selling the products in the European commodities market. Such an approach would have set them apart from many Bristol merchants at the time, for while the latter also wanted to exploit the overseas cod fisheries, they were still desperately searching for new markets for their cloth. The Portuguese, by contrast, wanted to expand their own fisheries westward and to "encourage English searches for alternative sources of fish in the western Atlantic, since the Icelandic fish trade had provided such an appreciable part of Portuguese imports."[161]

Both João and his associates would have known the advantages of permanent shore stations in the fishing business. Such "factories" enabled people to fish from early spring until very late in the fall and to supervise the stockfish while it was drying. The three Bristolmen, too, would have had every reason to share the swelling optimism about the huge cod available on those other shores, and they would have been as aware as the three Azoreans of how hard it was to find suitable year-round workers. Together, the six men may well have decided on a solution involving the Norse colony in Greenland—a colony long known to several Bristolmen.

To people so accustomed to using the labor and risking the lives of other people, this would have been an obvious move, given the many circumstances that argued in favor of it. A recurring theme in the annals of fifteenth- and sixteenth-century exploration and colonization is the ruthlessness and ingenuity the leaders displayed in their search for settlers and workers, and there is no reason to suppose that João Fernandes and his associates were different.

The three Bristolmen belonged, as we have seen, to the circle of merchants most intent on controlling North Atlantic exploitation and most likely to have maintained some contact with Greenland. They would have had access to pilots as well as to interpreters, and most important of all, they would have known that the Norse Greenlanders mastered all the necessary skills. They could hunt and prepare seal and other game of land and sea, maintain boats and fishing tackle, catch fish in fresh and salt water, prepare stockfish, and boil livers for train oil—and they knew how to survive under tough conditions. Housing would be no problem, either; all they needed, it seemed, was a heap of turf and stone to call home. The same was true of their sturdy domestic animals, who would have been a welcome addition to a new settlement.

The advantage of shipping both people and domestic animals the relatively short distance across the Davis Strait, with the current astern, would have been obvious to a man of João's experience—his voyages cannot have failed to make him aware that southern Greenland lay just across the large "bay" from Labrador. Many fewer provisions would be needed than if a colonizing voyage had to be organized all the way from Portugal, or even Bristol.

The biggest stumbling block would have been the Bristol merchants who regarded Greenland as "theirs" no matter how long it had been since their last call: probably Hugh Elyot, Robert Thorne the Elder, and some of their closest associates. The younger Thorne's 1527 map shows that these men evidently had fishing interests along a stretch of Labrador, which they also thought of as belonging to them, *before* John Cabot's 1497 voyage, and we have seen that they were active in tightening the Bristol trade monopolies just when João Fernandes and his two Azorean associates joined company with three other Bristolmen from the Elyot-Thorne circle.

It would hardly be cause for wonder if Elyot and Thorne quickly made short work of the 1501 Anglo-Portuguese syndicate by persuading Thomas Asshehurst and João's two Azorean companions to drop out of the scheme and join their own group. They had demonstrably already done so by the summer of 1502, when Francisco Fernandes and João Gonsalves were given pensions as a reward for having served as captains for the Bristol merchants "into the New Found Land"—several months *before* Hugh Elyot obtained his December 9 patent that excluded João Fernandes, Richard Warde, and John Thomas.

Another big problem with involving Greenlanders in an attempted settlement on the west coast of the Davis Strait would have been persuading them to join such a scheme of their own free will, for it was hardly feasible or profitable to raid those scattered and often secluded Greenland farmsteads for slaves. People would have to be talked into emigration by someone just as persuasive as Eirik the Red; someone who could play on their inherited knowledge about Vínland, Markland, and other desirable locations across the water, which modern ships and information now were bringing within reach again. Such persuasiveness, leadership, and organizational ability were the qualities that had enabled not only Eirik the Red, but people like John Cabot, the Corte Real brothers, and João Fernandes to arrange their voyages of discovery.

The Norse Greenlanders' lives were harsh even under optimum conditions, and for some time prior to 1500 they had probably been competing with the Eskimos for fish and game. Periods of extreme weather conditions would have exacerbated the erosion caused by the Norsemen's relentless stock farming, and chances are that the Greenlanders had further jeopardized their day-to-day existence by adjusting their traditional economy to the English demand for stockfish and train oil. But at the same time, there is no reason to suppose things were so bad that they had lost their ability to function either as individuals or as a society, or to make decisions as momentous as those made by their ancestors when new opportunities offered. They had eagerly responded to outside impulses in the past—as for example their ambitious adaptation of clothing fashions shows.

This combination of circumstances makes it likely that many of the remaining Greenlanders would have been affected by the new European expansion and seized the chance of a new and prosperous life elsewhere. Conditions in the Eastern Settlement would have had to be unsatisfactory, but not necessarily unspeakable, for a new colonizing venture to be an attractive option. Those who first colonized Greenland, for instance, can by no means have been the most desperate people in Iceland.

Unfortunately, the ones most likely to grasp such an opportunity, or to be invited, were the young and able-bodied, particularly males. These people in their prime are the ones a society can least afford to lose, especially a population as small and dependent on hard physical labor and group hunting as the Norse Greenlanders were. For the Eastern Settlement to lose the strongest and most fertile segment of their population at the very start of the sixteenth century would have been the beginning of the end, for it is clear from maps and documents that for the first several decades of the sixteenth century, the Eastern Settlement's isolation from the rest of Europe was as good as total. The major seafaring nations now focused on exploiting the new sea routes to the Americas and the Orient; the English search for a northwest passage *through* North America to Asia, which began with Sebastian Cabot's 1508 expedition from Bristol, clearly did not include stopovers in the Eastern Settlement; and Greenland's contact with the rest of Scandinavia remained severed. When the Danes finally sponsored the Englishman James Hall's expedition to their ancient colony in 1605, the only people found were Eskimos, so the notion arose that the Eastern Settlement must lie on the inaccessible east coast.

Two known circumstances point to the gradual petering-out of a truncated population rather than to a sudden, overwhelming disaster around 1500: the presence of the late-fifteenth-century "Burgundy cap" in the Herjolfsnes graveyard, and a report from a few decades later suggesting that a few remaining old Norse Greenlanders were dying with no one to bury them.

Around the year 1540, a man called Jon Greenlander because he had repeatedly drifted off to Greenland while sailing with German ships from Hamburg, reported that on one of those occasions his ship had entered a large, wide, and calm bay with many islands. The sailors had stayed away from the populated islands, of which there were several (there is no knowing whether the reference is to Eskimo or Norse habitations); they had also seen farms on the mainland. Dropping anchor near an unpopulated island, they had gone in their ship's boat to a small island where they went ashore. Here they found fishing huts, boathouses, and fish-drying racks just like in Iceland, as well as a dead man lying face down on the ground. On his head was a well-made cloth hood; the remainder of his clothes were made partly of homespun, partly of sealskin. Next to him lay a bent knife, very worn down by repeated sharpening, which Jon and his companions took with them as a souvenir. Björn Jonsson of Skardsá, who wrote down this story in his "Greenland Annals" around 1623–25, added that even in his own time many sensible people thought there still were some Norse colonists in Greenland, especially because pieces of ships built in the Greenland manner, with baleen lashings and coated with seal oil, were still washing ashore in Iceland.[162]

The eighteenth-century Norwegian missionary Hans Egede was also convinced that a small, forgotten Norse colony still existed in an Eastern Settlement that he and his contemporaries were convinced lay on the east coast of Greenland. Ironically, his first attempt to recolonize Greenland through "Hope Colony," which endured from 1721 to 1728 in the outermost parts of the fjords that cradled the remains of the Western Settlement, also ended in oblivion. The site was rediscovered in 1903. After their recent excavations there, the Danish archaeologists Hans Christian Gulløv and Hans Kapel concluded that this tiny settlement had succumbed because European technology was inadequate to the local challenges. They also observed that the local Eskimos must have known about the position of the colony all along, for they called the place Illueruunerit—"the place where there used to be houses."[163] We may marvel at Egede's and his successors' lack of information about the medieval Norse colonists, but a far more important question is why there had been such complete lack of official curiosity about Greenland in the interim.

Late in the summer of 1501, when João and his companions would have been setting sail for Greenland (if that is where they were heading first), King Hans was facing serious uprisings in both Sweden and Norway. The situation did not improve over the next couple of years.[164] It is hard to see how Hans could have remained completely untouched by the fever of discovery now taking hold of Europe, but Greenland and exploration would have been far from his mind at that time. Although Hans's young and energetic heir, Christian II, faced equal political difficulties, on a couple of occasions there were signs that he wanted to participate in European expansionism by reasserting his authority over Greenland. His chancellor Erik Valkendorf, who was also the Norwegian archbishop, may well have planted these seeds in his young monarch's head when returning from negotiations at the Burgundian court to arrange a marriage between Christian and Isabella, the daughter of King Philip of Spain.

Valkendorf was a well-traveled man, not only in the course of diplomatic missions, but also while overseeing his archbishopric's income, especially from the northern codfish trade. His reasons for wanting to reassert the Norwegian church's old authority over the Orkneys as well as Greenland were as complicated as the man himself, but they need no further analysis here, for the Greenland voyage he and Christian II planned came to nothing. We know that the plans must have been serious, however, for on June 17, 1514, the Danish crown learned that the pope had granted Christian's petition for indulgences for "those who voyage to the islands on the far side of the Polar Sea . . ." ("*Et primo de indulgentiis navigantibus ultra mare glaciale ad insulas concedendas . . .*").[165]

Christian's inflated ambitions concerning Greenland were matched only by his and the pope's ignorance about that distant country. At the Danish king's request, Pope Leo X in 1519 appointed a Minorite named Vincent Petersson, Christian's confessor, as bishop of Gardar. The reason given for the royal petition was that Christian intended to sail to Greenland with a mighty fleet and retrieve the inhabitants from heathendom—the pitiable creatures had been without a bishop for thirty years. Two years later, the out-of-favor Valkendorf was in Continental exile, and the king's sycophantic spies abroad reported back about both the archbishop and other matters, including the growing threat to Christian's Greenland from expanding Spanish activities in those waters.[166]

The king was by this time in such trouble with his subjects that Emperor Charles V called a meeting in Hamburg in the summer of 1524 to discuss Christian II's political problems, which were not improved by increasing rumors of his sympathy with Martin Luther.[167] Christian's queen was the sister of the emperor himself and of Queen Leonora of Portugal, and Christian was not shy about leaning on his influential relatives, whose peer he considered himself. As late as in October of 1525, he was corresponding amicably with Henry VIII of England.[168] This was precisely the period when Henry was pondering Cardinal Wolsey's 1521 proposal to send five ships on "a viage into the Newfound Iland"—an expedition that was attempted after a fashion in 1527, and proved unsuccessful.[169] Innumerable other letters to and from Christian and his relatives-by-marriage crossed the Continent in the same period. The remarkable thing is that not *one* of these letters mentions either North American or Greenland exploration. Either the various parties knew or cared nothing about each others' ambitions, which seems unlikely, or else they had no intention of revealing their information and plans. The blackout is in any case complete.

Total documentary silence surrounds the fate of not only the Norse Greenlanders, but João Fernandes, Richard Warde, and everybody else who may have entrusted their lives to a scheme that appears to have ended in disaster far from home. Even if their expedition did not sink to the bottom of the Davis Strait, no northern colonizing enterprise would have had much chance of succeeding at that early date. Records from a much later date, during early English colonization attempts in those latitudes, show that to clear the land was unexpectedly backbreaking work, and that the North American Indians were not suited to this or any other kind of slave labor. The cost of labor as well as of shipping the lumber home turned out to be prohibitive. The English had to learn these lessons the hard way, and we cannot blame those who first claimed land in those parts many years earlier if their bright hopes were untarnished by experience. Nor could they have guessed the magnitude of what turned out to be the the biggest problem of all for European settlers in that region, namely the weather: [170]

One basic obstacle to all early attempts to plan settlements in North America was the obstinate conviction of Europeans that climate in North America could be equated precisely with climate in western Europe. Since North America has a continental climate dominated by the great land mass that lies behind it, extremes of heat and cold as compared with western maritime Europe were unexpectedly great.

The early European voyages to eastern North America were seasonal ventures. The men spent their winters in Bristol, Galway, Lisbon, or the Azores, and therefore did not know how savage the winters were in those new-found lands. They saw only the promise awaiting any man who could get a royal charter that enabled him to stake a proper claim and build up a flourishing trade in codfish, train oil, lumber, furs, and other North Atlantic produce.

No archaeological finds on either side of the Davis Strait have been analyzed to test a hypothesis linking the Norse Greenlanders' disappearance with unrecorded early attempts at North American colonization that involved Bristol's familiarity with Norse Greenland, or with the documented association between the Bristolman Richard Warde and the Azorean explorer João Fernandes, who seem to have perished during a North Atlantic venture at the beginning of the sixteenth century. At best, the current archaeological and documentary evidence provides only circumstantial evidence for the possibility that it was no mere coincidence that the Norse Greenland colony came to an end just in those years when early North Atlantic exploration touched it so closely.

Archaeological information about the Labrador coast south of Hamilton Inlet during this period is scant.[171] Hamilton Inlet is at latitude 53°45′N, approximately the same latitude as Galway in western Ireland, so the coastline to the south of the inlet corresponds to the region associated with early cartographical references to the "Isle of Brazil" as well as with Norse "Markland." We can only hope that it may someday be possible to investigate this huge area better, since it may hold the key to some of the problems addressed in this book. Someday, too, archaeologists may find a firm explanation for the baffling presence of Basque tiles and earlier European material in even the oldest Thule archaeological sites around Hamilton Inlet.[172] And eventually, if Hans Kapel has his way, we shall perhaps know the origin of some of the glass beads found in old Thule Eskimo sites in Greenland and learn whether they were the same kind used by Portuguese explorers and traders elsewhere in the years immediately before and after 1500.[173]

We may even discover the source of one of C. L. Vebæk's unique finds in the churchyard at Ø149, the old nunnery in Narsarsuaq where he also unearthed the ancient sun compass. In Grave Field II, where only the most recent graves very near the surface were excavated, Vebæk found the remains of an adult female whose clothing was as decomposed as she, but which had been fastened along the left side under the arm by means of a "zipper." An arrangement of iron and bronze rings, closely spaced on both sides of the garment's opening, the "zipper" would only have needed a cord to interlock the rings and form a closure.[174] An archaeologist or a sharp-eyed art historian may someday solve the mystery of who had brought this idea—or the garment itself—to Greenland toward the end of the Norse period.

Perhaps archaeologists one day will find, along the vast stretches of Labrador, another "place where there used to be houses" bearing witness to a short-lived experiment based on hope, but defeated by the overwhelming odds of pitting man's ingenuity against the wiles of nature in this region. Such discoveries would be our only substitute for records that were never written about either the Norse Greenlanders or about "those who made discoveries [and] were ruined thereby" when they "steered northward, coasting the Bacallaos region and Labrador."[175] Ruin may have taken many forms. Death by starvation may have competed with death from the cold, or destruction may have been swift from exposure to new and deadly diseases such as syphilis.

The eerie Greenland scene of careful burials and deserted, tidy homesteads, so eloquently described by Joel Berglund, strongly suggests voluntary desertion of the Eastern Settlement. Neither those who left, nor those few who stayed behind, could possibly have foreseen Greenland's coming isolation just when contact with Europe appeared to be increasing, any more than their forebears could have predicted that shipping from Norway would cease.

There is no proof that those who went away were persuaded to do so by João Fernandes and his English-Portuguese expedition, or that the Bristol English had been solely responsible for maintaining contact with Norse Greenland in the fifteenth century until they established alternative fisheries on the other side of the Davis Strait. But both circumstantial evidence and common sense suggest that the Greenlanders, who had so clearly taken active part in the North Atlantic economic community throughout the fifteenth century, had remained opportunists to the end and joined the early-sixteenth-century European surge toward North America.

Reference
Matter

The Lawman
Thorstein Eyjolfsson
and His Descendants

Throughout the fifteenth century, when official contact with Greenland ceased and the English established themselves in Iceland while taking control of the northern sea lanes, the descendants of the powerful Icelandic chieftain Thorstein Eyjolfsson of Urd (including Thorstein Olafsson, the Hvalsey bridegroom of 1408, and his brother Bishop Arni) wove a dense web with other powerful North Iceland families to form a tight ruling class that seems to have avoided the economic hardships visited on their less fortunate fellow Icelanders as the Middle Ages drew to a close.

1.

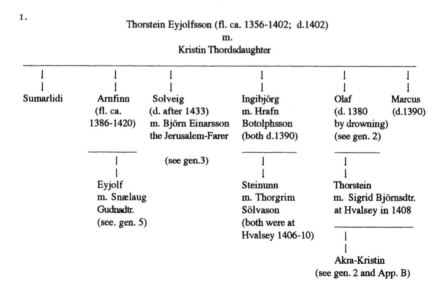

Between about 1356 and 1402, when he succumbed to the Black Death, Thorstein Eyjolfsson's career followed a pattern common among his peers: he served as either lawman or *hirðstjóri* for a number of years and also spent much time abroad.[1] Both at home and abroad he played for high stakes while enjoying the friendship of the Norwegian kings Hákon and Magnus and oiling connections from which his descendants benefited. Still loyal to King Magnus after the latter's imprisonment in 1365, he went abroad in 1367 to visit the king in captivity, but was himself captured by Lübeck men. Thanks to his high connections, he found himself back in Iceland a couple of years later, this time as lawman of the entire country.[2]

As Genealogy 1 shows, he found time to sire several children, of whom his daughter Solveig (m. Björn the Jerusalem-Farer) and his son Arnfinn figure prominently in the present book. Among his grandchildren (see Genealogy 2), four are of particular interest to us, namely Thorstein Olafsson, his brothers Arni and Hall, and Steinunn Hrafnsdaughter, whose lover was sentenced to be burned at Hvalsey in Greenland, as described in Chapter Six.

2.

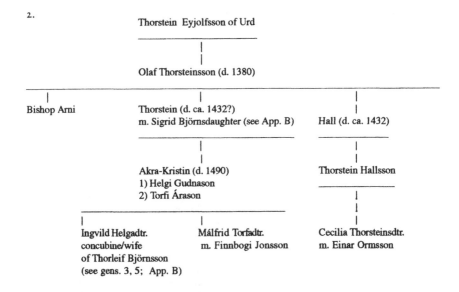

By the time they had reached adulthood, Thorstein Eyjolfsson's grandchildren were well accustomed to turbulence and danger. During the years 1380–81, Iceland suffered a bad smallpox epidemic; also in 1380, Thorstein, Arni, and Hall Olafsson lost their father (Olaf Thorsteinsson) to drowning. Their cousin Steinunn Hrafnsdaughter (see Genealogy 1) lost her parents and siblings when they were killed by a landslide in Langadal in 1389 or 1390; her uncle Marcus Thorsteinsson was killed that same year.[3]

Thorstein, Arni, and Hall enjoyed better luck. This was in no small part due to their (and Steinunn's) aunt, Solveig Thorsteinsdaughter, who worked through her husband Björn Einarsson the Jerusalem-Farer, as detailed in Chapter Six. The three Olafssons also stood to benefit from their kinship with Vatnsfjord-Kristin, Björn and Solveig's only surviving child (See Genealogy 3).

3.

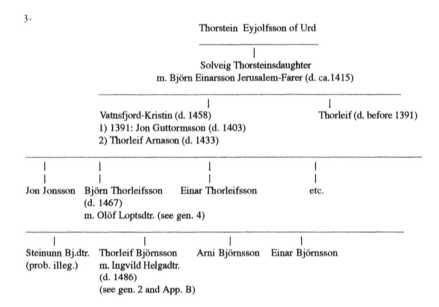

Thorstein Eyjolfsson of Urd

Solveig Thorsteinsdaughter
m. Björn Einarsson Jerusalem-Farer (d. ca.1415)

Vatnsfjord-Kristin (d. 1458)   Thorleif (d. before 1391)
1) 1391: Jon Guttormsson (d. 1403)
2) Thorleif Arnason (d. 1433)

Jon Jonsson Björn Thorleifsson   Einar Thorleifsson   etc.
             (d. 1467)
             m. Olöf Loptsdtr. (see gen. 4)

Steinunn Bj.dtr. Thorleif Björnsson   Arni Björnsson Einar Björnsson
(prob. illeg.)   m. Ingvild Helgadtr.
                  (d. 1486)
                  (see gen. 2 and App. B)

In 1391, Kristin Björnsdaughter was married off to the equally rich and well-connected Jon Guttormsson (see Genealogy 4), who died from the Black Death in 1402–3, while Kristin lived on until 1458.[4] The close ties between the two families continued, however, for the notorious and powerful Björn Thorleifsson, Vatnsfjord-Kristin's son by her second husband Thorleif Arnason, married Jon's niece Olöf Loptsdaughter (see Genealogies 3, 4, and 5), and they became the parents of Thorleif Björnsson, who finally married his concubine Ingvild Helgadaughter (see Appendix B).

4.

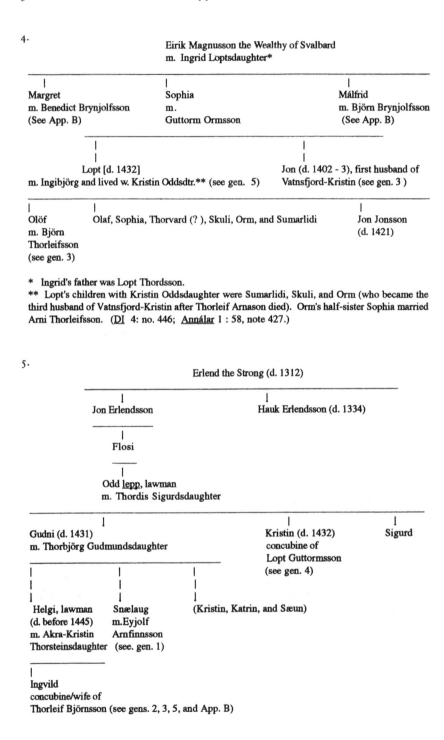

Eirik Magnusson the Wealthy of Svalbard
m. Ingrid Loptsdaughter*

Margret   Sophia   Málfrid
m. Benedict Brynjolfsson   m.   m. Björn Brynjolfsson
(See App. B)   Guttorm Ormsson   (See App. B)

Lopt [d. 1432]   Jon (d. 1402 - 3), first husband of
m. Ingibjörg and lived w. Kristin Oddsdtr.** (see gen. 5)   Vatnsfjord-Kristin (see gen. 3)

Olöf   Olaf, Sophia, Thorvard (?), Skuli, Orm, and Sumarlidi   Jon Jonsson
m. Björn   (d. 1421)
Thorleifsson
(see gen. 3)

* Ingrid's father was Lopt Thordsson.
** Lopt's children with Kristin Oddsdaughter were Sumarlidi, Skuli, and Orm (who became the
third husband of Vatnsfjord-Kristin after Thorleif Arnason died). Orm's half-sister Sophia married
Arni Thorleifsson. (DI 4: no. 446; Annálar 1 : 58, note 427.)

5.

Erlend the Strong (d. 1312)

Jon Erlendsson   Hauk Erlendsson (d. 1334)

Flosi

Odd lepp, lawman
m. Thordis Sigurdsdaughter

Gudni (d. 1431)   Kristin (d. 1432)   Sigurd
m. Thorbjörg Gudmundsdaughter   concubine of
                                         Lopt Guttormsson
                                         (see gen. 4)

Helgi, lawman   Snælaug   (Kristin, Katrin, and Sæun)
(d. before 1445)   m.Eyjolf
m. Akra-Kristin   Arnfinnsson
Thorsteinsdaughter (see. gen. 1)

Ingvild
concubine/wife of
Thorleif Björnsson (see gens. 2, 3, 5, and App. B)

Björn Thorleifsson was killed by the English in 1467. He was *hirðstjóri* at the time and had been knighted by the Danish king ten years earlier, so his murder made Anglo-Danish relations deteriorate further, as discussed in Chapter Eight. A two-year peace treaty in 1473 between Edward IV and Christian I sought to defuse the situation, but it got little help from Björn and Olöf's son Thorleif.[5]

Thorleif had at least thirteen children by Thorstein Olafsson's grand-daughter Ingvild Helgadaughter before he finally married this third cousin (see Appendix B). The liaison between Björn the Jerusalem-Farer's grand-son and Ingvild, the granddaughter of Thorstein Olafsson and Sigrid Björns-daughter, further tightened the connections among the various North Ice-land chieftain families discussed in this book.

It helps us understand the ease with which Thorstein Olafsson and his friends and descendants wielded power if we go back for a brief look at the careers of some of Thorstein's older relations, starting with his uncle Sumarlidi Thorsteinsson (see Genealogy 1). The Flatey Annals for 1387, the year Björn the Jerusalem-Farer returned from Greenland to Hvalfjord in Iceland with his four ships, noted cryptically: "The merchants in Hval-fjord and Sumarlidi met [or quarreled]. Later he [Sumarlidi] was engaged in various travels and enterprises." There is no mention of where Sumarlidi, another cog in the Icelandic power wheel, went in his pursuit of business. With an economy that may merely reflect recent Norwegian attempts to enforce the crown's restrictions on any trade with the Atlantic colonies that violated royal privileges and circumvented the Bergen Staple, the same an-nals tell us that in the summer of 1393, Sumarlidi went "abroad."[6] During the intervening years, he had engaged in his share of fights and property transactions, including a sale of land at Sauda to Sigrid Björnsdaughter's uncle, Benedict Brynjolfsson (see Appendix B), and he was reckoned one of the chief men in Iceland, just as were his father Thorstein Eyjolfsson and his brother Arnfinn.[7]

In 1386, Arnfinn Thorsteinsson had received land at Hálsi in Svarfadar-dal from his father, to which he added during the next few years as became a man in his position.[8] Especially during the turbulent years 1419–20, when the Icelanders were walking a tightrope between welcoming the En-glish merchants and decrying the violence of English fishermen, Arnfinn had an important part in Icelandic politics as lawman and *hirðstjóri*. Like so many of his relatives and peers, he played a complicated game and played it well—he was knighted, as was his son Eyjolf after him. By virtue of his own position and his family ties, Arnfinn knew as much as any man in Ice-land about the current situation in Greenland, about the advantages and disadvantages of the English presence in Iceland, and about power politics in Copenhagen. And both he and his son Eyjolf were firmly woven into the web of power and influence in Iceland. Eyjolf Arnfinnsson's wife was Snælaug Gudnadaughter (see Genealogy 5), whose grandfather Odd *lepp* had also been on the 1391 list of the most powerful men in Iceland. In 1467 their daughter Margret was married to Hrafn, son of the same Brand Halldorsson who had gone to Greenland with Thorstein Olafsson.[9]

Sumarlidi and Arnfinn Thorsteinsson's brother Olaf did not live long enough to make much mark on history, but Olaf's sons (see Genealogy 2) made up for their father's early demise. Hall Olafsson was too young to be on the 1391 list of great chieftains, but he had reached his stride by 1409, the same year his brother Thorstein took the precaution of obtaining written proof of his and Sigrid Björnsdaughter's marriage from the officialis at Gardar in Greenland. At the *Alþing* that year, Hall was one of the many chieftains who added their names to a document reaffirming in general terms that the Norwegian crown owned one quarter of the space aboard any ship going from Iceland to Norway after having made its first voyage *from* Norway (see Chapter Six).[10] We know that Björn the Jerusalem-Farer's friend, the *hirðstjóri* Vigfus Ivarsson, was able to grant exemptions to this agreement, and that others who signed the document and its transcripts also were friends or kinsmen of Hall, Arni, and Thorstein Olafsson.[11]

Like his uncle Arnfinn (Thorsteinsson), Hall Olafsson signed the 1419 and 1420 *Alþing* letters to King Eirik. As a descendant of Thorstein Eyjolfsson, he was also involved in the property claims which Thorleif Arnason made on behalf of his wife Vatnsfjord-Kristin Björnsdaughter (see Genealogy 3) in 1420 and 1421. Lawman Hrafn Gudmundsson appointed Hall one of the judges in the former case, and Hall's brother Thorstein, who by this time was *hirðstjóri*, made him a judge in the latter one.[12] Hall died around 1432, presumably of the smallpox epidemic scouring Iceland in 1431–32.[13]

Returning to Iceland after his time in Greenland and Norway, Hall's brother Thorstein Olafsson began his own magisterial career while his brother and uncle were both at the center of power, but—as noted in Chapter Seven—Thorstein's name does not appear on the 1419 and 1420 *Alþing* letters to King Eirik which Hall and Arnfinn had signed, although he was a full-fledged member of the North Iceland power elite at the time.[14]

Thorstein Olafsson may have died of the smallpox epidemic just like his brother Hall and many of his peers, for he does not appear in the records after 1431, when he was the lawman for southern and eastern Iceland and probably the chief instigator of the *Alþing* petition to King Eirik discussed in Chapter Seven.[15] The likelihood that he died in this epidemic is our chief clue to the identity of Arni Olafsson, the famous Skálholt bishop.

Not everyone would agree that Bishop Arni was the brother of Thorstein and Hall Olafsson. The point of departure in any discussion about Bishop Arni's background has always been the relationship between him and Helgi Gudnason (see Genealogy 5); the modern Icelandic historian Björn Thorsteinsson is representative of the prevailing view. He believes that little is known of Arni other than that he probably was of chieftain stock, and that his sister's son was Helgi Gudnason (the lawman in north and west Iceland from 1438 until 1443), who died before 1445.[16]

Although the lineage shown in Genealogy 5 is the likely one for this family, there is no complete agreement about Helgi Gudnason's pedigree. There is one incontestable fact about his family connections, however: he was the first husband of Akra-Kristin, the daughter of Thorstein Olafsson and Sigrid Björnsdaughter. This relationship, combined with the probability that Thorstein was dead by 1432, constitutes the real key to Bishop Arni's identity.

In two documents, from December 1435 and January 1436, witnesses declared that back in 1419, Bishop Arni Olafsson had given his "sister's son" Helgi Gudnason the farm Hvalsnes at Rosmhvalanes in northern Iceland. At the *Alþing* in the summer of 1436, the *hirðstjóri* Orm Loptsson and twelve judges appointed by him sided with Helgi in his dispute with Nikulas Snæbjarnarson over this farm.[17] Another surviving document shows that Ingunn Gunnarsdaughter had granted Arni full authority over Hvalsnes farm and all her other property in 1415, the same summer that Lopt Guttormsson (see Genealogy 4), Hall Olafsson, and six other men testified that they had witnessed the transfer of property to Arni by Sigrid Björnsdaughter's relatives Benedict Brynjolfsson and Margret Eiriksdaughter (see Appendix B).[18] On the basis of these sources, scholars have made convoluted attempts to find a likely Gudni who might have married the daughter of a likely Olaf and become brother-in-law to Bishop Arni, and who produced a chieftain son named Helgi. One fairly common assumption has been that Arni was the son of Olaf *toni* Thorleifsson, who died in 1393, and who might have had an unnamed sister who married Gudni Sæmundsson.[19]

In my view, a simpler and more reasonable explanation is that the judges in the 1435–36 property dispute had focused on Helgi Gudnason's *current* status. Thorstein Olafsson was quite likely dead by that time, but his widow Sigrid Björnsdaughter was still the "sister" (actually sister-in-law) of Bishop Arni. Since 1428 at least, Sigrid's daughter Akra-Kristin had been married to Helgi Gudnason, who was thus Sigrid's "son" (actually son-in-law).[20] The exact term would not have been important unless determining consanguinity was the legal issue. If "sister's son" is short for "sister-in-law's son-in-law," as I believe it is, Bishop Arni was the brother of Hall and Thorstein Olafsson and the cousin of Vatnsfjord-Kristin, as well as the grand-nephew of the *hirðstjóri* Arni Thordsson—for whom he was probably named.[21]

Such a background would explain why Arni appointed Björn the Jerusalem-Farer (his uncle-by-marriage) to be his ombudsman as *hirðstjóri* in 1414, before Arni himself arrived in Iceland in 1415. It would also explain the property transactions in the period 1415–19 that involved Bishop Arni and the families of Thorstein Olafsson, Björn the Jerusalem-Farer, Orm Loptsson and his son Guttorm (whose brother Jon was Vatnsfjord-Kristin's first husband), and the lawman Odd Thordsson *lepp*.[22] Above all, it would provide an answer to the question of why Thorstein Olafsson and his friends were not put on trial for having defrauded the crown when they arrived in Norway in 1410, fresh from their Greenland venture.

But if Bishop Arni was the son of Olaf Thorsteinsson, who were Helgi Gudnason's parents, and why would Bishop Arni have given him Hvalsnes farm before leaving Iceland in 1419—*if* indeed he had made the gift? There is no proof that the claims made during the 1435–36 property dispute were based on anything but the *plausibility* that just before Arni left Iceland (for good, as it turned out), he had given one of his many farms to a promising young brother of Snælaug Gudnadaughter. After all, she was married to Arni's cousin Eyjolf Arnfinnsson (see Genealogies 1 and 5), and Arni's relations with the family were so close that only a year earlier, in 1418, he and Snælaug's father Gudni had exchanged land while at the *Alþing*.[23]

Gudni's father (and Snælaug's grandfather; see Genealogy 5), the lawman Odd Thordsson *lepp*, traced his ancestry to Thorfinn Thordsson *karlsefni* and Gudrid Thorbjörnsdaughter, the first European colonizers of the New World, and was reckoned one of the great men in Iceland both in 1391 and in 1420.[24] His many grandchildren, impeccably married, remained members of the inner power circle, which also contained the descendants of Thorstein Olafsson and Sigrid Björnsdaughter (who will be discussed in Appendix B).[25]

Sigrid Björnsdaughter

The progenitors of Sigrid Björnsdaughter were at least as powerful as those of Thorstein Olafsson, whom she married at Hvalsey in Greenland in 1408. Her background warrants a closer look here, because it has largely been ignored by scholars studying the last recorded voyage between Greenland and Norway, who have primarily focused on the men involved. The landed wealth Sigrid inherited formed the basis for Thorstein's career in Iceland; it also made possible the strategic marriages of their daughter Akra-Kristin and her two daughters, Ingvild Helgadaughter and Málfrid Torfadaughter (see Genealogy 6).

6.

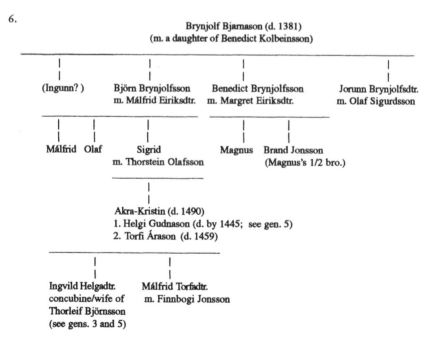

Brynjolf Bjarnason (d. 1381)
(m. a daughter of Benedict Kolbeinsson)

(Ingunn?)   Björn Brynjolfsson   Benedict Brynjolfsson   Jorunn Brynjolfsdtr.
              m. Málfrid Eiriksdtr.   m. Margret Eiriksdtr.   m. Olaf Sigurdsson

Málfrid Olaf   Sigrid   Magnus Brand Jonsson
            m. Thorstein Olafsson   (Magnus's 1/2 bro.)

Akra-Kristin (d. 1490)
1. Helgi Gudnason (d. by 1445; see gen. 5)
2. Torfi Árason (d. 1459)

Ingvild Helgadtr.   Málfrid Torfadtr.
concubine/wife of   m. Finnbogi Jonsson
Thorleif Björnsson
(see gens. 3 and 5)

It is a notable feature of Sigrid Björnsdaughter's family that her father and uncle—Björn and Benedict Brynjolfsson—as well as her grandfather Brynjolf Bjarnason were all called "the Wealthy" many years before mortality from the Black Death had placed large numbers of farms in the hands of a few people. Like Thorstein Olafsson's kin, Sigrid's relatives figure prominently in medieval Icelandic documents, not only because of their many recorded property transactions, but because their wealth, prominence, and power ensured that they were called upon to serve as lay judges or witnesses (often in matters involving friends or relatives), as financial managers for religious houses, and in other public and private offices.[1]

Sigrid's father, Björn Brynjolfsson, and his equally wealthy brother Benedict were reckoned among the chief men in Iceland in 1391, along with such notable contemporaries as the *hirðstjóri* Thorstein Eyjolfsson (see Appendix A) and his sons Sumarlidi and Arnfinn, and with Björn Einarsson the Jerusalem-Farer and Sigmund *hvítkollr*, Björn's traveling companion when he "drifted off" to Greenland.[2]

As male members of one of the most prominent families in North Iceland, Sigrid's grandfather (Brynjolf Björnsson) and his sons had close dealings with the lawman Thorstein Eyjolfsson and his kin years before Sigrid married Thorstein Olafsson in 1408—a fact that surely had some bearing on later events, especially since land transactions in that society were a serious business and not often entered into by people who did not know each other well. In 1386, Thorstein Eyjolfsson was involved in settling a dispute over a whale carcass to which Sigrid's father Björn had laid claim, and between 1391 and 1394 Sigrid's uncle, Benedict Brynjolfsson, completed the purchase of land at Sauda in Skog which Thorstein Eyjolfsson and his son Sumarlidi had owned together.[3]

Björn Brynjolfsson, father of the Hvalsey bride, was clearly pulling his own weight in their Skagafjord community by 1379, when he was one of the witnesses to a property transaction at Miklabær in Blönduhlid.[4] His father Brynjolf Björnsson, the wealthy owner of Great Akrar in Skagafjord, was still active at the time, including as financial adviser to Reynistead nunnery, but he died on February 14, 1381.[5] It was left to his son Björn to arrange his (Björn's) sister Jorunn's marriage to Olaf Sigurdsson. Björn discharged that office with the same care he brought to all his other financial transactions; he had the complicated business deal written up and properly witnessed.[6] It is no wonder that Sigrid Björnsdaughter's Hvalsey marriage to Thorstein Olafsson gave rise to repeated affidavits concerning that union, for both she and Thorstein came from families accustomed to having their business transactions witnessed and documented.

Björn Brynjolfsson made his daughter a wealthy woman in Iceland, quite apart from whatever she may have owned in Greenland. The property inventory for the church at South Akrar in Blönduhlid in the period 1382–ca. 1600 shows that Björn made generous donations to that church in 1392, and that the lands at Akrar, Grof, Gegnishól, Vellir, Mid-Grund, and South Grund were among his many farms at the time.[7]

At the end of 1392, he also formally granted his children Olaf, Sigrid, and Málfrid equal shares in their inheritance. A detailed document accompanied this distribution, with everything from boundary markers to driftage rights carefully described.[8] Among the lands Sigrid was to share with her siblings were those called South Akrar, Outer Akrar, and Brecka. The holding called Great Akrar clearly became Thorstein's principal seat, which suggests that by the time Thorstein arrived in Greenland, Sigrid had become the chief heir to her father's great estate. Her brother Olaf and her sister Málfrid are both likely to have died in the Black Death (1402–4), for Málfrid appears only in the document concerning her inheritance, and there is nothing specific in later records about Olaf (the name Olaf Björnsson is in itself not particularly rare). The usually well-informed Espolin demonstrated his time's paucity of knowledge about Sigrid's background when he reasoned that since Thorstein Olafsson (Sigrid's husband, as we now know) had his seat at Great Akrar, he must have been the son of Olaf Björnsson (who actually was Sigrid's brother).[9] Espolin's assumption that power and property should be traced through the male line was an attitude shared by many later scholars.

Another aspect of Björn Brynjolfsson's provisions for his children also has interesting implications: Sigrid was to have the farm Thorleiksstead, which had belonged to her mother, while there was no mention of a maternal inheritance for Olaf and Málfrid. Sigrid's mother, Málfrid Eiriksdaughter, came from a wealthy family, and Thorleiksstead in Blönduhlid, which henceforth was to be Sigrid's, was clearly a desirable property.[10]

Indeed, it is obvious that Thorstein Olafsson considered Thorleiksstead a pleasing by-product of his marriage to Sigrid, for he wanted to build a chapel there. On May 25, 1431, he got permission from Bishop Jon Vilhjalmsson of Holar to do so, in a letter that refers to Thorleiksstead as Thorstein's own property.[11] Sigrid and Thorstein's heirs found the property equally useful. In 1456, Akra-Kristin Thorsteinsdaughter's husband, Torfi Árason, used his share in Thorleiksstead to pay for a favor that had secured for him the office of lawman; in 1489, the aging Akra-Kristin sat at Thorleiksstead while engaged in selling off some of her land elsewhere; and when Kristin's wealth was to be distributed among her heirs, a meeting to discuss the matter was held at Thorleiksstead.[12]

There is no indication of why Björn Brynjolfsson decided to settle property on his children in 1392. He was alive both in 1394, when he witnessed a corody contract for Reynistead nunnery, and in May of 1396, when he helped witness an inventory of Holar See's property in Hjaltadal.[13] The exact year of his death is not known, but it is likely that he died in the Black Death, because he was not involved in the April 1405 negotiations at Hvalfjord over a sale of land involving Ingunn (Jorunn?) Brynjolfsdaughter, Benedict Brynjolfsson, and Björn Einarsson the Jerusalem-Farer, among others.[14]

The closeness implied here between Sigrid's family and Björn Einarsson, who went to Greenland *before* he earned the name "Jerusalem-Farer," suggests that he may well have had a hand in arranging Sigrid's first marriage in Greenland, but for reasons noted in Chapter Six, any property agreements made in conjunction with that marriage would have had to be spoken, not written ones.

Neither does the proof of his and Sigrid's wedding which Thorstein obtained in 1409, before leaving Greenland, contain a statement of financial arrangements—again in keeping with the need to conceal direct business transactions between two Norwegian colonies. The written sources are as silent about the deal hammered out at Hvalsey between Sigrid and Thorstein as the property transactions of their descendants are widely documented. There is also a noticeable lack of detail in the two subsequent Icelandic affidavits (dated 1414 and 1424) of their wedding, although the clear purpose of these documents was to make certain that any property transactions connected with the 1408 Hvalsey marriage were as legal as the marriage itself. The affidavit written in May of 1414 at Akrar is evidence of this—it was found bundled together with two other documents from 1414 (dated April 8 at Munkathverá in Eyjafjord, and April 23 at Holar) that concern complicated land transactions among the group of North Iceland chieftains to which Thorstein Olafsson belonged.[15]

The wealthy Sigrid was probably safe in Greenland when the Great Plague struck her native region with such terrible force that in mid-winter 1402–3 the North Icelanders made a public vow to fast, pray, and make donations to religious institutions.[16] If—as seems likely—her father, sister, and brother were among the many who perished at that time, Thorstein Olafsson would have brought her the news in 1406, and (as discussed in Chapter Six) he would certainly have been aware of her increased wealth.

When Sigrid returned to Iceland with Thorstein in 1411, she still had close relatives there, including her uncle Benedict Brynjolfsson (also called Benedict the Wealthy of Akrar). Benedict of Akrar (and owner of Sjáarborg, Espihol, and many other fine farms) was still counted among the chieftains in North Iceland in 1420, along with Sigrid's husband Thorstein and many of his kin.[17]

Presumably Benedict could handle the diminution of property he put up with in 1415, when nine men (including Thorstein's brother Hall Olafsson) testified that Benedict Brynjolfsson and his wife Margret Eiriksdaughter had handed over to Thorstein's other brother, Bishop Arni Olafsson of Skálholt, all the property Margret had inherited after her sister's sons and which they had inherited as legitimized sons of the priest Steinmod Thorsteinsson. The stated rationale for Benedict and Margret's largesse was that *sira* Steinmod had been the officialis at Holar (an office Bishop Arni now held) and still owed money both to the Holar See and to the archbishop; the transaction is in any event another interesting example of bookkeeping within this tightly knit chieftain class.[18]

Benedict must have died during the winter of 1420–21, for in the spring of 1421 his widow (Margret Eiriksdaughter) had to defend her right to property she claimed Björn the Jerusalem-Farer had sold to her husband. A complaint filed by the chieftain Thorleif Arnason on behalf of his wife Vatnsfjord-Kristin (see Appendix A, Genealogy 3) claimed that Margret was holding onto some fields and cattle that Kristin had inherited after Jon Jonsson (her son by her first marriage, who had died young), and which Jon had inherited from his father's mother (and Margret's sister) Sophie Eiriksdaughter, who in turn had that inheritance from her sisters Ása and Ingileif. The royal administrator charged with appointing judges for two hearings was none other than Thorstein Olafsson, related by blood or marriage to both parties in this convoluted dispute.[19]

Thorstein and Sigrid's daughter (Akra-Kristin Thorsteinsdaughter) and granddaughters (Ingvild Helgadaughter and Málfrid Torfadaughter) helped consolidate their circle's grip on wealth and power. Akra-Kristin was first married to the lawman Helgi Gudnason (see Appendix A, Genealogy 5) and then to Torfi Árason, who rose to prominence through a combination of domestic power-play and carefully cultivated relations with the Dano-Norwegian king. After a long struggle over consanguinity, Ingvild (Akra-Kristin's daughter by Helgi Gudnason) married Thorleif Björnsson, like herself a great-great-grandchild of Thorstein Eyjolfsson (See Appendix A). During his career, Thorleif served Bishop Andrés "of Gardar" while the latter sat as officialis at Skálholt, and he enjoyed the office of *hirðstjóri* for many years, as noted in Chapter Eight.[20]

Wealthy and accustomed to having their own way, Thorleif and Ingvild lived together despite the church's disapproval. In 1471, Bishop Svein of Skálholt granted the pair absolution for having had seven children together despite being third cousins, but neither the pious readings he assigned nor the fines the couple had to pay produced a change of heart, for in 1474 Bishop Svein gave his officialis authority to grant absolution to Thorleif and to confess both him and Ingvild for their latest child. After they had obtained a letter from the pope, King Christian I in 1477 gave them permission to marry despite being more closely related than the law permitted.

Their financial agreement was dated August 23, 1484, two years before Thorleif died.[21] The story of their perseverance does not quite constitute an Icelandic "Camelot," however, for in a document entitled *Witnisburdur millum Tholleifs og Ingvelldar um mein,* several people testify to the existence of a sexual relationship between Thorleif Björnsson and a second cousin of Ingvild's.[22]

After Akra-Kristin's death in 1490, Ingvild inherited one-third of her mother's property. Her brother-in-law, Thorleif's wily brother Einar Björnsson (see Appendix A, Genealogy 3), claimed he was entitled to another third.[23] Einar's greed supported his ambition, as demonstrated by a letter written at the *Alþing* the very next year (1491), when 25 men asked King Hans to make Einar Björnsson *hirðstjóri* of all Iceland.[24] They were led by Finnbogi Jonsson, who was married to Ingvild's sister Málfrid Torfadaughter, the heir to the remaining third of Akra-Kristin's great wealth.

Her wealth secured for Ingvild a respectable old age in a corody arrangement with the nunnery at Helgafell, where she would live not as a religious, but as a woman of rank with her own servants, bed linen, and other luxuries.[25] Wealth and power also settled at last the vexing question of legitimacy on the part of her children by Thorleif and ensured that they, too, would retain their place in society as Iceland moved into a period beyond the concern of this book.[26]

Overlapping Enterprises, ca. 1480-1510

	John Cabot connection			N. Atlantic fishing and trade			
Individual names	Greene's tenants	Voyages 1497–98	H. Elyot+ S. Cabot (1502+)	Iceland trade	Iberian trade	Anglo- Azorean	1480 & 1481
Ameryk, Richard[a]		(re pension)		?	x	(re fish '02)	(juror)
Asshehurst, Thomas			x		x	x	
Bradley, Thomas		x ('98)					
Clerk, Wm., Jr.	x			x	x	x	
Croft, Thomas							x
De la Fount, Wm.				x	x		x
Elyot, Hugh		? ('97)	x		x	x	
Fernandes, Francisco			x		x (?)	x	
Fernandes, João		? ('98)			x	x	
Forster, John, Jr.				x	?		
Gonsalves, João			x		x (?)	x	
Goodman, John				x	x		
Greene, Philip	——	?			x		(juror)
Jay, John, Jr.	x	? ('97+'98)		x	x	x	x
Lloyd, John				?	?		x
Shipward, John				x	x		
Spencer, Wm.[a]				x	x		x
Straunge, Robert				x	x		x
Thirkill, Lancelot		x ('98)				?	
Thomas, John	x				x	x	
Thorne, Nicholas (son R. Sr.)						x	
Thorne, Robert Sr.		? ('97)	x	x	x	x	x
Thorne, Robert Jr.					x	x	
Thorne, Thomas (Wm.'s son)			x			x	
Thorne, Wm. (bro. of R. Sr.)			x			x	
Warde, Richard					?	x	

[a] Listed as having an Icelandic servant in his household in 1484. A "John Eliot" was also on the list; he may possibly have been the father of Hugh Elyot.

Notes

ABBREVIATIONS

The following abbreviations are used in the Notes. For full forms of these and all shortened citations, see the Works Cited.

DI   *Diplomatarium Islandicum*
DN   *Diplomatarium Norvegicum*
GHM   *Grønlands Historiske Mindesmerker*
MoG   *Meddelelser om Grønland*
PRO   The Public Record Office, London

INTRODUCTION

1. "Grænlendingasaga," *Íslendingasögur*, pp.368–71;*Islenzkfornrit*4: 244–52.
2. As the Greenland map shows, a voyage from the Julianehaab region up to the Nuuk region would have a distinctly westerly trend.
3. Williamson, *Cabot Voyages*, p. 11.
4. Nørlund, "Buried."
5. Vandvik, *Latinske*, pp. 70–73, 177. The pope's letter is often supposed to be referring to the Greenlanders because of the implied lack of bread, but a notation made on the back shows that it concerns the Norwegians.
6. Morison, *European Discovery*, pp. 67–68.
7. Nansen, *Nord*, p. 361.
8. Hansen, "Anthropologica medici."
9. Fischer-Møller, "Mediaeval Norse Settlements"; Brøste and Fischer-Møller, "Mediaeval Norsemen"; H. Ingstad, *Land*, p. 309; Krogh, *Erik*, pp. 61–62.
10. One recent exception is H. C. Gulløv's article "Noua terra 1566," in which he takes issue with Sturtevant and Quinn's thesis in "This New Prey."
11. See, e.g., Quinn's assumption (*North America*, p. 114) that there were no more Norse colonists in Greenland when the English began their North Atlantic explorations at the end of the fifteenth century.

12. Skelton, Marston, and Painter, *Vinland Map*; Wallis, Maddison, Painter, Quinn, et al., "Strange Case," pp. 183–217.

13. Morison, *European Discovery*, p. 208n; Quinn, *England and the Discovery*, pp. 22–23.

14. Quinn, Quinn, and Hillier, eds., *New American*.

15. Quinn, *Explorers and Colonies*, p. 125.

16. Barkham, "Basque Whaling"; idem, *Los vascos*; Tuck, *Red Bay*. I am also indebted to Professor David B. Quinn for information he gave me during a conversation at the Anglo-American Conference of the Institute for Historical Research in London, July 9, 1992.

17. A. S. Ingstad, *Discovery*; H. Ingstad, *Norse Discovery*; idem, *Vesterveg*.

18. Andreasen and Arneborg, "Gården under sandet—undersøgelserne"; idem, "Gården under sandet. Nye nordboundersøgelser"; Arneborg and Berglund, *Gården under sandet . . . status november 1993*; H. C. Kapel, "Nyopdaget nordbogård."

19. Grønnow and Meldgaard, "De første," p. 143.

20. Roussell, "Farms," p. 11.

21. Nørlund, "Buried," pp. 14–19.

22. Taagholt and Bach, "Hvad foregår," p. 216.

23. Conversations with Jørgen Meldgaard and Jette Arneborg in Copenhagen, May 5, 1991.

24. Andreasen, "Langhus," p. 182.

25. See, e.g., Bowman, *Radiocarbon*. Bowman clarifies many of the principles and problems involved, including (pp. 20–25) the so-called marine reservoir effect, which is of particular importance to Greenland archaeologists.

26. Conversation with Jette Arneborg in Copenhagen, May 4, 1991.

27. Danish Polar Center, *Newsletter* no. 24 (1991), p. 25. In a follow-up telephone conversation with Jette Arneborg on May 27, 1993, she noted that the information for the years 1955–94 will be published as a book in the series *MoG, Man & Society* after being entered into a computerized database, and that the project will continue as a current, on-line research tool.

28. Grønnow, Meldgaard, and Berglund-Nielsen, "Aasivissuit," pp. 63–69.

29. Jansen, "Critical Account."

30. At the same site, Vebæk also found a complete circular disk, of either spruce or larch, with incised circles—possibly a half-finished sundial. "Church Topography," pp. 58–59, 65–71, 75; Thirslund and Vebæk, *Vikingernes Kompas*; Vebæk and Thirslund, *Viking Compass*.

31. Conversation with C. L. Vebæk in Copenhagen, May 4, 1991; Taylor, May, Lethbridge, and Motzo, "Norse Bearing Dial?"

32. Letter to the author from C. L. Vebæk, Oct. 23, 1991. Vebæk's recent monograph on Vatnahverfi is no. 17 in the series *MoG, Man & Society*; his monograph on site Ø17a is no. 18 in the same series.

33. Arneborg, Gulløv, and Hart-Hansen, "Menneske," pp. 39–41; conversation with Hans Kapel in Copenhagen, May 5, 1991.

CHAPTER ONE

1. Jakob Benediktsson gives an excellent overview of these redactions in Pulsiano, ed., *Medieval Scandinavia*, pp. 373–74.

2. All three works are published in the Icelandic series *Islenzk fornrit*, as well as in Vol. 1 of *Íslendinga sögur*. Several English translations exist; the selections in Jones, *Norse Atlantic Saga*, pp. 143–55 and pp. 186–235 are also useful.

3. Benediktsson in Pulsiano, ed., *Medieval Scandinavia*, pp. 332–33; Halldórsson, *Grænland*, pp. xiv–xv; idem, in Pulsiano, ed., *Medieval Scandinavia*, p. 240; Jones, *Norse Atlantic Saga*, pp. 304–5.

4. Halldórsson, *Grænland*, pp. 293–406; Jones, *Norse Atlantic Saga*, pp. 306–7, 310.

5. Halldórsson, *Grænland*, p. 297; Jones, *Norse Atlantic Saga*, p. 307.

6. Liestøl, "Runes," p. 232.

7. Ibid., pp. 232–33.

8. Jones, *Norse Atlantic Saga*, pp. 12–14.

9. Vebæk, "Church Topography," pp. 65–71; Vebæk and Thirslund, *Viking Compass*. The latter work also describes (p. 23) a triangular piece of steatite, engraved with a gnomon curve, which Vebæk found in 1949 during excavations at Ø71 in Vatnahverfi.

10. Thirslund in Vebæk, "Church Topography," pp. 65–71. A reconstruction of the dial was tested aboard the Viking ship replica *Gaia* on a voyage from Norway to North America in the late summer of 1991. Thirslund's article "Navigation" is the best recent summary in English concerning the use of this sun compass.

11. Conversation with Kari Ellen Gade, June 1991.

12. Foote, "Icelandic *sólarsteinn*." (See also *Kulturhistorisk leksikon*, 12, cols. 261–62.) Foote dismissed Carl V. Sølver's suggestion (*Vestervejen*, esp. pp. 118–19) that there might be a connection between Vebæk's wooden bearing dial and the "sunstone." Foote noted that according to literary evidence, the "sunstone" must be as smooth and round as the rocks found along the shore; it must be valuable enough to warrant mention in inventories or other accounts of property; it must obviously belong to the mineral kingdom; *and* it must serve some sort of navigational purpose—presumably by making it possible to locate the sun even in cloudy weather. He advanced the theory that the "sunstone" was a smooth, convex piece of quartz or other crystal capable of magnification and of gathering the sun's rays to form a burning point. Citing widely from other European literary sources to support this theory, he nevertheless was careful to observe that the known fragments of Icelandic medieval lapidaries make no references to crystalline rock used as a burning glass, and they do not employ the word *sólarsteinn*.

13. Thirslund, "Navigation," pp. 116–17; Jones, *Norse Atlantic Saga*, p. 13.

14. On the settlement-period farm Ø17a at Narssaq, Vebæk also found what may have been a stone bearing dial (H. Ingstad, *Land*, pp. 51–52). Concerning early sailors' portable instruments, it is worth noting that among the articles retrieved from Henry VIII's flagship, the *Mary Rose*, which went down off Ports-

mouth in 1545, there were pocket sundials (personal observation at the Maritime Museum, Greenwich, England).

15. *The King's Mirror*, p 93.

16. Foote's citation, p. 142, is to O. A. Johnsen and Jón Helgason, *Den store Saga om Olav den hellige* (1941), pp. 670–71. The passage in question was translated by J. Turville-Petre (*The Story of Rauð and His Sons* (1947), p. 24, as: "So the King had the sunstone held aloft, and observed where it cast out a beam."

17. *DI* 3, no. 594; Foote, "Icelandic *sólarsteinn*," p. 14, incl. n. 10; Karlsson, *Islandske originaldiplomer*, pp. 166–67.

18. *Íslendinga sögur*, pp. 326, 363; *Islenzk fornrit* 4: 197, 241.

19. *Íslendinga sögur*, pp. 78–82, 326–28, 363–64; *Islenzk fornrit* 4: 197–99, 241–42.

20. *Íslendinga sögur*, pp. 328, 364; *Islenzk fornrit* 4: 199, 242. See also Jones, *Norse Atlantic Saga*, pp. 73–75, 186, 209; Magnusson and Pálsson, trans. and eds., *Vinland Sagas*, pp. 49–50, 76–77. What little we know of Gunnbjörn's voyage comes from "Landnámabók" (The Book of the Settlements), ch. 14, in *Íslendinga sögur*.

21. For the story of Nadd-Odd, see "Landnámabók" in *Íslendinga sögur*, p. 25. See also Brøndsted, *Vikings*, pp. 61–62; Jones, *Norse Atlantic Saga*, pp. 37–41, 159.

22. The story of Snæbjörn: "Landnámabók" in *Íslendinga sögur*, pp. 112–16; Jones, *Norse Atlantic Saga*, pp. 169–72.

23. "Landnámabók," "Eiriks saga rauða," and "Grænlendinga saga" in *Íslendinga sögur*, pp. 80, 328–29.

24. See, e.g., Bruun, "Arkæologiske"; Nørlund and Stenberger, "Brattahlid"; Krogh, *Viking*.

25. Jones, *Norse Atlantic Saga*, pp. 36–37, 39, 130, 144, 156.

26. "Islendingabók" in *Íslendinga sögur*, p. 8; *GHM* 1: 168; Berglund, "Decline," pp. 109–35. For a discussion of the term Skræling, see Jones, *Norse Atlantic Saga*, pp. 92–93. The "loose translation" is mine.

27. Andreasen, "Nordbosager," pp. 135–36; Sørensen, "Pollenundersøgelser," pp. 296–304.

28. Bruun, "Oversigt"; Roussell, "Sandnes"; idem, "Farms"; Arneborg, "Nordboarkæologiske."

29. H. Ingstad, *Land*, p. 116.

30. *Íslendinga sögur*, pp. 366–71; *Islenzk fornrit* 4: 244–52.

31. H. Ingstad, "På jakt."

32. *Íslendinga sögur*, p. 370; *Islenzk fornrit* 4: 250.

33. Kleivan, "Eskimoenes," pp. 347–55.

34. *Íslendinga sögur*, pp. 370, 372; *Islenzk fornrit* 4: 250, 253.

35. Kari Ellen Gade, personal communication.

36. Magnusson and Pálsson, trans. and eds., *Vinland Sagas*, p. 58n.

37. *Íslendinga sögur*, p. 370; *Islenzk fornrit* 4: 251.

38. Jones, *Norse Atlantic Saga*, p. 124. A belt of mixed broadleaf and coniferous forests stretches northeastward from New England to the southern bank of the St. Lawrence, and the habitat indicated for *Zizania aquatica* is the same as that shown

for two kinds of wild grapes (*Vitis rotundifolia* and *V. riparia*), reaching northward virtually to the south shore of the St. Lawrence (Wernert, ed., *North American Wildlife*, pp. 400, 475).

39. Jones, *Norse Atlantic Saga*, p. 124; Koht, *Den eldste*, p. 92; Magnusson and Pálsson, trans. and eds., *Vinland Sagas*, p. 86n.

40. Wallace, "L'Anse aux Meadows," p. 39.

41. Jones, *Norse Atlantic Saga*, p. 76.

42. *Íslendinga sögur*, p. 371; *Islenzk fornrit* 4: 251.

43. Magnusson and Pálsson, trans. and eds., *Vinland Sagas*, p. 56; Jones, *Norse Atlantic Saga*, p. 193. *Eykt* may mean anything from the approximately three hours of work a farmhand might be expected to do at one stretch, to the time around 3:30 in the afternoon, while *dagmál* is the first meal of the day, at about 9 A.M. (*Norrøn ordbok*, pp. 72, 98).

44. Jones, *Norse Atlantic Saga*, pp. 124–25, 193.

45. *Íslendinga sögur*, pp. 374–76; *Islenzk fornrit* 4: 254–57.

46. Dumond, *Eskimos*, p. 141; H. Ingstad, *Norse Discovery*, pp. 289–90; Jones, *Norse Atlantic Saga*, p. 130; McGhee, "Contact," pp. 7–9; idem, "The Skraellings"; Wallace, "L'Anse aux Meadows," pp. 31–33.

47. *Íslendinga sögur*, pp. 355–56; *Islenzk fornrit* 4: 231–232.

48. *Íslendinga sögur*, pp. 340–43, 377–80; *Islenzk fornrit* 4: 214–17, 257–60.

49. *Íslendinga sögur*, pp. 340–43, 377–80; *Islenzk fornrit* 4: 214–17, 257–60. The other half of the farm originally belonged to another Thorstein, as both Vínland sagas agree. There is no record of how Thorstein Eiriksson had obtained his share. At a guess, Eirik the Red spotted this lovely site during his initial reconnaissance of Greenland, claimed it for himself and his heirs, and let another man have a half share in return for developing the farm while he himself resided at Brattahlid.

50. McGhee, "Contact," p. 13; Roussell, "Sandnes," pp. 106–8. See also text accompanying the exhibited arrowhead at the National Museum in Copenhagen. Jette Arneborg refers to this arrowhead in her Ph.D. thesis ("Kulturmødet") and in letters to me of Mar. 21 and Apr. 26, 1993. Like McGhee, she notes the work of William W. Fitzhugh, starting with "Environmental Archaeology and Cultural Systems in Hamilton Inlet, Labrador," *Smithsonian Contributions to Anthropology*, 16 (1972).

51. *Íslendinga sögur*, p. 381; *Islenzk fornrit* 4: 261.

52. *Íslendinga sögur*, pp. 358–59, 388–90; *Islenzk fornrit* 4: 236–37, 267–69.

53. Thjodhild's father Jörund was the son of Ulf Squint-Eye, while Ári was the grandson of Ulf Squint-Eye's son Atli the Red.

54. *Islandske Annaler*, p. lxv.

55. Arneborg, "Grønland," pp. 19–20; *Islandske Annaler*, pp. 213, 353, 403.

56. Andersen and Malmros, "Ship's Parts," pp. 118–22 (quote on p. 122).

57. Grønnow and Meldgaard, "De første," p. 125.

58. Andreasen and Arneborg, "Gården under sandet. Nye nordboundersøgelser," pp. 22, 26–29, 34, 41. The authors note (p. 41) that tests have not yet been performed on the lumber to determine species, probable place of origin, etc. In a letter to me dated Mar. 21, 1993, Arneborg advises that all the wood used at the site is driftwood.

59. *GHM* 3: 492; H. Ingstad, *Vesterveg*, pp. 102–3.

60. *GHM* 3: 492–93; Halldórsson, *Grænland*, pp. 48–55. The translations are mine.

61. Hall, *Life*; Fitzhugh and Olin, eds., *Archaeology*, pp. 5, 18, 23–24, 46, 48–54, 72, 76–77, 83–86, 93–96, 114–16, 126, 162, 166, 173–211; Fitzhugh, personal communication, Dec. 1994 and Jan. 1995.

62. Fitzhugh and Olin, eds., *Archaeology*, pp. 111–14.

63. Nørlund and Roussell, "Norse Ruins," p. 138. Jette Arneborg at the National Museum in Copenhagen kindly went through Nørlund's old field notes and photographs and found no reason to amend Nørlund's published description. In her report to me (Jan. 1995) she stressed that the Gardar skulls lay in a different pattern from those found in Baffin Island; it should be further noted that the two Baffin Island finds also differ from each other. The similarity among the three arrangements consists in the deliberate care with which they were left.

64. Nielsen, "Evidence"; Nørlund and Roussell, "Norse Ruins," pp. 142–44; Jette Arneborg, personal communication, Jan. 1995. See also Buchwald and Mosdal, "Meteoric Iron."

65. Wallace, "L'Anse aux Meadows," pp 35–37.

66. Hamre, *Erkebiskop*, pp. 51–52.

67. *Islandske Annaler*, p. 112; *GHM* 3: 6–9; Jónsson, "Grønlands gamle," p. 328; "Landnámabók," ch. 13; Roussell, "Sandnes," p. 28.

68. *Islandske Annaler*, pp. 320–22.

69. *Biskupa sögur* 1: 795.

70. See, e.g., Brøgger, *Vinlandsferdene*, pp. 36–37.

71. Vandvik, *Latinske dokument*, pp. 65–67 and 170–72. The translation is mine.

72. Bjørnbo, "Cartographia," pp. 68–80; Koht, *Den eldste*, pp. 9–11, 90–92; *The King's Mirror*, pp. 134–36.

73. *GHM* 3: 216–18; Jóhannesson, "Om Haf," pp. 17–28.

74. Bjørnbo, "Cartographia," p. 82. A recent essay on the geography of the North as seen through Icelandic legendary fiction notes: "The mediaeval Icelanders' notion of the known world between Newfoundland and Jerusalem is both well documented and fairly close to reality, as a result of the personal acquaintance with foreign regions made by Icelanders on their extensive journeys which they had undertaken ever since the ninth and tenth centuries. . . . Yet, despite the fact that the Scandinavians knew the North from first-hand experience, they still copied and quoted information about it from far less well-informed continental authorities for their more scholarly texts." (Simek, "Elusive," pp. 248–49.)

75. Egede, *Grønlandsbeskrivelse*, pp. 1–2. Egede also noted the general belief that in the northeast, Greenland was connected with Asia and "Tartary" all the way to Russia. A footnote says that Eskimos from Disko Island had told him Greenland must be an island, because there was such a strong current from the north that it helped keep ice away from the middle of the "ocean."

76. H. Ingstad, *Norse Discovery*, p. 253.

77. Holand, *Explorations*, is one example of such enthusiasm, which provokes

reactions like the flippant approach taken by Morison in *European Discovery*, vol. 1. For a more reasoned commentary, see McGhee, *Ancient Canada*, pp. 165–68.

78. McGhee, "Contact," pp. 15–21; idem, "The *Skraellings*," pp. 49–50.

79. The stone can be seen today in The National Museum of Copenhagen. See also Arneborg, "Contact," p. 28; idem, "Kulturmødet," pp. 108–9; Jones, *Norse Atlantic Saga*, p. 80. In "Contact," Arneborg refers to a personal 1991 communication from Marie Stoklund for the dating of this runestone. There is no hint of what happened to Erling, Bjarni, and Eindridi, or of which Settlement they came from.

80. Arneborg, "Kulturmødet."

81. See, e.g., Schledermann, "Notes," esp. p. 462.

82. Holtved, "Nûgdlît," pp. 89–94; Schledermann, "Ellesmere," p. 595; idem, "Norsemen," p. 60.

83. Arneborg, "Kulturmødet," esp. pp. 123–25, App. 2, p. 1 (she cites work done by E. Holtved, J. Meldgaard, R. McGhee, J. A. Tuck, W. Arundale, R. Jordan, and K. McCullough); Dumond, *Eskimos*, pp. 141–47.

84. McGhee, "Contact," p. 20; Schledermann, "Notes," p. 461; idem, "Norsemen," pp. 54–56.

85. J. Meldgaard, "Bopladsen Qajaa," pp. 191–205.

86. McGhee, "Contact," pp. 12–20. The topic is also discussed at length in Arneborg, "Kulturmødet."

87. Jones, *Norse Atlantic Saga*, p. 277.

88. Grønnow, Meldgaard, and Berglund-Nielsen, "Aasivissuit," p. 7.

89. Schledermann, "Nordbogenstande," pp. 223–25; idem, "Norsemen," p. 57.

90. Gulløv, "Eskimoens syn"; Schledermann, "Nordbogenstande"; idem, "Norsemen," p. 57.

91. Jones, *Norse Atlantic Saga*, p. 281; McGhee, "Contact," pp. 16–17; Mary-Rousselière, "Exploration," pp. 590–93.

92. Gulløv, "Eskimoens syn"; Schledermann, "Nordbogenstande," pp. 222–25; idem, "Norsemen," pp. 59–66; idem, "Preliminary Results"; idem, "Ellesmere Island," pp. 594, 600.

93. Gulløv, "Eskimoens syn"; Mathiassen, "Inugsuk," pp. 285–90, Plate XXII, items 3–5; idem, "Sermermiut," pp. 161–72.

94. Mathiassen, "Inugsuk," p. 284.

95. McGhee, "*Skraellings*," p. 50; Hart Hansen, Meldgaard, and Nordqvist, *Qilakitsoq*, pp. 20–22.

96. Holtved, "Arbejder," p. 192; Mathiassen, various reports in *MoG*, but esp. "Inugsuk," p. 295; Meldgaard, "Inuit-Nordboprojektet," pp. 160–62 (noting that there are actually remarkably few signs of mutual Norse-Eskimo influence and explaining the large culture gap as being in part due to racial prejudice on the part of the Norse); conversation with Hans Kapel in Copenhagen, May 5, 1991.

97. *GHM* 3: 238–43; Halldórsson, *Grænland*, pp. 53–55, 147 (Halldórsson thinks this compilation originated with Jón *lærði* Gudmundsson ca. 1623 and was revised by Björn ca. 1643); Jones, *Norse Atlantic Saga*, pp. 20, 80.

98. McGovern, "Economics," pp. 407–8.

CHAPTER TWO

1. *GHM* 3: 463; *Islandske Annaler*, p. 212.

2. There are examples of Greenland tombstones inscribed with Roman letters. On an almost complete tombstone found in the Herjolfsnes churchyard, large Roman letters announce "Her hvilir Hro[ar] Kolgrimss[on]" ("Here rests Hroar Kolgrimsson"). Clemmensen, "Kirkeruiner," pp. 355–58.

3. Karlsson, *Islandske originaldiplomer*, pp. xvi–viii.

4. *DN* 17: no. 849.

5. *DN* 17: nos. 850, 852.

6. Koht, *Den eldste*, pp. 92–94.

7. Jansen, "Critical Account," pp. 12–18; Koht, *Den eldste*, pp. 90–92. I translated the quote from Koht's New-Norwegian rendition of the Latin. See also Jones, *Norse Atlantic Saga*, pp. 85–86.

8. For a discussion of this work, see Steinnes, "Ikring Historia Norvegiae." The text can be found in Koht, *Den eldste*, pp. 1–53.

9. Koht, *Den eldste*, pp. 9–10 (I translated the quote from Koht's New-Norwegian rendition of the Latin); Jóhannesson, "Om Haf," p. 19.

10. *The King's Mirror*, pp. 134–37.

11. *GHM* 3: 264–367; Jóhannesson, "Om Haf," pp. 17–28; *The King's Mirror*, p. 138.

12. Frydendahl, "Sommerklimaet"; Jónsson, *Det gamle*, pp. 17–19; Wrigley, Ingram, and Farmer, eds., *Climate*.

13. *The King's Mirror*, p. 142.

14. Hall, *Viking Dig*, pp. 99–101.

15. Arneborg, "Nordboarkæologiske," pp. 3–4; Nørlund, "Buried," pp. 89–90, p. 87.

16. Hall, *Viking Dig*, pp. 81–101; Sørensen, "Pollenundersøgelser"; Fredskild and Humle, "Plant remains," p. 80.

17. Nørlund and Roussell, "Norse Ruins," p. 37; Vebæk, "Vatnahverfi" (1952), p. 114; Nørlund and Stenberger, "Brattahlid," pp. 64, 119; Roussell, "Sandnes," p. 151; idem, "Farms," pp. 190–95, 243.

18. Kowaleski, "Town," discusses products needed in medieval European markets.

19. Sørensen, "Pollenundersøgelser."

20. Koht, *Den eldste*, p. 89. I translated the quote from Koht's New-Norwegian rendition of the Latin.

21. See, e.g., Roussell, "Farms," p. 24.

22. Fredskild, "Agriculture," p. 385; Fredskild and Humle, "Plant Remains," p. 80; Hansen, "Using Climate," p. 47; Sørensen, "Pollenundersøgelser."

23. Henschen, *History*, p. 178.

24. Roussell, "Farms," esp. pp. 79–81, 159.

25. See Andreasen, "Langhus-ganghus."

26. Ibid.; Roussell, "Farms," pp. 79–81, 159.

27. McGovern and Bigelow, "Archaezoology," p. 85; letter to the author from C. L. Vebæk, Oct. 23, 1991.

28. Jansen, "Critical Account," pp. 81–83.

29. Vebæk and Thirslund, *Viking Compass*, p. 55; letter to the author from C. L. Vebæk, Nov. 18, 1992.

30. McGovern, "Bones," esp. pp. 197–209; McGovern and Bigelow, "Archaezoology," pp. 91–96.

31. McGovern and Bigelow, "Archaezoology," pp. 92–98; Arneborg, "Niaqussat."

32. McGovern and Bigelow, "Archaezoology," pp. 91–96; Vebæk, "Hunting." Naturally beached whales were also a valued source of food among the Norse. *Hrafns saga* (p. 24) tells of Ragnheid in Selárdal who sold a man named Thorvald twelve *vættir* (weights) of whalemeat at his request and made him promise to reciprocate the next time a whale drifted ashore in his own fjord. The saga writer added ominously: *"Fyrir þann hval galt þorvaldr aldri síðan"* ("Thorvald never paid for that whale later").

33. McGovern and Bigelow, "Archaezoology," pp. 91–96; Vebæk, "Hunting."

34. McCartney, "Nature," esp. p. 522.

35. McGovern, "Bones," esp. pp. 195–96; McGovern and Bigelow, "Archaezoology," pp. 96–97.

36. Vebæk, "Church Topography," pp. 71–72.

37. Cat bones have so far not been found in Norse Greenland middens either, but the remains of 110 mice which Vebæk and his team found at the bottom of a barrel at Ø71 indicate that there must have been a need for cats, which were common all over Scandinavia. Vebæk, "Vatnahverfi" (1952), p. 110. Dogs, pigs, and ravens could easily dispose of dead cats thrown on the midden after being skinned; the mere absence of identifiable cat bones cannot be taken as evidence that there were no cats in medieval Greenland.

38. Holm Olsen, "Helgøy Project," p. 96; *Kulturhistorisk Leksikon* 18: cols. 506–10 (by Odd Vollan).

39. Nørlund and Roussell describe such mill stones in "Norse Ruins," pp. 140–42.

40. McGovern, "Economics," pp. 410–11; McGovern and Bigelow, "Archaezoology," pp. 96–97. Regarding declining access to northern hunting grounds, McGovern notes that "more stratified collections must be studied before we can make such a statement with confidence."

41. McGovern and Bigelow, "Archaezoology."

42. See, e.g., Buchwald and Mosdal, "Meteoric Iron," esp. pp. 25–27.

43. C. Kapel and Nansen, "Forvildede tamfår," p. 24; Sadler, "Beetles."

44. Henschen, *History*, p. 149; Madsen, "Om Trikiner."

45. Hall, *Viking Dig*, p. 97.   46. "Orkneyinga saga," p. 109.

47. Jones, *Norse Atlantic Saga*, p. 87.   48. Ibid., pp. 70–71.

49. Henschen, *History*, pp. 108–10. The Leprosy Museum at St. Jørgens Hospital in Bergen, Norway, bears chilling witness to the impact of this terrible disease right into this century.

50. "Eiriks saga rauða," chs. 3, 6; "Grænlendinga saga," ch. 6 (*Íslendinga sögur*, pp. 332, 340–43, 377–80; *Islenzk fornrit* 4: 205, 214–17, 257–60); Henschen, *History*, p. 64.

51. Vebæk, "Church Topography," pp. 30–31, 40–42; idem, "Klostre," p. 198; Roussell, "Sandnes," p. 17.

52. Krogh, *Viking*, pp. 30–43.

53. Lynnerup, "Norse Settlers"; McGovern, "Economics," pp. 404–25.

54. Scott, Halffman, and Pedersen, "Dental Conditions," p. 199.

55. Lynnerup, "Norse Settlers"; Lynnerup, Frohlich, Arneborg, Alexandersen, and Hart Hansen, "Greenland Anthropology."

CHAPTER THREE

1. Koht, *Den eldste*, pp. 9–11; "Eiriks saga rauða" in *Íslendinga sögur*, pp. 336–40, and *Islenzk fornrit* 4: 209–14; "Kristni saga," in *Íslendinga sögur*, pp. 267–68.

2. Jones, *Norse Atlantic Saga*, p. 85n.

3. Meldgaard, "Tjodhildes." For a later discussion of the probability that this little church was the one built by Thjodhild, see Krogh, "Om Grønlands," pp. 294–96.

4. "Fóstbræðra saga," in *Íslendinga sögur*, pp. 223–24; Jones, *Norse Atlantic Saga*, p. 86.

5. "Fóstbræðra saga," in *Íslendinga sögur*, p. 229.

6. Clemmensen, "Kirkeruiner," p. 335; Nørlund and Roussell, "Norse Ruins," pp. 26–28; Roussell, "Farms," pp. 46–48. Although incontrovertible archaeological proof is lacking, the site has a number of small, indistinct ruins suggestive of the booths the Icelanders used during their annual stays at the Assembly Plain (*þingvellir*).

7. "Skáld-Helga saga," in *Íslendinga sögur*, pp. 413–39; Jónsson, "Grønlands gamle," p. 327.

8. In Norway and Iceland, the second lawman dated from 1277. See Gjerset, *History of Iceland*, pp. 213–30, for a summary in English of these late-thirteenth-century changes affecting Iceland.

9. Of chief importance here is Nørlund and Stenberger, "Brattahlid." See also Bruun, "Arkæologiske," pp. 283–99; Roussell, "Farms," pp. 42–45, 101, 118, 152–97.

10. "Grænlendinga þáttr" in *Íslendinga sögur*, p. 395; Jones, *Norse Atlantic Saga*, pp. 236–48.

11. Arneborg, "Roman Church," p. 145.

12. For a description in English of the early Icelandic tithing laws, see Byock, *Medieval Iceland*, pp. 91–95. For an excellent overview in Danish, see Skovgaard-Petersen, "Islandsk egenkirkevæsen."

13. *Islandske Annaler*, pp. 16–31, 320–22; *Norges gamle Love* 1: 439–41. The consecration took place at Lund because the Norwegians did not get their own archdiocese until 1154.

14. *GHM* 3: 6–9.

15. Ibid.; *Islandske Annaler*, pp. 16, 320–22; Jones, *Norse Atlantic Saga*, pp. 236–37.

16. Arneborg, "Roman Church," p. 148.

17. *Islandske Annaler*, pp. 61–67, 324.

18. *GHM* 3: 9; Helgason, *Islands Kirke*, pp. 106–12; *Islandske Annaler*, pp. 61, 322–24.

19. Bröste and Fischer-Møller, "Mediaeval Norsemen," pp. 4–9; Nørlund and Roussell, "Norse Ruins," pp. 32–53; Roussell, "Farms," pp. 46, 131–35.

20. Nørlund and Roussell, "Norse Ruins," pp. 26–28, 32–55.

21. *GHM* 3: 9–11; *Islandske Annaler*, pp. 324–25, 361.

22. When discussing Greenland's contact with the rest of the world in later years, it is necessary to keep in mind that nothing prevented the Greenlanders from continuing this shipbuilding practice for another three hundred years.

23. *GHM* 3: 8–9; *Islandske Annaler*, pp. 61, 120; Roussell, "Sandnes," pp. 100–101, 168–70.

24. *GHM* 3: 9–11; Nørlund and Roussell, "Norse Ruins," pp. 16–17.

25. *DN* 6: no. 10.

26. Krogh, "Grønlands middelalderlige"; Vebæk, "Church Topography," pp. 5–20.

27. Jansen, list of churches appended to "Critical Account"; Vebæk, "Church Topography," pp. 5–20; Roussell, "Farms," p. 135.

28. Roussell, "Farms," pp. 48, 107, 135, also figs. 27, 28, 74, 75.

29. Vebæk, "Church Topography," pp. 21–27.

30. Helgason, *Islands Kirke*, pp. 102–5, 115–18.

31. *Regesta Norvegica* 1: nos. 173, 199.

32. Helgason, *Islands Kirke*, pp. 133–39.

33. That shipping connections in the early thirteenth century were no worse is attested by the fact that Víga-Hauk Ormsson and his wife Hallbera, some time between 1203 and 1208, first went from Iceland to Norway and from there to Greenland. They were joined by their kinsman Magnus Markússon, who was equally anxious to turn his back on troubles in Iceland. ("Hrafns saga," text pp. 24–28, notes pp. xliv–xlv.

34. *GHM* 3: 11–13.

35. *DI* 3: nos. 15, 16 (*Biskupatál*); *DN* 17B: p. 282; *GHM* 3: 11–13.

36. The time required for letters to pass between the Norwegian archbishop and Rome was not unreasonable. A letter Jon of Nidaros wrote to the pope at the very end of 1278 brought a reply dated January 31, 1279. *Regesta Norvegica* 2: nos. 206–14.

37. *DN* 1: no. 28.

38. *DN* 6: no. 27.

39. Helgason, *Islands Kirke*, pp. 145–52.

40. *Regesta Norvegica* 1: nos. 468–469.

41. Helgason, *Islands Kirke*, p. 152; *Norges kongesagaer* 1: xiv–xvii.

42. *Norges kongesagaer* 4: 7–14.

43. *GHM* 3: 11–13; Helgason, *Islands Kirke*, pp. 152–54; Jones, *Norse Atlantic Saga*, pp. 68–69; *Norges kongesagaer* 4: 253–54.

44. Byock, *Medieval Iceland*, pp. 75–76. In the summer of 1262, the Icelanders

in the north and south decided at the *Alþing* to subject themselves to the Norwegian king (*DI* 1: no. 152). The Icelanders' covenant with the Norwegian king was drawn up the following year (*DI* 9: no. 2).

45. Gad, "Grønlands tilslutning"; *GHM* 3: 200–204; H. Ingstad, *Land*, pp. 226–27, 241; Jones, *Norse Atlantic Saga*, pp. 86–87.

46. Arneborg, "Grønland, udgangspunktet," pp. 16–17.

47. *DN* 15: no. 29; 17B: p. 283.

48. *DN* 18: no. 33.

49. *DN* 6: no. 9; 19: no. 281.

50. *Islandske Annaler*, pp. 328–30.

51. *Islandske Annaler*, p. 330.

52. *GHM* 3: 238–47. Björn Jónsson of Skardsá told this story, which he says he got from *Hauksbók*.

53. *Norske kongesagaer* 4: 311.

54. Authén Blom, *Kongemakt*, p. 137.

55. *GHM* 3: 13–15, p. 49n.

56. *GHM* 3: 13–15; *Islandske Annaler*, pp. 50, 337.

57. Helgason, *Islands Kirke*, p. 173.

58. *DN* 6: nos. 35–39.

59. *DN* 6: nos. 42–66; *Regesta Norvegica* 2: nos. 206–14.

60. Authén Blom, *Kongemakt*, p. 172.

61. Ibid., pp. 172–76; *Norges gamle Love* 2: 354, 462. Authén-Blom notes that both parties agreed that they *and* their successors would abide by the *Sættargjerð*. She also points out that it was only a matter of months before Magnus gave the archbishop an exempting privilege (*stedjebrev*), dated in Bergen on September 13, 1277 (*Norges gamle Love* 2: 481).

62. *Norsk Kulturleksikon* 5: 319.

63. *Regesta Norvegica* 2: nos. 292–95.

64. Ibid., nos. 295–96.

65. *DN* 17: nos. 871–77; 19: no. 310; *GHM* 3: 90–93; *Regesta Norvegica* 2: nos. 297, 298, 340, 342, 347.

66. *Regesta Norvegica* 2: no. 404.

67. *GHM* 3: 13–15, 90–93; *Islandske Annaler* pp. 50, 70–72, 338.

68. *DN* 17B: p. 205; *GHM* 3: 13–15. King Magnus's sons Eirik and Hákon were still so young that the actual government was in the hands of a Council of Regency. While the nobles of the Council soon forced Archbishop Jon into exile and put Canon Eindridi in his stead, Thord of Gardar was not consecrated until Archbishop Jörund succeeded Eindridi in 1288.

69. *Biskupa sögur* 1: 795. This story is mentioned in Chapter One in another context.

70. *GHM* 3: 13–15; Pálsson, "Landafundurinn."

71. *Norges gamle Love* 2: 170; 3: 134–35. King Magnus Eiriksson *smeyk* renewed Hákon's *Rettarbót* of 1302 in 1348.

72. *DI* 2: nos. 176, 177. See also *Norges gamle Love* 2: 354, concerning the 1277 concordat between King Magnus and Archbishop Jon *rauð*.

73. *DN* 17B: p. 221; 10: no. 9; *GHM* 3: 94. Arni's letter, which was written in

Norse rather than in Latin, survives in draft form. The midsummer date of the letter suggests that the bishop knew a long overdue ship was about to leave Bergen for Greenland.

74. *DN* 2: no. 91.

75. *DN* 10: no. 9; *GHM*, 3: 94.

76. Bishop Arni was not short of money. An affidavit from this period notes that a "foreigner" had received goods worth 100 pounds sterling from the Bergen bishop and promised to pay in full within seven days, after the bishop's representative had "called on him at home" and demanded the money. (*DN* 10: no. 11.)

77. *GHM* 3: 15–19, 94; *Islandske Annaler*, pp. 203, 341–43.

78. *DN* 3: nos. 73, 76–80, 99, 101; 4: nos. 97–103; 6: no. 71; 7: nos. 54, 59–62, 63, 72–73; 8: nos. 26–35; 9: no. 84; 10: no. 10; 17B: p. 289; *Islandske Annaler*, p. 151.

79. *DN* 1: nos. 113, 115, 120.

80. Authén Blom, *Kongemakt*, pp. 189–91, 444–45. She notes that this policy was even more important in the reigns of Magnus Eiriksson *smeyk* and Hákon VI, because they spent most of their time in Sweden and were dependent on having people loyal to them on the Norwegian Council.

81. *Islandske Annaler*, p. 203.

82. Ibid., pp. 151, 343.

83. Ibid., pp. 50–54, 73, 340–42. Henschen attributes the 1306 epidemic to smallpox spread from Denmark, where it had arrived sometime in the thirteenth century (*History*, p. 53).

84. *DN* 7: nos. 103, 104; Gad, "Grønlands tilslutning."

85. H. Ingstad, *Land*, p. 232; Keller, "Vikings," p. 138; Munch, *Pavelige Nuntiers*, pp. 25, 29.

86. *DN* 17 : no. 23.

87. Gad, "Grønlands tilslutning," pp. 259–72; Keller, "Vikings," p. 138. Keller (citing figures from *Regesta Norvegica* 4: nos. 488, 493, 496, 504–6, 518–21, 532–33) also shows the Greenland payment to have been slightly less than one-tenth that of Bergen's.

88. For a useful account of medieval Norwegian coinage, weights, and measures, see *Norsk Kulturhistorie* 5: 316–30.

89. *Kulturhistorisk leksikon* 4: col. 210.

90. *DN* 9: no. 100.

91. *DN* 2: no. 210; *Kulturhistorisk leksikon* 13: cols. 250–55.

92. *DN* 4: no. 182.

93. Authén Blom, *Kongemakt*, pp. 205, 387. The translation is mine.

94. *GHM* 3: 482–84; H. Ingstad, *Vesterveg*, pp. 102–3. See also Chapter One.

95. *DN* 19: no. 459.

96. *Audubon Society Encyclopedia*, pp. 274, 277; Stefansson, *The Three Voyages*, vol. 1, pp. xliii–xliv. Stefansson cites Müller-Röder, *Die Beizjagd und der Falkensport in alter und neuen Zeit* (Leipzig, 1906), p. 15.

97. *DN* 19: nos. 293, 493. King Edward was made well aware of what a choice gift a whale's head was. Back in 1223, Henry III had received a gift of falcons from King Hákon of Norway, with a promise of more when Hákon got them from the

birdcatchers he had sent to Iceland. When they returned with their catch two years later, Hákon sent another thirteen gyrfalcons—three of them white—to the English king, noting that he knew Henry's father and other ancestors prized Icelandic falcons more than gold or silver. (*Regesta Norvegica* 1: nos. 324, 326, 354.) These royal birdcatchers probably either went to Greenland themselves or waited for a transshipment from there. Not only were white falcons very, very rare in Iceland, but the king's men were gone for two years, not just one.

98. *DN* 8: nos. 96, 135.

99. Authén Blom, "Participation," esp. p. 387.

100. For the North Europeans, the charm of walrus ivory was that it was cheaper than elephant ivory. Until about 1500, well after the Portuguese had established coastal footholds in Africa, elephant ivory continued to reach Europe via the old trade routes up the African *east* coast and through the Mediterranean. Since gold, slaves, and spices were the principal concerns of the Portuguese at first, it took rather longer to develop new routes for the ivory trade. On narwhal tusks, see Pedersen, "Narhvalen." At the Museum of London in the summer of 1992, the text to a narwhal horn lent by the Wellcome Institute noted: "Until the late 17th century many English believed in the power of unicorn horn as a medicine and as a test for poisons. The ivory tusks of the narwhal were highly valued."

101. Authén Blom, "Participation," pp. 385–87. For the story of Ohthere, see Orosius, *History*, pp. 19–21 (Anglo-Saxon), 39–50 (English translation and notes). When King Alfred translated Orosius's work into Anglo-Saxon, he added several passages of his own, including the account of Ohthere's voyages to the White Sea and to Hedeby in Schleswig. This report may well have been given without an interpreter, for Anglo-Saxon seafaring expressions in particular were very similar to those used in Old Norse.

102. H. Ingstad, *Land*, p. 241.

103. Jones, *Norse Atlantic Saga*, p. 103.

104. Jónsson, *Det gamle Grønlands*, pp. 17–19.

105. *GHM* 3: 463.

106. *Islandske Annaler*, p. 212.

107. It was reasonable for Greenland's trading connections with Norway to be direct, without stopovers in Iceland, for the Icelanders needed the same commodities as the Greenlanders and could not furnish Greenland with anything useful that people there did not already have. Nørlund also uses this argument ("Buried," p. 246).

108. For example, Magnus V's *Rettarbót* of 1348 reiterated the prohibitions against foreigners sailing north of Bergen or to his tributary countries, and also revealed that a number of licenses had been issued up to that time. A much greater number was granted in the second half of the century, however. (Authén Blom, *Kongemakt*, p. 201; *Norges gamle Love* 2: no. 258.) Hákon Magnusson's 1360 *Rettarbót* (*DI* 9: no. 6) was similarly intended to demonstrate royal muscle.

109. This was especially true after 1343, when the Norwegian nobles tried to protect themselves against the unpopular King Magnus Eiriksson *smeyk* ("the ingratiating"), supposedly king of both Sweden and Norway until he died in 1374, by electing his son Hákon as king of Norway. *DN* 2: no. 258.

110. *DN* 8: nos. 127–28.

111. *Kulturhistorisk leksikon* 4: col. 211.

112. Arneborg, "Roman Church," p. 147; *DN* 8: nos. 128–35; Gad, "Grønlands tilslutning."

113. Arneborg, "Roman Church," p. 147; *DN* 5: no. 152; *GHM* 3: 886–89.

114. *DN* 17B: p. 206; *Kulturhistorisk leksikon* 12: col. 539.

115. *DN* 10: nos. 29, 36, 39.

116. *DN* 5: no. 152. The same summer Bishop Hákon sent Ivar Bárdarson off to Greenland, he allowed three other clergymen from his diocese to go abroad to study—two in Paris and one in England (*DN* 1: no. 273; 5: no. 149; 21: no. 61). Ivar's talents and ambitions seem to have been of a different stripe.

117. *Islandske Annaler*, p. 210. It is worth noting that Jon Eiriksson *skalli* never actually visited his bishopric.

118. *DN* 17B: pp. 282–83; *GHM* 3: 15–19.

119. Helgason, *Islands Kirke*, p. 185; Jones, *Norse Atlantic Saga*, p. 95; Oddsson, "Annalium in Islandia Farrago," pp. i–vii and 2. Since both Gisli and his father were Skálholt bishops, he may well have had access to documents that were lost when Skálholt Cathedral burned in 1630, and his assertions therefore cannot be dismissed out of hand. Nor can they be proved. It is quite possible that those archives once contained notes about the Greenlanders' dereliction of duty in the serious matter of tithes and taxes, of which Jon Sigurdsson of Skálholt would certainly have been told when he was abroad for his own consecration in 1343, the same year Jon *skalli* was made bishop of Gardar.

120. *DN* 4: no. 293; *GHM* 3: 115–16.

121. *DN* 4: no. 293; 17: no. 61.

122. Nørlund, "Buried," esp. pp. 54, 92. The dating of costumes is augmented by the text accompanying garments exhibited at the National Museum in Copenhagen. See also Chapter Two.

123. Arneborg, "Nordboerne"; *GHM* 3: 37; *Islandske Annaler*, p. 212.

124. *GHM* 3: 37; *Islandske Annaler*, pp. 213, 353.

125. *DN* 17B: pp. 282–83.

126. *GHM* 3: 19–21.

127. *GHM* 3: 15–19.

128. *GHM* 3: 15–19; *Islandske Annaler*, pp. 275–76, 353–55, 396, 404.

129. *Islandske Annaler*, p. 369.

130. Amorosi, Buckland, Ólafsson, Sadler, and Skidmore, "Site Status," pp. 172–73; Slack, *Impact*, pp. 7–9.

131. *Islandske Annaler*, p. 275.

132. Gottfried, *Black Death*, pp. 8, 57; Slack, *Impact*, pp. 7–9.

133. See, e.g., Meldgaard, "Inuit-Nordboprojektet," pp. 166–68.

134. Conversation with Jette Arneborg in Copenhagen, May 4, 1991.

135. *GHM* 3: 37–41, 142–59.

CHAPTER FOUR

1. Some historians of Greenland have wondered whether Ivar went back to Norway for a brief visit around 1344, for in a letter written that year (*DN* 17: no. 59), Pope Clement VI requested that the priest Ivar Bárdarson of Bergen diocese be given

the first available ecclesiastical benefice, with or without cure of souls, in that diocese, and he ordered the priests at the Church of the Twelve Apostles in Bergen, etc., to accept Ivar in that office. The letter does not describe a *fait accompli*; it merely suggests that Ivar's friends were looking out for his interests during his absence. It seems doubtful that Ivar would have undertaken the long voyage so soon after setting foot in Greenland, and that he would then go back to spend many more years at Gardar before returning to his sinecure at the Church of the Twelve Apostles.

2. Arneborg, "Nordboerne"; Keller, "Vikings," pp. 135–36.

3. In modern times, Ivar's "Description of Greenland" was published in Jónsson, "Grønlands gamle Topografi," in 1899, and then again in a carefully annotated monograph edition, *Det gamle Grønlands Beskrivelse,* in 1930. Centuries earlier it had been translated into Danish and other languages, including Dutch by none other than the explorer William Barents in 1594. The first English translation was printed in *Purchas his Pilgrimes.* Proof of Ivar's eventual return to Norway is a receipt (*DN* 4: no. 442) for Peter's Pence and other monies, which the papal nuncio gave Bishop Botolv of Stavanger on June 25, 1364. The receipt refers to "Ivarus Berderij . . . canonicus duodecim apostolorum Bergensis."

4. Jónsson, *Det gamle,* pp. 8–9.

5. McGovern, "Economics," pp. 406, 414–16.

6. *GHM* 3: 205–17.

7. Skovgaard-Petersen, "Islandsk egenkirkevæsen."

8. Ibid., pp. 231, 234, 240–56, 264–70, 294–96.

9. *DI* 2: no. 513.

10. Arneborg, "Roman Church," pp. 147–49. See also the discussion in Chapter Three.

11. Jónsson, *Det gamle,* p. 24.

12. Ibid., p. 27.

13. Berglund, "Kirke"; idem, "Decline," pp. 118–121; Krogh, *Viking,* p. 93; idem, "Bygdernes Kirker," p. 274; idem, *Erik,* p. 143; idem, "Gård," p. 242; McGovern, "Economics," pp. 428–29.

14. Arneborg, "Roman Church," pp. 148–49.

15. Nørlund, "Buried," p. 54.

16. Roussell, "Farms," pp. 190–96.

17. McGovern, "Economics," pp. 428–29.

18. The phrase "moribund isolation" is Berglund's; see Berglund, "Decline," p. 120.

19. *DN* 6: no. 527; 17: no. 759.

20. Jónsson, *Det gamle,* p. 43.

21. Vebæk, "Church Topography."

22. Bruun, "Arkæologiske," p. 452; Nørlund and Roussell, "Norse Ruins," pp. 144–45.

23. The Eskimos found these bell-metal pieces useful as hammer stones, among other things. They could also be put to good use by the Norse themselves, who mastered the art of metal-casting and needed appropriate material. Soapstone metal molds, intended for objects ranging from arrowheads to spindle whorls, have been found in various locations at Gardar as well as at Brattahlid (Bruun, "Arkæologiske," p. 448; Nørlund and Roussell, "Norse Ruins," pp. 146–48).

24. Nørlund and Roussell, "Norse Ruins," pp. 144–45, 149–50.

25. Andreasen and Arneborg, "Gården under sandet. Nye nordboundersø-gelser," pp. 39–40.

26. Delaney, *Celts*, p. 95.

27. Thomas, *Religion*, pp. 49–52.

28. *Islandske Annaler*, p. 289.

29. Magnusson and Forman, *Viking*, p. 41.

30. Stoklund, "Nordbokorsene."   31. Nørlund, "Buried," p. 205.

32. Ibid., pp. 60–71, 251.   33. Ibid., pp. 60–67.

34. Ibid. The wood-and-baleen box is also noteworthy for the hint it gives of Norse-Eskimo contact at that early date.

35. Nørlund and Roussell, "Norse Ruins," p. 137.

36. For a discussion of this aspect of peasant-based societies in Northern Europe in the Middle Ages, see Wickham, "Problems." I am grateful to Dr. Bernhard Soffer for calling this article to my attention.

37. Authén Blom, *Kongemakt*, p. 48; *DN* 11: no. 61; *Kulturhistorisk leksikon* 4: cols. 210–11; 17: cols. 651–55; 20: col. 446; *Norges gamle Love* 3: 74.

38. Jónsson, *Det gamle*, pp. 24–27.

39. *Kulturhistorisk leksikon* 17: cols. 651–55. There is no reason to suppose the ombudsmen were slack about collecting fines. In 1320, for example, King Magnus Eiriksson decreed that an ombudsman could keep one-third of what he collected. There are also many examples of ombudsmen's attempts to enhance their revenues in other ways.

40. Vandvik, *Latinske dokument*, pp. 42–51, 84–87, 142–56, 187.

41. Authén Blom, *Kongemakt*, pp. 34–41 (which notes that especially in the second half of the fourteenth century, letters of privilege commonly contained for-mulaic words such as "salvation," "grace," and "mercy"); *DN* 21: no. 83; *GHM* 3: 120–23. The king's letter exists only in a sixteenth-century copy of an odd trans-lation from Swedish into Danish, which phrases the purpose of the expedition thus (*DN* 21: no. 83): "*Att vi giøre dett i Heder till gud Och Vor Siells og forelldre skyld som udi Grønland haffver Christendom och Opphold thill Denne Dag oc vil end ey lade nederfalle om Vore Dage*" ("That We do this in honor of God and for the sake of Our soul and our Ancestors who are Christians and live in Greenland to this day and [whom] We will not abandon in Our own time"). See also H. Ingstad, *Norse Discovery*, pp. 378–79.

42. Arneborg, "Nordboerne"; *GHM* 3: 120–23. See also Chapter One.

43. Jónsson, *Det gamle*, pp. 29–30.

44. Conversation with Jette Arneborg in Copenhagen, May 4, 1991. See also Andreasen and Arneborg, "Gården under sandet—undersøgelserne," p. 11; Arne-borg and Berglund, *Gården*, pp. 1–6.

45. All the finds are discussed in Andreasen, "Nipaitsoq"; idem, "Nordbo-sager."

46. Mathiassen, "Sermermiut Excavations 1955," pp. 45–48.

47. Gulløv, "Eskimoens syn."

48. Arneborg, "Nordboerne," p. 304; idem, "Aqigssiaq," p. 217; idem, "Nord-boarkæologiens," p. 130.

49. Conversation with Jette Arneborg in Copenhagen, May 4, 1991; Arneborg,

"Nordboarkæologiens," p. 131. Arneborg refers to Peter Schledermann's unpublished Field Report to the Canada Council on the Inuit-Norse project.

50. Gulløv, "Eskimoens syn"; idem, "Kangeq"; Grønnow, M. Meldgaard, and Berglund-Nielsen, "Aasivissuit," p. 63. The greatest concentration of bones at Aasivissuit is at the level dated to the end of the fifteenth century.

51. Nansen, *Nord*, p. 370; H. Ingstad, *Land*, pp. 320–24.

52. Jette Arneborg, personal communication, April 1994; Arneborg and Berglund, *Gården*, p. 5; Jones, *Norse Atlantic Saga*, p. 167.

53. Dúason, *Landkönnun*; Oleson, *Early Voyages*. Oddsson, "Annalium," pp. i–vii, 2; see also the translation in Jones, *Norse Atlantic Saga*, p. 95. Jones (*Norse Atlantic Saga*, p. 279) roundly refutes both Gisli's story and the Dúason-Oleson theory of a fourteenth- and fifteenth-century Norse-Eskimo merger.

54. Andreasen, "Langhus-ganghus," pp. 181–82.

55. Andreasen, "Nordbosager," p. 135.

56. Arneborg, "Nordboerne"; idem, "Roman Church," pp. 147–48. The Norwegians were irate that King Magnus sat in Sweden and dictated to the Norwegians. In 1344 he had been forced to make his three-year-old son Hákon king of Norway under a Council of Regents. Hákon came of age in 1355, and soon afterward Magnus lost the Swedish throne also, to the German Albrecht.

57. *DN* 8: no. 157; *Islandske Annaler*, pp. 276–77.

58. Arneborg, "Nordboerne."

59. *Islandske Annaler*, p. 356.

60. *DN* 8: no. 170; 6: no. 248.

61. *DN* 5: no. 193. Magnus's priorities appear as questionable as his grasp on reality was tenuous. In June of 1350, for example, less than a year after the Black Death had begun its grim harvest in Norway, he had a summons (*DI* 2: no. 529) written in hard-hit Bergen, ordering eight prominent North Iceland farmers to take "the first ship leaving Iceland after they have heard or seen the letter," to account for themselves in a complaint against Bishop Orm Aslaksson of Holar.

62. *DN* 17B: pp. 282–83.

63. *DN* 12: no. 103; 17: nos. 208–9; 17B: p. 283; 19: no. 52; *GHM* 3: 27–33, 59; *Islandske Annaler*, pp. 227–28, 282, 364, 414.

64. *DN* 5: no. 268.

CHAPTER FIVE

1. P. Egede, *Efterretninger*, p. 254.

2. Berglund, "Decline," p. 118. The west coast of Norway, which has an environment as harsh as it is beautiful, has produced a large number of Norwegian emigrants to the United States. At the same time, farmers and fishermen with deep roots in the scraggy soil of windblown islands have more than once been known to resist relocation by well-intentioned modern authorities.

3. Matthews, "Archaeological," pp. 257–58.

4. H. Ingstad, *Norse Discovery*, p. 490.

5. Andreasen and Arneborg, "Gården under sandet—undersøgelserne 1991," pp. 12–13.

6. Berglund, "Decline," pp. 116–17; Fredskild, "Agriculture," p. 386.

7. Dansgaard, Johnsen, Clausen, and Gundestrup, "Stable Isotope," pp. 46–47.

8. Frydendahl, "Sommerklimaet." Frydendahl bases his conclusions both on the work of Hubert H. Lamb and on his own calculations.

9. Myhre, "Iron-Age Farm," p. 29; Salvesen, "Hoset," pp. 113–17.

10. Andreasen and Arneborg, "Gården under sandet—undersøgelserne 1991"; idem, "Gården under sandet. Nye nordboundersøgelser," pp. 22–24, 31, 43. This farm site is no. 555 in the new numbering system.

11. Roussell, "Farms," pp. 33, 59–62, 78–79.

12. Holm Jakobsen, "Soil Resources."

13. Hagen, "Man," pp. 15–16.

14. McGhee, "Archaeological Evidence," pp. 173–74.

15. Lamb, *Climate*, pp. 209–10; Rosenørn, Fabricius, Buch, and Horsted, "Isvinter."

16. H. Kapel, "Nyopdaget"; M. C. Parry, "Climatic Change," p. 320; Wrigley, Ingram, and Farmer, eds., *Climate*, pp. 12–13. See also the editors' Introduction to the last-named work.

17. Berglund, "Decline," esp. pp. 115–16; Wrigley, Ingram, and Farmer, eds., *Climate*, pp. 12–13; Danish Polar Center, *Newsletter*, no. 24 (1991), p. 18.

18. Arneborg, "Niaqussat"; McGovern and Bigelow, "Archaeozoology," pp. 92–98.

19. Bruun, "Oversigt," pp. 62–63.

20. Arneborg, letter of Mar. 21, 1993 (referring to recent studies of this bone material by Dr. Niels Lynnerup); J. Meldgaard, "Inuit-Nordboundersøgelsen, 1976"; idem, "Inuit-Nordboprojektet," p. 166.

21. Andreasen, "Nipaitsoq"; idem, "Nordbosager," pp. 135–37.

22. Andreasen, "Nipaitsoq," pp. 186–87; Møhl, "Ressourceudnyttelse."

23. Arneborg, letter of Feb. 2, 1993, in response to queries about the conclusions of Buckland, Sveinbjarnardóttir, Savory, McGovern, Skidmore, and Andreasen in "Norsemen."

24. Andreasen, "Nordbosager," pp. 135–143; conversation with Jette Arneborg in Copenhagen, May 4, 1991.

25. Cowgill, de Neergaard, and Griffiths, *Knives*, pp. 46–49, 139–41. A discussion (p. 47) of heraldic devices notes that unlike the vaguely heraldic "doodles" with which a leatherworker might decorate his wares, "[s]cabbards with arms unique to themselves, especially when only single shields, should be especially instructive, and there may be some significance in the object's provenance." Of the 55 "ordinaries of arms" (p. 48) shown on the various scabbards found in London, only one had the gyronny of eight associated with the Campbell arms.

26. Letter of Dec. 5, 1991, from James D. Galbraith, Deputy Keeper, Scottish Record Office, Edinburgh.

27. Johnston, *Heraldry*.

28. Quinn, *England and the Discovery*, pp. 21–22.

29. All the finds are discussed in Andreasen, "Nipaitsoq"; idem, "Nordbosager."

30. *Audubon Society Encyclopedia*, p. 277; *DN* 8: nos. 96, 135.

31. *DN* 19: nos. 305, 336, 379, 389–90; for details of the turmoil in Scotland at this period, see Mackie, *History*, pp. 35–45, 62–65, 79–80.

32. *DN* 19: no. 52.

33. Thorsteinsson, *Enska öldin*, pp. 24–26, 29–30, 265–67. Thorsteinsson also thinks the Englishman Thomas Gardner may have had access to records no longer extant when he wrote in 1754 that the eastern North Sea port of Dulwich had 36 ships trading as far away as Iceland during the reign of Edward I (1272–1307). See also *Encyclopaedia Britannica*, 15th ed., vol. 2 (under "Dunwich"), which reports the same story, noting that severe coastal erosion caused the eventual decline of Dunwich.

34. Foote and Wilson, *Viking Achievement*, p. 279; Graham-Campbell and Kidd, *Vikings*, p. 115; *Kulturhistorisk leksikon* 14: cols. 507–10.

35. Bruun, "Oversigt," pp. 98, 224; Gulløv, "Eskimoens syn," p. 229; idem, "The Eskimo's View," p. 124; Roussell, "Sandnes," p. 124.

36. Interview with Jørgen Meldgaard in Copenhagen, May 3, 1991.

37. Gulløv, "Eskimoens syn"; Mathiassen, "Inugsuk," Plate 22:5.

38. Roussell, "Sandnes," p. 124.

39. *Kulturhistorisk leksikon* 7: cols. 222–29.

40. Roussell, "Sandnes," pp. 151, 205, 243–44.

41. Ibid., pp. 60–72.

42. Andersen and Malmros, "Ship's Parts," p. 121; Roussell, "Sandnes," pp. 74–101.

43. Roussell, "Sandnes," p. 90.

44. Roussell, "Farms," pp. 13, 64, 171–74, 197, 215, 235, 262, 348.

45. Degerbøl, "Osseous Material"; Roussell, "Farms," pp. 66–69.

46. Roussell, "Farms," pp. 13–17, 29, 66, 179–89, 201, 225, 246–88.

47. Ibid., artifact no. 281.

48. Bruun, "Oversigt," p. 82; Roussell, "Farms," p. 98. This stretch of coast has a number of both Norse and Thule Eskimo house ruins and is dominated by the large mountain called Pisissarfik (The Shooting Place). According to Eskimo legend (Rink, *Eskimoiske Eventyr*, pp. 205–6), it got this name after a shooting contest that took place nearby, between a young Norseman and a young Eskimo who were longtime friends. The contest ended with the death of the Norseman.

49. Roussell, "Farms," pp. 32–33, 104–5, 132–35, 196–98, 221–22, 231, 251–56.

50. Fischer-Møller, "Mediaeval Norse."

51. Roussell, "Farms," pp. 52–53; idem, "Sandnes," pp. 12–14.

52. Moltke, "Greenland Runic"; Roussell, "Sandnes," p. 16. We do not know if this rune stick is a sample of priestly learning at Sandnes, nor for how long Sandnes or the other Western Settlement churches had ordained priests. Norwegian priests would have had to be quite keen on saving souls to end up here, and fresh manpower from Iceland became increasingly unlikely as foreign bishops became the rule there after 1345 and interest waned in educating native priests in the cathedral schools. (Helgason, *Islands Kirke*, p. 208.) If there was a school—either at Gardar or at the small Augustinian monastery at Tasermiutsiaq—for training native Norse Greenlanders to perform church offices, the academic standard may have left something to be desired.

53. Arneborg, "Nordboarkæologiske"; idem, "Vikingerne," p. 191; Roussell, "Sandnes," p. 117.

54. Roussell, "Sandnes," pp. 110–11, 117–120.
55. Ibid., pp. 105, 108.
56. Pedersen, "Ikâmiut"; Rosenørn, Fabricius, Buch, and Horsted, "Isvinter."
57. Garde, "Beskrivelse," pp. 3–4.
58. Taylor, "Letter."
59. Ibid., pp. 56–60.
60. Campbell, *Early Maps*, pp. 22–23; Nebenzahl, *Atlas*, pp. 126–29.
61. Taylor, "Letter," pp. 56–63.
62. Eisner, *Kalendarium*, pp. 2–3; Hakluyt, *Principall Navigations*, pp. 248–49; Taylor, "Letter," pp. 65–67.
63. Quinn, *Explorers*, p. 319; Ruddock, "John Day"; Taylor, "Letter," p. 67.
64. Quinn, *England and the Discovery*, pp. 82–84, 107–9; Skelton, Marston, and Painter, *Vinland Map*, p. 179; Taylor, "Letter," pp. 61–64, incl. note 11.
65. Taylor, "Letter," pp. 56–60.
66. Jónsson, "Grønlands gamle"; idem, *Det gamle*. For a good recent review of this topic, see Vebæk, "Church Topography," pp. 5–20.
67. Jónsson, *Det gamle*, pp. 17–19. Italics mine.
68. Taylor, "Letter," p. 65. Taylor notes that such references are often identified with the Malstroem at the Norwegian Lofoten Islands.
69. Fitzhugh, *Cultures in Contact*, pp. 23–26.

CHAPTER SIX

1. See, for example, *DN* 6: no. 247, dated June 17, 1360.
2. Gjerset, *History of Iceland*, p. 239; Helgason, *Islands Kirke*, p. 221.
3. *GHM* 3: 37–41; *Islandske Annaler*, pp. 285, 367–68.
4. Helgason, *Islands Kirke*, p. 221.
5. Berglund, "Decline," esp. p. 125, has useful comments on the Hanse effect on Bergen's Greenland trade.
6. Jónsson, *Det gamle*. See also the complete list of Greenland bishops by O. Kolsrud in *DN* 17B.
7. *DN* 17B: p. 283; *Islandske Annaler*, p. 229.
8. *GHM* 3: 17–33; *Islandske Annaler*, pp. 282, 354, 414.
9. *DN* 12: no. 103.
10. *GHM* 3: 451; *Islandske Annaler*, pp. 282, 364, 414.
11. Arneborg, "Nordboerne."
12. Conversations with C. L. Vebæk and Jette Arneborg in Copenhagen, May 2, 1991. Arneborg had recently been on reconnaissance in the Middle Settlement and noted that the Norse ruins there are in a uniformly bad state; it is impossible to say whether they are of a greater age and had been abandoned earlier than those in the rest of the Eastern Settlement.
13. McGhee, "Contact," p. 12; Rink, *Tales*, pp. 308–17.
14. Albrethsen and Keller, "Use of the Sæter"; Berglund, *Hvalsø*, pp. 36–37; *GHM* 3: 863; Holm, "Beskrivelser," p. 102, Table XXIc.
15. Mathiassen and Holtved, "Eskimo Archaeology," map, p. 87.
16. Ibid., p. 89.
17. Keller, "Vikings," p. 126. Joel Berglund cautions that since it is very hard to

date the Norse farms in Greenland, we do not know how many were occupied at a given time ("Decline," p. 113).

18. *DN* 6: nos. 282–83, 359; 17B: pp. 207–8.

19. Carus-Wilson, "Iceland Trade," pp. 157–59; Gjerset, *History of the Norwegian People*, p. 257.

20. Pastor, *History* 1: 141–45; 2: 11–19.

21. *DN* 17: nos. 351, 356–57, 361–62, 413, 971; Thorsteinsson, *Enska öldin*, pp. 134–35.

22. *DN* 17: no. 213.

23. *DN* 17B: p. 283; *GHM* 3: 129–30; *Islandske Annaler*, pp. 282, 365–66.

24. *DN* 17: nos. 177, 180, 183; 17B: pp. 209, 283; *Islandske Annaler*, pp. 282, 414.

25. *DN* 17: nos. 208–9, 219, 222; 17B: p. 284.

26. *DN* 17B: p. 284. The information about "Bishop Anders" is said to come from Claus Lyschander's *Den Grønlandske Chronica* (Copenhagen, 1606). Since there was an *officialis* named Eindride Andresson at Gardar in 1409, who will be discussed later in this chapter, Lyschander's information seems of doubtful value, though it is conceivable that "Andresson" could become "Anders."

27. *DN* 17: no. 168; 17B: p. 283.

28. *DN* 17: no. 351.

29. *DN* 17: nos. 356–57, 361–62, 379.

30. *DI* 3: no. 315; *GHM* 3: 123–27. The levy, *sekkjagjöld*, was repealed by Queen Margrethe in 1389.

31. Authén Blom, "Participation."

32. *Islandske Annaler*, pp. 282, 414.

33. *DN* 3: no. 451; 18: no. 33.

34. *DI* 3: no. 367; *DN* 18: no. 33.

35. Espólin, *Árbækur*, 2: 8.

36. *DN* 1: nos. 345, 458; 2: nos. 515–20; 21: no. 133.

37. *DI* 3: no. 367; *DN* 18: no.33.

38. Bjarnason, "Auðbrekku bréf," pp. 370–411; *Islandske Annaler*, pp. 282–83, 364–66, 413–15. Only the two last-mentioned annals specify that Björn "Jerusalem-Farer" Einarsson and Sigurd *hvítakoll* (White-Pate) were of the party; "Lögmanns-annáll" is so uninterested in Björn that it does not even mention his going to Norway in 1379 and again in 1388, the year after his return from Greenland. "Lögmanns-annáll," "Gottskálks annáll," and "Flatey annáll" all note that these four ships, which they called "Iceland-farers" (i.e. bound from Norway *to* Iceland), drifted off to Greenland and returned to Hvalsfjord in Iceland two years later, in 1387.

39. *GHM* 3: 435 (excerpt from Björn Jónsson's "Annals"); Johannesson, "Reisubók"; *Kulturhistorisk leksikon* 14: col. 28.

40. Bjarnason, "Auðbrekku bréf," pp. 304–8; *Islandske Annaler*, p. 288; *Kulturhistorisk leksikon* 14: col. 28.

41. *Islandske Annaler*, p. 287.

42. *DN* 19: nos. 535–55, 657–60, 667–706.

43. *DN* 11: no.110.

44. *Islandske Annaler*, p. 288.

45. *GHM* 3: 37–41; *Islandske Annaler*, pp. 288–89; Thorsteinsson, *Enska öl-din*, pp. 33–34. This story has a curious ending: Gudrun happily resumed living with her old husband, Snorri Torfason, after he had returned to Iceland via Norway in 1314. The *Icelandic Annals* make it clear that she was a woman of wealth and influence, as were both of her husbands. In 1399, Snorri and Gudrun had sold a considerable amount of land to Jon Jonsson, one of the Hvalsey visitors in 1406–10 (*DI* 3: no. 13).

46. *Islandske Annaler*, p. 289.

47. *Annálar 1400–1800*, 1: 13–20; *DI* 3: no. 632; 4: nos. 341, 372, 376, 638; 12: no. 13.

48. For information about Thorstein's literacy, see Karlsson, *Islandske original-diplomer*, p. liv and Document 171. For more information about Steinunn, see Appendix A.

49. *DI* 4: no. 638.

50. *GHM* 3: 37–41; *Islandske Annaler*, p. 288.

51. Berglund, "Decline."

52. Roussell, "Farms," pp. 34–41, 242, 260.

53. Berglund, *Hvalsø*, pp. 12–14.

54. Ibid., pp. 14, 31; Nørlund, "Buried," p. 54; Roussell, "Farms," pp. 124–25, 154, 190–96, 243.

55. *DI* 3: no. 398.

56. *DI* 4: no. 10.

57. *DI* 3: no. 597.

58. *DI* 3: nos. 597, 632; 4: no. 376; *GHM* 3: 145–59. According to Finn Magnusen, Bishop Odd Einarsson of Skálholt made verified transcripts of all three documents.

59. *DN* 13: no. 91.

60. *DN* 13: no. 64; 16: nos. 55, 62; 17: nos. 180, 356–57, 361, 431, 491; 17B: p. 284; *GHM* 3: 142–44, 154.

61. *Annálar 1400–1800* 1: 16; Thorsteinsson, *Enska öldin*, p. 269.

62. *Annálar 1400–1800* 1: 13.

63. *DI* 3: no. 599.

64. *DI* 3: nos. 600–602.

65. Espólin, *Árbækur* 2: 8; *DN* 18: no. 33; *Islandske Annaler*, pp. 289–90.

66. *DI* 16: no. 77; Thorsteinsson, *Enska öldin*, p. 47.

CHAPTER SEVEN

1. Espólin, *Árbækur* 2: Preface. Espólin (1769–1836), lawyer and historian, was a prominent civil servant in the north of Iceland for many years.

2. Quinn, *England and the Discovery*, p. 48; Thorsteinsson, *Enska öldin*, pp. 262–63, 274–76.

3. Carus-Wilson, *Overseas Trade*, pp. 5–9; idem, *Merchant Adventurers*.

4. Berglund, "Decline"; Quinn, *England and the Discovery*, p. 28.

5. Thorsteinsson, *Enska öldin*, p. 41.

6. *GHM* 3: 37–41; *Islandske Annaler*, p. 290.

7. *Annálar 1400–1800* 1: 17–20; Bjarnason, "Auðbrekku bréf," p. 407; *DI* 3:

nos. 626, 629, 633; *DN* 17: no. 368; Espólin, *Árbækur* 2: 8; *Islandske Annaler*, pp. 290–91; Thorsteinsson, *Enska öldin*, pp. 38, 46–49.

8. Bjarnason, "Auðbrekku bréf," pp. 404–7; *Islandske Annaler*, pp. 287, 290–91; Thorsteinsson, *Enska öldin*, p. 195. Examples of property transactions are in *DI* 3: nos. 637–38; 4: nos. 312–13, 322, 333.

9. Bjarnason, "Auðbrekku bréf," p. 407; *Islandske Annaler*, pp. 289–90.

10. *Islandske Annaler*, p. 290.

11. *Islandske Annaler*, p. 369; Thorsteinsson, *Enska öldin*, pp. 25–27; idem, "Íslands- og Grænlandssiglingar," pp. 15–16. Thorsteinsson cautions against assuming that the English brought the Black Death to Iceland in 1402. The contagion could just as easily have come via a foreign vessel in Bergen.

12. Carus-Wilson, "Iceland Trade," p. 159; Williamson, *Cabot Voyages*, p. 4.

13. Carus-Wilson, "Iceland Trade," pp. 159–60; *Kulturhistorisk leksikon* 22 (1976): cols. 151–52 (by B. Thorsteinsson).

14. Bjarnason, "Auðbrekku bréf," p. 407; *Islandske Annaler*, pp. 290–91; *Norske Samlinger*, p. 50; Thorsteinsson, *Enska öldin*, pp. 29–30, 38, 48–49.

15. *Kulturhistorisk leksikon* 9: col. 666 (by Lars Hamre).

16. Bertelsen, "Farm Mounds," p. 49 (citing the results of Gerd Stamsø Munch's research at Senja in western Norway); Holm Olsen, "Helgøy Project," pp. 86–101; Keller, "Vikings," p. 138; *Kulturhistorisk leksikon* 18: cols. 506–10 (by Odd Vollan).

17. Thorsteinsson, "Henry VIII," p. 67 (citing *DI* 16: no. 80; Rolls of Parliament, 4: 79).

18. *Annálar 1400–1800* 1: 19–20; *Islandske Annaler*, p. 291.

19. *Annálar 1400–1800* 1: 18–20; *Islandske Annaler*, p. 291.

20. *Islandske Annaler*, pp. 290–91; Thorsteinsson, "Íslands- og Grænlandssiglingar," pp. 28–30.

21. *DI* 3: nos. 597, 632; Thorsteinsson, *Enska öldin*, pp. 33–34.

22. Karlsson, *Islandske originaldiplomer*, pp. xxxii–iii, xxxviii, li.

23. Thorsteinsson, *Enska öldin*, pp. 76–77.

24. Halldórsson, *Grænland*, p. 297.

25. Thorsteinsson, *Enska öldin*, pp. 94–95, 195. See also Appendixes A and B.

26. Painter, "Matter," p. 192; Skelton, Marston, and Painter, *Vinland Map*, pp. v, 170 to end.

27. Wallis, Maddison, Painter, Quinn, et al., "Strange Case," p. 184. See also Chapter One.

28. I saw the "Vinland Map" firsthand when the Yale Library lent it for the British Museum's exhibit on "Fakes" in the summer of 1990. The legends are in Latin. I have used the translations provided by Helen Wallis in "Strange Case," p. 184.

29. Concerning pertinent saga redactions, see Jones, *Norse Atlantic Saga*, p. 306. Concerning the latest evidence that the "Vinland Map" is a fake, most likely made in Germany during the period 1933–41, see Seaver, "The 'Vinland Map': Who Made It, and Why? New Light on an Old Problem." *The Map Collector* 70 (Spring 1995), pp. 32–40.

30. *Kulturhistorisk leksikon* 12 (1967): col. 392 (by Jakob Benediksson); Thorsteinsson, *Enska öldin*, pp. 46–49.

31. *DI* 16: nos. 77–80; *Islandske Annaler*, pp. 291–93; Thorsteinsson, "Henry VIII," p. 67.

32. A lest is an old measuring unit that originally referred to a wagonload. "Burned silver" is distinguished from coined silver, which could be adulterated. *Annálar 1400–1800*, pp. 20–21; *Islandske Annaler*, pp. 291–92.

33. *DI* 4: nos. 340, 345; Thorsteinsson, *Enska öldin*, pp. 53–55.

34. *Annálar 1400–1800* 1: 22; *DI* 4: nos. 330, 331; Thorsteinsson, *Enska öldin*, pp. 52–53, 56.

35. *DI* 4: nos. 313, 333, 352, 355; Espólin, *Árbækur* 2: 16.

36. *DI* 4: no. 330.

37. *DI* 3: nos. 597 (1409), 630–32 (1414); 4: no. 376 (1424). See also Appendix B.

38. Concerning the price of cod, see Thorsteinsson, "Henry VIII," pp. 68–69.

39. *Islandske Annaler*, p. 291; *Kulturhistorisk leksikon* 20: cols. 151–52 (by Thorsteinsson); Thorsteinsson, "Íslands- og Grænlandssiglingar," pp. 19–20.

40. Thorsteinsson, "Henry VIII," pp. 72–73.

41. Nørlund, "Buried," pp. 179–80.

42. Nørlund, "Buried," pp.122–25, 149–51; Arneborg, Gulløv, and Hart-Hansen, "Menneske," p. 43.

43. Nørlund, "Buried," p. 251.

44. Carus-Wilson notes that at least eighteen of the many complaints made against the English for the period 1420–25 by King Eirik's representative Hannes Pálsson concerned disputes with Danish officials and alleged thefts of fish from them ("Iceland Trade," p. 165).

45. *Kulturhistorisk leksikon* 18: cols. 506–10 (by Odd Vollan).

46. Berglund, "Decline," p. 124; idem, *Hvalsø*, pp. 12–13.

47. Cowgill, de Neergaard, and Griffiths, *Knives*, pp. 88–89 and Fig. 87; Nørlund and Roussell, "Norse Ruins," pp. 92–94, 143–44 and Fig. 80c.

48. *DI* 4: no. 776; *DN* 6: no. 527. More recently, discussions have included the tale of the Angakkoq from Uunartoq, written down by Niels Egede and brought to general attention by Helge Ingstad (*Land*, pp. 329–32). According to this tale, some Eskimos wanted to settle near the Norse, who were unwilling at first, and who possessed many sorts of weapons. Amicable relations were eventually established. Three small ships came from the south and robbed and killed some Norse, who made two ships flee and caught the third. The Eskimos fled far inland. The following year, a whole fleet came to pillage and kill. When the same pirates returned the next year, the Eskimos headed inland again and took some children and women with them. They returned in the fall and found every farm burned and deserted. Nothing was then seen of the pirates for many years, until one of these "English privateers" returned and decided to trade with the Eskimos, the way they had done off and on ever since. Björn Thorsteinsson thinks that regardless of how much Egede or the storyteller may have shaped the tale, we must accept the likelihood of European attacks on the Eastern Settlement in the fifteenth century, when the English were attacking the Icelanders, Faroese, and Norwegians and wasting whole settlements where there were few people to defend themselves (*Enska öldin*, pp. 279–80).

49. The continuing lack of realistic knowledge about conditions in the north is

reflected in a 1464 receipt from the Roman Curia to Bishop Alf of Stavanger deftly placing that Norwegian city in Ireland. *DN* 17: nos. 515–18, 1085.

50. Pastor, *History* 2: pp. 74–75, 86–88.

51. *DI* 4: nos. 744, 748–58, 760–61, among others.

52. I have used the translation in Rey, "Gardar," pp. 331–32.

53. See, e.g., Gad, *Early History*, pp. 158–61.

54. See the information later in this chapter on German enterprise in Iceland; also Barkham, "Basque Exploration." Barkham calls it a "ridiculous legend," made up by historians depending solely on secondary sources, that the Basques chased whales farther and farther into the Atlantic "until they collided with North America." Basque whaling was in the first place "essentially coastal," and in the second place was not forced far from home in search of game in the later Middle Ages. The Biscay whale was nowhere near exterminated even in the sixteenth century.

55. Carus-Wilson, *Merchant Adventurers*, p. 6; Quinn, *England and the Discovery*, p. 48.

56. *DI* 4: no. 331.

57. *Annálar 1400–1800*, pp. 22–23.

58. *DI* 4: no. 333.

59. *DI* 4: nos. 331, 336, and p. 331; *Kulturhistorisk leksikon* 20: cols. 151–52 (by Thorsteinsson); Thorsteinsson, *Enska öldin*, pp. 262–63.

60. *DI* 4: no. 343.

61. *DI* 4: no. 341.

62. Thorsteinsson, *Enska öldin*, pp. 63–64.

63. *Annálar 1400–1800*, p. 23.

64. *Annálar 1400–1800*, p. 23; *DN* 1: nos. 670, 756; *Islandske Annaler*, p. 293.

65. Thorsteinsson, *Enska öldin*, pp. 65–66.

66. *DI* 4: no. 381; Thorsteinsson, "Íslands- og Grænlandssiglingar," pp. 33–34.

67. *Annálar 1400–1800*, pp. 24–25; *DI* 4: no. 381.

68. *DI* 4: no. 381; *GHM* 3: 152–54; Thorsteinsson, *Enska öldin*, p. 268. Brand showed his temper when he mortally wounded a man in a fight at the 1421 *Alþing* (*DI* 4: no. 348; *Islandske Annaler*, p. 293).

69. *DI* 4: no. 376.

70. *DI* 4: no. 380; 16: nos. 81–84; Thorsteinsson, *Enska öldin*, p. 78.

71. Carus-Wilson, "Iceland Trade," pp. 165–66.

72. Thorsteinsson, *Enska öldin*, pp. 65–66.

73. *DI* 4: no. 558.

74. Thorsteinsson, *Enska öldin*, pp. 102–3.

75. *DI* 16: no. 88; Thorsteinsson, *Enska öldin*, pp. 101–3.

76. *DI* 4: no. 328; Thorsteinsson, *Enska öldin*, pp. 101–3.

77. Carus-Wilson, "Iceland Trade," p. 167.

78. Carus-Wilson, "Iceland Trade," pp. 164–65; *DI* 4: nos. 343, 381; *DN* 20: 1: nos. 753, 749.

79. Carus-Wilson, "Iceland Trade," p. 163; idem, *Overseas Trade*, pp. 56–58.

80. Carus-Wilson, *Merchant Adventurers*, p. 6. Assuming a date of ca. 1424 for

the Bristolmen's debut in Iceland, Carus-Wilson extrapolates from the poem "Li-belle of Englyshe Polycye." Thorsteinsson notes ("Íslands- og Grænlandssiglingar," pp. 46–47) that it was not until sixty years later, in 1484, that Bristol ("Byrstofu") is mentioned in Icelandic sources (*DI* 7: no. 12). This lack of agreement shows the need for caution in depending on written sources alone to determine when Bristol joined in regular sailings to Iceland. It seems odd that it should have lagged almost thirty years behind rival cities.

81. Quinn, *England and the Discovery*, pp. 47–48; Thorsteinsson, "Íslands- og Grænlandssiglingar," pp. 46–47.

82. Carus-Wilson, "Iceland Trade," p. 166.

83. *DN* 1: nos. 620, 756; 20: no. 776.

84. Thorsteinsson, *Enska öldin*, pp. 98–99.

85. Carus-Wilson, *Merchant Adventurers*, p. 6.

86. Thorsteinsson, *Enska öldin*, pp. 262–63.

87. Quinn, *England and the Discovery*, p. 48; Thorsteinsson, *Enska öldin*, pp. 262–63, 274–76.

88. Hatcher, *Plague*, pp. 16–17, 27–30, 55–58; McNeill, *Plagues*, p. 169; Slack, *Impact*, pp. 30–32.

89. Veale, *English Fur Trade*, pp. 4–25, 136.

90. Kowaleski, "Town and Country," esp. pp. 63–68.

91. Carus-Wilson, *Medieval Merchant*, pp. 21–24.

92. *DN* 20: nos. 47–48, 771; Thorsteinsson, *Enska öldin*, pp. 90–93, 99; Trondhjems Sjøfartsmuseum (Norway), information pamphlet for visitors.

93. *DI* 16: nos. 86, 87, 90; Thorsteinsson, *Enska öldin*, p. 99.

94. *Islandske Annaler*, p. 294.

95. *DI* 8: no. 18; 9: no. 23.

96. *DI* 4: no. 501; Thorsteinsson, "Íslands- og Grænlandssiglingar," pp. 35–36.

97. *Annálar 1400–1800*, p. 25.

98. *DI* 16: no. 85.

99. *Annálar 1400–1800*, pp. 26–27.

100. *DI* 4: no. 401. See also Appendixes A and B.

101. *DI* 4: nos. 352, 355, 408; *Islandske Annaler*, p. 294.

102. *DI* 4: no. 501; *GHM* 3: 148–59; Quinn, *England and the Discovery*, p. 48; Thorsteinsson, *Enska öldin*, p. 268; idem, "Íslands- og Grænlandssiglingar," pp. 35–36.

103. Thorsteinsson, *Enska öldin*, pp. 83–85.

104. *Annálar 1400–1800*, pp. 26–27.

105. Thorsteinsson, *Enska öldin*, p. 96.

106. Thorsteinsson observes that this period of lawlessness (1430–31) involved rampaging men not only from Bishop Jon Gereksson of Skálholt's retinue, but also from the supporters of other priests and of lay chieftains (*Enska öldin*, p. 138).

107. *DI* 4: no. 506; *DN* 20: no. 789; *Kulturhistorisk leksikon* 20: cols. 151–52 (by Thorsteinsson); Thorsteinsson, *Enska öldin*, pp. 116–18.

108. *DI* 4: no. 506; *DN* 20: no. 789; Thorsteinsson, *Enska öldin*, pp. 111–19.

109. *Islandske Annaler*, p. 370.

110. *DI* 4: no. 501. See also Appendix B.

111. Thorsteinsson, *Enska öldin*, p. 112.

112. *DN* 17B: pp. 284–85.

113. *DI* 4: no. 558; *DN* 5: nos. 646–47; 6: no. 445; 20: nos. 799–800; Thorsteinsson, *Enska öldin*, pp. 106–11.

114. *DI* 4: nos. 602, 613; 8: no. 26; *DN* 17: nos. 514–21, 525, 527–28; 17B: p. 285 (Bartholomew "of Greenland" was serving the pope in Florence when Bishop Jon Vilhjalmsson arrived there); *GHM* 3: 163–65. See also Carus-Wilson, "Iceland Trade," p. 169; Pastor, *History* 2: 3–5; Thorsteinsson, *Enska öldin*, pp. 136–37, 144.

115. *Islandske Annaler*, p. 370.

116. *DI* 16: no. 107; Thorsteinsson, *Enska öldin*, p. 146.

117. *DN* 20: nos. 811–12, 814.

118. *DN* 20: nos. 811–12, 814, 816–19, 825.

119. Carus-Wilson, "Iceland Trade," p. 170; *DI* 16: no. 149; *DN* 17: nos. 556–60, 566; 17: p. 267; Thorsteinsson, *Enska öldin*, pp. 147–53.

120. Carus-Wilson, *Overseas Trade*, pp. 70–92, esp. pp. 71–72.

121. Thorsteinsson, *Enska öldin*, pp. 160–61.

122. *DI* 4: no. 645; *DN* 20: no. 825.   123. *DN* 16: no. 115–20.

124. *DN* 2: no. 741.   125. *DN* 2: no. 746.

126. *DN* 20: no. 829.   127. *DN* 5: no. 720.

128. *DN* 17B: p. 285.   129. *DN* 20: nos. 839, 841.

130. Carus-Wilson, *Overseas Trade*, p. 73 (citing Cal. Patent Rolls, 1441–46, p. 81); *DI* 16: no. 128.

131. Carus-Wilson, *Overseas Trade*, p. 81 (citing PRO Treaty Roll 126, m.13); *DI* 16: no. 133.

132. *DI* 4: nos. 715, 718; 16: no. 137; *DN* 20: no. 842.

133. *DI* 11: no. 11; *DN* 20: nos. 850–61.

134. Carus-Wilson, *Overseas Trade*, p. 87 (citing PRO Exch. K.R. Memoranda Rolls, Hilary, 28 Henry VI, m.8; Cal. Pat. Rolls 1446–52, p. 191); *DI* 16: no. 143.

135. *DI* 16: nos. 147, 151.

136. Thorsteinsson, *Enska öldin*, pp. 162, 164–65.

137. *DN* 17B: pp. 267–68; Thorsteinsson, *Enska öldin*, pp. 174–89.

138. *DN* 2: no. 789; 3: no. 810; 5: nos. 765, 768; 8: nos. 341–43, 345; 17: no. 1032, to list but a few of the many documents scattered in Marcellus's wake.

139. *Islandske Annaler*, p. 370.

140. *DI* 4; no. 778; 5: nos. 46, 54, 56, 93; Thorsteinsson, *Enska öldin*, pp. 183–84.

141. *DI* 5: no. 57.

142. *DI* 5: no. 175.

143. Thorsteinsson, *Enska öldin*, pp. 186–87.

144. In the course of a discussion-by-mail with Jette Arneborg about lumber imports in medieval Greenland, she noted (Mar. 21, 1993) that there is no real proof that the Greenlanders imported wood from Norway, just as there is no incontrovertible evidence of wood that could only have come from North America. There is no lack of interesting specimens to be analyzed, only of the funds and the manpower to have the analyses performed.

CHAPTER EIGHT

1. *DI* 16: no. 231; Thorsteinsson, "Henry VIII," p. 74.
2. Thorsteinsson, "Íslands- og Grænlandssiglingar," p. 47.
3. Quinn, *Explorers*, p. 209.
4. *DI* 5: no. 55.
5. *DI* 3: no. 771; 6: no. 152; 12: no. 19; Thorsteinsson, *Enska öldin*, p. 186.
6. *DI* 5: no. 58; 16: no. 152; *DN* 20: no. 866.
7. Carus-Wilson, *Overseas Trade*, pp. 94–97 (citing PRO Treaty Roll 133, m. 12).
8. Carus-Wilson, "Iceland Trade," pp. 178–79; idem, *Overseas Trade*, p. 9.
9. *DI* 5: no. 115.
10. *Diplomatarium Christierni Primi*, pp. 201–7; *DN* 3: no. 881.
11. Carus-Wilson, *Merchant Adventurers*, pp. 7, 11.
12. Examples are *DI* 16: no. 8 (concerning the cargo of ships going to Iceland from Hull and Scarborough) and cargo lists in Carus-Wilson, *Overseas Trade*, pp. 252–53.
13. *DI* 5: no. 138. See also Appendix B.
14. *DI* 11: nos. 12–15; Thorsteinsson, *Enska öldin*, pp. 186–87.
15. *DI* 5: no. 137.
16. *DI* 5: nos. 133, 136; Thorsteinsson, *Enska öldin*, pp. 190–94.
17. Pastor, *History* 2: 383 (citing *Danske Magazin* 1: 352; Jahn, *Danmarks Historie*, p. 259; L. Daae, *Kong Christian*, p. 112).
18. *DN* 17: no. 1047. In September of 1457, Christian I wrote to Francesco Sforza, duke of Milan, and boasted that he had conquered Sweden all the way to the borders of the Bulgars and the Russians (*DN* 17: no. 1053).
19. Carus-Wilson, *Overseas Trade*, pp. 120–27; *DI* 16: nos. 165, 169, 184, 197–98, 203, 205, 207, 214; Thorsteinsson, *Enska öldin*, pp. 174–75.
20. Carus-Wilson, *Overseas Trade*, p. 125 (citing PRO Treaty Roll 145, m. 27).
21. Carus-Wilson, *Overseas Trade*, pp. 137–38.
22. *DI* 5: no. 400; 16: no. 210; Thorsteinsson, "Henry VIII," p. 71.
23. *DI* 11: no. 19; 16: no. 216; Thorsteinsson, "Henry VIII," p. 71.
24. Thorsteinsson, "Íslands- og Grænlandssiglingar," pp. 49–50.
25. *DI* 5: no. 199; 11: no. 13; *GHM* 3: 184–85.
26. *DI* 5: nos. 175, 201, 225, 227; *DN* 17B: pp. 285–86.
27. *DN* 16: no. 231; 17: nos. 724–26, 1119. Langebæk's collection of seals in the Kongelige Geheime-Archiv (Copenhagen) has a drawing of a seal with this heading in his own hand: "Frater Jacobus Gadensis Episcopus. Dipl. Rost. 1487." The seal has a coat of arms with a large mussel-shell in the middle, surrounded by three arrows with turned-away points in a golden field; above is a bishop's mitre. The surrounding inscription: "Secretum Jacobi, Epi. Gadensis." (*GHM* 3: 187–91).
28. Thorsteinsson, "Íslands- og Grænlandssiglingar," p. 50.
29. *DI* 5: no. 377.
30. *DI* 10: no. 28; 16: no. 219; Thorsteinsson, *Enska öldin*, pp. 204–5.
31. *DI* 10: nos. 22, 23, 28; 16: nos. 215, 217, 219; Carus-Wilson, "Iceland

Trade," pp. 179–80; idem, *Overseas Trade*, pp. 136–37; Espólin, *Árbækur* 2: 66; Thorsteinsson, *Enska öldin*, pp. 207–13.

32. *DI* 5: no. 371.

33. *DI* 5: nos. 443, 446.

34. *DI* 5: p. 1086.

35. Quinn, *England and the Discovery*, pp. 48–49.

36. *DI* 5: nos. 22–25, 27; Carus-Wilson, "Iceland Trade," pp. 179–80.

37. Friedland, "Hanseatic League," p. 541.

38. *DI* 16: no. 220.

39. One account of these misconceptions is found in *GHM* 3: 473–81.

40. The letter can be found in "Diplomatarium Groenlandicum," pp. 5–6. I have translated the passage quoted from the original Dutch. Bobé, in translating the Dutch *velen kleynen schepen szunder bodem* into Danish as *mange smaa aabne Skibe* ("many small open ships"), has downplayed *szunder bodem*. Morison (*European Discovery*, p. 92) uses the common English interpretation, "many small ships without keels," attributing the translation to Nansen, *Northern Mists* 2: 122–33. I discussed the problem with Kari Ellen Gade in the German Department at Indiana University and Orrin W. Robinson III in the German Department at Stanford University and decided to translate these five words literally, as "many small ships without bottom [or floor]," because there is absolutely nothing in Grypp's letter to suggest that he had realistic perceptions about either Greenland or the Eskimos. "*Szunder bodem*" may have been intended to convey "without keel," but I doubt it. The word for "keel" is old and unambiguous in all the seafaring northern nations. It is certainly harder to imagine a ship without a bottom than one without a floor (floor boards) or a keel, but the real issue is that we cannot know what Grypp thought he was describing in a flight of fancy based on second-hand information.

41. Larsen, *Discovery*, pp. 29–33, 69–72, 88–91.

42. Morison, *European Discovery*, pp. 89–94, 108–9. Morison demonstrates (p. 89) that the map described by Grypp must have been Hieronymous Gourmont's map of Iceland, published in Paris in 1548. This map is also the obvious source of inspiration for Olaus Magnus's 1555 claim (see facsimile page on p. 91 of Morison) that Pining and Pothorst were notorious pirates, said to have been outlawed from all the northern kingdoms and to have made a pirates' nest on "Hvitserk," from which they made naval sorties in 1494, and where they had made a seamark and a compass. The information provided on the subject in *Purchas his Pilgrimes* is clearly even farther removed from reality.

43. Quinn, *England and the Discovery*, pp. 43–44. Williamson gave somewhat more credence to the idea of a joint Dano-Portuguese voyage circa 1472 (*Cabot Voyages*, p. 12).

44. Thorsteinsson, *Enska öldin*, p. 215.

45. Danstrup and Koch, *Danmarks Historie*, 5: 59–63, 65–72.

46. *DI* 6: no. 66; 11: no. 22.

47. *DI* 6: nos. 66–67; 10: nos. 23, 27; Thorsteinsson, "Íslands- og Grænlandssiglingar," pp. 65–66; idem, *Enska öldin*, pp. 222–28.

48. *DI* 16: no. 230.

49. Thorsteinsson, *Enska öldin*, 242–43.

50. *DI* 6: nos. 262–63; 11: nos. 27, 32–33, 36–38, 40–41; Thorsteinsson, "Henry VIII," p. 72.

51. Danstrup and Koch, *Danmarks Historie,* 5: 81–86.

52. *DI* 5: nos. 562, 652, and p. 1086; 6: nos. 101, 147, 159, 164, 208, 273, 467.

53. *DI* 7: no. 12; 11: nos. 34–35; 16: no. 235; Thorsteinsson, *Enska öldin,* pp. 232–34, 242–43.

54. *DI* 11: nos. 36, 37, 41, 42.

55. Thorsteinsson, *Enska öldin,* pp. 148–49, 244–48.

56. See, e.g., *DI* 6: nos. 559, 630.

57. *DI* 6: no. 617; 8: nos. 72, 73.

58. *DI* 7: nos. 499, 550; 16: no. 230 and pp. 445–46; Thorsteinsson, "Henry VIII," pp. 71–72; idem, *Enska öldin,* pp. 256–57.

59. *DI* 6: no. 633.

60. *DI* 5: no. 446; 6: no. 659; 7: no. 285.

61. Thorsteinsson, *Enska öldin,* pp. 251–52 (citing *DI* 16: nos. 444–45; Rymer's *Foedera* 12: 374).

62. *DI* 11: no. 35.

63. Quinn, *England and the Discovery,* pp. 48–49.

64. Thorsteinsson, *Enska öldin,* p. 292.

65. This segment of de la Peyrère's account is printed in Gad, *Grønlands historie,* p. 223. See also Kisbye Møller, "Isaac de la Peyrère." For background in English on de la Peyrère, see Lintot and Osborn, eds., *Collection,* pp. 363–406. Christian I died in 1481; Hans was crowned in 1483. It is worth noting that Ole Worm was a friend of the same Gísli Oddsson (1593–1632) who believed that the Greenlanders had turned heathen and gone to America in 1348. Gísli attended the University of Copenhagen for a couple of years. (Oddsson, "Annalium," pp. 1–2.)

66. *DI* 6: nos. 66, 67. My attention was called to these documents by Thorsteinsson, "Íslands- og Grænlandssiglingar," p. 48.

67. Quinn, *England and the Discovery,* pp. 49–50. In addition to giving credit to M. E. Williams, Quinn cites PRO, E., 179, 270, 54. He also notes that Martin Behaim's 1492 globe says the Icelanders sold their children to the English as slaves.

68. Quinn, *England and the Discovery,* p. 51.

69. Ibid., pp. 20–21.

70. Quinn, "Columbus," p. 281.

71. According to Thorsteinsson, customs records show that Iceland-farers returning to Bristol would stop in Ireland on the way home and top up their cargo if necessary ("Íslands- og Grænlandssiglingar," p. 68).

72. Quinn, *Ireland,* pp. 6–7.

73. Ibid., pp. 3–5; Sacks, *Widening Gate,* pp. 39–40; Morison, *Christopher Columbus,* p. 41; Carus-Wilson, *Medieval Merchant,* pp. 16–17.

74. Quinn, "Columbus," pp. 278–83.

75. Thorsteinsson, *Enska öldin,* p. 263; idem, "Íslands- og Grænlandssiglingar," p. 54. Thorsteinsson stresses that the peak Icelandic fishing season is in the spring, while the summer months, going into the autumn, constitute the main fishing season off southwestern Greenland. He warns against setting too much store by what Englishmen sending their ships abroad said about where their ships went

in the fifteenth century. Carus-Wilson also says that ships usually left England for Iceland between February and April ("Iceland Trade," p. 176).

76. Morison, *Christopher Columbus*, p. 41; Quinn, *Ireland*, p. 3. There are known instances of an Eskimo in his kayak having drifted off and been spotted in the British Isles, e.g., several times in the Orkneys in the period 1690–1728 during the so-called Little Ice Age, and once on the river Don near Aberdeen (Lamb, *Climate*, p. 210).

77. De la Roncière, *Carte*, pp. 7–8, 17–22.

78. Nebenzahl, *Atlas*, pp. 22–25; Pelletier, "Peut-on encore."

79. Quinn, *England and the Discovery*, pp. 60–62, 75–77; idem, "Columbus," pp. 278–97; idem, *Explorers*, pp. 302–4; Quinn, Quinn, and Hillier, eds., *New American* 1: 145; Wallis, "Is the Paris Map."

80. Skelton in Williamson, *Cabot Voyages*, p. 297.

81. De la Roncière, *Carte*, pp. 7–9.

82. Wallis, "Is the Paris Map."

83. I have borrowed my quotation from Quinn, "Columbus," p. 282 (attribution: Benjamin Keen, ed. and trans., *The Life of the Admiral Christopher Columbus by His Son Ferdinand*, 1959, p. 11). See also De la Roncière, *Carte*, p. 7, citing Fernando Columbus, fol. 9.

84. Both "latitudes" and "tides" are very satisfactorily tackled by Quinn in his closely argued article, "Columbus," pp. 282–83.

85. Morison, *Christopher Columbus*, p. 41.

86. Thorsteinsson, *Enska öldin*, p. 263.

87. Morison, *Christopher Columbus*, p. 45; idem, *European Discovery*, p. 288, note.

88. De la Roncière, *Carte*, p. 38.

89. Quinn, *England and the Discovery*, p. 59; Skelton, Marston, and Painter, *Vinland Map*, pp. 139, 166–67; Williamson, *Cabot Voyages*, pp. 29–30, 55–56.

90. Carus-Wilson, *Overseas Trade*, p. 148.

91. *DI* 5: no. 155; Thorsteinsson, *Enska öldin*, pp. 265–67.

92. De la Roncière, *Carte*, pp. 27–29; Quinn, *England and the Discovery*, pp. 60–62.

93. De la Roncière, *Carte*, p. 24; Quinn, Quinn, and Hillier, eds., *New American* 1: 85–88.

94. J. H. Parry, *Discovery*, pp. 52–53.

95. Grafton, *New Worlds*, is good background reading.

96. Williamson, *Cabot Voyages*, pp. 74–75; Wallis, "Is the Paris Map."

97. For a thorough mapping of the North Atlantic currents and prevailing wind patterns, see the *Oxford World Atlas*, p. 93.

98. McGuirk, "Ruysch World Map"; Nordenskiöld, *Facsimile Atlas*, Pl. 32 and text.

99. Quinn, *England and the Discovery*; Quinn, Quinn, and Hillier, eds., *New American* 1: p. 91; Ruddock, "Reputation," p. 98.

100. One such text was reconstructed by McGuirk ("Ruysch World Map," pp. 137–39). Located in the sea northwest of an erased depiction of Cuba, the text referred to the "Hyperboreans of Europe and Arompheia in Asia" who live "right up

to the place where the furthest latitudes of the world are. Where the days are six months in duration."

101. Bjørnbo, "Cartographia," p. 188. Recent archaeological research on volcanic activity in Iceland is well covered in *Norwegian Archaeological Review* 24 (1991): no. 1.

102. Bjørnbo, "Cartographia," p. 188; *Kulturhistorisk leksikon* 4: cols. 281–87 (by Authén Blom); 18: cols. 506–10 (by Odd Vollan).

103. Ptolemy, *Geographia*. Originals used: British Map Library copies 1 and 2, cataloged as C.1.d.5 and .6. The English translation of the quoted passage comes from Harrisse, *Discovery*, p. 304. Harrisse says that Ruysch claimed to have sailed along the 50th parallel, but this is a mistake. The Latin original says 53°N.

104. Harrisse, *Discovery*, pp. 178–79, 270.

105. Quinn, *Explorers*, p. 119.

106. *Calendar of State Papers: Letters etc. Between England and Spain*, 1: 202. No. 233 is a letter of March 5, 1499, from De Puebla to Queen Isabella, recommending forgiveness of Buxer's fine, since he wants to enter Isabella's service. Buxer had formerly been a servant to the Governor of the Prince of Wales and was now taking a parcel of letters from De Puebla to the Queen. Some of these letters appear to have been purloined.

107. H. Ingstad, *Vesterveg*, pp. 72, 148, 181.

108. J. H. Parry, *Discovery*, pp. 39–41, 174–82. See also Wallis and Robinson, eds., *Cartographical Innovations*, pp. 178–79.

109. Quinn, *North America*, pp. 88–90.

110. Carus-Wilson, *Merchant Adventurers*, pp. 15–16.

111. Quinn, "Columbus," p. 286; idem, *England and the Discovery*, pp. 7–9, 72–73; idem, *Explorers and Colonies*, pp. 119–21, 302–3; idem, *Ireland*, pp. 3–4; idem, *North America*, pp. 60–64; Quinn, Quinn, and Hillier, eds., *New American* 1: 91.

112. Quinn, "Columbus," p. 286.

113. Thorsteinsson, "Íslands- og Grænlandssiglingar," pp. 52–56.

114. Useful descriptions of local topography, ice conditions, and fishing may be found in H. Ingstad, *Land*, pp. 107, 116, 119, 132, 145, 155, 173, 183, 221. Ingstad describes (p. 183) his own experience of hauling up huge cod from the coast outside Sandwich Bay.

115. Carus-Wilson, *Overseas Trade*, pp. 216–17.

116. Quinn, *North America*, pp. 88–90.

117. Quinn, "Columbus," pp. 286–87; Quinn, Quinn, and Hillier, eds., *New American* 1: 91–92.

118. Carus-Wilson, *Overseas Trade*, pp. 218–89, 151–58, 161–65; Quinn, "Columbus," p. 287; idem, *England and the Discovery*, pp. 47, 56–57, 74; idem, *North America*, pp. 60–62; Quinn, Quinn, and Hillier, eds., *New American* 1: 91–92. For the Exchequer inquiry, Quinn cites PRO, E., 122/19, 16.

119. McGrath, "Bristol," p. 81; Quinn, *England and the Discovery*, pp. 72–73; idem, *North America*, pp. 62–64.

120. Thorsteinsson, *Enska öldin*, p. 291.

121. Letter of December 18, 1497, from Raimundo de Soncino to the Duke of

Milan. Printed in translation in Biggar, *Precursors*, pp. 19–20; Quinn, Quinn, and Hillier, eds., *New American* 1: 97; Williamson, *Maritime Enterprise*, pp. 56–58, idem, *Cabot Voyages*, pp. 209–11.

122. The John Day letter, found by L.-A. Vigneras, was first publicized in "New Light" and "Cape Breton Landfall." The translated passage is from Quinn, "Columbus," pp. 296–97. See also Morison, *European Discovery*, pp. 206–9; Quinn, Quinn, and Hillier, eds., *New American* 1: 99.

123. Biggar, *Precursors*, pp. 28–29; Mackie, *History*, p. 123; Quinn, Quinn, and Hillier, eds., *New American* 1: 101; Williamson, *Cabot Voyages*, p. 208.

124. *Calendar of State Papers: Spanish*, pp. 134, 141; *Calendar of State Papers: Venetian*, 1: 169, 269–70; Sneyd, *Relation*, pp. 13–16, 18, 64.

CHAPTER NINE

1. Gulløv, "Eskimoens syn," pp. 226–34; idem, "Eskimo's View," pp. 121–29.

2. Mathiassen, "Inugsuk," pp. 276, 289; Mathiassen and Holtved, "Contributions," pp. 110–18, Pl. 7:21.

3. Jette Arneborg, *Kulturmødet*, pp. 126–27.

4. Carus-Wilson, *Overseas Trade*, cargo list, p. 253; Tylecote, *History*, pp. 87–88.

5. Exhibition at the National Maritime Museum in Greenwich; Mathiassen and Holtved, "Contributions," p. 116, Pl. 6:11, and Pl. 7:22.

6. Nørlund, "Buried," pp. 165–66, 171–74, 179–83, Figs. 120–21, 123, and Pl. 30.

7. Carus-Wilson, *Merchant Adventurers*, pp. 15–16.

8. Nørlund, "Buried," pp. 240–41.

9. Ibid., pp. 128–31, no. 63; Peacock, *Costumes*, p. 26.

10. Vebæk, "Vatnahverfi" (1992), pp. 16, 45–70, 85–86, 90 (incl. Fig. 128), 108, and esp. the Register of Objects on 123.

11. Ibid., p. 108.

12. Ibid., pp. 19, 24–25, 82–86.

13. Ibid., pp. 82–86, 119–20.

14. Berglund, "Displacements," p. 151.

15. Blindheim, *Vikingtid*, pp. 15–21 and Fig. 1; display of old Norwegian iron-production methods at the Museum of Antiquities, Oslo University; *Kulturhistorisk Leksikon* 8: cols. 57–58 (by T. Dannevig-Hauge); letter of March 24, 1993, from Irmelin Martens, Institutt for Arkeologi, Kunsthistorie og Numismatikk, Oslo Universitet. Martens also consulted with Gerd Færden, an expert on iron from medieval Norwegian cities.

16. I am grateful to my son, David O. Seaver, for explaining many of the processes used by early smiths and foundries.

17. Tylecote, *History*, pp. 75–76, 103–4.

18. Schubert, *History*, pp. 102–10, 121–22, 145. He cites Carus-Wilson, *Overseas Trade*, pp. 171, 180, et seq.; also "The Libelle of Englyshe Polycye" (c. 1436) concerning the importance of metal and sea trade. Useful information on iron imports from Spain to England is also found in Childs, *Anglo-Castilian Trade*, pp. 62,

112–13, 118. Childs notes that especially the iron from the Basque provinces was of a very high quality, easily extracted, and so low in phosphorus that it lent itself to a profitable production of very malleable iron.

19. Nørlund and Roussell, "Norse Ruins," pp. 55–58, 78–83, 94, 109–12, 115–17, 144; McGovern, "Bones," esp. pp. 210–15.

20. Nørlund and Stenberger, "Brattahlid," esp. p. 55; Roussell, "Farms," pp. 42, 101, 118, 138, 197.

21. Holm, "Beskrivelser," p. 143. In a letter of June 4, 1993, Arneborg noted that Eskimos occupied the Herjolfsnes site after the Norse had left, and that later European artifacts have been associated with contact between Eskimos and Europeans in that settlement.

22. Stoklund, "Nordbokorsene," p. 106; *Collier's Encyclopedia* 13: 559 (C. W. Davis's article on "Jet"); *Encyclopaedia Britannica*, 11th ed., 15–16: 358–59. Yorkshire is also the modern world's chief commercial supplier of jet (*Columbia Encyclopedia,* p. 1082).

23. Nørlund, "Buried," pp. 54, 221, 236, 254, 255, 267; Roussell, "Farms," pp. 190–95.

24. For a succinct description in English of these ice conditions, see Garde, "Navigation," pp. 215–41.

25. Nørlund, "Buried," pp. 234–37.

26. A number of Latin transcripts and various translations are available. I have used the recent translation in Rey, "Gardar," pp. 332–33, and the Latin transcript in "Diplomatarium Groenlandicum" (ed. Bobé), pp. 3–4. The original citation is A. S. V. Fonds Alexander VI, Div., Arm. 29, vol. 50, fol. 23 and 24.

27. *DN* 17: nos. 754, 758, 759, 761, 762, 1147; 17B: p. 286. Bishop Mathias of Gardar is said to have been a *vicarius* for the bishop of Halberstadt in 1500 and 1506.

28. Bittles and Neel, "Costs." The quote is from p. 120. In a brief telephone consultation on Dec. 1, 1994, Dr. Neel said that in his view, the cause of the Greenlanders' eventual disappearance could not have been genetic deterioration.

29. McGovern, "Economics," pp. 404–29.

30. Hastrup, "Sæters."

31. Berglund, "Decline," esp. pp. 111, 122.

32. Keller, "Vikings," esp. pp. 138–40.

33. Berglund, "Decline."

34. McGovern and Bigelow, "Archaezoology," pp. 87–88.

35. Ibid., pp. 85–101.

36. McGovern, "Zooarchaeology," pp. 93–107, esp. pp. 97–98.

37. Fredskild, "Agriculture," pp. 387–89.

38. Fredskild, "Palaeobotanical Investigations."

39. Ibid.

40. Ibid., pp. 30–37. I am also indebted to Dr. Fredskild for his personal comments and suggestions on this topic.

41. Ibid., pp. 39–41.

42. Pang, "Climatic Impact." Dr. Pang also provided supplementary information about his research and conclusions on this topic, for which I am most grateful.

43. Dansgaard, "Bringer luftforureningen," p. 25; Dansgaard, Johnsen, Clausen, and Gundestrup, "Stable Isotope"; Dansgaard, Johnsen, Reeh, Gundestrup, et al., "Climatic Changes," pp. 24–27; Hammer, Clausen, and Dansgaard, "Greenland Ice Sheet."

44. Dansgaard, Johnsen, Reeh, Gundestrup, et al., "Climatic Changes," p. 26.

45. Salvesen, "Hoset Project," pp. 109–18, 146–49.

46. Ogilvie, "Climatic Changes," pp. 248–49.

47. Wrigley, Ingram, and Farmer, eds., *Climate*, pp. 12–13.

48. Nørlund, "Buried," pp. 237–45.

49. McGovern, "Economics," pp. 418–19.

50. Salomonsen, "Ornithological," p. 15.

51. Albrethsen and Keller, "Use of the Sæter," p. 95.

52. Mattox, "Fishing," pp. 2–3.

53. Ibid., pp. 28–29, 34, 69.

54. McGovern, "Economics," pp. 410–11; McGovern and Bigelow, "Archaezoology," pp. 96–97.

55. Quinn, *Explorers and Colonies*, pp. 316–17.

56. Van der Wee, *Growth* 2: 72.

57. Phillips, "Growth," p. 50.

58. According to the Norwegian scholar Reidar Bertelsen, "This shift is well documented in the historical literature." See Bertelsen, "Farm Mounds." The quote is from p. 49.

CHAPTER TEN

1. Francisco López de Gómara, *Historia de las Indias* (first published in Seville, 1553), as cited in Harrisse, *Discovery* 1: 131.

2. Harrisse, *Discovery* 1: 127–31.

3. Quinn, *North America*, p. 136.

4. Harrisse, *Discovery* 1: 60.

5. For the notions of clannish business interests and Italian merchants in Seville I am indebted to George Holmes, who read a paper entitled "Europe in 1492" at the Anglo-American Conference of Historians in London, on July 9, 1992. The theme of the conference, organized by the Institute for Historical Research, was "Europe and the Americas."

6. Larsen, *Discovery*, pp. 7–15. He cites Gómez Eannes de Azurara, *Chronica do descobrimento e conquista de Guiné*, Ch. 87; the interested reader should also see the full translation published by the Hakluyt Society as *The Chronicles of the Discovery and Conquest of Guinea* (2 vols.; London, 1876–99).

7. Larsen, *Discovery*, pp. 20–22. He cites *Diplomatarium Christierni I*, pp. 134–35, and notes that Henry died on November 13, 1460.

8. Fernández-Armesto, *Before Columbus*, pp. 187–88.

9. Phillips, "Growth," p. 50; Morison, *European Discovery* 1: 94–97; J. H. Parry, *Discovery*, pp. 52–53.

10. Phillips, "Growth," p. 38.

11. Fernández-Armesto, *Before Columbus*, pp. 11–42, 169–70, 199–201.

12. Ibid., pp. 198–200.

13. Ibid., pp. 207, 251; Quinn, *North America*, pp. 88–90; Quinn, Quinn, and Hillier, eds., *New American* 1: 85–86. Fernández-Armesto assumes that the voyage of discovery for which Fernão Dulmo of Terceira and his partner got a license in 1486 (Chapter Eight) was unsuccessful because the westerlies forced them to return to their starting point in the Azores.

14. Fernández-Armesto, *Before Columbus*, pp. 250–52; Nebenzahl, *Atlas*, pp. 2–5, 15 (Toscanelli's map is no longer extant; Germanus, as it happened, was also working in Florence); Williamson, *Cabot Voyages*, pp. 7–8, 10, 296.

15. Morison, *European Discovery* 1: 96–101; Quinn, *England and the Discovery*, p. 43; Quinn, Quinn, and Hillier, eds., *New American* 1: 81, 84; Williamson, *Cabot Voyages*, pp. 184–86.

16. Morison, *European Discovery* 1: 93; Quinn, *North America*, pp. 58–59, 65–66; Quinn, Quinn, and Hillier, eds., *New American* 1: 85–88; Vigneras's article on Gaspar Corte-Real in *Canadian Biographical Dictionary* 1: 234–36. Quinn and Morison refer to the writings of Gaspar Frutuoso, 1522–91, whom Morison calls "a notoriously unreliable collector of gossip." It was in 1486 that the Flemish settler Fernão Dulmo of Terceira and his partner Joham Affonso do Estreito of Madeira received their license for a voyage of discovery to "Island(s) or terra firma presumed to be the Island of Seven Cities" (see Chapter Eight).

17. Quinn, *England and the Discovery*, pp. 41–43.

18. Morison, *European Discovery* 1: 96–97.

19. Ibid., pp. 98–99.

20. Harrisse, *Discovery* 1: 60; Morison, *Christopher Columbus*, pp. 51–53; Nebenzahl, *Atlas*, pp. 18–19; Prestage, "Portuguese Expansion," pp. 231–32; Williamson, *Cabot Voyages*, pp. 8–9.

21. Morison, *European Discovery* 1: 213.

22. Cummings, Skelton, and Quinn, *Discovery*, p. 215.

23. Bjørnbo, "Cartographia," pp. 152–57.

24. Morison, *Christopher Columbus*, pp. 41–93; Quinn, *England and the Discovery*, pp. 45, 75–79.

25. Prestage, "Portuguese Expansion," pp. 171–98. When Vasco da Gama reached Calicut in 1499, and Cabral officially discovered Brazil on his outward voyage to India in 1500, Portuguese maritime triumph seemed complete. The very next year King Manoel began sending out an annual fleet to service the Portuguese East India trade (Skelton, *Prince Henry*, p. 57).

26. Nebenzahl, *Atlas*, pp. 34–35, 77; *Times Atlas of World Exploration*, pp. 49, 149.

27. Quinn, *North America*, p. 110; Williamson, *Cabot Voyages*, pp. 49, 120, 163–64.

28. Cortesão, "Pre-Columbian Discovery," pp. 29–30 (citing *Algunos documentos do Archivo Nacional da Torre do Tombo* [Lisbon, 1892], pp. 9, 14, 45); Crone, "Alleged Pre-Columbian."

29. Nebenzahl, *Atlas*, p. 15.

30. Quinn, *England and the Discovery*, pp. 51–52.

31. Quinn, *England and the Discovery*, p. 49; Williamson, *Cabot Voyages*, p. 14.

32. Quinn, *England and the Discovery*, p. 5 (citing PRO, Customs Account, Bristol, Sept. 29, 1492–Mar. 25, 1494, E. 122/20/9); Williamson, *Cabot Voyages*, pp. 14–15.

33. Morison, *European Discovery* 1: 158–59; Williamson, *Cabot Voyages*, pp. v–vi, 33, 37–41.

34. Quinn, Quinn, and Hillier, eds., *New American* 1: 93–94; Williamson, *Cabot Voyages*, pp. 48, 202–3.

35. Quinn, *North America*, p. 114.

36. For John Day's letter to Columbus, see Vigneras, "New Light" and "Cape Breton"; Quinn, "Columbus," pp. 296–97. See also Biggar, *Precursors*, pp. 28–29; Morison, *European Discovery* 1: 206–9; Quinn, Quinn, and Hillier, eds., *New American* 1: 99–101; Williamson, *Cabot Voyages*, pp. 23–24, 30, 38–39, 86, 89, 228–29 (including text of De Ayala's letter).

37. J. H. Parry, *Discovery*, pp. 181–88.

38. Quinn, *North America*, pp. 79–81; Parry, *Discovery*, p. 180. Parry notes that some fifteenth-century navigators knew there was such a thing as variation, i.e. the difference between the magnetic and geographical poles, but they usually regarded it as a constant. Our earliest surviving reference to *changes* in variations are in Columbus's journal of his 1492 voyage.

39. Carus-Wilson, *Overseas Trade*, pp. 218–89, 151–58, 161–65; Quinn, "Columbus," p. 287; idem, *England and the Discovery*, p. 47, pp. 56–57, 74; idem, *North America*, pp. 60–62; Quinn, Quinn, and Hillier eds., *New American* 1: 91–92 (for the Exchequer inquiry, Quinn cites PRO, E, 122/19, 16); Williamson, *Cabot Voyages*, p. 19.

40. Williamson, *Cabot Voyages*, pp. 47, 219.

41. Carus-Wilson, *Overseas Trade*, pp. 218–89, 151–58, 161–65; *Dictionary of Canadian Biography* 1: 386 (entry for John Jay, by Quinn); Quinn, "Columbus," p. 287; idem, *England and the Discovery*, pp. 47, 56–57, 74, 128; idem, *North America*, pp. 60–62, 294; Quinn, Quinn, and Hillier, eds., *New American* 1: 91–92; Ruddock, "Columbus," pp. 185–88; idem, "Reputation," pp. 97–98.

42. Williamson, *Cabot Voyages*, p. 48.

43. Quinn, *North America*, p. 115.

44. Morison, *European Discovery* 1: 159–60; Quinn, Quinn, and Hillier, eds., *New American* 1: 93; Williamson, *Cabot Voyages*, pp. 49–50, 204–5.

45. Williamson, *Cabot Voyages*, pp. 41, 46.

46. Vigneras, "New Light," p. 508; idem, "Cape Breton," pp. 222, 228.

47. *Dictionary of Canadian Biography* 1, entries on Hugh Elyot and Robert Thorne by Quinn (Elyot and Thorne Sr. were especially active from about 1480 to at least 1510); Hakluyt, *Principall Navigations* 1: 257; Quinn, *England and the Discovery*, p. 11, 122; idem, *Explorers*, pp. 121–22; Ruddock, "Reputation," p. 98 (citing PRO, E. 368/276, m. 11d); Williamson, *Cabot Voyages*, pp. 26–29, 247–48.

48. Quinn, *England and the Discovery*, p. 86.

49. Morison, *European Discovery* 1: 193–95, gives a useful account of the various elements in these controversies.

50. Morison, *European Discovery* 1: 169.

51. Vigneras, "New Light" and "Cape Breton."

52. Quinn, Quinn, and Hillier, eds., *New American* 1: 95; Williamson, *Cabot Voyages*, pp. 61–63, 76. Twentieth-century experience shows that until September, gales along the Labrador coast rarely last for more than about twelve hours. John Cabot must have had good information, but also a measure of good luck, for in those waters easterly winds, especially after July, often bring impenetrable fog accompanied by heavy Atlantic swells (Brøgger, *Vinlandsferdene*, p. 73).

53. Harrisse, *Discovery* 1: 17–23, 36; Morison, *European Discovery* 1: 174–80, 193; Williamson, *Cabot Voyages*, pp. 66 to end.

54. Williamson, *Cabot Voyages*, pp. 64–65, 68–82, 84.

55. Ibid., pp. 67–73.

56. Nebenzahl, *Atlas*, pp. 30–33 (pp. 32–33 show a large color reproduction of the La Cosa map); *Times Atlas of World Exploration*, pp. 11, 48–49, 252. As recently as 1987, Ricardo Cerezo Martínez, the Director of the Museo Naval in Madrid, which owns the La Cosa map, was not convinced that the work is a copy, not the original. Nor did he think that La Cosa would have had time to find out where John Cabot sailed ("Critiques").

57. Nebenzahl, *Atlas*, pp. 30–33.

58. Cummings, Skelton, and Quinn, *Discovery*, p. 52; Morison, *European Discovery* 1: 138–42; Nebenzahl, *Atlas*, pp. 30–33; Quinn, *England and the Discovery*, pp. 98–99.

59. Morison, *European Discovery* 1: 184–85.

60. For Sebastian Cabot's 1544 statement, see Quinn, Quinn, and Hillier, eds., *New American* 1: 95; Williamson, *Cabot Voyages*, p. 208. De Soncino's letter is in *Calendar of State Papers: Milan, 1385–1618*, pp. 336–37. A complete translation appears in Williamson, *Maritime Enterprise*, pp. 55–57; idem, *Cabot Voyages*, pp. 209–11.

61. Williamson, *Maritime Enterprise*, pp. 57; idem, *Cabot Voyages*, p. 211.

62. Williamson, *Maritime Enterprise*, pp. 54–56; idem, *Cabot Voyages*, pp. 207–8.

63. Quinn, Quinn, and Hillier, eds., *New American* 1: 99–100.

64. Ibid., pp. 95–102; Williamson, *Cabot Voyages*, p. 91–93, 211, 226–28.

65. Quinn, Quinn, and Hillier, eds., *New American* 1: 102; Williamson, *Cabot Voyages*, pp. 78–80, 101–4.

66. *Canadian Biographical Dictionary* 1: 641, entry on Lancelot Thirkill (by Quinn); Quinn, *England and the Discovery*, pp. 100–103; idem, *North America*, p. 121; Quinn, Quinn, and Hillier, eds., *New American* 1: 101–9; Williamson, *Cabot Voyages*, pp. 82, 101–13, 228–29.

67. Morison, *European Discovery*, p. 180.

68. *Canadian Biographical Dictionary* 1: 234–36, article on Gaspar Corte-Real by L.-A. Vigneras.

69. Phillips, "Growth," pp. 48–49.

70. Biggar, *Precursors*, pp. 35–37; Morison, *European Discovery*, pp. 213–17;

Quinn, *North America*, pp. 121–23; Quinn, Quinn, and Hillier, eds., *New American* 1: 146–47.

71. Biggar, *Precursors*, pp. 35–37; *Dictionary of Canadian Biography* 1: 234–36 (by Vigneras); Morison, *European Discovery* 1: 213–15; Quinn, *North America*, pp. 121–23; Quinn, Quinn, and Hillier, eds., *New American* 1: 146–47; Williamson, *Cabot Voyages*, pp. 118–19.

72. Morison, *European Discovery*, pp. 213–15; Quinn, *England and the Discovery*, pp. 115–16; idem, *North America*, pp. 123–24; Quinn, Quinn, and Hillier, eds., *New American* 1: 152 (the source of the quote, which is from De Góis); *Dictionary of Canadian Biography* 1: 234–36 (by Vigneras).

73. Cummings, Skelton, and Quinn, *Discovery*, p. 53.

74. Biggar, *Precursors*, pp. 64–67; Cummings, Skelton, and Quinn, *Discovery*, p. 53; Quinn, Quinn, and Hillier, eds., *New American* 1: 152; Williamson, *Cabot Voyages*, pp. 106–7, 116, 121.

75. Milano, *Carta*, pp. 96–97. Nobody named Cantino or Cantini is listed as an official emissary for the House of Ferrara, but whenever Cantino wrote to the Duke, he referred to himself as "Your humble servant."

76. Cummings, Skelton, and Quinn, *Discovery*, p. 53; Morison, *European Discovery* 1: 215–17; Quinn, Quinn, and Hillier, eds., *New American* 1: 115–16, 145; Williamson, *Cabot Voyages*, p. 229.

77. Biggar, *Precursors*, pp. 67–70; *Dictionary of Canadian Biography* 1: 236 (by Vigneras); Morison, *European Discovery*, p. 217; Quinn, Quinn, and Hillier, eds., *New American* 1: 151–52; Williamson, *Cabot Voyages*, p. 121.

78. For an especially good overview of these voyages, see *The Times Atlas of World History*, pp. 156–57.

79. Williamson, *Cabot Voyages*, p. 172.

80. Nebenzahl, *Atlas*, p. 34; Quinn, *Explorers and Colonies*, pp. 51–52. These strictures must be taken seriously. When Angelo Trevisa, secretary to the Venetian representative in Spain, wrote to the annalist Domenico Malpiero on August 10, 1501, about the voyage of Pedro Alvares Cabral, he noted that it was impossible to obtain a map showing the voyage, because the Portuguese king had imposed the death penalty on anyone who sent abroad any map made inside that country (Milano, *Carta*, p. 96).

81. Quinn, *Explorers and Colonies*, pp. 304–5.

82. Morison, *European Discovery* 1: 226. Morison translated the text.

83. Morison, *European Discovery*, pp. 217, 224–27; Nebenzahl, *Atlas*, pp. 34–37; Quinn, Quinn, and Hillier, eds., *New American* 1: 149; Williamson, *Cabot Voyages*, pp. 122–23, 309–10 (source of the quote).

84. De la Roncière, *Carte*, pp. 27–29; Quinn, *England and the Discovery*, pp. 60–62; Quinn, Quinn, and Hillier, eds., *New American* 1: 31, 145.

85. Biggar, *Precursors*, pp. xxiv, 94–96, 144–45; *Dictionary of Canadian Biography* 1: 236 (by Vigneras); Quinn, Quinn, and Hillier, eds., *New American* 1: 153–54, 4: 183–87.

86. Quinn, Quinn, and Hillier, eds., *New American* 1: 145, 153–54, 4: 183–87; Morison, *European Discovery* 1: 217; Vigneras, "Voyages of Diogo."

87. Biggar, *Precursors*, pp. 98–99; Morison, *European Discovery* 1: 210;

Quinn, Quinn, and Hillier, eds., *New American* 1: 154–55; Williamson, *Cabot Voyages*, p. 117.

88. Biggar, *Precursors*, pp. 100–102; Vigneras, "Voyages of Diogo."

89. Vigneras, "Voyages of Diogo."

90. Ibid. (citing *Boletim do Instituto Historico* 18 [1963]: 20–21, and *Actas do Congreso Internacional de História dos Descubrimentos*, 5, part 1: 175, for de Lima's work).

91. Ibid. (with references as in n. 90 above for de Lima's research). João Alvares Fagundes, from the Portuguese fishing town of Viana do Castelo, coasted along southern Newfoundland into the Gulf of St. Lawrence in 1520, "if not earlier." (Morison, *European Discovery* 1: 228–30).

92. Biggar, *Precursors*, pp. xxii–xxv; Cummings, Skelton, and Quinn, *Discovery*, p. 79; *Dictionary of Canadian Biography* 1: 303–4 (article on João Alvares Fagundes by Vigneras); Morison, *European Discovery* 1: 228–33, 248–49.

93. Vigneras, "Voyages of Diogo" (with references as in n. 90 above for de Lima's research).

94. Quinn, Quinn, and Hillier, eds., *New American* 4: 183–87; Vigneras, "Voyages of Diogo." Vigneras is convinced that Diogo and Manoel de Barcelos claimed lands "scattered on and off the shore of Cape Breton on the north coast of the Gulf of St. Lawrence and in Southern Labrador." He assumes that these locations were never actually settled, but that "they served as stations for the fishing and drying of cod in the spring and summer."

95. Quinn, *Explorers and Colonies*, pp. 121–22; Quinn, Quinn, and Hillier, eds., *New American* 1: 140–43.

96. *Canadian Biographical Dictionary* 1: 304–5 (article on João Fernandes by Arthur Davies); Carus-Wilson, *Overseas Trade*, pp. 236, 286 (citing PRO, E. 122/20/9); Morison, *European Discovery* 1: 210; Quinn, *England and the Discovery*, p. 55, 57; Williamson, *Cabot Voyages*, p. 118.

97. Biggar, *Precursors*, pp. 31–32; Quinn, Quinn, and Hillier, eds., *New American* 1: 145; Williamson, *Cabot Voyages*, p. 235.

98. The Corte Real patent is printed in Biggar, *Precursors*, pp. 35–37; Quinn, Quinn, and Hillier, eds., *New American* 1: 146–47.

99. Williamson (*Cabot Voyages*, p. 117) was convinced by Morison's arguments in *Portuguese Voyages*, pp. 51–68, that de Barcelos could not have gone exploring with João Fernandes in the mid-1490s. Neither of Morison's two reasons stands up to scrutiny, however. The first one, that he had found documentary evidence that the lands de Barcelos was chafing about in 1506 were not the same ones he had owned ca. 1495, is a non-argument. Morison's second reason, that his search of the registers in the Torre do Tombo of Lisbon failed to turn up a license to either de Barcelos or João Fernandes ca. 1495 is not proof one way or another of whether they had gone exploring, as opposed to attempting settlement or trade.

100. Ruddock, "John Day," p. 232.

101. Quinn, *North America*, p. 96.

102. Williamson, *Cabot Voyages*, p. 310.

103. *Canadian Biographical Dictionary* 1: 304–5 (article on João Fernandes by Arthur Davies); Hamy, *Catalog*, esp. Pl. 3; Williamson, *Cabot Voyages*, p. 310.

104. One map is in the British Museum: Add. MS 31316, fol. 5. It is so like the King-Hamy chart that Skelton thinks the two maps quite likely were by the same author and of approximately the same date. The other map, called "Kunstmann II" and dated as "post-1506," gives the name "Terra do Lavorador" to Greenland.

105. In a telephone conversation (May 18, 1993) with Dr. William Frank at the Huntington Library, he noted that nothing more definite could be said about the map's origin or date at that point.

106. Williamson, *Cabot Voyages*, p. 120.

107. Morison, *European Discovery*, p. 242; Williamson, *Cabot Voyages*, pp. 230–33 (a selection from Alonzo de Santa Cruz, *Islario General de todas las Islas del Mundo*). Note that Santa Cruz's manuscript was not printed until 1908. Even after historians and geographers realized that the *labrador* referred to on the Wolfenbüttel map was João Fernandes of Terceira, they have been divided on whether João himself experienced Greenland as a distinct "promontory" on the *eastern* side of the Davis Strait, or whether the cartographers were simply confused by all the new information they had to incorporate in their maps—a confusion in no way lessened by the lack of accurate surveying.

108. Williamson, *Cabot Voyages*, pp. 98–99, 121.

109. Ibid., pp. 309–17. The original of Maggiolo's 1516 map, too, is in the Huntington Library.

110. Nebenzahl, *Atlas*, pp. 58–60.

111. Bjørnbo, "Cartographia," pp. 177, 181; Williamson, *Cabot Voyages*, p. 121.

112. Williamson, *Cabot Voyages*, pp. 309–11.

113. See, for example, the warrant of October 1511 from Queen Joanna of Castile to John de Agramonte concerning an agreement with King Ferdinand for a voyage to Newfoundland. Queen Joanna thought there might be gold in the new lands and considered setting up a colony or a trading factory there (Biggar, *Precursors*, pp. 102–15).

114. Hakluyt, *Principal Navigations* (1903 MacLehose ed.), pp. 159–81 (Thorne's map is between pp. 176 and 177); Harrisse, *Discovery* 1: 19–23; Nebenzahl, *Atlas*, pp. 92–93; Williamson, *Cabot Voyages*, p. 116. Note that Thorne, Elyot, and Sebastian Cabot were all active in the Anglo-Azorean Syndicate *after* João had left it in 1502 (Quinn, Quinn, and Hillier, eds., *New American* 1: 103, 117–18).

115. Hakluyt, *Principall Navigations* (1965 facsimile ed.), pp. 252–56.

116. For the text of both documents, see Biggar, *Precursors*, pp. 40–59; Quinn, Quinn, and Hillier, eds., *New American* 1: 103–9; Williamson, *Cabot Voyages*, pp. 235–47.

117. Quinn, *England and the Discovery*, p. 16.

118. Williamson, *Cabot Voyages*, pp. 125–26, 243–45.

119. Quinn, Quinn, and Hillier, eds., *New American* 1: 103.

120. Quinn, *England and the Discovery*, pp. 114–15; idem, *North America*, pp. 124–25; Quinn, Quinn, and Hillier, eds., *New American* 1: 103.

121. Quinn, Quinn, and Hillier, eds., *New American* 1: 109; Williamson,

Cabot Voyages, pp. 127, 215. The original citation is to PRO, Daybook of the Treasurer of the Chamber, 1499–1502, E 101/415, 3 (Period Jan. 2–7, 1502).

122. Quinn, *England and the Discovery*, p. 121; Quinn, Quinn, and Hillier, eds., *New American* 1: 103; Williamson, *Cabot Voyages*, pp. 214–16.

123. Ruddock, "Reputation," p. 98 (citing PRO, Exchequer, Memoranda Roll, Lord Treasurer's Remembrancer, E 368/278, *Status et visus*, Trinity Term, 20 Henry VII, m. 2); Quinn, Quinn, and Hillier, eds., *New American* 1: 117–18.

124. Quinn, Quinn, and Hillier, eds., *New American* 1: 119–20.

125. Carus-Wilson, *Medieval Merchant*, p. xxviii; McGrath, *Merchant Venturers*, pp. 7–8; Sacks, *Widening Gate*, pp. 88–91, 160–64 (the quote is from p. 89).

126. Sacks, *Widening Gate*, p. 89.

127. McGrath, *Merchant Venturers*, pp. 7–8; Sacks, *Widening Gate*, pp. 89–90 and notes 10–12.

128. *Dictionary of Canadian Biography* 1 (article on Hugh Elyot by Quinn).

129. Sacks, *Widening Gate*, pp. 162–64.

130. *Dictionary of Canadian Biography* 1 (article on Hugh Elyot by Quinn).

131. Williamson, *Cabot Voyages*, pp. 247–48; Quinn, Quinn, and Hillier, eds., *New American* 1: 109.

132. Quinn, *North America*, pp. 125–26; Quinn, Quinn, and Hillier, eds., *New American* 1: 110; Ruddock, "Reputation," p. 98 (citing PRO. E 368/276, m.ll *d*).

133. Hudd, "Richard Ameryk," pp. 123, 128 (noting that Ameryk / Ap Meryke became sheriff of Bristol in 1503 and died during his year in office; he was then succeeded by none other than Robert Thorne); Quinn, Quinn, and Hillier, eds., *New American* 1: 117–18.

134. Quinn, Quinn, and Hillier, eds., *New American* 1: 110.

135. Ibid.; Williamson, *Cabot Voyages*, pp. 248–49.

136. Williamson, *Cabot Voyages*, pp. 222–23; Hakluyt, *Principall Navigations* (1965 facsimile ed.) 2: 515; Quinn, Quinn, and Hillier, eds., *New American* 1: 110. The natives in this case were most likely Indians; there is absolutely no reason to think they were Norse Greenlanders.

137. Quinn, *North America*, pp. 126–27; Quinn, Quinn, and Hillier, eds., *New American* 1: 103, 111–16. Quinn notes that the patent did not actually set aside the charters of 1496 and 1501; its chief novelty was a strict injunction against entering lands discovered by the Portuguese or by the subjects of other friendly princes.

138. The charter is printed in Biggar, *Precursors*, pp. 70–91; Quinn, Quinn, and Hillier, eds., *New American* 1: 111–16; Williamson, *Cabot Voyages*, pp. 52–61.

139. Williamson, *Cabot Voyages*, pp. 216, 262; Quinn, Quinn, and Hillier, eds., *New American* 1: 103, 116–17.

140. Quinn, *England and the Discovery*, p. 123; Quinn, Quinn, and Hillier, eds., *New American* 1: 117; Williamson, *Cabot Voyages*, p. 116.

141. Quinn, *North America*, p. 128; Quinn, Quinn, and Hillier, eds., *New American* 1: 117–18; Ruddock, "Reputation," pp. 97–98. We do not know if the Bristol ship on which the cartographer Ruysch went to the New World in 1502–4 may have been part of a growing fleet of fishing boats seeking their trans-Atlantic catch independently of Elyot and his circle.

142. Quinn, *North America*, pp. 131–32; Quinn, Quinn, and Hillier, eds., *New American* 1: 156–57.

143. Quinn, *England and the Discovery*, pp. 124, 133; idem, *North America*, pp. 128–30; Quinn, Quinn, and Hillier, eds., *New American* 1: 118–24; Ruddock, "Reputation," pp. 98–99; Williamson, *Cabot Voyages*, pp. 35–37, 50, 216, 262–64. Quinn argues convincingly that the "popyngais" (parrots) must have been specimens of the Carolina parakeet, whose range included part of New England. The bobcats (*Lynx rufus*) had an even wider range. While both the birds and the animals may have been obtained through trade with the Indians, Quinn thinks it probable that at least one of the expedition's ships ranged "well to the south along the mainland coast, past what are now the shores of the United States" (*North America*, pp. 128–29).

144. Quinn, *England and the Discovery*, p. 128. The spotty Bristol customs accounts that have survived (1512–13 and 1517–18) show not only Hugh Elyot, but John Thomas and Thomas Asshehurst trading with the Iberian peninsula. In 1524, Elyot still resided in Broad Street, as did one of the John Jays; John Thomas was still active as a merchant; and William Thorne was living in Pyle End.

145. Quinn, *North America*, pp. 129–30; Quinn, Quinn, and Hillier, eds., *New American* 1: 103; Ruddock, "Reputation," pp. 98–99 (citing PRO E 368/279).

146. Quinn, *England and the Discovery*, pp. 142–43; idem, *North America*, pp. 121, 132–33; Quinn, Quinn, and Hillier, eds., *New American* 1: 121.

147. Connell-Smith, "English Merchants," pp. 56–58; McGrath, "Bristol and America," pp. 93–94.

148. Hakluyt, *Principall Navigations* (1965 facsimile ed.), p. 252; Williamson, *Cabot Voyages*, p. 171.

149. Sacks, *Widening Gate*, pp. 69–70. At the Anglo-American Conference on British Studies in Denver, October 1992, Sacks explained this use of the Tolzey Court further and stressed the vast number of such "suits" at the end of any trading year.

150. Williamson, *Cabot Voyages*, pp. 262–64; Quinn, *England and the Discovery*, p. 125; idem, *North America*, pp. 128–29; Quinn, Quinn, and Hillier, eds., *New American* 1: 119–20.

151. Quinn, *England and the Discovery*, pp. 128–29.

152. Biggar, *Precursors*, pp. 96–97; Quinn, Quinn, and Hillier, eds., *New American* 1: 154.

153. Quinn, *North America*, pp. 104–5.

154. Cell, *Newfoundland*, pp. 5–7; Cummings, Skelton, and Quinn, *Discovery*, pp. 84–97; Dumond, *Eskimos*, p. 141; McGhee, "Contact," pp. 6–9; Sturtevant and Quinn, "New Prey," pp. 64–67.

155. Phillips, "Growth," p. 48, n. 21 (citing Godinho, *L'économie de l'empire portugais*, p. 18).

156. Hatcher, *Plague*, esp. pp. 27–30, 43, 55–58, 60–64; Slack, *Impact*, pp. 15–17, 56–68, 70–73 (note esp. graph in fig. 1, p. 71), 84–89, 112, 185–87; McNeill, *Plagues*, p. 169.

157. Sneyd, *Relation*, pp. 35, 86–89. People convicted of high treason were also

in a special position with regard to church sanctuaries, for in 1483 the king had obtained a papal bull allowing him to surround a church harboring such fugitives to prevent exit on any grounds at all (Sneyd, p. 87, with a 1483 citation to Rymer's *Foedera*).

158. Williamson, *Cabot Voyages*, pp. 130.

159. Quinn, *Explorers and Colonies*, pp. 153–58.

160. Phillips, "Growth," pp. 50, 79.

161. Quinn, *England and the Discovery*, pp. 49, 85.

162. *GHM* 3: 513–16.

163. Gulløv and Kapel, *Haabetz Colonie*, pp. 5–6, 20–22. Daniel Bruun demonstrated the early mission's location in 1903, partly on the basis of two eighteenth-century maps which other investigators had overlooked. Egede's own journals and letters from those first seven years are moving, horrifying, and very informative.

164. *DN* 8: nos. 451–53, 455, 457–66.

165. *DN* 17: nos. 1260, 1263; Hamre, *Erkebiskop*, pp. 47–48.

166. *DN* 1: no. 1059; 7: no. 558; 17: nos. 1184–86, 1273; Hamre, *Erkebiskop*, p. 48 (citing *Acta Pontificum Danica* 6: no. 4895, a letter written in Rome ca. 1521 by Klaus Pedersen, a canon from Lund).

167. *DN* 9: no. 532; 11: no. 395; 12: nos. 365–66.

168. *DN* 11: nos. 413, 461.

169. Biggar, *Precursors*, pp. xxv, xxx–xxxi, 134–42; Hakluyt, *Principall Navigations* (1965 facsimile ed.) 2: 517.

170. Quinn, *Explorers and Colonies*, pp. 163–64.

171. McGhee, "Contact," p. 8 (referring to work by William Fitzhugh).

172. Sturtevant and Quinn, "New Prey," pp. 64–67.

173. Interview with Hans Kapel in Grønlandssekretariatet (Copenhagen), May 3, 1991. Evaluating the provenance of such beads is far from simple. Kapel noted, for example, that beads were so highly valued by the Eskimos that they would hand them down for generations.

174. Vebæk, "Church Topography," pp. 40–42, 44–45, 58–59, 75, 79. Vebæk also retrieved a spherical bead of white glass from House 2, a small bead of blue glass outside House 9, and on the surface of House 2 a well-preserved, oblong iron tool of unknown purpose and definitely of neither Norse nor Eskimo origin. These items may simply have come from whalers any time after the first quarter of the sixteenth century, when Basque whalers were active in the lower Davis Strait.

175. Francisco López de Gómara, *Historia de las Indias* (first published in Seville, 1553), as cited in Harrisse, *Discovery*, 1: 131.

APPENDIX A

1. *DI* 5: p. 1088; Espólin, *Íslands Árbækur* 1: 82–84; *Islandske annaler*, p. 357.

2. Espólin, *Íslands Árbækur* 1: 91–98; *Islandske annaler*, pp. 225–28, 277–79, 358–62, 407–11.

3. Espólin, *Íslands Árbækur* 1: 102–5, 110; *Islandske annaler*, pp. 281, 284, 296, 364, 366, 413, 416.

4. *DI* 3: note p. 439; 5: Register: "Kristín Björnsdóttir Jorsalafare"; *Islandske annaler*, pp. 282, 364–65, 414.

5. *DI* 5: p. 848; 11: nos. 13, 14, 15; 16: no. 230.

6. *Islandske annaler*, pp. 415, 421.

7. Espólin, *Íslands Árbækur* 1: 111–12; see also Appendix B.

8. *DI* 3: nos. 336, 337, 341; 4: no. 12.

9. *DI* 5: 443.   10. *DI* 3: 599.

11. *DI* 3: 600–602.   12. *DI* 4: nos. 335, 355.

13. *DI* 5: 550; *Islandske annaler*, p. 370.

14. *DI* 4: nos. 313, 333, 352, 355; Espólin, *Íslands Árbækur* 2: 16.

15. *DI* 4: no. 506; *Islandske annaler*, p. 370; Thorsteinsson, *Enska öldin*, pp. 111–19.

16. Thorsteinsson, *Enska öldin*, pp. 46–47.

17. *DI* 4: nos. 592–93, 599.

18. *DI* 3: nos. 637–38.

19. *DI* 3: no. 534; 5: p. 910.

20. On Jan. 20, 1428, Thorolf Brandsson and his wife Gudrun Bjarnardaughter exchanged property with Akra-Kristin and her husband (*DI* 4: no. 401).

21. That is, if we may assume that Thorstein Eyjolfsson's wife was Kristin Thordsdaughter (Eyjolfsson), who on her mother's side was descended from Bishop Arni Thorlaksson. See, e.g., Arnorsson, "Smiður," pp. 30–31, 125–26.

22. *DI* 3: no. 638; 4: nos. 312–13, 322, and 333.

23. *DI* 4: no. 322.

24. Espólin, *Íslands Árbækur* 1: 112; 2: 16.

25. *DI* 3: pp. 493–96; 5: pp. 819, 837.

APPENDIX B

1. *DI* 3: nos. 226, 263, 359, 360, 376, 383–86; 4: nos. 16, 348, 567, 568; 5: nos. 586, 582, 587; 12: no. 11; Espólin, *Íslands Árbækur* 2: 4.

2. Espólin, *Íslands Árbækur* 1: 112.

3. *DI* 3: nos. 333, 411; 8: no. 11; 9: no. 13.

4. *DI* 3: pp. 336–37, no. 280.

5. *DI* 3: no. 305; Espólin, *Íslands Árbækur* 1: 104–6.

6. *DI* 4: no. 10.   7. *DI* 12: no. 10.

8. *DI* 3: no. 398.   9. Espólin, *Íslands Árbækur* 1: 115.

10. *DI* 6: no. 5.   11. *DI* 4: no. 501.

12. *DI* 5: no. 126; 6: nos. 578, 633.   13. *DI* 3: nos. 408, 511.

14. *DI* 3: no. 582.

15. *DI* 3: nos. 597 (1409), 630–32 (1414); 4: no. 376 (1424).

16. *DI* 9: no. 5.   17. Espólin, *Íslands Árbækur* 2: 16.

18. *DI* 3: no. 638.   19. *DI* 4: nos. 352, 355.

20. *DI* 5: p. 1086.

21. *DI* 5: nos. 562, 652; 5: p. 1086; 6: nos. 101, 147, 159, 164, 208, 273, 467.

22. *DI* 6: no. 669.   23. *DI* 6: no. 633.

24. *DI* 6: no. 659.   25. *DI* 7: nos. 366, 367.

26. *DI* 7: pp. 378–79.

Works Cited

The following journals occur frequently in the Works Cited. Rather than repeat full publication information with each citation, publication details (city, country as needed, and occasionally publisher) are given here:

Acta Archaeologica   Copenhagen: Munksgaard.
Acta Borealia   Tromsø, Norway: Novus.
Forskning i Grønland/tusaat   Copenhagen: Dansk Polarcenter.
Grønland   Odense, Denmark: Det grønlandske selskab.
Hikuin   Copenhagen: Hikuin.
Grønlandsk kultur- og samfundsforskning   Nuuk, Greenland.
MoG (Meddelelser om Grønland)   Copenhagen: Dansk Polarcenter. A monograph series in journals published by Commissionen for Ledelsen af de geologiske og geographiske Undersøgelser i Grønland. Note that volume numbers do not always follow chronologically.
MoG, Man and Society (Meddelelser om Grønland, Man & Society)   Copenhagen: Dansk Polarcenter. This monograph series supersedes the previous one, running concurrently with a straight science series.
Saga   Reykjavik: Tímarit sögufelagsins.

PRIMARY SOURCES

"'Accounts of Iseland [and Greenland], sent to Monsieur de la Mothe del Vayer' by La Peyrère (1644)." In Henry Lintot and John Osborn, eds., *A Collection of Voyages and Travels*. 3d ed., vol. 2. London, 1977.
Annálar 1400–1800. Vols. 1–5. Copenhagen: Hið íslenzka bókmenntafélag, 1922–61.
Biskupa sögur. Vols. 1–2. Copenhagen: Hið íslenzka bókmenntafélag, 1858–78.
Calendar of State Papers: Letters etc. between England and Spain. Vol. 1. London: Public Record Office, 1862.
Calendar of State Papers: Milan, 1385–1618. London: Public Record Office, 1912.

Calendar of State Papers: Spanish. Vol. 1 (1485–1509). London: Public Record Office, 1862.

Calendar of State Papers: Venetian. Vol. 1 (1202–1509). London: Public Record Office, 1864.

Diplomatarium Christierni Primi. Hans Knudsen, comp., C. F. Wegener, ed. Copenhagen, 1856.

"Diplomatarium Groenlandicum 1492–1814." Louis Bobé, ed. *MoG* 55 (3). Copenhagen, 1936.

Diplomatarium Islandicum. Vols. 1–16. Copenhagen and Reykjavik, 1857–1959.

Diplomatarium Norvegicum. Vols. 1–21. Oslo, 1849–1970.

"Eirik's Saga." In Magnus Magnusson and Hermann Pálsson, trans., *The Vinland Sagas*, pp. 73–105. Harmondsworth, Eng.: Penguin Books, 1965.

"Eiríks saga rauða." In *Islenzk fornrit*, 4: 194–238. Reykjavik: 1935.

"Eiríks saga rauða." In Guðni Jónsson, ed., *Íslendinga sögur* 1: 323–59. Reykjavik: 1968.

"Fóstbræðra saga." In *Islenzk fornrit* 6: 120–276. Reykjavik: 1935.

"Grænlendinga saga." In Guðni Jónsson, ed., *Íslendinga sögur* 1: 369–90. Reykjavik: 1968.

"Grænlendinga saga." In Magnus Magnusson and Hermann Pálsson, trans., *The Vinland Sagas*, pp. 47–72. Harmondsworth, Eng.: Penguin Books, 1965.

"Grænlendinga þáttr." In *Islenzk fornrit* 4: 272–92. Reykjavik: 1935.

"Grænlendinga þáttr." In Guðni Jónsson, ed., *Íslendinga sögur* 1: 391–411. Reykjavik: 1968.

Grønlands Historiske Mindesmerker. C. C. Rafn and Finn Magnusen, comps. and eds. Vol. 3. Copenhagen: De Kongelige Nordiske Oldstids-Selskab, 1845.

Hakluyt, Richard. *Principall Navigations of the English Nation.* 2 vols. Photolithographic facsimile of the 1589 edition, with an introduction by David B. Quinn and Raleigh Ashlin Skelton. Cambridge, Eng.: Hakluyt Society, 1965.

———. *The Principal Navigations . . . of the English Nation.* MacLehose ed. for the Hakluyt Society. Vol. 2. Glasgow: 1903.

Historia Norvegiae. In Halvdan Koht, *Den eldste Noregshistoria.* Gamalnorske Bokverk, vol. 19. Oslo: 1921.

Hrafns saga Sveinbjarnarsonar. Guðrún P. Helgadóttir, ed. Oxford: Clarendon Press, 1987.

Icelandic Annals. See *Islandske Annaler indtil 1578.*

Islandske Annaler indtil 1578. Gustav Storm, comp. and ed. Oslo: Norsk Historisk Kjeldeskrifts-Institutt, 1977. Reprint of 1888 edition.

"Íslendingabók." In Guðni Jónsson, ed., *Íslendinga sögur* 1: 1–20. Reykjavik: 1968.

Ivar Bárdarson, *see* Jónsson, Finnur, *under Secondary Sources below.*

The King's Mirror [Speculum regale]. Laurence Marcellus Larson, trans. New York: 1917.

"Kristni saga." In Guðni Jónsson, ed., *Íslendinga sögur* 1: 243–80. Reykjavik: 1968.

"Landnámabók." In Guðni Jónsson, ed., *Íslendinga sögur*, 1: 21–241. Reykjavik: 1968.

Norges gamle Love. Vols. 1–5. [Vols. 1–3: R. Keyser and P. A. Munch, eds.; vols. 4–5: Gustav Storm, ed]. Oslo: 1846–95.

Norges kongesagaer. Vols. 1–4. Finn Hødnebø and Hallvard Magerøy, eds. Oslo: Gyldendal, 1979.

Norske Samlinger. Christian C. A. Lange, ed. Oslo: 1852.

"Orkneyinga saga." Hermann Pálsson and Paul Edwards, trans. and eds. Harmondsworth, Eng.: Penguin Books, 1981.

Orosius. *King Alfred's Anglo-Saxon Version of the Compendious History of the World.* Joseph Bosworth, trans. and ed. London: Longman, Brown, Green and Longmans, 1859.

Ptolemy [Claudius Ptolemaeus]. *Geographia.* Rome: 1508. Originals used: British Map Library copies 1 and 2, cataloged as C.1.d.5 and .6.

Regesta Norvegica. Oslo: Norsk Historisk Kjeldeskriftfond, 1889–1979.

"Skáld-Helga saga." In Guðni Jónsson, ed., *Íslendinga sögur* 1: 413–39, Reykjavik: 1968.

The "Vinland Map." Property of Yale University Library, New Haven, Conn.

GENERAL REFERENCE WORKS

The Audubon Society Encyclopedia of North American Birds. John K. Terres, ed. New York: Knopf, 1980.

The Christopher Columbus Encyclopedia, vols. 1–2. Silvio A. Bedini, ed. New York: Simon and Schuster, 1992.

Collier's Encyclopedia. Vol. 13. New York: P. F. Collier, 1983.

The Columbia Encyclopedia. New York: Columbia University Press, 1963.

Dictionary of Canadian Biography. G. W. Brown, Marcel Trudel, and André Vachon, eds. Vol. 1. Toronto: 1965.

Encyclopaedia Britannica. Eleventh and fifteenth editions. London: Encyclopaedia Britannica, Inc., various years.

Kulturhistorisk leksikon for nordisk middelalder, 21 vols. + index, Copenhagen: 1956–78.

Norges Kulturhistorie. Ingrid Semmingsen, ed. Oslo: 1979–81.

Norsk biografisk leksikon. Oslo: Aschehoug, 1924–70.

Norrøn ordbok. Leiv Heggstad, Finn Hødnebø, and Erik Simensen, comps. Oslo: Det Norske Samlaget, 1975.

North American Wildlife. Susan J. Wernert, ed. Pleasantville, N.Y.: Reader's Digest, 1985.

Oxford World Atlas. Saul B. Cohen, ed. Oxford: Oxford University Press, 1973.

The Times Atlas of World History. Geoffrey Barraclough, ed. London: Hammond, 1978.

The Times Atlas of World Exploration. Felipe Fernández-Armesto, ed. London: HarperCollins, 1991.

SECONDARY SOURCES

Ahlenius, Karl. *Olaus Magnus och hans framställning af Nordens Geografi*. Uppsala, 1895.

Albrethsen, Svend E. "Sæters in the Norse Eastern Settlement of Østerbygden in Southwest Greenland." *Acta Borealia*, 1991, vol. 8: 15–28.

Albrethsen, Svend E., and Christian Keller. "The Use of the Sæter in Medieval Norse Farming in Greenland." *Arctic Anthropology* 23 (1986): 91–107.

Amorosi, Thomas, Paul C. Buckland, Guðmundur Ólafsson, Jon P. Sadler, and Peter Skidmore. "Site Status and the Palaeoecological Record: A Discussion of the Results from Bessastaðir, Iceland." In Christopher D. Morris and James D. Rackham, eds., *Norse and Later Settlement and Subsistence in the North Atlantic*, pp. 169–191. Glasgow: University of Glasgow Occasional Paper Series 1, 1992.

Andersen, Erik, and Claus Malmros. "Ship's Parts Found in the Viking Settlements in Greenland: Preliminary Assessments and Wood-diagnoses." In B. L. Clausen, ed., *Viking Voyages to North America*. Roskilde: The Viking Ship Museum, 1993.

Andreasen, Claus. "Langhus-ganghus-centraliseret gård." *Hikuin* 7 (1981): 179–84.

———. "Nipaitsoq og Vesterbygden." *Grønland* 30 (1982): 177–88.

———. "Nordbosager fra Vesterbygden på Grønland." *Hikuin* 6 (1980): 135–46.

Andreasen, Claus, and Jette Arneborg. "Gården under sandet—undersøgelserne 1991." *Forskning i Grønland/tusaat*, 1992, no. 1: 10–18.

———. "Gården under sandet. Nye nordboundersøgelser i Vesterbygden." In *Grønlandsk kultur- og samfundsforskning*, 1992: 11–49.

Andrews, K. R., W. P. Canny, and P. E. H. Hair, eds. *The Westward Enterprise: English Activities in Ireland, the Atlantic, and America ca. 1480–1650*. Liverpool: 1978.

Arneborg, Jette. "Aqigssiaq og nordboerne." *Grønland* 38 (1990): 213–19.

———. "Contact between Eskimos and Norsemen in Greenland." In Else Roesdal and Preben Meulengracht Sørensen, eds., *Beretning fra tolvte tværfaglige vikingesymposium, Aarhus Universitet 1993*, pp. 23–35. Aarhus (Denmark): Hikuin, 1993.

———. "Grønland, udgangspunktet for sejladserne til Nordamerika." In *Vikingernes sejlads til Nordamerika*, pp. 13–21. Roskilde: The Viking Ship Museum, 1992.

———. "Kulturmødet mellem nordboer og eskimoer" (The cultural encounter between Norsemen and Eskimos). Ph.D. dissertation, Copenhagen University, 1991. To be published in English translation as part of the series *MoG: Man & Society*, Copenhagen.

———. "The Niaqussat Excavations Reconsidered." *Acta Borealia*, 1991, vol. 8: 82–92.

———. "Nordboarkæologiske undersøgelser ved Kilaarsarfik i nordboernes vesterbygd." *Forskning i Grønland/tusaat*, 1985, no. 2: 2–9.

———. "Nordboarkæologiens historie—og fremtid." *Grønland* 37 (1989): 121–37.

————. "Nordboerne i Grønland." *Hikuin* 14 (1988): 297–310.

————. "The Roman Church in Norse Greenland." *Acta Archaeologica* 61 (1990): 142–50.

————. "Vikingerne i Nordatlanten." In Niels Lund, ed., *Norden og Europa i vikingetid og tidlig middelalder*, pp. 179–94. Copenhagen: Museum Tuscalunum, 1993.

Arneborg, Jette, and Joel Berglund. *Gården under sandet: Arkæeologiske undersøgelser af nordbogård i Grønlands Vesterbygd, Nuuk kommune, status november 1993*. Nuuk: Grønlands Nationalmuseum og Arkiv, 1993.

Arneborg, Jette, Hans Chr. Gulløv, and Jens P. Hart-Hansen. "Menneske og miljø i fortidens Grønland." *Forskning i Grønland/tusaat*, 1988, no. 1: 39–47.

Arnorsson, Einar. "Smiður Andrésson: Brót úr sögu 14. aldar." *Saga* 24 (1949).

Authén Blom, Grethe. *Kongemakt og privilegier i Norge inntil 1387*. Oslo: 1967.

————. "The Participation of the Kings in the Early Norwegian Sailing to Bjarmeland (Kola Peninsula and Russian Waters), and the Development of a Royal Policy Concerning the Northern Waters in the Middle Ages." *Arctic* 37 (1984): 385–88.

Bárdarson, Ivar. *See* Jónsson, Finnur.

Barkham, Selma Huxley. "The Basque Whaling Establishments in Labrador 1536–1632: A Summary." *Arctic* 37 (1984): 515–19.

————. "Basque Exploration and Discovery." In Silvio A. Bedini, ed., *The Christopher Columbus Encyclopedia* 1: 265–66. New York: Simon and Schuster, 1992.

————. *Los vascos en el marco Atlantico Norte: Siglos XVI y XVII*. Vol. 3 of the series *Itsasoa*, Enrique Ayerbe gen. ed. Bilbao: Etor, 1987.

Berglund, Joel. "The Decline of the Norse Settlements in Greenland." *Arctic Anthropology* 23 (1986): 109–35.

————. "Displacements in the Building-Over of the Eastern Settlement, Greenland." *Acta Archaeologica* 61 (1990): 151–57.

————. *Hvalsø—kirkeplads og stormandsgaard*. Julianehaab, Greenland: 1982.

————. "Kirke, Hal og Status." *Grønland* 30 (1982): 275–85.

Bertelsen, Reidar. "Farm Mounds in North Norway: A Review of Recent Research." *Norwegian Archaeological Review* 12 (1979): 48–56.

Biggar, Henry Percival. *The Precursors of Cartier, 1497–1534*. Publications of the Canadian Archives, no. 5. Ottawa: 1911.

Bittles, Alan H., and James V. Neel. "The Costs of Human Inbreeding and Their Implications for Variations at the DNA Level." *Nature Genetics*, 8, no. 2 (1994): 117–21.

Bjarnason, Einar. "Auðbrekku bréf og Vatnsfjarðarerfdir." *Saga* 37 (1962): 370–411.

Bjørnbo, Axel Anthon. "Cartographia Groenlandica." *MoG* 48. Copenhagen: 1912.

Blindheim, Charlotte. *Vikingtid*. Oslo: Universitetets Oldsaksamling, 1973.

Bowman, Sheridan. *Radiocarbon Dating*. London: British Museum Publications, 1990.

Brøgger, A. W. *Vinlandsferdene*. Oslo: 1937.

Brøndsted, Johannes. *The Vikings*. New York: Viking Penguin, 1965.

Brøste, K., and K. Fischer-Møller. "The Mediaeval Norsemen at Gardar: Anthropological Investigation." *MoG* 89 (3). Copenhagen: 1944.

Bruun, Daniel. "Arkæologiske Undersøgelser i Julianehaabs Distrikt." *MoG* 16. Copenhagen: 1917.

———. "Oversigt over Nordboruiner i Godthaab- og Frederikshaab-Distrikter." *MoG* 56 (3). Copenhagen: 1917.

Buchwald, Vagn Fabritius, and Gert Mosdal. "Meteoric Iron, Telluric Iron and Wrought Iron in Greenland." *MoG, Man & Society* 9. Copenhagen: 1985.

Buckland, Paul C., Gudrún Sveinbjarnardóttir, Diane Savory, Tom H. McGovern, Peter Skidmore, and Claus Andreasen. "Norsemen at Nipaitsoq, Greenland: A Palaeoecological Investigation." *Norwegian Archaeological Review* 16, no. 2 (1983): 86–98.

Byock, Jesse L. *Medieval Iceland*. Berkeley: University of California Press, 1988.

Campbell, Tony. *Early Maps*. New York: Abbeville Press, 1981.

Carus-Wilson, Eleanora Mary. "The Iceland Trade." In E. Power and M. M. Postan, eds., *Studies in English Trade in the Fifteenth Century*, pp. 155–82. London, 1933.

———. *Medieval Merchant Venturers*. London, 1954.

———. *The Merchant Adventurers of Bristol*. Bristol: Bristol Branch of the Historical Association, Local History Pamphlet 4, l962.

———. *The Overseas Trade of Bristol*. London: Merlin Press, l967.

Cell, Gillian T., ed. *Newfoundland Discovered*. London: Hakluyt Society, 1982.

Cerezo Martínez, Ricardo. "Les critiques à propos de la date de réalization—1500—et à l'authenticité de la carte de Juan de la Cosa: son refus." *Proceedings*, 12th International Conference on the History of Cartography. Paris: 1987.

Childs, Wendy R. *Anglo-Castilian Trade in the Later Middle Ages*. Manchester: Manchester University Press, 1978.

Clemmensen, Mogens. "Kirkeruiner fra Nordbotiden m.m. i Julianehaab Distrikt: Undersøgelsesrejse i Sommeren 1910." *MoG* 47 (8). Copenhagen: 1911.

Connell-Smith, G. "English Merchants Trading to the New World in the Early Sixteenth Century." *Bulletin of the Institute for Historical Research* (London), 23 (1950): 53–67.

Cortesão, Jaime. "The Pre-Columbian Discovery of America." *The Geographical Journal* (London), 89, no. 1 (1937): 29–42.

Cowgill, J., M. de Neergaard, and N. Griffiths. *Knives and Scabbards. Medieval Finds from Excavations in London*. Vol. 1. London: The Museum of London, 1987.

Crone, G. R. "The Alleged Pre-Columbian Discovery of America (a rebuttal of J. Cortesão)." *The Geographical Journal* (London), 89, no. 5 (1937): 455–60.

Cummings, W. P., R. A. Skelton, and D. B. Quinn. *The Discovery of North America*. London: 1971.

Cunnington, Cecil Willett. *Handbook of English Medieval Costumes*. London: 1968.

Danish Polar Center. *Newsletter*. Copenhagen: 1991.

Dansgaard, Willi. "Bringer luftforureningen torsken tilbage til Grønland?" *Forskning i Grønland/tusaat*, 1985, no. 1: 24–25.

Dansgaard, Willi, S. J. Johnsen, H. B. Clausen, and N. Gundestrup. "Stable Isotope Glaciology." *MoG* 197 (2). Copenhagen: 1973.

Dansgaard, Willi, S. J. Johnsen, N. Reeh, N. Gundestrup, H. B. Clausen, and C. U. Hammer. "Climatic Changes, Norsemen, and Modern Man." *Nature* 255 (1975): 24–27.

Danstrup, John, and Hal Koch, gen. eds. *Danmarks Historie.* Vol. 5: *De første Old-enborgerer, 1448–1533.* Copenhagen: Politikens Forlag, 1963.

Degerbøl, Magnus. "The Osseous Material from Austmannadal and Tungmera-lik." *MoG* 89 (1): 345–54. Copenhagen: 1941.

Delaney, Frank. *The Celts.* Boston: Little, Brown and Co., 1986.

De la Roncière, Charles. *La Carte de Christophe Colomb.* Paris: 1924.

Dúason, Jón. *Landkönnun og Landnám Íslendinga í Vesturheim.* 3 vols. Reyk-javik: 1941–48.

Dumond, Don E. *The Eskimos and Aleuts.* London: Thames and Hudson, 1987.

Egede, Hans. *Det Gamle Grønlands Perlustration eller Naturel-Historie.* Didrik Arup Seip, ed. Oslo: Det norske språk- og litteraturselskap, 1988. Facsimile ed.

———. *Grønlandsbeskrivelse 1741 og 1926* [Det gamle Grønlands Nye Perlustra-tion]. O. Solberg, ed. Oslo: 1926.

Egede, Poul. *Efterretninger om Grønland.* Copenhagen: H. C. Schroeder, 1787.

Ehrensvärd, Ulla. "Cartographical Representations of the Scandinavian Arctic Re-gions." *Arctic* 37 (1984): 552–56.

Eisner, Sigmund. *The Kalendarium of Nicholas of Lynn.* Athens: University of Georgia Press, 1980.

Espólin, Jón. *Íslands Árbækur.* Copenhagen: Íslenzka Bókmentafélag, 1821–55.

Feest, Christian F., ed. *Indians and Europe.* Aachen: 1987.

Fernández-Armesto, Felipe. *Before Columbus. Exploration and Colonization from the Mediterranean to the Atlantic, 1229–1492.* Philadelphia: University of Penn-sylvania Press, 1987.

Fischer-Møller, K. "The Mediaeval Norse Settlements in Greenland: Anthropologi-cal Investigations." *MoG* 89 (2): 3–81. Copenhagen: 1942.

Fitzhugh, William W., ed. *Cultures in Contact: The Impact of European Contacts on Native American Cultural Institutions, A.D. 1000–1800.* Washington, D.C.: Smithsonian Institution Press, 1985.

Fitzhugh, William W., and Jacqueline S. Olin, eds. *Archaeology of the Frobisher Voyages.* Washington, D.C.: Smithsonian Institution Press, 1993.

Foote, Peter G., "Icelandic *sólarsteinn* and the Medieval Background." In Michael Barnes, Hans Bekker-Nielsen, and Gerd Wolfgang Weber, eds., *Aurvandilstá,* pp. 140–54. Odense: 1984.

Foote, Peter, and David M. Wilson. *The Viking Achievement.* London: Sidgwick and Jackson, 1970.

Fredskild, Bent. "Agriculture in a Marginal Area: South Greenland from the Norse Landnam (A.D. 985) to the Present (1985)." In Hilary H. Birks, H. J. B. Birks, Peter Emil Kaland, and Dagfinn Moe, eds., *The Cultural Landscape: Past, Present and Future,* pp. 381–94. Cambridge, Eng.: Cambridge University Press, 1988.

———. "Palaeobotanical Investigations of Some Peat Deposits of Norse Age at Qagssiarssuk, South Greenland." *MoG* 204 (5): 1–41. Copenhagen: 1978.

Fredskild, Bent, and Lilli Humle. "Plant Remains from the Norse Farm Sandnes in the Western Settlement, Greenland." *Acta Borealia,* 1991, vol. 1: 69–81.

Friedland, Klaus. "The Hanseatic League and Hanse Towns in the Early Penetration of the North." *Arctic* 37 (1984): 539–43.

Frydendahl, Knud. "Sommerklimaet på Nordatlanten omkr. år 1000." In *Vikingernes sejlads til Nordamerika*, pp. 90–94. Roskilde: The Viking Ship Museum, 1992.

Gad, Finn. *The Early History of Greenland*. Vol. 1: *Earliest Times to 1700*. Ernst Dupont, trans. London: 1970.

———. "Grønlands tilslutning til Norgesvældet 1261." *Grønland* 12 (1964): 259–72.

———. *Grønlands historie*. Vols. 1–2. Copenhagen: l970–78.

Garde, T. V. "Beskrivelse af Expeditionen til Sydvestgrønland 1893." *MoG* 16. Copenhagen: 1894.

———. "The Navigation of Greenland." In M. Vahl, G. C. Amdrup, L. Bobé, and A. D. Jensen, eds. *Greenland*. Vols. 1–3. London: 1928–29.

Gísli Oddsson. *See* Oddsson, Gísli.

Gjerset, Knut. *History of Iceland*, London: 1924.

———. *History of the Norwegian People*. London: 1932.

Gottfried, Robert S. *The Black Death*. London: 1983.

Grafton, Anthony. *New Worlds, Ancient Texts. The Power of Tradition and the Shock of Discovery*. Cambridge, Mass.: Harvard University Press, 1992.

Graham-Campbell, James, and Dafydd Kidd. *The Vikings*. London: British Museum Publications, 1980.

Grønnow, Bjarne, and Morten Meldgaard. "De første Vestgrønlændere," *Grønland* 39 (1991): 103–44.

Grønnow, Bjarne, Morten Meldgaard, and Jørn Berglund-Nielsen. "Aasivissuit— The Great Summer Camp: Archaeological, Ethnographical, and Zoo-archaeological Studies of a Caribou-hunting Site in West Greenland." *MoG, Man & Society* 5. Copenhagen: 1983.

Gulløv, Hans Christian. "Eskimoens syn på europæeren—de såkaldte nordbodukker og andre tvivlsomme udskæringer." *Grønland* 30 (1982): 226–34.

———. "The Eskimo's View of the European: The So-called Norse Dolls and Other Questionable Carvings." Anne M. Jensen, trans. *Arctic Anthropology* 20 (1983): 121–29.

———. "Kangeq: Et uddrag af Grønlands historie." *Grønland* 24 (1976): 97–116.

———. "Noua terra 1566. Newfoundland, Labrador og Grønland i samtidens europæiske bevidsthed." *Grønland* 35 (1988): 129–46.

Gulløv, Hans Christian, and Hans Kapel. *Haabetz Colonie 1721–1728*. Ethnographical Series 16. Copenhagen: Publications of the National Museum, 1979.

Hagen, Anders. "Man and Nature: Reflections on Culture and Ecology." *Norwegian Archaeological Review* 5 (1972): 1–22.

Hall, Charles Francis. *Life with the Esquimaux*. Two volumes in one. London: Sampson, Low, Son, and Marston, 1864.

Hall, Richard. *The Viking Dig: The Excavations at York*. London: The Bodley Head, 1984.

Halldórsson, Ólafur. *Grænland i Miðaldaritum*. Reykjavik: 1978.

Hammer, C. U., H. B. Clausen, and W. Dansgaard. "Greenland Ice Sheet Evidence of Post-glacial Volcanism and Its Climatic Impact." *Nature* 288 (1980): 230–35.

Hamre, Lars. "Erik Valkendorf." In *Norsk Biografisk Leksikon* 17: 501–11. Oslo: 1970.

———. *Erkebiskop Erik Valkendorf. Trekk av hans liv og virke.* Oslo: 1943.

Hamy, T. J. E. *Catalog of Portolan Charts of the Fifteenth, Sixteenth, and Seventeenth Centuries Collected by Dr. T. J. E. Hamy: Sold at Auction in New York.* New York: 1912.

Hansen, Birger Ulf. "Using Climate and Vegetation Studies in Southern Greenland to Estimate the Material Resources During the Norse Period." *Acta Borealia,* 1990, vol. 1: 40–55.

Hansen, F. C. C. "Anthropologica medici: historica Grønlandiae antiquae." *MoG* 67 (3). Copenhagen: 1924.

Harrisse, Henry. *The Discovery of North America.* 2 vols. London: 1892.

Hart-Hansen, Jens Peder, Jørgen Meldgaard, and Jørgen Nordqvist. *Qilakitsoq: De grønlandske mumier fra 1400-tallet.* Copenhagen: 1985.

Hastrup, Kirsten. "Sæters in Iceland, 900–1600." *Acta Borealia,* 1989, no. 6: 72–85.

Hatcher, John. *Plague, Population and the English Economy, 1348-1530.* London: 1977.

Helgason, Jón. *Islands Kirke fra dens Grundlæggelse til Reformationen.* Copenhagen: 1925.

Henschen, Folke. *The History of Diseases.* Joan Tate, trans. London: 1966.

Holand, Hjalmar R. *Explorations in America Before Columbus.* New York: 1956.

Holm, G. F. "Beskrivelser af Ruiner i Julianehaabs Distrikt, undersøgte i Aaret 1880." *MoG* 6: 57–192. Copenhagen: 1883.

Holm Jakobsen, Bjarne. "Soil Resources and Soil Erosion in the Norse Settlement Area of Østerbygden in Southern Greenland." *Acta Borealia,* 1991, vol. 1: 56–68.

Holm Olsen, Inger Marie. "The Helgøy Project: Evidence from Farm Mounds: Economy and Settlement Pattern A.D. 1350–1600." *Norwegian Archaeological Review* 14 (1981): 86–101.

Holtved, Erik. "Arbejder og indtryk under to års ophold blandt Polareskimoene 1935–37." *Grønland* 29 (1981): 186–204.

———. "Nûgdlît. En forhistorisk boplads i Thule distriktet." *Grønland* 2 (1954): 89–94.

Hudd, A. E. "Richard Ameryk and the Name America." In H. P. R. Finberg, ed., *Gloucestershire Studies.* Leicester, Eng.: Leicester University Press, 1957.

Ingstad, Anne Stine. *The Discovery of a Norse Settlement in America: Excavations at L'Anse aux Meadows, Newfoundland, 1961–1968.* Oslo: Universitetsforlaget, 1977.

Ingstad, Helge. *Land Under the Pole Star.* London: Jonathan Cape, 1966.

———. *Vesterveg til Vinland.* Oslo: Gyldendal, 1965.

———. *The Norse Discovery of America.* Vol. 2. Oslo: Universitetsforlaget, 1985.

———. "På jakt efter sagaens Helluland." Article in the newspaper *Aftenposten* (Oslo), Dec. 27 and 28, 1971.

Jansen, Henrik M. "A Critical Account of the Written and Archaeological Sources' Evidence Concerning the Norse Settlements in Greenland." *MoG* 182 (4). Copenhagen: 1972.

Jóhannesson, Jón. "Om Haf Innan." *Saga*: Sögurit 24. Reykjavik: 1960–62.

———. "Reisubók Bjarnar Jorsalafára." *Skírnir* 119 (1945): 68–96.

Johnston, G. Harvey. *The Heraldry of the Campbells*. 2 vols. Edinburgh: 1920.

Jones, Gwyn. *The Norse Atlantic Saga*. 2d ed. Oxford: Oxford University Press, 1986.

Jónsson, Finnur [Ívar Bárdarson]. *Det gamle Grønlands Beskrivelse*. Copenhagen: 1930.

———. "Grønlands gamle Topografi efter Kilderne: Østerbygden og Vesterbygden." *MoG* 20. Copenhagen: 1899.

Jónsson, Guðni, ed. *Annálar og Nafnaskrá*. Reykjavik: Íslendingasagnaútgáfan, 1962.

Kapel, Christian, and Peter Nansen. "Forvildede tamfår i Grønland." *Forskning i Grønland/tusaat*, 1990, no. 3–4: 19–24.

Kapel, Hans C. "Nyopdaget nordbogård i Vesterbygden." *Forskning i Grønland/tusaat*, 1991, no. 1: 8–15.

Karlsson, Stefán. *Islandske originaldiplomer indtil 1450*. Editiones Arnamagnæanæ, Series A, vol. 7. Copenhagen: 1963.

Keller, Christian. "Vikings in the West Atlantic: A Model of Norse Greenlandic Medieval Society." *Acta Archaeologica* 61 (1990 [1991]): 126–46.

Kisbye Møller, J. "Isaac de la Peyrère: Relation du Groenlande." *Grønland* 29 (1981): 168–84.

Kleivan, Helge. "Eskimoenes skjebne på Labradors Østkyst." *Grønland* 5 (1957): 347–55.

Koht, Halvdan. *Den eldste Noregshistoria*. Gamalnorske Bokverk, vol. 19. Oslo: 1921.

Kowaleski, Maryanne. "Town and Country in Late Medieval England: The Hide and Leather Trade." In Penelope C. Corfield and Derek Keene, eds., *Work in Towns, 850–1850*, pp. 57–73. London: Leicester University Press, 1990.

Krogh, Knud. "Bygdernes Kirker: Kirkerne i de middelalderlige norrøne grønlandske bygder." *Grønland* 30 (1982): 263–74.

———. *Erik den Rødes Grønland*. Copenhagen: 1982.

———. "Om Grønlands middelalderlige kirkebygninger." In *Minnjar og Menntir: Festskrift til Kristján Eldjárn*, pp. 294–310. Reykjavik: 1976.

———. "Gård og kirke." *Hikuin* 9 (1983).

———. *Viking Greenland*. Copenhagen: 1967.

Lamb, H. H. *Climate, History and the Modern World*. London: 1982.

Larsen, Sofus. *The Discovery of North America Twenty Years Before Columbus*. London: 1925.

Liestøl, Aslak. "Runes." In Alexander Fenton and Hermann Pálsson, eds. *The Northern and Western Isles in the Viking World*. Edinburgh: John Donald, 1984.

Lintot, Henry, and John Osborn, eds. *A Collection of Voyages and Travels*. Vol. 2. London: 1977.

Lynnerup, N. "The Norse Settlers in Greenland: The Physical Anthropological Perspective." *Acta Borealia*, 1991, no. 1: 93–96.

Lynnerup, N., B. Frohlich, J. Arneborg, V. Alexandersen, and J. P. Hart-Hansen.

"Greenland Anthropology: Experiences with Computer Registration of Skeletal Remains." Proceedings of the Second Seminar of Nordic Physical Anthropology. *Institute of Archaeology Report Series* 46. Lund, Sweden: 1990.

Mackie, D. J. *A History of Scotland*. 2d. ed. New York: Dorset Press, 1978.

Madsen, Holger. "Om Trikiner i Grønland." *Grønland* 9 (1961): 81–92.

Magnusson, Magnus, and Hermann Pálsson, trans. and eds. *The Vinland Sagas: The Norse Discovery of America*. Harmondsworth, Eng.: Penguin Books, 1965.

Magnusson, Magnus, and Werner Forman. *Viking: Hammer of the North*. London: Orbis, 1976.

Mary-Rousselière, Guy. "Exploration and Evangelization of the Great Canadian North: Vikings, Coureurs des Bois, and Missionaries." *Arctic* 37 (1984): 590–602.

Mathiassen, Therkel. "Inugsuk, Mediaeval Eskimo Settlement in Upernivik District, West Greenland." *MoG* 77. Copenhagen: 1930.

———. "Sermermiut." *Grønland* 12 (1964): 161–73.

———. "The Sermermiut Excavations 1955." *MoG* 161 (3). Copenhagen: 1958.

Mathiassen, Therkel, and Erik Holtved. "Contributions to the Archaeology of Disko Bay." *MoG* 93 (2). Copenhagen: 1934.

———. "The Eskimo Archaeology of Julianehaab District." *MoG* 118 (1). Copenhagen: 1936.

Matthews, Barry. "Archaeological Sites in the Labrador-Ungava Peninsula: Cultural Origin and Climatic Significance." *Arctic* 28 (1975): 245–62.

Mattox, William G. "Fishing in West Greenland, 1910–1966: The Development of a New Native Industry." *MoG* 197 (1). Copenhagen: 1973.

McCartney, Allen P. "The Nature of Thule Eskimo Whale Use." *Arctic* 33 (1980): 517–41.

McGhee, Robert. *Ancient Canada*. Montreal: Canadian Museum of Civilization, 1989.

———. "Archaeological Evidence for Climate Change During the Last 5,000 Years." In T. M. L. Wrigley, M. J. Ingram, and G. Farmer, eds., *Climate and History. Studies in Past Climates and Their Impact on Man*. Cambridge, Eng.: Cambridge University Press, 1980.

———. "Contact Between Native North Americans and the Medieval Norse: A Review of the Evidence." *American Antiquity* 49 (1984): 4–26.

———. "The *Skraellings* of Vinland." In B. L. Clausen, ed., *Viking Voyages to North America*, pp. 43–53. Roskilde: The Viking Ship Museum, 1993.

McGovern, Thomas. "Bones, Buildings, and Boundaries: Palæoeconomic Approaches to Norse Greenland." In Christopher D. Morris and D. James Rackham, eds., *Norse and Later Settlement and Subsistence in the North Atlantic*, pp. 193–230. Department of Archeology, University of Glasgow, Occasional Paper Series No. 1. Glasgow: 1992.

———. "Economics of Extinction in Norse Greenland." In T. M. Wrigley, M. J. Ingram, and G. Farmer, eds., *Climate and History: Studies in Past Climates and Their Impact on Man*, pp. 404–34. Cambridge, Eng.: Cambridge University Press, 1980.

———. "Zooarchaeology of the Vatnahverfi." In C. L. Vebæk, "Vatnahverfi: An inland district of the Eastern Settlement in Greenland," pp. 93–107. *MoG, Man & Society*, 17. Copenhagen: 1992.

McGovern, Thomas, and G. F. Bigelow. "Archaezoology of the Norse Site Ø17a Narssaq District, Southwest Greenland." *Acta Borealia*, 1984, no. 1: 85–101.

McGrath, Patrick. *The Merchant Venturers of Bristol*. Bristol: 1975.

———. "Bristol and America 1480–1631." In K. R. Andrews, W. P. Canny, and P. E. H. Hair, eds., *The Westward Enterprise: English Activities in Ireland, the Atlantic, and America ca. 1480–1650*, pp. 81–102. Liverpool: 1978.

McGuirk, Donald L., Jr. "Ruysch World Map: Census and Commentary." *Imago Mundi* 41 (1989): 133–41.

McNeill, William H. *Plagues and Peoples*. New York: 1976.

Meldgaard, Jørgen. "Bopladsen Qajaa i Jakobshavn Isfjord." *Grønland* 39 (1991): 191–205.

———. "Inuit-Nordboprojektet. Arkæologiske undersøgelser i Vesterbygden i Grønland." In *Fra Nationalmuséets Arbejdsmark*, pp. 159–69. Copenhagen: 1977.

———. "Inuit-Nordboundersøgelsen, 1976." *Grønland* 24 (1976): 33–44.

———. "Tjodhildes kirke på Brattahlid." *Grønland* 12 (1964): 281–99.

Milano, Ernesto. *La Carta del Cantino*. Modena: 1991.

Moltke, Erik. "Greenland Runic Inscriptions I." *MoG* 88 (2): 223–32. Copenhagen: 1936.

Morison, Samuel Eliot. *Christopher Columbus, Mariner*. London: 1956.

———. *The European Discovery of America: The Northern Voyages*. Vol. 1. New York: Oxford University Press, 1971.

———. *Portuguese Voyages to America in the Fifteenth Century*. Cambridge, Mass.: 1940.

Munch, Peter Andreas. *Pavelige Nuntiers Regnskabe*. Oslo: 1864.

Myhre, Bjørn. "The Iron-Age Farm in Southwest Norway." *Norwegian Archaeological Review* 6 (1973): 14–29.

Møhl, Jeppe. "Ressourceudnyttelse fra norrøne og eskimoiske affaldslag belyst gennem knoglematerialet." *Grønland* 30 (1982): 286–95.

Nansen, Fridtjof. *Nord i Taakeheimen*. Oslo: 1911.

Nebenzahl, Kenneth. *Atlas of Columbus and the Great Discoveries*. Chicago: Rand McNally, 1990.

Nielsen, Niels. "Evidence on the Extraction of Iron in Greenland by the Norsemen." *MoG* 76: 193–213. Copenhagen, 1930.

Nordenskiöld, Nils A. E. *Facsimile Atlas to the Early History of Cartography*. New York: Kraus Reprint, 1961 [1889].

Nørlund, Poul. "Buried Norsemen at Herjolfsnes." *MoG* 67 (1). Copenhagen: 1924.

Nørlund, Poul, and Aage Roussell. "Norse Ruins at Gardar, the Episcopal Seat of Mediaeval Greenland." *MoG* 76 (1). Copenhagen: 1929.

Nørlund, Poul, and Mårten Stenberger. "Brattahlid." *MoG* 88 (1). Copenhagen: 1934.

Oddsson, Gísli. "Annalium in Islandia Farrago" and "De Mirabilibus Islandiae." Halldór Hermannsson, ed. In *Islandica* 10. Ithaca, N.Y.: 1917.

Ogilvie, A. E. G. "Climatic Changes in Iceland A.D. ca. 865 to 1598." *Acta Archaeologica* 61 (1990 [1991]): 233–51.

Oleson, Tryggvi J. *Early Voyages and Northern Approaches, 1000–1632.* London: The Canadian Centenary Series, 1964.

Painter, G. D. "The Matter of Authenticity." *The Geographical Journal* 140 (1974): 191–94.

Pálsson, Hermann. "Landafundurinn árið 1285." *Saga* 4 (1964): 53–69.

Pang, Kevin D. "Climatic Impact of the Mid-Fifteenth Century Kuwae Caldera Formation, as Reconstructed from Historical and Proxy Data." *Eos* 74 (1993): 106.

Parry, J. H. *The Discovery of the Sea.* London: Weidenfeld, 1975.

Parry, M. C. "Climatic Change and the Agricultural Frontier." In T. M. L. Wrigley, M. J. Ingram, and G. Farmer, eds., *Climate and History: Studies in Past Climates and Their Impact on Man.* Cambridge (England): Cambridge University Press, 1980.

Pastor, Ludwig. *The History of the Popes.* Frederick Ignatius Antrobus, ed. Vols. 1–2. London: John Hodges; Kegan Paul & Co., 1891.

Peacock, John. *Costumes, 1066–1966.* London: Thames and Hudson, 1986.

Pedersen, Alwin. "Narhvalen, grønlændernes højt værdsatte jagtvildt." *Grønland* 10 (1962): 464–71.

Pedersen, Erling. "Ikâmiut, Sukkertoppen Distrikt: Historisk strejflys over en nedlagt boplads." *Grønland* 14 (1966): 219–22.

Pelletier, Monique. "Peut-on encore affirmer que la BN possède la carte de Christophe Colomb?" *Revue de la Bibliothèque Nationale* 45 (1992): 22–25.

Phillips, Carla Rahn. "The Growth and Composition of Trade in the Iberian Empires, 1450–1750." In James D. Tracy, ed., *The Rise of Merchant Empires,* pp. 34–101. New York: Cambridge University Press, 1990.

Power, Eileen, and Postan, M. M., eds. *Studies in English Trade in the Fifteenth Century.* London: Studies in Economic and Social History 5, 1933.

Prestage, Edgar. "Portuguese Expansion Overseas, Its Causes and Results." In Edgar Prestage, ed., *Chapters in Anglo-Portuguese Relations.* London: 1935.

———. *The Portuguese Pioneers.* London: A. and C. Black, 1933.

Pulsiano, Phillip, ed. *Medieval Scandinavia.* New York: Garland Publishing, 1993.

Quinn, David Beers. "Columbus and the North: England, Iceland, and Ireland." *The William and Mary Quarterly,* Series 3: 49, no. 2 (1992): 278–97.

———. *England and the Discovery of America, 1481–1620.* London: Allen and Unwin, 1974.

———. *Explorers and Colonies: America, 1500–1625.* London: The Hambledon Press, 1990.

———. *Ireland and America: Their Early Associations, 1500–1640.* Liverpool: 1991.

———. *North America from Earliest Discoveries to First Settlements: The Norse Voyages to 1612.* London: Harper and Row, 1977.

Quinn, David Beers, Alison M. Quinn, and Susan Hillier, eds. *New American World: A Documentary History of North America to 1612.* 5 vols. New York: 1979.

Rey, L. "Gardar, the 'Diocese of Ice.'" *Arctic* 37, no. 4 (1984): 324–33.

Rink, Henry. *Eskimoiske Eventyr og Sagn*. Copenhagen: 1866.

———. *Tales and Traditions of the Eskimos*. Edinburgh: 1875.

Rosenørn, Stig, Jens Fabricius, Erik Buch, and Svend Aage Horsted. "Isvinter ved Vestgrønland: Klima, vestis, oceanografi og biologi." *Forskning i Grønland/tusaat* 1981, no. 4: 2–19.

Roussell, Aage. "Farms and Churches in the Mediaeval Norse Settlements of Greenland." With an Appendix by Magnus Degerbøl, "The Osseous Material from Austmannadal and Tungmeralik." *MoG* 89 (1). Copenhagen: 1941.

———. "Sandnes and the Neighbouring Farms." With an Appendix by Erik Molkte on "Greenland Runic Inscriptions I." *MoG* 88 (2). Copenhagen: 1936.

Ruddock, Alwyn A. "Columbus and Iceland: New Light on an Old Problem." *The Geographical Journal* 136 (2): 177–89. London: 1970.

———. "John Day of Bristol and the English Voyages Across the Atlantic Before 1497." *The Geographical Journal* 132, no. 2 (1966): 225–32.

———. "The Reputation of Sebastian Cabot." *Bulletin of the Institute for Historical Research* 47 (1974): 95–99.

Sacks, David Harris. *The Widening Gate: Bristol and the Atlantic Economy, 1450–1700*. Berkeley: University of California Press, 1991.

Sadler, J. "Beetles, Boats and Biogeography." *Acta Archaeologica* 61 (1990 [1991]): 199–211.

Salomonsen, Finn. "Ornithological and Ecological Studies in S.W. Greenland (59°46′–62°27′N. Lat.)." *MoG* 204 (6). Copenhagen: 1979.

Salvesen, Helge. "The Hoset Project." *Norwegian Archaeological Review* 10 (1977): 109–49.

Schledermann, Peter. "Ellesmere Island: Eskimo and Viking Finds in the High Arctic." *National Geographic* 159, no. 5 (1981): 574–601.

———. "Nordbogenstande fra Arktisk Canada" (Hans Christian Gulløv, trans.). *Grønland* 30 (1982): 218–25.

———. "Norsemen in the High Arctic?" In B. L. Clausen, ed., *Viking Voyages to North America*. Odense: The Viking Ship Museum, 1993.

———. "Notes on Norse Finds from the East Coast of Ellesmere Island, N.W.T." *Arctic* 33 (1980): 454–63.

———. "Preliminary Results of Archaeological Investigations in the Bache Peninsula Region, Ellesmere Island, NWT." *Arctic* 31 (1978): 459–74.

Schubert, John R. T. *History of the British Iron and Steel Industry, ca. 450 B.C.–A.D. 1775*. London: Routledge and Kegan Paul, 1957.

Scott, G. Richard, Carrin M. Halffman, and P. O. Pedersen. "Dental Conditions of Medieval Norsemen in the North Atlantic." *Acta Archaeologica* 62 (1991 [1992]): 183–207.

Seaver, Kirsten A. "The 'Vinland Map': Who Made It, and Why? New Light on an Old Problem." *The Map Collector* 70 (Spring 1995).

Simek, Rudolf. "Elusive Elysia or Which Way to Glæsisvellir? On the Geography of the North in Icelandic Legendary Fiction." In Rudolf Simek, Jónas Kristjánsson, and Hans Bekker-Nielsen, eds., *Sagnaskemmtun: Studies in Honour of Hermann Pálsson*, pp. 247–75. Vienna: 1986.

Skaare, Kolbjørn. "Skilling, alen og bismerpund." In *Norges Kulturhistorie* 5.

Skelton, R. A. *Prince Henry the Navigator and Portuguese Maritime Enterprise.* Catalogue of an Exhibition at the British Museum, Sept.-Oct. 1960. London: The British Museum.

Skelton, R. A., Thomas E. Marston, and George D. Painter. *The Vinland Map and the Tartar Relation.* New Haven, Conn., 1965.

Skovgaard-Petersen, Inge. "Islandsk egenkirkevæsen." *Scandia* 26 (1960): 230–96.

Slack, Paul. *The Impact of Plague in Tudor and Stuart England.* London: 1985.

Sneyd, Charlotte Augusta, trans. and ed. *A Relation . . . of the Island of England . . . About the Year 1500.* Camden Society (London), Series 1: 37 (1847).

Stefansson, Vilhjalmur, and Eloise McCaskill. *The Three Voyages of Martin Frobisher.* 2 vols. London: Argonaut Press, 1938.

Steinnes, Asgaut. "Ikring Historia Norvegiae." *Historisk Tidsskrift* 34: 1–61. Oslo: 1946–48.

Stoklund, Marie. "Nordbokorsene fra Grønland." In *Fra Nationalmuséets Arbejdsmark*, pp. 101–13. Copenhagen: The National Museum, 1983.

Sturtevant, William C., and David Beers Quinn. "This New Prey: Eskimos in Europe in 1567, 1576, and 1577." In Christian F. Feest, ed. *Indians and Europe.* Aachen: 1987.

Sølver, Carl V. *Vestervejen. Om Vikingernes Sejlads.* Copenhagen: 1954.

Sørensen, Ingrid. "Pollenundersøgelser i møddingen på Niaqussat." *Grønland* 30 (1982): 296–304.

Taagholt, Jørgen, and H. C. Bach. "Hvad foregår der af videnskabelig aktivitet i Grønland idag?" *Grønland* 23 (1975): 213–20.

Taylor, E. G. R. "A Letter Dated 1577 from Mercator to John Dee." *Imago Mundi* (Stockholm) 13 (1956): 56–67.

Taylor, E. G. R., W. E. May, T. C. Lethbridge, and R. B. Motzo. "A Norse Bearing Dial?" *Journal of the Institute of Navigation* 7 (1954): 78–84.

Thirslund, Søren. "Navigation by the Vikings on the Open Sea." In Birthe L. Clausen, ed., *Viking Voyages to North America*, pp. 109–17. Roskilde: The Viking Ship Museum, 1993.

Thirslund, S., and C. L. Vebæk. *Vikingernes Kompas: 1000-årig pejlskive fundet i Grønland.* Kronborg, Denmark: Handels- og Søfartsmuséet, 1990.

Thomas, Keith. *Religion and the Decline of Magic.* London: 1971.

Thorsteinsson, Björn. *Enska öldin í sögu íslendinga.* Reykjavik: 1970.

———. "Henry VIII and Iceland." *Saga-Book* 15: 67–101. London: 1957–59.

———. "Íslands- og Grænlandssiglingar Englendinga á 15. öld og fundur Norður-Ameríku." *Saga* 4–5 (1965–67): 3–72.

Tracy, James D., ed. *The Rise of Merchant Empires.* New York: Cambridge University Press, 1990.

Trondhjems Sjøfartsmuseum (The Trondheim Maritime Museum). Information pamphlet obtained on 1993 visit.

Tuck, James. *Red Bay, Labrador.* St. John's, Newfoundland: 1989.

Tylecote, R. F. *A History of Metallurgy.* London: 1992.

Vahl, M., G. C. Amdrup, L. Bobé, and A. D. Jensen, eds. *Greenland.* 3 vols. London: 1928–29.

Vandvik, Eirik. *Latinske dokument til norsk historie fram til år 1204.* Oslo: 1959.

Veale, Elspeth Mary. *The English Fur Trade.* Oxford: Clarendon Press, 1966.

Vebæk, Chr. Leif. "The Church Topography of the Eastern Settlement and the Excavation of the Benedictine Convent at Narsarsuaq in the Uunartoq Fjord." *MoG, Man & Society* 14. Copenhagen: 1991.

———. "Hunting on Land and at Sea and Fishing in Medieval Norse Greenland." *Acta Borealia* 8, no. 1 (1991): 5–14.

———. "Klostre i de grønlandske Nordbobygder." *Grønland* 5 (1953): 195–200.

———. "Vatnahverfi: An Inland District of the Eastern Settlement in Greenland." *MoG, Man & Society* 17. Copenhagen: 1992.

———. "Vatnahverfi: En middelalderlig bondebygd i Grønland." In *Fra Nationalmuséets Arbejdsmark*, pp. 101–14. Copenhagen: The National Museum, 1952.

Vebæk, Chr. Leif, and Søren Thirslund. *The Viking Compass Guided Norsemen First to America.* Skjern, Denmark: 1992.

Vigneras, L.-A. "The Cape Breton Landfall: 1494 or 1497. Note on a Letter from John Day." *The Canadian Historical Review* 38 (1957): 219–28.

———. "New Light on the 1497 Cabot Voyage to America." *The Hispanic-American Historical Review* 36 (1956): 503–9.

———. "The Voyages of Diogo and Manoel de Barcelos to Canada in the Sixteenth Century." *Terrae Incognitae* (Amsterdam) 5 (1973): 61–64.

Wallace, Birgitta Linderoth. "L'Anse aux Meadows, the Western Outpost." In Birthe L. Clausen, ed., *Viking Voyages to North America*, pp. 30–42. Roskilde: The Viking Ship Museum, 1993.

Wallis, Helen. "Is the Paris Map the Long-Sought Chart of Christopher Columbus?" *The Map Collector*, 1992 (Spring): 20–21. London: The British Map Library.

Wallis, Helen, F. R. Maddison, G. D. Painter, D. B. Quinn, et al. "The Strange Case of the Vinland Map." *The Geographical Journal* 140 (1974): 183–217.

Wallis, Helen, and Arthur H. Robinson, eds. *Cartographical Innovations: An International Handbook of Mapping Terms to 1900.* London: Map Collector Publications in Association with the International Cartographic Association, 1987.

Wee, Herman van der. *Growth of the Antwerp Market and the European Economy, 14th to 16th Century.* Vol. 2. Louvain: 1963.

Wickham, Chris. "Problems of Comparing Rural Societies in Early Medieval Western Europe." *Transactions of the Royal Historical Society*, Sixth Series, pp. 221–46. London: 1992.

Williamson, James A. *The Cabot Voyages and Bristol Discovery Under Henry VII.* With the cartography of the voyage by R. A. Skelton. Cambridge, Eng.: 1962.

———. *Maritime Enterprise, 1485–1558.* Oxford: 1913.

Wrigley, T. M. L., M. J. Ingram, and G. Farmer, eds. *Climate and History. Studies in Past Climates and Their Impact on Man.* Cambridge, Eng.: Cambridge University Press, 1980.

Index

In this index, an "f" after a number indicates a separate reference on the next page, and an "ff" indicates separate references on the next two pages. A continuous discussion over two or more pages is indicated by a span of page numbers, e.g., "57–59." *Passim* is used for a cluster of references in close but not consecutive sequence. In all subheadings below, the letters æ-ä will be listed at the end of the regular English alphabet, followed by the letters ø-ö and å-á. The letter ü will follow immediately upon the regular u. The medieval Norse are listed under their first names, while modern Icelandic writers appear under their patronymics. The following abbreviations appear with place names: E = England; G = Greenland; I = Iceland; N = Norway; ES = Eastern Settlement; WS = Western Settlement; NA = North America.

Abduction and captivity, 178, 193, 251, 297; of children, 179, 193, 355, 361; as component of piracy, 6, 13, 174–76, 180; for slavery, 193, 205ff, 258, 302–3, 309–10. *See also* Piracy
Absolution, *see* Excommunication and absolution
Adalbrand Helgason, 76
Adam of Bremen, 34, 45, 49, 210
Adaptation, 6, 12–13, 59f, 239–49, 252–53. *See also* Climatic factors; Isolation
Akrar (I), 155f, 163, 183, 190, 325f
Alþing (legislative and judicial assembly): in Greenland, 62f, 148, 340–42; in Iceland, 62ff, 169, 177, 183ff, 204; petitions from, 77, 157, 168–69, 176f, 184–85, 204, 320, 328
Ameralik (G), 109, 118, 126
Ameralla (G), 109, 120, 126
Amerindian peoples, *see under* Native Americans
Ameryk, Richard, 206, 222, 273, 297, 329
Ammassalik region (G), 19, 46, 211

Andreasen, Claus, 51–53, 95–98 *passim*, 114, 119f
Anglo-Azorean Syndicate, *see under* Bristol
Annálar (New Annals), 165, 178, 183f. *See also* Icelandic Annals
Antilia, *see* Brazil, Isle of
Archaeology: in Greenland, 2, 7–13 *passim*, 44–47 *passim*, 66–67, 95; in America, 9, 24, 30, 37–42 *passim*, 310–11; in Norway, 9, 115; obstacles to, 9–10, 54, 97, 115–20 *passim*, 130, 230–31, 241. *See also* Andreasen, Claus; Arneborg, Jette; Berglund, Joel; Bruun, Daniel; Gulløv, Hans Christian; Mathiassen, Therkel; McGovern, Thomas; Nørlund, Poul; Roussell, Aage; Skeletal remains; Vebæk, C. L.
Archbishops, *see* Norwegian archbishops
Archbishops, non-Norwegian, 45, 69
Architecture, *see* Houses and house types
Arms and armor, 12, 38–43 *passim*, 103, 108, 119–24 *passim*, 131, 184, 232, 302. *See also* Arrowheads; Harpoons and spears; Metals and metalworking

Arneborg, Jette, 11, 26, 55, 98, 114, 119, 131, 228, 335f, 351; photographs by, 20, 22, 116, 154; on Norse relations with Eskimo cultures, 37, 103–5, 141, 365; on communications between Norse Greenland and the rest of Europe, 63, 71, 87–88, 358; on Norse relations with Church of Rome, 64, 71, 93, 110–11

Arnfinn Thorsteinsson, 168, 176–77, 315–20 *passim*

Arngrímur Jónsson, 67

Arni (Greenland priest), 72

Arni Ólafsson, *see under* Bishops

Arpatsivik (G), *see* Hvalsey

Arrowheads, 11, 26, 54, 335, 346. *See also* Arms and armor

Art, *see* Carved images

Asia: as object of exploration, 213, 222, 236, 263–75 *passim*, 300, 307; North America mistaken for, 213–15, 254, 259, 265–76 *passim*. *See also* Maps and mapping

Asshehurst, Thomas, 291, 294–99 *passim*, 304–6 *passim*, 329

Atlakviða ("Lay of Atli"), 44

Austmannadal (G), 113f, 127–30 *passim*

Authén Blom, Grethe, 82, 342f

Azores, 213, 257–62 *passim*, 280–81, 287, 291–94 *passim*, 303. *See also* Terceira

Bacallaos, *see* Newfoundland Banks

Baffin Island, 23, 29–34 *passim*, 39f, 124

Balearic Islands, 257

Baltic Sea and Straits, 194–201 *passim*, 234

Baptism, *see* Religious services

Barkham, Selma H., 9, 356

Basques, 9, 176, 257, 356, 375

Bath houses, 58, 126

Beads, 12, 310, 375

Bearing dial, *see* Navigation

Bede (English historian and saint), 28

Behaim, Martin, 135, 261–62, 361

Belgium, *see* Low Countries

Benediktsson, Jakob, 15, 333

Beneventanus, Marcus, 214–17 *passim*

Bergen (N), 66, 71, 99, 111, 136, 141, 187; and Greenland trade, 71, 78–84 *passim*, 122f, 205, 238; as center of Norwegian colonial administration, 77–78, 84–86, 91, 102, 146–49 *passim*, 188; and relations with the crown, 78–85 *passim*, 102f, 132, 146, 150; as center for codfish trade, 82, 157, 165–67 *passim*, 182–85 *passim*, 196, 202–6 *passim*, 251,

319, 343; and relations with the Hanse, 83–84, 133, 139, 144, 182–85 *passim*, 205–6, 251; and Iceland trade, 150–51, 158–62 *passim*, 190, 202, 319; and relations with the English, 157, 182–85 *passim*. *See also* Björn Einarsson; Fishing and fish trade; Hanse; Ívar Bárdarson; Norwegian archbishops; Royal chapels; Thorstein Ólafsson

Berglund, Joel, 113, 119, 142, 153, 240–41, 252f, 311

Bertelsen, Reidar, 366

Bigelow, Gerald F., 54–57 *passim*, 241, 248–50 *passim*

Birds, *see* Diet; Falcons

Bishops, 6, 32–33, 72–74 *passim*, 77–78

—of Gardar (G) and "of Greenland": Arnald, 33, 64–65; Jón *knútr*, 64ff; Jón *smyrrill* Sverrifostri, 65–68 *passim*; Helgi, 68f; Nicholas, 69; Ólaf, 70–76 *passim*; Thord, 76–79, 342; Arni, 79, 85–91 *passim*, 149; Jón Eiriksson (*skalli*), 86–88 *passim*, 111; Alf, 111–12, 140–45 *passim*, 149; Henrik, 145; Jón, 145, 157; Berthold, 145, 156; Peter (of Strengnes), 145; Anders, 145; Georgius, 145; Peter Staras, 145; Johannes Petersson, 146; Jacob Treppe, 146, 157, 359; Andres, 157, 197–99 *passim*, 327; Bartholomew, 174, 186, 358; Gregorius, 188; Jacob, 198; Mathias Knutsson, 237–38, 365; Jacob Blaa, 238; Vincent Petersson, 309

—of Hólar (I): Ketil, 64; Brand, 65; Gudmund Árason, 69; Björn Hjaltason (*electus*), 69; Bótolf, 70; Heinrek, 70f; Jón Eiriksson (*skalli*), 88; Orm, 88, 348; Jón Vilhjamsson Craxton, 153, 168, 182–87 *passim*, 325, 358; Jón Bloxwich, 186–87; Gottskálk Keneksson, 190; Matthew, 190–97

—of Skálholt (I): Ísleif Gizurarson, 45, 49; Thorlak Runolfsson, 63–68 *passim*; Páll Jónsson, 65–68 *passim*; Magnus, 69; Magnus Gudmundsson (*electus*), 69; Sigvard, 70; Jón, 93, 345; Vilchin, 139; Arni Ólafsson, 158–69 *passim*, 176, 315–22 *passim*, 327; Marcellus, 175, 189–90, 195–99 *passim*; Jón Gereksson, 179, 184–86 *passim*, 356; Gottsvin Comhaer, 187–90 *passim*; Svein, 327; Odd Einarsson, 353. *See also* Bergen; Eirik Gnúpsson *upsi*; Episcopal representatives; Gísli Oddsson

Bittles, Alan H., 239

Bjarni Herjolfsson, 1, 17, 23, 165

Björn Brynjolfsson, 152–56 *passim*, 323–25

Björn Einarsson ("Jerusalem-Farer"), 71, 147–51 *passim*, 155–64 *passim*, 177, 195–99 *passim*, 315–25 *passim*, 352

Björn Jónsson from Skardsá, 29, 42, 67, 308, 337

Björn Thorleifsson, 150, 164, 194–99 *passim*, 317ff

Bjørnbo, Aksel Anton, 34–35, 167, 211, 262

Black Death, *see* Plague

Blubber and fish oil, 48, 218, 248, 305f. *See also* Diet; Fuel; Trade items

Bobé, Louis, 200

Bones, *see* McGovern, Thomas; Middens; Skeletal remains

Botanical research, *see* Fredskild, Bent

Bradley, Thomas, 274

Brand Halldórsson, 152, 163–65, 178, 199

Brattahlid (G), 7, 20–22 *passim*, 26, 50–53 *passim*, 62–65, 95, 102–3, 235, 243–45. *See also* Eirik the Red

Brazil, Isle of, 192, 211–23 *passim*, 257–61 *passim*, 266–71 *passim*, 276–80 *passim*, 290f, 310

Brendan, Saint, 208

Bristol (E), 159–60, 179f, 193, 205–8 *passim*, 234, 249, 295–96, 301, 356; fishing and trade from, 170, 179–82, 187–89, 193–98 *passim*, 214–29 *passim*, 264–72, 297–306 *passim*; exploration from, 180–81, 192, 217–24, 252, 268–74, 288–91; and Anglo-Azorean Syndicate, 192–93, 255, 267–69 *passim*, 283, 291–310 *passim*, 372; merchant adventurers of, 295–97. *See also* Cabot, John; Cabot, Sebastian; Elyot, Hugh; Fernandes, João; Textiles

Bronze, *see* Metals and metalworking

Bruun, Daniel, 97, 119, 124, 128, 375

Butter, 48, 82, 109, 194

Butternut (white walnut), 24

Burials, *see* Nørlund, Poul; Roussell, Aage; Rituals

Buxer, Thomas, 218, 363

Cabot, John, 1f, 205, 213, 222–23, 265–80 *passim*, 287–306 *passim*, 373

Cabot, Sebastian, 2, 266–72 *passim*, 287–301 *passim*, 307, 372

Cabral, Pedro Alvares, 263, 277, 367–70 *passim*

Campbell clan, 121–22, 131

Canary Islands, 213, 221, 257–60 *passim*, 264

Cantino, Alberto, 277–80, 380

Canynges, William, 187f, 193f

Cape Farewell (G), 170–72 *passim*, 201, 237, 275–79 *passim*, 285

Cape Verde Islands, 213, 257, 263

Carbon dating, *see* Dates and dating

Caribou, 21, 38, 48, 54f, 118ff, 128, 242. *See also* Diet; Hunting

Cartier, Jacques, 24, 303

Carus-Wilson, Eleanora Mary, 179, 220, 355f, 362

Carved images, 39–42 *passim*, 124–26, 131, 227–29 *passim*. *See also* Clothing; Symbols, Christian and pagan

Castile, 157–58

Caterpillars, 114–15

Cathay, *see* Asia

Cats, 56, 339

Cattle, *see* Livestock

Cartography, *see* Maps and mapping

Centralized farms, *see* Farms and farming; Houses and house types

Chain mail, *see* Arms and armor

Charles V, 309

Chess, *see* Games and gaming pieces

Children as captives, *see* Abduction and piracy

Chieftains, 48, 62–65, 70, 92–95, 101–2; in Iceland, 79, 140, 152, 158–62 *passim*, 168–74, 183–85. *See also* Family connections and kinship

Christian faith and practice, 61f, 68, 86–87, 91–102 *passim*, 107, 156, 174. *See also* Religious services; Rituals; Symbols, Christian and pagan

Church bells, *see* Metals and metalworking

Church construction in Greenland, 65–68, 154

Church farms, *see* Farms and farming

Church of Rome, 6, 69, 112, 139, 143–46, 182–83; establishment of, in the Far North, 33–36, 45, 61ff; later relations of, with Greenland, 44, 61–69 *passim*, 95–102 *passim*, 112, 139, 143, 174–76, 235–37 *passim*, 250. *See also* Bishops; Christian faith and practice; Church construction in Greenland; Clergy; Curia; Episcopal representatives; Parish churches; Norwegian Archbishops; Secular control; Tithes and tithing

Clavus, Claudius, 166–67, 215, 276

Clergy, 67–68, 74ff, 85f, 110ff, 183, 356; in Greenland, 6, 63, 67f, 95–101 *passim*, 111, 156, 238, 350; as participants in exploration ventures, 273–74, 299

Clerk, William, 267, 301, 329

Climatic factors, 6, 8, 21f, 53, 242, 310; in
farming, 51–55 *passim*, 115–19, 239–
48, 252–53, 306; in population growth
and losses, 77, 89, 115. *See also* Adaptation; Erosion and overgrazing; Fodder
and pasturage; Ice; Navigation
Clocks, *see* Navigation
Cloth, *see* Textiles
Clothing, 5, 9–12 *passim*, 39–42 *passim*,
47f, 77–78, 87, 124–26; as evidence of
Greenland's foreign contacts after 1400,
70–73, 125, 227–31, 252, 306f, 311. *See
also* Carved images; Textiles
Cnoyen, Jacobus, 133–37 *passim*
Coats of arms, 120–22, 131, 190, 195,
349, 359
Cod, 56f, 74, 118, 162, 186, 217, 247ff,
272–73; exploitation of, 151, 158–63
passim, 170–72 *passim*, 182, 187, 192,
209, 217, 257, 302; competition for,
162–63, 170, 176–87 *passim*, 203–6
passim, 222, 252; preservation of, 162,
172, 193, 220, 226, 237, 249, 305. *See
also* Bergen; Bristol; England; Fishing
and fish trade; Hanse; Iceland, Newfoundland Banks; Norwegian archbishops; Stockfish; Trade items; Trade restrictions
Coins and coinage, 74f, 80, 85, 343, 355.
See also Metals and metalworking
Colonization: of Iceland and Greenland, 1,
14f, 19–23, 307; of North America, 14,
26–27, 33–36 *passim*, 280, 302–6 *passim*, 322, 336; of Portuguese and Spanish
Atlantic islands, 213, 257f, 291f. *See
also* Eastern Settlement; Emigration;
Western Settlement
Columbus, Bartholomew, 208–9
Columbus, Christopher, 8, 134, 207–11,
222–23, 253ff, 259–71 *passim*, 280, 368
Columbus, Ferdinand, 134, 208
Communications, 2, 47, 132, 162, 170,
260–61, 302, 307–11, 341; between
Norway and Greenland, 2, 6f, 44, 61–77
passim, 81–90 *passim*, 132, 139f, 151,
157, 161; between Iceland and Greenland, 27, 63–66, 72f, 88, 151, 156, 169–
73, 180, 185, 191, 198–99; between
Norway and Iceland, 64–69 *passim*, 77,
81, 88–90, 139f, 160ff, 182; between
the British Isles and other North Atlantic
countries, 88, 100, 121–24, 137, 161f,
180–87 *passim*, 350; between the Nordic countries and Rome, 66, 69, 73–75,
341. *See also* Björn Einarsson; Bergen;

Bristol; Davis Strait; England; *Inventio
fortunata*; Norwegian archbishops; Por-
tugal; Spain; Thorstein Ólafsson; Trade
Compass, *see* Navigation
Consanguinity: and church policy concern-
ing marriage, 33–36 *passim*; and the de-
bate concerning genetic deterioration
among the Norse Greenlanders, 33–36
passim, 239
Convicts, use of, in early exploration, 273,
303–4, 374–75
Coopering, 38, 42
Copenhagen, 5, 10–12 *passim*, 47, 97,
182, 190f, 195, 199. *See also* Denmark;
Monarchs, Norwegian and Dano-
Norwegian
Copper, *see* Metals and metalworking
Corsica, 257
Corte Real, Gaspar, 213, 260–63 *passim*,
269, 274–87 *passim*, 292f, 303
Corte Real, João Vaz, 200, 259–62, 275f
Corte Real, Miguel, 261–63 *passim*, 274–
81 *passim*, 285–87 *passim*, 292f, 303
Corte Real, Vasco Annes, 261–63 *passim*,
274–81 *passim*
Cortesão, Jaime, 263–64
Cosmology and geography, *see* Maps and
mapping *and individual cartographers by
name*
Council of Regency (of Norwegian nobles),
75, 190, 202, 342f
Courts, *see* Law courts
Covenant of Union (1263), *see* Gamli
sáttmáli
Crantz, David, 165
Croft, Thomas, 220–22, 266, 329
Crone, G. R., 264
Crosses and crucifixes, *see* Symbols, Christian and pagan
Crown, Norwegian and Dano-Norwegian:
waning interest in Greenland of, 6, 66,
70, 76, 112, 139, 250, 257, 307; politics
and prerogatives of, 70–76 *passim*, 91,
148, 157–68 *passim*, 179–98 *passim*,
225. *See also* Bergen; Crown representatives; Hanse; Monarchs, Norwegian and
Dano-Norwegian
Crown representatives: in Iceland, 70f,
102–3, 157–58 *passim*, 176–79, 183,
192–204 *passim*, 355; in Greenland,
71ff, 85, 91, 102, 347; in Norway, 80,
102. *See also* Ívar Bárdarson; Pining,
Didrik
Curia, 34, 74, 110–12, 202, 263, 309; concerns of, for the Far North, 5, 33–36 *pas-*

sim, 45, 68f, 74ff, 80f, 87, 96; ignorance of, about the Far North, 87, 174–76, 309, 355–56. *See also* Church of Rome; Jón rauð; Norwegian archbishops; Popes
Currents and wind patterns, *see* Navigation

D'Ailly, Pierre, 210
Da Gama, Vasco, 257–77 *passim*, 367f
Dansgaard, Willy, 245–46
Dates and dating, 22, 38–42 *passim*, 54, 60, 67–68, 105; methods in, 11, 332; problems in, 15, 29, 72f, 142, 227, 233, 241
Davis Strait, 1, 22–42 *passim*, 107f, 124, 132, 165, 192, 215
Day, John, 34, 222–23, 266–73 *passim*
De Agramonte, John, 372
De Ayala, Dom Pedro, 223, 266, 271–74 *passim*
De Azurara, Gómez Eannes, 256
De Barcelos, Alfonso, 281
De Barcelos, Diogo, 281–82, 371
De Barcelos, Manoel, 281, 371
De Barcelos, Pedro, 281–84 *passim*, 371
De Barcelos Machado, Marcos, 281
De Covilhã, Pedro, 262
De Gómara, Francisco López, 254f
De Hürter, Jobst (father and son), 261
De la Cosa, Juan, 270
De la Fount, William, 220, 329
De la Peyrère, Isaac, 205, 251
De la Roncière, Charles, 208–13 *passim*, 279
De las Casas, Bartolomeo, 134
De Lima, Baptiste, 281–82
De Niveriis, Marcellus, 175, 189–90, 195–99 *passim*
De Puebla, Rodrigo Gonzales, 265–66, 363
De Santa Cruz, Alonzo, 287, 372
De Soncino, Raimondo, 272–74
De Tieve, Diogo, 260
Dee, John, 133–37 *passim*, 268f
Delaney, Frank, 98
Denmark, 39, 87f, 123, 144, 167, 182, 188, 201, 256, 307. *See also* Copenhagen; Crown, Norwegian and Dano-Norwegian; Monarchs, Norwegian and Dano-Norwegian
Denmark Strait, 170, 218, 247, 275, 284, 291
"Description of Greenland," *see* Ívar Bárdarson
Días, Bartolomeo, 262–64 *passim*
Diet, 21, 48–58 *passim*, 74, 120, 127, 162,

220–21, 241–42, 253. *See also* Fishing and fish trade; Grain; Malnutrition; McGovern, Thomas
Diseases (human and animal), 58–60, 130, 311, 339. *See also* Epidemics; Plague (bubonic and pneumonic); Skeletal remains
Disko Bay region (G), 26, 38, 41, 57, 124, 137, 227
Do Estreito, Joham Affonso, *see* Dulmo, Fernão
Dogs, 57f, 339
Dolls, *see* Carved images
Dowry, 94, 155
Drifting off-course, *see* Navigation
Driftwood, *see* Forests and forest products
Dúason, Jón, 108
Dulmo, Fernão, 213, 367

Eastern Settlement (G), 20–21, 33, 43, 63, 69, 102–4, 172; end of, 1f, 5–6, 47, 86, 224, 306–11; theories on decline of, 5–7, 12, 80–81, 95, 237–41; churches and clergy in, 6, 61–63, 67–69, 91–96, 156, 174–76; contact with Thule Eskimo people, 6, 101; excavations in, 11, 53, 55. *See also* Bergen; Brattahlid; Gardar; Herjolfsnes; Hvalsey; Ívar Bárdarson; Narsaq; Narsarsuaq; Western Settlement
Ecological problems, *see* Erosion and overgrazing
Economic fluctuations and inflation, 6–11 *passim*, 44, 76–89 *passim*, 96, 100, 112, 139–40, 156–59 *passim*, 182
Egede, Hans, 11, 35, 307, 375
Egede, Niels, 355
Egede, Poul, 113
Eiderdown, 48, 81, 109
Einar Björnsson, 204, 328
Einar Sokkason, 63–65
Einarsfjord (G), 62
Eindridi Andreasson, 156
Eindridi (Canon, later Archbishop, of Nidaros in Norway), 75, 342
Eindridi Erlendsson, 158, 165
Eirik Gnúpsson *upsi*, 32–33, 63, 165
Eirik the Red (Thorvaldsson), 1, 6, 17–27 *passim*, 54, 59–63 *passim*, 153, 165, 172, 211, 235, 253, 276, 306
"Eiriks saga rauða" (The Saga of Eirik the Red), 14f, 19f, 24–26, 61, 164, 236
Eiriksfjord (G), 20, 94
Eliot, John, 206
Ellesmere Island (NA), 38f, 115
Elyot, Hugh: and early American voyages, 268f, 288–90, 294–301 *passim*, 306,

329, 373; and Cabot family, 268, 294–301 *passim*, 329; and litigations of, 269, 295–96, 301–2; and Anglo-Azorean Syndicate, 294–99, 306, 373; and license of 1502, 297–98, 306, 373

Emigration, 13, 113–14, 131, 206, 251–53; to North America, 86, 96, 104–8 *passim*, 113–14, 306–11 *passim*, 348. *See also* Colonization

England, 88; and early voyages in the North Atlantic and Davis Strait, 5, 8, 13, 23, 124, 172, 180, 205–6, 259–62, 309; maritime hegemony of, 144, 171–73, 177–78, 182, 187–91, 197, 225–26; and relations with Denmark-Norway, 158, 177–79, 185–89, 193–205 *passim*, 268, 272; and relations with Iceland, 161–69 *passim*, 176–89 *passim*, 198–205 *passim*; and relations with Greenland, 169–76, 190–92, 223–25, 249–52; and relations with Portugal and Spain, 211–13, 223, 229, 260–64 *passim*, 268. *See also* Bristol; Fishing and fish trade; Hanse; *Inventio fortunatae*; Monarchs, English; Trade

Environmental problems, *see* Climatic factors; Erosion and overgrazing

Epidemics, 6, 59, 130, 140, 181, 185, 191–94 *passim*, 316, 320, 343. *See also* Plague (bubonic and pneumonic)

Episcopal representatives, 85–88 *passim*, 91, 97–99, 102–4, 156. *See also* Ívar Bárdarson

Eric the Red, *see* Eirik the Red

Erlend Philippusson, 147–49 *passim*, 158

Erosion and overgrazing, 6, 115–17 *passim*, 242–48, 306. *See also* Fredskild, Bent

Eskimos, 28, 46, 54f, 72, 113, 133–36 *passim*, 375; Dorset culture, 21, 37f; Thule culture, 21, 37f, 105–8 *passim*, 118, 124f, 172, 227–38, 308; relations of, with Norse Greenlanders, 6, 21, 97, 101–9, 138–43 *passim*, 156, 306, 337, 350, 355. *See also* Inuit-Norse Project of 1976–77; Native Americans

Espólin, Jón, 158, 325, 353

Excommunication and absolution, 75f, 98, 111

Eyvind the Easterner, 20

Fagundes, João Alvares, 282–83, 371

Falcons, 48, 82–85 *passim*, 122–23, 182, 343–44. *See also* Campbell clan; Trade items

Family connections and kinship: in rela-

tions among Norway and its Atlantic colonies, 1, 151–58 *passim*, 190–94 *passim*, 198–99; in early Bristol exploration, 2, 255; in early Norse exploration and colonization, 19–26 *passim*; in early Iberian exploration and colonization, 255, 261–62. *See also individual explorers and colonizers by name*

"Farm beneath the sand, the" (WS), 9, 28, 107, 115–17, 335

Farms and farming, 43, 51–53 *passim*, 114–20, 172, 240, 252–53; church farms, 53, 62, 67, 92–95, 101, 153. *See also* Houses and house types

Faroes, the, 69, 75–78 *passim*, 87f, 92, 111, 177ff, 194, 203, 241

Fernandes, Francisco, 291–302 *passim*, 306, 329

Fernandes, João: and Pedro de Barcelos, 281–87, 291–92, 371; and Bristol, 283, 287–305 *passim*, 329, 372; licenses granted to, 283–84, 291–94, 302, 373; and probable reasons for North American exploration, 283–93 *passim*, 302; and Anglo-Azorean business associates, 283, 291–309 *passim*; and the name Labrador, 285–94 *passim*, 372; and possible connection with Greenland, 285–91, 296, 303–11 *passim*. *See also* Maps and mapping

Fernández-Armesto, Felipe, 257f, 367

Fertility, 7

Festal halls, 95, 153f, 250

Finn Halldórsson, 78–79

Finnbogi Jónsson, 199, 204, 328

Finnmark (N), 179f, 188f, 193, 197, 217

Fischer-Møller, K., 128

Fish oil, *see* Blubber and fish oil

Fishing and fish trade, 5, 13, 118–20, 208–10, 217, 249–52, 262, 292; Norse participation in, 28, 32, 54–57 *passim*, 162, 172, 217; as component of farming, 43, 248. *See also* Bristol; Cod; England; Hanse; Newfoundland Banks; Norwegian archbishops; Portugal; Trade

Fitzhugh, William W., 31, 335

Flanders, *see* Low Countries

"Flatey Annals," *see* Icelandic Annals

Flateyjarbók (The Flatey Book), 15, 63, 67, 165

Flax, 48, 50, 130. *See also* Textiles

Fodder and pasturage, 20f, 56f, 114–19 *passim*, 242–48 *passim*, 253

Foods, *see* Diet

Foote, Peter, 18, 333

Forests and forest products, 126f, 271,

304; Norse Greenlandic sources of, 1, 23f, 27ff, 33–37 *passim*, 49ff, 108, 136ff, 248; Norse Greenlandic use of, 18, 28f, 49f, 335; wood types in, 28, 50f, 120, 127, 358

Forster, John, the Younger, 329

Forster, Stephen, 188, 193

"Fóstbrǽðra saga" (The Fosterbrothers' Saga), 62

France, 195, 202, 206, 220, 224, 234, 255f. *See also* Monarchs, European

Fredskild, Bent, 8, 243–53 *passim*

Friedland, Klaus, 199

Frobisher, Martin, 29–30

Frydendahl, Knud, 46, 115

Fuel, 21, 31, 48, 51

Fur and fur trade, 1, 32f, 37, 47f, 81–83, 138, 181f, 248–50, 304

Fǽrden, Gerd, 364

Gad, Finn, 71, 80

Gade, Kari Ellen, 17, 360

Galway, 205–8 *passim*, 214–19 *passim*, 261, 302, 310. *See also* Ireland

Games and gaming pieces, 40–42 *passim*, 58, 127

Gamli sáttmáli (Covenant of Union, 1263), 71–73, 77, 168, 342

Gardar Cathedral and See, 42, 61–65 *passim*, 85, 93–96, 111, 143, 156, 235

Gardar farm and festal hall, 50, 65, 93–95, 154, 234–35; as administrative center, 62f, 74, 108, 140, 153, 340. *See also* Ívar Bárdarson; Nørlund, Poul

Garde, T. V., 132

Genetic defects, 239. *See also* Skeletal remains

Genoa, 254, 258, 262–65 *passim*

Germanus, Donnus Nicolaus, 259

Germanus, Henricus Martellus, 167, 259

Germany, *see* Hanse

Gilbert, Sir Humphrey, 282

Giske (N), 158–61 *passim*

Gísli Andresson, 151, 163

Gísli Oddsson, 86, 96, 104–7 *passim*, 345, 361

Gizur Thorvaldsson, 70

Glass and pottery, 18, 48, 65, 87, 95, 126, 131, 153, 232–35 *passim*, 310

Goats, *see* Livestock

Gold, *see* Metals and metalworking

Gómes, Diogo, 219

Gonsalves, João, 282, 291–300 *passim*, 306, 329

Goodman, John, 329

"Gottskálk's Annals," *see* Icelandic Annals

Grain, 7, 24f, 47, 50, 57, 74, 152, 183, 187, 231, 238, 304

Grapes, 24f, 236

Grave goods, 41, 96–101 *passim*. *See also* Nørlund, Poul

Greene, Philip, 222, 266, 301, 329

Greenland, descriptions of, in early maps and texts, 45–49 *passim*, 166–67, 174–79 *passim*, 212–18, 277–79, 285–91, 331, 371. *See also* Bristol; Colonization; Eastern Settlement; Maps and mapping; Trade; Western Settlement

Grimsby (E), 58

Grypp, Carsten, 200–201, 360

"Grǽnlendinga saga" (The Saga of the Greenlanders), 14–26 *passim*, 165, 236

"Grǽnlendinga þáttr" (The Greenlanders' Tale), 63–64

Grǽnlandsannáll (Greenland Annals), *see* Björn Jónsson from Skardsá

Gudrid Thorbjarnardaughter, 26–27, 322

Gudrún Styrsdaughter, 151, 163, 352

Gulløv, Hans Christian, 39f, 105ff, 124f, 227–29 *passim*, 308, 329

Gunnbjarnarskerries, 19–20, 211

Gunnbjörn Ulfsson, *see* Gunnbjarnarskerries

Hakluyt, Richard, 134

Hall, Charles Francis, 29–31 *passim*

Hall, James, 307

Hall Ólafsson, 157–61 *passim*, 168, 177, 185, 315–22 *passim*

Halldór (Greenland priest), 42, 72

Halldórsson, Ólafur, 8, 15, 236

Halls, *see* Festal halls

Hamilton Inlet (NA) 310, 335

Hamre, Lars, 32

Hannes Pálsson, 177–79, 182, 355

Hanse, 176, 221, 225–26; in Norway, 78, 83, 139, 144, 162–65 *passim*, 182–85 *passim*, 202–6 *passim*, 251; in Iceland, 144, 199–205 *passim*, 225; in England, 182, 199, 203, 234. *See also* Pining, Didrik; Pothorst, Hans

Hansen, F. C. C., 7, 238

Harpoons and spears, 55f, 128, 131

Harrisse, Henry, 217, 254f, 270

Hastrup, Kirsten, 6, 240–41

Hauk Erlendsson, 15, 164

Hauksbók (Hauk's Book), 14f, 164

Hawks, *see* Falcons

Heathen practices, *see* Paganism

Hebrides, 72, 88, 92, 123, 207

Helgi Gudnason, 183, 199, 316–23 *passim*, 327

Helgi Thordsson, 62
Helluland (NA), *see* Baffin Island
Henry the Navigator, 256f, 366
Herjolfsnes (ES), 47, 62–87, 95, 109, 154, 170–72, 181–82, 234, 304. *See also* Nørlund, Poul
Hides and leather products, 75, 81f, 109, 181–82, 304
Historia Norvegiæ, 34, 45–46, 61
Holand, Hjalmar R., 36
Hólar Cathedral and See (I), 111
Holm, Gustav, 235
Holm Jakobsen, Bjarne, 117
Holsteinsborg region (G), 28, 32, 38, 57. *See also* Norðrseta
Holtved, Erik, 42, 142f, 228
Horses, *see* Livestock
Hoset (N), 246
Houses and house types, 11, 48–54, 65, 120, 154. *See also* Farms and farming
Hrafn Gudmundsson, 163, 320
Hrolf (d. 1295), 33, 76
Hull (E), 178ff, 196, 203–6 *passim*
Hunting, 14, 21, 28, 32, 36, 56, 127, 131, 138; as component of farming, 43, 119, 250–51. *See also* Diet; Fur and fur trade; Norðrseta
Huntington Library (Calif.), 285f, 372
Hvalsey (ES): wedding of Sigrid Björns-daughter and Thorstein Olafsson (1408), 5, 89, 151–56 *passim*, 163f, 168f, 191, 199, 233, 239, 249f, 320–26 *passim*, 353; church belonging to, 67, 153–54; farm and festal hall, 95, 142, 153f, 169–73 *passim*, 235
Hvítramannaland (NA?), 27
Hákon Jónsson, 149, 158
Hákon Sigurdsson, 158
"Hákonar saga Hákonarsonar" (The Saga of Hákon Hákonsson), 70–73 *passim*
Hålogaland (N), 35, 178ff, 189, 197, 209

Ice, 46–49, 83, 115–18 *passim*, 132, 180, 220, 236–38. *See also* Navigation
Ice core research, 8, 245–46
Iceland, 5, 19, 23, 75, 117; connections of, with Greenland, 1, 63, 114, 147, 151–58 *passim*, 169; connections of, with Norway and Denmark-Norway, 1, 63, 69–70, 110–11, 159, 177, 184, 336; early descriptions of, in maps and texts, 45–46, 49, 200, 209–18 *passim*, 262, 285–86, 360. *See also* Bishops; Björn Einarsson; Bristol; Colonization; Fishing and fish trade; Maps and mapping; Trade; Thorstein Ólafsson
Icelandic Annals, 28, 44, 59, 64–66 *pas-*

sim, 81–89 *passim*, 99, 130–41, 151, 157–61 *passim*, 246, 352f; *Annálar* (New Annals), 165, 178, 183f
Ikigaat (G), *see* Herjolfsnes
Illorssuit, V13a (WS), 117
Indians (North American), *see under* Native Americans
Ingimund Thorgeirsson, 66
Inglefield Land (NA), 37
Ingstad, Anne Stine, 24, 32
Ingstad, Helge, 9, 22–25 *passim*, 32, 35, 83, 107f, 114, 218, 355
Ingvild Helgadaughter, 194, 199, 203f, 316–19, 323, 327–28
Inheritance, *see* Property
Innussuk, *see* Eskimos; Native Americans
Inuit, *see* Eskimos; Native Americans
Inuit-Norse Project of 1976–77, 11, 55, 119f
Inventio fortunatae, 123–24, 132–37, 150, 262
Ireland, 123, 180ff, 193, 211, 220, 229, 269, 273, 290; monks from, 21; and North Atlantic trade, 207, 361. *See also* Galway
Iron, 54; sources of, 29–32 *passim*, 38, 57f, 138, 364–65; objects made of, 40–42 *passim*, 57f, 98, 120–22 *passim*, 142, 193, 228–33, 234, 311; production of, and "blooms," 29–32 *passim*, 57f. *See also* Arms and armor; Metals and metalworking; Tools
Íslendingabók (The Book of the Icelanders), 14f, 21
Isolation, 33, 118; as putative factor in the demise of Norse Greenland, 6, 13, 95, 100, 113, 138f, 143, 237–39, 252, 306–11 *passim*. *See also* Adaptation; Climatic factors; Communications
Italy, 257–60 *passim*
Ívar Bárdarson, 46; "Description of Greenland," 5, 62, 67, 84, 90–97 *passim*, 102–9, 136–43 *passim*, 153, 346; and voyage to the Western Settlement, 32, 102–14 *passim*, 131f, 229; and reasons for going to Greenland, 85–96 *passim*, 102, 154, 345; returns to Norway, 91, 98, 102, 111, 135–41 *passim*, 345–46
Ívar Vígfússon *holm*, 111
Ivory, 30–31, 37–39, 48, 57, 63–65, 80–83, 109, 241, 344. *See also* Carved images; Narwhal; Trade items; Walrus

Jansen, Henrik M., 11, 45
Jay, John (the Younger), 220, 266–67, 329
Jet, 235
Jóhanneson, Jón, 15, 161

Jón Biartzson, 158
Jón Eigilsson, 158
Jón Greenlander, 307–8
Jón Guttormsson, 164, 317f
Jón Jónsson, 152, 163, 353
Jón *rauð* ("the Red," Norwegian arch-
    bishop), 73–83 *passim*, 342. *See also*
    Norwegian archbishops
Jón Skolp, 200–201, 256–59 *passim*
Jones, Gwyn, 8, 15–18, 25, 38, 42, 59, 81
Jónsson, Finnur, 91, 104

Kalmar Union (1397), 144–46
Kapel, Hans, 10ff, 42, 308–10, 375
Karlsefni, *see* Thorfinn Thordsson
Keller, Christian, 6, 91, 240–41, 343
Kemys, Arthur, 273, 297
Kepken, Daniel, 195–99 *passim*
Ketilsfjord (G), 57, 97
Kielsen, Ove, 10
Kilaarsarfik (G), *see* Sandnes
King's Mirror, The, 34, 46–48, 66
Kinship, *see* Family connections and
    kinship
Knighthood, 190–95 *passim*, 319
Knives and daggers, *see* Arms and armor;
    Iron; Metals and metalworking
Kolbeinsson, Sigurd, 71
Kollgrim (burned as sorcerer), 99, 153f
Kowaleski, Maryanne, 181
Kristín Björnsdaughter (Vatnsfjord-
    Kristín), 150, 164–68, 317–20, 327
Kristín Thorsteinsdaughter (Akra-Kristín),
    183–85 *passim*, 190, 194, 198f, 204,
    315–28 *passim*, 376
"Kristni saga" (The Saga of Christianiza-
    tion), 61

La Cosa, Juan de, *see* De la Cosa, Juan
Laaland (Danish courtier), 256–57
Labrador (NA), 23ff, 30, 36, 113–14, 205,
    217–19 *passim*, 269. *See also* Fernandes,
    João; Forests and forest products;
    Markland
Landnámabók (The Book of the Settle-
    ments), 14, 107
L'Anse aux Meadows (NA), 9, 24f, 32,
    35, 114. *See also* Ingstad, Helge; New-
    foundland; Newfoundland Banks; Vín-
    land
Larsen, Helge, 6–7
Larsen, Sofus, 200–201, 254–55, 259
Latitude sailing, *see* Navigation
Latitudes and longitudes, calculations of,
    see Navigation
Law courts, 12, 62f, 102–3, 153, 221–22,
    301. *See also* Alþing; Lawmen

Law suits, 71, 148–49, 158, 221–22, 281–
    84 *passim*, 295–96, 301
Lawmen: in Greenland, 62f, 102–3; in Ice-
    land, 63, 102–3, 153; in Norway, 63,
    102–3, 140, 183, 204. *See also* Crown
    representatives
Lawspeakers, 62–63
Lay control, *see* Secular and lay control
Leather, *see* Hides and leather products
Legislation and law codes, 45, 62, 71–77
    passim, 92–93, 123, 151, 182, 251;
    Löngurettarbót (1450–51), 206f;
    Piningsdómur (1490), 204–6, 223, 269
Leif Eiriksson, 1, 6, 15f, 22–27, 61–62,
    164
Letters patent, *see* Licenses
"Libelle of Englyshe Polycye," 357, 364
Licenses, 371; for trade, 84, 150, 163, 167,
    177–78, 183, 188–97 *passim*, 204, 220;
    for discovery, 213, 254–55, 259–63
    passim
Liestøl, Aslak, 16
Lisbon, 207, 264f, 275f, 183, 302. *See also*
    Portugal
Literacy, 45, 66–68, 152, 163, 338, 350
Livestock, 9, 21, 27, 54–58 *passim*, 114–
    20, 172, 194, 235, 242; uses for, 48, 54,
    304–5; abandonment of, 104–9 *passim*,
    127, 282–83. *See also* Diet; Fodder and
    pasturage; McGovern, Thomas
Lloyd, John, 329
Logging, *see* Forests and forest products
London, 121, 173, 186f, 196, 205, 272f,
    299
Low Countries, 75, 80–82, 132–33, 194,
    202, 229, 256ff
Lumber, *see* Forests and forest products
Luther, Martin, 309
Lynn (E), 178ff
Lysufjord (WS), *see* Ameralik
"Lögmanns-annáll," *see* Icelandic Annals
Löngurettarbót (1450–51), 193, 206f. *See
    also* Legislation and law codes

Madeira Islands, 206, 213, 257f, 264
Maeshowe (Orkneys), 16
Maggiolo, Vesconte, 288
Magic and superstition, 39, 83, 99–100,
    110, 130, 153. *See also* Runes and runic
    inscriptions
Magnusen, Finn, 44, 353
Magnusson, Magnus, 25
Maine penny, the, 36
Malnutrition: as putative cause of the
    Norse Greenlanders' extinction, 5–8, 60,
    104, 113–20 *passim*, 242, 253, 311. *See
    also* Skeletal remains

Man, Isle of, 69, 72

Maps and mapping, 7f, 13, 24, 35, 134–37
passim, 164–67 passim, 200, 209, 260–
66 passim, 270, 360; Mercator world
map (1569), 133; Ruysch world map
(1508), 135, 214–18, 262, 267, 276,
280, 287, 362–63, 373; Ptolemy's Geographia (various eds.), 135, 167, 214,
259–62 passim; Claudius Clavus's maps
of the north (1427 and after), 166–67,
215, 276, 287; Henricus Martellus Germanus (ca. 1489), 169, 259–64 passim;
Cantino (1502), 213, 263, 277–80, 284;
Paris Map (1489–92), 208–17 passim,
262, 279–80; Catalan chart (Biblioteca
Ambrosiana, ca. 1480), 211–13, 221,
262, 276; Toscanelli (1470s), 259–61,
367; Behaim globe (1491–92), 261–62,
361; Pizzi (1424), 261; Cabot (1544),
270–72 passim; La Cosa (1500), 270–
71; Velho (1560–61), 282; King-Hamy
(ca. 1502), 285–87, 372; Wolfenbüttel,
287, 372; Thorne (1527), 288–90, 296,
306; Maggiolo (1516, 1511), 288; Oli-
veirana (ca. 1508–10), 288; Ribeiro
(1529), 288; Waldseemüller (1507), 300.
See also "Vinland Map"; and individual
cartographers by name

Marauders, see Abduction and piracy

Markland (NA), 23, 27f, 34, 108, 122,
136, 248. See also Forests and forest
products; Labrador

Martens, Irmelin, 233–34, 364

Mary Rose, 229, 333

Mary-Rousselière, Guy, 39

Mass, see Religious services

Mathiassen, Therkel, 11, 40ff, 125, 142f,
227ff

Matthews, Barry, 114

Mattox, William G., 247

McCartney, Allen P., 56

McGhee, Robert, 25f, 36–42 passim, 142

McGovern, Thomas, 6, 54–60 passim, 92–
95 passim, 235–42 passim, 247–50
passim

McGuirk, Donald L., 362–63

Mecca, 265

Medicine, 39, 83, 181, 344

Meldgaard, Jørgen, 11f, 120, 124–25, 232

Melville Bay (G), 38, 42

Mercator, Geraldus, 133–37 passim, 262

Merchant adventurers, see Bristol

Metals and metalworking, 97f, 107, 127,
228, 232–34, 249, 304, 311, 346; pewter, 18, 173, 235; gold, 32, 65, 74, 87,
258; silver; 32, 74f, 80, 120–22, 167,

190, 213, 274; bronze, 39ff, 232–34;
and casting of church bells, 40, 65, 97f,
142, 346. See also Arms and armor; Iron

Mice, 89, 339

Middens, 54ff, 95, 119–22 passim, 130,
241–42, 339. See also McGovern,
Thomas

Middle Settlement (G), 67, 351. See also
Eastern Settlement

Mills, 57, 133

Moltke, Erik, 54, 130

Monarchs, Continental: French, 195; Portuguese, 101, 196, 219, 256–57, 262–66
passim, 274–87 passim, 291–93, 309;
Spanish, 208, 218, 223, 263–66 passim,
273, 287, 308–9, 372. See also France;
Portugal; Spain

Monarchs, English: Edward I, 83; Edward
II, 83; Alfred, 83, 124, 344; Edward III,
122, 133; Henry V, 158, 165ff; Henry
VI, 179, 182, 186–89 passim, 193–96
passim, 231; Edward IV, 198f, 319; Richard III, 203; Henry VII, 204f, 262, 266–
73 passim, 287, 291–303 passim; Henry
VIII, 309; Henry III, 343–44. See also
England

Monarchs, Norwegian and Dano-
Norwegian, 62f, 69–70, 76, 81–182 passim, 316; Olaf Tryggvason, 15, 61, 165;
Olaf Haraldsson, 18; Eirik Magnusson
("Priest-Hater"), 33, 75–77, 342; Olaf
Kyrre, 36; Sigurd ("Jerusalem-Farer"),
63f; Hákon Hákonsson, 70–73, 343–44;
Fredrik II, 71; Hákon VI Magnusson,
71, 133, 144–46, 342ff; Magnus Hákonsson ("Law Mender"), 72–77 passim, 83,
342; Hákon V Magnusson, 77–79, 82,
102, 111; Magnus Eiriksson (smeyk),
81–85 passim, 103, 110–11, 122, 139,
343–48 passim; Christian I, 123, 189–
202 passim, 207, 212, 256f, 319, 327,
359–61 passim; Margrethe, 144–50 passim, 157–61 passim; Eirik of Pomerania,
144, 150f, 158–67 passim, 176–87 passim, 256, 320; Ólaf Hákonsson, 144;
Christopher of Bavaria, 187–89 passim;
Christian III, 200; Hans, 201–6 passim,
308, 361; Christian II, 308–9. See also
Crown politics and prerogatives; Crown
representatives; Sweden

Monasteries, see Religious houses

Monopolies, see Trade restrictions

Moors, 256

Morison, Samuel Eliot, 6ff, 200f, 211,
260–65 passim, 270–72, 280, 360, 371

Munch, P. A., 46

Myths and tales, 45f, 59, 105–8 *passim*, 142, 211, 215, 280, 355
Mäding, Heinrich, 204
Møhl, Jeppe, 9
Málfrid Björnsdaughter, 155, 323–25
Málfrid Torfadaughter, 194, 199, 204, 316, 323, 327f

Nansen, Fridtjof, 107, 113
Narsaq, Ø17a (ES), 12, 54–57 *passim*, 241–42, 248, 333
Narsarsuaq, Ø149 (ES), 12, 17, 59–60, 67–68, 97, 310, 375. *See also* Religious houses
Narwhal, 21, 37–39 *passim*, 48, 83, 97, 181, 249, 344. *See also* Ivory; Medicine; Trade items
Native Americans, 9, 21, 36–42 *passim*, 292; Amerindian peoples, 1, 25ff, 36, 272–74 *passim*, 280, 297–303 *passim*, 309, 372f; Dorset Eskimos, 25, 30f, 36–39 *passim*, 138; Thule Eskimos, 25, 31, 36–40 *passim*, 138, 310
Natural disasters and volcanic eruptions, 59, 139, 191–94 *passim*, 217, 245. *See also* Climatic factors
Natural resources, 8, 21–33 *passim*, 248, 271–72, 302–4 *passim*, 310, 334–35. *See also* Fishing and fish trade; Forests and forest products, Iron; Newfoundland Banks; Trade items
Navigation, 8, 161–62, 206–7, 219–20, 262–66 *passim*; currents and wind patterns in, 1, 16, 132, 214–18 *passim*, 247–49 *passim*, 258–60, 270, 305, 368; "drifting off" as excuse for ending up in Greenland, 5, 71, 146–51 *passim*, 157, 250; instruments used in, 12, 16–18, 25, 29, 132–33, 180, 219, 237, 270, 284, 329, 333–34; latitude sailing in, 16, 214–19 *passim*; sailing routes used in, 27, 46–47, 84, 132, 136f, 152, 170, 180–81, 206–9 *passim*, 217–21, 268–70, 284–85; climatic factors in, 46–47, 81–88 *passim*, 139f, 236–37, 362; hazards to, 46–47, 84, 115, 123, 132, 172, 180; calculations of latitudes and longitudes in, 210, 214–20 *passim*, 237, 263, 270, 290, 335; use of pilots in, 226, 266; compass deviation as obstacle to, 237, 266, 368. *See also* Ice
Nebenzahl, Kenneth, 208, 271, 278
Neel, James V., 239, 365
"New Annals," *see Icelandic Annals*
New Brunswick region (NA), 24f
Newfoundland (NA), 8–9, 24f, 36, 205,

214, 259–60, 265, 269. *See also* Bristol; England; Fishing and fish trade; Maps and mapping; Newfoundland Banks; Vínland
Newfoundland Banks, 8, 13, 181, 205, 214–22 *passim*, 252, 272, 283. *See also* Bristol; England; Fishing and fish trade; France; Portugal
Niaquusat, V48 (WS), 22, 55, 119, 239
Nicholas of Lynn, *see Inventio fortunatae*
Nidaros (N), *see* Norwegian archbishops; Trondheim
Nielsen, Nils, 31f
Nipaatsoq, V54 (WS), 22, 104, 115–22 *passim*
Njál's Saga, 16
Nordenskiöld, A. E., 214
Norðrseta (Greenland and Davis Strait), 21, 28–29, 32, 37, 57, 105, 131, 138, 227, 339; official voyage to, ca. 1260, 42, 72–73. *See also* Hunting
North America, discovery and early exploitation of: by Norse, 1f, 13–14, 22–33, 164, 236–37; by English and other Europeans, 1, 8, 114, 164, 172, 180. *See also* Asia; Bristol; England; Fishing and fish trade; France; Newfoundland Banks; Portugal; Vínland
Northwest Passage, search for, 267, 300, 307. *See also* Asia
Norway: general conditions in, 5f, 56f, 61, 74, 88–89, 139–44 *passim*; political and economic developments in, 27, 31f, 35f, 43–47 *passim*, 112–27 *passim*, 256, 308. *See also* Economic fluctuations and inflation; Monarchs, Norwegian and Dano-Norwegian; Norwegian archibishops; Norwegian nobles
Norwegian archbishops, 32–36 *passim*, 61, 66–69 *passim*, 92, 190, 197, 201, 246, 340–42 *passim*; and relations with Rome, 5, 67–82 *passim*, 87, 112, 143; and relations with Greenland, 6, 69–86 *passim*, 95, 143–45; and relations with Iceland, 69–72 *passim*; and the codfish trade, 74, 162, 217, 308; and relations with Bergen, 78–80, 85–86. *See also* Bishops; Clergy; Jón *rauð*; Valkendorf, Erik
Norwegian nobles: and the Council of Regency, 75, 190, 202, 342f
Nunes, Pedro, 266
Nunneries, *see* Religious houses
Nuremberg, 261f
Nutrition, *see* Diet
Nuuk region (G), 10–11, 105, 113, 118
Nørlund, Poul, 26, 67, 235–38 *passim*; ex-

cavations at Herjolfsnes, 2, 7–10 *passim*, 87, 95–101 *passim*, 170–73, 229–36 *passim*, 247, 307; excavations at Gardar, 31, 65, 97, 101, 173, 335

Oceanographic research, 8
Ogilvie, A. E. G., 246
Ohthere (Norwegian chieftain at King Alfred's court), 83, 124, 344
Oil, *see* Blubber and fish oil
Olaf (Haraldsson), Saint, *see* Monarchs, Norwegian and Dano-Norwegian
Ólaf Björnsson, 155
Ólaf Loptsson, 164–65, 195, 236
Olaus Magnus, 167, 200, 360
Óleson, Tryggvi, 108
Ólöf Loptsdaughter, 150, 164, 195–98 *passim*, 317ff
Ombudsmen, *see* Crown representatives; Episcopal representatives
Oral history, 16
Orkneys, 16, 68, 88, 123, 141, 145, 189, 194, 101, 308
Oslo (N), 87, 158, 165, 187
Ottar, *see* Ohthere
Overgrazing, *see* Erosion and overgrazing

Pang, Kevin D., 245ff, 365
Parasites, 58f
Parish system, introduction of, 91–94, 154
Parry, J. H., 8, 219, 368
Parry, M. C., 118
Pasqualigo, Lorenzo, 273f
Pasqualigo, Pietro, 274–77 *passim*
Pasturage, *see* Fodder and pasturage
Pelletier, Monique, 208
Permafrost, 117f
Philippa (English princess), 150, 256
Pigs, *see* Livestock
Pilgrimage, 150, 155, 188, 193, 202, 207
Pining, Didrik (the Elder), 199–205, 226, 256–59 *passim*, 360. *See also* Hanse
Pining, Didrik (the Younger), 205
Piningsdómur (1490), 204–6, 223, 269. *See also* Legislation and law codes
Piracy, 69, 131, 139ff, 156, 167–70 *passim*, 179–80, 195, 207, 226, 257. *See also* Abduction and captivity; Pining, Didrik (the Elder)
Plague (bubonic and pneumonic), 8, 174; in Norway and its Atlantic colonies, 81, 88–89, 104, 110f, 150, 155–62 *passim*, 316, 324–26, 348; in England, 88–89, 181, 234. *See also* Diseases (human and animal); Epidemics
Poetry and skalds, 12, 44, 62
Polar bears, 21, 39, 55–58 *passim*

Polo, Marco, 134, 265–68 *passim*
Popes: Alexander III, 5, 33–36 *passim*; Leo IX, 45; Innocent III, 68; Innocent IV, 69; Nicholas III, 74; Martin IV, 75, 81; Honorius IV, 76; John XXII, 80f; Clement VI, 87, 345; Nicholas V, 96, 174–79 *passim*, 189, 226, 237; Alexander VI, 96, 237–38; Gregory XI, 143; Boniface IX, 143; Alexander V, 144ff; John XXIII, 144–46 *passim*, 161; Martin V, 144, 182f; Clement VII, 145; Gregory XII, 146; Eugene IV, 174, 185f; Innocent VIII, 237; Leo X, 309. *See also* Curia
Populations, size of: in Greenland, 43, 59f, 80, 112, 143, 241, 252–53, 307; in Iceland, 59, 253; elsewhere, 80, 181f, 303–4
Porsild, Morten, 11, 124
Portugal, 176, 196, 202, 206f, 213, 219f, 303, 309f; and North Atlantic exploration and trade, 5, 8, 13, 23, 200–201, 213, 225, 255–64, 274–85, 373; and African and Asian exploration and trade, 101, 250, 256–63 *passim*, 275, 302, 367–70 *passim*; and Mediterranean trade, 257–58. *See also* Monarchs, Continental; Trade; *and individual explorers by name*
Pothorst, Hans, 199–201, 226, 256–59 *passim*, 369
Pottery, *see* Glass and pottery
Powell Knutsson, 103, 110–11
Property: of the church, 92–94 *passim*, 153, 354; bequests and sales of, 93, 354; inheritance of, 92–94, 123, 152–56 *passim*, 169, 185, 199, 204, 324–38; of the crown, 94, 102. *See also* Dowry
Ptolemy (Claudius Ptolemæus), 209f
Pynke, John, 206
Páll Hallvardsson, 156
Pálsson, Hermann, 16, 25, 76

Qaqortoq (G), *see* Hvalsey
Quinn, David B.: on pre-Columbian Atlantic discovery, 8–9, 201, 207–9, 213, 220f, 259f, 279–80; on Norse Greenland, 122, 134, 283; on fishing and fish trade, 180, 206, 361; on post-Columbian Atlantic discovery, 219, 255, 267–71 *passim*, 293, 373–74

Rats, 88–89
Reindeer, *see* Caribou
Religion, *see* Christian faith and practice; Church of Rome; Religious services
Religious houses: in Greenland, 12, 17,

67–68, 97, 310, 350; in Iceland, 19, 68, 324, 328; in Norway, 68, 111, 141; Ter Doest monastery, 75
Religious services, 66ff, 88, 98f, 156. *See also* Rituals
Rettarbót (1302), *see* Trade restrictions
Ribeiro, Diogo, 288
Richard (English merchant), 163, 167, 178
Rink, Henry, 142
Rituals, 19, 31, 95–101 *passim*, 253, 311, 335. *See also* Religious services
Robinson, Arthur H., 8
Robinson, Orrin W., III, 360
Rognvald, Earl of Orkney, 58–59
Roussell, Aage, 26, 32, 50–53, 66f, 97, 117f, 124–31, 154
Royal chapels, 78–79, 85, 91, 135, 345–46
Ruddock, Alwyn A., 134, 297, 300
Runes and runic inscriptions, 36, 44, 54, 66f; Kingittorsuaq runestone, 37, 99, 130, 337, 350. *See also* Literacy
Russia, 32, 81–83, 110, 178, 196
Ruysch, Johann, 135, 214–18

Sable Island (NA), 282f
Sabo, Debora, 39f
Sacks, David Harris, 301
Sailing routes, *see* Navigation
Salt, 221
Salvesen, Helge, 246
Sandnes (WS), 26, 47f, 63–67 *passim*, 119f, 124–31 *passim*, 229, 335; administrative importance of, 22, 26f, 32–33, 109
Sardinia, 257
Schellendorp, Stephan, 177f
Schledermann, Peter, 37ff
Scolvus, *see* Jón Skolp
Scotland, 69, 83, 120–23, 180, 194f, 223
Secular and lay control, 64, 68, 87, 92–96, 100–102, 112, 143, 154
Seals, 21, 32, 48, 54–58 *passim*, 118ff, 127, 242, 248–50. *See also* Diet; Trade items
Seaver, David O., 3–5, 49, 215
Selby, John, 178
Sermermiut (G), 40, 105
Seven Cities, Isle of the, *see* Brazil, Isle of
Seville, 255, 264, 288ff
Sharpening stones, 40, 105, 122
Sheep, *see* Livestock
Shetland, 88, 123, 161, 194, 201
Shipping, *see* Communications
Ships and shipbuilding, 29, 50, 66, 71, 108, 126–27, 131–38 *passim*, 248, 308, 341; advances in, 123, 161, 193, 220

Shipward, John, 329
Shipwrecks, 42, 64ff, 72, 147, 274
Siglufjord (G), 67, 97
Sigrid Björnsdaughter, 2, 151–64 *passim*, 168–73, 178, 183–85, 194, 199, 249f, 315–27 *passim*. *See also* Hvalsey; Thorstein Ólafsson
Sigrid Erlendsdaughter, 158
Sigurd Kolbeinsson, 147
Silver, *see* Metals and metalworking
Simek, Rudolf, 336
Skagafjord region (I), 27, 152, 160–64 *passim*, 178, 183–86 *passim*
Skalds, *see* Poetry and skalds
Skeletal remains, 7, 10–12, 59f, 120, 128, 232, 239, 332, 349; dental studies of, 60
Skelton, R. A., 209, 285, 372
Skovgaard-Petersen, Inge, 92–93
Skrælings, *see* Eskimos; Native Americans
Skuli Bárdarson, 70
"Skálholt Annals," *see* Icelandic Annals
Skálholt Cathedral and See (I), 44, 65, 86, 92, 111, 195
Skálholtsbók (The Skálholt Book), 15, 164
Slag, *see* Iron; Metals and metalworking
Slavery, *see* Abduction and captivity
Smithies, *see* Iron; Metals and metal-working
Snorri Sturluson, 70
Snorri Thorfinnsson, 27
Snorri Torfason, 151f, 157, 163, 353
Snæbjörn Galti, 19–20
Soapstone, 10, 18, 41, 120, 127
Sokki Thorisson, 63–65
Sólveig Thorsteinsdaughter, 150f, 161, 315–16. *See also* Björn Einarsson
Southampton (E), 160, 181, 207
Spain, 8, 206f, 218, 234, 303, 308–9; and early exploration, 23, 213, 223–25 *passim*, 254–58, 262–63, 275, 304, 372. *See also* Castile; Columbus, Christopher; Monarchs, Continental; Seville
Spencer, William, 206, 220, 265, 329
Spice, 257f, 267f, 273–75 *passim*, 304. *See also* Asia
St. Lawrence region (NA), 24f, 30, 272, 282, 303, 385
Stamsø Munch, Gerd, 354
Starvation, *see* Malnutrition
Stavanger (N), 79
Steinunn Hrafnsdaughter, 153, 215–17
Stenberger, Maårten, 235
Stockfish, 82, 160–65 *passim*, 169–72 *passim*, 184, 194, 221, 249–52 *passim*, 305f. *See also* Cod; Fishing and fish trade; Trade items
Stoklund, Marie, 99–100, 235, 337

Storehouses, 57, 128, 235
Straunge, Robert, 329
Sturla Thordarson, 14, 70
Sturlubók (Sturla's Book), 14
Sugar, 258, 283, 304
Sumarlidi Thorsteinsson, 315, 319f, 324
Sunstone (*sólarsteinn*), 16–19, 25. *See also* Navigation
Superstition, *see* Magic and superstition
Sutherland, Pat, 39
Sveinn Estridsson, 39
Sweden, 75f, 81, 123, 160, 185–88 *passim*, 202, 234, 308, 343, 359. *See also* Monarchs, Norwegian and Dano-Norwegian
Symbols, Christian and pagan, 10, 39f, 96–100 *passim*, 128–30
Sæmund Oddsson, 152, 156, 168
Sættargerð (1277), *see* Trade restrictions

Tales, *see* Myths and tales
Tasermiut (G), *see* Ketilsfjord
Taxes, *see* Tithes and taxes
Taylor, Eva G. R., 132–37 *passim*
Telles, Fernão, 259
Templars, 39
Ter Doest monastery, 75
Terceira, 259–62 *passim*, 281–83, 291, 304
Textiles, 38–42 *passim*, 47–50 *passim*, 57, 81–83 *passim*, 127ff, 142, 229; Bristol cloth, 230, 267, 283, 302–5 *passim*. *See also* Clothing
Thirkill, Launcelot, 274, 329
Thirslund, Søren, 17f
Thjodhild Jörundsdaughter, 19f, 27, 60f
Thomas, John, 266–67, 291–99 *passim*, 304–6 *passim*, 329
Thorbjörn Bárdarson, 152, 163
Thord Eigilsson, 44, 84–88 *passim*
Thord Jörundarson, 152, 163
Thord *kakali*, 70
Thorfinn Thordsson (Karlsefni), 15, 26–27, 63, 152, 164f, 236, 322
Thorgest of Haukadale, 19
Thorgrim Sölvason, 152f, 157
Thorkell *farserkr*, 153
Thorkell Leifsson, 62
Thorleif Arnason, 150, 177–78, 317, 327
Thorleif Björnsson, 198f, 202ff, 323, 327–28
Thorleiksstead (I), 155, 185, 325
Thorne, Robert, the Elder, 206, 265, 268–69, 289–90, 294–301 *passim*, 306, 329, 372
Thorne, Robert, the Younger, 269, 288–90, 294–96 *passim*, 300, 306, 329
Thorne, Thomas, 297, 329

Thorne, William, 294–301 *passim*, 329
Thorstein Eiriksson, 1, 6, 15f, 22, 26
Thorstein Eyjólfsson, 151, 195, 199, 315–20 *passim*, 324–27 *passim*
Thorstein Helmingsson, 152
Thorstein Ólafsson, 2, 147, 151–78 *passim*, 183–85, 190–94 *passim*, 198f, 224–25, 233–38 *passim*, 249f, 315–27. *See also* Hvalsey
Thorsteinsson, Björn, 157–70 *passim*, 177–85 *passim*, 195, 203, 210–12, 220f, 320, 350, 355f, 361
Thorvald Eiriksson, 1, 6, 15f, 22–26 *passim*
Thorvald Helgason, 76
Timekeeping, 16–19, 25
Tithes and taxes, 302, 340; in Norway and its Atlantic colonies, 47, 64, 71–87 *passim*, 91–96, 102, 109–15 *passim*, 140–46 *passim*, 184, 191, 251. *See also* Bergen; Crown representatives; Episcopal representatives; Norwegian archbishops; Stockfish
Tombstones, 67, 96, 338
Tools, 12, 57, 98, 127–31 *passim*, 233
Tordesillas, Treaty of (1494), 223, 263–64, 275–79 *passim*, 302
Torfi Árason, 190–99 *passim*, 316, 323, 327
Toscanelli, Paolo, 259–61 *passim*
Trade, 84, 158–73 *passim*, 178–86 *passim*, 193, 256–58; from Greenland before 1400, 39, 43, 47–48, 61, 71, 79–85 *passim*, 95, 139, 146; from Norway and Denmark, 47, 61, 71, 74, 82, 160; from Iceland, 71, 139, 146, 151, 158–60, 177–84, 201–5; from Greenland after 1400, 160–62, 169–73, 186ff, 191, 197, 223–25, 229–40 *passim*, 268–69, 306; from Spain and Portugal, 211–13, 229, 256–57. *See also* Trade items; Trade restrictions
Trade items, 221, 250, 344; from Norway, 27, 32, 47, 147–51 *passim;* from Greenland, 31, 38f, 48, 57, 80–85 *passim*, 138, 147–48, 160, 182, 240–41, 248–52; from North America, 32, 37, 48, 138; from Iceland, 147–48, 160, 194; from England, Ireland, and Scotland, 182, 220, 226–30 *passim*, 249, 267, 283. *See also* Natural resources; *and individual trade items by name*
Trade restrictions, 74, 81–84 *passim*, 123, 146–49 *passim*, 155–56, 160–62, 177–89 *passim*, 204–5, 264, 342–44. *See also* Licenses
Traditions, 12

Trondheim (N), 79–80, 156, 182, 190. *See also* Norwegian archbishops
Tunulliarfik (G), *see* Eiriksfjord
Turks, 257

Ujarassuit, V7 (WS), 67, 117f, 128
Umiivik, V15 (WS), 117
Umiviarssuk, V52a (WS), 66, 124–27 *passim*, 131
Undal, Peder Clausen, 44
Unicorns, *see* Narwhal
Units of measure, 355
Uunartoq (G), *see* Siglufjord

Valkendorf, Erik, 32, 82, 91, 104, 308–9
Vallarte (Danish courtier), 256f
Vandvik, Eirik, 33–36
Vatican Library, 44
Vatnahverfi (ES), 12, 62, 232–34, 242
Vebæk, Christen Leif, 12, 16f, 54–59 *passim*, 67–68, 97, 232–34, 242, 311, 333, 375
Veidarvísir ok borgaskipan, 34
Velho, Bartolomeuo, 282
Venice, 265, 273f
Vestmannaeyjar (I), *see* Westman Islands
Vígfús Ívarsson *holm*, 158, 163, 167, 320
Vigneras, L.-A., 274–75, 280–82, 371
Vínland (NA), 14, 23–28 *passim*, 33–36, 45, 62f, 124, 152, 164, 183, 199, 207, 236
"Vinland Map," 8, 164–65, 354
Vínland sagas, *see* "Eiriks saga rauða"; "Grænlendinga saga"
Virgil, Polydore, 274
Vogado, João, 260
Volcanic eruptions, *see* Natural disasters and volcanic eruptions
Von Damminn, Balthazar, 178, 182

Waldseemüller, Martin, 300
Walkendorf, Erik, *see* Valkendorf, Erik
Wallis, Helen, 8, 209, 214–17 *passim*, 354
Walrus, 21, 30–32, 37ff, 48, 56–58, 63, 83, 97, 130, 241, 248–50. *See also* Hunting; Ivory; Trade items

Warde, Richard, 291–310 *passim*, 329
Weapons, *see* Arms and armor; Harpoons and spears
Weather, *see* Climatic factors
Weaving, *see* Textiles
Western Isles, the, *see* Hebrides
Western Settlement: end of, 2, 5, 47, 57, 86, 96, 104, 137–38; theories on decline of, 5–7, 12, 80–81, 89; and contact with Thule Eskimo people, 6, 11, 103–9; excavations in, 9ff, 53, 55, 104, 124–31; early settlement of, 21–22, 109; and early North American exploration, 26, 33; population of, 43, 105–13 *passim*; and communication with the Eastern Settlement, 63, 102–4, 108–10 *passim*, 122, 248; churches and clergy in, 67–69, 128–31 *passim*; possible contact with non-Nordic Europeans, 124–26, 229. *See also* Eastern Settlement; "Farm beneath the sand"; Ívar Bárdarson; Niaquusat; Nipaatsoq; Sandnes; Ujarassuit; Umiviarssuk
Westman Islands (I), 161, 168, 176ff
Whales and whaling, 9, 21, 35, 55f, 83, 127, 138, 218, 339, 356; whales as gift objects, 83, 343. *See also* Trade items
Wheat, *see* Grain
Whetstones, *see* Sharpening stones
Williams, Mary E., 206
Williamson, James A., 2, 5, 265–70 *passim*, 274–78 *passim*, 285, 292, 300
Wind patterns, *see* Navigation
Wine, 88, 187f
Women's lives, 19f, 26–27, 57, 60f
Wood, *see* Forests and forest products
Worcestre, William, 220
Worm, Ole, 205, 361

York, town of (E), 47, 58
Yslond, William, 206, 265

Öxna-Thorir (Viking chieftain), 19

Ári Marsson, 27
Ári Thorgilsson, 15, 21
Ásmund *kastanrassi*, 66

Seaver, Kirsten A.
  The frozen echo: Greenland and the exploration of
  North America, ca. A.D. 1000–1500 / Kirsten A. Seaver.
    p. cm.
  Includes bibliographical references (p.   ) and index.
  ISBN 0-8047-2514-4 (cl.) : ISBN 0-8047-3161-6 (pbk.)
  1. Greenland—Discovery and exploration—Norse.
  2. North America—Discovery and exploration—Norse.
  I. Title.
  G760.S43   1995
  970.01'3—dc20   95-16605
                                                  CIP

Original printing 1996
Last figure below indicates year of this printing:

13 12 11 10 09